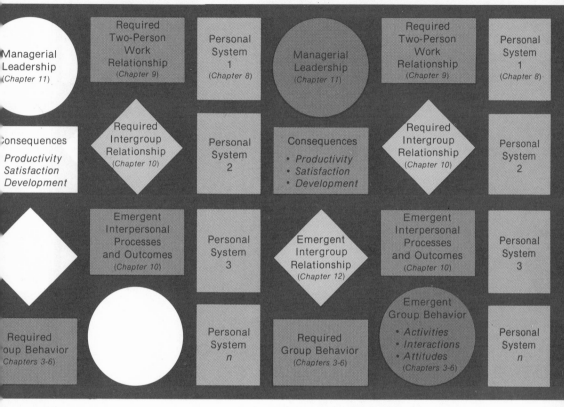

Environmental
Influences

EFFECTIVE BEHAVIOR
IN ORGANIZATIONS

**The Irwin Series in Management and
The Behavioral Sciences**

Consulting Editors
L. L. CUMMINGS and E. KIRBY WARREN

Advisory Editor
JOHN F. MEE

By

ALLAN R. COHEN
Associate Professor of Administration
and Director, M.B.A. Programs

STEPHEN L. FINK
Associate Dean and
Professor of Organizational Behavior

HERMAN GADON
Professor of Management

ROBIN D. WILLITS
Professor of Administration and Organization

with the collaboration of
Natasha Josefowitz
Lecturer in Organizational Behavior

The Whittemore School of Business and Economics,
University of New Hampshire

EFFECTIVE BEHAVIOR IN ORGANIZATIONS

Learning from the Interplay
of Cases, Concepts, and
Student Experiences

1976

RICHARD D. IRWIN, INC.   Homewood, Illinois   60430
Irwin-Dorsey International   Irwin-Dorsey Limited
Arundel, Sussex   Georgetown, Ontario
BN18 9AB   L7G 4B3

Photographs by Fred Bavendam.
Cover design by Ken Silvia.

First Printing, January 1976

ISBN 0-256-01773-5
Library of Congress Catalog Card No. 75–22678
Printed in the United States of America

*To all our colleagues in
Organizational Behavior who
have created a new and exciting
field by combining
social science knowledge with
organizational experience.
We hope that this book is a
further step in building a bridge
between theory and practice.*

PREFACE

THIS BOOK is designed for a basic introductory course in human behavior in organizations. The topics covered include individual behavior, interpersonal relationships, small groups, inter-group relations, leadership and change. All are dealt with in the context of diverse formal organizations (industrial, educational, governmental, health care, and so on). While previous courses in the social and/or behavioral sciences can be helpful, the book is written to be understood by the student with no prior exposure to the field.

Organizational behavior courses usually have at least several goals, including the mastery of a body of theory and research findings; improvements in analytical ability and decision-making capacity; clarification of student values; increased interpersonal and group skills; and development of leadership ability. While individual instructors may emphasize some goals more than others, ultimately all the goals converge toward educating for *action*, for enhanced student ability to be effective in an organization.

Thus we have based this book on the assumption that students best learn effective organizational behavior by practicing it on realistic problems or dilemmas, and then reflecting upon their efforts, utilizing concepts, theories, reasoning, and guidance. Having put ourselves in a similar position—facing many exquisite dilemmas in writing a useful textbook—we would like to make explicit the educational and organizational issues we wrestled with in preparing this package of materials. In our efforts, over the past ten years, to implement our premises in the classroom, we have encountered a number of issues similar to those reported by our colleagues in other schools. These include:

1. How can students be convinced that behavioral science theory can actually be useful and add to "common sense" in solving real organizational problems?
2. How do we help students prepare for action roles which contain ambiguity and uncertainty, and therefore need more than theoretical formulations to resolve?
3. How can students be taught to increase both their analytical abilities and their interactive skills?

4. Similarly, how can the gap be bridged between teaching cognitive content, such as theory and research findings, and teaching effective skills, usually through experience?
5. How do classroom teachers convey to inexperienced students the reality of the behavioral difficulties with which all members of organizations must cope? Students with little work experience tend to view organizational behavior as irrelevant or unnecessary despite repeated surveys made several years after graduation which indicate that in retrospect, administration students highly value behavioral courses and wish they had taken more.
6. How can students be helped to live with the uncertainty that goes with a subject matter in which the "right answer" partly depends on the values of the particular manager?
7. In short, how can existing knowledge about organizations, groups and individuals, be used to teach those subjects in a way that does justice to their complexity and uncertainty, yet universality?

This book is the result of our struggles with these knotty dilemmas. We have tried to pull together and integrate the polar approaches to teaching organizational behavior represented by former books. Our approach is a balanced one in which concepts and cognitive material are applied to actual problems, utilizing classroom processes which reinforce and illuminate the conceptual material.

We think of the classroom as a real organization, with genuine problems of leadership, structure, motivation, social pressure, interpersonal friction, etc., which parallel those in companies and elsewhere. Therefore, we try to integrate the textual material with the students' ongoing classroom experiences in analyzing cases, participating in simulations and exercises, working in groups, taking directions from a "supervisor," and so on.

To foster the integration of concepts and experiences, we have written the text material in an informal, personal style, using examples and illustrations from the students' world of classrooms and campus organizations as well as from business and nonprofit organizations. Similarly, the cases have been chosen to represent a cross section of organizational life, especially those situations with which students can readily identify, whether in the university, industry, health field, government agency, or other educational institutions. Many cases have been student written, furthering ease of identification. In addition, they were written with the book's central conceptual scheme in mind, so that there is sufficient data for practicing use of the analytical tools presented.

Sometimes it is difficult for students to grasp or retain theory in ways that permit easy application. Simply describing research findings or presenting a theory as developed by its author may leave the student to his or her own inexperienced devices to find ways of translating the ideas into more useful forms. What we have chosen to do throughout the book is to present as many concepts as possible in the form of situational *propositions* about behavior. We have found that propositional statements are more easily remembered and applied than unconnected strings of references, and that students readily adopt this format as a way of articulating their own insights and concepts. Rather than focus upon who did the research and what the research design was, we offer the insight from it in a tentative form that is immediately testable by the student on a problem being faced. While trying to insure that no major concepts were omitted or oversimplified, we tended to select those we believe most useful in analysis of actual problems. We also worked to integrate propositions with a central conceptual scheme, relating all chapters and topics in the book to one another.

In general, we have tried to organize the book so that a student *experiences* in the classroom a genuine organizational dilemma, with real consequences, while *analyzing* others (through a case) in a similar dilemma, using *concepts* or *research findings* about such problems. In this way, we hope to make the "medium" a reinforcing part of the conceptual "message."

Another way in which we have tried to demonstrate that the course material indeed is relevant to *any* future managers, is by the inclusion of more than the usual amount of material on power, influence, and conflict in organizations. These often neglected areas generate strong student interest and maintain perspective when the book focuses on collaboration, listening, or cohesion. If we expect students to adopt contingency thinking, choosing behavior appropriate to the situation, we must acknowledge those unpleasant aspects of organizations calling for defensiveness or "political maneuvering," as well as the more congenial territories with which organizational behavior has usually been concerned. We have often had to fight down our own unintentional tendency to sound as if openness and trust were always appropriate managerial behavior; in doing so we believe that we have made the book more balanced and theoretically sound.

December 1975

ALLAN R. COHEN
STEPHEN L. FINK
HERMAN GADON
ROBIN D. WILLITS

ACKNOWLEDGMENTS

WRITING THIS BOOK has made us more aware than ever of the inter-dependencies necessary to complete a complex task. It is with double gratitude, then, that we thank the large number of people who helped shape this book.

Seven of our colleagues, most of them former students in earlier versions of the course for which the book was written, tested rough drafts in the classroom and gave us valuable feedback. For this help we thank Pat Canavan, Cotton Cleveland, Harry Noel, Richard Pastor, Randy Webb, Maryann Wideson, and Mike Williams.

More than 1,000 students have used various drafts of the book, and for their responses, critical, constructive and occasionally even positive, we are extremely grateful. They invariably let us know when our elegant designs and crackling prose confounded their best efforts to understand what we intended for them to learn; without them we would not have been able to attain whatever clarity finally emerged.

The editorial advice and encouragement we received from Larry Cummings and Kirby Warren deserve special mention. They were able to make helpful suggestions from within our point of view and raise issues from other perspectives in the field which proved extremely useful. Even when we disagreed with their comments, we felt that they understood what we were trying to do and wanted to aid us in doing it better. That kind of editorial relationship is rare and we valued it highly.

We are also grateful to the organizers and participants of the Stanford-Berkeley Conference on Teaching Organizational Behavior. The stimulation received there was heady, and came at just the right time. Many ideas and dilemmas expressed there found their way into our thinking and writing.

Several secretaries overcame the mysteries of our handwriting and marked-up drafts, including Marylou Chag, Linda Fitzgerald, and Jennifer McKinnon. But for uncomplainingly coping with manuscript crises and deadlines, far beyond the call of duty, we give special thanks to Madeline Piper and Susan Gilman. In addition, Patricia Trow, as our graduate assistant, cheerfully completed a number of assignments which made our job easier.

We also thank Robert Bovenschulte and Michael Hartman for their unselfish sharing of ideas and advice.

Dean Jan Clee of the Whittemore School of Business and Economics and his administrative staff were also extremely supportive of our efforts, helping with logistics, teaching assignments, freedom to experiment, and all such things that academics sometimes only hope Dean's offices will provide.

Finally, we want to mention our wives and families. They are a living part of this book, and their contributions to it and us could never be fully catalogued. In each of these small organizations, countless observations, propositions, complexities, and analyses unfold and develop. For letting us be ourselves even when that entailed long absences for writing and meetings, to Joyce, Elaine, Lydia, and our children, our thanks and love.

December 1975

A.R.C.
S.L.F.
H.G.
R.D.W.

CONTENTS

CASES AND READINGS

EFFECTIVE BEHAVIOR
IN ORGANIZATIONS

*Much of what you can learn about
organizational behavior
is quite accessible;
it goes on around you
all the time.*

1

INTRODUCTION

WHAT DOES the term "organization" mean to you? Usually it arouses images of a fairly large collection of people with some kind of division of labor, bosses and workers, goals, a way of informing and controlling members, and so forth. It is natural, therefore, to first think of organizational behavior as a study of human activities in large corporations.

Yet much of what you can learn about organizational behavior is more accessible; it goes around you all the time. You are a member of a family; may live with other people; belong to some clubs, teams or committees; have a job involving others; eat and shop where people work; and so forth. The university itself is a large organization containing many smaller organizations: the fraternity or sorority, academic departments, business and other administrative offices. Even the classroom is an organization. You are in a position to see many of the main ingredients of organizational life in your everyday contacts. All of these groupings have implicit if not explicit goals, structures and policies. These in turn seek to direct behavior in certain ways. They shape people's interactions with each other and they are potentially a major source of an individual's productivity, satisfactions, and personal learning or development. In short, you have

3

immediately at hand some ready-made opportunities to study organizational behavior. We will try to help you learn to see and understand more of your living and working experiences.

The contents and format of this book are expressly designed to integrate "book knowledge" and immediate experience. In this way we hope to facilitate the process of putting learning to work and of applying knowledge where it has personal meaning. What better way to do this than to apply it to one's own experience?

Throughout this book you will be asked to analyze your own behavior in the classroom, your interactions with others, the pressures you experience both internally and externally (from your work group, the professor, and others), the climate in the classroom, and so forth. Analogies will be drawn with other organizational settings, either through student experience or the use of case studies. Theories and concepts will be introduced as tools for helping you to make sense out of your observations and experiences. In many respects, the objectives of this book and the course for which it is designed are aimed at creating the ability to learn from experience, in a circular process of extracting knowledge out of experience, testing that knowledge on new experience, extracting new learning, retesting, and so forth.

CENTRAL THEMES: LEARNING FROM DOING; THE MANAGER AS SCIENTIST

There are two central themes running through the book; one is the idea of "learning from doing" and the other the metaphor of "manager as scientist." With respect to the first, we believe that in order to learn how to *behave* effectively, rather than just *understand* behavior, it is necessary to be active and engaged. This calls for a different educational model from what you may be used to. Most college classrooms are not organized to give practice in action skills, but rather to enhance acquisition and understanding of material that may not have immediate direct application. In such classes the professor does most of the talking and grading, students listen, individually write notes and papers, take exams, answer some questions, and address most of their comments to the professor. But just as in a biology lab, where you have to *practice* dissecting a frog in order to learn the relevant skills, in a course designed to improve your organizational *effectiveness,* a more active student role is necessary.

A model of learning from *doing* is called for. It includes but goes beyond the premise that there are ideas, bodies of knowledge, or concepts that are important to remember. It assumes that learning to act occurs when you put these ideas, facts, or concepts to work in your life. This demands more than the ability to remember the contents and write them down on command. Ideally, it means learning to apply them to real-life situations and problems. Therefore, in a course in organizational behavior, the classroom needs to become a kind of learning laboratory in which you, the student, have the opportunity to test-out, practice, try, experiment with and utilize the variety of concepts and ideas that are the subject matter of the book. It means that as you proceed, you should try to see connections between what you are learning and your own behavior, as well as the behavior of individuals around you. Differences in class size and duration may limit the opportunity for such experiential learning during regular class hours. Nonetheless, when taking part in any organized activity, you can make observations and apply your conclusions to those relationships important to you in the classroom and outside.

One dilemma you are likely to face is the struggle to remain appropriately detached or objective while you are personally involved in the learning experience. In sociology this role is called "participant-observer;" it poses a dilemma because of the natural human tendency of a person to become *less* detached as he/she becomes more involved in a given situation. The fine line is difficult to identify; *too much detachment can minimize one's appreciation and understanding of another person or a set of interactions, but too much involvement can bias (even distort) one's perspective.*

The learning process you will use — alternating between experience and conceptualization — will also draw on our belief that a manager must operate like a scientist. We use this term cautiously, because it often conveys an image to people of a lonely man working in a laboratory, surrounded by test tubes, wearing thick glasses and a white coat, lost in thought about serious problems, and attempting to study them in an objective fashion. For some people "scientist" carries a very positive connotation; that is, someone who is objective, careful, systematic, and does things in a well-thought-out manner. For others, the connotation is a very negative one; it conveys the image of someone who is cold, distant, and often not too involved with other people. We do not intend to suggest either of these images; rather, we intend to capture an attitude about how to carry out day-to-day actions. What we mean by a *scientific attitude* in this respect is the process of sorting out (a) what is going on in one's relationships, (b) increasing the ability to predict likely outcomes of one's own and others' behaviors, and (c) thereby making more informed choices which can (d) be checked for results against expectations. *It is the act of comparing the intent of any one of our actions with the effect of that action, and then learning from it.* Such an attitude

---

There is absolutely no inevitability as long as there is a willingness to contemplate what is happening.

Marshall McLuhan

requires that you constantly question, examine, and evaluate the consequences of your actions so that you learn from both your failures and your successes.

Suppose you were asked to make recommendations about a strange, new sport, the rules for which you did not know. Can you imagine, for example, what the first tennis match you ever saw might be like? Some people dressed in abbreviated white costumes dash around hacking at a fuzzy sphere with a lollipop shaped stick, shouting about "love!" Yet sometimes when the sphere comes near them they step aside and do not wave their sticks, but appear to stare intently at some white lines on the ground. The participants stop and start quite suddenly, changing positions, throwing the sphere in the air and batting at it, crouching carefully or running rapidly toward the long webbed object hanging between the participants. Before you could ever offer sensible advice, you would have to *watch* carefully for any *patterns* to the game, *deduce the rules* (how long would it take you to figure out the scoring rules, that "love" meant no points, a certain number of points makes a "set," and so forth?), *test your assumptions* about how the game works *by predicting what will happen next* ("The first hitter aims for the opposite forecourt, so if I am correct about service rules, the second try must hit in that area or a point will be lost.") and slowly begin to *see the order in the apparent chaos.*

As you become increasingly sophisticated you could begin to draw conclusions about the internal workings and strategy of the game, making connections between when to rush the net, when to lob over an opponent's head, and so forth. Whether you systematically dissected the components of each stroke and its relation to opponent's weaknesses, or just observed until you had some hunches about what was likely to be effective, you would have to operate as a kind of scientist, gathering data, asking questions of it, forming tentative conclusions based on apparent patterns, testing those by more observation, and so on. In that way you would establish an order to the buzzing confusion you first experienced.

> *I'm not smart. I try to observe. Millions saw the apple fall but Newton was the one who asked why.*
>
>   Bernard Baruch

Trying to make sense out of an organization can be equally confusing, and even more challenging, since you are at the same time a part of what you are observing, affecting it, and affected by it. People at work don't often hold still for examination by impartial, detached observers, and they seldom behave by such explicit, pre-agreed rules as tennis players do.

Many of you who are reading this book have aspirations of becoming managers where you will hold down a position in a firm, company, institution, or perhaps in a community, where what you do has some impact upon the lives of other people. In that respect you will be managing other people, and making decisions which affect them. You may have some direct power over them in a supervisory capacity, or perhaps be engaged in some activity which plans and develops the objectives of an organization. Whatever may be the context of your role as a manager, you will need the skills of searching for patterns and connections, making predictions, testing out the consequences of an action or decision that you make, collecting information as to success, and modifying your actions accordingly. You will need to adopt and maintain an attitude of tentativeness; that is, a readiness to change your mind, to modify your views, to change your theory, to recognize your faults, to acknowledge your mistakes, and to take corrective action. Have you ever had, or seen, a boss who is so concerned about being right and so closed to feedback that he/she makes inappropriate decisions, saying, in effect, "Don't confuse me with the facts"? Such a person is, in our terms, a poor scientist and, therefore, a poor manager.

THE RELATIONSHIP BETWEEN THE BOOK DESIGN AND ASSUMPTIONS ABOUT MANAGERS

There are connections between the educational model of learning from doing and the concept of the manager as a scientist which can now be made explicit. Learning to become a manager requires the equivalent classroom experience of the laboratory in which students learn to become scientists. It requires activity and experimentation, a "hands on" approach to the territory being investigated. Just as a scientist-to-be asks questions, gathers data, tests, evaluates and retests, brings theories, concepts and intuition into the interpretation of the data, so the manager-to-be must practice these skills. Passivity is not a very efficient way to learn effective behavior.

> No man can reveal to you aught but that which already lies half asleep in the dawning of your knowledge . . . If he is indeed wise he does not bid you enter the house of his wisdom, but rather leads you to the threshold of your own mind.
>
> Kahlil Gibran
> The Prophet

As you progress through the book, examining and learning from your observations and experiences, you can build your own managerial theory in the form of sets of hypotheses and concepts—what we call *proposi-*

tions — that will help to guide your actions. An example of a **proposition** is the authors' belief that **Experiencing and analyzing behavior is likely to produce more learning of organizational skills than merely reading or hearing about it.** Such an idea can be tested and modified if necessary, then applied to other situations. Hopefully, the process of making propositions will aid in your development as a more effective manager, and as a more competent individual. You have a chance to develop a way of looking at people in organizations that goes beyond any specific information you acquire; the manager who has internalized the kind of *scientific attitude* we have discussed, should be able to continue learning in the changing situations facing him/her at work.

In summary, then, this book is concerned with the preparation of students who plan to become managers of people, and who will leave a course that uses it possessing skills in the following areas: (1) identifying problems, (2) understanding their origins, (3) predicting their consequences, (4) considering gains and losses of those consequences for the short- and long-run, and (5) possessing the willingness and capacity to choose well from among alternatives. In short, this book seeks to cultivate the rare qualities of insight, analysis, and judgment. Its emphasis is on knowledge utilization, the marriage of theory to practice, the development of managerial skills, and not just on the acquisition of knowledge for its own sake.

THREE PREMISES ABOUT LEARNING; THE CLASSROOM AS AN ORGANIZATION

In order to make the best possible use of the classroom as a source of learning about organizational behavior we make three important premises. These premises represent a major departure from the typical classroom model, but they are fundamental to our own. Our first premise, already discussed, is that *experiencing and analyzing behavior is likely to produce more learning than merely reading about it.*

Our second premise is that *just as at work where each member of a group has an impact on the way the group functions, in the classroom, all members of the course, students as well as instructor, influence and are influenced by the total climate and the network of relationships which develop during the course.*

Our third premise is that *each person in the class is a resource.* In order to maximize learning objectives, the class is faced with the problem of using all of its resources. Since use of these resources depends upon how members influence one another, the class and each individual in it has the potential opportunity and responsibility for examining the impact of different types of influence. Given these premises, the classroom itself can become the organizational setting for all members to learn about the meaning and impact of influence—their own and others. This is a core issue for any manager.

Thus the classroom is an analogue to the world of organizations. We claim that the situation in the classroom is not radically different from situations encountered in company board rooms or on the shop floor. The class is an organization with goals, structure, rewards and products; it must deal with such questions as: Who will have influence? How is it to be allocated? Who can give rewards and on what basis? How will decisions be made? How will task responsibilities be determined? How much independence and interdependence will members have? If you keep the commonalities in mind, you will see that the determinants of effectiveness in the classroom are applicable elsewhere.

> He that was only taught by himself had a fool to his master.
> Ben Jonson
> *Discoveries*

Since this book attempts to teach alternative forms of behavior in organizations, depending on the situation, the appropriate classroom organizational model is one where students share influence and accept the challenge of being responsible for the outcome of their own behavior in the course. Just as at work, we believe this will lead to a more productive and satisfying "organization" and a richer learning experience.

Certainly the instructor has a role which calls for special responsibilities. He/she is presumably a unique resource, a repository of knowledge, an accumulation of broader experience than the student. The student has less information about organizational behavior and may not know what his/her choices are. One of the instructor's responsibilities is to make information available which will increase the range of students' alternatives. At the same time, the student does know which of his/her own opinions and values, needs and puzzlements, must be taken into account if the course is to speak to real concerns. To be effective, the instructor must find out what is in the student's head. Thus, there needs to be a process of mutual exchange, search and discovery.

As part of his/her organizational responsibilities, the instructor draws up a set of requirements, which might include course objectives, assigned readings and cases, topical sequences, a suggested grading formula, and so forth. But within the limits of total system constraints—such as the requirement for grades—student responses may influence various aspects of the original plans.

Where influence is mutual, classroom activity will be sufficiently open-ended to provide opportunities to take advantage of learning from experience. Students and instructor must somehow cope with the uncertainties of reality, to follow behavior as it is generated in the classroom. By focusing on what is happening "here and now" and by finding evidence in the immediate context to support concepts, the situation provides opportunities for powerful reinforcement of learning.

If our assumptions about the impact of mutual influence are correct, you should be able to bear considerable responsibility for your education and also for the maintenance of the educational system. Given the opportunity to share influence, to be initiating rather than reactive, *we predict that you will feel more involved and committed, will become more independent as well as interdependent, will place greater value on internalization of knowledge, and that there will be an increase in innovative activities and of expansion of alternatives for teacher and student alike.* The results of our own efforts so far convince us that this is so. One of the most common organizational responses—at work and in the classroom—is for members to do only the minimum required of them. We hope that this book and the use of the classroom as a sample organization where influence is shared can lower the probability of your wanting to just get by, and increase your effort, learning and enjoyment.

TAKING A LOOK AT YOURSELF

It should be clear by now that this book will not be used only at an abstract level. While theories and concepts will be emphasized for their utility, you will actively use them and not passively commit them to memory. It should also be clear that you will be required to pay a great deal of attention to your own behavior, your own values and assumptions, and your own personal competence as it is reflected in your behavior in the classroom.

In those chapters concerned with interpersonal relations and the dynamics of behavior in groups, you will have an opportunity to take a good look at your impact on others in a task situation. In what respects is your behavior facilitative or *functional* to the group task? In what ways is it constraining or *dysfunctional?* How do your own values affect your involvement in an activity, your openness to others' ideas, or your approaches to problems described in case studies?

In chapters that focus primarily on individual behavior, you will find ample opportunity to learn about your own needs and abilities, your leadership potential and ways to increase and expand your own personal growth. Are you in touch with your leadership capacities and potential? If you take advantage of the opportunities afforded by this course, the payoff for you personally can be very high. You can become interpersonally more competent as well as a better manager-scientist.

NOTHING IS AS SIMPLE AS IT SEEMS

> *For every problem there is a solution which is simple, direct, and wrong.*
>   H. L. Mencken

If you long for a job in which all problems are easily defined, their causes are clear and known, decisions are simple, future events are quite predictable, and you can almost immediately find out whether you made the correct decision, you probably ought to think again about a managerial career. Organizational life is much too complex for a handful of rules, theories or slogans to be automatically applied to every problem. While the behavioral science theories and concepts in this book should be helpful to you in figuring out what is going on, or even in guiding an action, they are by no means sufficient for all problems you will encounter, nor easy to apply. They are more helpful than intuition alone, but they do not come with ten year, money-back guarantees.

For one thing, most behavior of any significance has multiple causes and multiple consequences. Thus, hasty, oversimplified diagnoses often miss the complexity of a situation and may lead to inappropriate action. For example, the decision-makers in a Massachusetts suburb decided that the *one* cause of so many accidents at a busy, five street intersection with no traffic lights and a supermarket on one corner, was "poor drivers." Therefore, they concluded that all they could do was to install an emergency phone on the corner to rapidly call the ambulance after an accident! Using oversimplified diagnoses of problems usually leads to similarly absurd "solutions."

Another problem facing managers is that they must make decisions under uncertain conditions, often before all the desired data are in. Quite often there is insufficient time for thorough study, or the roots of the problem are not accessible to the person who must decide. For example, employees are often afraid to tell *any* boss all they know, especially if what they say might include criticism of the boss. And even if they were to be completely open, they might not know fully their own motivations or other necessary information. Finally, the conditions at the time of the decision can change by the time it is implemented, so that what looks sensible at one time may seem foolish later. The energy crisis, which was accelerated by the Arab oil embargo in late 1973, made the auto manufacturers who were producing fancy gas guzzlers look bad, even though such cars had been popular when the decision to produce them had to be made.

Furthermore, the manager must not only make decisions under uncertainty, but also live with the consequences of those decisions. He/she does not have the luxury of leisurely tinkering with something inside a sealed vacuum flask and being able to put aside the experiment when it is not going well. Even deciding to do nothing is a decision which can affect a manager deeply, since that will not stop a chain of consequences from following, including changed perceptions of him/her by subordinates, colleagues, and boss.

Because the manager lives in a complex world of multiple causes and effects, makes decisions under uncertainty and must live with the consequences of decisions made under imperfect conditions, a specific ability is needed. It is the knack of thinking in terms of probable outcomes, rather than certain ones; of figuring and playing the odds. Anything the manager can do to predict likely outcomes more accurately, to increase the possibility of correct action, even when he/she cannot be *sure* about what will happen, is a great asset. If even "no decision" is a decision, the ability to take risks when outcomes are not certain becomes an important managerial attribute.

Thus, throughout the book you will be placed in a position of having to act and live through the consequences of each action or decision. For example, you may be asked to participate in group projects; if you decide not to say anything to the members of your group who shirk their responsibilities, for fear of hurting their feelings, you will be one of those who will live with the outcome. And conversely, should you decide to confront them, you would have another set of consequences to cope with. Which way you choose to handle such a dilemma, and which consequences you are willing to accept, depends upon your *own* personal values; no one else can tell you what is worth living with.

Through this continual process of being placed in organizational situations where you must make decisions about how to behave and then see what happens, your skills and organizational effectiveness should be improved. Quite often you will find that there is no *one* correct answer to the dilemmas or situations you are faced with. Since one person's meat can be another's poison, the "correct" solution will be quite different depending upon the values of the decider.

A MODEL FOR DECISION MAKING

The need to be clear about the desires of the person making a decision will be apparent throughout the book. The decision maker must find a way to assess what *demands the situation places* upon those involved, what solutions (and their consequences) would be *personally desirable* to him/her, and what the *possible alternatives* are which can accommodate both the situation and the decision maker.

Sometimes the particular task, the people involved in doing it, or the organizational context "calls for" or "demands" certain decisions and results. The head of the organizational unit may want a specified increase in productivity, or the task may call for a particular level of informational flow, or the employees may need some minimum amount of direction. *The situation itself is a powerful determinant of what is appropriate as a decision.*

On the other hand, the manager being a part of the situation and affected by it, cannot ignore his or her personal values in making the decision. As indicated earlier, what one manager might be happy to contend with another might find extremely unpleasant, and vice versa.

In the classroom organization, for example, every teacher has to make some decisions about an evaluation system, just as do managers of any organizational unit. In most universities there are some overall limits to the grading system imposed upon everyone, including the form in which they will be reported, the requirement that there be grades, sometimes the rough distribution among them, and so forth. *These are part of the demands of the situation.* Furthermore, the general pressures on students to perform, the requirements for work in other courses, and student attitudes about grading are also part of the situation which sets limits as to what the faculty member can do.

Nevertheless, the inclinations of the individual instructor are also an important factor in determining a grading system. Does he/she want grades to *entice* students or to *threaten* them into learning? Does he/she worry more about the student who might "beat the system" or the one who responds best to being trusted? How important does the instructor think it is to use grades for developmental feedback, so that students may improve performance, versus using grades to make final evaluations of what was learned? The teacher's own values cannot help but shape what decision is right for him/her.

Furthermore, between the demands of the situation and the values of the instructor there are many alternative ways of accommodating both. There are several variations between a complete honor system, with self-grading, and daily surprise quizzes. Often there is a certain amount of "wiggle-room" in organizations in which the decision maker can find a way to get close to what he/she wants even though the demands of the situation may not be completely favorable or "cooperative."

As a manager-scientist, it would be useful for you to be able to distinguish between what *is appropriate to the situation, what is personally desired* and *what alternatives are thus feasible.*

The rest of the course should give you ample opportunities for practicing. The text, cases, exercises and your instructor will try to help you clarify your own values and make better estimates of how well they will be served by what you do in a variety of human situations. While we would hardly claim that practice makes perfect, it should increase the probabilities of your being able to make sensible decisions which get you what you want, and enhance your ability to learn from experience.

The book is organized to help you approach decision making through

FIGURE 1–1
**The Interplay Between the Decision Maker and the
Problem Situation**

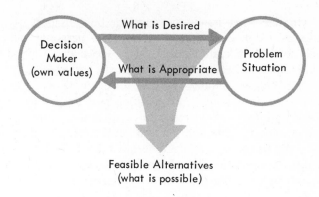

looking at various organizational areas a piece at a time. Chapter 2 provides an overview of organizations from a systems point of view, stressing the need to examine decisions in terms of their differing consequences for all the related people and groups affected by them. Chapters 3 through 6 deal with work groups and what you can do to understand and affect them positively.

Chapters 7 and 8 cover individual behavior. Chapter 7 focuses on the general needs and motivations which cause individual responses, while Chapter 8 looks at each unique person and the way in which his/her individuality shapes action.

Chapters 9 and 10 deal with relations between two people at work. Chapter 9 illuminates the kinds of relationships which are appropriate to particular work situations as well as the kinds of relationships individuals prefer, and how these perspectives mesh or conflict. Chapter 10 looks closely at the processes of relationships, paying special attention to how communication occurs or is blocked between people.

Chapter 11 then focuses more explicitly on leadership, providing ways of determining what kind of managerial behavior is appropriate to which situations.

Next, Chapter 12 examines relationships *between* groups, detailing the forces which lead to collaboration or conflict. And finally, Chapter 13 reviews all the other material in the book by helping you to determine change strategy as a manager.

The cases and exercises are all designed to put you in the position of a manager or organizational member who has to decide what is going on, what the situation calls for, what alternatives exist for resolving the problem(s) or dilemma(s) faced and ultimately, what consequences your values will permit you to accept. In the book, as in life, we do not expect perfect, easy solutions to present themselves very often; the chance to practice sorting out complexities and making informed choices can nevertheless be enjoyable if you will plunge wholeheartedly into doing it.

KEY CONCEPTS FROM CHAPTER 1

1. Basic Premise: Much of what you can learn about organizational behavior goes on around you *all the time.*
2. Central Themes:
    a. Learning from doing.
    b. The manager as scientist.
3. The Scientific Attitude is the act of comparing the intent of actions with their effects, and then learning from the process.
4. A decision-making model that considers:
    a. What is *appropriate* to the situation
       (task, people, organizational context).
    b. What is *possible.*
    c. What is *desired* by the individual(s)
       (values, goals, limits of tolerance).

SUGGESTED READINGS

Bennis, W. G. "Goals and Metagoals of Laboratory Training," *Human Relations Training News,* National Training Laboratories, Washington, D.C., 6, no. 3 (Fall 1962), pp. 1–4.

Berelson, B., and Steiner, G. *Human Behavior: An Inventory of Scientific Findings.* New York: Harcourt, Brace & World, 1964.

Bruyn, S. T. *The Human Perspective in Sociology.* Englewood Cliffs, N. J.: Prentice-Hall, Inc., 1966.

Farber, J. *The Student As Nigger.* New York: Pocket Books, 1970.

Gorman, A. H. *Teachers and Learners: The Interactive Process of Education.* Boston, Mass.: Allyn and Bacon, 1969.

Jamieson, D. W., and Thomas, K. W. "Power and Conflict in the Student-Teacher Relationship," JABS 10 (1974), 321–36.

McGregor, D. *The Professional Manager.* New York: McGraw-Hill Book Co., 1967.

Postman, N., and Weingartner, C. *Teaching As a Subversive Activity.* New York: Delacorte Press, 1969.

Rogers, C. R. *Freedom to Learn.* Columbus, Ohio: Charles E. Merrill Publishing Co., 1969.

Simon, H. A. *Administrative Behavior,* 2d Ed. New York: The Macmillan Company, 1957.

——— *The New Science of Management Decision.* New York: Harper & Row, Pubs., Inc., 1960.

A system is any set of mutually interdependent elements.

2

THE TOTAL ORGANIZATION AND THE CONCEPT OF SYSTEMS

WHY BOTHER to study organizations and the behavior of people in them? The answer is straightforward: There is almost no way you can avoid working for, dealing with, or being affected by organizations in modern life. Much of your food was probably grown on a large farm owned by a corporation, your education has been conducted in a variety of organizations, your health is probably attended to by someone in a group practice or at least affiliated with a hospital, you probably have been on a number of committees, your job will be in an organization, large or small, you will pay taxes to, be licensed and processed by various governmental organizations—and, as pointed out in Chapter 1, even your family is an organization of a special kind. Now, more than ever, "no man is an island."

Organizations are the inevitable consequence of attempting to solve complex problems. When a problem requires the efforts of more than one person, some kind of organization is necessary in order to get the work done. Whether the problem requires a few or many to work together—a pair of lumberjacks sawing logs or several hundred thousand employees to provide telephone service—the existence of an organization raises a series of fundamental questions or dilemmas which must be resolved in order to accomplish the organization's goals. Imagine what it takes to get any complex job done:

17

1. Goals must be determined, agreed upon and disseminated (goal setting).
2. Some way of making decisions about goals and all subsequent tasks must be found (decision making).
3. The various tasks necessary to achieve the goals must be divided and allocated (division of labor).
4. People who are willing to and capable of doing the tasks must be found, employed, trained and assigned to the tasks (recruiting).
5. Somehow timely information must be conveyed to those who need it to do their tasks (communications).
6. A way must be found to get organizational members to do the necessary work (motivation).
7. A way must be found to insure adequate performance of the tasks (control).
8. A way must be found to insure coordination of the tasks (coordination).
9. A way must be found to measure and modify all of the above when the conditions leading to the original goals change (environmental scanning and organizational mission).

Much of this book will be devoted to exploring aspects of these issues. The problems of trying to decide what an organization should do, who should do it, how they should divide work, coordinate efforts, and so forth, have provided challenges for thousands of years. Imagine the organization required to build the Pyramids in Egypt, or the aqueducts in the Holy Roman Empire. Even the first primitive hunting band somewhere had to decide who would do what, where they would hunt, what would happen to the hunter who was disabled, less skilled or uncooperative.

Over the centuries many ways of organizing people have been imagined. In large organizations the most frequent form is the bureaucratic hierarchy, usually represented by boxes and lines in a formal organization chart. The traditional organization chart often looks like a pyramid, with many people at the bottom of the chart and increasingly fewer at the top.

See Figure 2–1, which pictorially represents certain guidelines for how the traditional large organization will go about its work:

1. Decisions will be made by specified people, in a hierarchy which gives increasingly broader powers to those who are higher in the organization.
2. There will be a set of explicit rules governing the rights and duties of employees.
3. Labor will be divided into carefully prescribed jobs by specialty.

4. A set of procedures will govern how to deal with problems as they arise from the work.
5. Relationships will be impersonal, objective and fair.
6. Selection and promotion will be based on technical competence.

The chart implies who will have direct powers over the work activities of others, who is responsible for certain activities, and therefore who should talk to whom, and about what. The pyramidal model assumes that most problems can be foreseen in advance, logically dealt with by rules and regulations, and that positions higher in the chart indicate greater knowledge and competence as well as greater rights and powers.

The world, however, has not always arranged itself to fit this neat but oversimplified set of assumptions. Problems are not always predictable in advance; greater expertise about particular issues does not always reside in the person with the highest position in the organization. Necessary information may be possessed by those not directly interconnected on the chart, and they must interact directly or action will be unreasonably delayed. Human emotions cause bending or evasion of rules to suit individual goals. Informal relationships influence decision making even though supposedly banned by the organization.

In essence, the dynamic interconnections and interreactions among organizational members are not shown on most organization charts, and particularly are missing from the traditional pyramidal chart. Though a

FIGURE 2–1
Pyramidal Organization Chart

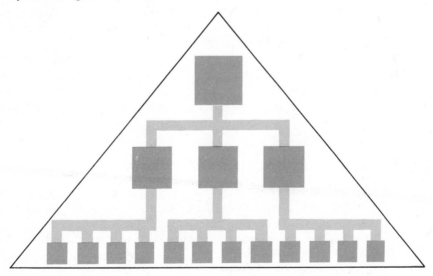

picture may be worth a thousand words, the snapshot of one aspect of an organization frozen into an organization chart can never capture the vibrant movement and groupings among members in an actual ongoing organization.

While numerous creative charts have been devised to represent the variety of organizational forms which have been invented to overcome some of the coordination problems described above, it is still necessary to find a way to discuss the interrelationships among organizational members. We need to see how individuals connect with one another to form groups, groups interact to form the organization, the organization interacts with its environment, and so on.

In order to be able to talk about organizational subparts and their relationships, we will need a special language which can enable us to see the parallels between the workings of groups and organizations of various sizes, purposes, membership, and so forth. We will want to be able to talk about commonalities (and differences) among a group of 12 assemblers in a factory, an entire insurance company, a team of teachers working out a curriculum, or a group of seven tax adjusters in a government revenue office. Though we do not want to throw out the everyday words like "group," "company," and "organization," we need a language that can incorporate all of these when necessary, and not be limited to the images associated with particular words. For example, the word "company" may imply private ownership, profits and, depending on one's orientation, either money-grubbing capitalists or efficient management. Yet even government-owned companies, such as municipal transit systems or those operating under public regulation, (for example, the phone companies), or a commune making candles as a means of support, must still deal with the same kinds of organizational issues outlined above.

Therefore, we shall utilize the language of social system analysis, which allows us to interchange the most general word "system" with "group" or "organization" when we wish to emphasize the similarities in diverse groupings. Furthermore, the word "system" emphasizes *interdependencies among subparts,* an advantage we will explain more fully below.

THE ELEMENTS AND BOUNDARIES OF A SYSTEM

A *system* is *any set of mutually interdependent elements.* Mutual interdependence means that a change in any one element causes some corresponding change in the others. An example of a simple physical system is the heating system in a house. It consists of a source of heat, a thermostat and a means of delivering heat to various parts of the house. Drops in temperature below a preset level cause the thermostat to send a signal to start the furnace, which delivers heat until the temperature rises in the house; this registers on the thermostat, which then turns off the furnace until the temperature drops again, and so on in a repetitive (and these days, increasingly expensive!) cycle. The constant interplay among these elements, mutually adjusting to maintain a roughly constant temperature in the house, demonstrates a system achieving *equilibrium*, in which the system parts are constantly tending towards a particular steady state.

> *The organism always works as a whole. We have not a liver or a heart. We are liver and heart and brain and so on. We are not a summation of parts, but a coordination . . . all these different bits that go into the making of an organism.*
>
> F. S. Perls
> *Gestalt Therapy Verbatim*

In order to achieve equilibrium, the system depends upon various *feedback* mechanisms. The thermostat cannot make the "decision" to turn the furnace on or off without "information" from the surrounding air. (Note Figure 2–2.) Imagine, for example, if a member of the household hung a coat over the thermostat. The feedback cycle would be disrupted; the thermostat would receive inaccurate information ("The room is very warm.") and would signal the furnace to shut off, irrespective of the actual temperature of the air (now blocked off by the coat) in the room. *The control mechanisms that maintain equilibrium in any system are dependent upon accurate feedback from various parts of the system and its surrounding environment.*

It is usually easy to identify the *boundaries* of a physical system in

FIGURE 2–2
Heating System in a Home

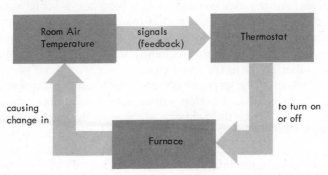

relation to the environment in which it exists. The heating system's three components are affected by external factors such as weather outdoors, quality of insulation in the house, temperature desired by the inhabitants, cost of fuel, and so forth, yet can be easily identified as separate from these other factors. Nevertheless, the heating system can also be seen, depending on one's interests, as a subpart of other larger systems which include these external factors: the lighting-heating-plumbing (support) system of the house, the house relative to other houses, a contributor to human pollution systems, and so forth. Thus how broadly or narrowly we bound a system is a strategic decision based on what will work for the problem(s) needing solution.

These issues (equilibrium, boundaries, and subsystems) are even more complex when looking at *human social* organizations.

A social system can also be seen as consisting of a set of mutually interdependent elements, which when viewed together as an organized whole, can be given a boundary separating the interrelated elements from their environment. For social systems the elements are *behavior* and *attitudes.* An interrelated set of behaviors (interactions and activities) and attitudes (perceptions, feelings, and values) comprise a social system.[1] Since interactions, or exchanges between people, are assumed to be connected with all other elements (by definition), and thus are observable and countable, they can be used to help draw boundaries around social systems. *Boundaries can* thus *be* operationally *defined by the relative number of interactions among any set of people.* For particular analytical purposes *a social system is any number of people who have relatively more interactions with one another than with others.*

Implicit in this definition is the notion that virtually any system is a subsystem in some larger system(s), since the system is delimited by *relative* numbers of interactions. Just as the house heating system for some purposes can be seen as the total system, say if checking out the accuracy of the thermostat, but for other purposes is a subsystem in a larger system, any group of people can be viewed from several perspectives. All the vice presidents in a bank are a social system in that they interact more with one another than with the tellers, but vice-presidents and tellers together form another system, since all employees interact with one another more frequently than with, for example, the employees of other banks in the same city.

And like the physical system, which tends toward equilibrium, social systems tend to develop self-adjusting behaviors which stabilize relationships, make the behavior of those in the system more predictable to members than it would be to others, and perpetuate the system's goals.

As you might guess, the larger the system in question, the more tenuous are the interdependencies. If we talk of the American people as

---

[1] These terms are our adaptations of the conceptual scheme of George Homans, elaborated more fully for small groups in Chapter 3.

a social system, it may well be true that the way you relate to classmates is affected by and affects the way parents treat children 2,000 miles away, but the connections are not readily traceable and may be unproveable anyway. For our purposes in this book, we will focus on social systems with more easily observable boundaries and interconnections.

For example, a very common, practical and often beautiful mutually-regulating social system is a mother and her breast-fed young child. The child's initial sucking signals the milk to begin producing, and the more the child sucks, the more is produced. Over several days the production stabilizes to meet the child's capacity, and remains there until the child grows and gets hungrier, when extra sucking calls forth a higher production level. This process continues until the child is fed some solid foods, which decrease its appetite for milk, decreasing the number and amount of nursings, which lowers milk production gradually towards weaning. Furthermore, during the nursing months, the mother and child become so finely tuned to one another that the mother's breasts remain relatively empty between feedings, but fill with milk at the baby's first hungry cry, even before sucking has begun. In addition, the softness of the baby's skin and the warmth of the mother's breasts reinforce each's enjoyment of the cradling position that goes with nursing, and provide strong, loving, protective bonds, which help generate the care from the mother needed by the baby and the responsiveness from the baby needed by the mother.

FUNCTIONAL AND DYSFUNCTIONAL ASPECTS OF A SYSTEM

While it seems a pity to introduce a discordant note into the mother-child relationship, we can use this same example to illustrate another important aspect of social systems thinking. The baby's hungry cry, so useful for notifying the mother that the baby wants feeding, and for stimulating the milk to "let down" into the breasts, can also have some less pleasant consequences. The mother and child usually are part of some other social systems, including some combinations of the father, other children, guests, and neighbors. The baby's cry, *functional* to feeding, can also serve to wake father at 4 A.M. (when he might be good company, but not much help), arouse jealousy in other children at the attention it gets, and irritate others trying to concentrate on sleep. Thus, the same behavior can be functional in one system but *dysfunctional* in some others. That is, it can serve a useful purpose in maintaining one system while having negative consequences for the maintenance of others.

Let us see how that can be true in a larger organizational setting. In most organizations those who reach executive ranks do so not only because of technical skill or knowledge, but also because their behavior "fits," that is, makes other executives comfortable to be with them.

Knowing how to behave at the country club, on the golf course, or in the executive dining room is often an important consideration in attaining promotion. (Of course, in another organization the settings in which "proper" behavior is judged might be different. Remember the informal touch football games that President Kennedy's closest aides just happened to love playing?) Selecting executives by how they fit socially into the higher echelon's particular pastimes can in the short run be highly functional for maintaining harmony. Especially where the potentials for conflict and disagreement are great, as they always are at the top of a large organization, it is much more comfortable to limit fights to those who are "one of our kind," whatever that kind happens to be.

Yet the consequences of using such criteria as part of the selection process can be, and have been, extremely dysfunctional for many groups shut out of the top ranks by color, sex, ethnicity, or background. There are surely many more talented leaders among blacks, women, Jews and non-Ivy League graduates than appear, for example, among the top ranks of most banks and insurance companies. Not only is the organization ultimately deprived of vast pools of talent and different points of view, but each of the groups are disproportionately kept from advancing, obtaining higher salaries and power.

Thus, what is, at least for a while, quite functional in one system, can be dysfunctional in others because they have different objectives. And, as is hinted at in the executive example, *the same behavior can be both functional (promoting harmony) and dysfunctional (reducing talent and diversity available) within a system.* Any act can be analyzed in terms of how well it serves to sustain over time, in relation to surrounding environments, the system(s) in which it occurs. The value one places on whether an act is dysfunctional or not depends on one's point of view. A functional behavior in a system one disagrees with can be considered "bad" (for example, teaching more effective surveillance tactics to the private police of a dictator) and a dysfunctional act in a system one disagrees with can be considered "good" (for example, a new assembly worker refusing to go along with the restrictive output of his work group and exposing them to management).

The Foreman   The foreman provides an illustration of the difficulty of being functional in all systems. In a modern plant he often is called the man-in-the-middle. This means that on the one hand management expects him to "get the work out from the workers" and push for higher production, while on the other hand the workers, some of whom the foreman has probably worked with as an equal, expect him to be "one-of-the-boys" and understand their problems in attaining, or reasons for not wanting to attain, higher production. Using the language of social systems, the foreman has membership in two different systems with conflicting goals; he finds this a difficult position. Often it can only be solved by withdrawal and depersonalization from the workers; in effect, by giving up his membership in their system. Or he may become extremely permissive with and protective of the workers; in effect, conspiring with them to keep undesirable information from flowing upwards. In this case, he has forfeited membership in the management system, or has at least tried to. Management may not be quite so willing to lose him and may, in fact, put even more pressure on him to increase production. Their efforts feed back on him and perpetuate the problem.

But beside the two group systems, management and workers, and the larger system — management, foreman, workers — the foreman's personality system is also involved. The foreman has some views of his own integrity, goals, and ambitions. If he were one kind of man he would be concerned about getting ahead in the organization, and would respond to the pressure from management by transmitting the pressure to the workers under him. Leaving aside for a moment the possible negative consequences this pressure might have on his ability to secure cooperation from the workers, we can say that the action "pressure on workers" would be functional both for the management system, insofar as it maintains it, and for the foreman's personality system. By conforming to management's desires, the foreman can also satisfy his own.

If, however, the foreman values highly the friendship of the men he works with, he may reject management's pressure completely, and behave as if his position were no different from the men under him. In this case, the pressure, which is functional for management because it maintains management's beliefs about "the nature of workers" and "management's right to manage," is dysfunctional for the foreman. To behave that way would not be consistent with his own values. Thus, the same act might be functional for one system, yet dysfunctional for another.

Here, however, as elsewhere, the situation may be even more complicated by unintended and unanticipated consequences, which can follow from any particular act. In the example above, management's pressure may be functional to the maintenance of what it believes about good managing, but may also be in part a *cause* for the need for pressure. Pressure applied repeatedly may cause workers to feel mistrusted, therefore resentful, therefore less cooperative, therefore "requiring" more pressure. The pressure becomes part of a larger system of interdependent relationships, in which management behavior towards workers is both cause and effect of worker behavior, and vice versa. Though the pressure may reinforce management solidarity by "confirming" its beliefs about workers, in the larger system, presumably designed to make profits for the enterprise as a whole, the pressure may not be as useful as it appears to management.

In short, there may be functional and dysfunctional effects of the same behavior; whether or not the behavior is functional depends on the sys-

tem in which one judges the behavior. Consequences unintended by the person often occur because too few or wrong systems are considered when anticipating results. One of the administrator's key tasks is to ensure that behavior which is functional for particular subsystems, but dysfunctional for the organization as a whole, is somehow modified so that the total organization does not suffer. This is easier said than done and much of this course will be aimed at giving you practice in making changes that do not backfire.

OPENNESS OF SYSTEMS AND TRANSFORMATION PROCESSES

Throughout this discussion of social systems we have only referred in passing to the environment of the system. In effect, we have talked as if the various systems used as examples were sealed off from their environments, more or less *closed* to outside influences. That was necessary to simplify discussion of a complex subject, but now that you have completely mastered the systems concept (!), we can go on to complicate matters a bit.

Ultimately, all organizations are open systems, that is, engaged in constant transactions with their environments, which usually consist of a number of other systems. An organization receives *inputs* from its surroundings, in the form of finances, raw materials, people, ideas, equipment, and so forth. It then does something to the inputs, in a *transformation process,* such as machining pieces, assembling parts, processing information, calculating numbers, building facilities, and treating patients. After these *internal operations* it sends some kind of finished *output* back into the environment, ranging from tangible products like automobiles and refrigerators, to changed people like recovered patients or educated students, to idea products like reports, analyses, or announcements. The outputs, in turn, become inputs to other systems.

FIGURE 2–3
An Open System

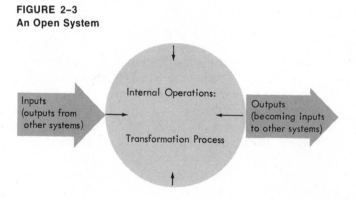

Since organizations are so interrelated with their environments, to remain in equilibrium they must make constant adjustments in the way they operate in order to take into account and cope with changes in inputs and demand for outputs. For example, when wool shortages send prices soaring in the carpet industry, substitutes, such as Acrilan, must be found and developed in order not to exceed the price range of most consumers. A marketing research firm might collect new data on attitudes from carefully defined groupings, and even redefine its sampling group as income levels and population movements shift. A government agency which is responsible for promoting foreign trade might stay in touch with changes in congressional laws, presidential policy, and foreign government attitudes in order to provide useful guidelines. On the output side, organizational systems need to stay aware of changes in demand, whether for compact cars, liberal arts graduates, or rented warehouse space. Drastic decreases in demand can easily threaten an organization's survival.

All of these environmental changes can and do affect the internal transformation process. *Any system will make adjustments in policies, rules, regulations and other operating behavior in order to attempt to survive and maintain itself in relation to its environment.*

> *A hen is only an egg's way of making another egg.*
> Samuel Butler
> *Life and Habit*

Though organizations often make mistakes, either in interpreting environmental changes or in attempting to compensate for them, the organization will attempt to do what is functional for its survival. One classic example was the March of Dimes organization shifting to other childhood diseases when polio, its original reason for existing, was conquered. Similarly, open *social* systems in organizations are very much affected by the environment around them. The attitudes members bring with them from the wider culture, the particular people who are available to join the system, economic conditions and their effects on member alternatives for employment, are all factors that affect behavior within the system. For example, when (1) jobs are readily available, (2) young college graduates are the main group of employees, and (3) there is widespread disillusionment with institutions in general, the ability of administrators successfully to give direct, arbitrary orders, without explanation, is likely to be considerably diminished.

Further, the minimum quality and quantity of work that is acceptable to whomever receives the social systems output will also affect internal operations. If the system is a total organization, the customers or clients will have considerable influence over the end products, and their response will often force internal adjustments fostering greater chances of survival.

If the system is a subsystem of an organization, like a work team on the shop floor, or a group of nursing administrators, its "clients" will be other parts of the organization, including management, and pressures for the appropriate quality and quantity of output will include everything from general disapproval and loss of privileges to reduced pay and threats of firing.

In general, then, any system must make at least minimal alterations in its internal operations, based on feedback from its environment, in order to survive. To increase the effectiveness of the system frequent and delicate adjustments are necessary; the more complex the system the more difficult the adjustments.

THE INTERCONNECTEDNESS OF SUBSYSTEMS AND LEVELS

While much of this book treats environmental facts as givens, or constants, in order to focus on internal relationships and their consequences, it is important to be aware of the connections of any of the systems we look at (small group, individual, interpersonal, leadership and intergroup) to the systems and subsystems surrounding them. The power in systems thinking lies in remembering to trace through what is connectable to what; to check to see if (1) a behavior that does not at first make sense can be seen to be functional to *some* system(s) and (2) a change in one aspect of a system will lead to other changes which are in the desired direction. Many a manager's greatest difficulties occur when he/she starts to solve a problem in one subsystem without seeing its connections and roots in a wider setting. Managers who forget to use the observation powers of scientists to test if they are addressing the right problem are like Americans traveling in a foreign country who speak English to a non-English speaking resident, and when not understood, repeat the same phrase over again, s-l-o-w-l-y and LOUDER.

For example, we have seen managers, excited by the management development tool, sensitivity training, try to solve problems of unclear and ambiguous job responsibilities by sending all their subordinates off to "bare their souls." After the executives have revealed their feelings about one another, gotten closer and pledged cooperation, the same squabbling over assignments and over territorial rights breaks out again because higher-level management fears delegating responsibility and has still not clarified what is expected of the subordinates. Not only do the original problems remain unsolved, but a potentially useful training tool for some situations gets a bad name.

It is important, therefore, periodically to shift focus from problem relationships within a subsystem to the links of that subsystem with others. For example, sometimes a fish is the last one to discover water, exactly because water is "always" there. The fish can spend its time worrying about its food and digestion as long as it is in the water and breathing automatically. Only when it is yanked out of the water does it notice its absence. With people as with fish, it often takes a catastrophe, (or an outside observer) to make visible the fundamental interconnections between the system and its environment. It is helpful, then, to occasionally take a detached view of puzzling behavior and ask *what function it is serving for whom,* rather than too quickly judge it harshly as irrelevant, wasteful, immoral, or foolish. Systems thinking encourages *understanding and acceptance of others' behavior,* at least as a first step in viewing organizations.

EQUILIBRIUM VERSUS CHANGE IN SYSTEMS

As indicated earlier, every system has a tendency to maintain a state of balance, or *equilibrium.* When the flow of raw materials into a manufacturing firm is balanced by the flow of products out of the company, that system can be described as maintaining a state of equilibrium. Should machinery break down, workers go on strike, poor planning occur, and so forth (all transformation processes), then the system gets thrown out of balance; management then devotes its attention to the re-establishment of equilibrium (repair the machinery, settle the strike, revise schedules, and so forth). The process is similar to the way the human body works, when it experiences stress from disease or accident. One or another subsystem (such as circulatory, autonomic, and respiratory), or a combination of them, mobilizes to re-establish the balance of survival-related processes. Remember the nursing infant? Note how crying occurs if the breast is withdrawn too soon, giving immediate feedback to the mother so that she will do what is necessary to restore equilibrium!

While the *survival* of a system depends upon its ability to maintain a basic state of equilibrium, its *development* often depends upon the ability to re-align aspects of its subsystems and modify its transformation processes; this makes dis-equilibrium at times inevitable and desirable. The infant cannot nurse forever; to survive he/she must change and adapt to the demands of a complex social environment. *In short, every system works toward an internal state of equilibrium by maintaining its existing balance of forces (the status quo); at the same time, every system struggles to respond to the pressures for change as the surrounding environment demands it.* The dilemma is obvious; equilibrium means comfort, lack of tension, the familiar, and so forth, while change means discomfort, tension, and the unfamiliar.

While you need not accept the status quo just because you understand its functions better, we suggest that you maintain a healthy respect for the resistance of systems to change as well as for the ability of system members to re-establish equilibrium when new inputs are attempted by managers. If every system changed continually, life would be just too confusing and unpredictable to act. One confirmation of this emerged from Freud's work; it was the realization that even neurotic behavior causing great pain to an individual will be clung to as long as it is providing more satisfaction to the person than the uncertain rewards of giving it up. In systems terms, if one of the interdependent elements gives at least partial satisfaction to the personality system, it may persist despite its partially dysfunctional consequences for the total system. In fact, the individual system may be sustaining or integrating itself by the very tension that exists between the functional and dysfunctional consequences of various elements.

Larger social systems, like individual systems, can persist for long periods of time with some dysfunctional elements; remember the managing system which was partly causing worker resistance as well as trying to overcome it? Groups, as well as individuals, may persist in behavior that is less than fully functional for the maintenance of the total system if partial satisfaction of some needs is being derived from the behavior. Present partial satisfactions are often preferred over uncertain future ones, because the costs involved in attaining new satisfactions may not seem worth the risk involved.

The known devil may indeed be better than the unproven angel; many systems have learned to cope effectively with "the devil," while comparatively few know what to do with angels when they are encountered! While it would be foolish to deliberately organize for dysfunctional consequences, it is not always easy to be rid of them once they are noticed. But since all administrators, (and certainly you) are on the side of the angels (by definition), you should at least be conscious of the workings of the systems you are trying to deal with or manage, and the reasons why so many devilish dysfunctionalities have managed to stay inside those systems for so long.

KEY CONCEPTS FROM CHAPTER 2

1. Fundamental issues for any organization to accomplish its work:
   a. Goals.
   b. Decision making.
   c. Division of labor.
   d. Recruiting.

      e. Communications.

      f. Motivation.

      g. Control.

      h. Coordination.

      i. Environmental scanning and organizational mission.

2. A system is any set of mutually interdependent elements; system and subsystems defined by respective *boundaries.*

3. A social system is defined by the relative number of interactions among its components.

4. Open systems:

      a. Seek to maintain equilibrium.

      b. Input from surroundings.

      c. Transformation process.

      d. Output into environment.

      e. Input to other systems.

5. Closed systems — sealed off from their environments.

SUGGESTED READINGS

Beckett, J. A. *Management Dynamics; The New Synthesis.* New York: McGraw-Hill Book Co., 1971.

Bertalanffy, L. von *General Systems Theory: Foundations, Development, Applications.* New York: George Braziller, Inc., 1968.

Churchman, C. West *The Systems Approach.* New York: Dell Publishing Co., 1968.

Drucker, Peter F. *Technology, Management and Society.* New York: Harper & Row Pubs., Inc., 1970.

Hall, R. H. *Organizations, Structure and Process.* Englewood Cliffs, N. J.: Prentice-Hall, Inc., 1972.

Katz, D., and Kahn, R. L. *The Social Psychology of Organizations.* New York: John Wiley & Sons, Inc., 1966.

Lawrence, P. R., and Lorsch, J. W. "Differentiation and Integration in Complex Organizations," *Administrative Science Quarterly.* 12 (1967) 2.

———— *Organization and Environment,* Boston, Mass., Division of Research, Graduate School of Business, Harvard University, 1967.

Leighton, A. H. "The Functional Point of View," *Human Relations in a Changing World.* New York: E. P. Dutton and Co., Inc., 1949, pp. 156–61.

Likert, R. *The Human Organization: Its Management and Value.* New York: McGraw-Hill Book Co., 1967.

Miles, R. E. *Theories of Management: Implications for Organizational Behavior and Development.* New York: McGraw-Hill Book Co., 1975.

Schein, Edgar H. *Organizational Psychology.* 2d ed., Englewood Cliffs, N. J.: Prentice-Hall, Inc., 1970.

Seiler, J. A. *Systems Analysis in Organizational Behavior.* Homewood, Ill.: Richard D. Irwin, Inc. and the Dorsey Press, 1967.

Woodward, J. *Industrial Organization: Theory and Practice.* Fair Lawn, N. J.: Oxford University Press, 1965.

The technology both sets limits on what social interactions and emergent behavior are possible and causes various interactions to occur. Even noise level affects the likelihood of social discourse.

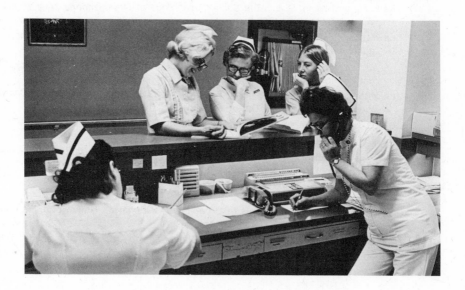

3

THE WORK GROUP   ONE of the most important and common types of subsystems in any organization is the work group. Though many students and managers think of organizations as consisting of a collection of individuals, each doing a separate and distinct job, much of the world's work is actually done in some kind of group. Even when the individual employee is not formally assigned to a clearly defined group of people, much of his/her work will likely be carried out in conjunction with a particular set of other people, and feelings of "being part of a group" will emerge. Even executives, who often like to think of themselves as "rugged individualists," seldom work alone or in isolation, and are members of

a top management team, many committees, task forces, study groups, and so forth, which directly affect their success or failure in the organization.

Yet it is not easy to work effectively in a group. Anyone who has ever had to coordinate activities and come to decisions in conjunction with several other people will remember at times having felt something like, "If only I could get rid of the others, I could do this job much better by myself, and save a lot of time, too!" Working together, at least in most Western, individualistic cultures, is not easily or automatically accomplished.

Why then is group work so recurrent? There are a variety of reasons; perhaps the most important is that few jobs can be done alone. It takes more than one person's energy, knowledge, skills and time to get most any complicated job done. Furthermore, when tasks are at all complex, a division of labor makes it possible to use individual efforts more systematically, and to take advantage of different talents and skills. A committee studying ways to cut fuel consumption in a company, for example, could have all members engage in the same research and discussion activities, but the complexities of the task make it desirable to divide up the work. One member might review technical literature, another survey the existing heating/cooling system, a third investigate what other companies have done, another check costs of conversion to alternate fuels, and so forth.

Yet in such a committee, as in other group activities where participants have different assignments from one another, activities must somehow be coordinated in order not to duplicate efforts, leave something undone, or work at cross purposes. Thus a group must find a way to allocate work, coordinate activities, define and agree upon goals, and then gain the commitments of members to carry out the group's work in a manner consistent with its objectives.

Groups also exist for another, more personal set of reasons. Even where a task does not call for coordinated effort, people working near one another often form relationships to fill social needs for conversation, companionship, or friendship. Human beings are social animals, and seem to need human association as much as they need food and drink; infants deprived of human contact do not develop well, even when properly clothed and fed. So groups often form for reasons above and beyond needs for task coordination. Indeed, for many members of work groups, individual needs for social relationship may be even more powerful in affecting behavior than organizational objectives.

Long before getting jobs, everyone has developed considerable experience with groups; they are the primary units of all social systems. Most people are born into a group—the family—and spend the greater part of their lives living, working, and playing in a wide variety of groups. When young, they belonged to gangs or clubs. As they grow up they tend to move into social settings where group belonging gives support, and provides avenues to do things they could not do by themselves. Thus it is not surprising that in the work world people continue to find groups to be a principal vehicle for carrying out tasks, not solely to seek superior organization goals through collective effort, but to meet individual needs as well.

What is more surprising is how difficult it is for groups in organizations to be effective and satisfying to their members. Occasionally this is caused by groups being utilized to do what could better be executed by one individual, as implied in the old joke: "A camel is a horse designed by a committee." More often, however, groups are just not run effectively; members do not know how to help the group take fullest advantage of its potential. We will address this issue in depth in Chapter 6 because we believe that the ability to help make a group function effectively can be learned and is worth learning. Thus we aim to help you improve both your *understanding* of how task groups work and your *skills* at getting what you want from the work groups of which you become a member.

Though many of the concepts we will introduce apply equally well to nonorganizational groups, we will focus on those that are task oriented because at least half of adult waking life is spent at work and most education does not give emphasis to this important area of concern. Nonwork applications of what is learned can be a personal bonus for mastering the course materials.

Since you have probably had some experience in groups, we can call upon your past experiences to bring to life the several concepts we need to build on. For example, you probably remember groups in which you played a dominant part and others in which you were more on the sidelines, times when you were part of the "in-group" and times when you were on the "outs." Perhaps you can think about some of the groups of which you are currently or have recently been a member. How are they organized? What is your place in them? Who controls them? Is there equality among members or a "pecking order?" These are the kinds of questions we will be addressing throughout the next few chapters.

It is the answer to these questions, among others, that will help to give you a better understanding of how groups function and what determines the effectiveness of a group in meeting its goals. As we go along, we will encourage you to use your own immediate and past experiences to validate the theories and concepts that will be introduced. Most of these concepts will also be directly applicable to the classroom setting and will help you to understand various aspects of your own experiences as the course unfolds. You should come out with a better sense of the consequences of your own membership in various groups, how your sense of individuality is affected, and how you can strike a balance among (1) your needs, (2) those of other individual members, and (3) the needs of the group as an entity.

HOW DO YOU KNOW WHEN A GROUP IS?

What exactly do we mean by a "group?" Is it any collection of individuals like strangers at a bus stop, or is it something more? As explained in Chapter 2, any social system is defined by the relative number of interactions among its components. Though the boundary can be drawn anywhere, depending on one's purpose, work groups often are clearly identifiable to others and to their own members. From now on we will use the word "group" to mean small face-to-face groups, consisting of more than 2 people and usually no more than 12 or 15. Such a group has an existence over an extended period of time, tends to see itself as separate and distinguishable from others around it, and has members who are mutually aware of their membership. As noted in the beginning of this chapter, some organizational groups are not formally defined as such, but function nevertheless as distinguishable units.

If a group appears to its members as a useful vehicle for meeting individual needs, then keeping relationships going among members of any group becomes an end in itself. This is why the size of the group is an important factor. If a group becomes too large, it is difficult for the members to maintain direct personal relations and there is an increasing chance of fragmentation into subgroups.

In summary, then, we can determine the existence of a group by noting its *size*, its *degree of differentiation from other groups*, the *existence of personal relations that have some duration, identification of the members with the group*, and often some *common goals*.

By defining groups in this way we include the following types:

1. Those groups which are permanent parts of an ongoing organization, like departments or work teams.
2. Temporary task groups like committees or special problem-solving groups whose life is compressed into a defined span of time.
3. Groups which are voluntarily formed purely for friendship or other social needs as noted earlier; these will not be our focus, but must be considered since they exist within and across types (1) and (2) above and directly influence these formal system groups.

You might like to note the characteristics of any groups of which you are a member and to share these with other students both within and outside of the groups in question. This process should give you a clearer sense of the existence of each group. It might also provide you with some perspective on the degree to which your memberships in a number of different groups at one time influence the pattern of your own life.

AN EFFECTIVE WORKING GROUP FEELS GOOD

No doubt you have been in a group that was really frustrating. Somehow things didn't quite click, the members did not seem to be able to put together their energies in useful ways, spirit was lacking, commitment and interest were low, issues were never resolved, and so on. If you have been fortunate, you may have at some time been in a group where the opposite was true; the group felt as if it was moving, growing, and achieving something. The members felt invigorated and mutually enhanced by one another. Everyone looked forward to being and working together. This all too rare kind of group experience leaves members with a good feeling, both about themselves and about groups in general. Despite the infrequent occurrence of such satisfying groups, we believe that many groups have the potential for becoming effective and exciting contexts for both work and social needs. And we assert that the more you understand about the workings of groups, the more competent you can become in making them into such settings.

THE NEED FOR SOME CONCEPTS

How do you begin sorting out all the components of what makes groups tick? As a manager–scientist, you need some tools to let you look at various aspects of what is going on in a work group, one piece at a time, and then fit the pieces together so that you can understand their interrelationships and effects upon one another. Though in actuality no social system sits still while you hold different parts constant, for analytical purposes we will take the liberty of talking as if various components of a work group can be separately examined. Only then can you begin to improve your ability to affect the behavior of the groups of which you are a member.

We will start by introducing a Basic Social System Conceptual Scheme which will help you to organize the pieces and put together the puzzle of why a group has developed in its particular way, and what might be done to alter its development. We will offer a series of propositions—tentative hypotheses—which you can use to explain the ways in which groups draw their members together and sort out their individual contributions. After looking at how groups integrate and differentiate their members (Chapters 4 and 5), we will discuss the concept of group effectiveness and how to judge the workings of a group under different conditions (Chapter 6). By then you should be more skilled in understanding what goes on in groups and have some better handles on how to explain the achievements of a successful group.

THE BASIC SOCIAL SYSTEM CONCEPTUAL SCHEME

In Chapter 2 you were introduced to the concept of a social system, consisting of two mutually interdependent elements: *behavior* and *attitudes*.[1] We will now look at groups in depth, expanding on the concepts to heighten their analytical usefulness. *Interactions—exchanges of words or objects among two or more members—*were mentioned as particularly crucial types of behavior since their frequency helps determine system boundaries, friendships and other feelings. Other types of behavior can be categorized as *activities—that which members do while they are in the group except for their interactions with other people—*such as operating a machine, writing on paper, issuing a license, and so forth. In addition to these kinds of work-related activities, there are likely to be a variety of non-work activities such as drinking coffee, listening to music, tapping a pipe on the table, and so forth.

Attitudes constitute the other category used for sorting out the parts of a social system. These can include neutral perceptions: ("Whenever I help Charley, he smiles."); feelings: ("I like my job."); or values: ("Nothing is more important than being honest in my dealings with the people I work with.") Perhaps the most important type of attitudes are those which members of any group inevitably develop about how members-in-good-standing *ought* to behave in that group. These attitudes we call *norms;* they are the cement which holds a group together, because they tell members exactly what behavior is believed desirable to foster the group's goals and maintain its existence. *Norms are group members' beliefs about what behavior is appropriate and attainable in a specific situation.* Behind every norm is the implicit statement: "Follow this norm because if you don't the group will be harmed somehow." For example, some common norms in student groups are: "Don't act as if you're trying to impress the person with authority" (as in, "Don't brown-nose the teacher"), "Don't act like a big deal," "Participate at least a little, but don't dominate the conversation," "Try not to say anything which will hurt other members' feelings." Can you see what members of a student group might perceive as the dangers if these norms were not followed?

Norms such as these are not always explicit; often they are understood implicitly (or assumed to be understood). Frequently the only way a norm is observable is by inadvertantly breaking it and seeing others' reactions. Norms can only be inferred from watching actual behavior,

---

[1] The balance of this chapter is our adaptation of the work of George C. Homans in *The Human Group,* and *Social Behavior: Its Elementary Forms.*

FIGURE 3–1
The Elements of a Social System
(all mutually interdependent)

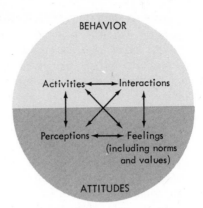

since they are not the behavior itself but the *beliefs* in members' minds about what behavior should be. Therefore, while behavior common to all members of a group usually indicates existence of a norm, it may also just be coincidental or customary. Some checking out of what members believe, or observing whether a nonconformer is punished, may be necessary to establish a norm's existence.

Since norms are not universal—in some executive groups, for example, it may be considered phoney *not* to try to impress the boss, or weak *not* to dominate conversations—each group develops its own norms which give the group its particular character. And very often, groups feel not only that their norms are useful ways of guiding members' behavior but are inevitable, correct and better than any possible alternatives. Thus violation of the norms by current members or even members of other groups is judged quite harshly.

Have you ever entered a new group and found that quite accidentally you have violated members' notions of "proper" behavior? One of the authors of this book was raised in a family where he was encouraged to give honest reactions to food served him. When he was offered fish at his prospective mother-in-law's house the first time he was invited there, he almost caused a major blowup by responding—as politely as he knew how—that he did not usually care for fish but would be willing to try a small portion. To a Southern housewife this was the height of inconsiderateness; in the author's family, taking what you did not like was considered to be a waste of good food.

At the New York Times the cub reporters sit in the last row of desks . . .; as they prove themselves they move up row by row. Beginning reporters who unknowingly sit at a vacant desk a row or two up from the back are politely but firmly told where they belong.

Kim Foltz
Harper's, July 1974

Another important type of attitudes is *values*. While *norms are shared ideas of "correct" behavior in the group, values are more fundamental notions of ideal behavior, usually unattainable because they are perfect ideals, but to be strived for.* Values are seldom explicit but very much shape how members interpret events and form expectations about behavior.

For example, in some groups members believe that it is "right" that individuals should always put group needs ahead of their own personal interests. Individuals are expected to subordinate their desires for the betterment of the total group. An extreme version of this value is found in the traditional families in India, where even marriage and career choice are made by elders with overall family benefit in mind. The extreme opposite of such values might be found in a contemporary American family where each child is taught from an early age to listen to his/her conscience and make choices accordingly.

In a work setting, such group values as "Get the work out no matter what," "Put the welfare of fellow workers ahead of the company's demands," "Don't let work spoil good relationships," or, "Everyone should look out for his own interests," strongly determine how members will behave.

Quite often, however, conflicting values may be held by various members of a group, or even by one member; this can cause serious tension at crucial times. For example, individual freedom and choice is a commonly held value, but so is the patriotic belief in "my country, right or wrong." In groups there are often values differences underlying questions of how important it is to talk through strong disagreements: "Majority rules" (so outvoted members should accept defeat gracefully) versus "peace at any price" (so dissatisfied members must somehow be placated). Later we will consider why groups made up of similar (if not some of the same) individuals may develop very different norms.

OBSERVING A SOCIAL SYSTEM

In your attempts as a manger-scientist to observe behavior, interactions, feelings, norms, and values in a group, and ultimately to analyze them for some kind of action, you will need to heighten your skills in both observation and inference. Activities and interactions can be observed directly, by watching, counting, noting both frequency and who is involved. Though accurate observation of activities is not easy, it is more straightforward than figuring out underlying group feelings, norms, and values. Norms are not written on members' foreheads for all to see, even though they govern behavior; they usually have to be inferred from what members say and do. For example, dirty looks and a crack about broken

down cars directed at a latecomer to a meeting can be reasonably inferred to mean that one norm is: Members are expected to be punctual.
A student who wears a tie and jacket to class when most students come in
jeans and denim shirts may get some comments which make him uncomfortable, even though there are no formal dress rules. Norms about dress
can then be deduced from both observations of what people are wearing
and how they react to someone who is dressed differently. Because norms
are so important for understanding groups, we need to find a way to discover where norms come from and how they operate to regulate group
behavior.

REQUIRED VERSUS EMERGENT BEHAVIOR

A helpful conceptual distinction in tracing the source of norms is to
separate out that part of a group's behavior and attitudes which is *required* or *given* by the larger system (organization) of which it is a part,
and that which emerges from the interactions of the group. The required
component (which we shall call the *required system*) usually centers on
the tasks assigned to the group: assemble so many parts per hour, sell
so many machines per month, visit so many welfare clients per week, and
so forth. Most organizations, however, also require certain other behavior and attitudes which are assumed to relate to effective carrying out
of the task. Usually, there are (1) some *required activities* like the
task-related ones above, (2) some *required interactions:* "Get the forms
from clerk A, inquire if there are any more, and after checking them over,
give agent C an assignment" and (3) some *required attitudes:* "Don't
be insolent when receiving instructions," or "Be loyal to our products,"
or "Don't make fun of the clients." These "requirements," are part of
the norms developed by the organization and are frequently called the
"formal system." They are usually contained in job descriptions and organizational rulebooks, and in orders from superiors, though sometimes
they are just seen as "part of the job" and are not spelled out. Often they
are strongly influenced by the technology and physical layout of the
group's working space; for example, if the person to whom you have to
give a report has a secretary sitting in an outer office, it will probably
be a requirement to interact with that secretary about the timing of your
visit with the person whom you want to see. Similarly, if two radio assemblers are working at benches which face each other, with parts in the
middle, a certain amount of interaction will be required to coordinate
efforts.

Inevitably, however, because people are social beings, with needs
greater and more complex than those of machines, a variety of behavior
and attitudes will begin to *emerge* and over time take on relatively stable

patterns. Making frequent appointments through a secretary leads to small talk, and slowly to some kind of relationship in which a greater amount of information, ideas, feelings are exchanged than a few informational questions about the boss's availability. The worker at the opposite bench, with whom coordination is necessary, ventures opinions and complaints, suggests having a coffee break together, slowly becomes a friend and perhaps visits you when you're sick. In these kinds of ways, a social system elaborates itself, leading to *emergent* and lasting behavior and attitudes that go way beyond what was originally required just to do the job. Some of what emerges will be elaboration on how to do the task, how much to produce, and so on, while the remainder will be related to purely social relationships such as who has coffee with whom, and who likes whom, *In both cases, it is this emergent (informal) system which gives a group its particular identity,* its view of who should do what, who should have influence, how close members should feel, and so forth.

FIGURE 3–2
Separating the Required from the Emergent System

Accordingly, it is this emergent system which often influences the performance of a group as much as, or more than, the required one. It is important to understand the significance and potency of emergent systems since they can outweigh even formal orders which are issued from above. Emergent social systems acquire their own life which is connected to but goes beyond what is required by the formal organization.

It is important to note that a well-developed emergent system with strong norms for behavior, can feel to any member as if the group-approved behavior is "required" of him/her. For example, if there is a strongly enforced emergent norm that "each member must produce at least 80 parts per hour," this may feel like a "requirement" to the new group member even though management may not formally require any particular hourly output. For our purposes behavior "demanded" by a group of its members is still called *emergent* provided that it is a result of group ideas rather than forced, organizational requirements imposed from outside the group.

BACKGROUND FACTORS

But how can we connect what emerges to what is required? Don't "personalities" and personal preferences make more difference than the requirements of the job? That indeed is a question worth exploring.

Personal Systems

People do bring something of their history with them when they enter a group. The values and feelings they have about what kind of behavior is proper, desirable, or possible get carried with them and influence how they react to what happens in the group, as well as whether or not they will choose to accept what happens. While we will explore in the chapters on individual behavior more about how individuals influence and are influenced by the world around them, at this stage of analysis we take personality characteristics as *givens* in each group. That is, the person arrives at the group with some set of attitudes which, when mixed with those of others, help create whatever emerges.

For our purposes, the individual in the group is also the "carrier" of the wider culture insofar as he/she brings along norms, values, and perceptions which get introduced into the group through the members. For example, there are widespread beliefs in the United States about the desirability of democratic procedures, especially among peers. If several members of a student study group carry these widely held beliefs, someone is likely to suggest that the group work without a formal leader, or

FIGURE 3–3
Connections of Personal Systems to Required and Emergent Systems

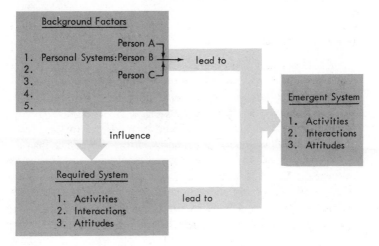

make decisions only by informal consensus. Since many members share such beliefs it is easy for the attitude from the wider culture to get accepted and adopted as a norm in the study group. What individuals have learned from the broader culture and their experiences in it become a (background) factor in determining the social system that will emerge in the group.

The set of attitudes a person brings to the group, the way the person sees him/her self and sees what is proper behavior, we call the "Personal System." The sum of all the individual members' personal systems is an important background factor needed to understand what emerges in a group. The personal systems combine with the job requirements to affect the emergent system.

Nevertheless, sometimes job requirements and/or the group's emergent system can be so powerful and overwhelming that even people with quite different personal systems will behave similarly when placed in the job. There is a tendency in organizations to over-credit individual personality defects for problems, and to underestimate the impact of job requirements.

When trying to trace the source of a group's particular emergent system, some questions you might ask about the personal systems of members are:

1.   How do individual members see themselves? Does that help explain the choices the group has made about how to make decisions, produce, relate to one another, and so forth?
2.   Why have members accepted or rejected the group's norms? What makes individual members receptive or resistant to the group's accepted way of doing things?
3.   Do the backgrounds of various members help explain why they initiated key or prominent events?

External Status

Another aspect of people outside of their personalities, which tends to be overlooked as an influence on what emerges in a group, is the person's position or status in other settings—home, community, social groups, organizations. The person's external (to the group) status influences how he/she sees him/her self and how others in the group see him/her. In general, **The higher a person's status outside a group, the higher a position or rank he/she will be accorded in a new group, at least at the beginning.** Does this fit with your experiences? In tracing the sources of the emergent system, you might ask how the members' external status relates to their positions within the group at different times. (The next chapter will look in greater detail at member positions in the group.)

Organizational Culture

In addition, a number of other factors condition what is brought into a group. The general culture of the organization in which the group exists influences the attitudes members come with. Whether the organization's climate is friendly or hostile, whether in general organization members are trusted and assumed to be motivated or suspected and considered irresponsible, whether disagreements are buried or encouraged, whether individuality is suppressed or fostered, and so forth, all make a difference to what people bring to the group. The organization's usual ways of handling such issues affect the beliefs and feelings with which members will approach a group. The emergent norms, for example, of a new task force in a generally benevolent and paternalistic company where no one gets fired, are likely to differ from a similar group in a very competitive, hostile corporation. In tracing the sources of the emergent system you might ask if any of the group's norms reflect the wider organization's culture and how the influence was transmitted.

Technology, Layout

Another important background determinant of emergent behavior can be grouped under the general label *technology*. This includes the kind of equipment used and the demands it makes upon group members for attentiveness, hours worked, activities with the equipment, interactions with others, individual judgment, and coordination of activities. The technology both sets limits on what social interactions and emergent behavior are possible and causes various interactions to occur. It affects what behavior can be required. Even noise level affects the likelihood of social discourse.

Similarly, the way in which the equipment and work space is physically laid out is a strong determinant of who is likely (and able) to talk with whom, and when. It is difficult to form a relationship with someone who must stay at a work station on the other side of a seven-foot-high machine; on the other hand, an open office with desks placed side by side makes conversation with neighbors easy.

The timing of work also makes a difference. Whether work comes in sporadic bursts or at a steady, measured pace affects opportunities for social relationships and sets limits on possible interactions. The timing of when shift members report and leave can be an important factor in communications and therefore important in the emergent system. Organizations which need around-the-clock coverage and high sharing of information (like hospitals) schedule differently from organizations which only work a second shift when there is great demand, and when the second shift's work is self-explanatory.

All of these factors, loosely grouped under technology, shape what is and can be required, and are usually fixed or determined in advance or outside of the group's existence. In turn, this will affect the emergent system. When trying to trace what emerges to technology, you might ask questions like:

1. What is the effect of the technology on which activities and interactions are required?
2. What is the nature of the group's technology in terms of numbers of people needed, when they must be in certain places, how much latitude they have in physical movement, variations of work methods used, judgment? How does all this affect how members feel?
3. What kinds of interactions and activities are made easy or not possible because of the layout, noise level, flow of work, and so forth?
4. What kind of expertise is required by the technology, and how does that affect who group members are, how they see one another, how they will be supervised, etc.?

Reward System

Just as technology is often determined apart from the particular members of the group, the organization's formal reward system—how it decides pay and position, and for what performance—is usually set before the group exists. The organization's reward system is a background factor that affects what is required and what emerges, as well as whether or not employees fully respond to offered rewards and punishments. In tracing emergent behavior to the reward system, you might ask how pay is determined and what effect that has on behavior, whether the pay system encourages competition or cooperation among members, whether good performance can be easily measured and rewarded, or bad performance measured and punished, and how that will affect emergent behavior.

All of the above factors—personal system, external status, organizational culture, technology, layout, and reward system—can be thought of as background factors, preconditions to the group's existence which help determine what will be required of members and also what emerges in their behavior. See Figure 3–4.

THE CONSEQUENCES OF EMERGENT SYSTEMS

All of what has been discussed so far in this chapter must be seen from the perspective of final results. The connections among background factors, required and emergent systems are important primarily in terms of the functionality or dysfunctionality of the consequences for the organization and its members. We can assess the consequences of what-

FIGURE 3–4
The Connection between Background Factors and the
Required and Emergent Systems

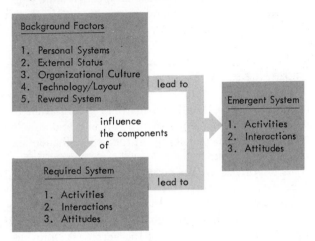

ever emergent system develops along several dimensions. Any work organization will be interested in *productivity:* How well the group does its required tasks, cost per unit of output, ability to meet deadlines, quality of output, and so on. Though many managers, particularly in small, private companies, maintain that productivity (and in turn profits) are all the consequences they care to know about, in fact few people with managerial responsibility actually operate only on this dimension.

For a variety of reasons managers also are interested in the satisfaction of members of their organization. While there is no necessary connection between satisfaction and productivity (a subject we will explore later), *the actual satisfaction people derive from their work and membership in a particular group is important enough in its effects on the people involved as well as on their productivity to merit close examination* in each situation we study. In fact, in some work groups, achieving satisfaction (close friendship, comfortable relations) may be the only dimension *members* are interested in. If you are in a class task group, you might like to try and check whether this proves to be true!

A third dimension to which we will also pay attention is that of *individual and group development/growth/learning. A group may be reasonably productive and satisfied but preventing its members from developing,* from learning anything that will increase *(a) their individual skills or abilities, (b) the range of resources available to the group, or (c) their ability to function effectively in changed circumstances.* For example, a student task group may be dividing up the work in a way that produces good reports but teaches members no new skills. An expert report writer may be doing most of the work, using already developed abilities but leaving other members under-utilized and unstretched.

Just as production is not necessarily correlated with satisfaction, group development can be independent of either. Conversely, development or learning can be occurring even when productivity and satisfaction are low. For example, even dissatisfied misfits in a job may be developing valuable skills; disgruntled employees often leave to start their own ventures, fueled by discontent and what they have learned from the job and others. As authors of this book we very much believe that the dimension of development and learning is important to assess along with the other two dimensions of productivity and satisfaction. Administrators who are concerned about the long-run enhancement of their organization's human resources will also value this dimension.

It is important to note again what was stated in Chapter 2, that it may not be possible in any given situation to achieve high performance on all three dimensions. An individual or group may make, or have to make tradeoffs among these dimensions. What to sacrifice for which benefits, is determined by the values of the person(s) choosing: Our concern is to make any action's likely consequences along all three dimensions more explicit in advance, so that choices can be more informed. But we will offer no magical or easy solutions guaranteeing wealth, happiness and growth to everyone.

We can complete Figure 3–4 then, by adding what we have just described. Whatever the emergent behavior and attitudes of a group, their functionality should be assessed along at least three dimensions: productivity, satisfaction and development. See Figure 3–5.

FIGURE 3–5
The Connection between Background Factors and the Required and Emergent Systems

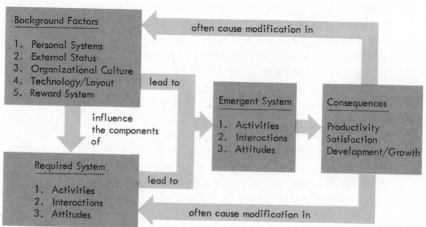

These consequences will then be judged by those members of an organization who feel responsible for performance; as you might guess, should they judge the consequences negatively, they are likely to make some changes in the required system. If productivity, for example is seen as too low, changes might be made in the type of equipment used, the pay system, the closeness of supervision, the personnel, or whatever those responsible assume to make a difference. Can you see that changes in the required system might in turn affect the emergent system, with new consequences for productivity, learning or satisfaction? Adjustments in one area will lead to responses in other areas until a new equilibrium is reached in the balance among the various components of the group.

All too often, unfortunately, the consequences of change are not those anticipated by the changer; tightening up on supervision might lead to sabotage rather than more productivity, for example — but that is worth closer attention and will be looked at again in the book's last chapter. For now we suggest you begin to get in the habit of sorting, as best you can, what you see in groups into the four categories we have suggested: Background Factors, Required System, Emergent System, and the Consequences for Productivity, Satisfaction and Development. Then try to trace the connections among them: What causes what, what seems to be associated with what, what seems unexplainable and needs more investigation?

THE RELATIONSHIPS BETWEEN REQUIRED AND EMERGENT SYSTEMS

It is important to note again that what emerges in groups will not necessarily be supportive of the required system; in fact, emergent behavior and attitudes may well be in conflict with the required tasks imposed from above or by the situation. Sometimes workgroups elaborate on ways to improve their performance, inventing improved methods, informally helping one another, and so forth. They even may develop an emergent system which compensates for deficiencies in the required system, as when norms develop in a paper mill that the nearest person to a paper break, regardless of formal position, immediately will start to rethread the paper in order to minimize waste. At other times, however, groups develop norms of limiting production, holding back effort, or even sabotaging the product.

A key challenge for you, will be to attempt to develop a series of propositions (hypotheses, generalizations) to predict when emergent systems are likely to be in conflict with the required system and when not. Can you trace what the relationships are between leadership style, technology, task requirements, member backgrounds, and so on, and the kind of system that emerges? The more useful the generalizations you can formulate, the more effective you can be in making informed managerial choices. And, of course, you need to be ready to modify your propositions when you come across contradictory evidence.

We are suggesting that it is often possible to predict likely emergent behavior if what is "given" by the situation—the background factors and the required system—are known in advance. Surprisingly to many students, the particular individuals in a situation may make less difference to what happens than the situation and its requirements. The demands of the task, technology, management style, and so forth, often can pull, as if by suction, behavior from a group regardless of who the particular members are. This is what is often referred to as the "office making the man," elevating its occupant and forcing growth in whomever fills the leadership role. Recent history with respect to the Presidency of the United States has proved, however, in a painfully glaring way, that occupying even the highest political office in no way *guarantees* particularly elevated behavior. The pulls are there, however, just as in any organizational situation, and often have induced more noble and strong behavior from Presidents than they had exhibited in earlier parts of their careers.

As you move through the course, try to notice if you are increasingly able to anticipate the kinds of behavior, norms, productivity, satisfaction, and so forth, to which a given set of requirements and background factors lead. We will try to help you improve your predictive abilities by what follows.

As an aid in helping you get started—to analyze cases, your own classroom group, the group you work in—the next chapters contain a series of propositions based on research, empirical observation and experience. We have tried to build them up in a logical sequence, and have also attempted to show how you can connect various pieces of what is observable with one another. That type of analysis goes beyond just using the concepts as fancy labels for behavior; it is a way of trying to *explain* what happens by referring to other, connected happenings. In that way, possible choice points, where your decision as a manager can make a difference to outcomes, should become visible.

KEY CONCEPTS FROM CHAPTER 3

1. A group can be defined by its:
    a. Size.
    b. Degree of autonomy.
    c. Differentiation from other groups.
    d. Interrelationships of some duration.
    e. Identification of members with the group.
    f. Common goals and symbols.

2. Behavior in group:
   a. Interactions.
   b. Activities.
3. Attitudes in group:
   a. Perceptions.
   b. Feelings.
   c. Norms.
   d. Values.
4. The Basic Social System Conceptual Scheme:
   a. Background factors:
      (1) Personal history.
      (2) Organizational culture.
      (3) Technology.
      (4) Layout.
      (5) Reward system.
   b. Required system.
   c. Emergent system.
   d. Outcomes: productivity, satisfaction, and development.

SUGGESTED READINGS

Bradford, L. P., and Mial, D. "When Is a Group?," *Educational Leadership* 21 (1963) 147–51.

Cartwright, D., and Zander, A. *Group Dynamics: Research and Theory.* New York: Harper & Row, 1953.

Hare, A. P. *Handbook of Small Group Research.* New York: The Free Press of Glencoe, Inc., Division of Crowell-Collier Publishing Company, 1962.

Homans, George C. *The Human Group.* New York: Harcourt, Brace & World, 1950.

_____ "Social Behavior as Exchange," *American Journal of Sociology* 63 (May 1958) 597–606.

_____ *Social Behavior: Its Elementary Forms.* New York: Harcourt, Brace, & World, 1961.

Luft, J. *Group Processes, An Introduction to Group Dynamics,* 2d ed. Palo Alto, Cal.: National Press Books, 1970.

Miller, J. G. "Living Systems: The Group," *Behavioral Science* 16 (1971) 302–98.

Napier, R. W., and Gershenfeld, M. K. *Groups: Theory and Experience.* Boston, Mass.: Houghton Mifflin Company, 1973.

Orth, C. D., III. *Social Structure and Learning Climate, The First Year at the Harvard Business School.* Boston, Mass.: Division of Research, Graduate School of Business Administration, Harvard University, 1963.

Shaw, M. E. *Group Dynamics: The Psychology of Small Group Behavior.* New York: McGraw-Hill Book Co., 1971.

Thibaut, John W., and Kelley, Harold *The Social Psychology of Groups.* New York: John Wiley & Sons, Inc., 1969.

Group cohesion will be increased by acceptance of a super-ordinate goal subscribed to by most members.

4

COHESIVENESS IN GROUPS
Integration

A CRUCIAL emergent factor in any work group is the degree to which members turn out to like each other and the group. A group that is close, tight and unified will behave differently, for better or worse, than one which is distant and fragmented. In this chapter we will look at *what* makes a group stick together. The functionality or consequences of sticking together for productivity, satisfaction and development, is ultimately a more important issue, but let us first try to understand what it is that pulls a group together. With a better understanding of the factors that lead to closeness, a manager is more likely to succeed in efforts to increase or decrease this important emergent characteristic of groups, should that be necessary.

In an effort to spell out the propositions about closeness, we begin with some elementary "building blocks" of relationships. While the first proposition looks obvious, it is often overlooked, and is important to those that come later. Remember from Chapter 3 that technology, work layout and the arrangement of space affect the chances of people talking with one another; we can restate that idea more formally:

The greater the opportunity/requirements for interaction, the greater the likelihood of interaction occurring.

That leads directly to the next proposition, which is fundamental to all human relationships:

The greater the interaction among people, the greater the likelihood of their developing positive feelings for one another.

And in turn:

The greater the positive feelings among people, the more frequently they will interact.

In other words, if you like someone, you will probably choose to spend more time with him/her than with someone you do not like.

These propositions must be modified or at least qualified under certain conditions; for example, when there are strong prior negative feelings on the part of one or more interactor, or when there are extreme status differences between those interacting, interaction may only increase prior feelings of dislike or distance and lead to avoidance or superficial contact. Furthermore, interactions cannot increase indefinitely; at some point they will level off and reach a kind of equilibrium, where both parties are either interacting enough to satisfy their needs, or are prevented by task requirements from interacting further. Can you think of other conditions under which these propositions would not be true?

While there are exceptions, these propositions are surprisingly applicable to many different situations, and have potent implications for managers. Consider different ways in which you might use them to design an organization. To resolve conflicts? To help make work more interesting? These simple propositions, when combined with others that follow (and which you develop yourself on the basis of your observations) can help explain the variety of emergent systems you will encounter in this book and elsewhere.

Required Interactions

Let us extend these propositions, utilizing the research that has been done on small groups, to show some of the connections that can be made among the components of the scheme we have outlined. The previous propositions suggest that once there is a work reason for people to interact, they will begin to do it more often and will develop some liking for one another beyond the original task reason for their interaction. Thus, **The greater the interactions required by the job, the more likely that** *social* **relationships and behavior will develop along with task relationships and behavior.** This is another way of describing the relationship between required and emergent interactions discussed in Chapter 3.

When members of a group begin to like one another and like being in the group, then the group will have attraction for the members and acceptance from the group will be seen as desirable by them. In other words, **The more attractive the group, the more *cohesive* will be its members.** As the emerging social relationships form, the group will develop norms — ideas about what behavior is expected of group members. **The more cohesive the group, the more eager individuals will be for membership, and thus the more likely they will be to conform to the group's norms.** Another way of saying this is that **The more cohesive the group, the more influence it has on its members.** Conversely, **The less certain and clear a group's norms and standards are, the less control it will have over its members.**

From the point of view of a total group, finding ways of getting members to feel attracted and willing to be influenced by the group is extremely desirable; a group can best reach its goals when it has everyone's allegiance and willingness to sacrifice personal desires on behalf of the group. From the individual's point of view, however, cohesion may be a mixed blessing in that there are personal costs in return for whatever may be the satisfactions of being an accepted member. The individual may have to forego preferred ways of relating to others, put out greater effort than is desired, or give more time and concern than is comfortable. In Chapter 7 we will explore more of the dilemma faced by the individual trying to decide how much to give up for the closeness offered by the group; we want to note for now, however, that while membership has a price for the individual, insofar as the participation of all members is necessary or valuable for achieving the *group's* goals, the creation of group cohesiveness is important.

Common Values and Goals

Since cohesion has such strong impact upon behavior in a group, it is useful to understand some of the ways in which it can be increased or decreased. We have already shown how cohesion is increased by frequent interaction, but there are a number of other factors which can affect it. For example, if members of a group come to it with attitudes, values and goals which happen to be fairly similar, it is much more likely that cohesion will rapidly occur. **The greater the similarity in member attitudes brought to the group as a background factor, the greater the likelihood of cohesion in a group.**

Super-Ordinate Goal

Along the same lines, when there is some kind of over-arching goal all group members aspire to, cohesion is likely to be increased. For example, there was for several years at one college a student organization which provided tutoring services to low-income children in three surrounding towns. Because most of the students who joined the organization had strong beliefs in the desirability of eventually changing the local school systems which created problems for low-income children in the first place, the organization was highly cohesive and friendly. Members usually sought each other out when at campus-wide events and felt great camaraderie. Thus, **Group cohesion will be increased by acceptance of a super-ordinate goal(s) subscribed to by most members.**

A Common Enemy

Similarly, you probably have had experience with another kind of superordinate goal, dislike for a common enemy. If people have the same enemy, they are likely to be friends; this general notion has long been used effectively by politicians in a number of countries to try to create a sense of national cohesion which overrides the variety of self-interests among different groups. And in a smaller group as well, **Group cohesion will be increased by the perceived existence of a common enemy.**

The common enemy may not necessarily be a hated enemy. Even friendly competition among groups usually has the effect of pushing group members to feel closer to one another. If by the time you read this you have already done a class exercise in groups, you may have noticed how the presence of other groups working on the same tasks seemed to cause people in your group to like one another more and perhaps even to begin to make "joking" comments about how much better your group was than the others. In Chapter 12 we will look more closely at relationships across groups, but for now it is important to note that the presence of competing or even potentially competing groups often makes members within groups feel closer to one another. In some classrooms this phenomenon is so powerful that even when a multigroup activity is conducted in which groups are *not* being compared to one another, group members still act as if it were a competitive situation and seem to feel cohesive just by being near other groups working on a similar activity. In other organizational settings, groups doing comparable work often exhibit the same kind of competitive tendencies, especially when performance is readily observable by all members. And accordingly, cohesion *within* groups increases.

Success in Achieving Goals

Another factor which can lead to greater feeling of liking among group members is for the group to be successful in achieving its goals at any particular time. If a group seems to be successful at getting what it wants, that makes the group more attractive to members, and seems to carry over in the way that members feel about one another. Thus, **Group cohesion will be increased by success in achieving the group's goals.** Do you see any impact from getting a good grade on the cohesion of classroom task groups?

A connected factor affecting group cohesion has to do with the relative position of the group in relation to other groups in the same overall organization. As you might expect, the higher the status of a particular group in relation to other groups, the more attractive it will seem to members. This is apparently true for everyone but Groucho Marx, who once said, "I wouldn't want to belong to any club which would have me as a member." But for others of us less witty or perceptive, **Group cohesion is increased in proportion to the status of the group relative to other groups in the system.**

Low External Interactions

A related issue from a somewhat opposite point of view, has to do with the amount of time that group members are required to spend away from the group. If group members, by the nature of their job, have to relate to many outsiders, (including others in the same organization but not in the group) they are less likely to feel strong allegiance to their own group. This is very often true of certain kinds of professional employees who spend a good portion of their time dealing with the problems of non-specialists in their organization, and who also spend time at professional meetings with people from other organizations, in order to keep up to date in their specialty, whether it is engineering, medicine, law, or whatever. Similarly, an organization's purchasing agent will often have to spend more time dealing with outsiders than fellow organization members, leading to reduced loyalty to his/her own department and organization. Thus, **Group cohesion will be increased when there are low numbers of external required interactions.**

Resolve Differences

While group success helps build feelings of closeness, it is also true that if a group has repeated problems with resolving differences among members, because of strong differences of opinion, values, or working style, the member-liking for one another will tend to decrease, even when the group manages to be successful. Thus, **The more easily and frequently member differences are settled in a way satisfactory to all members, the greater will be group cohesion.** Nevertheless, success, even if arrived at by a cantankerous process, can soothe many bad feelings. A winning group usually overlooks its differences; a losing group often finds fault with its members.

Availability of Resources

Finally, the way members feel about each other is frequently affected by the availability of resources to the whole group. When resources such as money, supplies, prestige or recognition are scarce, group members are likely to feel competitive with one another. Conversely, when there is an abundance of whatever resources the group needs, members are likely to see each other more charitably and therefore like each other more: **Group cohesion will increase under conditions of abundant resources.** For example, when the staff of an innovative health center saw government grants rolling in, they felt close to the other "pioneers" on the staff. When government money dried up and even weekly paychecks were in jeopardy, dissension and anger towards one another broke out.

CONSEQUENCES OF COHESION FOR PRODUCTIVITY, SATISFACTION, AND DEVELOPMENT

The preceding propositions all relate to group integration. The cohesiveness or attractiveness of a group and the power of its norms to regulate behavior are one major aspect of emergent systems and a factor that is important for diagnosing and predicting group behavior. As explained, cohesiveness is influenced by background factors, such as similarity in member attitudes, and by attributes of the required system, such as the necessity for interaction. By carefully tracing what is brought to the workgroup and what is required of it, it is possible to make sense of the degree of closeness that emerges.

While all of the above propositions have been phrased in terms of what positively increases cohesion, they are also intended to be reversible in terms of what decreases cohesion. At any given time, as a manager, you may wish to increase or decrease cohesion among a particular group and may be able to affect differing aspects of the conditions cited by the propositions. It requires a careful assessment of existing conditions to first decide in which direction cohesion should be pushed, and then how to do it.

> For example, the manager of a large department store was faced with customer complaints about waiting time for service. Upon investigation, he found that many of the full-time salespeople congregated near the fitting rooms for conversation. They enjoyed one another's company so much that they found it difficult to interrupt the gossip and joking to go wait on customers. The manager had to find a way to decrease the group's cohesion without creating major resentment that would interfere with selling enthusiasm. How might such a problem be approached?

Productivity

Since a cohesive group is one in which members adhere to the norms, it should not be surprising that in such a group, norms are likely to develop not only in regard to general behavior, but also about member productivity. The group will usually arrive at a strong sense of how much each member should produce, how much variation from that level will be tolerated, and then encourage the members to produce at or near that level. Whether production is measured in widgets/hour as in a manufacturing group, or in "sufficient hours spent preparing an analysis," as in a student task group, **The more cohesive the group, the more similar will be the output of individual members.**

Another way of looking at the effect of cohesiveness on productivity

> . . . the poor decision making performance of the men at those White House meetings might be akin to the lapses in judgement of ordinary citizens who become more concerned with retaining the approval of the fellow members of their work group than with coming up with good solutions to the tasks at hand.
>
> I. L. Janis
> Group Think

is in terms of how much effort members will make to see to it that the productivity norms, high or low, are followed. As you might expect, **The more cohesive the group, the more it will try to enforce compliance with its norms about productivity.** Cohesive groups will work hard to get members to increase output if it is lower than the group thinks appropriate, and also supply pressure to hold down the output of members who embarass the group by producing "too much."

You may remember from Chapter 3 that a group's idea of what is the proper amount to produce may be only vaguely related to higher management's or the rest of the organization's ideas of the proper amount. In general, if the group feels in sympathy with or supported by "higher management" (or those who define good performance) it will have a tendency to enforce a fairly high level of productivity on its members, and vice versa. Since a cohesive group will bring member productivity into line, **The greater the cohesion of the group, the higher productivity will be if the group supports the organization's goals and the lower productivity will be if the group resists the organization's goals.**

The group that sticks together can thus be irritatingly resistant to efforts to increase its productivity when, for whatever reason, it does not wish to raise output. But a cohesive group which wants to produce more will pull even its weaker members along quite effectively. What does this suggest to you, as a future manager, about your relationships to task groups reporting to you, and to the conditions under which their cohesiveness might be desirable?

Satisfaction

A cohesive group will, by definition, have a high overall level of satisfaction; presumably a group attractive to its members is satisfying. Individual members, however, may very much feel that the norms of the group call for behavior that is not easily given. Belonging to a close, co-hesive group can be a warm, supportive experience, but for some, the embrace of the group may feel a bit suffocating. Should that happen to many members of the group, its cohesiveness may well begin to suffer as members struggle to assert their own individuality. But the positive feel-ings from being a member of a cohesive group can be sufficient for some people to overcome even low pay, unpleasant physical conditions, harsh bosses, and so forth.

Development and Learning

A cohesive group can provide excellent opportunities for members to help and learn from one another. In fact, that can be part of what attracts members. The sharing of knowledge, skills and experiences can be very rewarding and growth promoting. Some groups, however, achieve cohe-sion only at the expense of individual growth. The group becomes so anxious to maintain a certain kind of harmony that it suppresses indi-vidual knowledge and differences for fear of making some members feel unequal or inadequate.

Cohesion achieved in this way may not hinder the group from produc-ing adequately, and may be reasonably satisfying to members who want the security of minimal competition and differences among peers, but can serve to "freeze" growth at a particular point. A student task group, for example, can see to it that everyone does his/her share of assignments, warmly socialize in and out of class, and support all members with liking and warmth, yet still prevent maximum individual learning. A quieter member who would learn valuable debating skills from being prodded to defend her ideas, may be allowed to make her contributions behind the scenes. Thus, she never is forced to practice new skills. Or an argumenta-tive member with a unique point of view might be cajoled into "not push-ing so hard, for the good of the group," and thus is never really faced with the consequences of his style, nor has a chance to think through and persuade others about his views.

On the other hand, if a group lacks cohesiveness, individual and group learning may be inhibited. It often takes at least a minimally supportive environment for members to take any risks in expressing ideas, defending unpopular views, and so forth. Therefore, the degree of cohesiveness in a group can have either positive or negative consequences for develop-ment; it takes careful analysis of the particular situation to assess the effects.

The next chapter explores further the connections between group co-hesion and effectiveness by looking at the other side of cohesiveness, that is, those forces which separate and differentiate group members. Even the most cohesive groups have differences among members which must be dealt with, and which have an impact on the group's productivity, satisfaction and development.

KEY CONCEPTS FROM CHAPTER 4

1. Propositions on Group Cohesiveness:
    a. The more interactions, the more positive feelings.
    b. The more positive feelings, the more interactions.
    c. The more attractive the group, the more cohesiveness.
    d. The more cohesive the group, the more eagerness for membership.
    e. The more eagerness for membership, the more conformity to group's norms.
        Therefore:
    f. The more cohesive the group, the more influence it has on its members.
    g. The less clear the group's norms, the less control it has over its members.
2. Group Cohesiveness increased by:
    a. Similarity in attitudes, values and goals.
    b. Existence of a common enemy.
    c. Acceptance of super-ordinate goals.
    d. Success in achieving goals.
    e. High status relative to other groups.
    f. Low number of required external interactions.
    g. Differences settled in satisfactory way to all members.
    h. Conditions of abundant resources.

SUGGESTED READINGS

Harvey, Jerry B.; and Boettger, C. Russell "Improving Communication Within A Managerial Work Group," *Journal of Applied Behavioral Science,* (March–April 1971) 154–79.

Homestead, Michael S. *The Small Group.* New York: Random House, Inc., 1969.

Napier, R. W., and Gershenfeld, M. K. *Groups: Theory and Experience.* Boston, Mass.: Houghton Mifflin Company, 1973.

Schachter, Stanley *The Psychology of Affiliation.* Stanford, Cal.: Stanford University Press, 1959.

Seashore, S. E. *Group Cohesiveness In the Industrial Work Group.* Ann Arbor, Mich.: Survey Research Center, Institute for Social Research, 1964.

Skinner, B. F. *Walden II.* New York: Macmillan Company, 1948.

Steele, Fred I. "Physical Settings and Social Interaction," *Physical Settings and Organization Development,* Reading, Mass.: Addison-Wesley Publishing Company, Inc., 1973.

Some members will be more listened to, or taken into account, than others, and in most groups, after awhile everyone knows reasonably accurately the relative standing of members in terms of influence.

5

DIFFERENTIATION IN GROUPS
Building Internal Structure as a Basis for Productivity

AFTER looking at integration—what it is that makes a group stick together and be attractive to members—it is important to examine the way groups sort out their members and differentiate them in terms of value to the group. Few groups have total equality among all members; some individuals obtain more respect and influence, some more liking, others less of one or the other. Over time a group will develop relative positions or "ranks" for its members; that is, members acquire different status from one another. In this chapter we will look at three key factors that determine the relative positions of group members: They are (1) status brought to the group from outside, (2) individual adherence to group norms, and (3) group related roles assumed by members. These factors contribute to individual member influence which ultimately influence group productivity, satisfaction and development.

The notions of status differences as something to observe and discuss often makes Americans uncomfortable because of their widespread professed beliefs about everyone being created equal, and the equally widespread general belief that differences among people working together should be minimized or ignored. The United States is one of a handful of countries where such beliefs are widely espoused. In most parts of the world the idea of some people being more worthy and esteemed than others, and of everyone having a rank or status

63

which can be precisely identified relative to all others, is accepted as obviously true.

While Americans acknowledge broad differences in status — doctor (professional) higher than garbage collector (blue-collar), professor higher than student (sometimes?) — the idea is resisted in groups of peers or those who see themselves as "about the same." The sameness usually refers to broad categories, such as "students," "middle managers," or "board members," and there is often resistance to the possibility that in fact, even in a group of peers, differences in status emerge, are identifiable, and have important consequences for the group and individuals in it.

For example, one of the most common norms students bring to task groups is, "we are all equal," which means that no one student member is supposed to be able to dominate others, tell them what to do or give orders. Yet it is clear that it would be extremely unlikely to have all members possessing equal skills in generating ideas, organizing, analyzing, writing, or interacting socially. As a result, once the group takes on some tasks, various members emerge with different status in the group.

> No two men can be half an hour together but one shall acquire an evident superiority over the other.
>
> Samuel Johnson
> in Boswell's *Life of Samuel Johnson*

Just which attributes of members will result in high ranking depends upon the norms and standards of the particular group; in some groups status goes to those who help most with the tasks, while in others, status goes to those who make members feel most comfortable and at ease. But inevitably, groups do develop some informal ranking of members, even if they do not discuss it directly. Though each group must be separately studied to see what the basis is for status in that group, in general, **Members who contribute most to task accomplishment are accorded the most *respect* in the group, while members who contribute most to social accomplishment (development of relationships) are accorded the most *liking* in the group.** A person's standing along these two dimensions of respect and liking will determine his/her overall status in the group, with the weights attached to each determined by the group's emergent norms and values.

INITIAL RANKING: STATUS CONGRUENCE

While over the long run status in a group emerges based on each member's contribution to whatever the group values, early status in a group is usually related to the status of each group member outside the group, as mentioned in Chapter 3 under background factors. In a statewide task force on the establishment of day care centers, for example, a member who is a pediatrician will usually be given more respect, at first, than a member who is a welfare mother (despite the possibility that the welfare mother may indeed know more about the needs of working parents and their children). In general, especially early in a group's life, **The higher the background factor of external status, the higher the emergent internal status of a group member.**

But it is not always obvious what attributes group members will use to rank status in the world outside the group. What some people consider high status attributes might not at all be seen that way by others, particularly if an attribute is not judged to be relevant to the group's purposes. For example, in the day care task force just mentioned, being a doctor will probably yield higher rank than being a welfare mother. But among a group of housing project residents organizing to request the establishment of day care facilities in their neighborhood, the welfare mother's experience with children and "the system," plus her membership on the statewide task force, might give her high status there. Similarly, a high status judge might be given little respect in a group which has crashed in the desert, if his/her survival skills are comparatively low. A mechanic might be given higher status in this situation even though he/she would be seen as lower status in other circumstances.

Furthermore, there can be many other factors that go into settling a person's status. We have been talking about profession, and by implication, income as two important factors, but there are others that often make a difference: Age, sex, education (where and how long), ethnicity, marital status, even region born in, and so forth. In student task groups, class standing, major subject and work experience are often important determinants, too, since careers are not yet established. Some of these factors are achievable by work and ability, such as education and profession, while others the person is born with or gets by just existing, such as age, sex, and ethnicity. Though the rankings may in no way be "fair" or just, especially to those who are low status, some kind of ranking exists everywhere. In many cultures, higher status goes to those who are older, male, married, highly educated, have high incomes, and are members of the dominant ethnic group. In any particular group, however, some of these factors might be reversed, as in these examples you may recognize: "Never trust anyone over 30," "ivory-tower, pointy-headed intellectuals," "fat cats," "male chauvinist pigs," and "honkies."

In general, **The higher a person is on all of these external dimensions (or other valued ones), the higher his/her emergent status within a group, and vice versa.** To any particular group, however, one factor may be seen as overriding all others; in certain organizations, for example, if you aren't a WASP (or whatever the dominant ethnic background), being high status on all the other factors will not make up for lack of status on that dimension.

Not only can we look at how high a person is on several status factors in order to estimate likely internal status, but we can also make some predictions about emergent behavior based on how consistent a person's status ranking is *across* factors. For example, some people are high or low in status on all factors; we call that *status congruency*.

If the pediatrician in our example were a 60 year old male, married and a descendent of someone who came over on the Mayflower, he would be congruent on all the status factors. Conversely, in New Hampshire at least, if the welfare mother were 20, French-Canadian, unmarried, unemployed and a high school dropout, she would be congruently low status. Can you envision the likely ranking of each within the day care task group? But suppose the pediatrician was a 28 year old black woman, just finishing her residency at a public hospital. Or that the welfare mother was a 33 year old professor's daughter, recently separated, graduate of Radcliffe College, temporarily on welfare because her husband was not sending support money and her three children under six years old left her unable to work? Can you see how the status factors of each would then be inconsistent with one another, "out-of-line," or *incongruent?* Can you imagine how difficult it might then be for the day-care task force members to "place" or rank each one? What might be their reaction?

FIGURE 5–1
Illustration of How Different People Can Be Ranked Along Several Status Dimensions

Person	Age	Sex	Education	Ethnicity	Profession	Income	
A ...	High	High	High	High	High	High	= High Status, Congruent
B ...	Low	Low	Low	Low	Low	Low	= Low Status, Congruent
C ...	Low	Low	High	High	High	High	= High Status, Incongruent
D ...	...	...	...	...	...	...	= etc.

THE BEHAVIOR OF HIGH STATUS MEMBERS

The status or rank of a group member may not be explicit or directly discussed by group members, but is usually inferrable from observing member behavior. In general, **Lower status members defer to higher status members, allowing higher status members to (a) initiate interactions, (b) make statements without being challenged, and (c) administer informal rewards or punishments. Higher status members will usually talk more, talk "for the group" in public situations, make more contacts with outsiders, and usually have the widest number of connections within the group.** Even body posture and seating arrangements can reflect status differences: Higher status members sit at or near the head of the conference table (or where they sit becomes the "head"); if the group is talking informally, they will be at the physical center of the grouping; they are looked at when others are speaking; and they tend to sit more erectly or confidently. In general, **The lower one's rank in a group, the more one defers to others, and vice versa.**

> *A principle of organization [necessary for] advanced social life . . . in higher vertebrates is the so-called ranking order. Under this rule every individual in the society knows which one is stronger and which weaker than itself, so that everyone can retreat from the stronger and expect submission from the weaker . . .*
>
> Konrad Lorenz
> *On Aggression*

Aside from external status, how do members arrive at their various informal positions in a group?

CONFORMITY TO NORMS AS A DETERMINANT OF EMERGENT STATUS

We have previously looked at the way norms emerge and how cohesiveness increases conformity to group norms. But no matter how attractive a group is, and no matter how much members wish to belong, it is almost never possible for every member to go along with all of a group's norms. Sometimes norms call for behavior beyond the capacity of individuals in the group, as for example, "Everyone should make creative contributions to the group's efforts." Some people have more of the skills that a group needs than do others, and when the norms call for those particular skills, they are at a natural advantage. If a student task group desires high grades, and must produce excellent written analyses to get them, the individual member who is good at performing such analysis and at writing clear conclusions will naturally be better able to conform to norms about contributing to the group's performance. Another member might be an excellent amateur carpenter, but not be valued as much in the group since such manual skills are not necessary to achieving high performance.

Other norms ask individuals to do what goes too strongly "against the grain," irritating the person's fundamental values and personality. For example, some groups ask that all members act humbly, even to the point of denying any needs for individual recognition. To a person raised with strong emphasis on individual competition and a belief in sinking or swimming on one's own best efforts, being modest about successes may be either impossible or seem too "wrong" to be tolerated, let alone tried.

For such a person, conformity to a norm of "humbleness" is a virtual impossibility, even if other aspects of the group make membership at-

tractive. In some more gentle, unjudging world, the inability or unwilling-
ness to conform to what are, after all, only one group's particular, idiosyn-
cratic norms, would go unpunished. The desirability, for example, of
false humility has not been proclaimed from on high as the one true way;
in fact, just around the corner, perhaps in our competitive individual's
family, sits a group with equal convictions about the rightness of savoring
glory when it is earned!

It is important to state explicitly that we are not talking about "con-
formists" versus "noncomformists" as absolute personality types; all
people have some group or groups to whose norms and values they conform, even when they are physically present elsewhere. The question is
only whether a person will (or can) conform to a *particular* group's norms
while a member. Nonconformity in that context is usually a sign of conformity to some other group's standards to which the "non-conformer"
still subscribes. If, when in Rome a person does not "do as the Romans
do," it is usually because he/she thinks that "doing as Americans/English/
Germans (select your own category) do" is better, nicer or more comfortable than going along with the present company.

Yet despite the fact that particular norms about productivity and other
kinds of behavior can vary sharply from group to group, each group's
ideas about proper behavior often become enshrined or "sacred," as if
there were no other possible way to behave and still be a good person.
Once a group has clear ideas about proper levels of productivity, for example, it will expend considerable energy trying to bring members who
deviate from them (hereafter referred to as *"deviants"*), into line. Thus,
**The more an individual group member fails to conform to the group's
norms, the more frequently negative sentiments will be expressed towards
him/her.**

The particular form of expression for negative sentiments can vary,
depending on the general style of group members and the particular norm
being enforced. Some groups may use sarcasm, irony and indirect hints to
let a member know he/she is not conforming properly, while other groups
may use nods, winks, facial mugging or "gentle love-taps" to admonish
deviating members. In the classic Hawthorne experiments[1], where the
relationship between social relations and productivity was first explored,
one work group was observed in which deviants who produced "too
much" were hit on the upper arm with the fist, a process called "binging."
This was a crude but effective way to see to it that no one person produced so much that management would start to ask why all workers could
not do the same each day.

Whatever the particular medium of expression, every group will have

---

[1] See F. J. Roethlisberger and W. J. Dickson, *Management and the Worker* (Cambridge,
Mass.: Harvard University Press, 1939).

ways of "punishing" its deviant members, and most will have at least some members who cannot or will not conform to its norms, leading to differences in rank. When the group expresses dislike for a member who isn't conforming, it often produces defensiveness or aggression in that member, which can in turn lead to greater punishment by the group and to new attempts to bring the member into line. After a while, however, the group will begin to ignore the deviant as if to punish him/her by withholding what the group sees as desirable relationships. **The less a member conforms to a group's norms, the greater will be the interaction directed at him/her for some time. Should the interaction fail to bring the member into conformity with the norms, interaction will sharply decrease.**

Conversely, the more closely a person conforms to the group's norms, and carries out the group's ideas of proper behavior, the better the person will be liked by other group members, and become what is called a "regular" member of the group. **The greater a member's conformity to the group's norms, the greater the group's liking for the member.**

The people who are best able to conform to the group's norms, because of skills, attributes, resources possessed by them — earned or otherwise — are likely to emerge as informal leaders in the group and be the most respected by other members. Just *what* the group values, varies from group to group and may not be fairly distributed among members. In one classic study, the most important attribute a member could have was being Irish, an attribute not easily acquired by non-Irish aspirants, but possessed by enough group members to make it crucial.[2] **The member(s) who conform most closely to a group's norms have the highest probability of emerging as informal leader(s) of the group.**

Interestingly, the informal leaders of a group can end up also having the most license to occasionally break the group's norms without punishment. It is as if a person builds up credits in the "liking and conformity-to-norms account" and thus can be the most free to "spend" the accumulated credit when he or she desires to. Thus we have to add the counter-proposition, **Informal group leaders may occasionally violate norms without punishment, provided that they have earned their leadership by general conformity to the group's norms.**

Many task groups, however, also have some members who refuse to have anything to do with the group's norms. The student, for example, who violates student norms by preparing for every class, reading all the suggested readings as well as the required readings in the course, challenging the teacher and filling up class time with questions and arguments, will often not be swayed by any punishments his/her classmates can generate and will thus be isolated from the student group. For those people

---

[2] A. Zaleznik, Christensen & Roethlisberger, *The Motivation, Productivity and Satisfaction of Workers* (Boston: Division of Research, Harvard Business School, 1958).

whose behavior is furthest from the norms of the particular group of which they are nominally a member, we use the term *"isolates."* As suggested earlier, those who fall between regulars and isolates we refer to as "deviants" in that they do not totally reject the norms of the group but neither do they totally conform to them.

EXTERNAL STATUS: HOW IT RELATES TO ACCEPTANCE OF GROUP NORMS

It is in the context of such categories as acceptance of norms that external status often makes a difference to internal membership. Insofar as having a certain ethnic background, age, educational attainment, and so forth, makes it likely that a person will share particular attitudes with others of the same background, external status allows group members to quickly "place" new group members. Of course, not *all* middle-aged, male, second-generation Lithuanian-Americans, for example, are the same in all of their beliefs, values and behaviors, nor are *all* sophomore women at, say, Vassar College the same. But within each category of people, common experiences and background can and often do lead towards common tendencies, especially as compared to other groups. Most Vassar sophomores are probably more like one another than they are like the Lithuanian-born males. Even when there are genuine differences among people within any one category, many outsiders *assume* commonalities — often by stereotypes. But apart from stereotypes, most people's values are based on how they were raised and their experiences thereafter, and various status factors do give shorthand hints at what a person's beliefs are *likely* to be. Thus though external status may not *accurately* reflect a person's beliefs, and may even sometimes be misleading, groups seem to rely on it in their early phases to "place" members.

When a group's norms are strongly held, it is often extremely difficult for anyone who wasn't raised from childhood with similar beliefs to go along. A Maine native, taught Yankee independence from birth, is likely to be upset and uncomfortable in a work group of immigrant Italians who believe in helping one another on and off the job, freely borrowing and lending money, tools and even food, and frequently stopping work to laugh and joke loudly together. The worker from Maine will probably not want or be able to go along with the others' norms and thus be isolated, while the member of the Italian subgroup who is most spontaneous and generous will probably be most respected. In some other group, the exact opposite could be true and the independent Downeaster would be most respected.

Whatever attributes a particular group treats as high status, external status and status congruence appear to have the following consequences for internal membership rank:

1. **High external status, congruent members tend to become regular members.** It is as if a group coalesces around those whose status when they come to the group is uniformly high. Perhaps the people who come with lower external status look to those with greater status to see how things are supposed to develop, thereby helping the high status congruent members become central.

2. **High status, incongruent members tend to become isolates.** Those who do not "fit" easily into one category create some confusion in others, causing neither respect nor liking. The result is often isolation, perhaps because the basically high status person will not as strongly "need" that particular group's approval.

3. **Low external status members, regardless of congruence, tend to become deviants.** Those whose overall status is low when they enter a group, seem to find difficulty in breaking free from the group, but cannot fully follow norms to become regulars. They are thus likely to perpetuate within the group the low status they arrive with.

SUBGROUPS AS A FORM OF DIFFERENTIATION

If group members are differentiated by how closely they adhere to group norms, there is a good possibility that they will form into subgroups based on their degree of conformity to the norms. In addition, other kinds of subgroupings often emerge on the basis of mutual personality attractions, previous friendships or common interests outside the group, shared positions on crucial issues, and so on. In a classroom task group, for example, subgroups may develop among those who are serious students, those who are fraternity/sorority members, the athletes, the campus activists, and others.

As soon as more than two people are in a group, the possibility exists of some of them joining up, and then taking sides. **The greater the number of people in a group, the more likely is subgroup division.** It is rare that a group does not develop some *cliques*.

For the manager-scientist the important issue is not whether subgroups exist but the basis for their formation and the resultant conse-

> *The worst cliques are those which consist of one man.*
> George Bernard Shaw

quences for group functioning. If the subgroups exist because of differing but complementary task abilities, they may be quite functional for accomplishing group goals. Even if based on more social considerations, they may or may not hinder communications among members, foster cooperation or conflict, prevent or facilitate accomplishment of tasks, increase or decrease satisfaction, and so forth. Though it is certainly easier to assess the consequences of subgroup formation than do anything about it, it is an important factor in determining member standing and resultant productivity, satisfaction and development.

You might like to think about what you could do to affect subgroupings which are getting in the way of a group accomplishing its goals. Can you use the propositions about interaction and liking, for example, to think of possible ways for easing subgroup solidarity or tension? Chapter 12 deals with relations among groups and will help you examine this issue on a larger scale but for now you can derive your own conclusions from what has already been presented.

Still another way to look at differences in member ranking within a group is through the concept of roles.

ROLES AS DIFFERENTIATORS OF GROUP MEMBERS

Can you imagine what life would be like if there were no predictability to anyone's behavior? How would you behave, for example, if you could never be sure of your father's reactions? Suppose you never knew who among your friends you could count on for cheering up, or blowing off steam, or talking through serious problems, or playing your favorite sport? Wouldn't life be chaotic if you had to make anew every single choice of behavior every time you saw another person? While the spontaneity of it all could be exciting, it might paralyze many of us and wear out the rest.

As people interact, however, individuals slowly arrive at patterned behavior, where each party begins to learn the other's likes and dislikes, needs, sensitive areas, and so forth, and can begin to accommodate to one another. A person comes to expect certain behavior and attitudes from others, and they come to expect particular behavior and attitudes from him/her. When you know the types of behavior, or pattern expected of you in a particular situation, you have learned a role, and automatically know what to do when in that situation. The way you then behave is not necessarily how you are in all situations, but is likely to be repeated by you whenever you are with that particular group of people or in that situation. This kind of "specialized" behavior is another way of differentiating members, resulting in a consistent place in the group for all who take on a patterned role. Here is an example of the role behavior of a faculty member in a business school:

At faculty meetings I find myself frequently raising challenging, possibly unanswerable questions about curriculum and educational philosophy, making my colleagues uncomfortable but sometimes forcing them to deal with issues on a more fundamental level. They now more-or-less expect this of me, that I'll take the role of the "resident radical," who tries to pull the rug out from under their assumptions, and thus they relate to me with a kind of stubborness which "pulls" even more questioning from me. Every group which discusses complex issues needs to have the status quo challenged; something about my personality lets me step in to fill that role, and the challenging function is thus taken care of.

But at another meeting I attend, where I am on the Board of Directors of a community health center, my behavior is quite different. Because there are many people on the board with low educational levels and little knowledge about organizations or health delivery systems, there is great need for expert information on how to set organizational goals and how to make decisions. Because I have some knowledge of these matters and am seen by other board members as a "business professor," at board meetings I tend to be much more in the role of "expert advice-giver" and "problem solver," so probably act more responsibly and less mischievously than at faculty meetings.

In each case, the group has a good sense of what to expect from me, and vice versa, which is convenient, and it saves considerable time and confusion about who will do what. Particular types of behavior are almost automatically called forth.

At the same time, having well-established roles also acts as a constraint on the choices made by me and the others. At faculty meetings it is hard for me to get in on proposing realistic solutions to curriculum problems, because others assume that if I am proposing something, it's probably too "far out." Conversely, by my questioning role I probably prevent others from being as critical and assumption-examining as they might like to be.

Similarly, there are times when I'd prefer to miss Health Center Board Meetings and relax with my family, or times when I would like to just joke around or toss out wild ideas, and many instances when I wish others would speak up more, but the responsibility of the role I'm in keeps me behaving in a helpful problem-solving way. And conversely, it is possible that some of the low-participating community members might feel freer to make constructive suggestions if I didn't pre-empt that role.

As with other kinds of deviance, behaving in ways not expected by others will cause discomfort in group members, and lead to attempts to force the person back into role. This can be uncomfortable for the individual trying to expand the role as well as for group members affected by the changes.

Thus, at the same time our various roles are convenient, they restrict our possible behaviors insofar as we choose to continue in them. Role behavior makes life more predictable, and constrained, by differentiating people according to particular behaviors expected of them and then reinforcing each role occupant for consistently taking that role.

Though the patterns may vary to a greater or lesser degree, work group members inevitably acquire roles bringing their own styles and preferences to the group's requirements. Members respond to the needs of the group with their own personal styles, and fairly rapidly begin to develop repetitive patterns of behavior. As group members notice one another's emerging patterns, they acquire expectations of how each person will behave, which reinforce whatever behavioral tendencies were exhibited, and soon a whole network of expectations is created which helps make each person's participation predictable.

Few people have either so limited a repertoire of possible behaviors within them, or so clear a notion of what they will not do, that they can completely resist responding to others' expectations of them. Whether the behavioral pattern originates from within or from the strong expectations of others, when a person is treated as if he/she were *supposed to* act in a certain way, frequently that person will begin to do so, that is, produce that expected pattern.

Conformity to expectations by others is not inevitable, of course, and sometimes people resist being drafted into roles that do not fit. In our classes, for example, we often see athletes, treated at first as if they are only "jocks" uninterested in learning, struggle not to accept such a demeaning role and to become contributing group members. Roles assigned on the basis of external characteristics, like sex, age or appearance are probably less difficult to resist than those based on actual behavior, but are by no means easy to escape. It takes a very determined person to continue to refuse to be what others expect of him/her, and such determination is rare. We will explore this question more closely in Chapters 8 and 10 especially in relation to conditions under which refusal is most likely. At present, we can say that for most people, concern with readily finding a comfortable place in a group makes acceptance of offered roles likely, if the roles are not too incongruent with how the person views him/herself.

For example, early in the life of a new group there will often be some uncomfortable silences, since members do not know one another and feel cautious about risking opinions without being sure of reactions. Inevitably, some member will become so uncomfortable with the silence that he/she will think up something to say just to ease the tension. It only takes a few such events to initiate expectations of the silence-breaker. In some groups, that member will then usually be expected to be an idea-initiator, and be appreciated for that. In another group with different needs, the silence-breaker might be seen as bidding for leadership and "assigned" (often unexplicitly) the role of "aspiring leader." Of course, the style and particular words used by the silence-breaker also make a difference as to how he/she will be perceived. If it is done with some humor, for example, that member may come to be seen as a great tension-releaser and be appreciatingly expected to take that role, that is, fulfill that function, whenever the atmosphere in the group becomes tense. On the other hand, the person who breaks silence by nervous chattering may not be so appreciated even when members notice and expect it.

In general, *roles in groups can be categorized by whether they serve to (1) help accomplish the group task (task-oriented), (2) help maintain good relationships among members (socially-oriented) or (3) express individual needs or goals unrelated to the group's purposes (self-oriented).*

Any role behavior reflects the person's personality and needs, but from the group point of view, the behavior will be seen as more valuable if it also fulfills a need of the group for getting the job done, or for sustaining satisfying relationships.

Furthermore, it is important to remember that one person might take on several of these roles, or that at different times several members might perform in the same role. How widely distributed and firmly established roles are, is an interesting indicator of the degree of crystallization or fluidity of a group's structure. Sometimes particular individuals acquire a "monopoly" on a role and no one else can take it, even though for the task at hand the other(s) would be best suited. **A group will be less effective if some or many capable members are prevented from taking needed roles.**

The following are roles which have been found to be useful and common in successful task groups:

Roles Related to Accomplishing the Group's Tasks:[3]

1. Idea initiator: Proposes tasks or goals, defines problems, suggests procedures or ideas for solving problems.
2. Information seeker: Requests facts, seeks information about a group concern, asks for expression of feelings, requests statements or estimates, solicits expressions of value, seeks suggestions and ideas.
3. Information Provider: Offers facts, provides information about a group concern, states beliefs about matters before the group, gives suggestions and ideas.
4. Problem Clarifier: Interprets ideas or suggestions, clears up confusion, defines terms, indicates alternatives and issues, gets group back on track.
5. Summarizer: Pulls together related ideas, restates suggestions after the group has discussed them, offers a decision or conclusion for the group to weigh.

---

[3] Adapted from R. F. Bales, *Interaction Process Analysis, A Method for the Study of Groups* (Reading, Mass.: Addison-Wesley Publishing Co., 1950).

6. Consensus tester: Asks to see if group is nearing decision, sends up "trial balloons" to test a possible conclusion.

Roles Related to the Group's Social Relationships:

1. Harmonizer (joker or soother):   Attempts to reconcile disagreements, reduces tension, gets members to explore differences.
2. Gate Keeper: Helps keep communication channels open, facilitates everyone's participation, suggests procedures that permit sharing of what members have to say.
3. Supporter: Exudes friendliness, warmth and responsiveness to others, encourages, supports, acknowledges and accepts others contributions.
4. Compromiser: When own idea or status is involved in a conflict, offers compromise, yielding of status, admitting error or modifying position in interest of maintaining group cohesion.
5. Standards monitor: Tests whether group is satisfied with way it is proceeding, points out explicit or implicit operating norms to see if they are desired.

The variety of self-oriented roles is endless. Some, like "group clown," may be tolerated or neglected, while others, like "wet blanket," or "bragger," may prove to be extremely annoying to other members and hinder group functioning. **In an effective task group, there will be a relatively low amount of self-oriented role behavior, and a balance between task- and social-related roles as necessary.**

The various roles that members take on become part of how they are ranked by the group. In some groups, idea initiators are most valued. As pointed out previously, high task contributors are usually respected, while high social contributors are usually liked, but each group will weigh the value of these patterns by its own standards and goals. **In general, the more a member fills both task and social roles, the higher will be his/her status in the group. Members who take only task or only social roles tend to become overspecialized; their emergent status then depends on how highly the group values their "specialty."**

INFLUENCE AS A RESULT OF RANK DIFFERENTIALS

No matter how egalitarian the ideals of a work group, it is unlikely that all members can contribute equally along those dimensions — task or social — that the group values. Even where external status is roughly equal, as the group interacts, some members will have better ideas, warmer personalities or whatever is seen as desirable. As others perceive these differential talents, their possessors will be allowed more say about what the group should do, directions it should take, how decisions should be made, and so forth. *This ability to affect the behavior of others in particular directions* we define as *influence*.

Whether it is explicitly acknowledged or not, as a result of external status, adherence to norms, and roles taken, every member will have some differential degree of influence on others in the group. Some members will be more listened to, or taken into account, than others, and in most groups, after awhile everyone knows reasonably accurately the relative standing of members in terms of influence. In student and other peer groups these differences are often denied, or at least talking about them is seen as taboo, for fear of hurting feelings. Nevertheless, differences inevitably exist and can be documented by an observer. Since internal influence in a group correlates with internal status, it can be noted by the same kinds of behaviors: deference, assertion, physical spacing, and so on. Just as the manager scientist will want to know about status differentials in groups, so will he/she want to be a careful observer of influence differentials, and how influence is acquired within a group.

In general, we can predict that **When a member has congruently high external status, conforms to the group's norms, fulfills task and social roles, he/she will be accorded high emergent status, and therefore have high influence within the group.** If some of these factors are different, an altered proposition would be necessary to predict amount of influence within the group. Can you assess the relative influence of members of task groups to which you belong, and then trace the influence to the factors discussed in this chapter?

The process of sorting out member influence and status is so important to a group's development that everything can be viewed from this perspective.[4] A group can be visualized as beginning with members sizing one another up and jockeying to find a satisfactory position in the group. The task work of the group will become the means for jostling or infighting until each member has a relative position or rank with which he/she is satisfied. Though not everyone can be simultaneously at the top in terms of influence, stability can be achieved when each member accepts the rank allotted him/her. If anyone is unhappy with his/her emergent position, new struggles will break out. The efforts to alter status then surface through attempts to more closely conform to norms, to change them, or to shift roles.

A group will not reach a stable equilibrium, where all its energies can be focused on its tasks, until its internal rankings are essentially accepted by all. Then a kind of cohesion can be reached. In this view, a group cannot be fully productive until it has arrived at a somewhat "crystallized" or accepted structure. Until differences of opinion about "proper" ranking

---

[4] This formulation was originally suggested by one of our students, Nfor Susungi.

are settled by the members of a group, it is less likely to be fully productive, since so much energy and attention must go into coping with individual restlessness.

On the other hand, **A structure which is too crystallized, where everyone "knows his place" only too well, can also have difficulties in producing, especially when tasks are changing and quick responsiveness is needed.**

When a member tries to change rank, his/her influence is tested; a successful alteration of position indicates that the person had more influence than he/she was being credited with, while an unsuccessful attempt confirms or lowers the person's position.

CONSEQUENCES OF MEMBER DIFFERENTIATION FOR PRODUCTIVITY, SATISFACTION, AND DEVELOPMENT

As indicated throughout this chapter, the rank and status of group members has important consequences for group productivity, satisfaction and development. In turn, how a member produces affects his/her rank.

In Chapter 4 we looked at how cohesiveness is connected to a group's production, pulling individual member output towards what the group's norms define as appropriate. Even noncohesive work groups, however, develop at least rough ideas about what is too much work and what is too little. Different groups have particular nicknames, richer than "deviants" or "isolates," for people who don't carry their own load, or for those who are so gifted or willing to work so hard that they make others look bad by their output. Those members who produce "too much" are often seen as "rate-busters," or as they are known in student circles, "curve-breakers." Conversely, "slackers," "gold-bricks," or "goof-offs" are those who just cannot or will not produce at a pace satisfactory to the particular group's members. In general, then, a person's standing in a group is partly determined by how closely he/she conforms to the group's norms, and is particularly affected by adherence to norms about individual output. Conversely, once a person's rank is established, a particular level of output is likely to follow.

An interesting irony of the above observations is that, **In a high producing group, the isolates and/or deviants are likely to be low producers, while in a group that holds down productivity, the isolates are likely to be high producers!** A person may choose not to conform because he/she doesn't want to work so hard or so little, or may be pushed into isolation out of inability to produce at about the group's desired rate. Similarly, a person who desires to be an accepted member will adjust productivity upward or downward to meet the group's norms. Whatever the cause, there is no doubt that rank within the group is connected to productivity.

A dramatic example of just how powerful a force is exerted upon members to produce according to group norms was reported in *Street Corner Society*, a detailed account of a group of young underemployed men who "hung around" together.[5] One of the valued skills in the group turned out to be bowling ability. But other qualities, such as social skills, intelligence and power of self-expression were dominant in giving members status; as you might expect, bowling expertise is not perfectly correlated with ability to argue well or talk to many people. One of the lower status members of the gang was the "best" bowler when measured by scores attained when bowling casually, but whenever the gang bowled competitively, his scores would inevitably fall below those of the gang's leaders!

The low status expert bowler may not have been fully aware of why he didn't do as well when with the others, but the pressure and razzing from the gang to have his "productivity" fall into line affected him enough to temporarily alter his ability to produce. In general, under competitive stress, the gang's bowling scores almost always perfectly reflected their relative status, even though some lower ranking members had more ability than they could deliver when being "kept in their places" by the others.

In a work group, some of the differentiation of members will follow from the task requirements. If various members are required to do different tasks, some group valuation of the respective worth of each task will probably emerge. Those who do jobs which the group sees as crucial to its success will probably be given higher status than others. When the group ranks members by the difficulty of the task each performs, the group is likely to be relatively high in output. Thus, **The more that member differentiation is based on task requirements, the more productive is the group likely to be.**

On the other hand, if member rank is largely based on external status the group is only likely to be high producing, if by coincidence the factors that determine external status are also those that would determine genuine contributions to the group's tasks. **The more that member differentiation is based on external status, the less productive is the group likely to be (unless external status happens to coincide with needed group skills).**

Summary Productivity Proposition

Differentiation, of course, need not be inconsistent with group cohesion. Though cohesive groups sometimes cling together and enforce false equality even when differentiation would be appropriate, a group can be both differentiated and attractive to members. A highly differen-

---

[5] William F. Whyte, *Street Corner Society,* rev. ed (Chicago: University of Chicago Press, 1955).

tiated group can be quite cohesive if all members believe that their positions accurately reflect their contributions, satisfy their needs, and lead to effective performance. In fact, if the group's tasks can best be done by each member *first* working on different aspects of the tasks and *then* coordinating individual efforts, the more differentiated *and* the more cohesive the group needs to be in order to produce at a high rate. Furthermore, if the group supports the organization's goals, it will pull the highest possible productivity from its members. **The greater the differentiation *and* cohesion of a group with norms supporting the organization's goals, the greater its productivity is likely to be.**

Satisfaction and Development

As suggested earlier, a group which is highly differentiated but in which each member accepts his/her status can be highly satisfied. Where differentiation, however, is a result of factors which some members do not accept as appropriate, considerable dissatisfaction can result. For example, if a work group automatically assigns low status to its female members, forcing them to do all the menial tasks and ignoring their contributions to the important jobs, there can only be general satisfaction if the women accept their lower ranking. If, however, as increasingly is the case, they want to be accorded whatever status they earn by merit, rather than automatically given low (or high) status merely because of sex, the group will have dissension and low satisfaction.

When group members take on roles and ranks that restrict them merely to doing what they know well, growth will naturally be limited. A group highly differentiated on the basis of adherence to norms which support maximum productivity, can be very efficient, but can limit chances for members to learn new jobs, try new skills or be creative about work processes. **If the group's tasks are routine, a rigid structure may be most productive, but least growth promoting. Tasks calling for creativity and responsiveness however, are not likely to be performed well by a rigidly differentiated group.** Furthermore, rigid differentiation is likely to be quite frustrating to members who want to learn and grow. For example, a group trying to think up a new commercial product, like a labor-saving small appliance, would have difficulty being imaginative if only the marketing person could give input on what customers might like, only the production manager could comment on how items can be built, and so forth. A free flow of ideas is called for regardless of the members' status and position, in order for the group to be creative.

On the other hand, an insufficiently differentiated group may be highly productive at creative tasks, stimulate great learning by members, but be anxiety provoking at the same time. The lack of clear positioning can cause considerable uncertainty and nervousness for some members, even while allowing them maximum opportunities for growth.

Finally, as you might expect by now, an under-differentiated group will probably be quite ineffective at performing routine tasks, thereby dragging down morale when results are poor, and probably leading to little growth except for those few members who can take advantage of the looseness to pursue their own ends.

The degree of differentiation and cohesion in a group, then, are important emergent outcomes of the way the group works together. They greatly affect a group's performance, satisfaction and learning. While we have tried to show how cohesion and differentiation come about, a more detailed look at how groups function as they go about their business can be useful in assessing their effectiveness. In the next chapter we examine more closely the working processes of groups, to help you more readily judge what is effective group behavior as it is occurring in the emergent system.

KEY CONCEPTS FROM CHAPTER 5

1. Overall status in group determined by:
   a. Respect: accorded to high task accomplishment.
   b. Liking: accorded to high social accomplishment.
2. Initial ranking:
   a. The higher the background factor of external status, the higher the emergent internal status of a group member.
3. Status:
   a. The higher a person is on dimensions valued by the group, the higher his/her status within the group (regular), and vice versa. Consistency of relative positions or dimensions determines degree of status congruence.
   b. Deviant: member who does not conform to group's norms; most negative attitudes expressed to that member.
   c. Isolate: conforms even less to group's norms; interactions with isolate very infrequent.
4. The more cohesive the group:
   a. The more similar member output.
   b. The more it will enforce compliance.
   c. The higher productivity will be if group supports management's goals.
   d. The lower productivity will be if the group resists management's goals.
5. The greater the number of people in a group, the more likely is subgroup formation.
6. Roles:
   a. Task-oriented
   b. Socially-oriented
   c. Self-oriented.

7. Influence:
   a. The ability to affect the behavior of others in particular directions.
   b. Affected by rank.
8. Differentiation and cohesion are related to productivity, satisfaction, and development.
   a. Relation to task requirements.
   b. Relation to external status.
   c. Relation to support of organization's goals.

SUGGESTED READINGS

Bales, R. F., and Strodtbeck, F. L. "Phases In Group Problem Solving," *Journal of Abnormal and Social Psychology,* 46 (1951) 485.

Grinnell, S. B. "The Informal Action Group: One Way to Collaborate in a University," *JABS* 5 (1969) 75–103.

Hollander, E. P. *Leaders, Groups and Influence.* New York: Oxford University Press, 1964.

Hopkins, T. H. *The Exercise of Influence in Small Groups.* Totowa, New Jersey: The Bedminster Press, 1964.

Kahn, R. L., Wolfe, D. M., Quinn, R. P., and Snoek, J. D. *Organizational Stress: Studies in Role Conflict and Ambiguity.* New York: John Wiley & Sons, Inc., 1964.

Maier, Norman R. F. "Assets and Liabilities in Problem Solving: The Need for an Integrated Function," *Psychological Review* 74 (1967) 244.

_____ "Male vs. Female Discussion Leaders," *Personnel Psychology* 23 (1970) 455–61.

Thompson, V. A. *Modern Organization.* New York: Alfred A. Knopf, 1961.

The smaller the group the fewer total resources there are available for work; however, it is easier to obtain full participation and coordination of individual effort.

6

DEVELOPING GROUP EFFECTIVENESS
Emergent Processes

Do you think you could tell from observing a group how well it is working? What criteria would you use? We have suggested you judge by the outcomes — productivity, member satisfaction and development. While these are the ultimate criteria of group effectiveness, it would be hard for a group to improve its operations as it went along if this were the only way to make judgments. To wait for the final outcomes to occur can be too late. Nor is progress toward those final outcomes necessarily an adequate basis for corrective action, since progress may become visible only when it is too late to take such action. Therefore, it is important for a group to have some basis for evaluating its emergent processes as it carries out a given task. The group needs to raise such questions as, "Are we working in the right way?" "Does everyone adequately understand his or her job?" "Are we avoiding important issues?" and "How do people feel about the objectives of the work?" To the extent that a group has available some set of criteria by which it can assess its processes, it is in a stronger position to improve the way it goes about a task.

The effectiveness of any group depends upon several factors. The presence of appropriate human and technological resources are background factors which establish both the possibilities and the limits for productive outcomes. Further, the policies and directives that make up the required system have direct influence over the effectiveness of a working group. Accordingly, most managers pay a great deal of attention to both background and required aspects of a work setting; they take great pains to select the right people for a job and to spell out job requirements and specifications. Yet the emergent processes of a work group, which are equally important, are often overlooked except when they overtly disrupt the work. Even when managers recognize the importance of dealing with emergent processes, they often lack a useful set of criteria by which to judge.

> For example, the top planning group of an aerospace firm was having a great deal of trouble producing useful plans. Their meetings often wandered from their stated agenda to rambling discussions of new books about youth in America, psychological interpretations of current events, etc. In the meantime corporate profits were steadily declining. Though the vice president for planning was not happy with the way the group worked, he would not risk pushing the group to examine its own processes, partly because he did not know how to judge them himself. Meetings got worse and worse, frustration grew and finally individual members began to quit for other jobs.

While Chapters 4 and 5 examined the emergent *properties* of a group (its structure or state, integration/differentiation, at any point in time), this chapter will focus upon the emergent *processes* (the dynamics) of a group as it functions. In short, the chapter will use a kind of social-psychological "microscope" to examine *how* a group operates.

As a starting point, we will look at issues faced by every working group, how these issues determine the criteria by which to evaluate the appropriateness of a given group's process, and how these evaluations need to take into account the particular situation of the group (for example, its purpose, size, composition, surrounding circumstances, and so forth). While it will not be possible to cover all the varieties of situations and show how the criteria apply in every case, we will give you a general sense of how to fit the two together. The bulk of the chapter uses two contrasting case examples to demonstrate how to consider situational factors when evaluating a group's process.

ISSUES FACING EVERY WORK GROUP

Every work group has to deal with the same general issues, regardless of whether it is a group of machinists on a shop floor, surgeons and nurses in an operating room, executives at a strategy meeting or students on a task force. It is the *way* in which a group goes about dealing with each of these issues and resolving the accompanying dilemmas that constitutes the group's emergent system and thus its effectiveness. While the dilemmas are similar for all groups, there are many possible ways of resolving them; and while groups vary in what the members consider desirable or preferable, different circumstances call for different approaches.

Figure 6–1 shows eleven issues facing every work group.[1] Corresponding to each issue we have listed sets of questions with which a group must cope. We suggest that you study the chart carefully, see how it applies to any group of which you are a member and evaluate how well that group has gone about dealing with the issues. Even before we go into detail on these eleven criteria of an effective group, you can probably discover some useful ways to apply them for yourself.

FIGURE 6–1
Issues Facing a Work Group

Issue	Questions
1. Atmosphere and relationships	What kinds of relationships should there be among members? How close and friendly, formal or informal?
2. Member participation	How much participation should be required of members? Some more than others? All equally? Are some members more needed than others?
3. Goal understanding and acceptance	How much do members need to *understand* group goals? How much do they need to *accept* or be *committed* to the goals? Everyone equally? Some more than others?
4. Listening and information sharing	How is information to be shared? Who needs to know what? Who should listen most to whom?
5. Handling disagreements and conflict	How should disagreements or conflicts be handled? To what extent should they be resolved? Brushed aside? Handled by dictate?

---

[1] A number of years ago, Douglas McGregor, a leading organizational theorist, described 11 criteria of an effective working group. While his studies were specific to certain kinds of groups (mainly executives), the issues inherent in McGregor's criteria serve as a useful framework for this chapter. See D. McGregor, *The Human Side of Enterprise.* (New York: McGraw-Hill, 1960).

FIGURE 6-1 *Continued*

Issue	*Questions*
6. Decision making	How should decisions be made? Consensus? Voting? One-man rule? Secret ballot?
7. Evaluation of member performance	How is evaluation to be managed? Everyone appraises everyone else? A few take the responsibility? Is it to be avoided?
8. Expressing feelings	How should feelings be expressed? Only about the task? Openly and directly?
9. Division of labor	How are task assignments to be made? Voluntarily? By discussion? By leaders?
10. Leadership	How should leadership *functions* be exercised? Shared? Elected? Appointed from outside?
11. Attention to process	How should the group monitor and improve its own process? Ongoing feedback from members? Formal procedures? Avoding direct discussion?

Every one of these issues can be related to some key aspect of a group's activities, interactions, attitudes and norms. In examining group process you might be looking at who is doing what, how he/she is doing it, who is interacting with whom, what seem to be the prevailing feelings, what kind of norm(s) has emerged in relation to a given issue, and so forth. Which of these questions demands attention depends entirely upon the particular situation, its complexity, its history, and so forth. For the sake of convenience throughout this chapter we will use the word "process" as a general term referring to any one or more of these emergent aspects of a group. It will be your job to determine *which* aspect of group "process" needs evaluation in any given set of circumstances. However, it is important to pay particular attention to group *norms,* since these govern the internal workings of a group. Because norms are difficult to change, their functionality needs to be examined as they emerge and before they become set in concrete. In fact, the eleven issues can be thought of as a classification system for group norms and therefore, serve as a systematic guide to their evaluation.

WHAT THE WORK SITUATION REQUIRES

There are many factors that can be used to determine differences in what kind of group process is appropriate to the job. We will focus on *five* which tend to have direct and important consequences. These are:

The size of the work group,
The distribution of resources (expertise) in the group,
The complexity and/or diversity of the task,
The time pressure on the group to produce,
The degree of task interdependence required.

As we discuss each of these factors we will generate propositions that describe the effects that each factor has on a work group. After we have discussed the factors, we will look at two examples which represent sharp contrasts in relation to all five of them. Then, using the examples as a point of reference, we will discuss each of the eleven criteria (Fig. 6–1) and see how they serve to describe effective working groups of very different kinds.

The Size of the Work Group

From your experience in groups of varying sizes, have you noticed how small groups have a different "feel" than large groups? The small group allows for closer relationships, a deeper knowledge of the members and a better sense of the whole picture at any given time. These are seen as advantages by many people and, consequently, they prefer working in a small group. Others are happier in a less intimate atmosphere, prefer the greater anonymity of the larger group and like the security of knowing there are more people to do the work and carry necessary group maintenance tasks.

Obviously, there has to be a trade-off in the various advantages of large versus small groups, many of which are primarily a matter of personal preference and many a matter of the inherent constraints posed by size. For example, it takes a greater effort and more formal procedures to make sure that everyone in a large group is fully informed in matters concerning them. It also takes more time and effort to coordinate the work of more people. While these issues influence the ease of conducting the group's operations, they may or may not detract from its ultimate effectiveness. Remember, our primary concern here has to do with the utilization of resources in carrying out a task. In this regard we can say that in most instances **The smaller the group the fewer total resources there are available for work; however, it is easier to obtain full participation and coordination of individual effort.** There may be rare exceptions to this proposition: John F. Kennedy once joked at a dinner of outstanding contributors to American life, "Never before have so many brains and talents been present in the same room at one time with the possible exception of the day when Thomas Jefferson dined alone!" Normally, however, fewer people mean fewer work resources, with the result that each carries a greater burden.

The Distribution of Resources (expertise) in the Group

Suppose an instructor assigned you to a group of students to work on a problem which involved the use of quantitative analysis. It's likely that you would depend upon the group member(s) who knew such methods best to take the most active part in the task. If the relevant abilities were evenly distributed among the members, the load would not fall upon any one or two individuals, but could be shared by all. The proposition in this regard follows very directly from the example. **The more evenly distributed are the resources (levels of expertise) of a group among its members, the more appropriate is total member participation.** This does not rule out the option of assigning specific jobs to only one or two members; it indicates only that the degree to which the assignments can appropriately be spread around depends upon the distribution of resources. It is as wasteful to give specific work to members who are unable to do that particular task as it is to ignore the most expert member.

The Complexity and/or Diversity of the Work

Suppose the task assigned in the example above were simply to determine the probability of occurrence of an event using some clearly specified information. While it would certainly take some ability to complete the assignment, it is likely that any one person who had studied probability could do it. If the assignment were much more complicated, like determining various production costs for a given product based upon information on manpower turnover, salary levels, overhead rates, market demand, and fluctuations in availability and costs of raw materials, the task might better be handled by the combined talents of several people. The proposition that follows from this is, **The greater the task complexity/diversity, the more appropriate it is to utilize the resources of a number of people.** It allows for the handling of a greater *amount* and *diversity* of information and in more complicated forms. Simple tasks call for simple information and fewer resources for completion.

In developing a plan of action for completing a complex task, groups are sometimes unable to work out every specific step ahead of time and to anticipate every contingency that might arise. Under such circumstances it becomes important for those who are implementing different aspects of the plan to "make the plan work" by adjusting and adapting to the contingencies encountered, and coordinating their alterations with those responsible for other parts of the plan. Yet this kind of creative and responsible behavior is not likely to be possible if the individual lacks knowledge about the rationale behind the plan, nor is he/she likely to be attentive to "making the plan work" if he/she lacks commitment to the plan. Thus another important proposition is: **The more likely it is that unexpected contingencies demanding immediate adaptation will occur in carrying out a task, the greater the need for members to have full information about the work plan's rationale, and be committed to the objectives of the plan.** Since the commitment to a course of action often rests on involvement in the development of the planned action and a consequent sense of ownership of the plan, a corollary proposition follows from the above: **The greater the need for individual members to make adjustments to a plan of action, the greater the need for them to share in the original planning and decision making.**

The Time Pressure on the Group to Produce

This issue poses a paradox. Very often when the time pressure is greatest, decisions are most critical. When decisions are most critical, the multiple resources of a group are most needed and thus the working process of that group is of greatest import. Yet the pressure to produce often makes it impossible to take the time to examine group process, even if it is operating poorly. Failure to take the time to look at process perpetuates that dysfunctional process; stopping to work on process eats up valuable time and can increase the stress with respect to the task. While either option is costly, the easiest time to work on group process issues is when there is adequate opportunity to deal with them fully; under pressure this is not likely to occur. Therefore, the proposition we suggest in this instance is that **The greater the time pressure, the less appropriate it is for the group to work on process issues.** One implication of this statement is that when time demands are at their lowest levels the group should examine its ways of working to prepare itself to deal more effectively with the periods of high pressure. When there are impending deadlines, a group needs to function well reflexively, though it is often only under pressure that group members realize what they have not settled! Thus it seems most useful to work on group processes early and on low-risk tasks where time is not crucial; then build on this base for key tasks and/or time constraints.

The Degree of Task Interdependence Required

A group of auto workers assembling a new car probably have their individual tasks pretty well routinized. They may talk a lot to each other, but it is not required in order to do the work. Their interactions depend more on personal preferences, mutual attractions, interests outside the task, and so forth; what we have called emergent factors. There is some degree of interdependence among the tasks each is performing because some jobs cannot proceed until others have been completed. However, the bases of the interdependence are clearcut and require relatively little exchange of information in an on-going manner. By way of contrast, a group of friends playing touch football constantly need to exchange information on strategy, weak spots in the other team, mistakes in their own play, and so on. These exchanges are demanded by the nature of their task almost from moment to moment. The player throwing a pass needs to be able to anticipate where the receiver will be and who will be blocking the onrushing opponents. Whether or not the auto workers ever develop any degree of friendship, mutual understanding seems only peripherally related to task accomplishment. In the case of the touch football team, it is extremely useful for the members to know a great deal about each other's abilities, as well as develop a sense of confidence in and support for each other. The degree of interdependence required leads to what we might call a *team* which goes a step beyond what we call a group.

The proposition that applies in this instance is, **The greater the degree of task interdependence required, the more important it is for group members to maintain continuing exchanges with and have knowledge of each other as persons.** The proposition refers primarily to task-related information. Whether or not personal friendships, as opposed to working colleagueships, develop in the course of the interactions is again a matter of member preferences and opportunities. It is not critical to the group's success, though likely when there is high interdependence. Think, for example, of the astronauts, whose very lives depend on one another's skill, knowledge and performance. It is not surprising that, at least while they work together, their families become close, spend time together and form relationships beyond what is directly required by work.

When You Put All the Factors Together

Each of the five factors can vary and can yield a tremendous variety of possible combinations. You find small groups with an imbalanced distribution of resources, working on simple tasks under high pressure, as in a group monitoring an automated chemical process; or large groups with high task interdependence working on complex tasks under little pressure, as in a corporate research lab. There are obviously too many possible combinations to explore each one. It might be useful and fun for you to generate different combinations and see if you can think of groups that fit; or you might take a look at some groups you know and see if you can describe them in terms of these five factors. Then later, as we discuss the kinds of group processes that are appropriate to a given set of circumstances, you can determine how those processes apply to your own examples. For illustration we will utilize two case examples of a highly contrasting nature. In this way we can highlight the importance of considering the situation when you determine what kind of group processes are appropriate.

THE CASE OF THE FACULTY GROUP

Suppose you were observing a group of seven faculty members working on the development of a new, interdisciplinary graduate program in the social sciences. Their individual backgrounds are varied, they are each highly knowledgeable in one or another area of social science and they are all considered to be competent teachers and scholars. The task before them involves many different specialties that need to be integrated, a lot of uncertainty about the outcomes of this type of educational venture, and a tremendous amount of material that needs to be prepared and reviewed in order to put together a proposal that can be accepted by colleagues and administrators. There is very little outside pressure to complete the proposal, so the group can take whatever time it wishes for the task. Since the entire concept of the program involves careful integration of all their ideas and expertise, every aspect of the work demands highly interdependent working relationships.

THE CASE OF THE RESTAURANT STAFF

Let's look at another group, one that is different from the first. It consists of 25 members of the staff of a high class restaurant. The group includes various levels of expertise from the head chef and maitre d' on down to the dishwashers and busboys, as well as wide variations in experience in a food service industry. The tasks themselves are not very complex, except for the chef's; each person has a clearly defined job with a very limited range of diversity. The restaurant has an excellent reputation to maintain and every member of the staff is under pressure to be on his or her toes at all times, paying attention to the quality of the food, the service, the cleanliness of the tables and floor, and so forth. While the job that any one person performs, especially at such levels as chef or maitre d', can affect the whole operation, each person's work is sharply enough differentiated so that much of it can be performed independently of the other employees. There are key points, however, where coordination is needed, in such matters as preparing orders in time, picking up food as it is ready to be served, getting tables cleared off fast enough to prepare for the next customer, and so on. But once a system has been devised, these are routine matters and do not require elaborate or intensive discussion and analysis by the staff at the time of execution.

HOW THE CRITERIA APPLY TO THE ISSUES FACING EACH GROUP

Atmosphere and Relationships

What seems most needed by the faculty group is an atmosphere of open exchange of ideas in a rather loose and nonconstraining setting. The more informal, close and friendly the relationships, the easier it will be for that kind of exchange to occur. An atmosphere of comfort and relaxation tends to facilitate the free flow of creative ideas.

While perhaps few people would prefer a formal, "strictly business" type of atmosphere, the restaurant setting seems to require something fairly close to that among the staff. Since the customers in this type of restaurant would probably desire a pleasant but deferential, welcoming atmosphere, the staff in this situation would need to strike a balance between the tight coordination among the tasks (the more formal aspects of the job) and the welcoming attitude conveyed to the customers (the more informal aspects). The two kinds of atmospheres are related; the nature of the tasks themselves calls for more business-like relationships, cordial and efficient, rather than close intimate ones.

Member Participation

A central question here is, "Does the level of participation of the members fit with their respective levels of task expertise?" It is not practical that in all situations everyone should share equally in the group's air time (though some groups might consider it ideologically desirable). Participation should depend upon the distribution of resources among the members. The faculty group is likely to require approximately equal participation from all its members. Each possesses a wide range of talents and knowledge relevant to the total task.

The restaurant staff, in contrast, is much more differentiated with respect to resources, experience and perspective on the task. Individuals at the level of head chef or maitre d' or host(ess) have a general sense of the total operation. They would need to participate more in the discussion of major plans or problems than, for example, the dishwashers or busboys (girls), whose jobs call for a much more circumscribed kind of involvement.

At the same time, it has been demonstrated many times over that **The greater the participation of members in resolving an issue, the greater their commitment to the decision.** From the point of view of productivity, the question becomes, "how *important* is a particular employee's commitment?" A person doing a routine, repetitive job may do no better being committed to it than one who just puts in time for money. Whether participation is then worthwhile on other grounds, like improved morale, is an issue for the manager.

Goal Understanding and Acceptance

It is difficult to perform a task if you don't understand it and it is difficult though not always impossible to do a *good* job if you don't feel committed to it. The level of understanding and acceptance required of any individual in a work group depends upon the scope of that person's responsibility. While he/she might *like* to know more, it may not be really required by the nature of the task.

In the faculty group all members share equal responsibility for the development of the program. It is important, therefore, that every member have a complete understanding of and feel a high level of commitment to the task goals. These goals are not likely to be clearcut and certain; consequently, understanding and acceptance are critical factors in the success of the work.

In the restaurant staff the importance of understanding and accepting the goals of the restaurant varies from person to person, depending upon the scope of his or her role in the task. The chef's knowledge and attitude can make a substantial difference in the quality of the food, but even a surly dishwasher can wash dishes. We're not suggesting that the attitude of the dishwasher is unimportant; we are saying that his/her understanding and acceptance of the goals of the restaurant are much less important to the success of the work effort than those of the chef or the maitre d'. The latter is really *required* by the situation; the former is not. Again, however, there has been some research suggesting that employees who are working on whole tasks, where they can see the final product, identify with the unit's goals, and be fully aware of their contribution to it, perform better. Organizing work so that even the dishwasher can do more challenging portions of the task is not always easy, but may be worth exploring.

Listening and Information Sharing

The principal question here is, "Do the members of the group pay attention to the ideas, opinions and knowlege of those members who possess the necessary expertise?" Since increasing numbers of tasks in our society require multiple resources, it has become more important over the years for people to learn how to build upon each other's knowledge and abilities. To do so they must be willing to listen to one another and to acknowledge the worth of each other's contribution to a job. This takes time and effort, but it pays off in several ways. First, it generally leads to better decisions, since maximum information is available and brought to bear upon an issue. Second, it generates greater task commitment, since ownership of the task is more widely shared. And third, it increases group cohesion, since members feel respected and supported.

In the faculty group the open and equal sharing of information and ideas is necessary to the task. The information, knowledge and special expertise are spread throughout the group and are relevant to the total task at almost any time. It is appropriate, in this case, that every member of the group be listened to by every other member virtually at all times.

For the restaurant staff the situation is a little different. While people prefer to be listened to, and feel good when they are, some situations simply do not call for it on a global basis. Again the chef, manager, maitre d' and possibly, the head waiter possess information and experience that gives greater weight to what they have to say. It is not a matter of devaluating the ideas of a kitchen worker; it is a matter of who has the most appropriate information and the best perspective on the particular work. These are the individuals whose opinions ought to carry the greatest weight. Often, of course, the person actually doing the work, no matter how far down in the organization, knows something that others more removed do not, and in such instances, should be given greater weight exactly because of his/her superior, first-hand knowledge. Too often, highly educated staff experts fail to find out what intuitive expertise exists among "operators" on the line.

Handling Disagreements

The question here is, "Does the group handle disagreements in such a way as to facilitate task accomplishment, or, at least prevent them from getting in the way of the task?" At one extreme a group might insist on talking through every disagreement until it is resolved; at the other extreme a group might tend to brush aside any form of disagreement. Rarely is either extreme appropriate to a work group (though the first might be for a therapy group). Although only a few people enjoy disagreements they are a fact of life. It is very rare that any group of people can all agree on everything. Interestingly enough, conflicts can be very *functional* to a task, especially when the task involves room for a wide variety of points of view.

In the case of the faculty group we would expect just such a situation; we would expect a lot of disagreement along the road to successful program development. It would be highly appropriate for that group to discuss and work its way through points of disagreement; it would be likely to improve the quality of the group's decisions and commitment to their implementation.

For the restaurant staff the situation is less open to wide variations of opinion. In fact, it is quite probable that the years of experience (assuming the presence of competence) of such people as the head chef, maitre d' or some of the more experienced waiters might be the appropriate basis for settling disputes regarding procedures, particularly when those disputes occur with or among less experienced staff. In contrast to the faculty group, it is also unlikely that a restaurant staff would have either the time or the desire to work through very many disagreements. They would need to be much more selective, work through those in which there was room for legitimate differences of opinion and rely upon expertise to settle the others.

Making Decisions

Decisions can be made democratically or autocratically; they can be made with the consent of all or by the dictates of a few. While most of us may identify with the democratic process, it is not always the most appropriate form of decision making in a group. Again leaving aside individual preferences, we can consider what kind of decision-making process is appropriate to a given situation. The faculty group represents the kind of situation that calls for decisions by consensus. There are several reasons for this. First, the uncertainties and complexities inherent in developing an academic program normally require a full mix of resources and a series of decisions that no one or two people can make. Researchers have shown that under conditions like the one cited here, group consensus tends to produce relatively high quality decisions. Second, decisions by consensus tend to result in a high level of commitment to the outcome. This would be a definite asset to a group of faculty attempting to start a new program.

In contrast, the restaurant staff would probably be an example of where consensus would be inappropriate for most decisions. Again, because of the size of the group and the wide discrepancies in experience, expertise, levels of responsibility, and so forth, the more important decisions would be best left to those who possess the necessary information and knowledge to make them. It would seldom make sense for a dishwasher to decide the chef's specials or for the cloakroom attendant to determine the best seating arrangement for a wedding party. Whatever the process of decision making, the central issue always has to do with making the best possible use of the resources and expertise present in a given group.

Evaluation of Member Performance

Performance appraisal is an important function of any task group. It is helpful for individuals to receive feedback on their work, positive or negative, in order for them to correct deficiencies and build on strengths.

Performance appraisal is most useful when it occurs close to the actual performance and comes from a knowledgeable source.

In the faculty group it would be most appropriate, personal inclinations aside, for members to offer frequent, direct and open praise and criticism of each other's ideas and actions relevant to the task. As peers, they are all useful sources of evaluation for each other.

In the restaurant staff, where the expertise is highly differentiated, work appraisals most appropriately occur from the top down. Remember, we are not talking about interpersonal feedback; that matter is covered in another chapter. We are talking about task performance only, where knowledge and experience determine the ability to offer constructive criticism. It must be acknowledged, however, that those at lower levels of an organization often do possess valuable observations about the performance of those in higher positions, and we by no means want to suggest that those with higher positions or greater learning should cut off criticism from below.

Another aspect of criticism has to do with readiness to receive it. In some groups such openness may be too painful for some members, no matter how needed. In that kind of situation, it may be better to withold even valid criticism, despite the loss of information entailed, because of the possibility of even more negative consequences. In general, however, it is our observation that people can usually take more than is frequently assumed, and in most groups we see greater error through overcaution than overbluntness.

Expressing Feelings

It is not hard to find people who argue that the expression of feelings has no place in a work setting. While that idea has been drilled into many in Western cultures, we feel it is constraining and unrealistic, given the emotional nature of the human being. The problem is how to establish some way of dealing with people's feelings about their work that *helps* the work effort and does not inappropriately drain off energy which is needed for task work. The expression of feelings and the process of dealing with the consequences can be painful, tiring and very time-consuming; but the failure to have them expressed and dealt with at all can ultimately be damaging to the members of a work group, as problems magnify under the pressure of witholding. Quite a dilemma!

Given the nature of the task and the size of their group, it seems appropriate for the faculty committee to express and deal with feelings in an ongoing way, openly and directly. The group cannot afford to "lose" any one member as a result of his or her feeling "turned off" to the task. Not only are each person's resources needed, but as we noted in Chapter 5, a disgruntled member can draw attention away from the task and hamper productivity. On occasions it means that the group will have to interrupt the task in order to discuss member feelings; it also means that the group members will need to take the responsibility to voice their feelings and to pay attention to those of others. It is not just negative feelings that require attention; the expression of joy, excitement and liking can be equally appropriate, in fact, crucial to a group's success.

In a group the size of the restaurant staff, with its mission, the expression of feelings becomes problematic. It would be more appropriate to utilize some planned procedures for gathering data on members' feeling about their work even though it may seem a bit mechanical. The data collection might be in the form of some impersonal questionnaires (though many people find these objectionable), or through scheduled interviews or group discussions outside of regular working hours. These latter approaches are generally found to be more comfortable for everyone concerned. The key difference between this situation and that of the faculty group is that the procedures for dealing with feelings normally have to be more planned and formalized. However, if they are built into the overall work environment, they are more appropriate than the looser and more spontaneous process that fits the faculty group situation.

Here again, as with expression of criticism, readiness to hear feelings affects what is possible. There are groups which are so tense about any emotion being openly expressed that no matter how great the need for such exchanges, they only lead to embarrassment and discomfort. Conversely, there are groups where personal needs for openness and closeness are so overwhelming that any encouragement of feeling expression leads to possibly satisfying but lengthy, non-work related personal discourses. Nevertheless, ways need to be found to get feelings known so they can be taken into account in doing the group's work.

Division of Labor

An effective group must be able to move from decisions to action, to role assignments, and to responsible carry-through. Nothing defeats a group more readily than failure to complete its promised action steps. One difficulty in this process is the fact that some assignments are more attractive than others; some are just plain drudgery. In a group such as the faculty group it is appropriate that some negotiation take place around task assignments. In this way the members can exercise some choice and still share equitably the "drudge" jobs, such as searching through piles of literature to see what other programs have done or composing letters of inquiry to other universities. Where special talent dictates, then the group can arrange its assignments to capitalize on that talent; where anyone can do a particular job, preferences can be exercised and roles can shift around as desired.

In the restaurant setting the jobs are much more specialized. Task assignments tend to be either predetermined or limited in range by the person's background and/or training. Negotiation of assignments would not be very appropriate to the situation, except on a very limited basis. A waiter might work in the kitchen on some occasions, or a maitre d' might have to act as head waiter at times. It is more appropriate that those individuals who possess the greatest knowledge of the work and whose expertise gives them the greatest legitimacy be the ones who carry the greatest weight in determining work assignments. It allows for the best matching of resources with jobs.

The Leadership Process

Here we are talking about leadership as a process, and we are limiting our discussion to that aspect of the leadership process that determines the way in which a group conducts itself. All the other dimensions we will leave to the chapter on leadership. The appropriate leadership process in a small group of equals (with respect to competence on the task) is one in which leadership is shared and changes as the task itself changes. At times it will be appropriate for some members to carry more influence than others; at other times the pattern will be different. What seems to be important is that the group legitimize this process in order to make the most of its resources. If, for example one member of the faculty group is especially good at expressing ideas in writing, his/her influence should carry more weight in the writeup of the proposal. Where any given social science specialty is being discussed, then the member most expert in that area should exert leadership.

The restaurant staff has more the appearance of a chain of command. The leadership functions are clearly defined by the tasks themselves and by the expertise of the individuals carrying out those tasks. As long as the levels of competence are congruent with the levels of authority, then the formal leadership pattern can be translated into an appropriate leadership process. If the group moves outside the boundaries of this process, as when a nonappointed leader attempts to exercise a great deal of influence, the group is put under a strain. The action of that person is not appropriate to the situation. There may very well be other factors that would justify such behavior, but we are confining ourselves to the process called for by the work situation. In short, the leadership process appropriate to the restaurant staff would be a relatively formal one determined by the experience and knowledge of the members, and one which would show little change over time.

Attention to Group Process

When a group is small and is operating in the kind of situation that is full of uncertainties, changing roles, open flow of information, and so forth, its working process tends to fluctuate all over the place. Frequent and deliberate stopping to look at the group's way of operating is highly appropriate for such a situation. In fact, it can make the difference between success and failure in the long run. There is always danger that the group will become overly engrossed in examining its own process, but that is normally a small price to pay compared to the time and effort wasted in operating ineffectively. The faculty group would need to look at itself from time to time, especially on those occasions when it was making little progress. Through a self-conscious examination of process the group can improve its use of member resources; it can establish a pattern of feedback to itself that helps it to build on strengths and correct deficiencies.

In a group of the size and nature of the faculty group there are several options for engaging in this kind of activity. One is to set aside a fixed amount of time at the end of each meeting to share perceptions and feelings about the way the group is working. Another method is to have a ground rule that permits discussion of process at any time a member deems it appropriate. This can interrupt the flow of work, but it has the advantage of dealing with issues as they occur. It also may be that the group will have to wait until it is really bogged down to get some reluctant members to accept the idea that talking about process and "personal feelings" is legitimate. Then a special "retreat" meeting may be acceptable. You could probably invent some of your own procedures for looking at group process; it would be useful for you to do so in any group in which you think it would be appropriate.

In a situation like that of the restaurant staff, an open discussion of group process does not fit. There are too many people, too many factors, too little time and not the kinds of fluctuations and uncertainties that make such an effort imperative. Those in the higher level positions need to pay attention to how things are going and need to gather data from all the staff who can bring issues to their attention. However, these procedures would have to be more formal and systematic in order to be useful. It would not be very appropriate to conduct process sessions of the kind that fit the faculty group.

Rarely, however, does a group not at some time, in some way, need to examine its process. An effective group will do this in a way that is as rapid and efficient as possible, but it can seldom be completely avoided without difficulties arising.

Now, let's summarize the whole picture comparing these two groups and the kinds of work situations they represent.

SUMMARY OF HOW THE CRITERIA APPLY TO EACH GROUP

The Faculty Group The group of faculty members working on a graduate program proposal can be described as:

A. A small group with

B.   Evenly distributed resources,
C.   Dealing with a complex and diverse task
D.   Under little external time pressure,
E.   But requiring a high level of interdependence.

Under these circumstances the appropriate group processes would tend to be as follows:

1.   Informal atmosphere with close friendly relationships.
2.   Full participation of all members equally.
3.   High level of goal understanding and acceptance on the part of every group member.
4.   Complete sharing of all information with every member listening to every other member.
5.   Disagreements discussed and resolved, not set aside.
6.   Decisions made by group consensus.
7.   Criticism of performance open and direct among all group members.
8.   Feeling about task expressed openly and directly.
9.   Task assignments made and accepted through discussion and negotiation; as voluntary as possible.
10. Leadership shared freely and changed along with corresponding changes in situational demands.
11. Group devotes significant blocks of time to the discussion of its own process.

The Restaurant Staff   The staff of the high-class restaurant can be described as:

A.   A large group with
B.   Highly differentiated resources
C.   Dealing with simple and narrow tasks, except for a few highly skilled jobs like chef,
D.   Under a high level of time pressure,
E.   With a relatively low level of task interdependence except at a few key points.

Under these circumstances the appropriate group processes would tend to be:

1.   Formal atmosphere with task-relevant relationships.
2.   Participation in discussions based upon expertise.
3.   Understanding and acceptance of goals related to level and scope of job responsibilities.
4.   Members obtain information from and listen to those other members possessing greater relevant knowledge.
5.   Only those disagreements directly interfering with task are dealt with; final resolution determined by those members with greatest expertise.

6. Decisions made by those with relevant level of knowledge and expertise.
7. Criticism of work made by those members with the requisite knowledge and experience.
8. Feelings expressed through prescribed procedures.
9. Assignments made by those members with greatest level of knowledge and expertise.
10. Leadership on any given aspect of task determined by the relevant knowledge and experience.
11. Very little time devoted to examining group process; procedures are devised by higher level members and carried out in a formal manner.

As you compare the two pictures just drawn, you might have some personal reactions to them. The first one portrays a kind of setting that many but not all people prefer, while the second has the ring of a small bureaucracy and may not be quite as attractive to you, though there are people who do prefer working in more structured, defined settings. Again we wish to remind you that what actually happens in any given situation is not just a matter of what the nature of the situation requires or calls for, it is also a matter of what other options are possible and what the members of any group might consider most desirable for them. The staff of the restaurant might very well *choose* to operate in a manner similar to that of the faculty group, but it would be fighting an uphill battle in the face of what the task situation demands. For example, try to imagine twenty-five people struggling to resolve all the disagreements which can occur in that large a number. How feasible would it be for such a group to arrive at a consensus on all issues? What would be the costs of ignoring the many years of experience and the levels of expertise that some individuals possess in order to widen and maximize member participation? And what would happen if everyone criticized everyone else and freely expressed all their feelings about every aspect of their work? Though such a set of choices might be made to work, it would consume extraordinary energy, and in the long run, it would be unlikely to get the work done effectively.

What both situations have in common is that they are maximizing the use of group member resources. They are appropriately different from each other in *how* they use their resources, but they can be equally high in the outcomes of productivity, worker satisfaction and development.

SOME VIABLE ALTERNATIVES

Are we saying that a group is "stuck" with a set of processes dictated by circumstances? No. We are saying that a given group needs to consider the nature of its circumstances in judging the effectiveness of its own processes. If it is a large group and applies small group standards, it will create difficulties for itself. And this same reasoning applies to each of the five conditions discussed earlier.

However, a group can *change* its circumstances. A large group can subdivide into smaller groups, each of which can utilize effective small group process criteria. Further, if the subdivisions equalize the levels of expertise in each subgrouping, then other criteria begin to change in their application. At the restaurant, for example, it may be that waiters in each area can usefully meet to discuss possible areas of cooperation, or chef, maitre d' and key waiters might periodically examine the way orders are transmitted. Some factors, like task complexity and required interdependence may be less subject to change, but even with these there is the possibility of exploring various forms of innovation and work variation. For example, individuals normally assigned to one kind of task can exchange jobs with others in order to learn a wider range of tasks.

We do consider it critical, however, that a work group, in order to be effective, remember to utilize its full range of resources. **If the task calls for differentiated levels of expertise in a group, then the effectiveness of that group's process will depend upon the degree to which it gives influence to appropriate members.** By way of contrast, **If the task calls for evenly distributed resources among the members of a group, then the effectiveness of the group's process will depend upon the degree to which influence is equally shared among the members.**

By the time you have read this you may have had sufficient experience in a classroom task group to be able to apply the various criteria to your own experience. Can you correlate how well your group has done on group assignments with the way you have been operating? What should you change? What seems to have worked well? Why?

The performance of your group depends on your ability to analyze the task demands, determine the appropriate set of processes, discuss how they vary from what you have been doing, and make whatever changes are necessary (consistent with your desires). As awkward as it may feel to discuss openly the way you have been making decisions, talking and listening to one another, handling disagreements, and so forth, it is in your collective interest to do so if you haven't already. The ability to find ways to correct a group's (or organization's or individual's) process is a crucial one which can serve you well throughout your organizational career.

KEY CONCEPTS FROM CHAPTER 6

1. Group effectiveness related to emergent processes.
2. Process issues faced by every work group:
   a. Atmosphere and relationships

      b. Member participation.
      c. Goal understanding and acceptance
      d. Listening and information sharing.
      e. Handling disagreements and conflicts.
      f. Decision making.
      g. Evaluation of member performance.
      h. Expressing feelings.
      i. Work assignments.
      j. Leadership
      k. Process evaluation

3. Factors affecting appropriateness of group process:
      a. Size
      b. Distribution of resources.
      c. Task complexity/diversity.
      d. Time pressure.
      e. Degree of interdependence.

4. The smaller the group, the fewer total resources and the more appropriate is participation by all.

5. The more evenly distributed the resources (expertise) the more appropriate is total member participation.

6. The greater the complexity/diversity, the more resources needed.

7. The greater the time pressure, the less time for process.

8. The greater the task interdependence, the greater the need for continuous exchanges and knowledge of each other on the part of group members.

9. The greater the member participation, the greater the level of commitment to goals.

SUGGESTED READINGS

Argyris, C. "T-Groups for Organizational Effectiveness," *Harvard Business Review* 42 (1964) 60–68.

Bales, R. F. *Interaction Process Analysis.* Cambridge, Mass.: Addison Wesley, 1950.

Campbell, J., and Dunnette, M. "Effectiveness of T-Group Experiences in Managerial Training and Development," *Psychological Bulletin* 70 (1968) 73–103.

Davis, J. H. *Group Performance.* Reading, Mass.: Addison-Wesley Publishing Company, Inc., 1969.

McGregor, D. *The Human Side of Enterprise.* New York: McGraw-Hill Book Co., 1960.

Miles, M. B. *Learning to Work in Groups, A Program Guide for Educational Leaders.* New York: Teachers College Press, Teachers College, Columbia University, 1959.

Patton, B. R., and Giffin, K. *Problem Solving Group Interaction.* New York: Harper & Row Pubs., Inc., 1973.

Rubin, I. M., and Beckhard, R. "Factors Affecting the Effectiveness of Health Teams," *Milbank Quarterly,* July, 1972.

Schein, E. *Process Consultation.* Reading, Mass. Addison-Wesley Publishing Company, Inc., 1969.

The intrinsic pleasure of conquering a complex task can be a powerful motivator quite apart from pay or praise received.

7

BASIC HUMAN NEEDS AND REWARDS

ONE MEMBER *of a student task group attends all meetings, but inevitably sits silently through the discussions. Though his grade depends partly on the contribution he makes to solving problems in the group and he has clearly done the necessary reading, he cannot be enticed, or bullied, into talking. He responds to all questions aimed at drawing him out with brief "yes" or "no" answers. When pressed for an opinion he mutters something like, "I agree with Harry." How would you explain and deal with his behavior?*

Joe Wexler is a 40 year old machinist who keeps getting fired from jobs.[1] In his current job he is once again heading for trouble. He keeps posting notices on the shop bulletin board, criticizing the company and its management practices, quoting poems and citing chess problems in order to "broaden horizons" among fellow workers. As chess champion of the city, he is clearly intelligent and able to see that his actions are provoking his boss; why does he continue to defy the requests to keep his notices down?

Throughout your life you have seen examples of people behaving in ways that do not make sense to you, that seem wrong, foolish, self defeating or totally

---

[1] "Howard Atkins and Joseph Wexler" case, copyright by President and Fellows, Harvard College.

incomprehensible. Sometimes you can shrug your shoulders and walk away, but as an organizational member, particularly one with managerial responsibilities, you cannot avoid dealing with difficult people. Furthermore, you can undoubtedly remember times when you were behaving in a way that seemed perfectly clear and logical to you, but was totally baffling to, or misunderstood by your parents, boss or friends. How to understand what is happening inside yourself or in another person is one of the most challenging, yet important, abilities you can acquire.

In the earlier chapters we looked at the needs of groups and organizational situations, focusing particularly on behavior that was appropriate to them. Now we will shift our attention to what is desired by individuals themselves, quite apart from what is called for by the external systems. One of our core premises is that for individuals much of organizational life requires balancing their own needs and desires with those of the organization. Sometimes it is possible to satisfy the person and the organization with the same action, and occasionally it is totally impossible to meet the needs of both. More often, people at work must find ways somehow to be true to themselves while still meeting organizational or group demands.

To illustrate how the individual is faced with a variety of choices for him or herself, we will take the Issues Facing a Work Group from the last chapter, and go through those showing the individual dilemmas each raises. A person joining a group goes through a series of possible choices about what joining will mean; in each case there is the possibility of (a) accepting the group's way of doing things, (b) trying to change it, or (c) refusing to go along with the particular behavior.

Group Issue	*Individual Dilemmas*
1. Atmosphere and relationship . . .	How friendly do I want to be? How close? Will others allow that?
2. Member participation	How much do I want to participate? Can I be as quiet/active as I'd like?
3. Goal understanding and acceptance	Are the group's goals compatible with mine? If I have different goals will there be a place for me? Should I seek a more compatible group or try to change my goals?
4. Listening and information sharing	Will I be able to get the information I need to do my work? To whom do I have to listen? Can I get others to listen to me?
5. Handling disagreements and conflict	How freely can I disagree? Will others disagree with me? Can I fight for what I believe in?

Group Issue	*Individual Dilemmas*
6. Decision making..............	Will I have a say in important decisions?
7. Criticism of member performance	Will I be able to tell others how they are doing? Who will tell me?
8. Expressing feelings	How open can I be about my feelings?
9. Division of labor	Who will decide what I do? How much say can I have over that?
10. Leadership...................	Will I be able to exert influence on the group? What happens if I try?
11. Attention to process	If I don't like the way we are doing things, can I say so?

The answers to these questions depend partly on the group's norms and operating procedures, and partly on the consequences one is willing to live with. As we have pointed out earlier, the behavior approved in one situation may be frowned upon in another; what we are interested in now is, given the external system's norms and values, what makes an individual respond in his or her particular way.

How does a person choose whether to go along with the group or organization, or even with another person? What motivates one person to willingly accept some group members doing almost nothing to contribute to solving group tasks, while another responds to the same problem with confrontation of the slackers, and still another fumes privately but only smiles in the group? How can we understand individual differences and similarities? With which of these following two quotes do you agree?

What is most personal is most general.

Carl Rogers[2]

Behavior is determined . . . by a personal, individual way of perceiving which is not identical to that of any other individual.

Combs & Snygg[3]

We will proceed on the assumption that *both* of the above contradictory statements are true. In some ways, we are all the same, stewing in the same juices, and we can understand particular behaviors through

---

[2] Carl Rogers, *On Becoming a Person* (Boston: Houghton Mifflin Co., 1961) p. 536.

[3] A. W. Combs and D. Snygg, *Individual Behavior* (New York: Harper & Bros., 1959) p. 19.

universal feelings and motives. In other ways, each of us represents a unique combination of elements, which adds spice to the universal stew, but makes prediction of behavior much more complicated.

For the manager–scientist, the problem is one of finding some useful concepts to guide his/her generalizations about people, other concepts to help understand the uniqueness of each person, and some guidelines to help know when to use which. That is not an easy task.

CHAPTERS 7 AND 8: FROM THE GENERAL TO THE PARTICULAR

In this chapter we will introduce you to some theories about human needs in general. Psychologists have many ways of categorizing human needs; we will use those which are most useful for understanding individual behavior at work. However, such theories tend to be quite broad and inclusive of wide variations in behavior. For example, we will refer to the "need for recognition" as a concept for understanding some aspects of behavior; while that notion might provide a possible insight into someone like Joe Wexler, the chess champ, it will fail to capture the particular *individual's* way of meeting that need. To understand the latter requires other frames of reference that tap into the individual's own world. Chapter 8 will be devoted to a concept we have found to be useful for understanding an individual's behavior, the *personal system.* It will be suggested as the stepping-stone into the world of another person, the key mechanism which modifies needs and produces particular behavior (See Fig. 7–1). Through it, we can come to understand and appreciate more fully the actions and attitudes of those around us.

FIGURE 7–1
The Personal System in Relation to Needs and Behavior

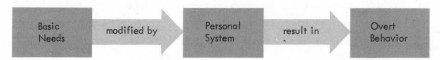

FUNDAMENTAL HUMAN NEEDS[4]

Survival Needs

The most uncomplicated behavior is found in infants. When they are hungry, thirsty or uncomfortable, they cry; when they are happy they smile or giggle; and when they are sleepy, they sleep. How simple a set of

---

[4] Much of this section is based upon the concepts of A. H. Maslow, F. Herzberg, R. White and D. McClelland. For references to the work of these authors, see the suggested reading lists at the end of this chapter and Chapter 8.

rules for predicting behavior! Through observing and studying infants psychologists have learned a great deal about the universal forces governing behavior; the infant's life is much less complicated than the adult's. Not many adults cry when hungry or thirsty; whether or not they cry when in pain depends upon what was learned as children. But at least people still smile and laugh when they are happy, and some people even go to sleep when they are sleepy. Although people tend to complicate the ways of meeting basic human needs, the needs still must be met; *survival* depends on it.

In order to survive, one must have enough air, water, food, protection from physical dangers, and so forth. The infant obviously is dependent upon others to have survival needs met; the best it can do is give some signals of hunger, thirst or discomfort. Fortunately, as mentioned above, the range of adult responses to the infant's signals requires little thought as to the uniqueness of the individual infant. Survival needs can be met in fairly universal ways. Even as they grow and mature people develop fairly similar methods of meeting these needs. Tastes and preferences develop, but the basic ingredients for survival are more or less universal.

Another characteristic of survival needs is that they demand relatively immediate gratification. Any parent will attest to that. The human organism will not tolerate deprivation of basic needs for very long without experiencing some level of threat. While you personally may not have had to endure prolonged periods of hunger or thirst or physical discomfort, can you see that even the fear of deprivation, let alone the experience of it, can act as a strong motivator?

Though increasing worldwide food shortages and ecological problems make the possibility less remote, contemporary organizations usually do not seem to be dealing directly with thirsty, hungry or physically uncomfortable employees. The fact is, however, that *indirectly* those issues are at the heart of organizational life. One reason why people work, and probably the most universal reason, is to survive, that is, to provide themselves with all the means necessary to guarantee adequate nourishment and protection from harm. And knowing this, it is possible for managers of organizations to expect people to exchange work effort for contribution to survival. While human motivation to work is certainly not governed solely by survival needs, it does seem to be based strongly enough upon them to account for the success of wage incentives, fringe benefits, pension plans, health benefits, and the whole myriad of programs typical of modern industry,

Those of you who have had to work undoubtedly can remember how important your paycheck was to you. People who are threatened about their survival will put up with almost any work conditions in order to earn the money necessary for food and shelter. Can you imagine yourself, however, spending your entire life in a job that satisfied only your basic needs? Most people seek something more from their work. What are some of the other sources of motivation?

Social Needs

Again we look to the developing infant for some clues. So far the little person has survived; he or she is adequately fed, clothed and protected. Not enough. We have already spoken of the human being as a social being; infants deprived of some basic minimal level of human contact do not grow in healthy ways. Normally the family provides the primary context for meeting the social needs of the infant, the needs for human contact and affection. The important ingredient is a kind of support base which provides a sense of belonging and the beginnings of feelings of personal worth. While the individual might survive the absence of such a support base, it is not likely to be a very healthy existence and can set the stage for a lifetime of desperately seeking a state of social belonging, or of apathetic withdrawal from human contact.

Like the survival needs, the social needs do not just disappear from the scene once provided for. They continue to exert important influences on individuals' behavior throughout their entire lives. Also, like the survival needs, when threatened they tend to prompt people into some kind of definite action. Think about those times when you have felt alone, isolated, deprived of the kinds of warmth and support that human contact alone can offer. You seek out your friends, or your family, or even casual acquaintances. When it gets really bad you may hang around a public place just to be in the presence of others, or you may even approach a total stranger to strike up a conversation.

> *No more fiendish punishment could be devised, were such a thing physically possible, than that one should be turned loose in society and remain absolutely unnoticed by all the members thereof.*
>
> William James
> *The Principles of Psychology XII*

Unlike the survival needs, the social needs do not seem to demand immediate gratification, at least among most adults. When necessary a person can await the return of a valued friend, although a letter or even just thinking about the other can provide some degree of comfort. Also, the social needs are expressed and satisfied in a greater number of ways than are the more basic survival needs. Look at the variety of social systems people live in, the differences in family relationships and the varying patterns of friendship and social groupings. In short, the social needs of people seem to have some relation to survival, but not quite the critical character of the needs for air, water, food, safety, and so forth. And while they exert powerful influence on all our behavior, they are subject to wide variations in styles.

For many years organizational managers paid little attention to the social needs of people. It was assumed that the economic reward of "a fair day's pay" would elicit a fair day's work, and that worker needs required no more attention. That assumption is only valid under certain limited conditions. Most people simply need more than just the pay for work, especially if they feel reasonably sure that they can get their needs for survival met elsewhere if necessary. In situations, however, where there are no other options for employment, human beings can be forced to work without any social interaction for very long stretches. Such a situation was observed by one of the authors at a very productive tile factory in India, which employed unskilled migrants from a poor region with severe chronic drought. Though workers in this factory stood face-to-face in groups of four, they were not allowed to speak to one another all day. The supervisor rigidly enforced the "no talking" rule, yet no one quit.

Nevertheless, over the years it has been discovered that worker productivity is usually governed to a great extent by their social relationships, a point we have already discussed in detail in earlier chapters. What we wish to bring out here pertains to the motivating forces behind those social interaction patterns. When permitted and/or encouraged, and when the physical setting does not constrain it, the social needs will make themselves visible. It is a process as inevitable as eating when you are hungry. When managers attempt to constrain social behavior beyond certain limits, the need does not disappear; it only gets coupled with frustration and seeks alternative outlets. For example, one factory erected a barricade between women employees seated opposite one another so as to discourage "distracting" conversation. This resulted in a significant increase in the number of trips the women made to the washroom! The smart manager–scientist is careful to look at the ways in which social behaviors may be functional or dysfunctional to the work effort. It is that distinction that enables him/her to provide ways to encourage the former and eliminate the latter.

Many of the cases you are studying in this book involve problems related to worker behavior that is a mix of work-related and social-related activities. It is often tempting to treat all social behavior as dysfunctional and, consequently, to recommend a hard line approach to eliminate it. We have already covered this issue with respect to the notions of required and emergent systems, the latter generally involving social behavior of one sort or another. Here we are re-emphasizing the same issue with the focus being human motivation. Arbitrarily curtailing all social behavior of workers not only overlooks the significance of emergent behavior but it goes counter to the very foundations of human needs.

So far we have talked about two fundamental sets of needs, those that affect survival and those that are of a social nature. Now we will go on to areas of motivation that appear a little later in the individual's developmental years. These areas are of major significance for the learning and growth of the individual.

Higher Level Needs

Most people are motivated by a range of needs that go well beyond survival and social belonging. They begin at a very early age to seek the approval and recognition of others and to seek a sense of personal respect that tells them that they are achieving something in this world, that they are leaving their mark on it in some way. For some people the route to self-esteem is through being productive, for others it lies in achieving higher and higher levels of prominence and recognition, and for some it comes through achieving authority and responsibility. It is through the satisfaction of these needs, particularly through work, that people feel adequate, and can grow and develop into fuller human beings.

Even beyond needs for achievement, recognition, responsibility, and so forth, there seems to be something more human beings each strive for, something which in some way reflects the inner potential inherent in each person. Such terms as "self-realization" or "self-actualization" have been used to identify this level of needs. Whatever one calls it, the reward for fulfilling any need at this level seems to be in the process itself and not necessarily in the responses of others. It is the doing, the engaging in the act itself that carries its own reward.

Another way of thinking about these kinds of accomplishments has been called the need for competence or mastery. Even very young children may spend hours attempting to master skills, aptitudes and abilities which are not directly connected to any safety or social rewards. Have you ever seen a baby practice pulling itself upright? As adults we still have the need to master new areas, whether work related or not. The intrinsic pleasure of conquering a complex task can be a powerful motivator quite apart from the pay or praise received. Hobbies can give pleasure just from engaging in them. Some people have jobs which involve high levels of creativity, imagination and problem solving ability, jobs which drive them to work very long hours without their even seeming to notice the effort. They can acknowledge the importance of the rewards which satisfy other needs, such as security of income, recognition by their organization, and so forth, but many insist that the overriding satisfaction is in the creative process itself. Can you think of activities, work or otherwise, which tend to absorb your time and energy for no other reason than the joy of engaging in them?

Other ways in which people meet needs for self-realization include learning and expanding knowledge, developing a philosophy of life, pursuing religious interests, and similar activities which yield a sense of self-expansion and growth. In recent years many people have "gone back to the soil," that is, they have discovered the sense of personal satisfaction and joy that lies in the process of raising plants, flowers, and crops of various sorts. It may be that the development of a total sense of appreciation for life and all its potential is the ultimate in self-realization.

If you examine the kinds of learning experiences you have had which have been the most personally rewarding, they are likely to be the ones that tap into the widest range of your needs, especially higher level ones. For some, the most satisfying learning, when they feel most engaged and alive, happens during a course or school experience. Too often, however, the most exciting learning only happens on your own. The satisfaction related to that kind of experience may be self-realization, a sense that you are realizing some inner potential for learning and growth.

When the time comes for you to pursue a career, it may be important for you to consider the full range of your own needs that can be met through work. Furthermore, if you ever become a manager who can influence the overall work environment, you may then need to remain aware of the great variety of human needs that may be fulfilled in that environment. In the next section we will look at the variations in needs as they pertain to different people, different circumstances and combinations of both. Though the connection between any concrete item of behavior and the needs leading to it may be obscure, almost anything a person does can be traced to the desire to satisfy some survival, social or higher order need.

Individual Variations in Human Needs

While all of the needs discussed — survival, social, self-esteem, mastery or self-actualization — appear to be universally operating for everyone some of the time, each person has different intensities of each need, and these intensities change in different situations. Some people, for example, are so preoccupied with gaining social acceptance that they hardly acknowledge or act on their other needs; it is as if they are "frozen" at one level of need and cannot unthaw enough to use the full range of human responses in them. Could that, for example, be a clue to understanding the silent group member, who, perhaps, so fears rejection that it becomes almost impossible to say anything which might be ridiculed?

There is controversy among psychologists about whether the needs discussed above, all exist simultaneously in people or are, indeed arranged in hierarchy.[5]

On the one hand, there is considerable evidence that a hierarchy does

---

[5] This controversy seems to reflect the principal difference between the points-of-view of Maslow and Herzberg, the former proposing the hierarchy model, the latter insisting that survival needs and growth needs ("motivators") exist along independent dimensions.

exist and that the lower level needs, that is, those that are more survival oriented, must be satisfied before the individual is able to devote energy to higher level needs. A frequently cited example is the starving man who is not likely to be concerned about his self-esteem until his belly is filled, as in the Indian company cited earlier. There is also evidence from the area of child development that supports this concern. Children who are deprived of basic satisfactions during the early years are often found to be limited in their degree of total psychological growth; they tend to remain insecure and survival oriented, even as adults.

On the other side of the issue are the many exceptions; examples of people who pay little attention to their basic needs, devoting their energies to intellectual or creative pursuits. There is also evidence from studies in organizations indicating that higher level needs may exist separately and alongside of survival needs. It has been shown that workers who are very unhappy with pay, working conditions, fringe benefits, and so forth, can still respond positively to improved opportunities for responsibility and advancement, as well as to a broadening of the work tasks themselves. Some researchers argue that the notion of a hierarchy is not especially relevant to the manager; the important thing to recognize is the significance of higher level human needs as critical motivators for work. They stress that an organization is seeing only a limited picture of human needs when it pays attention solely to such items as pay and working conditions (survival issues), to the exclusion of worker esteem, achievement, and opportunities for self-realization.

We can look at this issue in still another way. Whether or not *all* employees could potentially respond to work that is more challenging, complex and engaging, there are many who for whatever reasons, are prepared to settle for low responsibility and autonomy if pay is adequate and working conditions decent. Managers can choose, therefore, to seek out such people for routine work, see that they are well paid, and ignore any unmet needs at work. Conversely, they can find those who are most concerned with self-realization to do the more inventive, complex tasks and then give them scope for creativity. This kind of thinking fits the notion of appropriateness to the situation, at least in terms of short-term productivity.

But there are problems inherent in this approach. Even if sufficient people of each type could be found, (and that is becoming increasingly difficult as younger people come to expect more fulfillment from work) there is still the question of long-term development of the human resources of the organization. Is it possible that the managerial assumption of low worker motivation, leading to jobs which are purposely kept routine, forces workers to set their sights only on pay and other survival rewards? Is that reaction likely to be seen by managers as confirmation of "low motivation," which then locks in the very behavior that causes the problem? Is it important for employees to learn new skills and aptitudes or just to routinely perform what they already know? Is it desirable to keep satisfaction at the lowest acceptable level, ignoring social and higher needs which may be less visible? Will that gain the desired level of commitment, imagination, loyalty? Is it healthy for an organization to have most of its employees just going through the motions, leaving all responsibility and decisions to a few "higher ups?"

If you want more than a short-term adequate fit, then there are many ways to explore the design of work to meet a greater range of human needs. Jobs which require only robot-like, repetitive activities can be automated or redesigned to be more challenging. Parts of various jobs can be combined to enrich the work of any one employee. Jobs can be rotated to provide variety and change of pace. Workers can be given more responsibility and autonomy, through more delegation for decision-making, and opportunities to set their own working hours, work pace, and work methods.

All of these methods have costs associated with them and are partly dependent on the availability of employees who want to engage themselves in work rather than just putting in time to get the money to satisfy needs elsewhere. Some jobs do not lend themselves to redesign, or would be too expensive to change. Cost considerations will surely play a part in deciding whether to try to find security-oriented employees to fit existing routine work, or to change the nature of the work itself. But money (or short-term profits in profit making organizations) is not the only consideration when looking at the fit between motivation and work. The satisfaction and learning of organizational members have important consequences, too.

Summary Propositions

Regardless of whether or not we assume a strict hierarchy of needs, we can state that **There are a wide variety of human needs operating at work.** In order to motivate organizational members, some diagnosis must be made of which particular needs are most important and then a system of rewards (pay, responsibility, and so forth) developed to fit. **(1) The closer the fit between member needs and organization rewards, the higher productivity will be. (2) The higher the level of needs, the more varied the rewards necessary to achieve productivity, satisfaction and individual development. Conversely, the lower the level of needs, the less varied need be the rewards.**

THE MANAGER AND THE REWARD SYSTEM

How can managers learn to use rewards to accomplish their objectives? A social system maintains its existence by virtue of its ability to meet the needs of its members. The behavior of the members that contribute to the system must be reinforced, that is, rewarded, encouraged and supported. In an organization it is the manager who exercises principal control over the reward system; yet many managers fail to appreciate just how their own behavior and decisions may reinforce or discourage desired behavior on the part of employees.

BEHAVIOR IS GOVERNED BY OUTCOMES

It seems fairly obvious that **People tend to repeat behavior that is rewarded, avoid behavior that is punished and drop or forget behavior that produces neither.** In other words, the outcomes of one's actions play a major role in determining one's future actions. If one knows that putting in extra work hours leads to more money, one is likely to put in the extra time if more money is a current goal. If one knows that his/her pay will be docked for being late to work, the alarm clock is likely to be set with time to spare. If extra hard work goes unrewarded, it will probably soon fade from a person's repertoire in that situation.

As a manager, one is in a position to reward, punish or ignore many different kinds of behavior. The manager's choices will have important effects upon worker productivity, satisfaction and development, and ultimately upon the overall climate of the work environment. Given all the complexities of human behavior, some guidelines would be useful for improving your skills in managing behavior. While by no means exhaustive, the following represent six key principles:

1. Rewards usually work better than punishments.
2. Intrinsic rewards usually are more effective than extrinsic rewards.
3. Behavior that results in both reward and punishment produces conflict.
4. Feelings and perceptions become associated with outcomes.
5. Avoidance of outcomes and their associated feelings and perceptions are important determinants of behavior.
6. The timing of rewards is important to their effectiveness.

Reward versus Punishment

Although managers may give lip service to "the power of positive thinking," they often become more concerned about controlling than rewarding employees. For example, can you think of instructors who always seem to worry about students getting away with something? They are likely to offer more punishments for doing something wrong than rewards for doing something right. Such a pattern may or may not be very effective in bringing about productive behavior in either workers or students; it normally is not very satisfying or conducive to development.

While behavior that is ignored tends to disappear, behavior that is punished — either directly or by withholding anticipated rewards — is more likely to go underground, particularly if it is related to some important need. Imagine working at a routine monotonous job and getting punished for even talking to your co-workers. Does it eliminate your social needs? When the "punisher" is not present, the behavior is likely to appear and may then be rewarded by the responses of others, by the satisfaction of meeting the social need and even by the joy of "getting back at the boss." You can see how a manager can become trapped by building a control system based on punishment instead of a reward system based on positive incentives connected to basic needs.

Often you can get people to do what you want by using the threat of punishment for not doing it. It may only work, however, as long as you have a "captive" group of employees, that is, workers whose options are limited. If the shoe is on the other foot and you are forced to compete for good workers, rewards may be the only basis by which you will be able to retain your employees, much less get high productivity from them.

In short, then, the use of punishment to manage behavior *can* produce desired outcomes under certain conditions and, may even be appropriate (for example, when the behavior poses an immediate threat to the system). However, **Most behavior is more effectively managed by the use of rewards and positive incentives than by the use of punishment.**

Intrinsic or Extrinsic Rewards

Rewards that occur apart from the work process are called *extrinsic*. Pay, benefits, bonuses, special privileges, and so forth, are examples of extrinsic rewards. *Intrinsic* rewards are those that are built into the work itself, including such factors as a sense of accomplishment, a chance to be creative, or the challenge of the work. Extrinsic rewards require constant attention and revision on the part of management, while intrinsic rewards are more immediate outcomes of an individual's efforts. If you are taking a course in something you enjoy, one reward lies in the learning process itself. If the course is required and irrelevant to you, the only reward may be the grade, which is clearly extrinsic.

In most cases, **Intrinsic rewards are more effective and long lasting than extrinsic ones.** Job enrichment and enlargement seem to be methods of increasing the intrinsic rewards of work. The basic survival needs are appropriately met by extrinsic rewards, but the social and higher level needs are best met through intrinsic rewards. Look at the difference between a situation in which social interaction is a legitimate part of the work process (as in the car assembly teams at Saab and Volvo) and that in which it is treated as a "fringe benefit" of getting the work done (for example, a coffee break or company social event). The former tends to be more effective in terms of making multiple rewards intrinsic to the work;

the latter forces a separation between the task rewards and the social rewards, consequently reducing the payoff directly associated with the work.

Obviously, extrinsic rewards are part of any organization's performance incentives and, under certain conditions (monotonous work, non-changing technology and work patterns, and so forth) management needs to depend upon extrinsic factors to motivate employees. In general, when an extrinsic reward system is necessary, it is most likely to be effective under the following conditions:[6]

1. Important rewards can be tied to performance (i.e., important in the eyes of the employees).
2. Information pertaining to *how* rewards are given is open and public.
3. Management is willing to explain the system to employees.
4. There is adequate variation in the rewards to match varying needs and performance.
5. Performance can be measured.
6. Meaningful performance appraisal occurs.
7. A high level of trust exists between management and employees.

The absence of these conditions tends to breed lack of interest and suspicion about "the name of the game."

Multiple Outcomes of Behavior

Think how easy it would be to manage people if all you had to worry about were simple connections between behavior and rewards. However, as you well know from all the previous chapters, not all the rewards and punishments are in the hands of the manager. Peer relationships and a variety of personal factors also come into play. For example, a worker may get rewarded by the boss for being productive and punished by his/her co-workers for being a "rate buster." What happens then is that he/she gets caught between conflicting outcomes which definitely complicate choices. The two sources of reward seem to be mutually exclusive and contradictory. The worker's final choice will depend upon the relative strengths of the rewards and punishments related to each choice and the relative strengths of the needs involved.

A manager who is aware of potential conflicts of this kind has many options for dealing with them. In most respects his/her choice must consider the given situation. However, we can say, in general, that **It is better to add attractiveness to desired outcomes than it is to add threat to undesired alternatives.**

---

[6] From E. L. Lawler, *Motivation in Work Organizations* (Monterey, Cal.: Brooks/Cole Publishing Co., 1973).

Feelings and Perceptions about Outcomes

When you get rewarded for your behavior it usually makes you feel good (except when you have done something you are ashamed of, just to curry favor; then rewards may bring guilt). Generally, however, rewarded behavior itself becomes associated with good feelings. These feelings can be secondary rewards for the behavior and increase the chances of its occurrence. **The more positive the feelings one associates with a given kind of behavior, the more firmly entrenched that behavior becomes.** If you do something that gets you respect, liking, money and advancement (multiple payoffs), you are likely to place a high value on that behavior; it becomes associated not only with the positive outcomes but also with a range of good feelings about yourself. Your *perceptions* of various aspects of a situation (including people, surroundings, and so forth) which has rewarding outcomes, tend to become associated with the rewards. You tend to perceive the setting as a good place to work, the boss as a nice guy and your co-workers as good people to work with. Out of these perceptions grows your judgment about the climate of the organization. Can you think of ways in which getting a good grade on a paper can generalize by association to other aspects of a course, including the instructor, the text, other students and even the attractiveness of the classroom?

Avoidance Behavior

It doesn't take more than one burn to teach a child not to touch a hot stove. Even the sight of the stove can conjure up a strong enough fear to make the child avoid a second contact. In many ways adults behave like burnt children; a bad experience with some behavior leads to avoidance of that behavior and any circumstance associated with it. Of course, one person's bad experience may be another's pleasure; some few people (called masochists) learn to consider particular types of pain as rewarding. Regardless of what causes discomfort, however, if there is no way to avoid an unrewarding situation, then the person is forced to live with his/her anxieties. If, for example, your past performances on exams have not been rewarding, you probably would like to avoid future ones. Just the thought of another exam can raise your anxiety to an uncomfortable level.

One of the interesting aspects is the fact that **Avoidance behavior is itself rewarding; it reduces one's tensions and makes one feel better—at least for the moment.** Did you ever put off studying until the last moment, preferring to take your chances with how you might feel later? What about the employee who is afraid to ask the boss for a raise? He goes as far as the boss's door and then, with a sigh of relief, returns to his desk.

The price that you pay for avoidance behavior is that you often lose out on something else that you want. The employee mentioned above just may never get his/her raise until he/she has pushed open the boss's door and asked for the raise. Remember Snoopy's pal, Charlie Brown? He anguished over the Little Red-Headed Girl, but could never move himself beyond the fantasy of talking to her. He approached to a point, then turned back, only to experience the "reward" of reducing his tension. Can you think of different people or experiences that attracted you but generated such anxiety that in the final analysis you gave in to avoidance? What price did you pay? What effect did your behavior have on your feelings about yourself?

You probably know people who tend to make others anxious. Sometimes a manager, simply because of the power he/she possesses, is a source of fear for employees. If the manager's behavior tends to be punitive, then he/she is likely to generate avoidance behavior in employees. Many executives have been known to say, "My door is always open to my employees," only to wonder why few pass through that door, or worse yet, only to assume that the employees "have no problems."

As a manager you will often be in a position to affect your employees' tensions and fears in conscious ways; how you choose to do so can be a very important matter. You can maintain a high level of control through the use of punitive and withholding behavior. You may get people to do what you want, but at a price for you and for them. Avoidance behavior tends to develop consequences, leading to a climate of mistrust and secrecy, that are not very conducive to the development of human resources.

The Timing of Rewards

While intrinsic rewards are built into the work itself, extrinsic rewards normally occur some time after the task has been accomplished. *How much time* lapses between effort and reward and *how regular* the time intervals are can have important effects on behavior. As a student you must have experienced wide variations in the time intervals between exams and grades. Most students seem to prefer the shortest possible intervals. Can you also see how your study habits may also be related to the timing of exams? As long as you know in advance when tests will occur, and assuming that a good grade is a relevant reward, you can plan to do most of your studying just prior to the exams and put in the least effort just after them. But suppose the instructor uses surprise quizzes throughout the semester and you cannot predict when you will be tested? Chances are you will maintain a moderately high level of effort all the time, in part to maximize the odds of receiving a decent grade, but also to avoid the chance of being punished by failure.

Different organizations have different patterns of dispensing their rewards. While promotions, raises, bonuses, and the like, tend to occur at regular long-term intervals in most places, some organizations make these more or less directly contingent upon job performance; that is, the rewards are timed to reinforce their connection to performance. Where the connection is vague, which can occur when the rewards are poorly timed, employees can easily begin to wonder about the payoff for hard work.

Wages and salaries in most cases are governed by many more factors than just individual work output. However, where a person's income *is* a direct consequence of work produced (products sold, services provided, and so forth), then the timing of the income can have strong effects upon the work output. Regular predictable return encourages a high level of productivity; delays and uncertainties about payments can easily result in reduced performance. A salesperson working on a commission basis usually counts on receiving that commission within a short time of his/her having earned it. Can you see how important it can be for a company that depends upon high sales (and uses a commission system for its salespeople) to minimize the lapsed time between a sale and a commission?

While there are many ways to schedule rewards both in the classroom and in a work environment, and while there are considerable variations among people and circumstances, you may find the following guidelines useful:

1. **Predictable, frequent rewards that are directly connected to work behavior tend to result in a high overall level of performance.**

2. **Predictable but infrequent rewards that are directly connected to work behavior tend to result in peaks and valleys of performance; the peaks occur as the reward time is approached and the valleys occur just after the reward is received.**

3. **Unpredictable rewards that are directly connected to work behavior tend to result in moderately high overall levels of performance, but also in some dysfunctional anxiety.**

The first principle seems to be especially important when people are concerned about survival, as might be the case during economic hard times. **Regular frequent wages or salaries tend to be most functional for survival needs.** A business that is struggling to meet its payroll and may even be forced to owe its employees back pay is faced with an uncertain reward system. Depending upon the loyalty of the employees, the history of the company and the potential threats to its survival, management will need to pay special attention to alternative rewards in order to maintain productivity.

While the principles stated above tend to have general applicability, their relative importance (as in the example above) may vary with people and circumstances, and there may also be exceptions to one or more of them. Some people, for example, seem to have a high tolerance for uncertainty and are not bothered by unpredictable rewards.

How would you assess yourself? Do you see yourself as someone who functions best in a system of frequent regular rewards? Or do you operate best when you can anticipate the possibility of some "big payoff" despite the uncertainty of when that will occur? Your answers may suggest something about the kind of career or life style you choose. Also, as a future manager you will need to understand a variety of other people's preferences in order to make sure that your reward system leads to the highest levels of productivity, satisfaction and development. Even such a simple matter as the timing of rewards can make a critical difference in your success.

In the final analysis, however, you may not really understand the effects of the rewards and punishments you dispense unless you understand how these are *perceived* by their recipients. After downing an enormous meal, one witty Irishman proclaimed, "Thanks be for that little snack; some folks might have called it a meal!" To understand which is which, and for whom, you will need to look within individuals, into each's personal system. In the next chapter we will help you to find ways to translate the general concepts from this chapter into the unique worlds of individuals.

KEY CONCEPTS FROM CHAPTER 7

1. Group issues and individual dilemmas:
   a. Accepting the group's way of doing things.
   b. Trying to change it.
   c. Refusing to go along with particular behavior.
2. A. Basic needs (survival, social, higher level needs).
      modified by
   B. Personal system
      result in
   C. Overt Behavior.
3. The hierarchy of needs is individual, however there are tendencies which exist universally.
4. The closer the fit between member needs and organization rewards, the higher the productivity.
5. The higher the level of needs, the more varied can be the rewards to achieve productivity, satisfaction and development.
6. Behavior is governed by outcomes:
   a. Rewards better than punishments.
   b. Intrinsic rewards more effective than extrinsic.
   c. Conflict is produced by behavior which results in both reward and punishment.
   d. Feelings and perceptions associated with outcomes.
   e. Avoidance of outcomes is important determinant of behavior.
   f. Importance of the timing of rewards.

7. Frequent predictable rewards more effective than infrequent and unpredictable rewards.

SUGGESTED READINGS

Argyris, C. *Integrating the Individual and the Organization.* New York: John Wiley & Sons, Inc., 1964.

Bass, B. M. *Organizational Psychology.* Boston, Mass.: Allyn and Bacon, Inc., 1965.

Bennis, W. G., Berlew, D. E., Schein, E. H., Steele, F. I. "Some Interpersonal Aspects of Self-Confirmation," in Bennis, Berlew, Schein and Steele, *Interpersonal Dynamics.* 3d ed. Homewood, Ill.: The Dorsey Press, 1973, pp. 127–42.

Brown, R. *Social Psychology.* New York: The Free Press, a Division of the Macmillan Company, 1965.

Dunnette, Marvin D. *Work and Nonwork in the Year 2001.* Monterey, Cal.: Brooks/ Cole Publishing Co., 1973.

Gellerman, Saul W. *Motivation and Productivity.* New York: American Management Association, 1963.

Hellriegel, D. "The Four-Day Work Week: A Review and Assessment," *M.S.U. Business Topics,* 1974.

Herzberg, Frederick "One More Time: How Do You Motivate Employees?" *HBR* 46, (1968) 53–62.

_____ *Work and the Nature of Man.* Cleveland, Ohio: World Publishing Company, 1966.

_____ Mausner, B., Snyderman, B. *The Motivation to Work.* New York: John Wiley & Sons, 1959.

Lawler, Edward L. *Motivation in Work Organizations.* Monterey, Cal., Brooks/Cole Publishing Co., 1973.

_____ *Pay and Organizational Effectiveness: Psychological View.* McGraw-Hill Book Co., 1971.

Levinson, H., Price, C. R., Munden, K. J., Mandl, H. J., and Solley, C. M. *Men, Management, and Mental Health.* Cambridge, Mass.: Harvard University Press, 1963.

McClelland, David C. *The Achieving Society.* Princeton, N. J.: D. van Nostrand Company, Inc., 1961.

Maslow, A. *Motivation and Personality,* 2d ed. New York: Harper & Row, Pubs., Inc., 1970.

Myers, M. Scott "Who Are Your Motivated Workers?", *HBR* 42, (1964) 73–88.

Roethlisberger, F. J. and Dickson, W. *Management and the Worker.* Science Edition, New York: John Wiley & Sons, Inc., 1964.

Rogers, C. *On Becoming a Person.* Boston, Mass.: Houghton Mifflin Co., 1961.

Sayles, Leonard "Job Enrichment: Little That's New—and Right for the Wrong Reasons," Proceedings of the Industrial Relations Research Association, Madison, Wisconsin, 1973.

Vroom, V. *Work and Motivation.* New York: John Wiley & Sons, Inc., 1964.

Weiner, Norbert *The Human Use of Human Beings,* Garden City, N. Y.: Doubleday and Company, Inc., 1964.

White, R. W. *Lives in Progress.* New York: Holt, Rinehart and Winston, Inc., 1952.

A person's self-concept generally has enough internal consistency so that it is possible to infer various aspects of the person from other known aspects.

8

THE PERSONAL SYSTEM

IF YOU, as a potential manager, wish to understand the behavior of another individual, you will have to go beyond concepts that simply apply to "most people" and to needs in general. It is necessary to develop some insights into the unique ways in which each person operates from his or her own frame of reference. To understand someone whose behavior is puzzling, surprising or contrary to your expectations requires a way of getting inside that person, seeing the world as he/she does. **From within, an individual's behavior makes sense, is understandable and reasonable, even when not clear from outside.**

You'll remember that in discussing group behavior we differentiated between those aspects of a group that we can directly *observe*, that is, the activities and interactions, and those which we can only *infer* from our observations, that is, the feelings, norms, and so forth. To understand and explain the latter we showed how it is necessary to get *inside* the frame of reference of the group itself. In Chapter 6 we offered a set of dimensions for examining the inner workings of a group so that we could better understand its effectiveness (or lack of) in meeting its goals. As stated then, we put a microscope on the group processes.

What we will now do is put a similar microscope on the *individual*. We mentioned that important factors determining group behavior are the backgrounds of the members, that is, their *personal*

127

systems. We will discuss the various components of a personal system which seem to be most useful in understanding a person's behavior.

Many psychologists argue that we should stick to observables and leave alone the "black box," that is, what goes on inside the person. To them inference is, at best, crude speculation far removed from real measurable data. They claim that we do the human being an injustice to fill up the black box with vague concepts, insisting that it is enough to study overt behavior and to make our predictions from that.

There is a great deal of validity to the position of behaviorists, and managers cannot afford to overlook it. The fact is, the best predictor of future behavior *is* previous behavior. When you hire somebody for a job, the key questions you ask pertain to *prior performance.* When you decide to promote someone you are usually making a prediction that his/her future behavior is likely to be consistent with past behavior. It is possible for a manager to hire, fire, promote, and make job changes quite effectively using only performance data (observable behavior) as his/her criteria. Whether or not he/she ever *understands* the behavior, that is, can explain *why* it occurs, is another matter entirely, a matter which requires that we *do* develop some ways of explaining what goes on inside that so-called black box.

We do not expect to turn you into a psychologist, nor do we think that a manager must be an expert on all the intricacies of human behavior. The individual is so complex anyway, perhaps even more than the social systems he/she creates, that even so-called experts seldom lay claim to "the answers." What we do hope to provide for you is a way to appreciate some of the inner workings of a person (including yourself) and some tools for organizing your picture of an individual so that you can understand and explain and more effectively predict behavior, not just classify it. While it is not easy to make useful inferences about things which cannot be directly observed, people tend to do it anyway. How often do you find yourself interpreting the motives of another person or labeling people in categories based upon some "quick diagnosis" you've made? Perhaps if you study and apply some of the following concepts you will improve your ability to make such judgments or at the very least slow down the process of coming to conclusions which tend to filter future inputs and lock in false definitions.

It is not easy to see how the world looks to someone else; few of us have been very well trained in such empathic skills. Fortunately, there are some ways of getting clues about how a person sees him/herself and how that is affecting behavior.

In the pages that follow we will take a careful look at the personal system as an important modifier of human needs. We begin by providing an overall scheme showing where the personal system fits into the total sequence of events that determine the behavior of an individual. We have already covered the topic of basic human needs and have pointed out that the connection between needs and actions is a very complicated one involving all the variations of individual personality. Without going into detail just yet, we can say that the general sequence is that shown in Figure 8–1. While the personal system is only one factor in this sequence, it is the most complex one and the one which carries the key to understanding individual behavior. It is that critical link to understanding a person's expectancies regarding his/her actions in a given situation; the expectancies are then the immediate preludes to actions.

FIGURE 8–1
The Connection between Needs and Actions

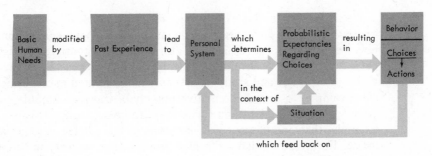

THE STRUCTURE OF THE PERSONAL SYSTEM

The personal system is structured around four basic subsystems plus a derived subsystem that exerts a unifying force on the others. The basic subsystems are:

Personal Goals.
Competencies.
Beliefs.
Values.

The unifying force is the *self concept.*

It is important to keep in mind that we are still thinking in systems terms, that is, we recognize that the various aspects of an individual are all interrelated. Growth and change in any one component of the personal system always affects the others. Let's examine each of these components.

FIGURE 8–2
The Personal System

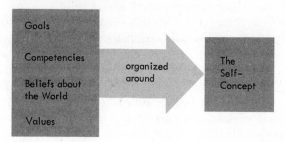

Personal Goals

Goals are those objects or events in the future which we strive for in order to meet our basic needs. A given goal (for example, a high income) may be related to several needs (for example, security, prestige, and achievement). Also, several goals (for example, success as a writer, generating new ideas and studying art) may all be related to one basic need, (for example, to actualize creative potential). Can you identify some of your goals as a student and relate them to basic needs? It is likely, for example, that one of your primary goals in this course is to get a good grade. For some students the high grade means security in school, for others it means achievement, and still others see the grade as only one of many goals related to learning and self-actualization. In a work situation such things as promotions, salary increases and the like serve as goals for employees. While these goals clearly tap into one or another basic need, the connections vary from one personal system to another. The task of a manager involves maintaining compatibility among the goals of individuals, those of subparts of the organization, and those of the total system.

If you were to list your various goals you could probably arrange them in some rough order of importance. Like the hierarchy of universal needs, a person tends to have a hierarchy of personal goals. Having a hierarchy helps one to set priorities and to resolve internal conflicts between goals. An example of an internal conflict might be the person whose goals include both rapid advancement in a career and also having a close family. Both require high levels of commitment, but frequently pull a person in opposite directions. Currently, women increasingly are faced with this particular dilemma and, for some, priorities are changing dramatically.

If you knew nothing else about a person except his/her goals, you could probably explain significant aspects of his/her behavior. From the other side, it's often fairly easy to infer someone's goal(s) by observing his/her behavior. As a manager you will almost always be concerned about the individual goals of those you work with, in particular as they pertain to your own goals and those of the larger system.

One of the paradoxes of life is that people sometimes don't know what their goals are until they've reached them. Have you ever had the experience of realizing how much you wanted something only *after* you got it? A person's concept of him/herself often makes it difficult to recognize certain aspects of his/her own personal system. Later in this chapter we will examine just how the self-concept can both include and block out parts of a person's total personal system.

How well people can meet their goals depends in part upon the *competencies* they have developed, which we will discuss next.

Competencies

Competencies are the areas of knowledge, ability and skill that increase an individual's effectiveness in dealing with the world. People are not born with competencies; they must *learn* them, though each person has varied natural capacities in different areas. Since the learning process is time and energy consuming, people tend to have a great investment in their competencies. While one may at times be willing and able to modify one's goals in a given situation, it is more difficult to alter competencies; new learning and change take time. Each person tends to be good at particular activities and strives constantly to reinforce these by engaging in behaviors that utilize them. When circumstances either block one from doing what one is good at, or demand functioning in areas that do not fit competencies, then a person experiences some degree of threat.

A person does not always see his/her own competencies as others do. Managers often "surprise" their employees by telling them what a fine job (or poor job) they are doing. While it is possible to predict performance from an external assessment of a person's competence, to *understand* a person's behavior usually requires knowing his/her *own* view of the competencies.

Take the perpetually silent group member, for example. Though there can be many reasons for a person staying silent, one such student explained that he saw himself as hardworking but not very intelligent, and he greatly feared making a fool of himself in front of the group. At the beginning he thought he would play it safe for awhile and then slowly get in; but once the group noticed his silence, he felt the possibility of "screwing up" was even greater, since anything he said would stand out more and be carefully evaluated. As someone who "couldn't stand being laughed at" it was better to have the group confused about his silence than "sure he wasn't smart enough." And even when he had something useful to say, which was often since he believed himself to be conscientious and thus always prepared well, the words would freeze in his throat. When someone was "nice" to him he felt all the more embarrassed for not contributing, and when he was confronted about it, he was sure he had been correct about the danger of being ridiculed. In effect, he became boxed into the role of "noncontributing member" by both his own fears and the emergent expectations of the group members. While the box was mostly of his own making, it appeared quite different when seen from inside than when examined from without.

In general, we can say that competencies form an important part of the personal system. To the extent that an individual can find ways to translate his/her competencies into effective behavior, he/she experiences reinforcement of them. **The wider the range of one's competencies, the more likely one is to find avenues for their fulfillment. The narrower the range, the more limited one feels in coping with the world, and the more limited one is in the possible range of goals one can attain in life.**

Beliefs

Beliefs are ideas people have about the world and how it operates. Everyone has beliefs about people, human nature, what life is all about, what the business world is like, what professors are like, and so on. A person brings his/her beliefs into every situation and seeks to confirm those that fit the situation. Sometimes events do not support one's beliefs and one is surprised (pleasantly at times, and unhappily at others); if the disconfirmation is very strong, one becomes defensive, disparaging, resistant, and so forth. People like to have events support their beliefs; it makes them feel "right"; it helps them to maintain a stable "fix" on the world. Can you think of some beliefs that you brought into this course? Did you believe, for example, that you could only learn from the professor, not from yourself and your peers? Was that confirmed or disconfirmed? Did you have some preconceived ideas about how groups function? What happened to these ideas?

One of the dilemmas posed by a person's beliefs is the fact that they often become *self-fulfilling prophecies*. Somehow people have a way of making things happen (even bad things), that they believe "always happen." Have you ever experienced the feeling that you failed in a task mainly because you expected to fail? The satisfaction you gain, of course, is knowing that you were right in the first place, a small, but concrete consolation! When beliefs like this creep into the self-concept, as we shall see later on, a person experiences the dilemma of "being right" versus "being successful."

Managers can trap themselves into a set of beliefs that are dysfunctional but self-confirming. Some years ago Douglas McGregor (whom you already know from Chapter 6) described two distinctly different sets of managerial beliefs. One set, which he labeled "Theory X," includes assumptions such as:

1. The average human being has an inherent dislike of work and will avoid it if he can.
2. Most people need to be coerced, controlled, directed, threatened with punishment to get them to put forth adequate effort toward the achievement of organizational objectives.
3. The average human being prefers to be directed, wishes to avoid responsibility, has relatively little ambition, wants security above all. (From Chapter 3.)[1]

The other set of assumptions, which he labelled Theory Y, includes the following:

1. The expenditure of physical and mental effort in work is as natural as play or rest.
2. Man will exercise self-direction and self-control in the service of objectives to which he is committed.
3. Commitment to objectives is a function of the rewards associated with their achievement.
4. The average human being learns, under proper conditions, not only to accept but to seek responsibility. (From Chapter 4)[2]

How do your beliefs compare with those in Theory X and Theory Y? Can you apply them directly to the classroom scene? Which beliefs do you think your instructor holds? What about other instructors? Can you infer which set of beliefs are held from the behavior you see? Can you, for example, see how believing Theory Y can lead to toughness and high expectations in one situation, but gentle prodding in another? Managers very often confirm their assumptions by treating people in ways that bring out the very behavior they expect, thus confirming what they believed in the first place. Have you ever had your parents treat you "like a child" and then find yourself behaving like a child? What about the teacher who believes that students will cheat if they are not watched carefully? That often leads to extensive controls, which students resent. Thus the minute the teacher stops "watchdogging," cheating will occur. On the other hand, the manager who is willing to delegate more responsibility often discovers, lo and behold, that people are capable of taking it. Obviously, this is not always the case; there will always be people (workers, students, and others) who do seem to operate best in a Theory X framework and others who do best in a Theory Y setting. *No one set of beliefs is valid for all situations.* The competent manager-scientist is

---

[1] D. McGregor, *The Human Side of Enterprise* (New York: McGraw-Hill Book Co., 1960).

[2] Ibid.

open to all possibilities, all kinds of people and all kinds of situations. His/her beliefs remain tentative, always subject to testing and revision.

One way of looking at the concept of "theory" is to view it as a set of beliefs, but ones that have been developed from systematic observation and research. Just as any beliefs tend to guide a person's behavior, the manager-scientist uses theory to guide his/her behavior in relation to members of an organization. And just as the validity of many beliefs depends upon the circumstances, the theories of a manager are most useful when they are open to the *contingencies* of the situation.

In the next section we will discuss the core of people's beliefs, namely, *values*.

Values

Values tend to form the foundation of a person's character. While some of one's values may change over the course of a lifetime, they do tend to remain fairly deeply entrenched in one's personality. A person develops a sense of right or wrong, good or bad, beginning quite early in life. Many of one's ideas change through the teenage years, but as mature adults, one tends to hold on to and defend some basic core within us which tells one *what is really important in life and basic to one as an individual*. Examples of values would be such ideas as:

a. Always being honest with others.
b. Always standing on your own two feet and not burdening others with your problems.
c. Always facing up to life's difficulties and not running away.
d. Never deliberately hurting another's feelings.
e. Never letting anyone feel you have not lived up to your responsibilities.
f. Always doing your best at any activity you try.
g. Never going "overboard" about interests.
h. Never allowing anyone to get ahead of you.
i. Never putting your faith in individuals, only institutions.

These are the kinds of attitudes that a person normally refuses to violate; they determine people's integrity as individuals. Following one's values enhances the basic sense of personal worth; failing to follow them causes guilt, shame and self-doubt.

Values also tend to exist in a hierarchy. Some are likely to be somewhat more critical than others. When a person experiences a value-conflict this hierarchical arrangement often helps him/her to make a decision. For example, a particular tax inspector needs help solving an audit; he believes in standing on his own two feet, so he does not want to seek help. But he also believes that it is even *more* important to arrive at a fair settlement, so he goes beyond his independence values and consults with an expert colleague.

Often value conflicts are very hard to resolve. For example, imagine yourself in a position where you must fire an employee for being absent too much due to alcoholism. One of your values is to always be honest and another is to always be kind. How would you balance these values against one another? Can you find a way to honor them both? For some people being honest with the person might be felt as an unkind act, or being kind to the person a dishonest act. Perhaps you can think of examples in your own life where you found yourself in a values conflict. It is in situations like that where not only does the way one sees oneself guide behavior, but also gets *forged,* making future choices more consistent with one's most deeply held values.

In short, we can say that the area of personal values serves as the principal governing body of the personal system. **The individual is enhanced by behavior that reinforces values, less affected by behavior that is not value-laden, and violated by behavior that is not consistent with his/her deeply held values. The value-component of the personal system can limit the range of goals, competencies and beliefs allowable, and it tends to evoke the strongest defensive behavior when under threat or challenge.**

THE SELF-CONCEPT

The general consistency of the personal system is organized by the individual's *self-concept; that is, the way the person sees him/herself.* The self-concept reflects the person's own unique way of organizing his/her goals, competencies, beliefs and values. Competencies are normally developed in order to meet goals, which in turn must fit with beliefs and values. For example, a man who decides to become an accountant is likely to be someone who sees himself as methodical, believes in the fallibility of people, and is dedicated to the values of being orderly and cautious. His manner of behavior is likely to be quiet and sober, his dress fairly inconspicuous and his car somewhat conservative. In short, **A person's self-concept generally has enough internal consistency so that it is possible to infer various aspects of the person from other known aspects.**

People strive to maintain their concepts of themselves by engaging in behavior that is consistent with their goals, competencies, beliefs and values as they see them, even to the point of pain or failure to achieve stated goals. Insofar as an individual succeeds in confirming his/her self-concept, he/she experiences a basic sense of adequacy and worth. Sometimes a person becomes so highly invested in protecting his/her self-concept that he/she begins to have difficulty in seeing him/herself as others do. This can lead to defensive behavior and to interpersonal con-

> *I am healthy and strong. I am honest and frugal. I am conscientious. I am indus-
> trious, reticent and modest. I am always friendly. I make no great demands. My
> ways are winning and natural. Everyone likes me. I can deal with everything. I
> am here for everyone. My love of order and cleanliness has never given reason
> for complaint. My knowledge is above average. Everything I am asked to do, I do
> perfectly. Anyone can provide the desired information about me. I am peace-
> loving and have an untarnished record. I am not one of those who start a big hue
> and cry over every little thing. I am calm, dutiful and receptive. I can become
> enthusiastic about every worthy cause. I would like to get ahead. I would like to
> learn. I would like to be useful. I have a concept of length, height, and breadth.
> I know what matters. I treat objects with feeling. I have already become used to
> everything. I am better. I am well. I am ready to die. My head feels light. I can
> finally be left alone. I would like to put my best foot forward. I don't accuse any-
> one. I laugh a lot. I can make heads and tails of everything. I have no unusual
> characteristics. I don't show my upper gums when I laugh. I have no scar under
> the right eye and no birthmark under the left ear. I am no public menace. I would
> like to be a member. I would like to cooperate. I am proud of what has been
> achieved so far. I am taken care of for the moment. I am prepared to be interro-
> gated. A new part of my life lies ahead of me. That is my right hand, that is my left
> hand. If worst comes to worst, I can hide under the furniture. It was always my
> wish to be with it.*
>
> Peter Handke
> *Kaspar**

flicts, issues which we will go into later in this chapter and again in Chapters 9 and 10.

**People also strive to enhance their self-concepts by learning and by
developing themselves toward some "ideal self."** This tendency can often
pose a dilemma for the individual. To enhance one's self-concept may
mean change in some aspects of it; and to change one's self-concept runs
counter to the tendency to maintain and/or protect it. It is a struggle between the security of knowing what one is and the risk of becoming something more. However, while a person may often feel comfortable with the
idea of simply "being what he/she is," most people do strive to live up to
their ideal selves as much as possible. To the extent that the ideal self is
not too discrepant from the perceived self, it serves as an incentive to
learn and grow. When the discrepancy is too great, the person is likely to
suffer from a lack of self-acceptance, which in turn leads to self-doubt
and then to behavior which, sadly enough, tends to confirm the low self-
concept.

Sometimes, as we've stated earlier, people engage in behavior which,
from an outside perspective, seems puzzling and even self-defeating.

---

* A play translated by Michael Roloff. Published in the U.S.A. by Farrar, Straus &
Giroux, Inc., New York, 1969, and published abroad by Eyre Methuen, Ltd., London,
1972. Reproduced with permission.

Perhaps you have known a student who is capable of doing outstanding work in his/her courses, but settles for B's by exerting minimal effort. From your own perspective you might wonder what is gained by that behavior. You know that the student sees him/herself as bright; how could "settling for a B" confirm that? From inside, that student's reasoning might go as follows:

> I don't need to get A's to prove I'm smart; look how easily I can get B's with hardly any effort.

It seems that **Behavior which appears illogical or self-defeating from an outside perspective usually makes sense when viewed from inside; people generally make choices that are consistent with their self-concepts.**

THE SELF-CONCEPT AND BEHAVIOR

In the remainder of the chapter we will discuss how the personal system, as organized around the self-concept, determines the behavior of the individual. We will first examine the ways in which the norms and role obligations of a given situation can combine with an individual's self-concept to exert powerful influences over behavior. Then we will discuss the effects of a person's expectancies (positive and negative) regarding the probable consequences of his/her choices upon the actual behavior. Finally, we will discuss some of the broad implications of an individual's choices with respect to careers, life style and the development of a basic sense of one's own adequacy and worth in this world. Our intent is to help you to gain some insights and perspectives on yourself, as well as to facilitate your knowledge of others, whether as a future manager or as a member of any social system.

FIGURE 8-3
How Behavior Results from Expectancies as Influenced by the Self-Concept

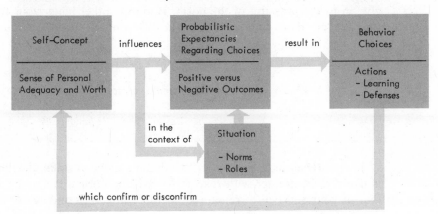

The basic proposition that underlies this section is that, **All other things being equal, the behavior most likely to occur in a given situation is that which the individual expects to best maintain and/or enhance his/her self-concept.** Figure 8-3 shows the ways in which behavior and self-concept are linked; it also summarizes the concepts and issues we will cover (as stated above) and can serve as a map for the remainder of the chapter.

Norms and the Self-Concept

One of the reasons a group may become cohesive is because it confirms the members' self-concepts; its *norms* are congruent with the members' values and beliefs, provide for the exercising of their competencies, and support the achievement of personal goals. Obviously, one of the reasons why a group's norms are what they are is because of the self-concepts of its members, which were brought to the group in the first place. However, because of variations in member needs and self-concepts, it is very unusual to find a group in which *all* the norms support *all* self-concepts at *all* times. Also, since people tend to be members of many different groups during their lives, they experience wide variations in the degree to which their self-concepts are supported by the norms that are present in a given situation. While a person may seek out settings that are likely to be self-confirming, it is very difficult to avoid completely situations in which the pressure to conform to norms conflicts with some aspect of the person's self-concept.

You have undoubtedly experienced times when those around you seem to be pressuring you into behaving in a way that runs counter to some aspect of your self-concept. For example, in a social gathering it is not uncommon for some kind of norm to develop in relation to drinking. Your goal may be to stick to soft drinks, but if you have no basic value opposed to drinking alcohol, the chances are fairly good that you will give in to the pressure of the norm. If, on the other hand, your feelings run deeper, then your resistance to the pressure will obviously be greater.

> *What a dependency if you want everybody to love you!*
>
> F. S. Perls
> *Gestalt Theory Verbatim* p. 36

In a work setting, where your livelihood may be at stake, the dilemma is likely to be greater with respect to resisting norms. It may be important to your survival to remain a "member in good standing" of a work group. What normally happens, then, is that **Norm pressures which go only against goals tend to result in conformity, while pressures that go against competencies, beliefs and/or values are likely to result in deviance or isolation.** The norms of a group are equivalent to the values of the individual; they are the respective "oughts" of their systems; as such they are resistant to change. **Conflicts between group and individual at the values level tend to be irreconcilable, at least without major sacrifice on the part of either the individual or the group.**

In one classroom workgroup a norm had developed to do the least work possible yet still get a "decent" grade. All of the students in the group liked the idea and supported the norm except one. Her goal in the class was to learn as much as possible, and she believed it important and right to give an all-out effort on every project. The rest of the group members were afraid that she would have enough influence (since she was the most knowledgeable member) to change the developing norm. They put more pressure on her, only to get back more resistance. She went from group deviant to group isolate, eventually not attending meetings of the group and doing most of the coursework on her own. Her concept of herself as a "good student" was so basic that she could not bring herself to violate it, even though the situation called for her to attempt exerting influence on the group.

The willingness to conform to group norms, therefore, **is a product of the closeness of the norms to one's self-concept.** The costs and benefits of conforming must be weighed against the costs and benefits of deviating. Sometimes the choice will be obviously toward conforming; sometimes it will involve a hard struggle; and sometimes the individual reaches a point beyond which he/she cannot comply. Can you think of instances in which each of these was true? How did you manage your own cost/benefit equation?

You should not, however, overlook the importance of the fact that it is partly through membership in groups that you can acquire and practice new competencies, enhance your goals by collaborating with others, and test the validity of many of your beliefs. Either quick compliance to norms or quick rejection of them can offer very little opportunity to learn and grow. It may be that those instances in which you are forced to *struggle* with the choice are the ones that benefit you the most.

Roles and the Self-Concept

In Chapter 5 we discussed how the behavior of group members evolved into various role patterns. We showed how these roles are an important part of the group structure and how their fulfillment is critical to the group's development. The emphasis at that point was on the ways in which role behavior served the group's operations, rather than on the attractiveness of roles from the perspective of the individual's own frame of reference. At this point we will re-examine the concept of roles as related to the concept of self.

You will remember that a role is made up of a particular set of behaviors and attitudes that accompany a given position in a social system. Roles serve to confirm or disconfirm the self-concepts of those who occupy them, as well as provide ways for individuals to broaden their self-concepts. For example, in most task groups in which leadership is allowed to emerge freely as the group develops, it is those individuals who see themselves as leaders among their peers who most readily take on the leadership roles. Insofar as the group supports this, the individual is able to reaffirm his/her self-concept via the behaviors associated with the role. The role is likely to be consistent with the person's goals ("I want to be a leader."), beliefs ("A group needs leadership."), competencies ("I know how to pull a group together."), and values ("It is of the utmost importance to get the work out; I know how to do it so I should take the initiative.") In other cases individuals who might wish to be leaders, but doubt their competencies, can, with some help and a little push, try out leadership roles until they have broadened their self-concepts to include that kind of role, at least in some situations.

No matter how a particular role is defined by a boss, peers, tradition, and so forth, **It is the individual's own unique perception of the role obligations that determines his/her reaction to the prospect of adopting the role. To the extent that a role is perceived to be congruent with the self-concept, the individual is inclined to adopt it; to the extent that a role is perceived to be incongruent with any aspect of the self-concept, the individual is inclined to reject it.**

An example with important implications for society relates to women and the roles they choose. As more and more women reject the self-concept of constant "supporters of men," they increasingly resist the kinds of roles that accompany such a position in society. The issue goes well beyond a matter of goals; it clearly pertains to the competencies of women as compared with men in almost all fields of work, and it is, without doubt, a basic matter of beliefs and values, especially in a society that espouses equality.

This issue has appeared more frequently in the classroom as more women students enter courses in management and administration. Tradition tended to draw the female students into various secondary roles in task groups. They often fell right into the "secretarial role" and into other roles of a supportive and maintenance nature, including, sometimes, making sure that the group was well nurtured. Somehow, it was never a male student who determined that the group needed homemade brownies at its meetings. Recently, many women students have overtly rejected the secretarial role, some with more vigor than others. Even though the fulfillment of such a role is highly functional for the group, it may be equally dysfunctional for the person asked to fill it. Obviously this issue is not a clear cut one, especially for many women who have built major aspects of their self-concepts upon role behaviors that, while not fostering their own growth, have been important sources of self-confirmation. It is not easy for anyone to give up behaviors which are comfortable, even if limiting.

Because roles are important vehicles for giving order and consistency to a person's behavior in a social system, they often serve as a source of support for a person's basic sense of adequacy. People derive their sense of adequacy by doing the things at which they are competent and by learning to be competent at the things they value. Everytime a person is faced with a situation that goes beyond his/her competence he/she feels a blow to the self-concept, to a sense of personal adequacy; everytime an individual experiences success in some activity, he/she enhances his/her sense of adequacy and confirms his/her concept of him/herself as a competent individual.

To the extent that an individual can build his/her life around roles that enhance competencies, he/she will develop a basic sense of adequacy. To the extent that an individual finds him/herself cast into roles that conflict with or fail to utilize competencies, he/she will tend to develop a sense of inadequacy. Obviously, very few people can structure their lives so that their various roles are all congruent with their self-concepts; everyone has to do the drudgery jobs at one time or another. There is little self-confirmation in doing dishes, taking out garbage, balancing the checkbook, straightening up your workplace, and so forth. But these things have to be done, and most people at least have the competence to do them. The problems occur when a person feels pressured to do things that do not fit with his/her competencies, at least as seen from "inside," or when the person feels constrained by circumstances from exercising the competencies he/she possesses. Imagine yourself in a job in which all your previous training has little use. You see others in the organization doing things that you know you could do as well or better, but the role you are cast into in the system does not allow you to engage in any of those activities. That can be more than frustrating; it could even be degrading. Then again, imagine what it might be like to be assigned to a job long before you are ready for it, only to perform at a mediocre level. This is hardly conducive to developing a sense of personal adequacy.

> One of the authors interviewed a 50 year old man who had once been president of his own company but was now one of a number of executives in a small manufacturing firm. He still had a concept of himself as "top man" and frequently made decisions that were later countermanded by the chief

executive of the company. Making his own decision would serve to reinforce the concept of himself he held in the old role as president, but created
problems in his present situation. Regardless of the quality of the decision,
being overruled served to reinforce the former president's subordinate
role in the firm. He had a great deal of difficulty accepting that role, since
the behavior that went with it failed to reinforce his own sense of competency as a manager, resulting in a loss of his sense of personal adequacy.
This once high-level executive spent a great deal of his time telling stories
about the good old days when he found himself making really tough
decisions.

Sometimes a role conflict can go very deep and hit on matters of personal worth. This happens when a role calls for a kind of behavior that
the person believes is wrong. Since most positions in an organization
entail multiple roles, especially as one moves up the hierarchy of the
system, most people, at one time or another, are called upon to adopt a
role that goes against their personal values. For example, at some time
an executive may be assigned to be the "hatchet man" in a situation needing strong action. On the one hand, while his/her values as related to the
total system might support such a decision, a concern for employee security might not support it. Though learning to live with that kind of
problem may be a useful aid to executive success, the price that is paid
for violating one's own values may appear later, as insomnia, ulcers,
nervous conditions, and so forth. Or, it may lead to a shift in the violated
values. It depends on how deep they and the beliefs which support them
are. The important thing for you to look at now is the relationship between your values and the ways in which various roles may call upon
you to behave inconsistently with your self-concept. **To the extent that
an individual adopts roles that support his/her values, the individual experiences him/herself as worthwhile: To the extent that the individual violates these values, he/she doubts his/her personal worth.**

Expectancies

Usually before you make a choice you appraise the situation and decide which alternatives are likely to result in self enhancement. Few
people like to waste their efforts and even fewer wish to engage in behavior that goes against their goals, beliefs, and so forth. To deal with the
matter of choosing the best course of action in a situation your appraisal
takes the form of a kind of prediction—"The chances are that if I do thus
and so, I will achieve what I want." You make a statement (implicit or
explicit) of your expectancy regarding the probable outcome. It's like
being your own personal scientist, making hypotheses, testing them out,
revising them when they prove wrong, and holding on to the ones that
prove accurate.

As stated earlier, the behavior most likely to occur is that which the person *expects* to most enhance his/her self-concept. When the expectancy and the self-concept fit together in relation to some behavior, no dilemma is experienced. But what happens when an anticipated outcome involves some risk to self, yet no alternatives exist to meet your goals? For example, say you have a concept of yourself as bright and as capable of putting your ideas into words very clearly. Your goal is to be outspoken in a classroom so that you can have some reaction to your ideas from the instructor. You now find yourself in a class in which the instructor refuses to entertain questions until he completes his lectures; but you always find that there is no time left for discussion at the end of the class. You can choose to keep your mouth shut, expecting a negative reaction should you speak up, or you can say something anyway in order to move towards your goal. In order for anyone to predict what you are likely to do would require that they know: (*a*) the strength of your goal to speak out; (*b*) your expectancy regarding the negative consequences of speaking out; and (*c*) your expectancy regarding the positive and negative consequences for your self-concept in not speaking out. Obviously, predicting an individual's behavior is not a simple matter, but we can offer a few guidelines for making predictions. These guidelines will also be useful to you when you attempt to formulate sets of personal propositions.

GUIDELINE PROPOSITIONS FOR PREDICTING INDIVIDUAL BEHAVIOR

1. **The more strongly an individual predicts that a particular behavior will be rewarding, the more likely it is to occur.**
2. **The greater a perceived competency, the more likely it is to be utilized; the more limited an individual's range of competencies, the more likely is an existing competency to be used regardless of situational appropriateness.**
3. **The greater the strength of expectancy regarding the effects of a given behavior, the more likely that behavior is to occur, and vice versa.**
4. **To the extent that a particular behavior is perceived to be positively related to the maintenance and enhancement of the self-concept, the behavior is likely to become an ongoing part of the individual's repertoire and vice versa.**

DEFENSIVE BEHAVIOR

In many cases the maintenance of the self-concept depends upon the retention of certain beliefs, even when these are no longer valid by external standards. Former Senator Joseph McCarthy had an image of himself as a great crusader who would rid the world of communism. To maintain this image he held the belief that communists were hiding behind every bush, which, in turn, justified his looking for them under every rock and leaf. Even when "hard facts" failed to support McCarthy's claims, he never changed his beliefs; they were too precious to his self-concept.

The following case illustrates vividly the bind into which a normally competent manager can get himself. It is not atypical in this day and age, when organizations grow and change faster than a manager's self-concept can.

> The chief executive of a small manufacturing company in England had been the one to build the organization right from its beginnings, when there were only a few dozen employees. He believed that it was important for a manager to be close to his employees, to be seen down on the shop floor, lending support and interest to the work effort. He made daily trips through the small plant talking to the men and offering help wherever it was needed. He was competent in his style of managing, the men knew him well, and he really enjoyed working in this way. Over the years the company grew rapidly to nearly 600 employees. The chief executive continued to make his appearances on the shop floor, but these were more sporadic and less personal, since there was more territory to cover and many new people. Most of the new employees did not know him personally, did not understand why he showed up and could not predict when he would appear. Consequently they became fearful of this behavior. Unfortunately, the executive was not aware of these fears; he continued to assume that he was generating the same welcome response he received in the early days. It was obvious that he had a great investment in continuing this behavior, since it was intimately connected with his concept of himself as a friendly, informal, personally concerned executive.
>
> At a meeting of the top management team one day, a subordinate who wanted to be helpful informed the executive that his travels around the plant were generating a great deal of fear and mistrust. The executive dismissed the idea as nonsense, insisting that the men in the plant really enjoyed the visits from the boss. After a few persistent attempts by the manager to convince the executive otherwise, the latter finally reacted with a violent outburst, stating that people who were afraid of him were simply stupid and did not understand his intent. The manager gave up, puzzled about why his helpful information was so badly received.

This example illustrates how data that appears to another as pertaining only to someone's expectancies may, in fact, cut very deeply into the core of that person's self-concept. The information not only challenged the executive's goals, it also implied to him that he was violating his own beliefs and values, as well as behaving incompetently as a manager. The example also illustrates the capacity of individuals to block out disconfirming data that is too threatening to the self-concept.

When anyone encounters data that does not gibe with his/her self-concept, defensive behavior is likely. The data may be denied, projected on to someone else, twisted to have a more acceptable meaning or attacked as invalid. A person's defenses protect him/her from being too uncomfortable, from having to change too rapidly, from too easily letting go of the view he/she has built up about him/herself and how the world works. Yet insofar as defenses prevent new data from being incorporated, evaluated and responded to, they keep a person from learning and growing. The problem for you as a manager-scientist is how to recognize defensiveness in yourself and others, and how to respond to it in a way that increases the likelihood of learning and decreases the rejection of new information and ideas.

In summary, we can offer the following propositions:

1. **The greater the threat of information or events to a person's self-concept, the greater the likelihood of a defensive response and vice versa.**
2. **The more defensive a person's response, the less the likelihood of learning and growth.**
3. **Refusal to accept disconfirming data, regardless of the form which the refusal takes, is an indicator of defensive reactions.**
4. **When an individual is defensive, another's behavior which allows the defenses to be lowered, rather than attempts to tear them down, increases the likelihood of learning.**[3]

This last proposition circles back to the first; responses which do not threaten another's self-concept are most likely to reduce defensiveness. If you can sense what another person values, what is important to how he/she defines him/herself, you can back off from whatever is threatening the self-concept and allow the other more elbowroom.

Part of the problem of allowing in sufficient new data to learn, has to do with the comfort of behavior that is already known. There is inevitably tension between the desire to expand one's knowledge and repertoire of behavior, and the desire to stick with the familiar. Where do you come out in this human dilemma? Do you see yourself as someone who usually prefers new experiences, or as a person who likes the familiar, tried and true? Can you formulate a proposition or two which describes how you personally deal with the contradictory desires for growth and security?

---

[3] For greater elaboration of these ideas, see Roger Harrison, *Defenses and the Need to Know,* in the Case section of this volume.

BECOMING AWARE OF YOUR OWN PERSONAL PROPOSITIONS

Though we do not propose that you carry around an ever ready list of propositions about yourself, we do believe that it is worth the effort for anyone to try to clarify the bases upon which choices are made. Since the way you see yourself determines your behavior, it is useful to make explicit how you are viewing yourself. Not only can that ease your decision-making, it can help you understand better the implicit personal propositions by which others operate. Finally, assumptions that are specifically spelled out are more easily evaluated; sometimes when you see your own assumptions clearly, the need for minor alterations becomes apparent.

One possible way to become more aware of your own personal propositions is to use a series of incomplete sentences. Make up a list of phrases that represent the kinds of situations you frequently are faced with. For example, you might use such phrases as:

Whenever I have a job to do that I don't like, I tend to . . .

When I am in competition with others, I tend to . . .

When I want someone to like me, I tend to . . .

When I am afraid of failing, I tend to . . .

If I try my hardest, I tend to . . .

If I am true to my own values in a group, I will . . .

If you just let your thoughts fill in the incomplete sides of the sentences, without any censoring, you can get to some of the ways in which your self-concept is determining your expectations and, thus, your behavior, in both positive and negative directions.

Another way of approaching clarity about your working propositions is to try to state the underlying assumption behind each of your most frequent concerns as a person. For example, if you avoid much interaction with group members because you worry about being hurt in relationships the underlying premise might be:

"If I am vulnerable and let others get too close, they will hurt me." If you always act warm and friendly to everyone, whether or not you mean it, the premise might be:

"If I don't make people feel I like them they may attack me." Another kind of premise, related to competence feelings, could be stated,

"If I ever let myself be caught unprepared, I will be extremely embarrassed." The opposite might go: "If I try my hardest and then don't do well, I will be more disappointed than if I do just enough to get by."

Underlying most of your behavior will be propositions of the sort just mentioned; can you list those which most frequently seem to control your behavior? Once stated, it can be useful to then assess under what conditions each statement is likely to be true, and under what conditions it may be inaccurate. Often people learn something useful about behavior and themselves and then overgeneralize it, acting as if it were *always* true, and ignoring the conditions which led to the learning in the first place. By now we hope you will see that specifying the conditions under which any statement is valid, is a vital part of making more sensible choices of behavior.

LIFE CHOICES

The ice cream lovers among the readers of this book will recognize that in some respects, life is like a trip to an ice cream parlor. There are so many flavors from which to choose, that any choice can seem incredibly difficult, especially given the limits of one's stomach and purse. Some people enter the parlor with their minds made up and their eyes closed to all the alternative flavors. "If vanilla was good before, it will be good enough now." Others decide to include several flavors so as to avoid too narrow a choice, eating more than they need to maximize the opportunities available. And still others gaze longingly at all the flavors, feeling overwhelmed, possibly hoping that someone else might make the choice for them. Perhaps the saddest outcome is when a person finally makes a choice and while eating the ice cream continues to think about the other flavors he/she *might* have chosen. Is there a better way to kill the enjoyment?

Can you see how many aspects of life are like the imaginary ice cream parlor? Choices about careers, schools, courses, professors, what movie to go to, whether or not to join a fraternity or sorority, and if so, which one, involve similar struggles. At least with ice cream you can always go back the next day and choose another flavor. Such areas as careers, marriage, and so forth, are not as easy to change the next day; they generally involve more long-term commitments. If people are uncertain about such choices, they often try to avoid making them.

> *When choosing between two evils, I always like to take the one I've never tried before.*
>
> Mae West
> in *Klondike Annie*

The fact is, every choice is usually a decision to rule out other alternatives. Although some people manage to "have their cake and eat it too," most people are forced to leave behind the many unopened doors. You can try to keep all your options open at all times, but you will pay a price.

Like the child who wonders if strawberry would taste better while he/she eats chocolate, the joy of the chosen experience is diminished.

If you think about the lives of the people whom you most admire, you can probably identify some theme running through each, a theme that reflects a chosen *direction* to life. The psychoanalyst, Victor Frankl, discovered, as a result of painful years in a Nazi concentration camp, that the survival and growth of the individual depends in part upon his/her ability to identify *meaning* in every experience. He was, in fact, one of the few survivors of the Nazi tortures, and he attributes this to his absolute *commitment to meaning in every moment* of his own existence.[4]

To avoid choice altogether is to avoid commitment to anything or anyone. Perhaps a child can afford to permit all choices to be made for him/her as long as the world is a place that he/she can trust. You may even know adults whose roles in life seem to involve being passive and helpless, remaining relatively uncommitted to anything or anyone. The payoff for them, of course, is that they can never be held responsible in the long run, since they never made any choices or commitment in the first place.

> *I'm giving you a definite maybe.*
> Samuel Goldwyn

To make a choice is to make a commitment. How one does or does not live up to one's commitments is another matter. But it does seem to follow, from what is known about human growth and development, that *active choice* resulting in *active commitment* tends to foster maturation of the self-concept. This is not to suggest that commitment to a decision never means re-examining that decision. That would be foolhardy. You can never know all the possible outcomes of any given choice. Even trying a new flavor of ice cream involves *some* uncertainty as to whether or not you will like it.

Important choices always involve some measure of risk to the self. Fear of taking risk can lead to fear of making important choices. And, making a commitment usually involves some degree of risk regarding one's ability to live up to that commitment. Therefore, fear of disappointing others can lead to avoidance of commitment.

Can you apply some of these ideas to yourself? Are there central themes running through your personal propositions that reflect your basic attitudes toward making important choices, making commitments

---

[4] V. Frankl, *From Death-Camp to Existentialism* (Boston: Beacon Press, 1959).

and taking risks? Such themes are basic to managerial behavior, where you are always required to make choices, make commitments and, often, take risks.

KEY CONCEPTS FROM CHAPTER 8

1. A. Basic human needs
      modified by
   B. Past experience
      lead to
   C. Personal system (in the context or a situation)
      which determines
   D. Expectancies regarding choices
      resulting in
   E. Behavior—choices—actions,
      which feed back on the Personal System.

2. The Structure of the Personal System:
   a. Personal goals
   b. Competencies
   c. Beliefs
   d. Values
      organized around
   e. Self-concept.

3. A. Expectancies—Regarding choices (positive vs. negative outcomes)
      result in
   B. Behavior—Choices (actions, learning, defenses)
      which confirm or disconfirm the self-concept.

4. Self-Concept and Norms:
   a. The willingness to conform to group norms is a product of the closeness of the norms to one's self-concept.
   b. Costs and benefits of conforming weighed against costs and benefits of deviating.

5. Self-Concept and Roles:
   a. To the extent that a role is perceived as congruent with the self-concept, inclination is to adopt it.
   b. To the extent it is seen as incongruent with any aspect of the self-concept, inclination is to reject it.
   c. To the extent roles are adopted that support values, one experiences self as worthwhile.
   d. To the extent that one violates these values, one doubts personal worth.

6. To predict behavior one would have to know:
   a. The strength of the goals directing the particular behavior.
   b. The expectancies regarding the positive and the negative consequences from the environment.
   c. The expectancies regarding the positive and negative consequences to the self-concept.

7. Defensive Behavior:
   a. The greater the threat to a person's self-concept, the greater the defensive response.
   b. The greater the threat to a person's self-concept, the less learning and growth.
   c. Important to attempt to find a nonthreatening alternative.

SUGGESTED READINGS

Allport, G., Vernon, P., and Linsey, G. *Study of Values,* 3d ed. Boston: Houghton Mifflin Co., 1960.

"America's Growing Anti-Business Mood," *Business Week* (June 17, 1972) 89–91, 103, 116.

Charles, A. W. "The Self-Concept in Management," *S.A.M. Advanced Management Journal* (April 1971) 32–38.

Combs, A., and Snygg, D. *Individual Behavior.* New York: Harper & Brothers, 1959.

Dill, W. R., Hilton, T. L., and Reitman, W. R. *The New Managers, Patterns of Behavior and Development.* Englewood Cliffs, N. J.: Prentice-Hall, Inc., 1962.

Fayerweather, J. *The Overseas Executive.* Syracuse, N. Y.: Syracuse University Press, 1959.

Fleischman, E., and Peters, D. "Interpersonal Values, Leadership Attitudes and Managerial Success," *Personnel Psychology* 15 (1962) 127–43.

Frankl, V. *From Death Camp to Existentialism.* Boston, Mass.: Beacon Press, 1959.

Guth, W. T., and Taquiri, R. "Personal Values and Corporate Strategies," *Harvard Business Review* 45 (1965) 123–32.

Hackamack, L., and Solid, A. "The Woman Executive," *Business Horizons* 15 (1972) 89–93.

Kelby, G. A. *The Psychology of Personal Constructs.* New York: Norton, 1955.

Lazarus, Richard S. *Patterns of Adjustment and Human Effectiveness.* New York: McGraw-Hill Book Co., 1969.

McGregor, D. *The Human Side of Enterprise.* New York: McGraw-Hill Book Co., 1960.

Morse, John J., and Lorsch, J. W. "Beyond Theory Y," *HBR,* (May-June 1970) 61–68.

Orth, C., and Jacobs, F. "Women in Management: Pattern for Change," *Harvard Business Review,* 49 (1971) 139–47.

Petit, T. A. *The Moral Crisis in Management.* New York: McGraw-Hill Book Co., 1967.

Rago, James J. Jr. "The Unmentionable: Our Own Behavioral Difficulties," *Business Horizons* (August 1971) 59–68.

Scott, W. A. *Values and Organizations.* Chicago, Ill.: Rand McNally and Co., 1965.

Simon, S. B., Howe, L. W., and Kirschenbaum, H. *Values and Clarification.* New York: Hart Publishing Co., Inc., 1972.

Sofer, C. *Men in Mid-Career.* Cambridge: Cambridge University Press, 1970.

Terkel, Studs *Working.* New York: Pantheon Books, 1974.

Toeffler, Alvin *Future Shock.* New York: Random House, Inc., 1970.

Walton, C. C. *Corporate Social Responsibilities.* Belmont, Cal.: Wadsworth Publishing Co., Inc., 1967.

White, R. W. "The Process of Natural Growth," in Lawrence, P. R. & Seiler, J. A., *Organizational Behavior and Administration.* Homewood, Ill.: Richard D. Irwin, Inc., 1965.

Whyte, W. H. Jr. *The Organization Man.* Garden City, N. Y.: Doubleday, 1957.

In a work setting a frequently occurring relationship is one in which one worker is training another (perhaps a newcomer) how to do a job.

9

THE TWO-PERSON WORK RELATIONSHIP
Background and Required Factors

THOSE with organizational responsibility usually say that people problems account for most of their headaches. As one top executive put it in exasperation, "If it weren't for the people in this place, we'd be a helluva lot better off." It seems that the formation of working relationships is a central issue for any organization.

In this chapter we are going to look at various aspects of relations between individuals and at the kinds of relationships that are appropriate to different work situations. In Chapter 10 we will look at some of the underlying processes of a two-person relationship, as well as at the outcomes of these processes. It goes without saying that interpersonal relations occur at *all* levels in an organization; in fact, an organization can be thought of as consisting of a *network of interconnected relationships*. Almost all work in organizations involves the combined efforts of many individuals.

Wherever two people get together to do a job, plan a social gathering, or just have fun, the outcome depends on *how they get along*. If they bicker, backbite, build grudges, or avoid one another, they are less likely to be productive, to be satisfied or to grow than if they enjoy being together, are mutually supportive and appreciative of one another's abilities. In a work setting where you may be *required* to work with somebody not of your own choosing, you may have added difficulties with which to cope. Hopefully, however, you can learn to understand and improve your work relationships, whether or not they are ones you might otherwise freely choose.

While some jobs are carried out in relative isolation and remain little affected by interpersonal factors, most work either requires or encourages interaction among individuals. **The more a job requires two people to work together, the more important is the kind of working relationship that develops.** Even where the interaction is only peripheral to the task, the relationship can still become a source of satisfaction or frustration, and thus affect the total work effort in important ways. Think about some of the jobs you have held. What do you remember about them? Often the most important aspects will be the people you worked with, either because they were a source of help and enjoyment on the job or because they got in your way and made life miserable for you. These issues are often just as critical in an organization as the nature of the work itself. Good interpersonal relations support the work effort; bad ones can kill it.

Most people struggle with such questions as, "How do I have more impact?" "How do I get people to respect me or like me?" "How do I move others to be more productive?" "How do I get myself noticed by certain people?" "Why don't my intentions come off quite the way I want?" "Why don't others see a situation the way I do?" Can the necessary skills be learned in order to deal with some of these issues? Insofar as you *evoke* responses in other people and they in turn evoke them in you, there is an opening wedge. By understanding your impact on others and practicing new behavior, you can gain some control over your relationships, and can build interpersonal competence. This is a basic ingredient of effective management.

> . . . *it's not what you do, Ben. It's who you know and the smile on your face! It's contacts, Ben, contacts! The whole wealth of Alaska passes over the lunch table at the Commodore Hotel, and that's the wonder . . ., a man can end with diamonds . . . on the basis of being liked!*
>
> Willy Loman to the apparition of his brother, in
> *Death of a Salesman*, by Arthur Miller

It is in this context that the usually bitter observation, "it isn't what you know, but who you know, that counts," is accurate. Being interpersonally competent, able to make effective relationships, *is* indeed part of what an organizational member should know. In a "network of relationships" the person who cannot meet others and build working relationships carries a heavy handicap.

THE SOCIAL SYSTEMS SCHEMA AS APPLIED TO THE
INTERPERSONAL RELATIONSHIP

In many ways the two person relationship is simply the smallest form of a group. Consequently, much of what you have already learned about group behavior will be relevant to the two-person work relationship. Also, what you learn in this chapter and the next should provide additional insights into the dynamics of a group. Both contexts involve communication processes, role relationships, status differences, expectations for behavior, degrees of liking and respect, and, ultimately, consequences for productivity, satisfaction and development.

As a framework for the two chapters, we will use the conceptual scheme used for discussing the work group. We will look at the nature of the work situation as it determines the required work relationship; then we will discuss how the backgrounds of the two people combine with the required work relationship to produce interpersonal processes and outcomes that have consequences for productivity, satisfaction and development. This framework is diagrammed in Figure 9–1.

The Task Situation

Two people working on simple, routine, independent tasks at opposite ends of a room have no work-related reason and little opportunity to develop a relationship. Two people working side-by-side on interrelated

FIGURE 9–1
The Social System Schema as Applied to Interpersonal Relationships

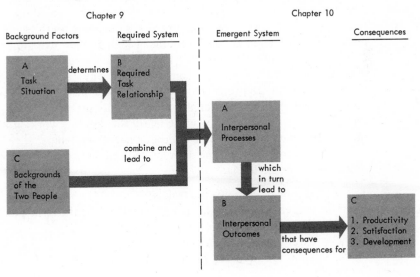

parts of the same job have a greater need and greater opportunity for developing a working relationship. In short, two of the critical aspects of a work situation that influence the kind of relationship that is required of two people are (1) *Task interdependence* and (2) *Opportunities for interaction.*

There are varying degrees of task interdependence, depending upon the complexity of the work, and varying kinds of interactions, depending upon the amount and type of information that has to be exchanged.

Imagine yourself at a soft drink bottling plant. One of the workers is inspecting racks of empty bottles, checking for chips or cracks. When a defective bottle is spotted it is his/her job to remove it from the rack before it goes past. If the bottles get knocked over in the process, then the worker is supposed to throw a switch that stops the movement of the bottles so that he/she can stand them all up again. It is a simple task to perform, it does not change over time, there are no risk factors involved, merely the simple judgment: defective/not defective. It does not call for any interaction with the person nearby and the outcome of the work is obvious and certain. In short, the job requires no relationship between any two people who may be performing it. The only exception might be when a new worker comes on; then it would seem to be appropriate for one of the other workers to familiarize the new person with the task and to serve as a temporary helper.

Contrast the above situation with that of the director of education at a private residential treatment center for disturbed children. He/she is concerned with assessing the needs of 38 children, designing individualized educational programs which will also be therapeutic, finding, selecting and supervising staff to carry out the programs, and so forth. There are new issues emerging constantly and new territory to be entered in almost every case. The director is dealing with the whole gamut of human factors and is constantly faced with his/her own impact on the children and staff. The director needs to have frequent contact with teachers in order to maintain consistency in ways of handling children as well as guarantee proper individual attention. Finally, there is uncertainty in each situation; outcomes are not easily predicted, and involve a great deal of risk and guesswork. Clearly this kind of work situation requires a broad range of possible interpersonal relationships.

The inspector's job and the director's job can be contrasted along several dimensions including:

1. How simple or complex the task is;
2. The degree to which the people involved in the task possess differential expertise;
3. The extent to which human factors (feelings, attitudes, behaviors of people) are involved in the work, as opposed to technical factors alone;

4. The frequency of human interaction or contact fostered by the task situation; and

5. The degree of certainty with which the outcomes of actions can be predicted.

Normally, a work situation which is simple, is equally familiar to both workers, is low in human factors, demands little interaction, and has high certainty of outcomes calls for a minimal interpersonal relationship. In contrast, a work situation that is complex, is unfamiliar to one of the workers, is high in human factors, demands a great deal of interaction and has a high degree of uncertainty with respect to outcomes, calls for a much broader type of interpersonal relationship. Obviously there are all kinds of situations in between the two extremes and, therefore, a variety of relationships which might fit the different situations. In the next section we will discuss some of these.

Four Kinds of Required Work Relationships[1]

For the sake of simplicity we will discuss *four* types of relationships that are directly relevant to a work setting. Each type calls for a different degree of interdependence between the people involved and is appropriate for a different kind of situation. Keep in mind that these are not pure types and that at different times a given relationship may combine them or change from one to another.

The first and most fundamental kind of relation for any job we call the *minimal task relationship*. In the minimal task relationship each person's behavior and the exchange of information are determined strictly by the specific demands of the task and its accompanying roles. An example is the operating room nurse and the surgeon. Normally, the only exchange between them pertains to the surgeon's need for instruments and the sharing of information pertaining to the welfare of the patient. No more complex a relationship is called for in order to effectively complete the work.

The second kind of work relationship we call *reality-testing*. It is one in which each individual checks out with the other his/her perceptions or interpretations of (*a*) the nature of the overall task (i.e., the realities of the situation) and (*b*) the effects of his/her own actions on the task (i.e., how effective or competent he/she is being). An example is two workers on a paper-making machine; the feeder at one end needs to know how the paper is coming out at the other end so that appropriate adjustments can be made. Various hand signals or brief phone conversa-

---

[1] Based upon concepts presented in W. G. Bennis, D. E. Berlew, E. H. Schein, and F. I. Steele, *Interpersonal Dynamics,* 3d ed. (Homewood, Ill.: The Dorsey Press, 1973) pp. 495–518.

tions (the machine is long and noisy) are exchanged to get the proper thickness and tensileness of paper. Two managers comparing their assessments of employees is another example of a reality-testing relationship.

The third kind of work relationship we refer to as a *controlling/influencing* relationship. In this instance one person serves as a source of control or guidance to the other and has a special influence over the other's behavior. Some common examples of this include a teacher–student, parent–child, superior–subordinate and therapist–patient relationship. In the work setting a frequently occurring relationship of this type would be one in which one worker is training another (perhaps a newcomer); another example would be a supervisory relationship in which one person possesses greater expertise than the other.

The fourth kind of relationship we refer to as the *colleague* relationship. It is one in which the two individuals have developed a liking and a concern for each other's welfare. It occurs above and beyond the strict requirements of the task, but is functional for facilitating open exchange. A colleague relationship is appropriate for peers who are collaborating on a complex task. (Remember the faculty group in Chapter 6?) Ideas bubble back and forth; work goes on during some social occasions and social talk sometimes occurs during work.

Some managers insist that one can never mix business with friendship; others take the opposite view, that one cannot work successfully with another person unless close, friendly relations are maintained. As you might suspect, both points of view contain some grain of truth, but neither is valid for all situations. In fact, it is safe to say that no one type of interpersonal relationship is appropriate to every work situation, even though the minimal task aspect of relationships will almost always be one component. In general, we can say that **The greater the degree of interdependence between two people's jobs, the more the required task relationship needs to extend beyond minimal task.**

Furthermore, **The more such factors as complexity, differential expertise, human problems, frequent interaction, uncertainty, and so forth, are part of the situation, the more the relationship needs to encompass elements of all four types of relationships.**

Each type of work relationship leads to different outcomes. The result of a good minimal task oriented relationship is competent performance, which is normally a principal objective of the organization. A poor relationship of this type leads to very visible output problems that demand direct attention. The outcome of a good reality-testing relationship is development and confirmation of the individuals' interpretations of the situation and reinforcement of their self-concepts. Failures in this type of relationship tend to produce lowered self-esteem and distorted pictures of the nature of the overall task situation. The outcome of an effective controlling/influencing relationship is *improved performance* on the part of the person being influenced and *satisfaction* on the part of the controller. An ineffective relationship in this area tends to result in less than adequate competence on the part of the worker (subordinate) and increasing dependency of that person on the controller (superior). With respect to colleague relationships, effectiveness leads to all the above outcomes, as well as to *solidarity,* which can serve as an important support base for both people. If the colleague relationship fails to develop well, the outcome is often one that includes alienation, hostility, and/or ambivalence on the part of one or both persons.

It is clear, then, that interpersonal relationships can strongly affect a work situation. If a task calls for all four kinds of work relationships to be present, their effectiveness can result in competent performance, reality confirmation, learning and solidarity; in contrast, their ineffectiveness can result in poor output, low self-esteem, distortions of reality, dependency and alienation.

What the Two People Bring to the Job

Personal Systems   We have already devoted considerable attention to the importance of personal systems as background factors in group behavior. In Chapter 8 we discussed in detail the various components of a personal system, in particular the self-concept. In the present chapter *the respective personal systems of two people are viewed as major determinants of their emergent relationship,* particularly in the context of the required system. The "fit" between their respective goals, competencies, beliefs, values and self-concepts is an important basis for explaining the quality of interactions between any two individuals.

It should not be surprising that when given the opportunity, people tend to build relationships with those who have similar values, beliefs, abilities and goals. Birds of a feather do flock together; the chances of speaking "the same language" make communication easier and more comfortable. In some circumstances, however, opposites attract. This is especially true when the opposite qualities are complementary to one another—when one person's skills fill vital gaps in the other's repertoire of skills, or when the values of one are attractive because they somehow suggest a way past the other's flat sides.

The most desirable kind of relationship is one which permits the exercise of choices, generates feelings of competence and produces confirmation of cherished values. Anyone would prefer relationships which reinforce all aspects of the self, although each aspect usually has a different priority. Goals are open to compromise; it is usually possible to accept alternative ways of doing things in a relationship, providing that they don't seriously threaten either the sense of competence or fundamental beliefs or values. Competencies are less open to compromise, but they are learnable, again provided that they are consistent with values. Values and beliefs normally are not negotiable; they go very deep and pertain to the integrity of the individual.

Can you think of examples of relationships in your own life which you would classify as the most and least satisfying? In all probability, the most rewarding ones gave you self-confirmation, while the least rewarding ones had the opposite effect. In any current relationship in which you are experiencing problems, it might be useful for you to diagnose the levels at which the problems exist. Are they primarily goal conflicts? If so, the chances are fairly good that you can work them out. However, if they reflect more basic differences in beliefs or values, the problem is likely to be harder to settle. Resolution of conflict in any work relationship depends upon the level of the personal system the conflict taps into.

The required task relationship can be another source of difficulty. An individual, for example, having a limited concept of his/her abilities, may find any relationship beyond minimal task somewhat threatening. Or someone who is used to seeing him/herself exclusively in the role of "boss," may have problems with a colleague type of relationship. Therefore, it is important for you as a manager to pay attention to the kinds of working relationships you demand of your employees and how your requirements fit with their personal systems. While you cannot constantly redefine work relationships just to suit workers' preferences, some awareness of these contingencies may save you a great deal of aggravation in the long run.

In the next section we will look at another background factor, the preferred styles of interacting that individuals possess. While these styles reflect various aspects of the personal systems of people, they do deserve special attention in their own right, since certain interaction styles seem to be appropriate to particular kinds of work relationships, and some work relationships tend to demand a wider range of interaction styles than others.

Four Styles of Interaction Individuals Prefer[2]   Almost no one behaves in exactly the same way in every situation; some settings and people call forth different behavior than do other. Only a very brave, or disturbed person would treat his boss, mother and lover with the same kinds and style of interactions. But almost everyone does have a preferred or dominant interaction style of some sort, a style which fits his/her self-concept, a style with which he/she feels most comfortable. When given the opportunity, that style will be used for interaction with other organizational members. For example, a woman principal of a school saw herself as ambitious, confident, extremely capable and honest. When at school

---

[2] Based upon concepts developed by W. F. Hill, *Hill Interaction Matrix* (Los Angeles: Youth Study Center, University of Southern California, 1965).

board or other community meetings she related to others in an open, challenging way. She did this even when others were more cautious and guarded in their styles.

While it is difficult to describe interaction styles, we will use four general categories to make discussion manageable. Remember that a person will probably at one time or another use all four styles, but prefer or tend to rely upon one more than the others. As you consider each of the styles we describe, you might try to picture yourself in various settings that seem to pull that particular way of interacting from you. Some people are very different at home, at work, with friends, on a date, and so forth. Others show only slight variations from their "usual" style. See where you fit in.

The first style involves *Conventional-Polite* forms of exchange, those that are governed mainly by social convention and what is normally considered "acceptable and polite" behavior. When any two people meet for the first time they are likely to start in this style; some people, however, prefer to keep as many relationships as possible that way. Their conversation tends to remain at an impersonal and cordial level and its content stays within the bounds of what is easiest to talk about.

A second style of interaction we call *Speculative-Tentative*. The person who prefers this kind of interaction examines, questions and evaluates everything and everyone in a careful manner, usually with the intent of trying to learn and understand. His/her conclusions tend to be tentative and open to modification, with fixed positions seldom taken. What is discussed this way may be anything from the task at hand to the relationship itself. The main quality of the interaction process generated by this style is an open flow of exchanges which are seldom emotionally loaded or threatening. In many ways this style of interaction has some of the low-key quality of the Conventional-Polite type of interaction. It is what you would expect in a discussion about future careers, for example, where exploration of a great deal of data, thoughtfulness, generation of alternatives and their consequences are all appropriate.

A third style of interaction is called *Aggressive-Argumentative*. It is when a person vigorously takes fixed positions on issues, and pushes his/her own arguments. The person's feelings tend to be strong while listening tends to be poor. This style often results in dominance. Interactions with such a person can be stimulating or frustrating, depending on the other's preferences; either way, the interactions are seldom dull and require high energy responses.

The fourth style of interaction is called *Expressive-Confronting*. It is one in which the person using it expresses openly and directly what he/she thinks and feels about situations and people. People who relate in this way often develop very close working relationships and intimate friendships. The range of feelings expressed is very wide and varies from anger to tenderness—whatever is actually being felt. People who find Expressive-Confronting interactions personally rewarding vary considerably regarding how often, and with whom, they consider such interactions desirable, but they usually try to get there in a relationship as rapidly as possible.

Fit between Styles   Apart from what is called for by the job itself, people who prefer one or another of these four styles fit compatibly with those who prefer some of the remaining styles but generate friction when with others. For example, the person who naturally prefers conventional-polite forms of interactions will probably be made exceedingly uncomfortable by the person who loves an expressive-confronting style, but may feel quite at ease with a speculative-tentative person. The confident female principal, for example, often intimidated teachers who preferred that interaction with women remain "proper" and "polite."

While almost anyone will respond partly to the situation, as when two strangers meet and both use a conventional-polite style, when there is *ambiguity* in the situation, people see and define it largely from their own respective frames of reference. Thus, to a proper New Englander the fifth year of knowing someone may be too early for open warmth and expressiveness, while to a Southern Californian five minutes of polite but friendly conversation may be seen as enough to begin some self-revelation.

Similarly, the same desires and feelings may be expressed quite differently, depending on the preferred styles of those involved. Two "expressives" might show genuine liking by grand and sweeping statements, strong pledges of caring and lots of hugging or back-slapping, while two "conventionals" might never use the actual words, "I like you" but show it through thoughtful gestures, like remembering to send a birthday card, inquiring after a sick relative, and so forth.

Nevertheless, much behavior is affected by the situation and its requirements as well as by the desires or preferences of those in it. To better understand what interpersonal behavior is appropriate under which work conditions, we turn now to task requirements and their impact on relationships.

How Interaction Styles Combine with Types of Relationships

How do these styles—conventional, argumentative, tentative and expressive,—work when they bump up against the types of relationships called for by task situations—minimal task, reality-testing, controlling/influencing and colleagueship? What desired styles fit best with which appropriate types of relationships? What happens if there is a mismatch?

The matrix below (Figure 9–2) shows the various combinations of interaction styles and work relationships possible. Basically, the matrix reflects two important ideas:

1. The more complex a work relationship tends to be, the wider the range of interaction styles that seem to be needed by the individuals (as indicated by all light shaded areas in the figure).[3]
2. Each type of work relationship tends to call forth a specific interactive style more than others (dark shaded areas).

The first point represents a critical issue for many managers who aspire to higher and higher positions in an organization. So often a person trained to do a specific kind of work (for example, a research lab technician), which may require little interaction with others beyond a minimal task level, gets promoted to a managerial position, only to be confronted with his/her limited range of interaction styles. A high-pressured negotiating session, for example, may require aggressive-argumentative behavior and the person simply cannot do it. He/she may attempt to handle things in the accustomed polite or possibly speculative manner more characteristic of "the old job" (in the research lab).

Of course, the opposite extreme is also possible. Have you known people who seem to be expressive and confronting no matter what the circumstances? It's as though they have an overdeveloped need to *relate!*

FIGURE 9–2
Combinations of Interaction Styles and Work Relationships

Types of Work Relationships

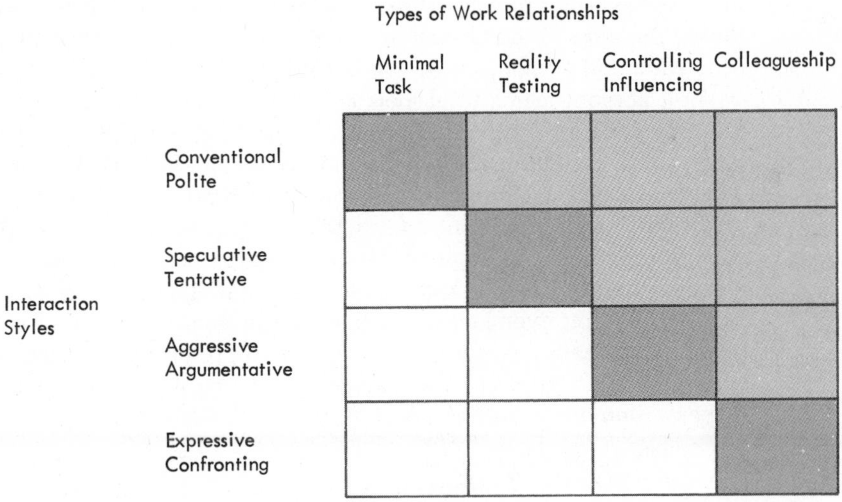

_____
[3] That is, as you read across the top of the matrix from left to right, each type of work relationship calls for more of the interaction styles.

Even the most routine, impersonal tasks get converted into rituals of personal devotion.

It should be obvious that no one style of interaction is suitable for all work relationships. Having a wide repertoire of styles can help you to adapt effectively to the demands of a complex work environment. Now, let's take a brief look at how specific kinds of work relationships tend to demand certain interaction styles. We'll discuss only a few examples, since you can probably see for yourself ways in which the two dimensions of the matrix fit together.

When a minimal task relationship is appropriate to the job, for example, people with conventional-polite preferred styles will probably make the easiest accommodation to the situation and to one another. Little more than information exchange is expected, emotional investment is at a minimum, and self-disclosure is low; easy comfort will be likely.

Similarly, when colleagueship is called for, those who prefer an expressive-confronting style will fit the situation easiest. Any team working on complex, engaging work, with high interdependence, will function better with people who have open, direct and honest interaction styles. A group of firemen, for example, is most effective when, as often happens, the members not only work together closely, but also live in the same neighborhood, socialize with one another's families, and in general provide all kinds of support for one another. Or a new astronaut who prefers the distance of conventional/polite interactions may find it difficult to adapt to the close quarters and life-and-death interdependence that describes a group of astronauts in space. In short, the further away from these "matches" a combination is on the chart, the greater the likelihood of tension and conflict in the relationship.

As a person begins to associate interaction styles with specific kinds of work relationships, he/she may develop preferences for one or another kind of relationship. What you bring to any new work situation will include learned preferences from previous work experience; and these preferences may pertain to a particular type of work relationship. Given what you perceive to be your own preferred interactive style(s), can you identify the kind of work relationship(s) that would probably suit you best? Have you ever had the experience of being required to work in a relationship that does not fit with your own preferences? What were the consequences? Note this experience of a young man working for a summer as a plumber's assistant:

> I was assigned to an older, very experienced man who was used to working alone. The boss assigned the man to teach me whatever skills were needed on the job. I was eager to learn; he did not know how to teach or help me and preferred not to try. I tried to be friends with the man; he felt that friendships had no place in a work setting. At times when I thought he had overlooked something on the job, I pointed this out. It only made him angry;

he thought I was questioning his ability to do the job. I finally settled for doing simple jobs that I could figure out for myself. I initiated very little conversation with him, except at lunch or over coffee, when it was "all right." He was satisfied; I was not.

The relationship had elements of incompatibility between required and desired relationships and between the preferred interaction styles of the two people involved. The assistant's need for a controlling/influencing type of relationship did not match the minimal task relationship preferred by the plumber; and the aggressive-argumentative style of the assistant conflicted with the conventional-polite style of the older man. We can also see how behind the desired relationships different levels of the self-concept were affected. The rejection of friendship or colleagueship at work by the older man was a matter of beliefs or values and probably was unchangeable. The assistant's desire for colleagueship was probably less a matter of values than a goal; thus, he was able to adapt. The plumber's lack of competence to teach and be helpful was a matter that could not have made him feel good about himself. Similarly, the assistant must have felt inadequate, wanting to be shown what to do so that he could gradually undertake more interesting assignments and not be totally dependent.

The issue of respective goals was something for the two individuals to negotiate. It is possible that if the older man had had the competence to teach the assistant, then he might have been more open to the latter's observations and "trouble shooting." While the younger man was not specifically assigned to that role, it was one that might have been both helpful and desirable in the relationship, though not strictly necessary.

In summary, we can offer the following propositions:

1. **To the extent that a required work relationship is compatible with the preferred interaction styles of both persons assigned to it, the relationship will be accepted.**
2. **To the extent that a required work relationship is incompatible with the preferred interaction styles of either or both persons assigned to it, the relationship will be resisted; the degree of resistance will depend upon the level of the personal system or self-concept affected in either or both individuals.**

In Chapter 10 we will examine what actually happens in a relationship once the two people begin to interact. We will look first at interpersonal processes and then at the outcomes of these processes.

Before proceeding, however, we suggest that you examine Figure 9–3 as a way of reviewing what we have covered so far. The left-hand side of the figure is filled in with the concepts of Chapter 9; the right hand side will be completed in Chapter 10.

FIGURE 9–3
Background Factors and Required System Effects on Interpersonal Relationships

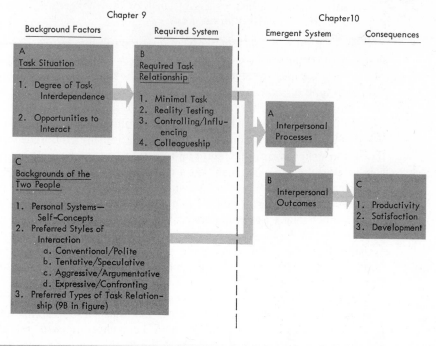

KEY CONCEPTS FROM CHAPTER 9

1. The Social System Schema as applied to the interpersonal relationship:
    a. The task situation
        determines
    b. The required task relationship
        which combine with
    c. Background of the two people
        and lead to
    d. Interpersonal processes
        which in turn lead to
    e. Interpersonal outcomes
        that have consequences for
    f. Productivity, satisfaction and development.
2. Work Situation:
    a. Task interdependence.
    b. Opportunities for interaction.
        (1) How simple or complex is the task.
        (2) Degree of differential expertise.
        (3) Human and/or technical factors.
        (4) Frequency of interaction required by task.
        (5) Degree of certainty in outcome prediction.

3. Four types of required work relationships:
   a. Minimal task.
   b. Reality-testing.
   c. Controlling/Influencing.
   d. Colleagueship
4. No one type of interpersonal relationship is appropriate to every work situation.
5. The greater the degree of interdependence between two people's jobs the more a required task relationship needs to extend beyond minimal task.
6. The more complex the task, the more the relationship needs to encompass elements of all four types of relationship.
7. Determinants of the emergent relationship
   a. Personal systems of the two people.
   b. Their preferred styles of interaction.
      (1) conventional-polite
      (2) speculative-tentative
      (3) aggressive-argumentative
      (4) expressive-confronting
   c. The fit between styles of the two people.
8. Each type of work relationship tends to call forth a specific interactive style more than others.
9. Compatibility of styles leads to an accepted relationship.
10. Incompatibility leads to resistance, tension and conflict.

SUGGESTED READINGS

Goffman, E. *The Presentation of Self in Everyday Life.* Garden City, N. Y.: Doubleday and Co., Inc., 1959.

Hill, W. F. *Hill Interaction Matrix.* Los Angeles, California: Youth Study Center, University of Southern California, 1965.

Kahn, R. L., Wolfe, D. M., Quinn, R. P., and Snoek, J. Diedrich *Organizational Stress: Studies in Role Conflict and Ambiguity.* New York: John Wiley & Sons, Inc., 1964.

Leader, G. C. "Interpersonally Skillful Bank Officers View Their Behavior" *JABS* 9 (1973) 484–97.

Schutz, W. C. *FIRO: A Three-Dimensional Theory of Interpersonal Behavior.* New York: Rinehart, 1958.

———— "Interpersonal Underworld," *Harvard Business Review* 36 (1958) 123–35.

Messages are transmitted by more than words; content and especially feelings are transmitted by gestures, voice intonations, facial expressions, body posture, and so forth.

10

THE TWO-PERSON WORK RELATIONSHIP
Emergent Processes and Outcomes

IN CHAPTER 9 we looked at the background and required factors which affect interpersonal relationships. Now we turn to an examination of the results of those factors. We begin with the difficulties inherent in any communications between people.

INTERPERSONAL PROCESSES

The Nature of Human Communication

What happens when one person talks to another? The process is so complicated that it is a wonder that anyone ever understands and gets understood. This section will include a description of the communication process and the factors that ease or hinder understanding.

Communication between people involves an exchange of (a) the content of what is being discussed, (b) feelings about the subject matter at hand, and (c) feelings about the other person.

The same exchange can be seen another way: what speaker A says is modified by B's self-concept (which includes how B interprets A's self-concept). For example, A is B's boss. B has had many troubles in the past with people in authority—parents, teachers, bosses. He sees himself as having been misunderstood and unappreciated by them. A is in a hurry, doesn't know B's background, so calls over his shoulder on the way by, "Hey, lend a hand, will

FIGURE 10–1
Three Levels of Exchange between Speaker and Listener

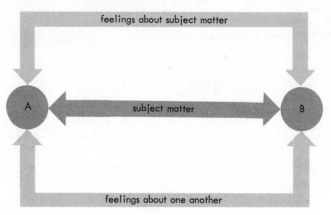

you?" B hears this as a criticism, reddens and mutters to himself at the "attack." (See Fig. 10–2).

This gets even more complicated as the self-concept of each alters the way messages are sent as compared to the actual feelings of the speaker. That is, A is feeling angry at B's apparent uncooperativeness and wants to reprimand B, but A sees himself as a kind person, so he tries to soften the blow through indirection; instead of saying what he feels—"You infuriate me when you sit there doodling while I work hard"—he says, "Isn't it amazing how some people just can't cooperate with others?" B, who sees himself as an intelligent person, eager to be helpful when he gets an original idea, but sees A as typically aggressive and impatient, feels puzzled about where A's remarks concerning cooperation come from, misses the feeling, and replies to the content, "Well it depends on

FIGURE 10–2
Other's Statements are Modified by Receiver's Self-Concept

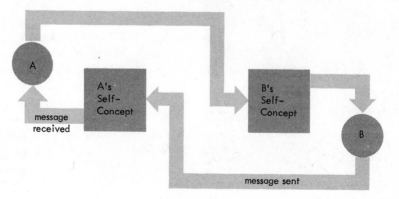

FIGURE 10-3
Self-Concepts and Perceptions of Other Filter Messages In and Out

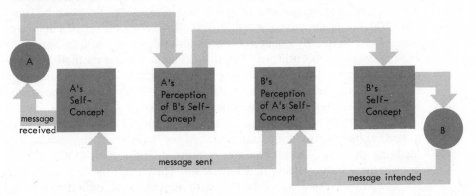

the people involved, but I don't think cooperation is so difficult." A starts to steam, B senses it, but doesn't know why; the relationship begins to deteriorate. (See Figure 10-3).

The potentials for difficulties are great. Let us take a closer look at the barriers to communication.

Barriers to Communication

The Nature of Human Perception and Cognition   The first barrier to communication is a result of the nature of all human perception. What a person sees and hears tends to be selective and to involve a degree of distortion shaped by the person's self-concept; *one perceives what one needs or expects to perceive.* For example, a good accountant can glance at a page full of figures and almost see mistakes "jump out." The correct numbers are barely seen; those that don't fit are noticed. Remember the story about the tailor who finally met his idol, President Kennedy? When asked what the president was like, he replied, "Oh, I'd say a 42 long with a slight slope to the right shoulder." An organization having difficulty will be seen by the production, marketing and accounting managers differently; each is likely to perceive the area he/she is most familiar with as needing the most resources but doing the best job.

This selective process can be functional; it saves time, allows people to concentrate on what's really important, and can help them perceive the meaning in incomplete messages, words, and so forth. On the other hand, distortion and selection can be dysfunctional; expecting the boss to be aloof and distant, for example, can make his nervousness or shyness seem cold, and "confirm" what was expected. When natural perceptual processes keep people from seeing what would be useful to see, they can create real difficulties.

In addition, since any mental concept is an abstraction, and, therefore, a simplification of reality, distortion is an inevitable part of committing experience to memory. Humans fit experience into pre-existing conceptions, discarding details and lumping things together. This can be functional (just as is selective perception); it allows the creation of a degree of order from chaos. By equating new experiences with old ones, previous experiences can be utilized. But this efficient sorting method also has potential dangers: the new can be overly distorted to fit pre-existing concepts, ignoring important details, failing to discriminate differences, and resulting in stereotyping rather than accuracy.

Characteristics of Language   The very nature of language constitutes a second barrier to communication. Many words are imprecise. The meaning of "level" to a carpenter is quite different than to a landscape contractor who is putting in a new lawn. How many is "a few?" Does "right away" mean drop the bucket with molten metal, or first pour it and then start the next job?

Many words have multiple meanings; miscommunication occurs when the two parties apply different interpretations. The purchasing agent who orders track spikes to repair the railroad siding may be surprised to receive a pair of running shoes. "Write," "right (correct)," "right (not left)," and "Wright" all sound the same, right? Sometimes words have different meanings to different subcultures of the country. Have you ever ordered a "milkshake" in Boston? To get ice cream, as in other parts of the country, you must order a "frappe." And don't ask for a "Boston cooler;" you have to call it a "root beer float." Similarly, a machinist's caliper measures diameter, whereas a nurseryman's caliper measures circumference! And what kind of "nursery" do you mean, anyway?

The fact that words are imprecise and have multiple meanings has become an even greater threat to communication as society has become more interconnected and mobile. The possibility of contact with someone with a different background and, hence, a different way of using words has increased. The fact that words are imprecise and have several meanings is also one reason why jargon develops. Jargon at its best is designed to avoid ambiguity and, when used for this purpose, can be helpful. On the other hand, "P. req." for purchase requisition, "M.I." for myocardial infarction (heart attack) and "social systems" for groups and organizations can be unintelligible to the outsider, even when efficient for the insider.

Finally, words have an emotional coloring that influence the communication process, because they trigger mental associations and emotional responses. Consider the following: "I want a large slab of slaughtered cow" versus "I would like the king-size cut of prime roast beef;" "let us hear the egghead's comments" versus "let us be informed by the expert intellectual." The words "slaughtered cow" conjure up many distasteful images that do not enhance people's appetites, even though they may, in fact, be more precise than the term "prime roast beef." Often it is the emotional color that is communicated rather than the intended meaning. The first time you hear an intern call an elderly patient, for whom no treatment is possible, a "crock," it is not likely to be easy to respond neutrally.

Multiple Channels   Messages are transmitted by more than words; content and especially feelings are transmitted by gestures, voice intonations, facial expressions, body posture, and so forth. All these media (elements) for messages go into the same communications package. The package is a clear one when the messages sent are consistent with one another. This occurs when everything fits together; when the nonverbal enriches the verbal, when the "music" fits the words. When a facial expression or a gesture or a tone of voice doesn't seem to match the words, "static" is created. Have you seen someone get red in the face, pound the table and declare, "What do you mean I'm angry?" That is giving off mixed messages; communication is incongruent. The words and music don't go together; it's like a love song sung to a march tempo. Since nonverbal messages tend to be ambiguous in meaning, thereby leaving room for interpretation by the other person, misunderstanding is possible. An embarrassed smile can easily be seen as implying agreement when it really means, "I'm too embarrassed to say how ridiculous I think your idea is." Frowns of concentration may be seen as disapproval, and so forth.

The State of Mind of the Two People   When a person is feeling any strong emotions—anger, fear, defensiveness, and so forth, it is very difficult to *listen* to another person. What usually happens is that A's emotion triggers a similar emotion in B; then both have trouble listening to the other. For example, an aggressive-argumentative exchange often contains emotionally charged, defensive kinds of messages. Effective communication becomes blocked, the tensions increase, and the whole cycle escalates. Is this kind of pattern familiar to you? It is likely that everyone has faced similar problems and could benefit from learning how to change the quality of a communication process when it is blocked, defensive and nonsupportive of the participants.

When possible differences in mental set, emotional state, channels used, words chosen, and so forth, are added together it becomes apparent how difficult it would be for the message sent to be the same as the message received. How many times have you argued about what was "really" said in a conversation? Each person "*knows* what *I* said" and each "*knows* what *I* heard," even though both are sure the other is wrong. Some degree of distortion seems inevitable in communication.

It Takes Both People for Communication to Work

One person alone cannot establish effective communication; he/she has no means of checking out whether or not the intended message was the received one. Because of the probability that some distortion will take place, good communication requires an exchange of messages, a two-way process. For A to disclose something to B without knowing how it was received is only half the process. And the more important the disclosure is to A, the more vital it is for A to check out its reception. Many exchanges, especially around work routines and the like, require a minimum amount of checking out; they are least subject to distortion. But even these communications can, if badly managed, lead to misunderstandings that may become more significant and require a great deal of clarifying. *An accumulation of little miscommunications often builds into a major source of conflict between two people.*

This is not to suggest that every message you send to another person requires a response or acknowledgment from that person, and vice versa. Very often a simple nod of the head or observing the subsequent behavior of the other person is enough to complete the process. But **As a task becomes more complex, as a relationship requires more avenues and frequency of communication, it calls for more attention to whatever processes ensure accuracy of communication.** This principle becomes doubly important when there is some degree of tension in the situation. **The key to more effective listening is the willingness to listen, and respond appropriately, to the feelings being expressed as well as the content.** An acceptance of the existence of feelings, and the legitimacy of the other person having them, even when you don't agree, usually eases the tension created when a person feels misunderstood or put down by the listener, and allows a focus on whatever is generating the original feelings.[1]

The following are some examples of the kinds of interpersonal communication problems which frequently occur:

Ambiguous Communications: The Mixed Message   This kind of problem occurs when several channels are in operation at the same time and they are not completely in tune with each other. One channel may be sending a message that is different from or contradictory to another, making the message difficult to understand. For example, the words are polite, or even friendly, but the tone of voice is angry or hostile (as might be the case with sarcasm). Another example is when the words are a question, but the manner of expression is an assertion. Have you heard someone say, "Don't you think that . . . ?", when he/she really means, "I think that you should . . ." Such ambiguous communication is likely to occur when a manager is trying to behave in a participative manner with subordinates, but really wants to maintain absolute control over outcomes.

Incomplete Communication: The Throwaway Line   This kind of communication occurs when enough of a message is sent to indicate the presence of an issue, but not enough to make clear what the issue really is or

---

[1] For a more detailed view of these and other listening skills, we refer you to Richard Farson and Carl Rogers, *Active Listening,* in the Case section of this volume.

how serious it is. For example, in the middle of discussing one issue, a reference is made to another problem, but it is offhand and passed over very quickly. It can be a very disruptive kind of behavior. Note the following example:

> An executive had the habit of referring off-handedly to extraneous issues during important meetings, when the issues could not be discussed appropriately. On one occasion, when discussing union relations, he said to one of his managers, "Though I was pleased with the way you handled the shop steward when he said the company is anti-union, I didn't like your interrupting me in the middle of my sentence in front of him, but never mind that now . . ." The target of the throw-away line (as it is sometimes called in the theater) was taken off guard by the comment, and found it difficult to concentrate on the issue at hand; he worried about the implication of having displeased his boss.

This kind of communication tends to raise anxiety and leave the recipient in the unfortunate position of having to fill in the rest of the message with his/her own fantasies, which often are worse than the actual situation.

Nonverbal Signals: The Person's Emotional State   Watch a busy executive going about his or her business; note the speed of movement, facial expression, posture, and so forth. It doesn't take much to interpret rapid pace, furrowed brow and thrust-out chin as, "I am harassed and under pressure; don't bother me with trivial matters." Most people communicate something of this sort when feeling overworked. At times, however, such nonverbal behavior can creep into a person's everyday style to the point where he/she appears harassed even when not. If one is unaware of the unintended message, it is a blindspot that can leave one puzzled by the reactions of others to it. In the example just given, the person may wonder why people don't come around to talk over problems even when they would be welcome. Are you aware of the kinds of signals expressed in your nonverbal behavior? Does your characteristic body posture say "I like myself" or "I feel insignificant?" Does your facial expression usually suggest anger, fear, curiosity, or what? Do you sit in a way which says "don't approach me" or "I am receptive to new relationships and ideas"? This may be an area worth exploring with your fellow students or co-workers. Though you can sometimes guess at how you are seen by observing the way others react to you, asking for feedback is probably the best way to find out, though not always the most comfortable.

So don't listen to the words, just listen to what the voice tells you, what the movements tell you, what the posture tells you, what the image tells you.

F. S. Perls
Gestalt Theory Verbatim p. 57

Nonverbal Signals: The Secret Society While nonverbal communication goes on all the time, often two people develop "special" signals to each other, such as a knowing look, nod or smile, a warning of threat, a smile of support, and many other signs and gestures. These forms of communication can be very handy or convenient, and they also tend to confirm the solidarity of the relationship. However, they also may convey a sense of a "secret society" with its own special language; this is likely to wall off others and be dysfunctional to outside relationships. In some situations, this type of communication is very important. For example, in negotiation sessions it is important to know how others on your side feel about things as they happen, without openly conferring. But even in these situations, it heightens feelings of exclusion and can have negative consequences, too.

With these aspects and difficulties of communication in mind, we can summarize with the following working proposition: **The greater the (a) complexity of a subject, (b) importance of a subject to the parties involved and (c) feelings aroused by the subject, the greater the possibilities for distortion, and, therefore, the greater the need for each to check with the other what has been heard and said.**

You can probably understand by now why so many managers tend to classify human relations difficulties as "communication problems." While the phrase is often just a catchall to reduce things to their simplest possible form, and can cover up the problem more than illuminate it, the observation is not too far off the mark. It is hard for people to understand one another. And while accurate understanding in no way guarantees agreement, there is little advantage in trying to sort out relationships through the additional static of unclear messages. It is worth the effort to practice listening to feelings as well as words, and to check out meanings when clarity is not certain. Effective communication is a basic step in building relationships.

Feelings of the Individuals

Every relationship has the potential for confirming or dis-confirming the participants' self-concepts. Whatever is sought in the relationship — whether it is liking, respect, or influence — a satisfying relationship confirms people's view of themselves and makes them feel good about who they believe they are. When two people agree in their goals, it makes them both feel supported; when they affirm each other's competencies, they feel a sense of adequacy; and when they reinforce each other's beliefs and values, they each feel worthy. **A relationship that makes each person feel supported, adequate and worthy will generally lead to mutual feelings of closeness, warmth and trust. By way of contrast, a relationship that makes each person feel unsupported, inadequate and unworthy will generally lead to mutual feelings of distance, coldness and suspicion.**

The terms *closeness* (versus distance), *warmth* (versus coldness) and *trust* (versus suspicion) take on different meanings in different kinds of relationships. Closeness and warmth are mainly a matter of degree. For example, a minimal task relationship would certainly not draw two people as close nor generate as many warm feelings as would a colleagueship; the stakes are different in each case. But even a minimal task relationship in which each person experiences self-confirmation can lead to some degree of closeness and warmth.

Trust

With respect to trust the situation is more complex; trust is a central issue in all human relationships both within and outside of organizations. Trust can refer to several aspects of a relationship: (1) how much confidence you have in the other's competence and ability to do whatever needs doing, (2) how sound you believe the other's judgment to be, (3) your belief in the extent to which the other is willing to be helpful to you and (4) how certain you are that the other has genuine concern for your welfare rather than any desire to harm you.

Since trust can refer to any or all of these areas, it is useful to be clear about which area you mean when you use the concept, and helpful to check what others mean by it. "I don't trust you" is a very different statement when it means, "Your lack of carpentry skills make me doubt whether you can build that chest," than when it means, "I think you would drop it on my toes at the first opportunity." Remember Theory X and Theory Y from Chapter 7? They are sets of beliefs which express greater or lesser trust in the motives of others.

While deep and all-encompassing trust may not be called for in a work situation, when it does emerge it can make work easier. It does this by way of forming the basis for greater *openness* in the relationship on all fronts. For example, two close friends probably will feel greater freedom to be open and honest in task-related areas than two relative strangers. The two friends are more likely to be willing to take *risks* with one another, that is, to say things that may be critical or revealing, in the belief that the other person will hear it accurately and not use it in a destructive way. While the level of trust in a relationship can develop gradually through the course of interactions over time, very often it takes some kind of risky behavior in relation to the other person to build trust at the deepest levels. That is, to deepen a relationship requires that someone take initiative in trusting the other—say, to do a really tough part of a joint task—before he/she can be certain of the consequences. If neither will take the risk of trusting, at least a little, the relationship remains at the same level of caution and suspicion.

On the other hand, when someone violates trust, especially when it has involved some personal risk, the relationship is usually damaged. The effect may be temporary or permanent, depending upon how deeply the violation affected the self-concept. It is easier to forgive a co-worker who goofed up some piece of the job or whose interpretation of a task was grossly in error, than it is to forgive a friend or close colleague for taking an action that puts one in a bad light with others.

In general, then, **The greater the trust one has in another's competence, judgment, helpfulness or concern, the more open one will be about matters relating to that aspect(s) of the relationship. In turn, the more one feels trusted, the easier it is to be open.**

Blind Spots and the Need for Feedback

The development of a relationship involves the behavior of both parties; to make it easier to look at the interconnection, see Figure 10–4. It shows the relationship from the perspective of each person and also what the combinations of their separate perspectives produce. From each person's vantage point there are aspects of the relationship that are *known*, (that each is aware of) and aspects that are *not known*. What both persons are aware of (upper left box) are those things that have been shared openly; what neither person is aware of (lower right box) are those things that have not made their appearance in the relationship, the future unknowns that may or may not emerge. The other two boxes are the ones that determine the direction in which the relationship is to develop, if it develops at all. They include those aspects of the relationship that one person or the other is aware of, but not both. What person A alone is aware of (has not shared with person B) in the relationship we call B's "blind spots" (and vice versa). The blind spots can be positive or negative in nature, but as long as they remain hidden from one person or the other, they tend to serve as obstacles to the development of a mutually enhancing relationship. **The fewer the number of blind spots one has, the greater the understanding of one's impact on others, and the greater the opportunity to choose alternative behaviors.** It is discouraging and a handicap to be misunderstood or misjudged on the basis of some behavior or mannerism of which one is not aware; you can't change what you do not know about.

In order for anyone to improve performance, please another or change self-defeating behavior, it is necessary to be aware of the impact one is having on the other(s). Since everyone can best alter mistakes or unintentional consequences *with* information on the impact of his/her behavior, rather than without it, telling a person how he/she is coming across is a kind of gift. It is the feedback of data which cannot be acquired nearly so effectively, if at all, in any other way. The feedback process, in which information is given on the consequences of certain actions, is central to any human relationship in which learning is desired or necessary. For

FIGURE 10–4
Model of a Two Person Relationship

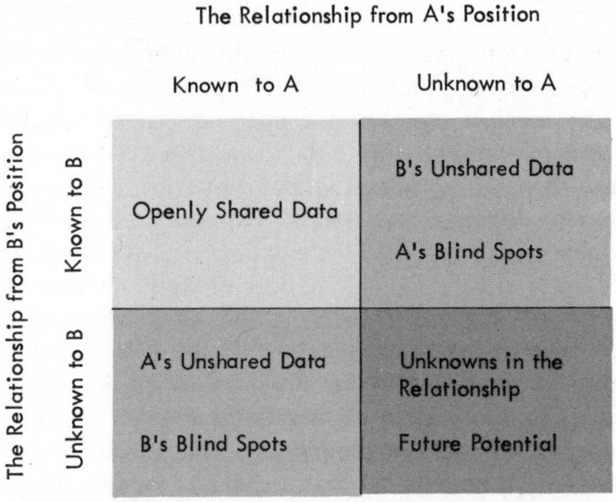

The Relationship from A's Position

		Known to A	Unknown to A
The Relationship from B's Position	Known to B	Openly Shared Data	B's Unshared Data A's Blind Spots
	Unknown to B	A's Unshared Data B's Blind Spots	Unknowns in the Relationship Future Potential

Note: This model is a modification of the "Johari Window," a concept presented in *Group Processes* by J. Luft (Palo Alto: National Press Books, 1970).

example, if a group member's constant jokes bother you, making it hard to take even his/her valuable contributions seriously, you prevent that person from learning how to be more effective if you do not tell him/her.

> *If someone criticizes me I am not any less because of that. . . . Before I thought I was actually fighting for my own self-worth; that is why I so desperately wanted people to like me. I thought their liking me was a comment on me, but it was a comment on them.*
>
> Hugh Prather
> *Notes to Myself,*
> (Moab, Utah: Real People Press, 1970)

But there is a dilemma in all of this. If trust is required for openness, and feedback is a form of openness that can be risky, (since the receiver may not welcome it as intended), how can you get others to give you the feedback you need? How can you build sufficient trust towards you to allow others to take the risk of telling you how you come across? Declaring your trustworthiness does not often work; the person who feels a risk will not easily accept testimonials! Usually it requires that you go first, taking the risk of disclosing something about yourself—your perceptions, feelings, concerns, and so forth. Self-disclosure builds trust. But self-disclosure can also be risky; it may not be received as intended, or may be used against the discloser. Consider the following example.

> The production manager and sales manager of a record player manufacturer must write a joint report to their boss on whether or not to produce a new quadrophonic model. The sales manager's job will be made easier if the model is added to the line; her salespeople want to be able to meet competition with "up-to-date" models even though sales will not at first be too high. The production manager's job will be made more difficult if the newly designed machine is put into production, since there are already quality problems with the existing level of production. If the wrong decision is made, it will be costly to both of them. Do they work together to examine all aspects of the problem, or does each hold back information unfavorable to their respective positions? If the sales manager admits that she has doubts about the market potential of quadrophonic sets and suspects the sales staff is only using lack of them as an excuse for poor efforts, will the production manager pounce on that and force a negative decision? Conversely, if he tells her that a special assembly line could be set up to minimize disruption to present production, will she take advantage of that to force a positive decision? Would either use the other's revelation to look good to the boss? Can they build sufficient trust to be able to share *all* the needed inputs and come to a sensible decision in which each does what is best for the company, regardless of personal inconvenience? The degree of trust, openness and closeness between them will have crucial ramifications for the company—and for their relationship in the future.

In general, we can say that:

1.   The greater the extent of openness in self-disclosure and feedback, the greater will be the resulting level of trust.
2.   The greater the level of openness that is required, the greater the level of risk experienced.
3.   The greater the level of risk required, the greater the level of trust that is needed for openness.
4.   The closer that self-disclosure and/or feedback come to the core of the self-concept, the greater the level of risk that is experienced and the higher the level of trust necessary for openness.

You need trust in order to take the risk of being open. But it is hard to develop sufficient trust until you do take the risk of being open. If the risk is positively responded to, the first critical step in building trust is established; if not, then you are left only with the satisfaction of knowing that you had the courage to take the risk. Risking mistakenly can be disastrous; risking too cautiously can be isolating.

Furthermore, it is occasionally necessary to work together with someone whom you do not trust; finding a way to get the job done without either making yourself vulnerable or offending the other person is a valuable skill to acquire. While open, trusting relationships are freeing and satisfying, plunging into acting as if the other person will respond in kind, just because you would prefer it, is like diving into a new swimming place without checking for rocks beneath the surface. Conversely, assuming that *all* water is loaded with sharks can rob you of a great deal of pleasure.

Unfortunately, it is almost impossible to develop guidelines for judging when it is worth risking openness and trust. As in other human situations you have to decide whether the expected gains are sufficiently greater than the potential losses to be worth the possibility of a failure.

The choices you make regarding interpersonal processes (to trust, to risk, to disclose, to be open, and so forth) can have important effects upon the liking, respect and role relationships that finally emerge. The remainder of the chapter will be devoted to these outcomes, with some concluding propositions regarding the consequences for productivity, satisfaction and development in a relationship.

OUTCOMES OF INTERPERSONAL RELATIONSHIPS

Liking and Respect

It's possible for two people to work together, even productively, without developing much liking or respect for one another. In a minimal task relationship this probably poses little problem, at least for getting the work done. However, as discussed in Chapter 7, most people have more needs than those that pertain only to the task; therefore, few people would find a work relationship that lacks liking and respect very desirable for long.

Liking is normally related to the personal and social aspects of a relationship. If the quality of communication between two people is such that feelings of closeness, warmth and trust develop, the outcome will, obviously, be liking. Even if the task does not require such interpersonal communication, if the individuals themselves desire it, their backgrounds are compatible and the opportunities for interaction are present, then the chances are good that their relationship will result in liking. Any one of these factors, however, can affect the outcome. For example, in one company two members of a management team had very similar styles of interacting; both were aggressive and argumentative. Their interpersonal process was terrible; neither could listen to nor understand the other. Consequently, they maintained a kind of distance, coolness and mistrust that resulted in mutual dislike. While they did, in fact, respect each other's abilities in the job, their dislike made work unpleasant for the entire team.

In a work relationship, mutual respect normally occurs as a result of the recognition of one another's competencies. Can you think of people whom you hold in esteem because of their abilities? Are they all people you also like? As discussed in Chapter 5, feelings of respect may not be consistent with liking. The example above illustrates this point. Furthermore, co-workers may develop a high level of task-related trust, but never feel close or warm on a more personal level. And while their processes of communication may be poor when feelings are involved, the two people may be perfectly capable of exchanging needed information about the work as the situation requires it.

In short, we can say that:

1. In a minimal task relationship, liking and respect need only be minimal in order to get the task done.
2. The degree of liking needed in a task relationship depends upon the preferences of the individuals, but also tends to be more appropriate to relationships that extend beyond the minimal task level.
3. The degree of respect needed in a task relationship increases as task interdependence increases and as the differentiated abilities of each person are required for satisfactory completion of the job.
4. To the extent that personal closeness, warmth and trust emerge, liking will result.
5. To the extent that task-related trust emerges, respect will result.

While it may, at times, seem difficult to be both liked and respected, the two outcomes are not mutually exclusive. The assumption that they are, in fact, can result in the unfortunate situation in which a manager says, "I'd rather be respected than liked; at least I'll get the job done." Have you ever heard this or a similar expression? What is unfortunate about it is the fact that such a manager limits the range of his own interpersonal competence and, consequently, may remain unresponsive to the needs of many employees. Insofar as a job requires more than a minimal task relationship, the development of *both* liking and respect can have important consequences for productivity, satisfaction and development. Let's examine these consequences in the form of some propositions.

Propositions Linking Liking and Respect to Productivity, Satisfaction and Development   While the connections are neither simple nor direct, since many other variables need to be considered, there does (except for minimal task) seem to be some very general relationship between liking and respect on the one hand and productivity, satisfaction and development on the other. We will list the propositions without elaboration; you yourself ought to be able to apply them to your own experience and to examples you may study.

1. When liking and respect are both high, productivity, satisfaction and development tend to be enhanced.
2. When liking and respect are both low, productivity, satisfaction and development tend to be reduced.
3. When liking is high and respect is low, productivity tends to be reduced,

satisfaction tends to be enhanced and development may be affected either way.

4. **When liking is low and respect is high, productivity tends to be enhanced, satisfaction tends to be reduced, and development may be affected either way.**

Keep in mind that these statements represent very general tendencies; that is, when all other things are equal, then the factors of liking and respect can provide predictive guidelines to productivity, satisfaction and development. A deeper understanding of the connections, especially in regard to development in a relationship, can be obtained by examining the quality of the patterned role relationships that emerge between two people. We will look at these next.

Patterned Role Relationships

Throughout this chapter we have implicitly and explicitly raised questions about the connection between what one person wants and how that affects and is affected by what another person wants. For a relationship to continue, there needs to be some kind of mutual accommodation of each to the other, some *reciprocity* between what each gives and gets.

Just as roles develop among group members to fulfill particular group functions, and are selected by individuals in line with their self-concepts, people often develop interpersonal role relationships at work.

The norm that it is obligatory to roughly "pay back" what one has "received" is almost universal, and operates between individuals, groups, organizations, or even societies. Though disputes can arise about whether what one party offers is sufficient to repay the other's original "gift" (How many "thank you's" does it take to satisfy your friend of the opposite sex that you really liked the sweater?), virtually everyone accepts that everything should somehow be repaid. Gratefulness for help, dinner invitation for dinner invitation, warmth for kindnesses; whatever the currency, mutual satisfaction of debts over time is necessary to sustain an equal relationship. And failure to repay either leads to breaking off the relationship or continued obligations and status differentials.

> *Friendship is seldom lasting but between equals. . . . Benefits which cannot be repaid and obligations which cannot be discharged are not commonly found to increase affection; they excite gratitude indeed and heighten veneration, but commonly take away that easy freedom and familiarity of intercourse without which . . . there cannot be friendship.*
>
> Samuel Johnson
> *The Rambler* No. 64.

"Noblesse oblige" or taking care of those who are less fortunate, is a way of dealing with unequal abilities to repay, though even in that type of relationship, deference, loyalty and gratitude are expected in return for more durable goods.

This universal *norm of reciprocity* serves to stabilize relationships, to bring them into a steady state which allows predictability and continuity. You may remember that the taking of *roles* serves much the same function. When behavior becomes patterned, meeting the expectations of others in a particular social system, everyone has a clear idea of what to expect and how to treat others. Each person develops a set pattern of behavior which provides something for the other, and as long as what is provided is desired, the relationship is easy to maintain. A member of an organization, by virtue of accepting a position in it, will find that others have expectations about the type of relationships deemed appropriate for someone in that role. Just as the plumber had some ideas about what kind of interpersonal behavior a plumber's assistant should exhibit, organizational members develop expectations which the role occupant cannot easily ignore, despite personal preferences which might be different. It takes a while for each party to alter expectations and preferences to fit the other.

In order for a work relationship to be sustained at anything more than the absolute minimum required by the task, or for a nonrequired relationship to continue, some mutually satisfactory role relationship will have to emerge.

The role relationships people establish with others become important sources of stability in their lives; they count on them to help maintain personal identity, a basic sense of adequacy and a sense of worth. Yet, once established, role relationships become very difficult to break out of, even when they no longer are fully desired, or are preventing needed growth and change. For example, think about the kinds of role relationships you have with members of that familiar organization, your family. How much have these changed as you have grown older? Do you find yourself getting drawn into some of your "old behavior" everytime you visit your parents? Well-developed role patterns are very hard to break. They tend to determine and shape a great deal of our behavior, and when they are outmoded, they serve to constrain a great many more satisfying possibilities in the relationships. Here is a 36 year old professional person describing his relationship with his 27 year old brother:

> When I get together with my youngest brother, I automatically fall into "older-brother" behavior, giving advice (that he may or may not want), looking after him, paying the check when we eat out, etc. Even though I try to treat him like the full-fledged adult he is, old habits are hard to break, and I slide into my most familiar and well-practiced role with him. He, in turn, falls into playing "kid brother," asking advice, appearing a bit unsure of

himself, letting me initiate, etc. We have a well-established role relationship which is convenient because it lets each of us know in advance a lot about how the other is likely to behave and react, and it saves considerable time and confusion each time we see each other.

At the same time, by definition, it also restricts each of our possible choices. Unless we are willing to make the other uncomfortable and challenge mutual expectations, he cannot really be assertive with me and I cannot easily be helpless, confused or needy with him. So at the same time that our roles are convenient, they also constrain our behavior as long as we choose to continue them.

Another example was observed at a large urban hospital.

> The director of nursing, an attractive woman, had allowed the male administrators to treat her as a "dumb blonde," pleasant but not very smart. Their discomfort at the possibility that she might be beautiful *and* competent led them to treat her that way; her discomfort at upsetting their expectations and possibly being seen as an "aggressive bitch," led her to play along.
>
> At a training session with her female assistant director, she was confronted about this behavior, and began to practice using her considerable analytical abilities. Shortly after, she was at a meeting of her peers, male directors of other departments. Someone made a snide comment about something in her jurisdiction; she came back with a fast, concise and powerful rebuttal. When all the dropped jaws were restored to the astonished faces, one of the men said, "I'm glad to see that your nice legs haven't been affected by your brains," a not very subtle attempt to get her back in role. She had to struggle hard to continue making contributions; eventually she left the hospital for a similar job where she could start fresh.

Have you ever experienced a similar dilemma? It is a problem that frequently occurs when you attempt to change your behavior toward another person, exactly *because* the relationship is reciprocal. You can decide, "From now on I'm going to be different with so-and-so." Then when you try it, "so-and-so" either resists the change, thinks you're crazy, or simply overlooks your "new behavior" as a temporary phenomenon. Psychotherapists struggle with this issue when they seek to bring about change in a client's behavior, and other key people in the client's life continue to cast him or her into the old roles. As a gag song put it, "I Can't Get Adjusted to the You That Got Adjusted to Me." Sometimes even when a person changes in ways that you find desirable, it can be difficult to begin treating that person in new ways! It means building whole new role relationships, which also means changing some of your own behavior to match the other person's. In short, to establish a new role requires stepping out of an old one. That isn't easy.

Can you see the implications of this problem for individuals who want to move upward in an organization? Every promotion or job change calls for new role relationships or altered ones with former colleagues and superiors. It can create great problems to become the supervisor of someone who formerly trained or managed you; how does one change from "promising young trainee" to "responsible executive?" Not everyone can easily let go of established patterns.

Role-Casting[2] If all the world were really a stage, as Shakespeare said, and you could each compose your own scripts for the players in your life, imagine how easy it would be to get people to do what you wanted them to do. For whatever roles you yourself wished to play you could cast others into roles that support and complement your own. You could make people see you as you wish to be seen, understand you, love you, respect you and so on. After all, you would be in charge not only of your own roles but of theirs as well; in that dreamland there would be no interpersonal hassles and misunderstandings, only smooth, consistent and mutually supportive relationships. How easy it would be for a manager; he/she would be totally in charge of every situation.

But alas, not only is life not that way, but it could not work anyway. Who would do the casting of roles for whom? Teachers for students? Or vice versa? Managers for workers? Workers for managers? Would you want someone to "write *your* script?" Few people would, and yet they constantly struggle with all the interpersonal issues that a playwright designs into a play. They cast themselves into roles and seek to evoke reactions in others that confirm those roles. At some level they *do* try to write the script for others. It's similar to casting roles in a play; the actions of one character call for certain kinds of reactions in other characters in order for their respective roles to make sense. And since reciprocity is likely to be the tie which links related roles together, *changing your own behavior may indeed be likely to induce changes in the behavior of another.* If you start treating your parents as if they were serious adult friends and as if you were also a mature adult, they will have to somehow accommodate to the alterations in your behavior. If the co-worker who avoids responsibility is treated responsibly, and expected to come through when needed, he/she may in fact be less likely to let you down than otherwise.

Insofar as a relationship exists in which both parties feel connected to one another, there is potential leverage for affecting the other's behavior by altering your own. Though the pulls are likely to be great to get back into the old roles, it is worth exploring whether a role relationship which is giving you trouble can be redefined into a new set of reciprocal roles through your own initiative. When that works, it can be very freeing and can lead to greater influence over the work environment you are in.

In short, the patterned role relationships that emerge in a work en-

---

[2] We are indebted to Professor Iain Mangham of the University of Bath, England, for introducing us to the concept of role-casting.

vironment have important consequences for productivity, satisfaction and development. While certain kinds of fixed patterns can enhance both productivity and satisfaction, as when the various aspects of two people's jobs are reciprocal, the developmental aspects of a relationship normally pertain to learning and change. When two people learn from one another, when they are able to create new role patterns as tasks and needs demand them, then the relationship will enhance all three outcomes, especially development. While work relationships of this kind may be rare and difficult to build, they are indeed worth the effort in the long run. We hope that the concepts and examples offered in this and the previous chapter will aid you in your own quest for growth-promoting work relationships.

Summary

Figure 10–5 illustrates the total picture we have covered in Chapters 9 and 10. It should be obvious by now just how complicated a two-person relationship can be; hopefully we have provided a coherent picture by following the sequence of factors shown in the chart. For your own practice, you might attempt to trace some relationships with which you are familiar through the sequence; you can go in either direction. For example, you might begin with the outcomes and try to analyze how they came about. By working your way back through processes, looking at the required relationship (if it's a work context), considering the backgrounds and circumstances, you might be able to explain the relationship

FIGURE 10–5

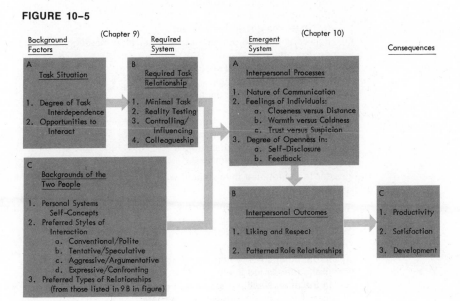

in some depth. Were the outcomes predictable from any of the factors identified in the scheme? Possibly you can use this approach in a forward direction, that is, to predict the probable outcomes of some current interpersonal relationships as you see them emerging.

By developing your diagnostic skills in this fashion, you can identify ways to alter the interpersonal processes to improve the relationship. If you can develop such interpersonal skill, you can't help but become a better manager of your own relationships and, if it's ever required of you, a better manager of other people's work relationships.

As stated earlier in this chapter, interpersonal competence is a basic ingredient of effective management; it makes a critical difference in how much *influence* you may exercise in relation to peers, superiors and subordinates. In the next chapter we will show just how the leadership in an organization is fundamentally a process of influence. You will be able to judge for yourself just how the interpersonal factors covered in this chapter constitute important background factors for leadership effectiveness.

KEY CONCEPTS FROM CHAPTER 10

1. Interpersonal Processes:
   a. Quality of communication.
      (1) Levels of exchange between speaker and listener:
         (a) Feelings about subject matter.
         (b) Subject matter.
         (c) Feelings about one another.
      (2) Self-concepts and perceptions of other filter messages in and out.
   b. Barriers to communication.
      (1) Selective hearing and seeing.
      (2) Imprecision of language.
      (3) Multiple channels (verbal and non-verbal).
      (4) State of mind.
      (5) Mixed messages.
      (6) Incomplete communication.
      (7) Unconscious non-verbal signals.
      (8) Conscious non-verbal signals.
2. The greater the emotional involvement with a subject, the greater the likelihood of distortion.
3. Feeling supported, adequate and worthy leads to closeness, warmth and trust in a relationship:
   a. Closeness and warmth, a matter of degree
   b. Trust
      (1) In the other's competence and ability.
      (2) In the other's judgment.
      (3) In the other's willingness to be helpful.
      (4) In the other's concern for your welfare.

      c. Trust leads to openness which permits risk-taking as in self-disclosure and feedback.

4. Model of a Two Person Relationship:
   a. Shared data with each other.
   b. Blind spots in each.
   c. Future potential for both.
5. To the extent that personal closeness, warmth and trust emerge, liking will result.
6. To the extent that task-related trust emerges, respect will result.
7. Correlations of liking and respect with productivity, satisfaction and development.
8. Norm of reciprocity stabilizes relationships.
9. Fixed patterns of role casting allows predicability and continuity as long as it is still desired; to break the pattern demands new, mutually influencing behavior.

SUGGESTED READINGS

Bennis, Warren, Berlew, David, Schein, Edgar, and Steele, Fred I. *Interpersonal Dynamics.* 3d ed. Homewood, Ill.: The Dorsey Press, 1973.

Davis, Keith "Grape Vine Communication Among Lower and Middle Managers," *Personnel Journal* (April 1969) 269–72.

Egan, G. *Face To Face.* Monterey, Cal.: Brooks/Cole Publishing Co., 1973.

Hall, Edward T. *The Silent Language.* Greenwich, Conn.: Faucett Publications Inc., 1959.

Giffin, K., and Patton, B. R. *Personal Communication in Human Relations.* Columbus, Ohio: Charles E. Merrill Publishing Co., 1974.

Haney, W. V. *Communication: Pattern and Incidence,* Homewood, Ill.: Richard D. Irwin, Inc., 1960.

Harris, Thomas A. *I'm OK, You're OK.* New York: Harper and Row Publishers, 1967.

Jongeward, D. *Everybody Wins: Transactional Analysis Applied to Organizations.* Reading, Mass.: Addison-Wesley Publishing Co., 1973.

Jourard, S. M. *The Transparent Self,* rev. ed. New York: D. Van Nostrand Company, 1971.

Luft, J. *Group Processes.* Palo Alto, Cal.: National Press Books, 1970.

Maslow, A. H. *Eupsychian Management.* Homewood, Ill.: Richard D. Irwin, Inc. and the Dorsey Press, 1965.

Rogers, Carl *On Becoming A Person,* Boston: Houghton Mifflin, 1961. Chapter 3, pp. 39–58, "The Characteristics of a Helping Relationship."

Walton, R. E. "Interpersonal Confrontation and Basic Third Party Functions: A Case Study." *JABS* 4 (1968) 327–44.

———— *Interpersonal Peacemaking: Confrontations and Third-Party Consultation.* Reading, Mass.: Addison-Wesley Publishing Co., Inc., 1969.

Zaleznik, A., and Moment, D. *The Dynamics of Interpersonal Behavior.* New York: John Wiley & Sons, Inc., 1964.

The greater the differential knowledge of the leader, the more appropriate will be unilateral control.

11

LEADERSHIP
Exerting Influence

THE TOPIC of leadership has fascinated people through the ages. After much discussion and research, the pursuit of a universal definition of effective leadership is still intriguing, but elusive. The world awaits definitive answers to such questions as: What makes a good leader? Who can be a leader? Can anyone be a leader? Can leadership skills be taught? What makes followers follow? What are the limits to leadership?

Social science researchers for years pursued the notion that there must be some common qualities shared by all leaders. Many long lists of sterling qualities (for example, aggressiveness, wisdom, charisma, courage, and so forth) have been generated, but have not

been found to apply to all leaders in all situations. To be effective, a leader's qualities must relate somehow to the situation he/she is in and to the nature of the followers. This view is consistent with the situational approach taken throughout this book, yet is just barely beginning to be widely accepted. The belief that General Patton, Mahatma Gandhi, Vince Lombardi, Golda Meir and Martin Luther King must have exactly the same qualities does not easily fade away.

The only qualities which researchers have been able to isolate as usually possessed by leaders are (1) a certain amount of energy, (2) a moderate level of intelligence, (3) some sociability and (4) some degree of self-confidence. However, the possession of these qualities does not guarantee that one will become a leader; nor does the absence of any one of them rule out the possibility of becoming a leader. It is, therefore, important to emphasize that *the potential for leadership may be assumed to be widely distributed among the general population.*

What kind of leadership behavior works when, and who should do it, is our topic for exploration in this chapter.

LEADERSHIP AS INFLUENCE

A great deal of the confusion about leaders and leadership arises from the assumption that there is or can be, only *one* leader for each group or organization. By personalizing leadership, discussion gets bogged down in a morass of personality factors, feelings about authority, connotations of giving and receiving orders, and so forth. It is more useful to think of leadership as a *process,* in which the involved parties *influence* one another in particular ways. *Influence is any act or potential act which affects the behavior of another person(s).* Let's look at the implications of using the concept.

First of all, influence cannot happen in isolation from others; it takes at least two to "tangle," just as with interpersonal relationships. The person who wants to influence must find someone to influence. Secondly, if you think about it carefully, you will see that only in the most extreme situations could *one* person in an influence transaction have *all* the influence, that is, affect the other's behavior without being affected in turn by the other's reaction. The machinist who leaps to attention when his boss gives an order, the secretary who bursts into tears when she feels that a request to work late is unreasonable, the student who challenges an assignment due the day after vacation, all exert influence on the person trying to influence them.

Cooperating humbly, for example, affects the person who is asking for cooperation and "pulls" more of the same from him/her. As Gandhi showed so well in India, humble, passive *non*cooperation can have a profound influence on those giving orders. Even the person who follows directions he/she knows are wrong, out of fear of being fired or punished, has influence on the behavior of the tyrant, allowing further exploitation and mistakes, since the directions were not resisted.

We must be careful, then, to remember that influence only succeeds in moving others in desired directions when the *net* influence, the amount of A's influence on B compared with B's influence on A, is greater. In the classroom or on the job, students and workers can be less *or* more influential than teachers and supervisors. *Leadership is net influence in a direction desired by the person possessing it.*

To understand this process better, we need to look at various types of influence. One important aspect of influence is whether or not it is formal or informal, part of a job's definition or acquired in some other way. *Formal influence is influence prescribed for the holder of an "office" or position in a particular social system.* The coach of a team has formal influence in initiating practice sessions, selecting starting players and substitutes, and so forth. *Informal influence is influence not prescribed for the office holder, but nevertheless affecting other members of the social system.* On the same team, for example, there may be several players whose advice other players and even the coach seek, on such matters as techniques and strategy against opponents. Though by position the players have no special influence alloted them, their knowledge and/or personal attractiveness and magnetism gives them influence anyway.

In addition to the distinction between formal and informal influence, we need to add the concepts of legitimacy and illegitimacy. *Legitimate influence is influence which is exerted by a person who is seen as having the right to do so by those influenced.* Conversely, *illegitimate influence is influence which is exerted by a person not seen as having the right to do so by those being influenced.* The basis for considering an influencer as legitimate may be (1) a positive assessment of his/her personal qualities, such as competence, experience, age; and/or (2) the acceptance of the process, such as election, appointment or automatic succession, by which the person acquired a role calling for the exercise of influence. Legitimacy will usually be seen to be limited to areas within the scope of the system and its goals. For example, the boss may legitimately give orders about how to sell a machine, but not about where to go on vacation. But within the scope of the organization, orders, requests, and directions will be seen as proper when they come from someone who has personal qualities considered appropriate or has acquired an office by an approved process.

On the other hand, even in the army, where soldiers are taught to "salute the uniform, not the man," a soldier will refuse to follow direct orders under a variety of circumstances, for example, if the commanding officer has disruptive personality characteristics or has acquired his office in objectionable ways, such as perceived favoritism. Furthermore, when influence is not seen as acquired legitimately, soldiers and other subordinates have many ways of subverting any orders from a person whose influence they do not accept, such as dragging their heels by following literally all rules in the books.

Since having formal influence does not insure legitimacy, nor having informal influence insure illegitimacy, it is useful to combine the two categories into the four possible combinations, as shown in Figure 11–1.

FIGURE 11–1
Types of Influence

	Formal	Informal
Legitimate	1	2
Illegitimate	3	4

By looking at the combinations we can see the ways in which influence is exercised. *Formal-legitimate influence* is what is usually meant when people say "X has the authority" to enforce particular behaviors. It *is the influence which is both prescribed for the holder of an office in a social system and seen as his/her right to exert by the other members of it.* A large part of leadership in organizations involves formal-legitimate influence by someone who has been assigned a role with supervisory responsibilities and who can use organizational means to reward or punish subordinates. The right to hire, fire, promote and adjust pay, reinforces this kind of influence.

Since most people who accept jobs in an organization are reasonably willing to accept directions from their "boss" on job-related matters, legitimacy is often taken for granted and assumed to go with any formal role. During such times as the student strikes in the late 1960s and early 1970s, or the rebellions of workers in France, it becomes evident that the legitimacy of those with formal organizational positions is precarious and rests upon the attitudes of the "followers." Students challenged the rights of professors to determine subject matter, give exams and grades, hire and fire colleagues, and exerted influence on other activities which had traditionally been seen as part of faculty prerogatives. Much of the work of organizations gets done because there is a considerable amount of legitimacy granted to those in formal positions, but that is by no means the only kind of leadership exerted.

A great deal of influence is based upon knowledge, expertise (whether perceived or real), or personal charm. *This informal-legitimate influence by a member of a social system, stands apart from the prescribed influence of his/her office but is accepted as within one's rights by the others in the system.* It is not predictable from organization charts, but is essential to organizational functioning. Some people know things or behave in charismatic ways that others value, regardless of position, and are given influence accordingly. The rewards and punishments available to this kind of influencer are more personal; that is, he/she can give or withhold important information and/or support.

Leadership in classroom groups is often exclusively of the "expert" kind, with the most knowledgeable member(s) of the group gradually becoming respected and listened to even when there is no formal leader. In fact, among many student groups, only a person with recognized expertise can take, or be given leadership, and then only for particular matters. There is a widespread student norm that no peer should give orders or directions to another student, so that even those students put in leadership roles by a class exercise often hold back from initiating directions.

Conversely, when a fellow student makes a "grab for power," it will usually be resisted by other students. Sometimes such a person quickly has volunteered for a leadership role before others dare to, and is allowed to take it, despite feelings that "it isn't right"; in that case the student has *formal-illegitimate influence,* which may not last long, unless he/she is seen as helping the group reach its goals. Similarly, in organizations where members are accustomed to having considerable say in matters affecting them, the boss' decision to create a new position located between him/her and the others ("because the work load is too heavy for me"), can result in resentment towards *whomever* is put in that new job, and lead to only grudging cooperation. If that person, however, has the formal authorization to administer some organizational rewards and punishments, he/she may end up with considerable influence anyway.

Finally, *the person who by personal access to some valued rewards, or more likely, feared punishments, gets influence over others, is using informal-illegitimate influence.* Physical threats by a fellow worker can coerce compliance which would otherwise be refused, as can special relationships with higher-ups. In one school system, for example, the music director forced principals to release students for week-long band trips and to arrange schedules to suit his convenience by maintaining a close relationship with several powerful school board members. He thus obtained more influence over principals than was called for by his position or was seen as his right by them. Though he obtained compliance, he also created considerable resentment, and was constantly criticized by the principals behind his back.

POWER

The capacity to utilize influence is "power." (Often "power" and "influence" are used interchangeably). People who have the ability to exert one or more of the four types of influence have power, which can be used toward the organization's ends or towards subgroup or individual goals, including those which are in direct opposition to organizational goals. As suggested earlier, no one is completely without influence, but some people have more net influence than others and hence more power.

In general, **The more legitimate one is perceived to be, the greater the likelihood of compliance with one's attempts to influence, and the less resentment at going along.** Power goes to those who are seen as having a right to it. Conversely, the less legitimate forms of influence breed resistance and resentment, though they will probably enhance the power of someone who already possesses other kinds of legitimate influence.

Informal influence is often necessary for those with formal influence if they want more than begrudging cooperation; when a formally designated leader does not have some knowledge seen as helpful by subordinates, it will be difficult to secure more than token compliance. As organizations become more complex and technically demanding, more people in leadership positions do *not* have the technical expertise necessary to gain influence beyond that of their own job description, making it hard for them to get full cooperation from those who know more than they do about some other aspects of the job. They must then find ways of gaining informal influence through their own personal attractiveness and their ability to make friendly relationships — or they must settle for a low power position relative to their subordinates.

> *. . . mercenaries knew that to do Cyrus [King of Persia] good service paid better than any monthly wage. Indeed, whenever anyone carried out effectively a job which he had assigned, he never allowed his good work to go unrewarded. Consequently . . . Cyrus got the best officers for any kind of job.*
>
> Xenophon
> *The Persian Expedition*
> (Translated by Rex Warren)

Overall, **The more a person has access to controlling rewards and punishments, the greater his/her power.** Thus a person who can give the formal rewards or use the formal punishments of an organization — hiring, firing, promoting, adjusting salary, allocating choice assignments or space, giving recommendations, and so forth, *and* give informal rewards or punishments, such as help, information, liking — will have the most power. Just what the rewards and punishments are depends on the organization and the perceptions of those in it, but whatever it is that people value or fear, those who control it will have power to influence behavior.

In summary, **The more types of influence a person exerts, the greater his/her power.**

Regardless of the source of power, its possession tends to lead toward certain consequences. These can be stated in the following propositions:

1. **The more power attributed to a person, the more he/she is the recipient of:**
   a. **communication,**
   b. **solicitous behavior, and**
   c. **deference by others seeking power.**
2. **The more a person is treated as though he/she has power, the greater will be his/her self-esteem.**
3. **The more power attributed to a person, the more that person will tend to view others with power as a reference point.**
4. **Those with high attributed power are attracted to and communicate more with others with high attributed power than with those who have low attributed power.**[1]

By examining these propositions, you can see why it is often said that power corrupts. The entire constellation of behavior and relationships that follow from the possession of influence generates a cycle in which people with high power tend to become more and more differentiated from those with low power, even though each is dependent upon the other. The person with power has it only because it is given to him/her by others. It ends the moment those who are doing the giving choose not to do so. A leader is a leader only so long as there are followers. It certainly raises the question of who really possesses the power, the one who leads or those being led.

There go my people. I must find out where they are going so I can lead them.

Anonymous

Many political leaders have been known to shift their attention and allegiance from their constituencies to their fellow politicians. The same thing can happen in an organization, especially as people climb increasingly higher in the hierarchy. Are you familiar with instances in which an emergent social leader in a group was appointed formal leader by the system, thus enhancing his/her degree of influence? Very often the individual is then seen to "change;" he/she is seen as less friendly to "us mere workers," and as playing up to the powers that be. This frequently happens as people find themselves in new leadership roles, having influence over people in areas never before experienced.

---

[1] For further elaboration of these propositions, see B. Berelson and G. Steiner, *Human Behavior: An Inventory of Scientific Findings* (New York: Harcourt, Brace and World, Inc., 1964).

It is not uncommon for those who have power to be not very well liked; as noted in the group chapters the group members who contribute most to getting tasks accomplished are usually most respected but seldom most liked. Informal task leaders often have to trade liking for respect; while occasionally someone can get both, most often **The more a leader strives for popularity, the less effective he/she becomes as task leader. Also, the more the leader strives to maintain task-leadership, the more he/she will lose popularity.** Can you think of any conditions where these propositions would not be true? How important each factor is in comparison with the other depends upon the nature of the situation and the person involved in the leadership role. For some situations and/or people, task maintenance function must take priority over social maintenance; in other situations and/or for other individuals, the opposite might be true. The important thing to keep in mind is that there is more than one option and that there may be some tradeoffs in each.

But *why* does this dilemma occur? Why is it so difficult to mix these functions? For one thing, not many people are really good at both; as a result, the task leader is likely to be someone who has the best skills or abilities related to the task (as it should be) and the social leader is often the most attractive person in the group. If that's the case then other group members tend to become dependent upon the task leader and may even see him/her as superior to the rest of the group. While this may generate respect for that individual, it also tends to breed resentment. As a result, whenever the task leader pressures others into working, while they may feel grateful for the direction, they also may feel resentful, annoyed and resistant to the task. This sequence of events is not inevitable, but it occurs frequently enough to warrant particular attention. We have also found it to be characteristic of a great many work groups in our classes. Can you apply it to your own experience?

MANAGERS AS FORMAL LEGITIMATE LEADERS: MANAGERIAL CHOICES

The kind of dilemmas we have been discussing are especially applicable to group members who exercise informal-legitimate influence. When a person acquires influence as a peer, difficulties arise around balancing relationships and work. Though a formally appointed leader also has to deal with this issue, holding a position which is organizationally defined as "above" the group in responsibility and authority involves a more complex set of choices. As a future manager, you will want to know what formally designated "Managers" do, that is, how they carry out their responsibilities.

For the rest of this chapter, we will focus on the manager and his/her choices about what functions to perform, what style of leadership to use,

FIGURE 11–2
Illustration of Managerial Choices Discussed in This Chapter

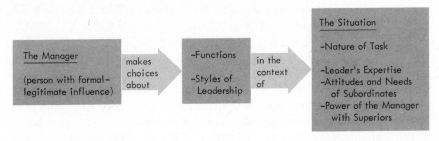

and how these choices are made in the context of a given set of conditions, including the nature of the task, the leader's expertise, the attitudes and needs of subordinates, and the power of the manager in relation to superiors. Figure 11–2 shows the sequential relationship among these variables.

Managerial Functions

We begin by looking at the set of functions that every manager must perform, indicating some of the more specific activities that comprise each.

The manager's functions fall into three related groupings. One group, *Interpersonal,* involves building and maintaining contacts and relationships with a variety of people located both inside and outside his/her organizational unit. A second group, *Informational,* involves gathering

FIGURE 11–3
The Interrelationships among Managerial Functions

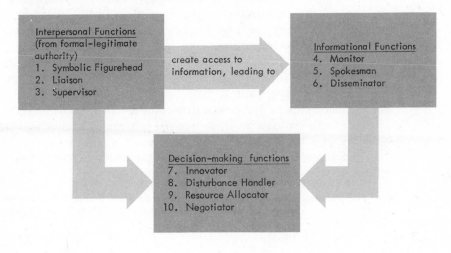

and disseminating information inside the unit and to and from the external environment. The third group, *Decision Making,* involves making a range of decisions pertaining to internal operating practices and to exchanges with other units of the organization as well as the outside world.[2]

As may be evident from the above, these groupings are interrelated; in accomplishing one function, the manager often will make progress on another. For example, while building a relationship with the manager of another unit of the organization, the manager typically will be gathering and sharing information. Furthermore, the information which a manager gains while carrying out an informational function may be crucial to his/her capability in carrying out the decision-making functions effectively. Let us now consider these interrelated functions in greater detail.

The Interpersonal Functions   The manager relates to people both within and outside of his/her own subsystem. Often students of leadership concentrate on the internal relationships of managers and think of their relationships with "outsiders" as nonessential or peripheral to the job. But some of the most important activities in which a manager engages involve building relationships with people other than subordinates.

One such function is that of *symbolic figurehead.* It entails carrying out certain social, legal, inspirational and ceremonial duties which simply go with being the head of an organizational system. The manager's function is largely representational, serving to symbolize his/her organization to the rest of the world. **The higher in the organization a manager's position, the greater will be the time spent in the symbolic figurehead function.**

Closely related to this function is that of *liaison.* In carrying out the liaison function the manager gives and receives information and favors in order to learn what is going on elsewhere that can be useful within the unit. Making contacts with people and then maintaining them are important, time-consuming activities, but necessary if the manager is to stay informed on organizational politics, on new opportunities, on changes in demand for the organization's outputs, and so forth. Furthermore, the contacts make it possible to exchange other favors, when necessary, facilitating internal operations.

The remaining interpersonal function is that of *supervisor,* a function one readily associates with managing. It entails hiring, training, motivating, evaluating and rewarding subordinates. In carrying out this function the manager tries to find a way to blend individual needs and concerns with the organization's goals, so that the subordinates remain committed to doing what is necessary to meet the system's objectives.

The interpersonal functions in which the manager relates to relevant others serve to give him/her an important advantage:

---

[2] The managerial functions described here are an adaptation of managerial roles described by Henry Mintzberg, *The Nature of Managerial Work* (New York: Harper & Row, 1973).

Through [them] the manager gains access to privileged information and he emerges as the "nerve center" of his organization. He alone has formal access to every subordinate in his own organization, and he has unique access to a variety of outsiders, many of whom are nerve centers of their own organizations. Thus the manager is his organization's information generalist, that person best informed about its operations and environment.[3]

Informational Functions   The interpersonal functions, then, lead to *informational functions,* which channel information into and out of the manager's unit. By serving as a *monitor* of information from sources within and outside of the unit, the manager keeps up-to-date on the climate he/she is operating in. The activities include designing ways of collecting information (formally and informally), reading reports, questioning contacts and subordinates, observing others' activities, and so forth.

In turn, the manager has the function of *disseminator,* passing relevant information on to subordinates. Since the manager will often be the only one in a unit with access to some information, this job is important and requires good judgment in terms of what information to pass along and to whom. It requires such activities as *telling, announcing, memo writing, and telephoning.*

In addition to the internal dissemination function, there is an important *spokesman* function, which entails transmitting information outside the unit. This includes *informing liaison contacts and others who influence the unit, lobbying, announcing, and so forth.*

Decision making Functions   As a consequence of his/her formal position and access to information, the manager performs several functions which involve making strategic decisions for the unit.

The *innovator* function calls for initiating and designing changes in the way the unit operates. In carrying out this task, the manager *diagnoses trends, envisions possibilities, plans improvements, invents programs and other solutions,* and in general *promotes innovation.*

A related decision making function is that of *disturbance handler.* Here the manager takes charge and makes decisions when nonroutine disturbances call for responses which individual subordinates cannot devise. The manager functions as the generalist problem solver, putting out fires as they arise, either as a result of subordinates' inability to anticipate and handle difficulties or as a consequence of innovations. **The lower the level of a manager in the organizational hierarchy, the greater will be the time spent on disturbance handling and other decision-making functions.** The need at lower levels of an organization is for maintaining the daily workflow, so these functions are predominant there.

Another decision-making function is that of *resource allocator.* The manager parcels out his/her unit's resources through a series of decisions

---

[3] Mintzberg, ibid.

on how members will spend time, materials and funds as well as how they can utilize formal-legitimate influence. Resource allocation involves *deciding among proposals, controlling subordinate latitude, setting priorities, authorizing expenditures, and so forth.*

Finally, the manager serves as *negotiator* for important decisions involving other organizations. Negotiating involves *bargaining, trading, compromising, collaborating, avoiding, and other similar activities.*

Typically, the negotiating function builds upon several of the other managerial functions. In representing the unit, the manager serves as *symbolic figurehead,* and *spokesman,* summarizing the organization's views. The negotiation will result in *resource allocation,* as something is given up or obtained from outside.

In brief, the ten functions comprise the job of the formal-legitimate officeholder:

> . . . the manager must design the work of his organization, monitor its internal and external environment, initiate change when desirable, and renew stability when faced with a disturbance. The manager must lead his subordinates to work effectively for the organization, and he must provide them with special information, some of which he gains through the network of contacts that he develops. In addition, the manager must perform a number of "housekeeping" duties, including informing outsiders, serving as figurehead, and leading major negotiations.[4]

Some of the ten managerial functions differ, one from another, on the basis of whether their focus is internal or external as shown in Figure 11–4. This serves to emphasize the point that a manager "stands between his organizational unit and its environment,"[5] and his functions include looking outward to what is happening in other parts of the total organization and the environment as well as downward at what subordinates do.

While each of these functions is important, it is not always imperative that only the manager carry them out. Within an organization there may be individuals who can do some of the particular functions more effectively than the manager in charge. Subordinates can take responsibility in these areas as well as managers give it. If, for example, a manager is not very effective at public speaking when carrying out the spokesman function, he/she may want to delegate some of the necessary activities to a good speaker on the staff. Similarly, it may be appropriate for a staff member to initiate delegation by offering his/her services and not merely waiting for the manager to give it.

Those activities, however, which require special, current information to perform well, may not be easily delegatable, unless others in the organization have high access to it. Nevertheless, most managers will be flooded with demands for their time and attention, and must choose care-

---

4 Mintzberg, ibid.

5 Ibid.

FIGURE 11–4
Focus of Managerial Functions Relative to the System

	Internal	External
Interpersonal		
1. Symbolic Figurehead	X	X
2. Liaison		X
3. Supervisor	X	
Informational		
4. Monitor	X	X
5. Disseminator	X	
6. Spokesman		X
Decision-Making		
7. Innovator	X	X
8. Disturbance Handler	X	X
9. Resource Allocator	X	
10. Negotiator		X

fully which roles and functions to emphasize. There will seldom be enough time to stay in contact with all information sources, inspire and direct all subordinates, cope with all disturbances and needs for innovation, and so forth. The choice between another 15 minutes working on a problem in the office, a quick stroll through the plant to get a feel for morale, or an early arrival at a meeting with other executives in order to pick up some scraps of information about an upcoming crisis, will constantly have to be made. The way in which the manager chooses to spend time determines his/her relative emphasis on the ten roles, all of which are necessary and demanding. Success as a manager depends in part on the ability to correctly choose among roles, and on the capacity to perform each of the roles well when necessary.

We have been looking at the nature of leadership as an influence process, and at the various roles and functions a manager must fill. We turn now to a look at *how* a manager should do his job and under what conditions particular functions and styles are appropriate.

HOW LEADERSHIP IS EXERCISED; ALTERNATIVE STYLES

There are many ways to categorize leadership styles. One familiar classification distinguishes among autocratic, democratic and laissez-faire approaches; another contrasts authoritarian with humanistic styles; yet another might compare "strictly business" with human relations approaches; the traditional paternalistic has been contrasted with the routinized bureaucratic and the more fluid "organic-adaptive," and so on. Different writers have different schemes; what we have chosen to do is spell out several underlying dimensions along which leaders can differ in carrying out their functions. Each leadership style is composed of a combination of positions along each of these dimensions. The particular labels for styles are less important than an understanding of the choices leaders can make in how they perform their roles.

As in the chapters on interpersonal relations, we assume that each person is likely to have a *preferred* leadership style which he/she will opt for whenever possible, but that this should be tempered by what is *appropriate* to the organizational situation. We will be as explicit as possible about what leadership behavior is called for under which circumstances, though the possibilities are complex.

There are five dimensions we will use to describe how a leader might carry out his/her leadership functions.

1. Retaining control versus sharing control.
2. High task-concern versus low task-concern.
3. High person-concern versus low person-concern.
4. Using formal system versus using informal system.
5. Cautious versus venturous.

Retaining versus Sharing Control

One crucial dimension of leadership style is the degree of control exerted on the behavior of others. How much latitude is given to others to make their own decisions, to vary from standard procedures, rules and regulations? How much information is shared with them? How free are they to question advice or orders, or to initiate ideas? How closely are they supervised; are they constantly watched or is their performance only checked periodically? In short, are they encouraged to try to influence the way work is done? For any particular problem, the amount of control retained by the manager can vary considerably. Figure 11–5 shows the choices a manager can make about how much influence to share with subordinates.

FIGURE 11–5
Managerial Choices of How Much Influence to Share with Subordinates for Each Problem.

Group Problems	*Individual Problems*
1. You solve the problem or make the decision yourself, using information available to you at the time.	1. You solve the problem or make the decision by yourself, using information available to you at the time.
2. You obtain the necessary infor-	2. You obtain the necessary infor-

FIGURE 11–5 Continued

Group Problems	*Individual Problems*
mation from your subordinates, then decide the solution to the problem yourself. You may or may not tell your subordinates what the problem is in getting the information from them. The role played by your subordinates in making the decision is clearly one of providing the necessary information to you, rather than generating or evaluating alternative solutions.	mation from your subordinate, then decide on the solution to the problem yourself. You may or may not tell the subordinate what the problem is in getting the information from him. His role in making the decision is clearly one of providing the necessary information to you, rather than generating or evaluating alternative solutions.

3. You share the problem with the relevant subordinates individually, getting their ideas and suggestions without bringing them together as a group. Then *you* make the decision, which may or may not reflect your subordinates' influence.

3. You share the problem with your subordinate, getting his ideas and suggestions. Then you make a decision, which may or may not reflect his influence.

4. You share the problem with your subordinates as a group, obtaining their collective ideas and suggestions. Then you make the decision, which may or may not reflect your subordinates' influence.

4. You share the problem with your subordinate, and together you analyze the problem and arrive at a mutually agreeable solution.

5. You share the problem with your subordinates as a group. Together you generate and evaluate alternatives and attempt to reach agreement (consensus) on a solution. Your role is much like that of chairman. You do not try to influence the group to adopt "your" solution, and you are willing to accept and implement any solution which has the support of the entire group.

5. You delegate the problem to your subordinate, providing him with any relevant information that you possess, but giving him responsibility for solving the problem by himself. You may or may not request him to tell you what solution he has reached.

Adapted from V. Vroom and P. Yetton, *Leadership and Decision-Making* (Pittsburgh: University of Pittsburgh Press, 1973).

High Task-Concern versus Low Task-Concern

While getting the work done is the essence of any leader's role, more or less attention can be paid to quantity of output, quality of work done, meeting deadlines, meeting output, expectations of other subsystems, improving performance in general. Managers can vary from constant preoccupation with output to negligible concern over it. Focus on task is often contrasted with focus on the morale and welfare of people doing the task, though they need not be contradictory. For example, the supervisor of the credit department in a bank had to see to it that at least one employee stayed late each Friday to complete certain forms. At first he made a list on which he arbitrarily rotated the assignment. When the employees complained, he had to use a method which gave them more say over the decision. It is often possible, therefore, to maintain a high level of task-concern, without necessarily sacrificing the involvement and feelings of those affected.

High Concern for People versus Low Concern for People

How much attention does the leader pay to the personal feelings and attitudes of others? Does he/she provide a warm, supportive working climate, or an impersonal one? Are nontask-related concerns of others noted, responded to, or sympathized with? How open is the leader about his/her human concerns, feelings, etc.? How much are others treated as people instead of as objects of production? Some managers focus all their attention on the effects of actions on the morale of those in their units, while others ignore it completely; clearly, there are many options in between these extremes.

High Use of Formal Procedures versus High Use of Informal Procedures

How much does the leader rely on predetermined rules, regulations and procedures? How standardized does he/she try to make the work routine? How many formal rules are made and enforced? How often does the manager improvise responses to problems rather than rely on established policy? Although formal procedures are usually intended to cover as many contingencies as possible, obviously no pre-established system can, in fact, anticipate them all.

Cautious versus Venturous

How venturesome are the leader's actions and decisions? How much risk is involved in decisions; how willing is the leader to make decisions that involve high risk? How visible is the leader willing to be to other parts of the organization and its environments? In other words, how bold is the leader? As you will see, the degree of boldness demanded of a leader varies from one situation to another.

Can you use these five dimensions to think about leadership in your classroom task group, in jobs you have held or organizations to which you have belonged? What kinds of choices have you made along these dimensions when you had leadership responsibilities? Do you tend towards one "style," i.e., a repeated cluster of similar choices? If your usual style has been "authoritarian," for example, you might have kept tight control over subordinates, been highly concerned with tasks but shown low people concern, used some formal rules and taken high risks in your decisions. Whatever your usual style, were there occasions when you chose to lead in a quite different way because the situation seemed to call for it? And most important, have you noticed any differential results of particular choices you or others have made on these dimensions? Has any one style seemed to work better than another? Did something work in one situation but not another? For example, when should a manager make a quick, unilateral decision and when should everyone be involved? It is these latter kinds of questions we will deal with next. For example, how does the general manager of a drug company decide how to get his production, purchasing and sales managers to cooperate in reducing inventories during a recession? Should he worry about their feelings, involve them in proposing solutions, develop some clear guidelines for them to cut inventories? Or how does the administrator of a hospital get the radiology department to cut down patient waiting-time for X rays? When patients sit waiting in the hallway for three hours while a technically interesting case is studied, how does the administrator deal with the stubborn but powerful chief radiologist? Can the administrator give a direct order to speed up? Can he offend the chief? What should he take into account in deciding? In order to deal with the endless series of dilemmas like these, it is necessary for a leader or manager to consider a number of situational factors.

FACTORS INVOLVED IN DETERMINING APPROPRIATE LEADERSHIP CHOICES

While it is probably easier to analyze what makes particular leadership styles effective than it is to actually *be* a good leader, there are a bewildering array of factors to keep in mind. We will isolate a number of situational aspects which should be taken into account in making appropriate leadership choices, but it is not possible to account for every contingency. Some of the important factors follow.

The Nature of the Task Situation

Some jobs are very stable and predictable. Their processes are not subject to rapid technological change, the need for their output is established and constant and rapid decisions are not necessary. Under these conditions, it is not especially effective to give great autonomy to subordinates. **The more predictable the nature of the task situation, the more appropriate will be tight control, formal, standardized procedures and cautiousness as leadership choices.** The converse is true for work that is less predictable in nature.

The Expertise of the Leader (as related to the competence of the subordinates)

A factor which is often related to the rate of change in the nature of the job is the amount of expert knowledge of the work possessed by the formal leader. When the leader clearly knows a great deal more about the work than any other members of the unit, whether through technical expertise or knowledge of the environment and its demands, it is costly to spend a lot of time asking for opinions, improvising methods and sharing control. **The greater the differential knowledge of the leader, the more appropriate will be unilateral control.** The converse is true for situations where those doing the work have knowledge equal to or greater than the leader, as is often the case for jobs requiring high technical input. The director of a research lab, for example, may supervise Ph.D. specialists who know much more about some aspects of a problem than he/she does; tight control and formal procedures would be self-defeating in that situation. On the other hand, small businessmen or leaders active in the entrepreneurial role often are so invested in what they are doing (emotionally even more than financially), and so immersed in their vision of what is possible, that they literally can do any job in the organization better than anyone else. In those situations high task-concern and low sharing of influence is probably appropriate, if not inevitable.

The Attitudes and Needs of Subordinates

The amount of challenge or routine in a job often attracts people whose motivations match job requirements. When subordinates like problem-solving and difficult assignments, are dedicated to the work and enjoy independence (i.e., are operating on higher level needs), different leadership choices are called for than when they are passive, dependent and threatened. **In general, the greater subordinates' needs for autonomy and independence, the less tight control by the leader is appropriate, and vice versa.**

On the other hand, as suggested in Chapter 7 on individual motivation, while close supervision of those operating on lower level needs may be productive in the short run, there are organizational and human consequences for satisfaction and learning which also need to be taken into account. This connects to the issue of concern for people versus concern for task. Some researchers have claimed that high concern for both is always most effective, and in general, either is ignored only at the leader's peril. But in some situations, at least temporarily, one should probably take precedence over the other.

For those organizational members who have high needs for independence and love challenging tasks, high person-concern may be a bit superfluous. Leaving them alone to get on with the work, in a cordial way, can be very effective. At the other extreme, with subordinates who are operating on survival needs, warmth and support may not be necessary (though much appreciated if given).

Most organizational members, however, will be affected by a wider range of needs, including those for social approval, and will be quite responsive to a supportive climate. **Where the work itself is not especially challenging or intrinsically fascinating, but those doing it are not threatened about survival, high concern for people along with high concern for task is appropriate.**

The Power of the Leader

For convenience we have been talking about "the leader" as if it were always one person, with formal-legitimate influence and sufficient power to do whatever is needed. But the actual power of the leader, or of those aspiring to perform leadership functions, is a very important factor in determining appropriate leadership style. Even the supervisor or manager who is formally and legitimately in that position will have varying amounts of influence with subordinates, superiors and peers respectively. Leaders who have considerable influence with their superiors, for example, can take more risks in the decisions they make, vary more from formal procedures, and will receive greater support from subordinates than those who do not. **The greater the "upward" influence of a leader, the less it is necessary to share control with subordinates.** Effective shared influence, however, is likely to increase the upward influence of a leader, since it can yield a solid support base when trying to persuade superiors. The leader who does not have clout with higher-ups or other outsiders must be cautious in changing formal procedures, and spend time building support among subordinates in order to have a stronger base of influence; thus, more sharing of control and concern for people will be appropriate. A common mistake for leaders of dissident groups is to become so caught up in fighting those with power that group members are ignored or not given much say; in a showdown the group members may not stand solidly behind the leader because they have not been "brought along."

Any leader with low legitimacy must worry about similar problems. It is not very effective to go around barking orders if those who are supposed to follow them do not accept your right to issue them. If legitimacy will not, or cannot, be conferred from an organizational superior, then it must be earned; involving others, giving warmth and support and taking low risks is then most appropriate. A successful risky decision can break through to a new level of respect from subordinates; a failure can cause a bad case of terminal influence.

> *All authority belongs to the people.*
> Thomas Jefferson

In some settings an organization's traditions and culture will not legitimize influence when it is attempted in a style considered inappropriate. Faculty members in universities, for example, often only accept administrator influence when administrators do not behave in a controlling, cold way. Conversely, in some companies, anything less than a gruff set of orders given as commands will be seen as weak and, therefore, unenforceable. In either type of organization stylistic choices are limited by member willingness to give power only to those using particular influence modes.

With so many possible stylistic choices to make, and so many situational factors to take into account, it is hard for an aspiring leader to sort out what to do when. For example, in general, less influence should be shared when subordinates are unconcerned about or unaffected by the decision and when they have less expertise than the manager. Greater sharing of influence should be used when subordinates' support and cooperation is needed, their knowledge is essential, or their commitment necessary because they must carry out the decision.[6] These guidelines must then be incorporated with task and people concern, and venturousness. Let's examine two contrasting situations.

EXAMPLE 1: THE PERSONNEL RECORD OFFICE

An experienced personnel officer is in charge of a group of six people whose job it is to go through the record of every new departing employee of the company and to transfer certain kinds of information on to index

---

[6] V. Vroom and P. Yetton, *Leadership and Decision-Making* (Pittsburgh: University of Pittsburgh Press, 1973).

cards. They work in a large insurance company in which there is a high rate of employee turnover. Consequently, the work-load is heavy and very steady. With a few exceptions, the people in this work group have been there for some years and the work is fairly routine for them, even when some special judgment is required. Some of the newer workers need occasional help, but mostly to answer simple procedural questions. The records themselves vary in quality and ease with which they can be understood; there are variations from department to department and supervisor to supervisor. Certain departments and supervisors are preferred and certain others are to be avoided. Therefore, one of the tasks is to divide the "plums" from the "prunes" in a way that is fair to everyone. The supervisor does that job.

The central leadership function in this case is one of maintenance and control over the flow of work. If it gets bogged down, then there is an accumulation of records which creates complaints from the vice president of personnel. Although he is a little more experienced than the others, the supervisor does not have any special expertise that others do not share. He normally answers the questions of the newer people, but in his absence several other employees can answer the questions just as well. He was appointed to his job because of seniority and demonstrated competence.

Because he has been there the longest, the supervisor of the records office carries sufficient influence among the workers to have the final say in any matter of controversy (of which there are few). Although he is not the most popular person there, his relations with the others are friendly and he is given a fair amount of personal respect.

The supervisor's style of leadership is fairly formal; he has developed detailed established procedures and requires employees to follow them. Any departure from these could create a minor furor. He gives his main attention to the task at hand, does not concern himself very much with the feelings or attitudes of the other employees, except when there is an obvious problem, and he is able to rely upon the abilities of others to help keep the work moving. Finally, we can describe his style as cautious, since he is careful not to take upon himself any decisions that go outside the bounds of what is already prescribed.

The leadership conditions in this case are simple to describe. The main roles of the supervisor are as *monitor* and *resource allocator,* with most attention going to maintaining and controlling the work flow. The situation is *routine and clear.* From what we know about what kinds of leadership fit what kinds of circumstances, the match in this case seems to be an appropriate one. The supervisor has a *moderate amount of influence,* which is all that is needed to keep work moving in its normal, routine way. He has the influence because he is accepted as the *formal-legitimate* supervisor of the group and because his relations with the other em-

ployees are adequate, given the relatively low level of personal commitment required by the task. His leadership style is also attuned to the situation. He shares a *little* of the *control* with the group members who
possess the required expertise; he maintains a *high level of task-concern,*
since the system demands accuracy and speed; he maintains only a *moderate level of person-concern,* enough just to keep tabs on serious problems, but not to the degree to which it might distract his attention from
the task; he sticks to the *formal procedures,* which are adequate for
completing the bulk of the work load; and he maintains *caution,* which
keeps him and his department out of trouble.

A Change in Requirements

What might happen if some of the factors involved were changed?
Suppose, for example, the insurance company's operations research
group decided to introduce the use of computers into the personnel records office and wanted the workers to punch their information on IBM
cards, and learn how to read printout sheets. The supervisor is called in
and trained in the use of the new system; then he is sent back to introduce it to his department members. We now have a very different situation from the previous one. It involves the *initiation* of a new *technology,*
which makes the situation *nonroutine.* Since it is likely that the workers
will feel some anxieties about their ability to learn the new methods and
since they are for the moment dependent upon the supervisor's expertise, it calls for a different kind of leadership. Now he needs a high
level of influence, which he may be able to get through his newly acquired expertise, provided that the others recognize it. With personal
tensions running high, he now needs to maintain a high level of person-
concern along with a very high level of task-concern. For the time being
he may need to retain control, which makes sense in terms of his special
knowledge and would also be functional in dealing with the anxieties of
the clerks. The emphasis upon formal prescribed procedures continues
to be appropriate for that portion of the work determined by the needs
of the computer system, but now the situation requires a little more venturousness on the part of the supervisor with respect to helping the
workers figure out how to make the new methods work.

The Effects of Changed Requirements on Leadership

Can you see how changing circumstances results in changing leadership requirements? If the supervisor in the case were not capable of or
interested in learning the new technology or training others, the company
would have been forced to consider changing the person in the leadership
role. When technology changes rapidly, difficulties arise. Suppose, for

example, the supervisor in the case just described were unable, even with full support, to handle the computer methods, but the company felt obliged to keep him in the supervisory role because of his seniority. Can you imagine how difficult it would have been for everyone concerned? His legitimacy would probably disappear and, with it, his influence as a leader. The increasing demand for management development programs springs from this kind of problem, namely, the need to maintain and upgrade knowledge and expertise in areas that require changing leadership.

EXAMPLE 2: THE COMMUNITY ENVIRONMENTAL GROUP

A small group of citizens in a suburban area had become deeply concerned about the rapid growth of industry in their area. The pollution problems had grown to the point where many families were considering the possibility of moving away. The latest crisis centered around plans for expansion on the part of a plastics firm, one of the worst offenders in the region.

One evening a group of a dozen people meeting in one of their homes decided to create a citizens' organization in the hope of building total community opposition to the company's planned expansion. They realized that they faced a major undertaking with many constraints. As a voluntary organization they would have to depend upon the willingness of people to offer their time and efforts outside of their normal working hours. They needed to recruit more people, identify special resources in the area, raise money, get out publicity and information to the community, and on and on and on. Obviously they needed leadership; the question was *who* could lead this kind of operation and what would be the best way to do it. No one seemed eager for the job. Finally, one of the women in the group, a pleasant, hard-working mother of four children, reluctantly offered to take on the leadership role. The rest of the group, with great relief, concurred with the idea. The new leader saw her job as gathering information, making phone calls, setting dates for meetings, asking for volunteers to help do important jobs like contacting community leaders who might support the effort, and so forth.

She wanted to make the organization as visible as possible as rapidly as possible, but only in ways that would attract membership, not result in the group getting a reputation as a bunch of troublemakers. Therefore, she decided that it would be very important not to offend anyone; she had to build friendly relations wherever she went. With the help of a few other volunteers she pushed ahead to build the organization. They began making the phone calls, contacting newspaper and television people to ask for coverage, writing up pieces to be duplicated and circulated door to door, and so forth.

Their campaign met with only minimal success. People wanted to know *who* they were, what existing organization they represented, what they really knew about pollution to begin with, what facts they had about the actual expansion plans of the plastics company, and many more questions that they had difficulty answering. Somehow the organization was not developing as the group had hoped and as the leader had planned it. Before we examine why this was so, see if you can diagnose the problem yourself. See if you can spell out the leadership issues in the case and decide what was or was not appropriate for the circumstances.

In many respects this case illustrates one of the more difficult kinds of leadership problems. In fact, it probably goes beyond what any one person could normally handle as a leader. The situation calls for great skills in the roles of symbolic figurehead, innovator, coordinator/leader, liaison, spokesman, negotiator; action must be taken on many fronts; and the situation is *turbulent* (or changing) and full of *uncertain outcomes*. Do you think *you* could handle it?

The appropriate leader for those circumstances would have to possess *a high degree of influence, a high level of expertise* and possess (or be able to build) *good working relations* with the organization members. With respect to style of leadership, the person would have to *retain control* until the organization became solidly established, maintain a *very high level of task-concern* and *high level of person-concern,* the former for obvious reasons, the latter because of the unusually high level of commitment needed in voluntary organizations. The leader would have to operate in a very *informal manner,* since there are no established procedures; and, finally, a *venturous approach* is needed, since there is no way to predict what might be behind all the doors that have to be opened.

As you can see, the person who had the leadership job in this case was not the best suited to the situation. One option she had was to draw in people who possessed the necessary expertise and abilities to compensate for what she lacked. Her own role might have been more focused on liaison work than some of the other needed roles and functions; that is also vital to an organization like the one just described. She might have been appropriate for that aspect of the leadership role, but clearly other resources were needed to meet the multitude of other demands.

As a way of summarizing what the two cases illustrate, let's see what kinds of propositions would apply. The proposition that would fit the personnel records case would go as follows:

In a work situation that calls for *monitoring and resource allocation roles* for a *work process* under *routine conditions,* with *employees who do not need high autonomy,* the appropriate leader would be someone *designated by the system, having moderate influence* and minimally *adequate leader-member relations;* the appropriate style for that leader would be to moderately *share control,* maintain a *high level of task-concern,* a mod-

erate level of person-concern, operate by *formal established procedures* and take *little risk.*

The proposition that would fit the community group case would go as follows:

In a work situation that calls for *innovative and other initiating roles* in relation to all aspects of the job, under *turbulent (nonroutine) conditions,* with *high subordinate independence,* the appropriate leader would be someone with *high influence, high expertise,* and very *good leader–member relations;* the appropriate style would be to *retain control* but involve many others, maintain a *high level of task-concern,* a *high level of person-concern,* operate by *informal, improvised procedures* and take *high risk.*

THE CONDITIONS UNDER WHICH PARTICIPATIVE METHODS ARE APPROPRIATE

As you realize by now, each time one of the factors is changed, the proposition that applies also changes to some extent. Thus, you, yourself, will have to take on the task of generating propositions that fit the various combinations of factors you may encounter. If you understand the steps in doing that, then you have mastered a way of conceptualizing the leadership process, one which will be more useful to you than any simple fixed rules about what leaders should or should not do.

As the two cases indicate, however, there may be clusters of managerial behavior which are appropriate in changing or stable situations. Though no situation you encounter is likely to have all of these elements the same, they frequently go together.

Many managers struggle with the issue of how to balance an emphasis upon "getting the job done" with the importance of involving employees in the processes of decision-making. The question seems to be, "How much time can I afford to spend informing and discussing matters with my employees if it cuts into valuable work time?" Or the question might be phrased in sharper terms like, "Who's running the show, me or my workers?" In general, **Leadership which fully involves those being led in decision making ("participative," "employee-centered") is most effective under the following conditions:**

a. **Decisions are nonroutine.**
b. **Nonstandardized information is flowing in or must be gathered through subordinates.**
c. **Actions are not being taken under severe time pressure.**
d. **Subordinates feel the need for independence, see participation as legitimate, can work without close supervision, will take the organization's goals into account, and can effect the implementation of decisions by acceptance or rejection of them.**

It should be obvious how a significant change in any one of these conditions can challenge the appropriateness of participative leadership. Time becomes an important factor when the environment demands rapid responses, or when the leader feels rushed and pressured. Ironically, unless the need for decisions is extremely urgent, it may be most functional to thoroughly talk through decisions when they are most pressing and important; it requires great skill to prevent premature closure of discussion when the wolf, real or imagined, is at the door.

Subordinate readiness is also a crucial issue, only briefly mentioned earlier. Have you ever been faced with a situation in which responsibility was thrown in your lap and you did not consider yourself competent to handle it? A leader who fails to consider the "state-of-readiness" of employees, with respect to sharing leadership responsibilities, can easily create more problems by pushing this approach than if he/she were to exercise more unilateral control. Under conditions where employees prefer to have the legitimate leader give the orders and feel the need for close supervision, participative leadership is likely to be highly dysfunctional.

Thus, when the opposite conditions are true, that is, **When decisions are routine, actions are being taken under severe time pressure, information is standardized and subordinates are dependent, more controlling forms of leadership are appropriate.** But to complicate the matter further, within any one organization the conditions surrounding each decision may vary. For example, subordinates may accept being controlled on some issues but not on others; some issues will need immediate decisions while others can be discussed at great length, and so forth. Effective leadership will fit not only the general situation but also the particular circumstances of each decision. That requires great flexibility and responsiveness as well as a genuinely "scientific" attitude on the part of the manager who is trying to decide how much participation by subordinates is appropriate, and when.

It may not always be possible, however, to adjust your behavior to the demands of the situation. As yet there are no agreed-upon limits to human flexibility. Individuals vary in their ability to change behavior; it may well be that when you face a situation demanding a style which is not natural to your personality, the best option is to find another person to do it, change jobs, or work at restructuring the situation to fit your strengths. Your own capacity to learn new behavior is thus an additional factor to consider when choosing a leadership style.

Similarly, the same factors which determine leadership *style,* also can affect which managerial functions should be emphasized. When the environment demands rapid responses and considerable attention, the manager is likely to spend more time on external functions, such as spokesman and negotiator, and less on the internal ones, such as supervisor. Conversely, when the manager's subordinates have less expertise than is needed to perform their tasks, and only the manager can supply what is missing, greater emphasis may be placed internally on coaching and training. Again, however, individual flexibility serves to limit how easily a manager can *choose* what to do.

LEADERSHIP AND VALUES

Unfortunately, there is even more to leadership than a determination of what will work when and an assessment of whether you can do what is called for. The fundamental question has to do with how you personally feel about the exercise of power. "Power" is one of the few dirty words left in our society. Accusing a person of needing power is usually an insult, while "you need love" is a gesture of caring. Yet everyone needs power in order to feel effective and adequate, and insofar as influence requires mutuality, everyone has some. Many people, especially students who want to become managers, try to gain power through leadership roles at every opportunity and look down on anyone who is not interested in constantly enhancing power. For such power seekers, some time spent thinking about their motives in wanting power, and the uses to which they intend to put it when a fair measure has been acquired, would be worthwhile.

> *They who are in highest places, and have the most power, have the least liberty, because they are most observed.*
>
> John Tillotson
> *Reflections*

On the other hand, many others, including even a few managerial students, fear leadership and its burdens, and consequently refrain from exercising more than passive influence. Though some influence is inescapable, since even silence has consequences on other system members, such "power avoiders" either define themselves as helpless and powerless or backpedal when responsibility hovers near. "It's good to have a leader because then I'll have someone to blame when things go wrong," is the widely held counterfoil to the belief that "no game is worth playing if I'm not the captain," (or at least struggling to become the captain's replacement). Those who shy away from leadership might profitably contemplate the costs of anyone holding back his/her full strength, and what the world would be like if everyone played it so safe.

The values question arises in another way. Even if a controlling, task centered, "authoritarian" leadership style works best in some situations with some people, do you want to (1) put yourself in such situations, (2) accept the conditions as fixed rather than trying to change them so that other styles become more appropriate, (3) focus on short-term results rather than long-term development of subordinates, or (4) live with the consequences of a society in which people who work best under an authoritarian style are kept dependent, passive and submissive? Are you willing to do what is necessary to maximize productivity regardless of the human costs?

Conversely, if a more influence-sharing, person-centered style is appropriate to get the work out, would you be willing to give up some control to get the best results? Could you respond to those you work with in a genuinely warm and supportive way, even when you would prefer that they do what you want without questioning everything? Could you risk your own job by allowing others the optimal amount of influence?

Trying to follow a contingency model as a manager–scientist does not automatically make that leadership role easier; even when you can figure out *what* to do and whether you can do it, you still have to decide whether you *want* to do it. The garden of roses we never promised you is unfortunately strewn with thorns, and there is no simple way through it. There are hard choices at every turning.

In Chapter 13 on managing organizational change, we will look at the strategies available to organizational members to influence the behavior of others in desired directions. Even the perfectly appropriate style of leadership must be applied somewhere in the organization, and we will explore that crucial part of a manager's job there.

KEY CONCEPTS FROM CHAPTER 11

1. Influence is an act or potential act which affects the behavior of another person or persons:
   a. Formal influence: prescribed by office or position.
   b. Informal influence: affecting others through expertise or personal attractiveness.
   c. Legitimate influence: seen by those being influenced as having right to do so.
   d. Illegitimate influence: seen by those being influenced as not having right to do so.
2. Power is the capacity to utilize influence:
   a. The more access to controlling rewards and punishments, the greater the power.
   b. The more types of influence one exerts, the greater the power.
   c. The greater one's power, the more one is the recipient of:
      (1) Communication.
      (2) Solicitous behavior.
      (3) Deference.
   d. The greater one's power:
      (1) The higher one's self-esteem.
      (2) The more one sees others with power as a reference point.
      (3) The more one is attracted to others with power.

3. Managerial choices:
   a. The manager (person with formal-legitimate influence) makes choices about
   b. Functions and styles of Leadership in the context of
   c. The situation, including:
      (1) Nature of the task situation.
      (2) Attitudes and needs of subordinates.
      (3) Power of the manager with superiors.
4. Manager's interpersonal functions create access to information which leads to
5. Informational functions which allow for
6. Decision making functions.
7. Preferred leadership style tempered by what is appropriate to the situation.
8. Dimensions of leadership style:
   a. Control: retaining versus sharing.
   b. Task Concern: high versus low.
   c. Person Concern: high versus low.
   d. System: formal versus informal.
   e. Actions and decisions: cautious versus venturous.
9. Controlling forms of leadership most appropriate when:
   a. Decisions routine.
   b. Severe time pressure.
   c. Information standardized.
   d. Subordinates dependent.
10. Participative leadership most appropriate when:
    a. Decisions non-routine.
    b. Little time pressure.
    c. Nonstandardized (requires judgment) information.
    d. Subordinates independent.

SUGGESTED READINGS

Berelson, B., and Steiner, G., *Human Behavior: An Inventory of Scientific Findings.* New York: Harcourt, Brace & World, Inc., 1964.

Berle, A. A. *Power.* New York: Harcourt Brace and World, Inc., 1969.

Blake, R. R., and Mouton, J. S. *The Managerial Grid.* Houston: Gulf Publishing Company, 1964.

Bragg, J. E., and Andrews, I. R. "Participative Decision Making: An Experimental Study in a Hospital" *JABS* 9 (1973) 727–35.

"G.E. Strikers, Back Their Leaders," *Business Week,* (November 8, 1969) 107.

Dalton, M. *Men Who Manage.* New York: John Wiley & Sons, Inc., 1959.

Dowling, William F. Jr.; and Sayles, Leonard R. *How Managers Motivate: The Imperatives of Supervision.* New York: McGraw-Hill Book Co., 1971.

Fiedler, Fred *A Theory of Leadership Effectiveness.* New York: McGraw-Hill Book Co., 1967.

_____ "The Trouble With Leadership Training Is That It Doesn't Train Leaders," *Psychology Today* 6 (1973) 23.

_____ and Chemers, M. *Leadership and Effective Management.* Glenview, Ill.: Scott, Foresman & Co., 1974.

Fleischman, E., and Hunt, J. *Current Developments in the Study of Leadership.* Carbondale, Ill.: Southern Illinois University Press, 1963.

French, J. R. P. Jr., Raven, B. "The Bases of Social Power," in D. Cartwright and A. Zander, Eds., *Group Dynamics: Research and Theory.* New York: Harper & Row, 1960, pp. 607–23.

Hoffer, Eric "The Working Man Looks at His Boss," *Harpers* (March 1954).

Hunt, J., and Larson, L. *Contingency Approaches to Leadership.* Carbondale, Ill.: Southern Illinois University Press, 1974.

Jennings, E. E. *An Anatomy of Leadership — Princes, Heros, and Supermen.* New York: McGraw-Hill Book Co., 1960.

King, D., and Bass, B. *Leadership, Power and Influence.* Lafayette, Ind.: Herman C. Krannert Graduate School of Industrial Administration, Purdue University, 1970.

Leavitt, H. J. *Managerial Psychology,* 2d ed. Chicago: The University of Chicago Press, 1964.

MacGregor, D. *Leadership and Motivation.* Cambridge, Mass.: The M.I.T. Press, 1966.

_____ *The Professional Manager.* New York: McGraw-Hill Book Co., 1967.

Maslow, Abraham *Eupsychian Management.* Homewood, Ill.: Richard D. Irwin Inc. and the Dorsey Press, 1965.

Miles, Raymond and Ritchey, J. B. "Participative Management: Quality vs. Quantity," *California Management Review* (Summer 1971) 48–56.

Milgrim, Stanley "Behavioral Study of Obedience," *Journal of Abnormal and Social Psychology* 67 (1963) 371–78.

Mintzberg, H. *The Nature of Managerial Work.* New York, N.Y.: Harper & Row, 1973.

Mockler, Robert J. "Situational Theory of Management," *Harvard Business Review* (May–June 1971) 146–55.

Porter, Lyman W.; and Lawlor, Edward E. III *Managerial Attitudes and Performance.* Homewood, Ill.: Richard D. Irwin, Inc., 1968.

Ready, R. K. *The Administrator's Job.* New York: McGraw-Hill Book Co., 1967.

Sayles, L. R. *Managerial Behavior.* New York: McGraw-Hill Book Co., 1964.

Strauss, G. "Some Notes on Power Equalization." in Leavitt, H. J. *The Social Science of Organizations,* Englewood Cliffs, N.J.: Prentice-Hall, Inc., 1963.

Tannenbaum, R., and Schmidt, W. "How to Choose A Leadership Style," *Harvard Business Review* 36 (1958) 95–101.

Vroom, V., and Yetton, P. *Leadership and Decision-Making.* Pittsburgh: University of Pittsburgh Press, 1973.

White, R., and Lippitt, R. "Leader Behavior and Member Reaction in three Social Climates," *Group Dynamics: Research and Theory.* 3d ed. D. Cartwright and A. Zander, eds. New York: Harper & Row, Inc., 1967, pp. 318–36.

Zaleznik, A. "The Human Dilemmas of Leadership," *Harvard Business Review* 41, no. 4, (July–August 1963).

If the work is carried out in such a way that one group cannot begin its task until another has completed its work, then you can see the critical nature of interdependence.

12

RELATIONS AMONG GROUPS IN THE ORGANIZATION

SINCE virtually every large organization requires some division of labor, it is usually necessary to have departments, branches, divisions, units, teams, and so forth, to accomplish the various tasks. Helping the individual subsystems do their parts and insuring that their work is integrated towards the goals of the organization as a whole, is a key way in which a manager determines the system's overall effectiveness.

When the organization has groups doing tasks which differ from one another in terms of complexity, rate of change of the technology used, skills needed, length of time it takes to complete the task, and so forth, then the job of coordinating the subunits becomes a major managerial undertaking.

In general, **The more differentiated the tasks necessary to accomplish the organization's work, the more appropriate it is to create separate subsystems for doing each task.** And as you might expect, **Each subunit works best when organized in a way that fits the demands of its task.** The subunit's structure, personnel, operating style and leadership should be matched to its particular tasks; in other words, **When the background factors and required system "fit" the unit's goals, it is most likely to be effective.**

Even when subunit organization is not perfectly matched to task, there is a tendency for the group to acquire an identity that is at least partly reflective of the type of work it does, the skills needed to do it, who the members are, the technology involved, the rate of change in the group's environment, and so forth.

Think about a classroom task group in relation to other groups. You can sense a kind of group identity which the members seek to maintain and enhance; it's like a group self-concept. The members have probably developed some distinct goals and preferences in working style, such as how to use their time, how task-oriented they wish to be, and how personal and close they permit members to become. They are likely to have some sense of the group's competencies, such as how well it discusses problems, how effectively it maintains participation, and so forth. And the group surely has a set of beliefs and values reflected in its norms, ideals and rules for what kinds of behaviors are acceptable or not. It is no different in any organization; **Work groups tend to develop a group concept which they strive to maintain and enhance.**

Furthermore, **The more cohesive the group, the clearer and more strongly felt is the identity likely to be to group members.** As you may recall, in Chapter 4 we offered a number of propositions on the factors that increase a group's cohesiveness, including common values and goals, a common enemy, high required interactions, and low interactions required outside the group.

And we also postulated that the more cohesive the group, the more closely members would conform to the group's norms. Thus, when a group emergent system which is attractive to members develops out of what is required to get the work done, the group's way of doing things is likely to be seen by members not only as appropriate but also as extremely desirable and valuable. The *group's* "self-concept" becomes worth protecting.

INTERVIEWER: *Did you have national anthems?*
2000 YEAR OLD MAN: *It was very fragmented. It wasn't nations; it was caves. Each cave had a national anthem.*
INTERVIEWER: *Do you remember the national anthem of your cave?*
2000 YEAR OLD MAN: *I certainly do; I'll never forget it. You don't forget a national anthem in a minute.*
INTERVIEWER: *Let me hear it, sir.*
2000 YEAR OLD MAN (SINGING): *Let them all go to hell except cave 76.*

From album, *The 2000 Year Old Man*
by Carl Reiner & Mel Brooks

VARIATIONS IN GROUP IDENTITY

What are some of the ways in which group "identities" may differ? How do differing emergent systems compare with one another? You will already have observed many groups in cases, in class and at work, and seen that they have different ways of doing things. In order to examine the reasons why groups sometimes have difficulty working together, we need to suggest a few important dimensions on which work groups often differ, to add to those discussed in Chapter 6 on group effectiveness.

Time Horizon

One important way in which group members in organizations may differ is in their view of time. There are certain kinds of tasks that tend to call for a relatively short-term time horizon and others that call for a long-term time horizon. These task "demands" transcend the fact that we all have different preferences for work pace. Basic research, for example, is not a process that can easily be hurried along and it tends to require a rather distant time horizon. Competitive sales, on the other hand, normally calls for rapid decisions and a series of short-term check points on the way to long-range objectives. **The time horizon tends to be shortest for those tasks that require immediate feedback and have outcomes that can provide such feedback; the time horizon tends to be longest for those tasks whose relevant outcomes and, consequently, sources of feedback are more delayed.** You can see how people in a marketing division of a company can measure their successes in terms of immediate sales and how inevitable it is that they would operate out of a relatively short time horizon. If, however, such sales commit other divisions of the system to delivery times that are incompatible with their own time horizons, some degree of conflict is bound to ensue. Research and development people, for example, may find such commitments impossible to meet and foreign to their concepts of how their work should be carried out. Each group is likely to deal with time issues in its own way, and believe in the "correctness" of its procedures and assumptions. Since "time" is so much a part of everything in organizational life it is often taken for granted. Often groups with different time horizons have difficulty understanding one another.

Background Factors

Other things being equal, we know that it is natural for people to gravitate into groups that reinforce their values. Most voluntary groups form on that basis, and their cohesiveness can be directly attributed to the fact that membership serves to reinforce basic personal values. While work groups in most organizations do not form on a voluntary basis, it is safe to say that the more differentiated a work group's task the more likely will members be recruited who share *common background factors*. These may include education, professional identity, ethnic grouping, race, religion, common interests, and so forth. **The more similar are members' background factors the clearer will the group's identity tend to be.** Since in most organizations the division of labor is based upon specialized task and skill areas, work groups at all levels of the system will tend to be composed of people with similar backgrounds, at least in regard to a given skill area.

Perspective on the Task

Some units have jobs which keep members narrowly focused upon one aspect of the work. An extreme example would be on an assembly line, where the workers put the same kind of bolt in the same kind of hole all day long, never getting to see the end product or even some of the subassemblies. Contrast that task to one involving a quality check on the final product; the perspective of each is very different with respect to the scope of the task.

The broader the perspective on the task, the greater will be member awareness of task-group interdependencies and the greater will be their concern for the total effort. Normally the higher a unit is in the hierarchy, the greater the likelihood of members seeing the "big picture," i.e., the overall relation of subunits and their connections to organizational goals. Members of lower level units often focus only on their particular set of tasks, with less sense of the context in which they are operating. But this difference in perspective is not limited to differences in hierarchical level. It can vary with the unit's required interactions with outside subsystems; **The greater the number of interactions required with other subsystems, the**

broader is a subsystem's task perspective likely to be. In any event, there can be distinct differences in member orientation and task perspective.

Attitudes toward Authority and Internal Structure

As you may recall from the chapters on leadership (11) and group effectiveness (6), the amount of control and participation in a group should be related to the group's needs in accomplishing its tasks. Groups where expertise is widely distributed and needed for the solution of complex, changing problems require a more participative, free-wheeling, noncontrolling style of operation than those where task requirements are clear and expertise strongly differentiated.

Groups develop over time, then, quite different notions about the proper style of leadership, the appropriate amount of latitude for individual decision-making and involvement, and for allowable amounts of initiative. Can you see how groups which differ along these dimensions might view one another with less than full approval?

Summary

Thus, in terms of (*a*) attitudes towards time, authority and structure, (*b*) perspective on tasks and (*c*) common values, organizational subsystems can and do differ. Each develops its own identity in coping with the tasks assigned to it. That identity is the group equivalent of individual self-concept; the more cohesive the group, the greater the members' commitment to preserving and enhancing its identity, and the more likely members are to see the group's way of doing things as correct, valuable, and superior to other groups' ways. Finally, insofar as group organization should follow from and be appropriate to the group's tasks, **The more differentiated a subsystem's tasks, the more effective it will be when its identity (or way of operating) is also differentiated from the identities of other subsystems.**

THE PRICE OF APPROPRIATE DIFFERENTIATION

Unfortunately, however, as you by now may have anticipated, **The clearer and more distinct a subsystem's identity, the more need will there be for coordination with other subsystems, but the more difficult will that be.** Insofar as differentiated groups carry on interdependent tasks there is a need for coordination among them. And the greater the degree of interdependence, the more important is the coordination.

In order for there to be effective intergroup coordination:

1. Each group must be aware of its own functions in relation to those of other groups;
2. Each group must be willing to maintain communication links with the other groups;
3. Each group must be willing to accept the legitimacy of the needs of the other groups; and
4. Each group must be willing to meet its own needs within the framework of the total system.

But a group with a sharply differentiated identity is likely to resist any form of coordination that conflicts with its identity. **The extent of a group's resistance to coordination with other groups will be directly related to the degree to which the required interactions conflict with the group's basic norms, ideals and values.**

Just as with individuals and relationships, **To the extent that a group perceives a relationship with another group as enhancing to its own identity, it will strive to develop and maintain that relationship. To the extent that a group perceives a relationship with another group as in some way threatening to its own identity, it will strive to resist or avoid that relationship.** In those instances in an organization where the nature of the task *requires* a working relationship between any two groups, these propositions become extremely important. **The more an intergroup relationship requires activities and interactions that are compatible with the identities of the groups involved, the more effective will that relationship be; the more it requires activities and interactions that are contradictory to the identities of either or both groups, the more that relationship will be a source of conflict.**

GROUP STATUS

We have been examining the sources of group identity as they follow from task differentiation, and showing how the differentiation can lead to difficulties. But there is another aspect to a group's identity which is important for understanding coordination problems.

It is inevitable that in assigning jobs to various subsystems, an organization will confer differing amounts of legitimate influence to groups. Some subsystems will be expected to give orders to and initiate interaction with others; other subsystems will be expected to wait for initiatives from subsystems doing different jobs. This allocation of influence will usually be based on the flow of work, though it may not have a very explicit rationale. Whatever the reasoning behind the particular way power is allocated, **The more legitimate power a group has within the system, the more freedom it has to initiate actions and the more other less powerful groups are dependent upon it to initiate actions.** The marketing department in one firm might have the right to decide what products will be tested and sold, while the production department has to go along despite its reservations. In another organization, the financial group might be given the power to exert control over operating departments, to insure adequate returns. But the formal, legitimate power of groups is not the only determinant of influence. The informal social system, as usual, has an important part to play.

INFORMAL GROUP STATUS IN THE SYSTEM

We have already pointed out in the chapter about leadership that influence in an organization is based upon both formal position and informal status, the latter being determined by a variety of factors, including education, social status of a given profession or occupation, special abilities, "who you know," how important the work is to the overall organization, and seniority. Just as some individuals in an organization seem to carry more informal influence than they have been formally assigned because they have been around for a long time or do a very special kind of work, it is not unusual for a particular subsystem to possess informal influence and status that far exceeds what is formally designated to it.

A common example of this is the case of technical staff in industry. While they do not normally possess the designated, formal authority of line people, who are responsible for the operations of the firm, their special expertise and advanced degrees often give them an informal status that carries a great deal of influence with top management. Or it may lead them to *see* themselves as higher status and therefore as having more influence than they are formally assigned. It becomes an intergroup problem when line people and staff people compete for influence and control because legitimacy is in dispute. Take the case of efficiency experts coming into a department to study its operations and make recommendations for improving that department. It doesn't take much imagination to see how the outside experts can be seen as the "enemy," since they pose the threat of carrying more influence than the organizational chart indicates. Similarly, within a university, power is delegated from the board of trustees to the administration, but informal status is attributed to the faculty, who are seen as the backbone of the educational process. Who carries the most weight and with whom? Struggles around this kind of issue can generate great tension and serious questions about what outcomes are functional for the *total* system as opposed to any one of the competing subsystems.

The more informal status a group has within the system, the more freedom it has to initiate actions and the more other lower status groups are dependent upon it to initiate actions. With the exception of the *source* (formal versus informal) of influence, this proposition is a repeat of the previous one. When a group has both legitimate power and informal status (for example, a medical staff running a hospital, engineers with advanced degrees managing a manufacturing company, and so forth) one major source of intergroup conflict is eliminated. But most large organizations tend to promote people on the basis of demonstrated managerial competence, which may or may not have anything to do with technical expertise. High status *professionals* often tend to view "mere administrators" as having less status, and, therefore, as not legitimately able to control the professionals even though the organization chart assigns the administrators formal authority.

In short, the existence of the two important sources of influence frequently results in incongruencies in intergroup relations. These incongruencies exist when a group possesses higher legitimate power than other groups but lower informal status, or vice versa. **An incongruency between legitimate power and status tends to result in confusion about which group can exercise the greater freedom to take actions that affect the other and which group "has the right" to initiate interactions with the other.** Can the university faculty decide to limit class sizes without considering the registration and facility problems that such an action poses? Can the administration decide to expand the university for financial reasons without obtaining faculty consent? Can the quality control expert stop production over the protests of the production manager? And when serious conflicts occur, how can one group initiate action without in some way affecting the identity of the other group?

An Example of How Status Affects Relations among Groups

Let's look at some examples of how these concepts come to life in a familiar setting.

For many years the principal professional groups involved in the field of mental health have been psychologists, psychiatrists and social workers. Almost any mental health setting is likely to employ people from each of these professions. The history of the relationships among these groups has been full of change and conflict, and illustrative of the above propositions. At one time the hierarchy was fairly distinct and, for the most part, accepted by all three groups. The psychiatrist, possessor of a medical degree and specialized expertise. was considered the senior person; each of the other groups, with its own special expertise, was relegated to a secondary position. The social worker was responsible for family contacts and placement, as well as for individual casework under the supervision of the psychiatrist. The psychologist was mainly concerned with diagnostic testing and evaluation, consultation with the psychiatrist and possibly some direct treatment of patients under the supervision of the psychiatrist.

As concepts of mental health changed, became less defined in medical terms and more in social terms, and as the quality and level of education changed in each profession, the identity of each and, consequently, their relationship with each other, also changed. Social workers became more competent to perform direct treatment and, thus, demanded more autonomy as professionals. Psychologists also received more training in the practice of psychotherapy and, along with the status associated with a Ph.D., pushed for total autonomy from the control of their psychiatric colleagues.

It was inevitable that in those institutions where the required interactions were a carryover from the "old days," psychologists and social workers were likely to exhibit some resistance. On the other side of the coin, in those settings where the relationships were "modernized" by allowing psychologists and/or social workers the autonomy they demanded, psychiatrists showed their own resistance. Whichever way it went, one or more groups experienced some degree of threat to their respective identities. Since, in any given setting, effective patient care is in part dependent upon how well the three professions work together, it takes little imagination to see the possible consequences of the conflicts among these three groups. The patients and the system paid the biggest price; but each group was determined to protect its identity and status.

CHOOSING BETWEEN CONFLICT AND COOPERATION

For the manager, whether or not to attempt to do something about subsystems in conflict depends upon an assessment of the functionality of the dispute for the total organization. While conflict can be costly, as in the above example, in some cases it is a necessary part of achieving full consideration of legitimately differing viewpoints. Without conflict among subsystems, the total needs of the organization might be ignored in favor of the highest status subsystem's needs, or pushed aside by the more powerful subgroups. Allowing or even encouraging conflict by greater differentiation of group ways of working, may be the only way to achieve some balance among subsystems which would each like to maximize its own effectiveness regardless of the consequences for the whole organization.

For example, while the survival of a company might depend upon rapid sales pricing decisions, it may also be crucial for the company to maintain a reputation for quality products and service. If the quality control, engineering, and service departments all took the same short-term view as the sales department, and in order to speed up decisions exercised very little control over their individual employees, they might get along better with sales, but shortchange long-term quality. Only if the respective subgroups are properly differentiated, encouraged to fully express their respective points of view, and allowed to struggle with the tradeoffs between keeping prices down and quality up, will a proper balance be achieved.

Where intergroup problems surface as wasteful conflict, they need to be approached in terms of reducing conflict and building cooperation; where problems are created by disproportionate dominance of one subsystem, they need to be treated with measures to further differentiate subgroups and/or increase open conflict among the groups. In short, conflict can be a result of genuine differences in group values which are reflected in disputes about desired system goals, in which case they may be functional and necessary for the total system. Without thorough discussion, the total system may be harmed. On the other hand, when conflict is a result of the group identification that often occurs with differentiated groups, and goes beyond legitimate disagreements into stereotyping, sniping, and sabotaging, it can be very dysfunctional for the total system. Energy gets used which could be better focused on the actual tasks.

Conversely, cooperation can be functional or dysfunctional for the total system, depending on whether it reflects genuine integration of efforts or covering up of disagreements which need to be aired in order to arrive at balanced decisions. And as noted in Chapter 2, there are times when it is not possible to produce functional consequences for all subsystems as well as for the total system. Imperfection is a price that often must be lived with in a complex organization.

TYPES OF INTERDEPENDENCE

The importance of intergroup cooperation versus conflict depends upon the degree and kind of interdependence of the work groups involved. If, for example, the work of each subsystem contributes to the productivity or welfare of the total system but is not directly related to that of the other, there are very few, if any, coordination issues. This is sometimes called *"pooled interdependence."* The various subdivisions of a large department store (housewares, sporting goods, clothing, and so forth) might be a familiar example of pooled interdependence. Each can try to maximize its own sales effectiveness without hurting other units.

However, if the work is carried out in such a way that one group cannot begin its task until another has completed its work, then you can see the critical nature of interdependence. This type is called *"serial interdependence"*; it is typical of assembly line operations, construction companies, printing firms, and even health services where treatment at one point in the system depends upon diagnostic tests at another earlier point in the system.

The most complex kind of interdependence occurs when work groups need to exchange information on a continuing basis; this is called *"reciprocal interdependence."* In the development of plans for a new car model for example, it is necessary for designers, engineers, market researchers and production experts to exchange information and ideas over and over so that the final product is both innovative and sound.

You can probably see for yourself how the manager's job will vary with each of the three kinds of situations described above. In the case of pooled interdependence he/she needs to make sure that each of the various groups maintains a satisfactory level of output but no one group is in a position to hold up the work of any other. With serial interdependence and reciprocal interdependence, the task is more complex and difficult. In fact, very few modern-day work patterns have the simplicity of pooled interdependence alone; a great many have elements of all three types. Take, for example, a research and development firm in which scientists, engineers, designers, production specialists, and so forth, all need to coordinate their efforts. The later stages of product manufacturing and testing are dependent upon the earlier stages of invention and development; the research chemists need to be aware of the manufacturing constraints and the manufacturing people must understand the time it takes to develop new ideas. The overall process requires ongoing information exchange among the various groups, and it is all oriented toward the goals of the total system.

You can appreciate by now just how important it is for a manager to understand and develop competence in dealing with intergroup relations. Whether the fostering of conflict or cooperation is called for, it is important that the manager understand the need for differentiated subsystems, the likelihood of their developing diverse identities or cultures, and the need for methods to resolve wasteful conflict when greater coordination is needed to achieve serial or reciprocal interdependence. Similarly, he/she should know some methods to achieve greater differentiation when too much harmony is creating imbalances.

> For example, one of the major international oil companies established foreign regional divisions, each of which was to attempt capture of a significant portion of a regional market. At the same time, the company headquarters insisted upon having final say on prices of products to new customers. Problems occurred when regional sales people needed rapid decisions in order to make a sale and were delayed by the policy of checking back with headquarters. The regional people felt that they were in the best position to know the local scene and ought to be able to take action as that scene demanded; the headquarters people insisted that their perspective was more worldwide and that they were in a better position to evaluate the going price on the world market. Both groups were right, but neither could acknowledge the legitimacy of the other's viewpoint. The longer the conflict went on, the more it got complicated with stereotypes, sabotage, miscommunications and the like.

We'll describe how the issue got resolved later in this chapter when we discuss approaches to intergroup problems. Do you think you could come up with some approaches of your own? It could be useful to then try to compare your approach with the one that was used in the actual situation.

THE PROBLEM WITH STRONG GROUP IDENTITY

In instances like the one at the oil company, in which two groups are competing or in conflict with one another, **Members of a differentiated, cohesive group with a strong sense of its own identity, will show the following tendencies:**

1. **Perception of their own group as "better" than the other group.**
2. **An upgrading of their own ideas and a downgrading of the other group's ideas.**
3. **An overestimation of their own competence and an underestimation of the competence of the other group.**
4. **Overvaluation of their own leader(s) and undervaluation of the other group's leader(s).**
5. **Avoidance or limiting of interactions and communication with the other group.**
6. **Distortion of information about the other group in ways that cast the other group in an unfavorable light.**
7. **Mistrust of the members of the other group.**

> *"When you're a Jet you're a Jet all the way,*
> *From your first cigarette to your last dying day.*
> *When you're a Jet, if the spit hits the fan*
> *You've got brothers around,*
> *You're a family man.*
> *You're never alone,*
> *You're never disconnected,*
> *You're home with your own*
> *When company's expected,*
> *You're well protected.*
> *Then you are set with a capital "J,"*
> *Which you'll never forget*
> *Till they cart you away.*
> *When you're a Jet, you stay a Jet."*
>
> Stephen Sondheim
> Lyrics, *West Side Story*

Perhaps you can recognize some or all of these tendencies from your own experience. Intergroup rivalries in school, competing gangs in the neighborhood, and organized team sports are all familiar examples. More troublesome, of course, are situations involving race relations, political and military conflicts and the like. These are more dramatic, dangerous manifestations of the same issues. But even within formal organizations these tendencies occur whenever two working units find themselves interdependent and in conflict. The more either or both groups see the conflict as a threat to group identity, the more evident these tendencies become and the more difficult it is to achieve resolution.

THE FOUNDATIONS OF INTERGROUP COOPERATION

How, then, can cooperation be built when it is necessary? As you study the following propositions on the foundation of intergroup cooperation, see if you can recognize their parallel from the chapters on group behavior. In fact, the fundamental proposition is almost identical in both cases.

The more frequent the interaction between any two groups, the greater the tendency to cooperate with each other. However, as in the case of interactions among members of a group, it is important to qualify the above proposition as follows:

To the extent that there is frequent and open information flow among groups in a system, common goals are more likely to develop.

And add to this proposition the following one:

The more groups recognize and accept common goals, the more likely they are to cooperate.

These propositions are basic to the effective management of all intergroup relations in an organization. To the extent that a manager uses a "divide and rule" approach by preventing open exchanges of information among working units, he/she risks intergroup competition and conflict, possibly to the serious detriment of the total system. Where task interdependence necessitates cooperation, the act of bringing key managers together frequently, and encouraging constant flow of communications among various interdependent work units, increases the likelihood of ongoing cooperation and goal achievement.

Since we also know that **The more groups share a common source of threat, the more likely they are to cooperate,** it becomes crucial for a manager to avoid becoming that "common source of threat." In competitive fields the common source of threat, obviously, must be the outside competition. Here is where an effective manager can mobilize cooperative effort by making certain that any source of threat serving to bind groups together lies *outside* the system and does not have divisive effects inside the system.

There are three additional propositions that help to complete the foundation for intergroup cooperation.

The more groups share common responsibility for problem-solving and for decision-making, the more likely they are to cooperate.

The more groups are able to establish joint memberships, the more likely they are to cooperate.

The more groups are willing to share and discuss their perceptions of each other, the more likely they are to cooperate.

THE NORM OF RECIPROCITY

In order for the propositions stated above to be translated into effective strategies for managing intergroup operations, the various groups involved need to recognize the significance of their interrelationships. Each needs to recognize that its own identity can be enhanced by its contribution to another group, and each needs to recognize the obligations for a return contribution. This kind of "fair exchange" principle increases *mutual* functionality and is also functional to the system. This is part of the "norm of reciprocity" discussed in Chapter 10, and it is often considered to be a critical factor in maximizing interdependence.

An example of this norm in operation occurs in many business schools, where several groupings of faculty, each from a different discipline, make decisions on curriculum content. With respect to each group's sense of its own importance it might be functional for it to dominate the decisions, but that would lead to an imbalanced program. The finance people would push for more finance courses, the marketing people for more marketing courses, the behavioral scientists for more organizational behavior courses, and so forth. If the faculty can establish a norm of reciprocity, then it is possible for each group to enhance the other, with the net result being a broad and balanced set of courses and a program that is functional for the school and the students.

On the other hand, if the groups are too understanding of the others, they may not demand the proper time for their own subject! Reciprocity can also become a form of "you scratch my back and I'll scratch yours," or "live and let live," which avoids tough priority decisions by giving everyone a bit of the goodies, deserved or not. It can be as dysfunctional to a total system to secure false peace as to fight endless battles.

METHODS FOR MAXIMIZING INTERGROUP COOPERATION

When greater cooperation is called for, there are several techniques which can help foster it. Listed below are six basic strategies for maximizing intergroup cooperation. These approaches are both preventive and curative; that is, each may serve as a means of establishing intergroup cooperation from the start or as a means of resolving intergroup problems or conflicts that have already developed. Obviously, the more these strategies are in operation the fewer problems are likely to develop, but few, if any, organizations are free from intergroup problems no matter how well they implement these approaches.

The six strategies are as follows:

1. Overlapping or multiple group membership.
2. Liaison or linkage people.
3. Joint task forces.
4. Joint group meetings
5. Job exchanges across groups.
6. Physical proximity.

Let's examine each of these approaches and see the advantages and disadvantages of each. Keep in mind that different situations call for different strategies and also that combinations of two or more of the approaches are often appropriate. Each of the six strategies is directly or indirectly derivable from the propositions stated in the previous section.

Overlapping or Multiple Group Memberships

In most organizations it is not unusual to be a member of more than one work group at any given time. A department manager, for example, is a member of both his/her own department and that group of people identifiable as department heads. A manager may also be assigned to a committee or task force in which he/she is required to represent the interests of his/her own department on some matter of planning, policy, budget decisions, and so forth. This type of multiple group membership has the obvious advantages of keeping the several groups in contact with one another, helping the manager to coordinate efforts of the different groups, helping him/her to see various perspectives, time horizons, and styles of operating, as well as facilitating a total system perspective. In all these respects such an approach is functional.

One of the problems, however, is the fact that multiple group membership can trap a person between the norms or goals of conflicting groups. For example, a committee or task force will tend to develop its own identity as it continues to meet. Every member becomes subject to the emergent norms and pressures of the "new group," and may, at times, be faced with the dilemma of choosing between the interests of his/her "home group" and those of the "new group." To the extent that he/she maintains absolute loyalty to the interests of the home group ("We'll get every dollar we can for our department, no matter how hard we have to fight,") he/she may hang up the new group; insofar as he/she succumbs to the pressures and influence of the new group ("We have to cut our budget for the sake of the other departments"), the home group can accuse the manager of forsaking the department.

This dilemma may be further complicated by the fact that the more frequently the individual meets and interacts with the members of both groups, the more difficult becomes the loyalty bind. Remember, this often tends to occur in the absence of other sources of interaction between members of the two groups, in which case the individual (manager in our example) is the principal link between the groups. As a manager becomes more aware of the legitimacy of the views and needs of other groups, via committee membership, and as he/she interacts more frequently with the members of the committee, there will develop greater mutual liking and respect. The individual becomes most acutely aware of his/her loyalty bind when: (*a*) he/she attempts to explain and defend each group's position to the other group, and (*b*) each group increases pressure on the individual to hold firm and maintain loyalty.

In addition, the more the individual representing a group embodies the norms and values of that group, the greater will be the bind in the face of conflicting pressures. And the more *cohesive* that group is, the more pressure it will exert to take an unyielding position.

In short, the multiple group memberships generally experienced by managers in large organizations can serve important functions in maintaining intergroup interdependence, but they also have built into them some serious obstacles related to conflicting pressures from the different groups. Some of the difficulties, however, can be offset by implementing additional approaches for intergroup interactions, as you will see in the next few pages.

Liaison or Linkage People

Over the years as organizations have faced increasing complexities and uncertainties, it has become more important for them to be able to process information and make decisions rapidly. The classical chain of command has become obsolete in many areas of work. It simply cannot manage the demand for flexibility and responsiveness to change and uncertainty. It has become more imperative than ever for groups in a system to maintain a fairly constant and open flow of important information. As a result, heavy demands are made upon managers to serve as the critical information links for the various subunits of the system. But managers have their limits and, in modern society, can easily suffer from overload problems.

One important development that has occurred in response to this problem is the creation of liaison or linkage people for the groups in the organization. These individuals, or sometimes groups of individuals, are not normally identified with any one operational unit nor do they carry any specific task responsibilities. Their role is simply (and it may not be so simple) to coordinate the efforts of various work groups, to facilitate the necessary exchanges of information and to help keep each unit apprised of the related activities of other units.

The advantages of utilizing liaisons who are not identified with existing work groups lie in their relative neutrality with respect to group pressures, their immunity from the sanctions of any single group and their relative freedom to move back and forth in the system as the task demands it. One disadvantage, of course, lies in their lack of legitimate "clout" to make things happen. However, through demonstrated competence they can develop a great deal of informal influence.

Linking people and groups work best when their emergent norms and attitudes towards time, structure, authority, and so forth fall approximately halfway between those of the groups being linked. If either group sees the linking people as too similar to the other group, the rejected group members are likely to feel ganged up on or misunderstood.

Joint Task Forces

The creation of a joint task force composed of members of different work groups, even groups that have experienced some conflicts, tends to be a very powerful and effective way of breaking down sharp lines between groups. Each member of the task force enters the new group with the security and support of members of the old group, but it generally follows that the interactions among the members across old group lines tends to generate liking and respect that eventually supersedes old group differences. Certainly some loyalty binds will be experienced and certainly the old group will never quite be the same. But the payoff in terms of greater productivity, mutual group enhancement and a wider perspective for all individuals can more than compensate for the loss of "the way it used to be."

Joint Group Meetings

Meetings of total groups with one another go even further than joint task forces to break down barriers. Obviously, a small task force can get more work done, but there are times when it is appropriate for all the members of two or more work groups to meet together in a face-to-face situation. If there has been a history of conflicts between the groups, for example, it is likely that each has built up stereotypes of the other. Since stereotypes tend to be maintained in the absence of real data and direct contact, the logical step is to bring the groups together in a setting that will facilitate interaction. Under such circumstances groups normally find it difficult to maintain the stereotypes and the related conflicts.

Remember the oil company situation described earlier? The regional people had developed very negative stereotypes of the headquarters people, and vice versa. Since they were several thousand miles apart and had never even met each other, with the exception of a few of the top level managers, it was inevitable that their differences and their stereotypes would become fixed.

The strategy that was employed as a first step to resolving the conflict was for each group to explicitly state its perceptions of the other and then to begin sharing these perceptions in a series of meetings designed to force a great deal of direct interaction. As you might guess, the stereotypes did not hold up for very long, the members of both groups began to perceive each other as individuals and to both like and respect one another. The joint meeting provided the necessary vehicle for the groups to recognize and accept their interdependence.

Since meetings of all the members were too expensive and time-consuming to hold very often, they created several joint task forces whose purpose it was to stay on top of problems and decisions affecting both groups. They also agreed to have certain individuals serve as liaison persons whose job it was to maintain a constant and rapid flow of information from the region to headquarters and back.

Whereas previously the managers were carrying the burden of all the problems and complaints and were, consequently, caught in the middle, the use of the above strategies for promoting inter-group cooperation ultimately removed a very dysfunctional load from the managers' backs.

Job Exchanges across Groups

It isn't very often that you find people from different departments exchanging jobs. You might even wonder how that makes sense. But it is difficult to appreciate another person's position until you've had a chance to walk in his/her shoes. Judgments about the behavior of other people are usually from outside the situation. If that situation happens to involve the other person's membership in another group, judgment can be colored by previous perceptions of that group. Also, it may be difficult to understand how it feels to be a member of that other group. By exchanging members chances are increased that members of both groups can appreciate the needs and operations of the other. It has the same kind of benefits as a cultural exchange.

In one large physical rehabilitation hospital the chief of occupational therapy exchanged jobs with the chief of physical therapy for two weeks. This action established a pattern for cooperation between the two departments that had never before existed. Members of the two departments increased their contacts and began to learn many skills from each other. Whereas the relationship between the two departments had been built upon rivalry, with each trying to demonstrate its greater value to the patients, the outcome of the job exchange was each group's recognition of its own and the other's unique but interrelated contribution to the welfare of the patient.

Physical Proximity

Perhaps all too obvious, but certainly not to be overlooked, is the importance of physical distance in the relations between groups. If two work groups are in different buildings the chances for interaction are minimal during the normal working hours. The best that can be hoped for is linkage people, joint task forces, occasional joint meetings, and the like. Given what we have already stated in regard to these strategies, we certainly do not underestimate their effect. But sometimes there is simply no substitute for frequent ongoing exchanges, both task related and of a social nature. None of the previous approaches allows much room for emergent social interactions among the members of the different groups. Each strategy is task related and normally has limited time boundaries. **To the extent that two working groups maintain a close physical proximity on a day-to-day basis, interactions are likely to develop that will enhance intergroup cooperation and minimize intergroup conflict.** Perhaps each of the other approaches is a poor approximation of this one, but necessary because of the great variety of organizational constraints that dictate physical separation (for example, job specialization, the technology of the work, and so forth). However, all too often managers overlook the obvious; the physical placement of people at work can have a major effect upon their performance. The physical proximity of working groups can be a significant factor in establishing their cooperation.

IMPLICATIONS FOR ORGANIZATIONAL CHANGE

As you will see in Chapter 13, groups can be important leverage points for bringing about change in an organization. The need for change is often related to the general issue of system interdependence and specifically to problems of intergroup cooperation. Any of the strategies for increasing cooperation represents a significant intervention into the system, whether utilized to resolve an existing conflict or as a means of minimizing the potential for future conflict. Even organizational change efforts that are not directly intended to affect the relationships among work groups more often than not do have some important impact on them. As you read through the chapter on organizational change it would be useful to keep in mind the basic propositions related to intergroup cooperation and see how they relate to the basic concepts and strategies for change.

KEY CONCEPTS FROM CHAPTER 12

1. The more differentiated the tasks necessary to accomplish the work, the more appropriate it is to create subsystems.

2. Variations in group identity:
   a. Time horizon.
   b. Background factors.
   c. Perspective on the task.
   d. Attitudes towards authority.

3. Intergroup coordination depends on:
   a. Awareness of own function in relation to others.
   b. Maintenance of communication links with others.
   c. Acceptance of legitimacy of the needs of others.
   d. Willingness to meet own needs within the framework of the total structure.

4. The degree of resistance to the above is related to resulting conflict with the group's basic norms, ideals, values.

5. Groups may have formal or informal status.

6. Groups may have legitimate or illegitimate power.

7. Cooperation and conflict may be either functional or dysfunctional to the total system.

8. Types of interdependence:
   a. Pooled.
   b. Serial.
   c. Reciprocal.

9. Problems with strong group identity:
   a. Seeing one's group as better than other(s).
   b. Seeing one's ideas as better than other(s).
   c. Over estimation of own competence.
   d. Over evaluation of one's leader(s).
   e. Avoidance of interaction with other group.
   f. Distortion of information about other group.
   g. Mistrust of the members of the other group.

10. The foundation of intergroup cooperation:
    a. Frequent interactions.
    b. Frequent and open information flow.
    c. Development and acceptance of common goals.
    d. Sharing a common source of threat.
    e. Shared common responsibility.
    f. Ability to establish joint memberships.
    g. Willingness to share and discuss perceptions of each other.

11. The norm of reciprocity maximizes interdependence.

12. Methods for maximizing intergroup cooperation:
    a. Overlapping or multiple group membership.
    b. Liaison people.
    c. Joint task forces.
    d. Joint group meetings.
    e. Job exchanges.
    f. Physical proximity.

SUGGESTED READINGS

Blake, Robert R., Shepard, H. A., and Mouton, Jane   *Managing Intergroup Conflict in Industry.* Houston, Texas: Gulf Publishing Co., 1964.

_____ and Jane S. Mouton   "Reactions to Intergroup Competition under Win-Lose Competition," *Management Science* (July 1961) 420–25.

_____   "Over-evaluation of Own Group's Product in Intergroup Competition," *Journal of Abnormal and Social Psychology* 64, (3) (1962) 237–38.

Boulding, K.   *Conflict Management in Organizations.* Ann Arbor: Foundation for Research on Human Behavior, 1961.

Coser, L. A.   *The Functions of Social Conflict.* New York: The Free Press, Division of Macmillan Company, 1956.

Gouldner, A.   "The Role of the Norm of Reciprocity in Social Stabilization," *Amer. Sociological Rev.* 25 (1960) 161–78.

Kelley, Joe   "Make Conflict Work For You," *HBR* (July–August 1970) 103–13.

Lawrence, P. R., and Lorsch, J. W.   *Organization and Environment—Managing Differentiation and Integration.* Cambridge, Mass.: Division of Research, Graduate School of Business Administration, Harvard University, 1967.

Lorsch, J. W., and Lawrence, P. R.   *Managing Group and Intergroup Relations.* Homewood, Ill., Richard D. Irwin, Inc. and The Dorsey Press, 1972, pp. 285–304.

Rice, A. K.   "Individual Group and Intergroup Behavior," *Human Relations* 22 (1969) 565–84.

Schelling, T. C.   *The Strategy of Conflict.* Oxford, England: Oxford University Press, 1960.

Scott, W. G.   *The Management of Conflict.* Homewood, Ill., Richard D. Irwin, Inc., 1965.

Thomas, J. M., and Bennis, W. G., eds.   *Management of Change and Conflict.* Baltimore, Md.: Penguin Books, 1972.

Thompson, James D.   *Organizations in Action.* New York: McGraw-Hill Book Co., 1967.

Walton, R. E.   "Third Party Roles in Interdepartmental Conflict," *Industrial Relations* 7 (1967) 24–43.

_____ and Dutton, J. M.   "The Management of Interdepartmental Conflict," *Adm. Science Quarterly* 14 (1969) 73–84.

*People usually decide to make a
change when things are not going
the way they would like.*

13

THE MANAGER AS THE INITIATOR OF CHANGE IN THE ORGANIZATION

THIS FINAL chapter in the book is intended to serve two purposes. First, it deals with the general topic of organizational change, discussing the issues related to identifying the need for change, various approaches to the issues, and specific methods and techniques designed to implement change in an organization. In addition, the chapter also provides an overview of the entire book by referring to the various perspectives and concepts presented in the previous chapters as they prove to be relevant to the issue of change.

HOW DO YOU KNOW WHEN CHANGE IS NEEDED?

People usually decide to make a change when things are not going the way they would like. If your car engine runs poorly, you may change the spark plugs; if you find yourself short of money before the next pay check, you may need to change your spending habits; if members of your family are constantly bickering, you may decide to change the patterns of interaction; and so forth. From the perspective of a manager, the need for change usually occurs when there is a problem related to *productivity, satisfaction,* and/or *development* in the system. It may be that the output of goods and services has fallen below expected levels, that an atmosphere of discouragement has emerged, that agency clients are protesting slow service, that

245

people in the system are not learning and developing needed skills and abilities, or some combination of these. Even when the need for change is identified, it is possible for a manager to close his/her eyes and hope that the pressure for it will blow away; but such a stance more often than not will result in the manager becoming the passive victim of the change rather than its planner and initiator. We assume that as future managers, you will want to be as much in control as possible over what goes on around you.

This chapter will provide concepts and tools to help you assume a more activist stance. Even for those who may never be faced with initiating a major organizational change, you still must deal with personnel coming and going, new forms of problems in daily work, unusual requests from outside a given work unit or from outside the system itself, and so forth. In that sense, an organization is like any living organism; it can decay or deteriorate over time without constant maintenance and rebuilding. Your ability (1) to anticipate the need for change, as opposed to reacting after the fact, (2) to diagnose the nature of the change that is required, rather than respond with the first thing that comes to mind, and (3) to make an intelligent choice of action steps, rather than find the fastest way to escape the problem, can be the ultimate basis of your success.

Unfortunately, it is exceedingly difficult to manage change so as to produce desired results. Most people, groups and organizations have remarkable resiliency, and like the child's bottom-weighted, rubber, punching clown, tend to return to the starting point as soon as the pressure is off. Furthermore, because of the interdependence of subsystems, a change in one place often pops up unexpectedly elsewhere, as shown in Chapter 2. It is not surprising that many people who have launched change projects give up in frustration and wonder why they did not "leave well enough alone."

As a member of an organization it is not easy to change something in a desired direction without (a) eventual reversion to the previous state, (b) consequences somewhere in the organization that you did not anticipate or (c) negative consequences cropping up which you did not intend.

Throughout the book, problems with change at different levels of the organization have been *implicit* in the analytical tools presented. For example, the social system conceptual scheme, indicating connections between consequences of the emergent system and alterations in the required system or background factors, points toward various focal points for change efforts.

We turn now to an *explicit* overview of the strategy for initiating change and for dealing with conflict. No single chapter, book or course can make you an expert on managing change. We will be looking at how changes, even those which are aimed at technical processes, often create positive or negative consequences for the people in the organization. Insofar as it takes people to perform the internal transformation processes of the organizations, their reactions to changes are of great interest to the manager. Further, we will offer some guidelines on changing behavior in ways that produce the least resistance and greatest chance of implementation and continuation. What we shall try to do is give you a sense of the various points at which a manager can intervene to accomplish his/her goals, the variety of tools available for making desired changes, some sense of what tools might be appropriate for solving various kinds of problems, and at what point in the organization they should be applied.

WHERE TO START

One way to think about starting points for change is implicit in the organization of this book, by the numbers of people involved. Change may be aimed at the individual, pair, small group, two or more groups, the total organization—or at leaders themselves. The target for change efforts will depend upon a number of factors.

1. Where is the tension in the system?
2. How interconnected is the unit (person, group, and so forth) having the problem with other organizational units?
3. To what extent does the organization operate as a hierarchy?
4. Where in the system is there the most readiness for change?

Let's examine each of these questions in some detail.

Where Is the Tension?

It is often easier to get people to change when they are experiencing a moderate amount of discomfort. Those who are content with the way things are will resist changes which might increase tension; those who are suffering a great deal sometimes cling to the status quo because it is the only certainty they can identify. In classroom task groups, for example, you may have noticed that those individuals who are satisfied with the grades they are receiving resist efforts to change the way the group makes decisions, allocates work, and so on. At the other extreme, perhaps surprisingly, members who are very upset with their performance also may resist change. They often seem to freeze in unproductive patterns, repeating the same fruitless behavior even though it does not help. A poor performer may continue to miss many classes or prepare poorly for discussions, even though it is clear from outside that a change in these areas would be helpful. Have you ever seen someone who is worried about failing a math course continue to avoid doing practice problems? Great tension can create as much resistance to change as lack of it does. Thus, it is not always the system with the greatest need or the greatest pain which is most receptive to change efforts. **In general, those who are experiencing moderate discomfort and tension are most amenable to change.** The tension can then serve as an impetus for change rather than as a signal for defensiveness.

How Interconnected Is the Problem Unit with Other Organizational Units?

Though ultimately all parts of an organization are interrelated, some units are relatively independent compared to others. For example, a research and development laboratory located miles away from the main offices and plant of a manufacturing company can probably change rules on dress and working hours more easily and with less repercussions, than could the assembly department at the plant. When an organizational unit is relatively independent because of location, power, structure, or task, changes are easier to implement. Thus **The greater the autonomy of an organizational subsystem, the more readily can changes be implemented, and the less will changes there cause problems for the rest of the organization.**

To What Extent Does the Organization Operate as a Hierarchy?

In strongly hierarchical organizations, where control tends to be tight and top-down, changes which do not have the support of those at the head of the organization are likely to be short lived. While the tension may be felt at lower levels of the organization, insofar as changes below will have effects on higher levels the support of those with the formal legitimate power must be acquired. It is disheartening and a waste of time to initiate change efforts that are squashed just as they begin to work, because higher-ups are made uncomfortable by them. **The more hierarchical the organization, the higher the change efforts have to be aimed, or legitimized. In turn, the greater the autonomy of the subunit, the less important will be support from higher levels in the organization.** We should note, however, that this does not imply that change in nonhierarchical organizations is necessarily *easier* to bring about; rather, it is meant to guide the focus of change efforts.

Where Is the Most Readiness and Receptivity to Change?

From one point of view, starting points are not so important, since a change in any one aspect of the organization is likely to affect other possible starting points anyhow. For example, if you are trying to get a non-cooperative individual to make a greater work contribution, and the difficulties are caused by his attitude towards the individually-oriented reward system and your controlling leadership style, you can begin trying to change his attitude, say, by having conferences with him trying to show him the consequences of his negative feelings. But as soon as he begins to respond, your leadership style will be affected and the reward system will somehow have to respond to his new behavior. Conversely, if you start by changing the reward system to more directly encourage his cooperation, his attitudes are likely to change accordingly, and you will be able to lead in a different, perhaps less controlling way.

Nevertheless, it is worth thinking through the questions of *leverage:* where would a change effort yield maximum payoff for the effort? As a manager it is useful to follow the principles of judo; rather than going against the resistance, go with it, so that a small amount of effort results in a proportionately large amount of movement.

Organizationally, this concept has two implications: **To initiate change, first try to determine where there is already inclination for movement in the desired direction, and then start with that aspect of the problem which is least likely to be directly resisted.** In the above example it may well be easier to start with changing the reward system in a way that encourages

FIGURE 13–1
A Way of Diagnosing Where to Attempt Change

	Functional	Dysfunctional
Easily subject to change	A. Support	C. Concentrate
Not easily subject to change	B. Protect	D. Box off

Source: From a lecture presented by Steven J. Ruma, June 1971, Bethel, Me.

A. Behavior which is functional to the system being examined, but easily subject to change, needs to be encouraged and supported.
B. Behavior which is functional and not subject to change can be relatively ignored, or protected from distorting influences.
C. Behavior which is dysfunctional but subject to change is where the biggest payoffs are and therefore where the greatest energy should be directed. (The reward system in the example we have been looking at may well be more subject to change, at least at first, than the attitude of the individual.)
D. Behavior which is dysfunctional but not easily subject to change probably needs to be adapted to, accepted and boxed off. Pouring energy into pushing on unmovable mountains is not the best way to spend time, unless you enjoy hernias or ulcers.

and pays off for cooperation, than to lecture at the individual who already feels angry.

In analyzing the point of greatest leverage, it can be helpful to look at the functionality or dysfunctionality to the system of the behavior in question, and the degree to which it is subject to change. The possible combinations are represented in Figure 13–1.

A corollary of the arguments presented in Figure 13–1 is that **Change should always be initiated with the minimum amount of pressure necessary to accomplish the objectives.** Since pressure usually breeds counter-pressure, its use in excess of what is mandatory just invites problems.

Managers attempting change sometimes forget that there are emergent *social* systems which will also be affected by even "pure" technological changes or other alterations in the required system. A new set of machines for producing a product with less manual labor may force new social groupings, violating existing friendships and relationships. This can create resistance aimed at the machinery or at the management, apparently irrationally, since physical "working conditions" are improved. Those involved may be "unappreciative" when what is troubling them is their discomfort at altered relationships. Often those affected do not even consciously realize the source of their resistance, or may feel embarrassed to state it directly.

On the other hand, change initiators who are sensitive to individual and group feelings often overlook possibilities to change the background or required system factors which are causing the problems. Such people-centered efforts can stimulate individuals and create great enthusiasm, but result in frustration when the basic problems remain.

> For example, a large corporation decided that it would have increasing problems if junior managers were not given more developmental training by their supervisors. The president of the company made an impassioned speech to all executives, explaining how important long term development of subordinates was to the company. Even those executives, however, who were very positive about training subordinates soon found out that their annual bonuses depended only on the quarterly profitability of their units. Since developing subordinates took considerable time away from activities that could directly affect profits, and had only long term payoffs, all such activities were soon given mere lip service. Not until the executive bonus system was revised to reward developmental activities along with profits did serious developmental activities begin.

> Similarly, in the 1950s, International Harvester developed an excellent Human Relations Training program for supervisors; by the end of the program supervisor attitudes were measurably different. When they got back on the jobs, however, many of their bosses ridiculed their learnings because the more considerate behavior taught in the program violated the organization's norms for leaders. Within six months not only had the new behavior

disappeared, but supervisors were less satisfied and effective than before the training.

This lesson has had to be relearned more times than many managers would care to remember: **To produce lasting changes, related subsystems must also be altered to support the initial changes.** Those subsystems which will be most affected by changes and/or have the most power over the changing subsystem require attention too.

BEGINNING THE CHANGE PROCESS

Perhaps the first factor to remember in beginning change efforts is that **Diagnosis should precede action.** Stated directly this point sounds obvious, but is nonetheless important. Because those in managerial positions are often harassed and results-oriented, they sometimes let impatience push them towards attempting solutions before the problem is clear. By now you have analyzed many problems where there were multiple, often hidden causes for dysfunctional behavior. In organizations, as in life, there is seldom one, simple, obvious cause for human problems. Some way of collecting data about the dimensions of the problem requiring change is inevitably necessary. Whether by interview, observation, questionnaire or analysis of records, data on the social system aspects of the problem should be gathered and analyzed before solutions are determined.

In general, **The most effective way to insure that change is implemented is to involve those affected by it in determining what it should be.** Even the collection of data is best done in collaboration with those who will be affected by the changes. If those affected are involved in diagnosis of the data and formulation of proposed solutions, successful implementation is more likely. Even the lowest level worker may have important contributions to make to solve an organizational problem of which he/she is a part; an elegant solution imposed from above which is not "owned" or accepted is not so elegant after all. The world's wastebaskets are filled with brilliant but unused recommendations.

There are many situations, however, where full participation is not possible or appropriate. If, for example, the problem is with employees who are incapable of improving their own performance, even after training, and they must inevitably be replaced, participation is probably not very appropriate even though it might be desirable from the employee's point of view. **When the necessary changes involve an opposing group(s) or individual(s) already committed to using illegitimate power to resist the changes, offers of involvement will probably be perceived as weakness and taken advantage of, or as a trick and resented.** As suggested in earlier chapters, **Participation and collaboration call for some basic level of trust in order to work; caution, distance, and legalistic negotiations are more**

appropriate when there is very low trust and/or high suspicion. Can you think of other situations where participation of those affected by the change would not be effective in achieving implementation?

Finally, one more related factor in beginning a change effort is that **Plans ought to be tentative and subject to alteration as feedback is received.** Working out every detail of a change in advance, then plowing ahead regardless of responses along the way, is a fairly good recipe for creating unnecessary resistance. Most people do not like to feel powerless, overwhelmed and ignored; if their legitimate objections and observations are belittled because they do not fit the master plan you have developed they are unlikely to help make the changes successful. Again, this sounds obvious, but people with a vision, as you will be when you want to change something, often treat every negative reaction as a nuisance rather than as helpful data necessary for achieving a *workable* plan.

THE ACTION-RESEARCH MODEL

The tentativeness and diagnostic activities called for above suggest that an action-research methodology is most appropriate for a planned change effort. Action-research begins with an identified problem. Data is then gathered in a way that allows a diagnosis which can produce a tentative solution, which is then implemented with the assumption that it is likely to cause new or unforseen problems, that will in turn need to be evaluated, defined, diagnosed, and so forth. Thus, action-research methods assume a constantly evolving interplay between solutions, results and new solutions. Figure 13–2 depicts the flow of steps in the model.

FIGURE 13–2
Action-Research Cycle

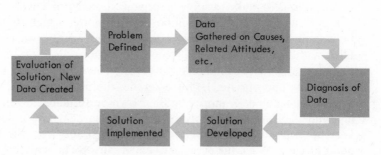

This model is a general one applicable to solving any kind of problem in an ongoing organization. It depends upon a sensible definition of the problem and the collection of relevant data, but to do that requires some preliminary way of thinking about diagnosis which can help sort out the root causes and interconnections among the complex factors likely to underlie any interesting problem. To help you organize the way you think about change problems we will show how the social system conceptual scheme used throughout the book can provide a useful diagnostic framework for organizational change. We have already noted that problems of productivity, satisfaction or development can occur in any one or more subsystems of the total system.

FIGURE 13–3
Change Problems Can Occur in Any Subsystem

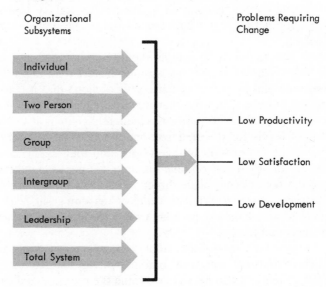

DIAGNOSTIC AIDS

Let's examine some procedures for tracing a problem back to its sources. Suppose, for example, a work group is having productivity problems because of insufficient resources. Efforts to improve its working *process* would probably be to no avail and, in fact, could complicate the problem even further. Suppose a manager is overloaded with work and cannot keep up with the pressure. It could easily be assumed that the wrong man has been chosen for the job when the problem is the way work is organized. You can probably think of many examples of how a misdiagnosis could lead to inappropriate and even destructive consequences. Remember, a symptom can have many possible causes; any physician will attest to the dangers of treating symptoms without knowing the underlying causes. It is the same thing for a manager who is attempting to make changes intended to eliminate a problem and/or to improve the system; treating the symptom without understanding the problem can easily "substitute a headache for an upset stomach."

The social system conceptual scheme provides a useful way of sorting causes of problems into manageable categories. Problems always surface in the emergent system (by definition), but their cause(s) may be in the background factors, required system *or* emergent system. For example, failure of a work group to solve its problems effectively may be due to a lack of proper technical training for the job (background factor), unclear task requirements (required system), or decision-making processes which ignore valuable member contributions (emergent system). One of the ways to approach a diagnosis of a change problem, then, is to sort the factors leading to it into the social system categories used throughout the book — background factors, required and emergent system.

In general, these categories should be examined sequentially for establishing a plan of attack. **Background factors tend to set limits on both the required and emergent systems.** It is obvious that it is useless to require people to behave in ways that are outside their range of competencies and then expect them to perform adequately. Nor is it sensible to establish output levels for the organization, or one of its subunits, which demand resources not present in the system, and then expect adequate performance. For any organizational function it is possible to list numerous background factors that place direct constraints upon both the required and emergent systems. What this line of reasoning suggests is that **The first point of attack on any problem calling for change is a consideration of the background factors.**

If you have established that there are appropriate and adequate resources and that these are combined in ways suited to the organizational tasks, *then* you can move to examine the required and emergent systems with some degree of confidence that therein lies the cause(s) of the problem.

Since emergent behavior is governed by complex factors normally outside the direct control of a manager, strategies aimed at various aspects of the emergent system tend to be complex, uncertain and time-consuming. Consequently, it makes sense to look next at the required system, at such matters as task definitions, work allocation, work patterns and routines, and who reports to whom. A manager is in a position to act directly upon these factors; **The required system tends to be the most directly and immediately within the control of management.**

Again we remind you of the possible importance of the involvement of those most directly affected by the change effort. Emergent systems can sabotage required systems; people who resent changes in their required work patterns can be very inventive about undermining the objectives of the change. Therefore, even though it is more direct and, perhaps, easier to change the required system do not overlook consequences in areas of the emergent system.

Furthermore, a direct action at one point in the organization tends to

FIGURE 13-4
Steps in Problem Diagnosis

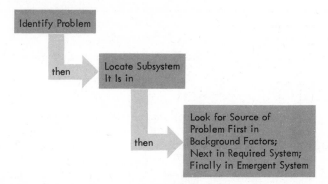

reverberate at other points. For example, it may seem simple enough to redefine an individual's job if the diagnosis calls for that; however, that redefinition might affect a task relationship, thus calling for a realignment of roles. Again, there seems to be no way to poke the system at point A without producing some reactions at points B and C.

If you, as a manager, can determine that you have the appropriate resources (background factors) and task definitions (required system), then you can more confidently look for the sources of a problem in the emergent system. It is similar to a physician ruling out several diagnoses before arriving at a final one. The importance of such a process of elimination is that strategies for change in the emergent system normally require in-depth data gathering and long-range procedures, and they often generate the greatest resistance. Thus interventions on the emergent system ought to be undertaken with caution, when other options are not appropriate.

While it is impossible to offer definitive diagnoses of the causes of emergent human problems out of their unique contexts, we have prepared Fig. 13-5 with illustrative examples of causes of problems which are often associated with the various size subsystems. It shows some possible causes of problems within each subsystem, with variations for whether the cause is in the background factors, emergent or required system. The examples of causes are meant to indicate possible diagnoses, not instant answers. More important is the process of examining the underlying issues in a systematic way. Here is an example of how the chart might be used.

> A student group is having difficulty in producing high quality case analyses despite seemingly endless hours of effort. Clearly, some change is needed. Looking across those cells in Figure 13-5 in the row corresponding to the "group" subsystem, you can see that several possibilities exist: (1) the group may simply lack the intellectual resources to do the work (background factors); (2) the task requirements may not have been adequately

FIGURE 13–5
Possible Underlying Causes of Organizational Problems Requiring Change

(1) When the
Locus of the
Problem Is: and (2) The Source of the Problem Is in the:

	Background Factors	Required System	Emergent System
		then (3) The Causes Might Be:	
Individual	Poor match of individual with job; selection or promotion problem.	Task too easy or too difficult; poor job definition.	Job fails to fulfill range of needs; little chance for learning.
Two Person	Personality clash; conflict in basic styles, values, and so forth.	Poor role differentiation and/or integration in job description.	Misunderstandings, failure to deal with differences in preferences; unresolved feelings.
Group	Insufficient resources; poor group composition for cohesion; bad physical setup.	Task requirements poorly defined; role relationships unclear or inappropriate.	Poor working process in one or more of the 11 areas related to effectiveness.
Intergroup	Status and power conflicts of two professions; physical distance.	Conflict on task perspective; required interaction contrary to background factors.	Conflicting group styles; dysfunctional competition.
Leadership	Poor selection and promotion decisions. Poor training and preparation.	Overload of responsibility; inappropriate reporting procedures.	Individual not liked and/or respected; in conflict with other sources of power.
Total System	Geographic setting; limited labor market; physical conditions.	System goals inappropriate or poorly defined; inappropriate output levels.	General climate of malaise, suspicion, anxiety, pressure, and so forth.

explained to the members (required system); or (3) the group may have failed to develop the kinds of working processes that result in good analysis (emergent system). Obviously, all three of these factors may be operating, and each demands a different kind of remedy.

This rough guide to diagnosing the causes of organizational problems can help you focus on where action is needed. How to overcome each difficulty is not always obvious even once it is identified. We turn now to a brief survey of widely used change methods, as a way of suggesting the range of approaches which have been developed in the constant struggle by managers to maintain effective organizations.

METHODS OF ORGANIZATIONAL CHANGE

Since there is an endless variety of change methods available to managers and organizational experts, we can only discuss a limited number in this chapter. What we have chosen to do is to provide you with examples of strategies aimed at the background, required and emergent systems, and at the various size groupings (individual, two person, and so forth). Thus, we have organized the remainder of the chapter into three main sections: (a) change methods related to background factors, (b) those that focus upon the required system and (c) those which address the emergent system most directly. Within each section we offer examples of methods that focus on each size subsystem. Also, to facilitate the presentation and organization of the material in each section, we provide a chart which serves as a map for our discussion.

Methods for Changing Background Factors

Figure 13–6 shows five general methods of change that deal directly with background factors; the focal point of each method is also identified.

FIGURE 13–6
Methods of Changing Background Factors

Method of Change	Focal Point
1. Personnel changes	Individual
	Two person relationship
	Group
	Leadership
2. Training and education	Individual
	Leadership
3. Technology and layout	Any level
4. Incentive plans	Individual
	Group
5. Background culture	Total system

The focal point is not to be confused with the parts of the system that might be affected by the change; it simply refers to the place where the direct action is taken. The overall effects of any change action can spread to many subsystems of the organization.

Personnel Changes   One of the crucial background factors in any work situation is the personal histories and resultant attitudes of the individuals concerned. Some change strategies are aimed at having an impact on what individuals bring to the situation and on which individuals are in the situation. The most direct way of affecting that is to replace individuals whose backgrounds cause difficulties with those who have appropriate skills, attitudes and experiences.

Though this method has been used at least since Adam and Eve were removed for failing to follow direct orders, it is not uncomplicated in practice. Firing or displacing people can cause difficulties in a variety of ways. The insecurity level of others may be raised, leading to greater defensiveness or decreased morale (though in some cases possibly to improved performance); unions may form or react negatively; legal problems may develop; work may be fouled up until a suitable replacement is found, brought in and prepared, and so forth. Furthermore, there is no automatic guarantee that the replacement will be more suitable than the predecessor. Nevertheless, at times, the wrong person(s) is in a job that is otherwise well designed, and only replacement will solve the problem. If that is so, then the original selection procedures may need examination and attention, to reduce the likelihood of the same problem arising again.

In some instances, the problem may be related more to a poor *combination* of people in a two person relationship, in a group or in a superior–subordinate relationship. The individuals involved may be perfectly competent for their work, but when put together they produce dysfunctional behavior. Obviously, one option is to fire one or more individuals, but a more functional option, in terms of organizational resources, is to re-combine the people into more compatible groupings or pairs. The diagnosis of "personality clash" fits this example; there can be basic values or style differences which are not likely to be resolved.

Another approach that many organizations have used is a system of executive assessment (often using elaborate psychological tests) to identify leadership potential. It is not uncommon to find key decisions about promotion based upon these techniques. While their validity has been called into question by many organizational experts, these approaches have met with enough success to warrant their continued, and apparently increased, utilization.

Training and Education   Other ways have been developed to change individual perceptions, attitudes or skills. A great deal of what goes on in organizational training programs is aimed at the individual, with the assumption that improved knowledge or attitudes will get translated into organizational payoff. Programs designed specifically to change individual behavior and interpersonal skills have been widely offered within organizations and by outside consultants, universities and training firms. For example, training in achievement motivation has been developed by Harvard psychologist David McClelland. His research indicated high correlation of need for achievement with entrepreneurship, so he and his associates developed a training program which they claim can alter individual motivation.

Many organizations pay particular attention to the training and development of their managers. They institute leadership training programs that focus upon the learning of managerial skills considered vital to effective leadership. Some of these programs operate on a year-round basis in the form of in-service education and many occur in the form of intensive workshops designed to focus upon specific skills and methods. When successful, such programs can have a significant effect upon the competence that a manager brings to his or her job, with obvious implications for the emergent behavior of people under that manager.

Another kind of behavioral training, aimed at improving a person's interpersonal competence, is called sensitivity training or T- (for training) groups. In an unstructured group setting, participants learn about the basic dynamics of how groups work, receive feedback on their own behavior in the group and its impact on others, and have the opportunity to practice new behaviors in a controlled situation. Many variations of the original T-group have developed. Some have focused more on what goes on within each individual member so that self-concept and the personal system are clarified or altered. Others have concentrated on group process phenomena, attempting to improve the ability of individuals to understand, predict, evaluate and change the way groups work. Still others have worked on particular aspects of behavior, like the use of power and influence, leadership skills, listening ability, and giving and receiving feedback.

Insofar as these kinds of training utilize experience based methods, they often have strong emotional effects on the participants. But these individually-oriented techniques suffer from some of the same difficulties of traditional training programs. First, even when measurable changes occur during training, they often fade out back on the job if not supported there. Second, new knowledge which for any reason cannot be utilized can be very frustrating, leading to anger, decreased morale or even departure from the organization for hopefully greener pastures. Third, those who receive such intense training experiences and like it, often become impatient with nonparticipants who do not sympathize with or cannot understand the participant's enthusiasm. Some rivalry can result between the "elite" few who are in the know and the "unenlightened masses." Thus, an individual may bring to the work situation some new behaviors that are functional for a situation *outside* the work setting but dysfunctional to others on the job.

Technology and Work Layout   Another background factor which can be changed to affect behavior is technology and/or work layout. Though all too often changes in technology ignore the consequences for social interaction, some sophisticated change efforts have consciously altered the existing technology to result in more satisfactory relationships and productivity. For example, both Saab and Volvo have experimented with the assembly line, reducing the monotony, isolation and repetitiveness to work, in an effort to allow group pride and interaction around whole tasks. These experiments are extremely expensive, involving huge capital expenditures, but have been undertaken because of labor force shortages and difficulties which hampered production.

Another series of experiments emanated from researchers at the Tavistock Institute in London. The method and organization of mining coal was changed to allow miners a more satisfying pattern of interaction and work, again allowing workers to gain the satisfaction of completing a whole task. Similar changes were made in weaving sheds in India. These large-scale changes in technology were made with explicit social system results in mind, and have been quite successful.

A technological or work layout change need not be so elaborate in order to have substantial impacts on emergent behavior. Waitresses and cooks who were always fighting about unclear orders, differing priorities and mistakes, began to get along much better when a rotating spindle on which written orders could be clipped was introduced.[1] Thus a problem which seemed to be wholly within the individuals involved was solved by a mechanical device, which altered interaction patterns in a way that fit existing attitudes and allowed differences to be easily checked and settled. Another simple change action can be the physical relocation of interdependent work groups to facilitate information flow, a method discussed in the previous chapter.

Technological changes can be very potent in yielding positive results, but are often expensive, demand extensive revisions in the required system and lead to unpredictable emergent behavior. As many organizations have discovered with dismay, a change which looks simple and could be helpful, may produce an unanticipated series of negative reactions in many related subsystems. Few companies, for example, have easily made the transition from a manual accounting system to a computerized one, even though great benefits were anticipated. The people who had to make the new equipment work often reacted with less than enthusiasm.

---

[1] Elias H. Porter, "The Parable of the Spindle," *Harvard Business Review,* vol. 40, no. 3 (May–June 1962).

The wise manager tries carefully to predict likely consequences of any change in technology or layout before beginning!

Incentive Plans   An organization's reward system is a background factor which can have a great impact on behavior when altered, but requires considerable thought first. People in organizations tend to do what will be rewarded (in the currency they value, which usually includes, but is not limited to pay) and tend not to bother doing what goes unrewarded, even though it may be appropriate to the organization's goals. Therefore dramatic changes in behavior can often be accomplished through this indirect mechanism. It is not always easy, however, to be certain just what factors organizational members will consider to be rewarding, so that what particular changes to make may not be obvious. Numerous incentive schemes have faltered because they either did not fully anticipate the behaviors which would result from how productivity was calculated and rewarded, or take into account the social patterns existing and their value to organizational members.

An individual incentive plan which fosters competition among cohesive group members may well be sabotaged by resentful members. In our classes, for example, if we force students to rate each other's contributions to group products, and insist that all members not be given the same grade, many groups devise ways of "beating the system," for example by rotating grades among members, using the minimum grade spread allowed, giving only one member a different grade on each project, and so forth. When the groups feel cohesive, an accurate grade reward for effort is worth less to them than the preservation of harmony.

Furthermore, change in the reward system for any one subsystem will inevitably have consequences for those in other subsystems. Therefore, even when localized changes produce desired results, the organizational ramifications may create difficulties. If one group, for example, responds to a new pay incentive system by increasing production considerably, thereby earning pay perceived by others as "too high," the original change may end up getting scuttled despite its effectiveness.

Furthermore, only a few executives are likely to have sufficient power to avoid difficulty among subgroups by changing the reward system for the entire organization. When that power is available, it can lead to desired behavioral changes without any direct, personal change efforts and the resultant resistances.

Background Culture   The final background factor we will discuss is the culture of the organization, that is, the customary way of doing things, attitudes and values that are "in the air," affecting everyone. Though ultimately any lasting system-wide behavioral change must affect the organization's culture, the overall culture is the most resistant aspect of any social system. The organization's attitudes about authority and how it should be used, interpersonal style, conflict, and so forth, will condition and affect all other changes – even what is seen as possible to change – and therefore require special attention. The approach to changing the organization's culture, however, may have to begin with changes in areas that are more directly manageable. But any change effort will benefit from being considered in terms of its effects on the overall culture of the organization, and planned to either fit that total picture or change crucial aspects of it.

Roger Harrison, for example, in his work in Europe, found that change efforts based on open expression of feelings were often resisted by executives from companies with cultures that strongly discourage such "emotionality." He developed new methods for altering behavior in conflict situations utilizing negotiations about role obligations. These methods were more compatible with the organizational backgrounds from which the executives came.[2]

If however, openness about feelings would have been functional for the organization, his methods would have had little impact on changing the culture which forbids that type of communication. Some other way of affecting the culture, rather than adapting to it, would be necessary – perhaps beginning with an intense group experience for the top executives which might directly question existing beliefs and attitudes. But as noted, direct attempts to change attitudes often increase resistance.

Ultimately, changing an organization's culture may require efforts along several fronts, utilizing a variety of approaches and supported from the top of the hierarchy. Since such efforts are expensive, require deep commitment from top executives who may not be fully comfortable with what behavior is required of them in a changed culture, and take several years to filter through the organization, you can see why such changes are difficult and rare.

Of course, one factor that determines the culture of any organization is its location or setting. A manufacturing plant located in South America may produce the same products as a similar plant in the United States, but the behavior of people in the respective settings will be very different because of obvious differences in the cultures of the two geographic areas. Even regional differences within the United States often determine differences in the culture of the same kinds of organizations in the different locations. For example, the rapid impersonal pace of a big city environment tends to carry over into any system located there. Move that system to a rural area where the pace is slower and the prevailing attitudes of people are different, and some very obvious differences within the organization itself may be observed.

---

[2] Roger Harrison, "When Power Conflicts Trigger Team Spirit," *European Business*, Spring 1972.

Methods for Changing the Required System

Figure 13–7 summarizes the different approaches we will discuss.

FIGURE 13–7
Methods of Changing the Required System

Method of Change	*Focal Point*
1. Revision of job descriptions	Individual
and work relationships	Interpersonal
Reporting relationships	Intergroup
Task role assignments	Leadership
Managerial responsibility	Group
2. Job modification	Individual
Job narrowing	Two person relation
Job enlargement	Group
Job enrichment	
3. Reformulation of	Total system
work objectives	

Revision of Job Description and Work Relationships   Job descriptions and organizational work relationships are two important determinants of behavior and interactions, and often a starting place for change efforts. Examining a job description to see if responsibilities are clear, boundaries sufficiently well defined, organizational authority adequate, job activities which need interaction or coordination with others spelled out, and then making appropriate changes, can result in markedly different behavior. A person who is not sure of what to do may perform so badly that he/she appears to be totally incompetent. With responsibilities clarified the same person may be able to do excellent work. Similarly, an alteration in who a person or group takes orders from can make a substantial difference in job performance. Changing the organizational level at which decisions are made, whether closer to the actual problem or closer to the top of the organization, can also have a significant impact on behavior.

These techniques of job analysis, centralization or decentralization of decision-making, and similar restructuring have great appeal to change experts because they appear to be rational and logical; there is no doubt that such structural changes can positively affect performance. But blueprints do not a bluebird make; human beings are remarkably inventive at getting around formal directions and plans. Organization charts and job descriptions, even when clear and relatively sophisticated, cannot take all contingencies and relationships into account. A certain amount of good will is necessary to effectively implement any structure. And conversely, even a sloppy, illogical structure can be made to work if those involved want it to. The attitudes people bring to the situation affect their response to any formal structure. Nevertheless, insofar as the structure determines interactions, and these in turn lead to positive feelings, and so forth, structural changes can affect attitudes as well as be affected by them. When lack of clarity or poor utilization of resources within the organization is at the heart of a behavioral problem, the methods described above can be extremely useful.

Job Modification   Job requirements can also be the focus for change when the required activities, interactions and attitudes are too difficult or too simple for the people in the system. Work that asks more of people than they are capable of giving may need to be broken into less complex or less demanding activities, so that others can do part of what is needed, or rules and procedures may need to be established in order to simplify decision-making.

> In recent years, for example, a number of ways have been developed to make physicians' jobs less demanding, so that they can best utilize their expertise. The physician's assistant and nurse practitioner are new roles carved out of the total job of diagnosing and treating patients, to free the doctor from the more routine but time consuming aspects of the job. The physician's assistant may be trained to treat certain common, non-serious problems, like colds, coughs, and so forth, and to recognize more serious conditions which must be seen by the doctor.

In the same way, assembly lines and other routinized forms of doing work can be used to make a job simple enough for a relatively unskilled person to do. Carried to the extreme, some jobs can be broken down into such simple, repetitive activities that machines can perform equally well. When trained manpower is scarce or very expensive, and unemployment high so that few alternatives exist for employees, such methods can be effective.

On the other hand, overly mechanical simple work can lead to boredom, lack of commitment, alienation or sabotage, and the most elaborate change efforts have been geared to countering these effects. As mentioned in Chapter 7, a variety of ways have been invented to try to make work more interesting, in the hopes of gaining improved performance and satisfaction. Job rotation, enlargement and enrichment are all ways of making work more challenging. While the technology may remain the same, work is divided differently to provide more variety, challenge, and satisfaction, which, hopefully, leads to greater productivity.

Reformulation of Objectives   Every individual and combination of people in an organization work toward certain objectives. Those objectives in turn fit into the broader framework of the total organization's objectives. Often the specific objectives at one level of the system may be out of phase or incongruent with those at another level and/or with those of the total system. This kind of problem calls for a reformulation of organizational objectives at one or another level in order to re-establish the necessary congruence for system interdependence. The focal point of such an approach may begin at any level, but it must also touch directly upon all others.

A specific approach called "management by objectives" has been developed in recent years. Its broad philosophy states, in essence, that worker and manager performance can best be evaluated in terms of their degree of success in meeting specifically defined organizational objectives. These objectives (a) pertain directly to and may be defined by each individual in the system, (b) demand coordination at a group and intergroup level, and, (c) must be reflective of the overall organizational goals. When utilized effectively, management by objectives can be an important vehicle for encouraging individuals to take responsibility for their own performance and provides them with the measuring sticks to do that.

The method requires each employee to set objectives for some time period and then negotiate agreement on these with the employee's supervisor. Performance is then judged by how close to the objectives the individual comes within that time period, rather than on more intangible personal characteristics or global judgments about the person's worth. The process of defining and agreeing upon objectives represents an attempt both to plan effectively and to generate commitment on the part of the employee to reach the goals.

The principle of management by objectives is sensible and almost inevitably practiced in some form or other, even if not formally adopted; however, its practice can be difficult or abused. If performance is to be judged by agreed-upon objectives, then the objectives stated must somehow be measurable; this can eliminate some important but not easily defined variables. *The more specific are the objectives, the more easily is performance measured, but the more likely it is that subtle factors will be ignored.* Furthermore, many managers use management by objectives without first securing the initiative and agreement of both those who are judging and those who are to be judged by the objectives. If the subordinates are not really committed to the objectives on which they will be judged, their performance is not likely to be as effective as it might otherwise be.

Methods for Changing the Emergent System

In one sense, all change is ultimately aimed at the emergent system. It is in emergent behavior that problems present themselves and require attention. However, some change strategies begin by directly attacking emergent behavior, even if ultimate solutions demand attention to background factors and/or the required system. Figure 13–8 refers to several different approaches to change in emergent factors.

FIGURE 13–8
Methods of Changing Emergent Factors

Method of Change	Focal Point
1. Counseling	Individual leadership
2. Third party consultation	Two person relation
3. Task group training, team building	Group
4. Intergroup confrontation	Intergroup relation
5. Survey feedback	Total system
6. Executive planning and confrontation sessions	Total system

Counseling　　Many organizations provide individual help to employees who may be experiencing difficulties in handling work demands or who may be generally unhappy in their work. Often the physical and/or psychological pressures of a given type of work can prove to be highly stressful; counseling is one way to help an individual learn ways of handling tensions and, whenever possible, of minimizing their adverse consequences. When a problem is more directly related to interpersonal or social factors, the counseling is likely to focus upon the individual's behavior, self-concept and general attitude. Presumably, the use of counseling as a method of organizational change pertains to emergent behavior, that is, problems that the work situation brought out in the individual. While some organizations may offer help for problems that employees *bring* to the situation (for example, personality problems, alcoholism, marital difficulties, and so on), most places advise such individuals to seek help from outside resources.

In a more positive way, individual counseling as a vehicle for leadership development can be a potent source of change. Many executives rely heavily upon the support and guidance of a trusted colleague, specialist or consultant. Through such a process the individual manager can become more aware of his/her own goals, develop increased managerial competence, and learn how to maintain an integration of his/her personal beliefs and values with the goals of the organization.

Third Party Consultation　　An extension of the counseling process occurs when two people encounter difficulties in working together and seek the help of a third party to resolve the issue(s). It is a technique that has been in existence for a very long time; examples include friends helping friends, marriage counseling, clergy offering advice to prospective marriage partners, and so forth. (Of course, when the help is not requested it might be called third-party interference.) In a work setting the helper might be a peer, a supervisor or some other objective person. The choice of third party consultant should be dictated by the demands of the situation and the mutual preferences of the two people needing the help.

Even when there is not a problem as such, there is usually room for improvement in any working relationship. In this regard, a manager always has the option, possibly even the obligation, and hopefully the skills to help his/her subordinates to improve their productivity, satisfaction and development by improving their work relationships. Such a proactive stance is more likely to facilitate a healthy work environment than would the more passive attitude of waiting until a problem occurs before taking action.

Task-Group Training: Process Consultation and Team Building Out of the experiences of T-groups (mentioned earlier) have developed several variations of task-group training or team building. In most of these methods, people who work together on a day-to-day basis are taught directly to work together more effectively. A team-building effort might examine the ways in which the group members collaborate or compete, the way they make decisions, the way they set agenda items, the amount of openness with which members relate to one another, and so forth. The person introducing change might observe regular meetings and make observations about the group's process, or might take the group away for a working retreat where processes are directly examined.

The most sophisticated versions of team building, however, do not assume that all the problems arise from the group's emergent behavior, but may be traced back to background factors, such as the company's culture and reward system, or to the required system and the way in which it determines influence and interactions. The advantage of team-building efforts is that once changes are accepted by the group, group members themselves can reinforce the new patterns of behavior and individuals are not left isolated as they might be after T-group or other such forms of training. A team that has developed sufficient levels of trust will be able to work on whatever problems arise in a self-correcting way that allows for changes in structure or technology as well as changes in member behavior.

Even a successful team-building effort, however, can still create problems for members of adjoining subsystems or with those higher in the organizational hierarchy. The team which works well together may ignore outside interests and demands or see as inferior other groups which do not seem to be working so well. This can cause resentment or jealousy, creating problems in other parts of the system.

Intergroup Confrontation As you might expect, methods have also been developed for dealing with problems between groups. In Chapter 12 you were introduced to some of the kinds of issues that lead to conflict between groups; re-emphasized here are those methods which work on finding ways to resolve conflicts between groups. Several mechanisms for structurally interweaving group members have been invented to allow diffusion of group boundaries, thereby lowering rivalry and commitment to each group's own preferred way of doing things. Direct exchanges of members, a new linking group made up of some members from each of the original groups, whether individually elected or selected by all groups together, and the utilization of independent judges or arbitrators, are all ways of resolving difficulties between groups. As you will have seen during the intergroup section of the course, the inherent problem with these kinds of solutions is that those who form a new, supposedly independent, group are likely to maintain allegiance to their own group, and, therefore have difficulties dealing with each other. Alternatively, they may link together into an independent system which then has trouble getting support from the individual groups. A more direct way of trying to deal with feelings among group members has its roots in the T-group but is more structured and controlled. In the *intergroup confrontation laboratory* groups exchange their collective opinion about how they see themselves and how they think the other group sees them, and then work on the accuracy and stereotyping contained therein. Though risky and highly charged, this method can break through mutual hostilities, particularly when there are not fundamental value differences between the groups but only inaccurate perceptions.

When direct confrontational methods work, whether between individuals or groups, it is because increased and more accurate communication is an appropriate solution to a problem involving some form of misperceptions. At other times, however, increased accuracy of communication can lead to further distancing among the involved parties, especially when it becomes clear that there are fundamental value differences which cannot be negotiated away. **In general, the more the problems among subsystems are based on value differences, the more appropriate are methods which involve arms-length, formal and legalistic negotiations rather than greater openness and trust.** When differing subsystems have high suspicions of each other and little trust, the most that can be hoped for is some kind of agreement to demarcate territories, live and let live within those boundaries and then formulate specific rigid and observable contracts on a point-by-point basis as needed. It is naive to try to shortcut this process by methods which encourage openness, honesty and vulnerability. Similarly, when problems can be resolved by better understanding and clarity, it is "paranoid" to be willing to only deal in legalistic and distinct contractual terms.

The methodology for dealing with any two subsystems in conflict is worth spelling out in some detail: (1) the first phase of conflict resolution calls for a thorough understanding of each party's position. This can only be done if differences are brought out and made explicit, even at the risk of polarization, rather than minimized and papered over. The more clearly and dramatically differences are stated, the greater are the chances that individual members of each subsystem will begin to raise questions about the strength and unambiguity of their group's positions. Furthermore, unless subsystem members feel that they have had a chance to state their position clearly and be understood by conflicting subsystems, they will find it hard to acknowledge the possibility of not being 100 percent right. (2) Once differences are looked at in bold relief, then the opposing subsystems can begin to point out perceived inaccuracies in other group perceptions. As noted earlier, where differences are great and value-based, tough bargaining leading to contractual relationships is appropriate. It is vital to have a contract for each side to do specific activities under particular conditions, composed in a way that allows each to observe whether or not the terms of the contract are being honored. If, however, the differences are not fundamental and based on values, a more direct and trusting collaboration can be developed. Any attempt to minimize a genuine set of differences may lead very rapidly towards each side believing that the other is behaving suspiciously, and then the conflicts are quickly renewed.

Survey Feedback   There's a paradox in all change efforts. On the one hand, those aimed at changing subsystems suffer from the problems mentioned many times by now, namely unintended consequences for other subsystems in the organization. On the other hand, efforts aimed at changing the *total* organization, particularly when it is a fairly large and complex one, often are so general and impersonal that they have very little impact on day-to-day behavior within a given subsystem. Ideally, then, the total change effort has to somehow deal with that paradox. A method is needed which first collects data about total system problems at a given time, allows diagnosis by those at the head of the organization as to priorities in solving the problems, and then tackles problems in order of importance. One useful way of approaching such total system change is the survey-feedback method developed at the University of Michigan. A lengthy questionnaire on employee attitudes and perceptions of the organization is administered, tabulated, and the anonymous (with respect to individuals) results fed back by departments. When followed up with specific action plans in each department, utilizing some of the methods described earlier, this can be an effective way to begin a total system change effort.

Executive Planning and Confrontation Sessions   Another method, pioneered by Richard Beckhard,[3] is called the confrontation meeting. A

---

[3] R. Beckhard, "The Confrontation Meeting," *Harvard Business Review,* vol. 45 (1967), pp. 149–55.

large cross section of organizational executives are brought together for a concentrated period of time, such as one day, assigned to small work groups and asked to develop lists of organizational problems needing solution. When the groups have reported their lists, priorities are set for working on problems, various groups are given the responsibility to work on them and deadlines are set for producing proposed solutions. Again, considerable follow-up is needed, utilizing some of the methods described earlier, such as team building, process consultation or individual counseling, but this kind of "shock-treatment" can be an excellent catalyst for generating energy to produce change. These methods, and other comparable ones, all follow the general action–research cycle described earlier on a somewhat more grand scale.

The underlying assumption of such change attempts is that the collection of data around problems, or even the generation of lists of problems, acts as a disconfirming and unfreezing process which creates sufficient tension to motivate commitment towards change. However, if our earlier proposition about the greatest change following moderate amounts of tension is valid, then in some organizations, methods which produce less tension may be called for. For example, methods which utilize "vision building," in which organizational members imagine and spell out what the organization might be like at some future period, and then work back from there to develop plans on how to get to where they think it might best be, can be used when data about current problems might prove so overwhelmingly threatening that it would paralyze action. It can also be used when there is insufficient tension in the present circumstances to arouse the desire to make needed long-term changes.

Another variation of this type of method is called *open system planning*. It involves top executives in thinking through the organization's relationships with its various environments and then developing a plan to maximize the effectiveness of each subsystem's transactions with its dominant environment(s).[4]

All such total organization methods run the danger of mobilizing considerable enthusiasm for change all at once, and then creating frustration when the actual results take a long time, which inevitably they do. Aroused expectations which are unmet may be considerably more dysfunctional than never raising expectations in the first place. Whether or not one is willing to take that risk is very much a matter of personal desires. Nevertheless, if organizations are to remain adaptive, they must find ways of gaining commitment to whatever changes are necessary to keep the organization working toward its goals.

---

[4] C. Krone, "Open Systems Planning: Redesign." *Human Systems Development Study Center Working Paper #74–6*. University of California Graduate School of Management, 1972.

AN OVERVIEW ON ORGANIZATIONAL CHANGE

We suspect that it might be a difficult task for you to develop an overall perspective on organizational change. The problems are many and complex, the procedures for diagnosis are loaded with uncertainties and pitfalls, and the methods of change are too complicated and varied to organize into a handy package. We hope that by our using the social systems conceptual scheme as a framework for the chapter, we helped you to appreciate the importance of asking many questions before arriving at a diagnosis of a problem and before selecting a change method that will be *appropriate* to the situation.

All too often, when change is needed, the presence of tension or anxiety makes it difficult to go through a systematic, careful series of diagnostic steps. It seems easier, perhaps even desirable to grab the first "treatment" that comes along. That is why in the history of organizational change there have been many sales pitches for one or another "elixir." Got a problem? Use Dr. Fixit's All-Purpose Employee Productivity Kit. While this may sound exaggerated, it is more the rule than the exception to find advocates of particularized methods touting claims of success no matter what the change problem. We caution you, as prospective managers, to maintain some degree of scientific skepticism; this is what can make the difference between an ordinary manager and a manager scientist.

Ultimately, however, no matter how astute you are as an observer of organizational culture, norms, and behavior, or how shrewd at assessing organizational change techniques, you will be making choices which reflect your own values, your best assessment of what consequences you are willing to live with. We wish you valid predictions, good judgment, and informed choices in your managerial career.

KEY CONCEPTS FROM CHAPTER 13

1. Need for change when problems occur with respect to production, satisfaction and/or development.
2. A manager can be the passive victim of change or its initiator and planner.
3. Target for change depends on following factors:
   a. Identification of the tension in the system.
   b. Identification of the interconnection of the problem person or groups with other units.
   c. Identification of the operating hierarchy.
   d. Identification of place or point with most readiness for change.

4. Those experiencing moderate discomfort and tension make system most amenable to change.

5. The more hierarchical the organization, the higher the change effort will have to be aimed.

6. The more autonomy in the subunit, the less important will be support from higher levels.

7. The more autonomy in the subunit, the easier to implement change.

8. Change should involve minimum amounts of force:
    a. Force breeds counter force, excess use invites problems.
    b. Diagnosis should precede action.
        (1) Is the behavior functional or dysfunctional?
        (2) Is it easily or not easily subject to change?
    c. For lasting change, subsystems must also be altered.
    d. Ownership through participation in diagnosis and action will help commitment and implementation of change.
    e. Flexibility through tentativeness permits feedback.

9. Action-research cycle:
    a. Constantly evolving interplay between solutions, results and new solutions.
    b. Problem defined leads to
    c. Data gathered on causes, related attitudes, etc., leads to
    d. Diagnosis of data leads to
    e. Solution developed leads to
    f. Solution implementation leads to
    g. Evaluation of solution; new data created leads to
    h. Redefinition of the problem(s).

10. Identification of problem:
    a. Locate subsystem it is in.
        (1) Look for source of problem.
            (a) First in background factors.
            (b) Next in required system.
            (c) Finally in emergent system.

11. Methods of changing background factors:
    a. Personnel change.
    b. Training and education.
    c. Technology and layout.
    d. Incentive plans.
    e. Background culture.

12. Methods of changing the required system:
    a. Revision of job descriptions and work relationships.
    b. Job modification.
    c. Reformulation of objectives.

13. Methods of changing the emergent system:
    a. Counseling.
    b. Third party consultation.
    c. Task group training: team building.
    d. Intergroup confrontation: Dealing with two subsystems in conflict through understanding of each other's position; pointing out of perceived inaccuracies in other group's position.
    e. Survey feedback.
    f. Executive planning and confrontation sessions.

SUGGESTED READINGS

Ammer, Dean S. "What Businessmen Expect From The 1970's," *HBR* (January–February 1971) 41–52.

Ansoff, H. Igor, and Brandenburg, R. G. "The General Manager of the Future," *California Management Review* (Spring 1969) 61–72.

Argyris, C. *Intervention Theory and Method.* Reading, Mass.: Addison-Wesley Publishing Co., Inc., 1970.

_____ *Management and Organizational Development.* New York: McGraw-Hill Book Co., 1971.

Beckhard, Richard *Organization Development: Strategies and Models.* Reading, Mass.: Addison-Wesley Publishing Co., Inc., 1969.

Benne, K. D. "Changes in Institutions and the Role of the Change Agent," in Lawrence, P. & Seiler, J., *Organizational Behavior and Administration,* rev. ed. Homewood, Ill.: Richard D. Irwin, Inc., 1965, pp. 952–59.

Bennis, W. *Organizational Development: Its Nature, Origins and Prospects.* Reading, Mass.: Addison-Wesley Publishing Co., Inc., 1969.

_____ *Changing Organizations.* New York: John Wiley & Sons, Inc., 1966.

Bennis, Warren G.; Benne, Kenneth D.; and Chin, Robert, eds. *The Planning of Change.* New York: Holt, Rinehart and Winston, Inc., 1964.

_____ and Slater, P. E. *The Temporary Society.* New York: Harper & Row, Pubs., Inc., 1968.

Bowers, David G. "O.D. Techniques and Their Results in 23 Organizations: The Michigan ICL Study," *The Journal of Applied Behavioral Science* 9 (January 1973) 21–43.

Bradford, Leland P.; Gibb, Jack R.; and Benne, Kenneth D., eds. *T-Group Theory and Laboratory Method.* New York: John Wiley & Sons, Inc., 1964.

Coch, L., and French, John R. Jr. "Overcoming Resistance To Change," *Human Relations Journal* 1 (1948) 512–32.

Cooper, C., and Mangham, I., eds. *T-Groups: A Survey of Research.* New York: John Wiley & Sons, Inc., 1971.

Davis, Sheldon A. "An Organic Problem Solving Method of Organizational Change," *Journal of Applied Behavioral Science* 3 (1967) 3–21.

Fiedler, F. "Engineer the Job to Fit the Manager," *Harvard Business Review* 43 (1965) 115–22.

Gardner, J. H. *Self-Renewal.* New York: Harper & Row, Pubs., Inc., 1964.

Greiner, L. E. "Antecedents of Planned Organizational Change," *JABS* 3 (1967) 51–85.

Harrison, Roger "When Power Conflicts Trigger Team Spirit," *European Business,* Spring 1972.

Hill, Michael "The Manager As Change Agent," *Personnel Journal* (January 1971) 60–63.

Humble, John W. *Management by Objectives and Action.* London: McGraw-Hill Publishing Co., Ltd., 1970.

Huse, E. F. *Organization Development and Change.* St. Paul, Minn.: West Publishing Co., 1975.

Jenks, R. S. "An Action-Research Approach to Organizational Change," *JABS* 6 (1970) 131–50.

Judson, A. S. *A Manager's Guide to Making Changes.* London, England: John Wiley and Sons, Ltd., 1966.

Katz, Daniel, and Georgopoulus, Basil S. "Organizations in a Changing World," *Journal of Applied Behavioral Science* (June 1971) 342–70.

Lawrence, Paul "How to Deal with Resistance to Change," *HBR* (January–February 1969) 4–5, 8–12, 166–76.

Lawrence, P. R., and Lorsch, J. W. *Developing Organizations: Diagnoses and Action.* Reading, Mass.: Addison-Wesley Publishing Co., Inc., 1969.

Leavitt, H. J. *New Perspectives in Organization Research.* New York: John Wiley & Sons, Inc., 1964.

Levinson, Harry. "Management by Whose Objectives," *HBR* (July–August 1970) 125–34.

Margulies, N., and Raia, A. P. *Organization Development: Values, Process and Technology.* New York: McGraw-Hill Book Co., 1972.

Morse, N., and Reimer, E. "Experimental Change of A Major Organization Variable," *Journal of Abnormal and Social Psychology* 52 (1956) 120–29.

Odiorne, George S. *Management By Objectives.* New York: Pittman Publishing Corp., 1965.

Rubin, I.; Plovnick, M.; and Fry, R. "Initiating Planned Change in Health Care Systems," *Journal Applied Behavioral Science* 10 (1974) 107–24.

Schein, E. H. *Process Consultation: Its Role in Organization.* Reading, Mass.: Addison-Wesley Publishing Co., Inc., 1969.

Schmahl, J. A. *Experiment in Change.* New York: The Macmillan Company, 1966.

Schon, Donald "Managing the Technological Innovation," *Harvard Business Review* (May–June 1969) 156–67.

_____ *Technology and Change.* New York: Delacorte Press, 1967.

Cases and Readings

Cases in this book not otherwise noted were prepared by various individuals with the guidance of the authors. We are grateful to these individuals and organizations for their assistance. For reasons of preserving the anonymity of the organizations involved in the cases, we list the individuals' names below, and gratefully acknowledge their contribution in this manner.

John Barry
Barbara A. Corriveau
Mary Ellen D'Antonio
Janet M. Delaney
Paul P. Hebert
Steve Lippman
Robert P. Lopilado
E. Thorn Mead
Donna S. Miller
Gary Mongeon
The New Hampshire
Sandra Seiler
Nfor N. Susungi
Cynthia L. Thompson
Peter Weinbaum
David Whall
Charles E. Winn

Active Listening*

By Carl B. Rogers and Richard E. Farson

THE MEANING OF ACTIVE LISTENING

ONE basic responsibility of the supervisor or executive is the development, adjustment, and integration of individual employees. He tries to develop employee potential, delegate responsibility, and achieve co-operation. To do so, he must have, among other abilities, the ability to listen intelligently and carefully to those with whom he works.

There are, however, many kinds of listening skills. The lawyer, for example, when questioning a witness, listens for contradictions, irrelevancies, errors, and weaknesses. But this is not the kind of listening skill we are concerned with. The lawyer usually is not listening in order to help the witness adjust or cooperate or produce. On the other hand, we will be concerned with listening skills which *will help* employees gain a clearer understanding of their situations, take responsibility, and co-operate with each other.

Two Examples

The kind of listening we have in mind is called "active listening." It is called "active" because the listener has a very definite responsibility. He does not passively absorb the words which are spoken to him. He actively tries to grasp the facts and the feelings in what he hears, and he tries, by his listening, to help the speaker work out his own problems.

To get a fuller picture of what is meant by active listening, let us consider two different approaches to the same work problem.

---

* Reproduced by permission, The University of Chicago, Industrial Relations Center.

Example No. 1

FOREMAN: Hey, Al, I don't get this production order. We can't handle this run today. What do they think we are?

SUPERVISOR: But that's the order. So get it out as soon as you can. We're under terrific pressure this week.

FOREMAN: Don't they know we're behind schedule already because of that press breakdown?

SUPERVISOR: Look, Kelly, I don't decide what goes on upstairs. I just have to see that the work gets out, and that's what I'm gonna do.

FOREMAN: The guys aren't gonna like this.

SUPERVISOR: That's something you'll have to work out with them, not me.

Example No. 2

FOREMAN: Hey, Ross, I don't get this production order. We can't handle this run today. What do they think we are?

SUPERVISOR: Sounds like you're pretty sore about it, Kelly.

FOREMAN: I sure am. We were just about getting back to schedule after that press breakdown. Now this comes along.

SUPERVISOR: As if you didn't have enough work to do, huh?

FOREMAN: Yeah. I don't know how I'm gonna tell the guys about this.

SUPERVISOR: Hate to face 'em with it now, is that it?

FOREMAN: I really do. They're under a real strain today. Seems like everything we do around here is rush, rush.

SUPERVISOR: I guess you feel like it's unfair to load anything more on them.

FOREMAN: Well, yeah. I know there must be plenty of pressure on everybody up the line, but—well, if that's the way it is—guess I'd better get the word to 'em.

There are obviously many differences between these two examples. The main one, however, is that Ross, the supervisor in the second example, is using the active-listening approach. He is listening and responding in a way that makes it clear that he appreciates both the meaning and the feeling behind what Kelly is saying.

Active listening does not necessarily mean long sessions spent listening to grievances, personal or otherwise. It is simply a way of approaching those problems which arise out of the usual day-to-day events of any job.

To be effective, active listening must be firmly grounded in the basic attitudes of the user. We cannot employ it as a technique if our fundamental attitudes are in conflict with its basic concepts. If we try, our behavior will be empty and sterile, and our associates will be quick to recognize this. Until we can demonstrate a spirit which genuinely respects the potential worth of the individual, which considers his sights and trusts his capacity for self-direction, we cannot begin to be effective listeners.

What We Achieve by Listening

Active listening is an important way to bring about changes in people. Despite the popular notion that listening is a passive approach, clinical and research evidence clearly shows that sensitive listening is a most effective agent for individual personality change and group development. Listening brings about changes in people's attitudes toward themselves and others; it also brings about changes in their basic values and personal philosophy. People who have been listened to in this new and special way become more emotionally mature, more open to their experiences, less defensive, more democratic, and less authoritarian.

When people are listened to sensitively, they tend to listen to themselves with more care and to make clear exactly what they are feeling and thinking. Group members tend to listen more to each other, to become less argumentative, more ready to incorporate other points of view. Because listening reduces the threat of having one's ideas criticized, the person is better able to see them for what they are and is more likely to feel that his contributions are worthwhile.

Not the least important result of listening is the change that takes place within the listener himself. Besides providing more information than any other activity, listening builds deep, positive relationships and tends to alter constructively the attitudes of the listener. Listening is a growth experience.

These, then, are some of the worthwhile results we can expect from active listening. But how do we go about this kind of listening? How do we become active listeners?

HOW TO LISTEN

Active listening aims to bring about changes in people. To achieve this end, it relies upon definite techniques—things to do and things to avoid doing. Before discussing these techniques, however, we should first understand why they are effective. To do so, we must understand how the individual personality develops.

The Growth of the Individual

Through all of our lives, from early childhood on, we have learned to think of ourselves in certain very definite ways. We have built up pictures of ourselves. Sometimes these self-pictures are pretty realistic, but at other times they are not. For example, an overage, overweight lady may fancy herself a youthful, ravishing siren, or an awkward teen-ager regard himself as a star athlete.

All of us have experiences which fit the way we need to think about ourselves. These we accept. But it is much harder to accept experiences which don't fit. And sometimes, if it is very important for us to hang on to this self-picture, we don't accept or admit these experiences at all.

These self-pictures are not necessarily attractive. A man, for example, may regard himself as incompetent and worthless. He may feel that he is doing his job poorly in spite of favorable appraisals by the company. As long as he has these feelings about himself, he must deny any experiences which would seem not to fit this self-picture — in this case any that might indicate to him that he is competent. It is so necessary for him to maintain this self-picture that he is threatened by anything which would tend to change it. Thus, when the company raises his salary, it may seem to him only additional proof that he is a fraud. He must hold onto this self-picture, because, bad or good, it's the only thing he has by which he can identify himself.

This is why direct attempts to change this individual or change his self-picture are particularly threatening. He is forced to defend himself or to completely deny the experience. This denial of experience and defense of the self-picture tend to bring on rigidity of behavior and create difficulties in personal adjustment.

The active-listening approach, on the other hand, does not present a threat to the individual's self-picture. He does not have to defend it. He is able to explore it, see it for what it is, and make his own decision about how realistic it is. And he is then in a position to change.

If I want to help a man reduce his defensiveness and become more adaptive, I must try to remove the threat of myself as his potential changer. As long as the atmosphere is threatening, there can be no effective communication. So I must create a climate which is neither critical, evaluative, nor moralizing. It must be an atmosphere of equality and freedom, permissiveness and understanding, acceptance and warmth. It is in this climate and this climate only that the individual feels safe enough to incorporate new experiences and new values into his concept of himself. Let's see how active listening helps to create this climate.

What to Avoid

When we encounter a person with a problem our usual response is to try to change his way of looking at things — to get him to see his situation the way we see it or would like him to see it. We plead, reason, scold, encourage, insult, prod — anything to bring about a change in the desired direction, that is, in the direction we want him to travel. What we seldom realize, however, is that, under these circumstances, we are usually responding to *our own* needs to see the world in certain ways. It is always difficult for us to tolerate and understand actions which are different from the ways in which *we* believe *we* should act. If, however, we can free ourselves from the need to influence and direct others in our own paths, we enable ourselves to listen with understanding and thereby employ the most potent available agent of change.

One problem the listener faces is that of responding to demands for decisions, judgments, and evaluations. He is constantly called upon to agree or disagree with someone or something. Yet, as he well knows, the question or challenge frequently is a masked expression of feelings or needs which the speaker is far more anxious to communicate than he is to have the surface questions answered. Because he cannot speak these feelings openly, the speaker must disguise them to himself and to others in an acceptable form. To illustrate, let us examine some typical questions and the types of answers that might best elicit the feelings beneath them.

Employee's Question	*Listener's Answer*
Just whose responsibility is the toolroom?	Do you feel that someone is challenging your authority in there?
Don't you think younger able people should be promoted before senior but less able ones?	It seems to you they should, I take it.
What does the super expect us to do about those broken-down machines?	You're pretty disgusted with those machines, aren't you?
Don't you think I've improved over the last review period?	Sounds as if you feel like you've really picked up over these last few months.

These responses recognize the questions but leave the way open for the employee to say what is really bothering him. They allow the listener to participate in the problem or situation without shouldering all responsibility for decision making or actions. This is a process of thinking *with* people instead of *for* or *about* them.

Passing judgment, whether critical or favorable, makes free expression difficult. Similarly, advice and information are almost always seen as efforts to change a person and thus serve as barriers to his self-expression and the development of a creative relationship. Moreover, advice is seldom taken, and information hardly ever utilized. The eager young trainee probably will not become patient just because he is advised that "the road to success in business is a long, difficult one, and you must be patient." And it is no more helpful for him to learn that "only one out of a hundred trainees reaches a top management position."

Interestingly, it is a difficult lesson to learn that positive *evaluations* are sometimes as blocking as negative ones. It is almost as destructive to the freedom of a relationship to tell a person that he is good or capable or right, as to tell him otherwise. To evaluate him positively may make it more difficult for him to tell of the faults that distress him or the ways in which he believes he is not competent.

Encouragement also may be seen as an attempt to motivate the speaker in certain directions or hold him off, rather than as support. "I'm sure everything will work out O.K." is not a helpful response to the person who is deeply discouraged about a problem.

In other words, most of the techniques and devices common to human relationships are found to be of little use in establishing the type of relationship we are seeking here.

What to Do

Just what does active listening entail, then? Basically, it requires that we get inside the speaker, that we grasp, *from his point of view,* just what it is he is communicating to us. More than that, we must convey to the speaker that we are seeing things from his point of view. To listen actively, then, means that there are several things we must do.

Listen for Total Meaning Any message a person tries to get across usually has two components: the *content* of the message and the *feeling* or attitude underlying this content. Both are important; both give the message *meaning*. It is this total meaning of the message that we try to understand. For example, a machinist comes to his foreman and says, "I've finished that lathe setup." This message has obvious content and perhaps calls upon the foreman for another work assignment. Suppose, on the other hand, that he says, "Well, I'm finally finished with that damned lathe setup." The content is the same, but the total meaning of the message has changed—and changed in an important way for both the foreman and the worker. Here sensitive listening can facilitate the relationship. Suppose the foreman were to respond by simply giving another work assignment. Would the employee feel that he had gotten his total message across? Would he feel free to talk to his foreman? Will he feel better about his job, more anxious to do good work on the next assignment?

Now, on the other hand, suppose the foreman were to respond with, "Glad to have it over with, huh?" or "Had a pretty rough time of it?" or "Guess you don't feel like doing anything like that again," or anything else that tells the worker that he heard and understands. It doesn't necessarily mean that the next work assignment need be changed or that he must spend an hour listening to the worker complain about the setup problems he encountered. He may do a number of things differently in the light of the new information he has from the worker—but not necessarily. It's just that extra sensitivity on the part of the foreman which can transform an average working climate into a good one.

Respond to Feelings   In some instances, the content is far less important than the feeling which underlies it. To catch the full flavor or meaning of the message, one must respond particularly to the feeling component. If, for instance, our machinist had said, "I'd like to melt this lathe down and make paper clips out of it," responding to content would be obviously absurd. But to respond to his disgust or anger in trying to work with his lathe recognizes the meaning of this message. There are various shadings of these components in the meaning of any message. Each time, the listener must try to remain sensitive to the total meaning the message has to the speaker. What is he trying to tell me? What does this mean to him? How does he see this situation?

Note All Cues   Not all communication is verbal. The speaker's words alone don't tell us everything he is communicating. And hence, truly sensitive listening requires that we become aware of several kinds of communication besides verbal. The way in which a speaker hesitates in his speech can tell us much about his feelings. So, too, can the inflection of his voice. He may stress certain points loudly and clearly and may mumble others. We should also note such things as the person's facial expressions, body posture, hand movements, eye movements, and breathing. All of these help to convey his total message.

What We Communicate by Listening

The first reaction of most people when they consider listening as a possible method for dealing with human beings is that listening cannot be sufficient in itself. Because it is passive, they feel, listening does not communicate anything to the speaker. Actually, nothing could be farther from the truth.

By consistently listening to a speaker, you are conveying the idea that: "I'm interested in you as a person, and I think that what you feel is important. I respect your thoughts, and even if I don't agree with them, I know that they are valid for you. I feel sure that you have a contribution to make. I'm not trying to change you or evaluate you. I just want to understand you. I think you're worth listening to, and I want you to know that I'm the kind of a person you can talk to."

The subtle but most important aspect of this is that it is the *demonstration* of the message that works. While it is most difficult to convince someone that you respect him by *telling* him so, you are much more likely to get this message across by really *behaving* that way — by actually *having* and *demonstrating* respect for this person. Listening does this most effectively.

Like other behavior, listening behavior is contagious. This has implications for all communication problems, whether between two people or within a large organization. To ensure good communication between associates up and down the line, one must first take the responsibility for setting a pattern of listening. Just as one learns that anger is usually met with anger, argument with argument, and deception with deception, one can learn that listening can be met with listening. Every person who feels responsibility in a situation can set the tone of the interaction, and the important lesson in this is that any behavior exhibited by one person will eventually be responded to with similar behavior in the other person.

It is far more difficult to stimulate constructive behavior in another person but far more profitable. Listening is one of these constructive behaviors, but if one's attitude is to "wait out" the speaker rather than really listen to him, it will fail. The one who consistently listens with understanding, however, is the one who eventually is most likely to be listened to. If you really want to be heard and understood by another, you can develop him as a potential listener, ready for new ideas, provided you can first develop yourself in these ways and sincerely listen with understanding and respect.

Testing for Understanding

Because understanding another person is actually far more difficult than it at first seems, it is important to test constantly your ability to see the world in the way the speaker sees it. You can do this by reflecting in your own words what the speaker seems to mean by his words and actions. His response to this will tell you whether or not he feels understood. A good rule of thumb is to assume that you never really understand until you can communicate this understanding to the other's satisfaction.

Here is an experiment to test your skill in listening. The next time you become involved in a lively or controversial discussion with another person, stop for a moment and suggest that you adopt this ground rule for continued discussion: Before either participant in the discussion can make a point or express an opinion of his own, he must first restate aloud the previous point or position of the other person. This restatement must be in his own words (merely parroting the words of another does not prove that one has understood but only that he has heard the words). The restatement must be accurate enough to satisfy the speaker before the listener can be allowed to speak for himself.

This is something you could try in your own discussion group. Have someone express himself on some topic of emotional concern to the group. Then, before another member expresses his own feelings and thought, he must rephrase the *meaning* expressed by the previous speaker to that individual's satisfaction. Note the changes in the emotional climate and in the quality of the discussion when you try this.

PROBLEMS IN ACTIVE LISTENING

Active listening is not an easy skill to acquire. It demands practice. Perhaps more important, it may require changes in our own basic attitudes. These changes come slowly and sometimes with considerable difficulty. Let us look at some of the major problems in active listening and what can be done to overcome them.

The Personal Risk

To be effective at all in active listening, one must have a sincere interest in the speaker. We all live in glass houses as far as our attitudes are concerned. They always show through. And if we are only making a pretense of interest in the speaker, he will quickly pick this up, either consciously or unconsciously. And once he does, he will no longer express himself freely.

Active listening carries a strong element of personal risk. If we manage to accomplish what we are describing here—to sense deeply the feeling of another person, to understand the meaning his experiences have for him, to see the world as he sees it—we risk being changed ourselves. For example, if we permit ourselves to listen our way into the psychological life of a labor leader or agitator—to get the meaning which life has for him—we risk coming to see the world as he sees it. It is threatening to give up, even momentarily, what we believe and start thinking in someone else's terms. It takes a great deal of inner security and courage to be able to risk one's self in understanding another.

For the supervisor, the courage to take another's point of view generally means that he must see *himself* through another's eyes—he must be able to see himself as others see him. To do this may sometimes be unpleasant, but it is far more *difficult* than unpleasant. We are so accustomed to viewing ourselves in certain ways—to seeing and hearing only what we want to see and hear—that it is extremely difficult for a person to free himself from his needs to see things these ways.

Developing an attitude of sincere interest in the speaker is thus no easy task. It can be developed only by being willing to risk seeing the world from the speaker's point of view. If we have a number of such experiences, however, they will shape an attitude which will allow us to be truly genuine in our interest in the speaker.

Hostile Expressions

The listener will often hear negative, hostile expressions directed at himself. Such expressions are always hard to listen to. No one likes to hear hostile words. And it is not easy to get to the point where one is strong enough to permit these attacks without finding it necessary to defend oneself or retaliate.

Because we all fear that people will crumble under the attack of genuine negative feelings, we tend to perpetuate an attitude of pseudo peace. It is as if we cannot tolerate conflict at all for fear of the damage it could do to us, to the situation, to the others involved. But of course the real damage is done to all these by the denial and suppression of negative feelings.

Out-of-place Expressions

There is also the problem of out-of-place expressions — expressions dealing with behavior which is not usually acceptable in our society. In the extreme forms that present themselves before psychotherapists, expressions of sexual perversity or homicidal fantasies are often found blocking to the listener because of their obvious threatening quality. At less extreme levels, we all find unnatural or inappropriate behavior difficult to handle. That is, anything from an off-color story told in mixed company to a man weeping is likely to produce a problem situation.

In any face-to-face situation, we will find instances of this type which will momentarily, if not permanently, block any communication. In business and industry, any expressions of weakness or incompetency will generally be regarded as unacceptable and therefore will block good two-way communication. For example, it is difficult to listen to a supervisor tell of his feelings of failure in being able to "take charge" of a situation in his department, because *all* administrators are supposed to be able to "take charge."

Accepting Positive Feelings

It is both interesting and perplexing to note that negative or hostile feelings or expressions are much easier to deal with in any face-to-face relationship than are truly and deeply positive feelings. This is especially true for the businessman, because the culture expects him to be independent, bold, clever, and aggressive and manifest no feelings of warmth, gentleness, and intimacy. He therefore comes to regard these feelings as soft and inappropriate. But no matter how they are regarded, they remain a human need. The denial of these feelings in himself and his associates does not get the executive out of the problem of dealing with them. They simply become veiled and confused. If recognized, they would work for the total effort; unrecognized, they work against it.

Emotional Danger Signals

The listener's own emotions are sometimes a barrier to active listening. When emotions are at their height, which is when listening is most necessary, it is most difficult to set aside one's own concerns and be understanding. Our emotions are often our own worst enemies when we try to become listeners. The more involved and invested we are in a particular situation or problem, the less we are likely to be willing or able to listen to the feelings and attitudes of others. That is, the more we find it necessary to respond to our own needs, the less we are able to respond to the needs of another. Let us look at some of the main danger signals that warn us that our emotions may be interfering with our listening.

Defensiveness   The points about which one is most vocal and dogmatic, the points which one is most anxious to impose on others — these are always the points one is trying to talk oneself into believing. So one danger signal becomes apparent when you find yourself stressing a point or trying to convince another. It is at these times that you are likely to be less secure and consequently less able to listen.

Resentment of Opposition   It is always easier to listen to an idea which is similar to one of your own than to an opposing view. Sometimes, in order to clear the air, it is helpful to pause for a moment when you feel your ideas and position being challenged, reflect on the situation, and express your concern to the speaker.

Clash of Personalities   Here again, our experience has consistently shown us that the genuine expression of feelings on the part of the listener will be more helpful in developing a sound relationship than the suppression of them. This is so whether the feelings be resentment, hostility, threat, or admiration. A basically honest relationship, whatever the nature of it, is the most productive of all. The other party becomes secure when he learns that the listener can express his feelings honestly and openly to him. We should keep this in mind when we begin to fear a clash of personalities in the listening relationship. Otherwise, fear of our own emotions will choke off full expression of feelings.

Listening to Ourselves

To listen to oneself is a prerequisite for listening to others. And it is often an effective means of dealing with the problems we have outlined above. When we are most aroused, excited, and demanding, we are least able to understand our own feelings and attitudes. Yet, in dealing with the problems of others, it becomes most important to be sure of one's own position, values, and needs.

The ability to recognize and understand the meaning which a particular episode has for you, with all the feelings which it stimulates in you, and the ability to express this meaning when you find it getting in the way of active listening will clear the air and enable you once again to be free to listen. That is, if some person or situation touches off feelings within you which tend to block your attempts to listen with understanding, begin listening to yourself. It is much more helpful in developing effective relationships to avoid suppressing these feelings. Speak them out as clearly as you can, and try to enlist the other person as a listener to your feelings. A person's listening ability is limited by his ability to listen to himself.

ACTIVE LISTENING AND COMPANY GOALS

How can listening improve production?

We're in business, and it's a rugged, fast, competitive affair. How are we going to find time to counsel our employees?

We have to concern ourselves with organizational problems first.

We can't afford to spend all day listening when there's a job to be done.

What's morale got to do with production?

Sometimes we have to sacrifice an individual for the good of the rest of the people in the company.

Those of us who are trying to advance the listening approach in industry hear these comments frequently. And because they are so honest and legitimate, they pose a real problem. Unfortunately, the answers are not so clear-cut as the questions.

Individual Importance

One answer is based on an assumption that is central to the listening approach. That assumption is: The kind of behavior which helps the individual will eventually be the best thing that could be done for the group. Or saying it another way: The things that are best for the individual are best for the company. This is a conviction of ours, based on our experience in psychology and education. The research evidence from industry is only beginning to come in. We find that putting the group first, at the expense of the individual, besides being an uncomfortable individual experience, does *not* unify the group. In fact, it tends to make the group less a group. The members become anxious and suspicious.

We are not at all sure in just what ways the group does benefit from a concern demonstrated for an individual, but we have several strong leads. One is that the group feels more secure when an individual is being listened to and provided for with concern and sensitivity. And we assume that a secure group will ultimately be a better group. When each individual feels that he need not fear exposing himself to the group, he is likely to contribute more freely and spontaneously. When the leader of a group responds to the individual, puts the individual first, the other members of the group will follow suit, and the group will come to act as a unit in recognizing and responding to the needs of a particular member. This positive, constructive action seems to be a much more satisfying experience for a group than the experience of dispensing with a member.

Listening and Production

Whether listening or any other activity designed to better human relations in an industry actually raises production—whether morale has a definite relationship to production—is not known for sure. There are some who frankly hold that there is no relationship to be expected between morale and production—that production often depends upon the social misfit, the eccentric, or the isolate. And there are some who simply choose to work in a climate of cooperation and harmony, in a high-morale group, quite aside from the question of increased production.

A report from the Survey Research Center[1] at the University of Michigan on research conducted at the Prudential Life Insurance Company lists seven findings relating to production and morale. First-line supervisors in high-production work groups were found to differ from those in low-production work groups in that they:

1. Are under less close supervision from their own supervisors.
2. Place less direct emphasis upon production as the goal.
3. Encourage employee participation in the making of decisions.
4. Are more employee-centered.
5. Spend more of their time in supervision and less in straight production work.
6. Have a greater feeling of confidence in their supervisory roles.
7. Feel that they know where they stand with the company.

After mentioning that other dimensions of morale, such as identification with the company, intrinsic job satisfaction, and satisfaction with job status, were not found significantly related to productivity, the report goes on to suggest the following psychological interpretation:

> People are more effectively motivated when they are given some degree of freedom in the way in which they do their work than when every action is prescribed in advance. They do better when some degree of decision mak-

---

[1] "Productivity, Supervision, and Employee Morale," *Human Relations*, Series I. Report 1, Survey Research Center, University of Michigan, Ann Arbor, Mich.

ing about their jobs is possible than when all decisions are made for them. They respond more adequately when they are treated as personalities than as cogs in a machine. In short, if the ego motivations of self-determination, of self-expression, of a sense of personal worth can be tapped, the individual can be more effectively energized. The use of external sanctions or pressuring for production may work to some degree, but not to the extent that the more internalized motives do. When the individual comes to identify himself with his job and with the work of his group, human resources are much more fully utilized in the production process.

The Survey Research Center has also conducted studies among workers in other industries. In discussing the results of these studies, Robert L. Kahn writes:

> In the studies of clerical workers, railroad workers, and workers in heavy industry, the supervisors with the better production records gave a larger proportion of their time to supervisory functions, especially to the interpersonal aspects of their jobs. The supervisors of the lower-producing sections were more likely to spend their time in tasks which the men themselves were performing, or in the paperwork aspects of their jobs.[2]

Maximum Creativeness

There may never be enough research evidence to satisfy everyone on this question. But speaking from a business point of view, in terms of the problem of developing resources for production, the maximum creativeness and productive effort of the human beings in the organization are the richest untapped source of power still existing. The difference between the maximum productive capacity of people and that output which industry is now realizing is immense. We simply suggest that this maximum capacity might be closer to realization if we sought to release the motivation that already exists within people rather than try to stimulate them externally.

This releasing of the individual is made possible, first of all, by sensitive listening, with respect and understanding. Listening is a beginning toward making the individual feel himself worthy of making contributions, and this could result in a very dynamic and productive organization. Competitive business is never too rugged or too busy to take time to procure the most efficient technological advances or to develop rich raw-material resources. But these in comparison to the resources that are already within the people in the plant are paltry. This is industry's major procurement problem.

G. L. Clements, president of Jewel Tea Co., Inc., in talking about the collaborative approach to management, says:

---

[2] Robert L. Kahn, "The Human Factors Underlying Industrial Productivity," *Michigan Business Review,* November, 1952.

We feel that this type of approach recognizes that there is a secret ballot going on at all times among the people in any business. They vote for or against their supervisors. A favorable vote for the supervisor shows up in the cooperation, teamwork, understanding, and production of the group. To win this secret ballot, each supervisor must share the problems of his group and work for them.[3]

The decision to spend time listening to his employees is a decision each supervisor or executive has to make for himself. Executives seldom have much to do with products or processes. They have to deal with people who must in turn deal with people who will deal with products or processes. The higher one goes up the line, the more one will be concerned with human relations problems, simply because people are all one has to work with. The minute we take a man from his bench and make him a foreman, he is removed from the basic production of goods and now must begin relating to individuals instead of nuts and bolts. People are different from things, and our foreman is called upon for a different line of skills completely. His new tasks call upon him to be a special kind of person. The development of himself as a listener is a first step in becoming this special person.

---

[3] G. L. Clements, "Time for 'Democracy in Action' at the Executive Level," address given before the AMA Personnel Conference, Feb. 28, 1951.

Anderson Manufacturing and Development Co.*

"HAM" WILSON looked at the public relations man across his desk with irritation. Then, with his characteristic self-control in dealing with company colonels, he suppressed the quick words that were on his tongue.

It has been a rough morning—a morning of hard, disciplined argument over promotional copy for the new compacting machine. While Ham had become visibly upset and impatient to end the session, the PR

---

* This case was prepared by Walter Milne under the direction of Professors A. H. Rubinstein and H. A. Shepard for courses in management of research and development conducted at the School of Industrial Management, Massachusetts Institute of Technology, Cambridge, Massachusetts, and is used with Dr. Shepard's permission.

man kept smiling, stubbornly fighting it out one point at a time. Ham disliked him intensely.

Although Anderson Manufacturing and Development had not had a PR man long, this guy was surely making up for lost time. Little by little he had taken under his wing everything that had anything to do with business development and promotion. He was young—somewhere in his early thirties, maybe four or five years older than Ham himself—and in spite of his smiling, driving assurance, technically ignorant. He didn't even understand what was basically new in the compactor, Ham thought with resentment.

Ham was proud of his compactor. He had directed its development from the beginning. The original concept had been tossed to him as a kind of challenge by his boss, the chief engineer, and Ham had given it long hours of exploratory thought and work on his own. And then he had become excited about it, sold it hard, and management had bought it. They had given him a tight budget and time schedule and he had made it. He felt damn good about that machine.

"You keep approaching this copy in the wrong way, Ham," the PR man was saying.

"This is aimed at the guys who are holding the money bags and you keep criticizing everything as though we were writing a technical report. I don't want to misrepresent your baby, believe me, but I'm trying to sell it. We've put a lot of money into its development and we're going to put a lot more into its promotion. Now we've got to sell it. I need good copy. Everybody upstairs wants good copy."

Ham was tempted to tell him what everybody upstairs could do, but checked himself again. He stared blankly at the copy, convinced that he was still right: it stunk. Worse, it seemed to border on dishonesty in some of its implications.

"What I would like to do," Ham finally said to PR, "is to have a chance to talk to the boss before we make a final decision on this. I don't want to let it go through as it stands on my own say-so."

"O.K., Ham," said PR, "but remember that I have to get final copy to the printer by the end of the week. I think what we've got right now is all right," he added, "and I certainly wouldn't want to see it watered down any more."

PR left as he had come—smiling, self-sufficient, and with hearty good words.

What a joker, Ham thought to himself. He wondered how a guy like that could live with himself, how he could do Anderson Manufacturing any real good. Apparently he did—at any rate he sat upstairs in a big room in executive row.

By way of contrast, Ham looked around his own little cubby. His battered desk and chair, and one visitor's chair, all but filled it. "The

Conference Room," the boys called it. He laughed, and then lost his laugh when a knock at the door reminded him that he had asked Holden to see him as soon as PR had left.

Bill Holden came in, easy and relaxed as always, and slouched into the chair at Ham's desk. He was a bright, young D.Sc. whom Ham himself had hired. But there were times when he wished he hadn't—and this was one of the times.

"Bill," Ham began, "I've just had a rough time with PR and I'm not going to beat around the bush. When your test results weren't in last Friday, you promised me—quite literally promised me—that we'd have 'em first thing this morning. And we don't have 'em. We practically rescheduled the whole program so that you could do some additional work with the physics group, and now you haven't made the new schedule. What are we going to do about it?"

"I know I promised to have them today, Ham," said Holden, "and believe me, I was shooting for it. The physics group work just took more time than I had expected. We're on some pretty fundamental stuff, and Dr. Maul asked me to do some library work on it. The whole thing just ran beyond our original expectations."

"Bill," snapped Ham, "your attitude confuses me; honestly, it does. I don't doubt that the physics group is doing important work, but you knew damn well that you were assigned part-time to my B project. And you know that when I juggled the schedule I was doing it to give you a break—you, personally. I never should have done it, but you practically pleaded with me and promised that you would come through on schedule. What do you think we're doing here anyway?"

Ham was flushed and angry, but Holden let it roll off easily.

"I suppose we're doing a lot of different things," Holden said in a tone that seemed half apology, half challenge. "The Chief was talking to me just the other day about the importance of the physics group work and about what a vital part I could play in it. You know it's pretty fundamental stuff, and frankly, that's why it appealed to me. It's well related to my previous experience—some of my doctoral work. I thought that's why you rearranged the schedule."

"Bill," said Ham, "you're talking nonsense and you know it. If all my men felt the way you do about the job, about fitting their work into the pattern, why the whole lab would fall apart."

"Well the whole thing seemed reasonable to me," said Holden. "After all, we're working for the same boss and good results in one place ought to be just as good as good results in another."

"Bill," said Ham in a rising voice, "you know damn well that's not so. Honestly, you're talking as though you were still a schoolboy and it didn't matter what you did—as though you didn't have responsibility to anyone else."

"But I've done good work," said Holden.

"I know it, and everybody knows it," interrupted Ham. "You've been here what—two, three years? During that time you've had more good ideas than anybody else on the lot. You're a good man, and the Chief has given you a pretty free rein. That's why I can't understand this. You try to run your affairs like a one-man band, but this lab is not being run the way you think it is."

Holden just kept looking at Ham.

"Everybody seems to think I've been doing O.K," Holden repeated defensively. "I've always tried to do my best."

"Sure you have," said Ham, "but you run around this place as though we were subsidized like the Royal Academy. You know we're not subsidized by anybody—we're organized to make money, and in order to make money we've got to push the stuff out the door. It matters a hell of a lot to me whether we do or not, because if we don't, it means my neck."

Ham looked at Holden and Holden looked at the floor and there was a long silence.

Ham liked Holden, but he was also a little envious of him, for Holden had the *big* degree. He also had brains. In fact, he had been good for the lab, Ham had to admit, even though he never worried much about meeting a schedule.

But hell, he said to himself as Holden looked up, I have to worry about a schedule even if Bill would rather be doing other things. Sometimes, he thought, I'd rather be doing other things myself.

"Bill," said Ham, finally cutting into the long silence, "I'm sorry I lost my temper. I've never blown my stack like this before. I was wrong in doing it now."

"I'm sorry too, Ham," said Holden. "You make me feel as though I've let you down personally. You've been very decent with me and I certainly didn't mean to let you down. If you want me to finish off the test runs. . . ."

"No, no need," interrupted Ham, a little wearily.

"When I didn't have the final figures this morning, I took what you'd already done and passed it on to Porter. He's got one of his boys finishing it out. The Chief expected a report before this, but he hasn't been pressing me for it."

Ham doddled for a minute on his scratch pad, and then went on:

"This is no life and death matter as you well know, Bill, and I'm sorry I acted as though it were. The point is not so much that you fouled up this schedule, but that you've fouled up for still another time. Anybody can understand missing once in a while, but it never seems to bother you that you have a reputation for never worrying about time. It would bother me. Every time I miss a schedule it bothers me."

Ham doodled again.

"You certainly know the things I've been saying are right, Bill," he said. "I think we should forget it for now, but let's understand that something's got to be done. I'll speak to the Chief as soon as I can, and we'll see what's to be done."

Holden backed out awkwardly, muttering apologies. As soon as he had left, Ham picked up the phone and called the Chief. The conversation was brief: Ham had a couple of problems he'd like to talk about; could he see the Chief sometime soon? "Sure" was the response—in about an hour, for lunch. Fine; done.

At lunch, the Chief characteristically opened right up with a hearty, "What's on your mind, Ham?" He asked it with a smile—a big, genuine, ready smile.

"Well, Chief, I had kind of a bad morning."

"I heard about it," said the Chief.

Ham didn't conceal his surprise. So PR had run to see the Chief, Ham thought. PR had tried to load the dice. That was a lousy trick.

"From PR?" Ham asked.

"No," said the Chief, looking hard at Ham, "from Bill Holden. He was in to see me right after he left your office. He told me the whole story. And as a matter of fact, Ham, there's a part of the story you don't know: Holden's being assigned to Doc Maul's group as part of a general reorganization that's been approved by the board."

Ham started, and he listened uneasily as the Chief began to explain. The reorganization was to involve the whole works. The lab was to be split into three groups. The Chief was to have over-all charge, but the company was going to appoint an assistant chief engineer who would be responsible for some forty engineers and as many nonprofessionals. Doc Maul was going to direct a smaller group on some of the more fundamental work. This was going to be a low-pressure group.

"Maul's group may not work out at all," the Chief went on, "but we're going to give it a try. It won't be much different from the way the physics group has operated anyway.

"This is where Holden fits in. He's to be a research associate—which, as you know, is a new title with us—Maul's right-hand man. Holden knows about this and he's happy about it. I think one of the reasons he stopped into my office today was to check on whether you knew it, and of course, you didn't.

"What happened was that Maul jumped the gun in telling Holden what his duties were to be, and Holden jumped the gun in acting like a research associate. He realizes that and he's sorry."

The Chief looked at Ham with an apologetic smile.

"I was going to tell you all this at the end of the week, Ham, after the executive committee had formally approved our plans. But let's forget Holden and get right down to brass tacks. Let's see what this is going to mean on our side of things."

Ham's uneasiness increased as the Chief went over things in more detail.

Maul was to become head scientist, he said. The Chief himself was to pick up two assistants. One of the two was to have the title assistant chief engineer. He would work in parallel with the Chief and have charge of about a third of the groups. The other new appointment was to be assistant to the chief engineer—a kind of leg man for the Chief.

"Now how do you fit into all this, Ham?" the Chief asked rhetorically. Ham took a big bite of pie and gestured his curiosity.

"We have discussed this whole thing pretty thoroughly," the Chief went on, "and we've looked at all the men we've got and we've talked to some from outside in an exploratory way. After looking and talking, we're well decided we want you to be assistant chief engineer."

Ham grinned. This felt good. Here he'd been working his fanny off and up to now, he thought, there hadn't been any gold stars on his report card. This really felt good.

"Actually, Ham," the Chief was saying, "you've been doing a big part of this job already. You know our procedures and you've proved you can keep on top of things. Whatever may have happened this morning I'd read as just a bad day. The record shows you work well with the men and keep them happy and push the stuff out."

Ham thought to himself that this was right. He had been doing part of this job all along. It had started nearly two years ago when Maul was out sick and the Chief began to dump things in his lap. And when Maul came back, the lab started to grow and the Chief kept handing him things. There was no formal pattern—it was one of those things that had just developed.

Still there had been plenty of time to participate in project work, too. Ham thought of the compactor. He had lived with that thing night and day. And that had been a good part of the setup as it was. Whenever something had come along that he had wanted to jump into, the Chief had always said to go ahead. And he had jumped into the compactor with both feet. That's the only way to do, Ham thought, when you really want to get something done.

The Chief was now talking specifics about the new job.

It would mean a substantial raise—about 15 per cent. Better still, it would mean participation in the bonus plan. It would mean a big new office. And it would mean a lot of little things: a private secretary, a membership in the executive's club, office expenses for journals and magazines—a whole new potful of the niceties of life.

Ham had an impulse to jump up and shake the Chief's hand and to rush out and call his wife, who had taken the youngsters on a two weeks' trip to her mother's. But the impulse was only a quick flash. It passed and was replaced by something like fear. This wasn't something Ham wanted to jump into—not just like that anyway.

As the Chief went through the slow, deliberate ritual of filling and lighting his pipe, Ham expressed his thanks for being considered for the position. But while he said the right things fully and fluently, he thought of reasons for delaying his decision.

He thought of the reports, the judgments, the budgets, the people. He thought of sweating out one project while you were worrying about the next. And strangely enough, he thought of PR.

He thought of PR because there was a guy he never wanted to be, a guy who was a kind of Mr. Management Merry-go-round in person. He wondered briefly if some day PR would wake up and realize he'd been running his whole life without ever catching up to anything. He wondered if some day after it was too late PR would wish he hadn't run so hard and so fast.

There was a pause during which the Chief looked searchingly at Ham.

"You're thinking this is a pretty big decision, Ham?" the Chief asked.

Ham nodded. "A very big decision," he said with emphasis.

"I agree," said the Chief, "and naturally no one wants you to make a snap judgment about it. The vice president told me to tell you to take your time. Personally, I want you to take a good hard look at it.

"We both know," the Chief added, "that you did a whale of a fine job with the compactor, and it may be that that's the kind of thing you ought to stick with, that that's the kind of thing you really want. You've got to balance that equation for yourself, Ham. I emphasize this because if you do take the new appointment—and it's got a lot to offer—you ought to realize that you'll be completely away from the bench.

"When you sold me on the compactor," the Chief went on, "we arranged things so that you could see it through yourself. That wouldn't be likely to happen again. Of course, you'll sit on top of these things and you'll take pride in these accomplishments, but in a different way—an entirely different way."

The Chief stopped talking and scratched a match to relight his pipe. Ham stirred his second cup of coffee.

"I understand what you're saying all right," said Ham, "and, believe me, I have very mixed feelings about it. I'm tempted by the new job—naturally—and I feel very flattered by the offer. But I do know that I like the purely technical side of things. And I know that if I took the new job I'd want to keep up in my field."

The Chief smiled at Ham as he waited for him to go on.

"I've enjoyed the courses I've been taking at the Institute," Ham continued, "and I'm satisfied that they've done me a lot of good. If I took this appointment, I'd keep working for my degree—just as I have been—one course at a time. And I'd probably sit in on some seminars. In fact I'd try to keep up technically in every way I could."

The Chief smiled again and then spoke quickly and earnestly:

"You can sell yourself on that line of argument pretty easily, Ham," said the Chief, "because it makes so much good sense on the face of it. But I'll give you long odds that it won't work that way. I don't want to be discouraging, but the older you get the harder it gets. It's hard to find the time — even harder to find the energy.

"Believe me," added the Chief with a wry smile, "I know. I went through it myself."

Ham thought about this. He thought of how little he really knew about the Chief. He did know he had been a top turbine man. And he knew the Chief had once won the Stalworthy medal "for outstanding contributions to turbine development." Not much of a medal, maybe, Ham thought, but still a medal — a symbol of achievement and recognition. Yet the Chief had traded this away for a stock-bonus deal with the Anderson company. Ham wondered if he had any regrets. He wished he knew.

"The fact is," Ham heard himself saying a little apologetically, "I'd rather thought that this year I might have a go at the degree on a half-time basis. You remember that we talked about this last year and you said then that the company would sponsor me."

"I did say that, Ham," replied the Chief, "and I'm sure that we can still do it if that's what you want."

"Well, I'm not sure at all," said Ham, "but I have a tentative program worked out and I've lined up a thesis."

"If this is what you want, Ham," returned the Chief, "I'd be the first to say Godspeed. My only advice would be to encourage you to pick a good thesis project. There are a lot of awfully facile theses written in that department, and I wouldn't want to see you fall into that kind of trap."

"As a matter of fact," Ham answered quickly, "I've got a pretty exciting project in prospect. Werner wants me to work with him, and you know his work. This could mean a lot for me professionally. There's no denying I would like that. I think anybody would."

"Ham," said the Chief quietly, "I understand your feelings perfectly, and I won't try to dissuade you if that's what you really want. You've got some good projects under your belt here, and a good job with Werner would never hurt you."

The Chief paused and brushed a few tobacco crumbs from the table-cloth to the floor.

"If I decide to finish up the degree on a half-time basis," Ham asked, "will I prejudice my chances here at the lab?"

"Ham, you know better than that, I hope," replied the Chief. "I'm with you either way. And as far as the people upstairs go, forget it. There's no problem there."

The Chief brushed at a last elusive crumb of tobacco.

"No, you won't prejudice your future, Ham," he added, "but it will be a different kind of future."

The Chief looked at Ham for a minute. Then he knocked his pipe on the ashtray and looked at his watch. The lunch was over.

*   *   *   *   *

When Ham returned to his desk he sat down with the uneasy feeling that he hadn't been demonstrative enough in thanking the Chief for the opportunity he'd been offered. But he was interrupted by an unexpected call from Jack Masters, an old classmate and a fraternity brother of Ham's at the Institute. Jack was in town on business and their brief, hearty conversation quickly closed with arrangements for dinner at Ham's club.

As Ham cradled the phone, he let his mind savor past memories. He was glad Jack was in town, he decided. Jack was a real solid citizen. It would be good to see him.

During the next two hours, Ham tried to put some final changes into his annual report, which was due next week. It was not until long past midafternoon that he became aware that only his hands were busy with the papers in front of him. His mind was still churning with confusion over the decision that lay ahead. With a gesture of disgust, he pushed the papers to the back of his desk and left the office. Without real purpose, he walked the length of A wing until he stopped at the cell where George Porter was finishing up the tests that Holden should have done. Porter and one of his technicians were running things with a quiet, easy competency. Ham liked George — everybody did.

"How are things going?" Ham called. Porter grinned and held up a finger asking him to wait a minute. Ham waved an O.K.

Ham never thought about George Porter much, but he thought about him now as he waited. He thought about him, because he suddenly realized that Porter wasn't so very much different from him. Of course, he was twenty years older, but he had the same kind of background, the same kind of education. And Porter, Ham thought to himself, was a guy in a well-worn groove. For the first time, this realization worried him.

Back before the war, George Porter and one of the founders of the Anderson company had run a little one-horse shop. And there Porter had helped develop one of the basic patents that had brought Anderson Manufacturing into being. But Porter had never grown away from the first project. Not that he didn't keep improving it, for he did. Just last month, for instance, he had finished making changes that would let it be tied in with a computer-controlled line. A new series of Air Force contract orders had already come in on that development. That's the way Porter's baby was: high quality and custom-built, and the military kept it well fed.

"Just about winding up, Ham," said Porter, coming out of the open cell. "It all went very easily, no troubles at all. The data look good."

Ham took the clipboard and scanned the data, plotting them mentally against the earlier runs. "They do look good," he said.

Porter, pleased, turned back to his technician. "They look good, Al," he shouted, and the technician grinned.

Ham thrust his hands into his pockets and leaned back against the wall as Porter and the technician kept feeding in the adjustments on the last run. Ham thought about Porter some more. He thought about how helpful Porter had been to him when he first joined the lab. Ham had been in Porter's group then, and they had been quite close for a while.

Ham recalled his first visit to Porter's home. Porter lived in the country, and he farmed a little. It wasn't much of a farm, Ham supposed: a couple of hundred chickens, a cow, a small garden. He remembered how impressed he'd been that first night that everything they'd eaten—from the very tasty salad to the peach dessert—had been grown right there. Ham hadn't seen much of the Porters recently, for Ham's wife ran their social life, and she didn't care for the Porters. He was sorry, for he rather liked George and his rawboned, easygoing wife.

Porter came out of the test cell and took the clipboard from Ham to record the data on the final run.

Funny, Porter's doing this job himself, Ham thought. After all, the tests were routine enough and a couple of technicians could have handled the job if company policy hadn't required that an engineer be present. But Porter could have covered this requisite by having one of his young engineers do the job. Yet he didn't, for that's the way Porter was—he never passed anything on to anybody else. He would worry, he once told Ham, that it wasn't being done right if he wasn't out there on the job. As Ham thought about this, he concluded that any worries Porter had were mighty little worries.

When the last run was completed, Ham took the clipboard again and looked at the final readings. They were right on the button.

"We'll all get the Anderson A of Approval for this one," Ham said, and Porter and the technician laughed at this reference to a standing company joke. Ham surprised himself by laughing, too.

"Flip you fellows for a coke," he said. "Odd man pays." Porter laughed again.

"You know, Ham," he said, "that's probably the thousandth time you've tried to match me for a coke, and I've never taken you up on it. Not today, either."

Ham smiled, threw back a friendly insult, and then added that the cokes were on him. While Ham was getting them, Porter and the technician shut down the machine. Then they all lounged back on the bench beside the test cell, drank their cokes, and talked. They talked trivia, and

Ham didn't say much. But Porter and the technician talked easily, sharing a rough kind of camaraderie.

Ham finished his bottle first, exchanged pleasantries with the two men, and walked on down the wing. As he turned the corner to his office, he looked back to see Porter and the technician closing down for the day. Although he couldn't tell for sure, he thought Porter was whistling. Ham watched him for a minute, and then almost imperceptibly shrugged his shoulders and walked slowly back to his office.

* * * * *

Ham met Jack Masters that evening in the lobby of the Engineer's Club. They exchanged quick greetings and went directly to the bar. It was a solid, comfortable bar, a good place to talk.

Over the first drink, Masters carried the conversation. He renewed old times, talked about new prospects. Masters was a good talker, and Ham enjoyed listening to him. He hadn't changed much, Ham thought, except that he was a little heavier, a little less volatile.

Masters was with National Company and had been in their New York office for nearly two years. He talked objectively and happily about his job. It seemed like a good deal, and Ham said so two or three times.

"Believe me, Ham," Masters kept saying in self-deprecation, "I'm nobody in the company."

Over the second drink, Ham edged the talk around to his own prospects. Masters was immediately interested. He asked the right questions and drew out the right details. He understood Ham's doubts quickly enough and as quickly dismissed them.

"Hell, Ham," he said, as they went in to dinner, "you don't have a problem, you have an opportunity. You've been doing part of this job already and you like it well enough—that ought to be all you need. I had to cut a lot of bait before I got this kind of bite."

"What do you mean, you 'had to cut bait'?" Ham asked. He was curious. And he was more than curious, for he was searching eagerly for any patterns of experience he might be able to match against his own.

Masters explained that after he'd been in National's Dallas operation for nearly three years, he began to have an almost panicky fear that he was stagnating. His jobs had become routine, and so had his raises. Masters had decided right then, as he put it, to fight his way out of the corner he was in. He did it by broadening himself technically. He did it by very deliberately avoiding getting stuck in the same kind of job too many times. He did it by smelling out every opportunity that was in the wind.

The break had come when his boss, an assistant to the chief engineer, went overseas to set up a new production facility in the Near East. This man's going left a kind of administrative vacuum which the company decided not to fill. But Masters flew into it and picked up every responsibility he could. He made himself a kind of communications center. And when the assistant's leave was extended, Masters was appointed acting assistant in Dallas. Then, before the first man returned, he was transferred to Jersey and then to New York.

"Well, your story's something like mine in some ways," said Ham, "only I didn't consciously try to bring anything off the way you did."

"That may be," said Masters, "but I think we all do this kind of thinking, whether it's conscious or not. Personally, I like to plan things out quite deliberately, for then you have more control over them. That just seems like a matter of good sense to me."

"What you're saying," said Ham with a laugh, "makes me feel a little like a country boy who's somehow getting along only because he's luckier than he ought to be. You're arguing that a guy has to be an opportunist to get ahead."

"Nothing opportunistic about it at all," Masters interrupted. "It's rather a question of creating opportunity, and certainly a question of taking opportunity whenever it comes along. Take this new job of yours — if you don't take it, somebody else will. That's the way I look at things."

"Maybe I'm just quibbling," said Ham, "so let's say I'm ready to buy your argument. This is not what really bothers me anyway. What bothers me is how do you know you ought to get out of technical work; how do you convince yourself that you ought to throw it all away?"

Masters explained it very readily in terms of money and status. He told Ham that he had analyzed National Company as thoroughly as though he were going to invest a couple of million dollars in it. This was only good sense, he said, for there he was, investing his whole life in it. And his analysis showed that all the glory in National Company went to the guys in the management seats — all the glory, all the money, and all the status. He also discovered that more than half the top men in National had come up out of research and development in the first place, and so he decided that the odds were all in favor of his trying the same thing.

"Right now," Masters said, as though clinching the argument, "I'm making half again as much as the guys who came into the lab with me and stayed there. And I'm more flexible," he added. "I can do more things and I'm worth more to the company."

Ham bristled a bit at this. The implication was that the man on the bench was some inferior kind of character, and he found himself resenting it. The argument was also clearly something of a personal challenge.

"All this may have been pretty clear-cut in your case, Jack," said Ham, "but I don't think it is in mine. You're with a big outfit — maybe that's where I should be, but I'm not — and I've got to look at my own situation. You fellows at National talk about millions the way we talk about thousands.

"Let's say I look at this thing pragmatically," Ham went on, "and I would agree with you that maybe this has been in my thinking all along. From a practical standpoint, I would say that you can afford to be secure and happy about your choice because your company is fat. If I were with National, I might feel the same way. You don't have to worry about finding your next job."

"You don't mean that," said Masters. "You know darn well that if I didn't do my job today, I'd be out on my can tomorrow. We're not running a philanthropy any more than you are."

"No, that's not what I mean," Ham rejoined. "What I mean is that you're insulated from all the wear and tear that affects a guy like me. You're not going to mess your job and you're not going out on your can. But I might."

Ham was wound up now.

"When the Chief talked to me today, Jack," he said, "he quoted a lot of figures about the progress of the company. But I'll be frank with you— we run on government contracts—we couldn't keep our shop open six months without the military."

Ham disclosed that one of his own projects had had a prospective government contract cut right out from under it and some of the engineers had been let go. Ham worried that this might happen to the whole kit and caboodle. Then what would happen to the little guy low down on the management ladder, he asked?

"Would I go to you, to National Company, and say won't you please take me on? Would I say I'm a helluva good man even though I haven't any patents to prove it. Would I say I'm loyal and I need the work and if you take me on you'll never regret it?"

Ham was talking at Masters now rather than to him. He wasn't stopping for answers.

"The way I see it," he argued, "if I stick to the technical part of R&E, I've got money in the bank. I'm negotiable. I can go to anybody in the industry, and I can say here's what I've got and here's what I've done, and they can see it right away."

Ham stopped to sign the dinner checks and to order a second cup of coffee. He looked across at Masters again and apologized for his rush of words. He slowed himself down.

Maybe some of these arguments were pretty tenuous, he agreed, but there were other things. There was the plain and simple joy of accomplishment in good project work, for instance.

Ham had written Masters about the compactor, and now he was speaking feelingly about it. That was the kind of thing a guy had to immerse himself in and that was one of the joys he was talking about. If you went into administration full time, you kissed that sort of thing good-by. And you lost something pretty substantial.

Ham let Masters chew over this point while they finished their coffee. Then they went out to the reading room, where they sat in a couple of comfortable chairs and flicked their cigarette ashes into the fireplace.

After a while Ham said: "Jack, I've been thinking pretty seriously about going back for my doctorate on a half-time basis. The company will sponsor me and Professor Werner wants me to do my thesis under him."

"Well," said Masters, "I remember that you wrote me about a year ago to say that you were thinking about it. I wrote back and urged you to forget it, and I thought you had given it up."

Masters blew a few smoke rings and thoughtfully watched them flatten out and lose their shape.

"If you do go back on a half-time schedule, will you use your compactor for a thesis?" he asked Ham.

"No, I can't," said Ham, "the machine isn't really mine. I guess I didn't tell you that."

Ham explained that a friend of Bill Holden's—a local man—had come up with the basic concept. Holden had brought him around to see the Chief as a kind of personal favor.

"But believe me," Ham added quickly, "there was plenty wrong with that machine when we first saw it. The inventor didn't have a sound idea of the basic processes involved. In fact, the odds on this thing's paying off looked so slim that nobody really wanted to touch it. But then I came up with a process that made it look better, and we worked like hell on it, and now we've got something that's really good."

Masters took a last drag on his cigarette and flipped it into the fireplace.

"Suppose you do go back for this degree of yours on a half-time basis," he asked Ham, "what's going to become of it?"

"Why, just what I've been saying," said Ham. "In the first place I think it's a good move, just from a practical point of view."

"I don't," Masters countered. "I think you're kidding yourself. Look at this guy Holden, for example. He's already *at* where you're only going to be. And all the time you're sweating out the earn-while-you-learn routine, he'll be jogging along piling up points. And then when you come back full-time and give it the old college try to catch up, you'll find that all the heroes have already been made."

"Well, maybe you're right," laughed Ham, "but why couldn't I look around just the way you did, only from an R&D point of view? I might just look around for the spot where the R&D man is well off, and then I'd aim for that and try to hit it."

"You won't find it," said Masters with emphasis. "I laugh at this because I think of our annual report in which we say solemn things about basic R&D being the prime mover of everything that comes down the pike, and we publicly pat its little head and sing hymns of praise. And I'm telling you — off the record and as a friend — that all of this is hypocritical as hell. It's like a bad scenario with half the lines stolen from 'The Life of Louis Pasteur.' I don't know who we think we're kidding — unless it's all the sweet old ladies who own most of our stock."

"That's pretty typical of some high-powered wheel in public relations," Ham laughed. And he laughed again recalling his morning meeting with PR over the promotional piece on the compactor.

"And maybe," Ham added with a smile, "this is a pretty good 'for instance' for my argument that by and large you'll find more honest substance in lab work than anywhere else on the lot."

"I won't argue that you won't find muttonheads in management," said Masters, "but you know darn well that you find them in the lab, too."

Ham nodded his agreement.

"You take the guys on the bench," Masters went on, "and you can pick among them qualitatively. And you know that on any team you've got a few with damn good brains. But you know also that you've got some other good brains seeing things through. It's not just the turn of the wheel that sends one group up and another group down. There are guys seeing things through all along the line. And some of them take plenty of risks."

Ham thought that this was right, too. He had bought a risk, he thought, when he had sold the Chief on the compactor. They had looked at him and said, "O.K., it's your baby." It was a money down, win or lose proposition; luckily he'd won.

In contrast, Ham thought of Holden and Holden's new appointment. This was a different kind of deal. The company would carry Holden as a kind of overhead. It was like a sweeps ticket; maybe they'd get their money back and maybe they wouldn't. The whole psychology of the thing was different.

Ham also thought of the pleasure he'd found in "seeing things through" for some of the men and some of the projects the Chief had assigned to him. There was a sense of accomplishment in this, too, he thought.

"Jack," Ham finally said, "I haven't been trying to give you an argument to deny what you might call the joys of management. I've tasted some of them, and I've found that I liked them. It's just that I have very mixed feelings, and I've been trying to see it from all sides.

"And you know," he added after a pause, "I honestly feel that I'm almost ready to decide to take the job."

Masters looked at Ham and smiled broadly with sheer delight.

"Ham," he said, "that's the most sensible thing your befuddled old brain has produced tonight. Let's have a nightcap on it before you lose it."

As they had their nightcap, they talked about their families and they made vague arrangements about getting together again "soon." When they had finished, Ham drove Masters back to his hotel. They were tired and they rode most of the way in silence. It was not until Masters shook hands on leaving that he returned again to Ham's decision.

"Ham," he said, "maybe I've got more faith in your company than you have, but I think it's a comer. And I think in this new job you've got a helluva fine opportunity to grow with it. Frankly, I think you'd be a sucker to do anything else. Do yourself a favor and take the job."

"Jack, I'm almost ready to think I will," said Ham, as he waved good-by. And maybe I will, he thought, as he drove the long fifteen miles to Cooperstown. He was glad he had seen Jack, he decided as he turned into his drive. It had been good to talk with him.

The next morning at the plant Ham sat for a long time with his annual report again. And again he stared idly at the pages, thinking and worrying, especially worrying. He wished that he could avoid the decision altogether, that the Chief or somebody else would come up with some inevitabilities as to why it could go only one way or another.

As Ham sat worrying, his mail arrived. It provided something of a diversion, and he was grateful for its coming. He spotted among the usual run of internal mail a letter from the Society. He read it with mounting disbelief, and then read it again to make sure. There was no mistaking what it said: his paper on the compactor had won the Society's annual George Peabody Award for the best paper of the year by a young engineer. In stiff, formal phrases the letter sent congratulations from the president of the Society and outlined the Awards Night program at which the Peabody Medal would be presented.

Ham grinned, and the grin grew into a big bubble of elation. Quickly he tucked the letter in his pocket and hurried down the wing to see the Chief. The Chief was in, and he shared Ham's delight as he offered hearty congratulations. He also called the vice president with the news while Ham was still in the office. Ham could hear the vice president's voice gather enthusiasm and begin to dominate the conversation. He couldn't make out the words, but the sounds were friendly.

"He says that you're to make the Society's schedule," said the Chief as he hung up, "and that your wife is to go with you if she can. And he wants you to take any extra time you may need on either side of the meeting—all at company expense, of course."

Ham felt good. It was nice to have these guys in your corner.

"You're not to let the new job make the slightest bit of difference in planning your schedule around this award," the Chief added.

Ham's bubble burst. There was no escaping the thing.

"He also says," the Chief went on, "that he would like to have an answer by the twenty-seventh, if possible. Now that they've made up their minds to move on this, they want to go ahead as quickly as possible."

Ham felt a sudden emptiness in his stomach. "Sure, Chief," he said, "by the twenty-seventh. I ought to have an answer all right, I've already given it a lot of thought."

"And Ham," said the Chief, smiling, "one last thing: be sure to get in touch with PR on this award so that we can exploit it as fully as possible for the company."

Ham nodded and said he would. He added a few words of personal thanks to the Chief and left. He wanted to get back to his office as quickly as possible. He wanted to come to grips with this thing. He wanted to get it settled.

As he hurried past the physics lab, he saw Holden—cup of coffee in hand—sitting at one of the tables, talking animatedly with Dr. Maul. As Ham neared his own cubby, he saw Porter lounging near the door, waiting for him with the formal report on yesterday's run. And as Ham drew nearer, he could hear that Porter was whistling.

Anne Bogan*

We're on the thirty-second floor of a skyscraper, the office of a corporation president. She is his private secretary. The view of the river, railroad yards, bridges, and the city's skyline is astonishing.

"I've been an executive secretary for eight years. However, this is the first time I've been on the corporate end of things, working for the president. I found it a new experience. I love it and I feel I'm learning a lot."

I BECOME very impatient with dreamers. I respect the doers more than the dreamers. So many people, it seems to me, talk about all the things they want to do. They only talk without accomplishing anything. The drifters are worse than the dreamers. Ones who really have no goals, no aspirations at all, just live from day to day . . .

I enjoy one thing more than anything else on this job. That's the association I have with the other executives, not only my boss. There's a tremendous difference in the way they treat me than what I've known before.

They treat me more as . . . on the executive level. They consult me on things, and I enjoy this. It stimulates me.

I know myself well enough to know that I've always enjoyed men more than women. Usually I can judge them very quickly when I meet a woman. I can't judge men that quickly. I seek out the few women I think I will enjoy. The others, I get along with all right, but I feel no basic interest. I don't really enjoy having lunch with them and so on.

You can tell just from conversation what they talk about. It's quite easy. It's also very easy to tell which girls are going to last around the office and which ones aren't. Interest in their work. Many of them aren't, they just don't dig in. They're more interested in chatting in the washroom. I don't know if that's a change from other years. There's always been some who are really not especially career-minded, but they have to give a little bit and try a little harder. The others get by on as little as possible.

I feel like I'm sharing somewhat of the business life of the men. So I think I'm much happier as the secretary to an executive than I would be in some woman's field, where I could perhaps make more money. But it wouldn't be an extension of a successful executive. I'm perfectly happy in my status.

She came from a small town in Indiana and married at eighteen. She had graduated from high school and began working immediately for the town's large company. "My husband was a construction worker. We lived in a trailer, we moved around a lot. There's a lot of community living in that situation and I grew pretty tired of it. You can get involved, you can become too friendly with people when you live too close. A lot of time can be wasted. It was years before I started doing this."

I have dinner with businessmen and enjoy this very much. I like the background music in some of these restaurants. It's soothing and it also adds a little warmth and doesn't disturb the conversation. I like the atmosphere and the caliber of people that usually you see and run into. People who have made it.

I think if I've been at all successful with men, it's because I'm a good listener and interested in their world. I enjoy it, I don't become bored with it. They tell me about their personal life too. Family problems, financial, and the problems of raising children. Most of the ones I'm referring to are divorced. In looking through the years they were married, I can see this is what probably happened. I know if I were the wife, I would be interested in their work. I feel the wife of an executive would be a better wife had she been a secretary first. As a secretary, you learn to adjust to the boss's moods. Many marriages would be happier if the wife would do that.

The Bagel Hockey Case

THE CAFETERIA for the Toronto Training Academy (TTA) was located on the first floor of the school's main residential hall. The cafeteria was open seven days each week. It consisted of a short order grill, a salad and delicatessen bar, a soda fountain and a hot meals counter, although the latter was not operated on weekends. It was heavily utilized by the students and by others during the week for food and as a social center. On weekends its use was rather limited since many TTA students were commuters and others left campus for the weekend. What business there was tended to come in spurts due in part to the use of the building for special workshops and other group activities.

During the weekend the cafeteria employed a different crew of workers than during the week. All seven of the weekend employees were students except for the cashier who was a housewife in her mid-30s. Two of the employees were attending high school; the senior Student Supervisor was from a two year business college, and the remaining three workers were from TTA.

Ernie Slim, the senior Student Supervisor, had been employed at the cafeteria for four years, a long period of employment for the cafeteria, and had worked his way up from grill attendant to his supervisory position. He was a shy, friendly character who rarely worked directly with the public but spent most of his time in the back room making food preparations for take-out and banquet orders. Henry Delano, the junior Student Supervisor, was more personable with the customers, often standing and chatting with them. He spent most of his day walking around overseeing the other employees, sometimes helping them when they found themselves bogged down with orders, or working the grill and fountain positions by himself while others took breaks. Having had no previous experience before beginning the job, Henry was often forced to rely on employees below him to explain tasks.

Two male students usually worked the grill, and during slow hours of the day they were required to work in the dishroom. Two female students worked the fountain and deli-bar and during slow hours bused cafeteria tables. The cashier's job only required her to attend the register and at the end of the day determine the total income. This position was always occupied, even during week days, by an older, more mature woman.

All worked under the general regulations of the cafeteria which required that all employees be neatly and cleanly attired. Girls were to wear hairnets and blue smocks over skirts; while boys had to wear white work shirts and paper hats. Sideburns were not permitted to extend below the ear lobe, and beards were not allowed. Mustaches had to be neat and closely trimmed, not extending beyond the width of the upper lip. Good sanitary practices were expected of all employees, and these regulations included the statement: "loud talking, singing, whistling, or horseplay will not be tolerated." A pay differential was established depending upon the individual's position, time employed, and whether or not the student had purchased a meal ticket. Weekend and weekday employees were on the same wage scale, and the pay range for grill and fountain employees was between $1.80 and $2.50 an hour, while supervisors received anywhere between $4.00 and $5.00 an hour. Except for the supervisors, the job was not considered a very desirable one, and, in fact, it had been a last-resort choice by every weekend employee.

Since the cafeteria was open from 12:30 to 7:00 on weekends, only one shift of workers was needed. All weekend employees worked on an eight hour day and were allowed a half hour for dinner and given a fifteen minute coffee break. These breaks were given at the discretion of the supervisors, but employees felt free to ask for them if they thought business was slow enough.

Scheduling, hiring, and firing were all done by the cafeteria manager, Mrs. Laraby, a middle aged women who had been manager for five years. She worked a 40-hour week, Monday through Friday, and rarely came into the cafeteria on weekends, unless there was a special banquet to be set up. As manager, she encouraged a relaxed working atmosphere but expected each employee to be responsible for his or her job and to observe strictly the regulations of the cafeteria. Although she was firm about what she expected of her workers, Mrs. Laraby was willing to listen to any problems encountered by the employees. As a result, they respected Mrs. Laraby and felt comfortable enough in her presence to joke with her, although they were careful not to, whenever her boss was around.

Grill products were of the hamburger and hot dog variety; the fountain's main business was ice cream cones; while the deli-bar served salads, desserts, and cold sandwiches, most of which had been made during the week and were now in the "staling" process. All beverage machines were self-service. A customer passed down the food line and paid the cashier located at the end of the line.

During the weekends, no large quantity food preparation was done, leaving the large kitchen area desolate and open to all employees. This large back room was blocked from the customer's view by walls which separated it from the food service area. (See Exhibit 1).

All employees performed the essential tasks which their jobs demanded of them, but without much enthusiasm. The working atmosphere was extremely relaxed and lenient, and since the work was menial, there was a flexible set-up in which almost everyone could operate in another's position. Frequently, the fountain person helped out the grill individual, and vice versa. However, a large portion of the working day passed with only a few customers trickling in. There was little opportunity to converse with friends coming through the food line, as was commonplace during the weekdays. This left the employees with much idle time.

The employees were close in age and shared common interests. Many friendships were formed. Supervisors were treated as equals, and joked and fooled around with the others. In the back room (kitchen), as time allowed, the male employees including the supervisors often engaged in a game of floor hockey, using brooms as sticks and a stale bagel as a puck. The crew also participated in other sports. One was "baseball" played with a spatula and a hard boiled egg. Another was "King of the Eggs." This game was particularly popular with the female employees. The idea was to find the "king egg" in a batch of hard boiled eggs destined to be used eventually in egg salad. The game required two players. Each chose an egg, then one party held her egg firmly in one hand while the other person used her egg to hit the immobile egg. The player whose egg withstood the impact without cracking was declared the winner and continued to challenge any other potential players. Of all the games, only baseball ruined any appreciable quantity of usable food.

There had never been any crackdown attempts on this behavior, which occurred only on weekends when the large kitchen was not in use and there were no older supervisors or managers present.

Participation in these events was left up to the individual, but the usual participants included the three male student workers and the supervisor. The fountain girls took part in games such as the egg cracking less fre-

EXHIBIT 1

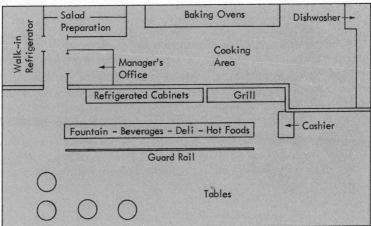

quently while the cashier never participated in any events but read during long intervals between customers. The general attitude of all employees toward these tournaments was favorable, except, as a fountain employee put it, "when you get stuck doing all the work while the others are out back having fun." On occasion, when employees were engaged in these tournaments, business picked up in the food service area. Then, the one or two individuals left attending the fountain or grill were swamped with orders, finding it impossible to leave their jobs and notify the others in the back room of the customer influx. It placed a lot of pressure on these workers and if this happened it meant that customers waited a long period of time for their orders.

One Sunday, during a normal midday lull, the three men and the supervisor were deep into a game of bagel hockey in the back room. The participants were totally involved in their fun and did not notice that there was an influx of customers, that the other attendants were overwhelmed at both grill and fountain, and that the cashier was busy at her register. On this particular occasion, Mrs. Laraby, the cafeteria manager, decided to pick up a book she had left in her office. Entering through the cafeteria, she first came upon the swamped employees, then proceeding to enter the back room, she discovered an exuberant hockey game in progress!

Banana Time Case*

THIS PAPER undertakes description and exploratory analysis of the social interaction which took place within a small work group of factory machine operatives during a two-month period of participant observation.

My fellow operatives and I spent our long days of simple, repetitive work in relative isolation from other employees of the factory. Our line of machines was sealed off from other work areas of the plant by the four walls of the clicking room. The one door of this room was usually closed. Even when it was kept open, during periods of hot weather, the consequences were not social, it opened on an uninhibited storage room of the

* Excerpted from Donald F. Roy, " 'Banana Time,' Job Satisfaction and Informal Interaction." Reproduced by permission of Society for Applied Anthropology from *Human Organization,* vol. 18, no. 4 (1960).

shipping department. Not even the sounds of work activity going on elsewhere in the factory carried to this isolated work place. There were occasional contacts with outside employees, usually on matters connected with the work, but, with the exception of the daily calls of one fellow who came to pick up finished materials for the next step in processing, such visits were sporadic and infrequent.

The clickers were of the genus punching machines; of mechanical construction similar to that of the better-known punch presses, their leading features were hammer and block. The hammer, or punching head, was approximately eight inches by twelve inches at its flat striking surface. The descent upon the block was initially forced by the operator, who exerted pressure on a handle attached to the side of the hammer head. A few inches of travel downward established electrical connection for a sharp, power-driven blow. The hammer also traveled, by manual guidance, in a horizontal plane to and from, and in an arc around, the central column of the machine. Thus the operator, up to the point of establishing electrical connections for the sudden and irrevocable downward thrust, had flexibility in maneuvering his instrument over the larger surface of the block. The latter, approximately twenty-four inches wide, eighteen inches deep, and ten inches thick, was made, like a butcher's block, of inlaid hardwood, it was set in the machine at a convenient waist height. On it the operator placed his materials, one sheet at a time if leather, stacks of sheets if plastic, to be cut with steel dies of assorted sizes and shapes. The particular die in use would be moved, by hand, from spot to spot over the materials each time a cut was made, less frequently materials would be shifted on the block as the operator saw need for such adjustment.

Introduction to the new job, with its relatively simple machine skills and work routines, was accomplished with what proved to be, in my experience, an all-time minimum of job training. The clicking machine assigned to me was situated at one end of the row. Here the superintendent and one of the operators gave a few brief demonstrations, accompanied by bits of advice which included a warning to keep hands clear of the descending hammer. After a short practice period, at the end of which the superintendent expressed satisfaction with progress and potentialities, I was left to develop my learning curve with no other supervision than that afforded by members of the work group. Further advice and assistance did come, from time to time, from my fellow operatives, sometimes upon request, sometimes unsolicited.

THE WORK GROUP

Absorbed at first in three related goals of improving my clicking skill, increasing my rate of output, and keeping my left hand unclicked, I paid little attention to my fellow operatives save to observe that they were friendly, middle-aged, foreign born, full of advice, and very talkative. Their names, according to the way they addressed each other, were George, Ike, and Sammy. George, a stocky fellow in his late fifties, operated the machine at the opposite end of the line; he, I later discovered, had emigrated in early youth from a country in Southeastern Europe. Ike, stationed at George's left, was tall, slender, in his early fifties, and Jewish; he had come from Eastern Europe in his youth. Sammy, number three man in the line, and my neighbor, was heavy set, in his late fifties, and Jewish; he had escaped from a country in Eastern Europe just before Hitler's legions had moved in. All three men had been downwardly mobile as to occupation in recent years. George and Sammy had been proprietors of small businesses; the former had been "wiped out" when his uninsured establishment burned down; the latter had been entrepreneuring on a small scale before he left all behind him to flee the Germans. According to his account, Ike had left a highly skilled trade which he had practiced for years in Chicago.

THE WORK

It was evident to me, before my first workday drew to a weary close, that my clicking career was going to be a grim process of fighting the clock, the particular timepiece in this situation being an old-fashioned alarm clock which ticked away on a shelf near George's machine. I had struggled through many dreary rounds with the minutes and hours during the various phases of my industrial experience, but never had I been confronted with such a dismal combination of working conditions as the extra-long workday, the infinitesimal cerebral excitation, and the extreme limitation of physical movement. The contrast with a recent stint in the California oil fields was striking. This was no eight-hour day of racing hither and yon over desert and foothills with a rollicking crew of "roustabouts" on a variety of repair missions at oil wells, pipelines, and storage tanks. Here there were no afternoon dallyings to search the sands for horned toads, tarantulas, and rattlesnakes, or to climb old wooden derricks for raven's nests, with an eye out, of course, for the telltale streak of dust in the distance which gave ample warning of the approach of the boss. This was standing all day in one spot beside three old codgers in a dingy room looking out through barred windows at the bare walls of a brick warehouse, leg movements largely restricted to the shifting of body weight from one foot to the other, hand and arm movements confined, for the most part, to a simple repetitive sequence of place the die, – punch the clicker, – place the die, – punch the clicker, and intellectual activity reduced to computing the hours to quitting time. It is true that from time to time a fresh stack of sheets would have to be substituted for the clicked-out old one, but the stack would have been prepared by someone else, and the exchange would be only a minute or two in the making. Now and then a box of finished work would have to be moved back out of the way, and an empty box brought up, but the moving back and the bringing up involved only a step or two. And there was the half hour for lunch, and occasional trips to the lavatory or the drinking fountain to break up the day into digestible parts. But after each momentary respite, hammer and die were moving again: click, – move die, – click, – move die.

I developed a game of work. The game developed was quite simple, so elementary, in fact, that its playing was reminiscent of rainy-day pre-occupations in childhood, when attention could be centered by the hour on colored bits of things of assorted sizes and shapes. But this adult activity was not mere pottering and piddling; what it lacked in the earlier imaginative content, it made up for in clean-cut structure. Fundamentally involved were: (a) variation in color of the materials cut, (b) variation in shapes of the dies used, and (c) a process called "scraping the block." The basic procedure which ordered the particular combination of components employed could be stated in the form: "As soon as I do so many of these, I'll click some brown ones." And, with success in attaining the objective of working with brown materials, a new goal of "I'll get to do the white ones" might be set. Or the new goal might involve switching dies.

INFORMAL SOCIAL ACTIVITY OF THE WORK GROUP: TIMES AND THEMES

I began to take serious note of the social activity going on around me; my attentiveness to this activity came with growing involvement in it. What I heard at first, before I started to listen, was a stream of discon-nected bits of communication which did not make much sense. Foreign accents were strong and referents were not joined to coherent contexts of meaning. It was just "jabbering." What I saw at first, before I began to observe, was occasional flurries of horseplay that was so simple and unvarying in pattern and so childish in quality that they made no strong bid for attention. For example, Ike would regularly switch off the power at Sammy's machine whenever Sammy made a trip to the lavatory or the drinking fountain. Correlatively, Sammy invariably fell victim to the plot by making an attempt to operate his clicking hammer after returning to the shop. And, as the simple pattern went, this blind stumbling into the trap was always followed by indignation and reproach from Sammy, smirking satisfaction from Ike, and mild paternal scolding from George. My interest in this procedure was at first confined to wondering when Ike would weary of his tedious joke or when Sammy would learn to check his power switch before trying the hammer.

Most of the breaks in the daily series were designated as "times" in the parlance of the clicker operators, and they featured the consumption of food or drink of one sort or another. There was coffee time, peach time, banana time, fish time, coke time, and, of course, lunch time. Other interruptions, which formed part of the series but were not verbally recognized as times, were window time, pickup time, and the staggered quitting times of Sammy and Ike. These latter unnamed times did not involve the partaking of refreshments.

My attention was first drawn to this times business during my first week of employment when I was encouraged to join in the sharing of two peaches. It was Sammy who provided the peaches; he drew them from his lunch box after making the announcement, "Peach time!" On this first occasion I refused the proffered fruit, but thereafter regularly consumed my half peach. Sammy continued to provide the peaches and to make the "Peach time!" announcement, although there were days when Ike would remind him that it was peach time, urging him to hurry up with the mid-morning snack. Ike invariably complained about the quality of the fruit, and his complaints fed the fires of continued banter between peach donor and critical recipient. I did find the fruit a bit on the scrubby side but felt, before I achieved insight into the function of peach time, that Ike was showing poor manners by looking a gift horse in the mouth. I wondered why Sammy continued to share his peaches with such an ingrate.

Banana time followed peach time by approximately an hour. Sammy again provided the refreshments, namely, one banana. There was, however, no four-way sharing of Sammy's banana. Ike would gulp it down by himself after surreptitiously extracting it from Sammy's lunch box, kept on a shelf behind Sammy's work station. Each morning, after making the snatch, Ike would call out, "Banana time!" and proceed to down his prize while Sammy made futile protests and denunciations. George would join in with mild remonstrances, sometimes scolding Sammy for making so much fuss. The banana was one which Sammy brought for his own consumption at lunch time; he never did get to eat his banana, but kept bringing one for his lunch. At first this daily theft startled and amazed me. Then I grew to look forward to the daily seizure and the verbal interaction which followed.

Window time came next. It followed banana time as a regular consequence of Ike's castigation by the indignant Sammy. After "taking" repeated references to himself as a person badly lacking in morality and character, Ike would "finally" retaliate by opening the window which faced Sammy's machine, to let the "cold air" blow in on Sammy. The slandering which would, in its echolalic repetition, wear down Ike's patience and forbearance usually took the form of the invidious comparison: "George is a good daddy. Ike is a bad man! A very bad man!" Opening the window would take a little time to accomplish and would involve a great deal of verbal interplay between Ike and Sammy, both before and after the event. Ike would threaten, make feints toward the window, then finally open it. Sammy would protest, argue, and make claims that the air blowing in on him would give him a cold; he would eventually have to leave his machine to close the window. Sometimes the weather was slightly chilly, and the draft from the window unpleasant, but cool or hot, windy or still, window time arrived each day. (I assume that it was originally a cold season development.) George's part in this interplay, in spite of the "good daddy" laudations, was to encourage Ike in his window work. He would stress the tonic values of fresh air and chide Sammy for his unappreciativeness.

Themes

To put flesh, so to speak, on this interactional frame of times, my work group had developed various "themes" of verbal interplay which had become standardized in their repetition. These topics of conversation ranged in quality from an extreme of nonsensical chatter to another extreme of serious discourse. Unlike the times, these themes flowed one into the other in no particular sequence of predictability. Serious conversation could suddenly melt into horseplay, and vice versa. In the middle of a serious discussion on the high cost of living, Ike might drop a weight behind the easily startled Sammy, or hit him over the head with a dusty paper sack. Interaction would immediately drop to a low comedy exchange of slaps, threats, guffaws, and disapprobations which would invariably include a ten-minute echolalia of "Ike is a bad man, a very bad man! George is a good daddy, a very fine man!" Or, on the other hand, a stream of such invidious comparisons as followed a surreptitious switching-off of Sammy's machine by the playful Ike might merge suddenly into a discussion of the pros and cons of saving for one's funeral.

"Kidding themes" were usually started by George or Ike, and Sammy was usually the butt of the joke. Sometimes Ike would have to "take it," seldom George. One favorite kidding theme involved Sammy's alleged receipt of $100 a month from his son. The points stressed were that Sammy did not have to work long hours, or did not have to work at all, because he had a son to support him. George would always point out that he sent money to his daughter; she did not send money to him. Sammy received occasional calls from his wife, and his claim that these calls were requests to shop for groceries on the way home were greeted with feigned disbelief. Sammy was ribbed for being closely watched, bossed, and henpecked by his wife, and the expression, "Are you man or mouse?" became an echolalic utterance, used both in and out of the original context.

Serious themes included the relating of major misfortunes suffered in the past by group members. George referred again and again to the loss, by fire, of his business establishment. Ike's chief complaints centered around a chronically ill wife who had undergone various operations and periods of hospital care. Ike spoke with discouragement of the expenses attendant upon hiring a housekeeper for himself and his children; he referred with disappointment and disgust to a teen-age son, an inept lad who "couldn't even fix his own lunch. He couldn't even make himself a sandwich!" Sammy's reminiscences centered on the loss of a flourishing business when he had to flee Europe ahead of Nazi invasion.

There was one theme of especially solemn import, the "professor theme." This theme might also be termed "George's daughter's marriage theme," for the recent marriage of George's only child was inextricably bound up with George's connection with higher learning. The daughter had married the son of a professor who instructed in one of the local colleges. This professor theme was not in the strictest sense a conversation piece; when the subject came up George did all the talking. The two Jewish operatives remained silent as they listened with deep respect, if not actual awe, to George's accounts of the Big Wedding which, including the wedding pictures, entailed an expense of $1,000. It was monologue, but there was listening, there was communication, the sacred communication of a temple, when George told of going for Sunday afternoon walks on the Midway with the professor, or of joining the professor for a Sunday dinner. Whenever he spoke of the professor, his daughter, the wedding, or even of the new son-in-law, who remained for the most part in the background, a sort of incidental like the wedding cake, George was complete master of the interaction. His manner, in speaking to the rank-and-file of clicker operators, was indeed that of master deigning to notice his underlings. I came to the conclusion that it was the professor connection, not the straw-boss-ship or the extra nickel an hour, which provided the fount of George's superior status in the group.

Barbara Herrick*

She is thirty; single. Her title is script supervisor/producer at a large advertising agency; working out of its Los Angeles office. She is also a vice president. Her accounts are primarily in food and cosmetics. "There's a myth: a woman is expected to be a food writer because she is assumed to know those things and a man doesn't. However, some of the best copy on razors and Volkswagens has been written by women."

She has won several awards and considerable recognition for her commercials. "You have to be absolutely on target, dramatic and fast. You have to be aware of legal restrictions. The FTC gets tougher and tougher. You must understand budgetary matters: will it cost a million or can it be shot in a studio in one day?"

She came off a Kansas farm, one of four daughters. "During high school, I worked as a typist and was an extremely good one. I was compulsive about doing every tiny job very well." She graduated from the University of Missouri. According to Department of Labor statistics, she is in the upper one percent bracket of working women.

In her Beverly Hills apartment are paintings, sculpted works, recordings (classic, folk, jazz, and rock), and many books, most of them obviously well thumbed.

MEN IN my office doing similar work were being promoted, given raises and titles. Since I had done the bulk of the work, I made a stand and was promoted too. I needed the title, because clients figured that I'm just a face-man.

A face-man is a person who looks good, speaks well, and presents the work. I look well, I speak well, and I'm pleasant to have around after the business is over with—if they acknowledge me in business. We go to the lounge and have drinks. I can drink with the men but remain a lady. (Laughs.)

That's sort of my tacit business responsibility, although this has never been said to me directly. I know this is why I travel alone for the company a great deal. They don't anticipate any problems with my behavior. I equate it with being the good nigger.

On first meeting, I'm frequently taken for the secretary, you know, traveling with the boss. I'm here to keep somebody happy. Then I'm in-

* From S. Terkel, *Working*. Copyright © 1972, 1974 by Studs Terkel. Reprinted by permission of Pantheon Books, a division of Random House, Inc.

troduced as the writer. One said to me after the meeting was over and the drinking had started, "When I first saw you, I figured you were a—you know. I never knew you were the person *writing* this all the time." (Laughs.) Is it a married woman working for extra money? Is it a lesbian? Is it some higher-up's mistress?

I'm probably one of the ten highest paid people in the agency. It would cause tremendous hard feelings if, say, I work with a man who's paid less. If a remark is made at a bar—"You make so much money, you could buy and sell me"—I toss it off, right? He's trying to find out. He can't equate me as a rival. They wonder where to put me, they wonder what my salary is.

Buy and sell me—yeah, there are a lot of phrases that show the reversal of roles. What comes to mind is swearing at a meeting. New clients are often very uptight. They feel they can't make any innuendos that might be suggestive. They don't know how to treat me. They don't know whether to acknowledge me as a woman or as another neuter person who's doing a job for them.

The first time, they don't look at me. At the first three meetings of this one client, if I would ask a direct question, they would answer and look at my boss or another man in the room. Even around the conference table. I don't attempt to be—the glasses, the bun, and totally asexual. That isn't the way I am. It's obvious that I'm a woman and enjoy being a woman. I'n not overly provocative either. It's the thin, good nigger line that I have to toe.

I've developed a sixth sense about this. If a client will say, "Are you married?" I will often say yes, because that's the easiest way to deal with him if he needs that category for me. If it's more acceptable to him to have a young, attractive married woman in a business position comparable to his, terrific. It doesn't bother me. It makes me safer. He'll never be challenged. He can say, "She'd be sensational. I'd love to get her. I could show her what a real man is, but she's married." It's a way out for him.

Or there's the mistress thing: well, she's sleeping with the boss. That's acceptable to them. Or she's a frustrated, compulsive castrator. That's a category. Or lesbian. If I had short hair, wore suits, and talked in a gruff voice, that would be more acceptable than I am. It's when I transcend their labels, they don't quite know what to do. If someone wants a quick label and says, "I'll bet you're a big women's libber, aren't you?" I say, "Yeah, yeah." They have to place me.

I travel a lot. That's what gets very funny. We had a meeting in Montreal. It was one of those bride's magazines, honeymoon-type resorts, with heart-shaped beds and the heated pool. I was there for three days with nine men. All day long we were enclosed in this conference room. The agency account man went with me. I was to talk about the new products, using slides and movies. There were about sixty men in the conference room. I had to leave in such a hurry, I still had my gaucho pants and boots on.

The presentation went on for an hour and a half. There was tittering and giggling for about forty minutes. Then you'd hear the shift in the audience. They got interested in what I was saying. Afterwards they had lunch sent up. Some of them never did talk to me. Others were interested in my life. They would say things like, "Have you read *The Sensuous Woman?*" (Laughs.) They didn't really want to know. If they were even more obvious, they probably would have said, "Say, did you hear the one about the farmer's daughter?" I'd have replied, "Of course, I'm one myself."

The night before, there was a rehearsal. Afterwards the account man suggested we go back to the hotel, have a nightcap, and get to bed early. It was a 9:00 A.M. meeting. We were sitting at the bar and he said, "Of course, you'll be staying in my room." I said, "What? I have a room." He said, "I just assumed. You're here and I'm here and we're both grown up." I said, "You assumed? You never even asked me whether I wanted to." My feelings obviously meant nothing to him. Apparently it was what you *did* if you're out of town and the woman is anything but a harelip and you're ready to go. His assumption was incredible.

We used to joke about him in the office. We'd call him Mr. Straight, because he was Mr. Straight. Very short hair, never grew sideburns, never wore wide ties, never, never swore, never would pick up an innuendo, super-super-conservative. No one would know, you see?

Mr. Straight is a man who'd never invite me to have a drink after work. He would never invite me to lunch alone. Would never, never make an overture to me. It was simply the fact that we were out of town and who would know? That poor son of a bitch had no notion what he was doing to my ego. I didn't want to destroy his. We had to work together the next day and continue to work together.

The excuse I gave is one I use many times. "Once when I was much younger and innocent, I slept with an account man. The guy turned out to be a bastard. I got a big reputation and he made my life miserable because he had a loose mouth. And even though you're a terrifically nice guy and I'd like to sleep with you, I feel I can't. It's my policy. I'm older and wiser now. I don't do it. You have to understand that." It worked. I could never say to him, "You don't even understand how you insulted me."

It's the always-having-to-please conditioning. I don't want to make any enemies. Only of late, because I'm getting more secure and I'm valued by the agency, am I able to get mad at men and say, "Fuck off!" But still I have to keep egos unruffled, smooth things over . . . I still work with him and he never mentioned it again.

He'll occasionally touch my arm or catch my eye: We're really sym-
patico, aren't we baby? There may be twelve men and me sitting at a
meeting and they can't call on one of the girls or the receptionist, he'd
say, "Let's have some coffee, Barbara. Make mine black." I'm the
waitress. I go do it because it's easier than to protest. If he'd known my
salary is more than his I doubt that he'd have acted that way in Denver—
or here.

Part of the resentment toward me and my salary is that I don't have a
mortgage on a home in the Valley and three kids who have to go to private schools and a wife who spends at Saks, and you never know when
you're going to lose your job in this business. Say, we're having a con-
vivial drink among peers and we start grousing. I'm not allowed to
grouse with the best of them. They say, "Oh, you? What do you need
money for? You're a single woman. You've got the world by the balls."
I hear that all the time.

If I'm being paid a lot of attention to, say by someone to whom I'm
attracted, and we've done a job and we're in New York together for a
week's stretch, we're in the same hotel, suppose I want to sleep with
him? Why not? Here's my great double standard. You never hear it said
about a man in my capacity—"He sleeps around." It would only be to his
glory. It's expected, if he's there with a model, starlet, or secretary. In
my case, I constantly worry about that. If I want to, I must be very careful. That's what I'm railing against.

This last shoot, it was an exasperating shot. It took hours. We were
there all day. It was exhausting, frustrating. Between takes, the camera
man, a darling man, would come back to where I was standing and put
his arms around me. I didn't think anything of it. We're hardly fucking
on the set. It was his way of relaxing. I hear a comment later that night
from the director: "You ought to watch your behavior on the set with the
camera man." I said, *"Me* watch it? Fuck that! Let *him* watch it." He
was hired by me. I could fire him if I didn't like him. Why *me,* you see?
I have to watch.

Clients. I get calls in my hotel room: "I want to discuss something
about production today that didn't go right." I know what that means. I
try to fend it off. I'm on this tightrope. I don't want to get into a drunken
scene ever with a client and to literally shove him away. That's not going
to do me any good. The only smart thing I can do is avoid that sort of
scene. The way I avoid it is by suggesting an early morning breakfast
meeting. I always have to make excuses: "I drank too much and my stomach is really upset, so I couldn't do it right now. We'll do it in the morning." Sometimes I'd like to say, "Fuck off, I know what you want."

*"I've had a secretary for the last three years. I hesitate to use her . . . I
won't ask her to do typing. It's hard for me to use her as I was used. She's*

bright and could be much more than a secretary. So I give her research assignments, things to look up, which might be fun for her. Rather than just say, 'Here, type this.'

"I'm an interesting figure to her. She says, 'When I think of Women's Lib I don't think of Germaine Greer or Kate Millett. I think of you.' She sees my life as a lot more glamorous than it really is. She admires the externals. She admires the apartment, the traveling. We shot two commercials just recently, one in Mexico, one in Nassau. Then I was in New York to edit them. That's three weeks. She takes care of all my travel details. She knows the company gave me an advance of well over a thousand dollars. I'm put up in fine hotels, travel first class. I can spend ninety dollars at a dinner for two or three. I suppose it is something— little Barbara from a Kansas farm, and Christ! look where I am. But I don't think of it, which is a funny thing."

It used to be the token black at a big agency was very safe because he always had to be there. Now I'm definitely the token woman. In the current economic climate, I'm one of the few writers at my salary level getting job offers. Unemployment is high right now among people who do what I do. Yet I get calls: "Will you come and write on feminine hygiene products?" Another, involving a food account: "We need you, we'll pay you thirty grand and a contract. Be the answer for Such-an-such Foods." I'm ideal because I'm young enough to have four or five solid years of experience behind me. I know how to handle myself or I wouldn't be where I am.

I'm very secure right now. But when someone says to me, "You don't have to worry," he's wrong. In a profession where I absolutely cannot age, I cannot be doing this at thirty-eight. For the next years, until I get too old, my future's secure in a very insecure business. It's like a race horse or a show horse. Although I'm holding the job on talent and responsibility, I got here partly because I'm attractive and it's a big kick for a client to know that for three days in Montreal there's going to be this young brunette, who's very good, mind you. I don't know how they talk about me, but I'd guess: "She's very good, but to look at her you'd never know it. She's a knockout."

I have a fear of hanging on past my usefulness. I've seen desperate women out of jobs, who come around with their samples, which is the way all of us get jobs. A lot of women have been cut. Women who had soft jobs in an agency for years and are making maybe fifteen thousand. In the current slump, this person is cut and some bright young kid from a college, who'll work for seven grand a year, comes in and works late every night.

Talk about gaps. In a room with a twenty-two-year-old, there are areas in which I'm altogether lost. But not being a status-quo-type person, I've always thought ahead enough to keep pace with what's new. I certainly don't feel my usefulness as a writer is coming to an end. I'm talking strictly in terms of physical aging. (Laughs.) It's such a young business, not just the consumer part. It's young in terms of appearances. The client expects agency people, especially on the creative end, to dress a certain way, to be very fashionable. I haven't seen many women in any executive capacity age gracefully.

The bellbottoms, the beads, beards, and sideburns, that's the easy, superficial way to feel part of the takeover culture. It's true also in terms of writing. What kind of music do you put behind the commercial? It's ridiculous to expect a sheltered forty-two-year-old to anticipate progressive rock. The danger of aging, beyond touch, out of reach with the younger market . . .

The part I hate—it's funny. (Pause.) Most people in the business are delighted to present their work and get praise for it—and the credit and the laughter and everything in the commercial. I always hate that part. Deep down, I feel demeaned. Don't question the adjectives, don't argue, if it's a cologne or a shampoo. I know, 'cause I buy 'em myself. I'm the biggest sucker for buying an expensively packaged hoax thing. Face cream at eight dollars. And I sell and convince.

I used Erik Satie music for a cologne thing. The clients didn't know Satie from Roger Williams. I'm very good at what I do, dilettantism. I go into my act: we call it dog and pony time, show time, tap dance. We laugh about it. He says, "Oh, that's beautiful, exactly right. How much will it cost us?" I say, "The music will cost you three grand. Those two commercials you want to do in Mexico and Nassau, that's forty grand. There's no way I can bring it in for less." I'm this young woman, saying, "Give me forty thousand dollars of your money and I will go away to Mexico and Nassau and bring you back a commercial and you'll love it." It's blind faith.

Do I ever question what I'm selling? (A soft laugh.) All the time. I know a writer who quit a job equivalent to mine. She was making a lot of money, well thought of. She was working on a consumer finance account. It's blue collar and black. She made this big stand. I said to her, in private, "I agree with you, but why is this your test case? You've been selling a cosmetic for years that is nothing but mineral oil and women are paying eight dollars for it. You've been selling a cake mix that you know is so full of preservatives that it would kill every rat in the lab. Why all of a sudden . . . ?"

If you're in the business, you're in the business, the _____ business! You're a hustler. But because you're witty and glib . . . I've never pretended this is the best writing I can do. Every advertising writer has a novel in his drawer. Few of them ever do it.

I don't think what I do is necessary or that it performs a service. If it's a very fine product—and I've worked on some of those—I love it. It's when you get into that awful area of hope, cosmetics—you're just selling image and a hope. It's like the arthritis cure or cancer—quackery. You're saying to a lady, "Because this oil comes from the algae at the bottom of the sea, you're going to have a timeless face." It's a crock of _____! I know it's part of my job. I do it. If I make the big stand my friend made, I'd lose my job. Can't do it. I'm expected to write whatever assignment I'm given. It's whorish. I haven't written enough to know what kind of writer I am. I suspect, rather than a writer, I'm a good reader. I think I'd make a good editor. I have read so many short stories that I bet I could turn out a better anthology than anybody's done yet, in certain categories. I remember, I appreciate, I have a feeling I could . . .

POSTSCRIPT: *Shortly afterward she was battling an ulcer.*

Ben Reed*

BEN REED, 27, graduated from State University in June 1959, with a B.A. degree in psychology.

Shortly after graduation he took a job as assistant office manager with the Acme Medical Association, a group health insurance organization. His salary was $5,000 per year. As assistant office manager he was responsible for supervising approximately forty female office employees who performed sorting, totaling, and recording operations concerning medical claims charged against Acme.

The office workers were situated at several rows of desks in a large open room. As assistant manager, Ben Reed had a desk in the same room but off to one side of the desks of the girls. His immediate supervisor, Mr. Charles Grayson, the office manager, had been with Acme for twenty years and had risen to his present position from a beginning job as a clerical assistant. During his career at Acme, he had watched the company grow and progress, and often referred to the increase in employees under his supervision with a great deal of pride.

* From Harry R. Knudson, Jr., *Human Elements of Administration*, copyright © 1963, Holt, Rinehart and Winston, Inc., Reprinted with the permission of Holt, Rinehart and Winston, publishers.

According to Ben Reed, his work at Acme was not especially challenging. In describing his job, he stated that his main duties were to
check the timecards of the office workers each morning, to make sure that
everything was in order, and to answer questions concerning claims that
the girls might bring to him. In addition, he did special statistical studies
at the request of the controller's office or Mr. Grayson. These studies
were infrequent, and during his first four months with Acme, Ben participated in only two such studies. He estimated that on the average he
actually "worked" no more than one or two hours a day.

Partially because of some courses he had taken at the University, Ben
Reed had some strong convictions concerning the supervision of the
office employees. He was concerned about the situation at Acme for two
reasons: (a) the high turnover of office employees—which averaged
about 48 per cent per year and, (b) the apathy of many of the girls toward
their work. He realized that he was new in the organization but nevertheless felt obligated to make some suggestions which he felt would improve
the situation with regard to the office force. Mr. Grayson, his immediate
superior, often did not agree with these suggestions.

For example, in order to utilize partially his unproductive time, Ben
suggested that as he had had several courses in physiology as a premed
student before transferring to psychology, it might be helpful if he could
spend an hour or two a week in instructing the office staff in some of the
basic fundamentals of physiology. The nature of the work was such that
knowledge of the various functions and systems of the body would, he
felt, be helpful in speeding up the sorting and processing of claims that
came in. Ben suggested to Mr. Grayson that he would be happy to conduct these informal classes as a part of his regular duties. Mr. Grayson,
however, did not feel this was a good suggestion and did not permit Ben
to go through with his idea.

Ben also had a disagreement with Mr. Grayson over the handling of
the case of Doris Martin. Doris, a clerk-typist, approached Ben one day
while Mr. Grayson was out of the office to report that she was sick and
desired to go home. Ben made the necessary arrangements for her to have
the rest of the day off. When Mr. Grayson heard of this incident he was
very upset. He told Ben that he did not have the authority to make these
kinds of decisions and that he, Mr. Grayson, would make all such decisions in the future. Although Ben felt that, because of his position as assistant office manager, because Mr. Grayson was not in the office at the
time the situation occurred, and because Doris Martin was obviously
sick, he had made a good decision, he let the matter drop.

On December 10, 1959, Mr. Robert Colvin, Controller of Acme
Medical Association, called Ben into his office to discuss plans for a new
electronic data processing installation that the company was considering
putting in to speed up the processing of claims. He spent about two and

one-half hours with Ben explaining the proposed system and concluded the interview by stating that he felt that as new men often had good ideas for improvement, he would welcome any thoughts that Ben might have.

Ben was enthusiastic about Mr. Colvin's approaching him, and spent several hours that night at home working out a plan that would permit the new process to be installed in his area with a minimum of difficulty. He submitted his ideas to Mr. Colvin the next morning.

Mr. Colvin was very much impressed with Ben's ideas and immediately called a meeting of several of the officials of Acme, including Mr. Grayson, to review Ben's plan. This meeting was held during the early afternoon of December 11. About 3:00 P.M., Mr. Grayson entered the area in which the girls' and Ben's desks were located, approached Ben's desks, and slammed the folder containing Ben's plans down on the desk, exclaiming, "What in the hell is this?" Before Ben could reply, Mr. Grayson commenced in a loud voice to lecture on the necessity of going through channels when submitting reports, ideas, and suggestions. His remarks attracted the attention of the office girls, most of whom stopped work to watch the disturbance. Ben Reed interrupted Mr. Grayson to suggest that they might continue their discussion in Mr. Grayson's office which was glass-enclosed and out of earshot of the girls. Mr. Grayson snatched the folder from Ben's desk and stalked into his office, Ben following.

The discussion in Mr. Grayson's office consisted mainly of a continuation of Mr. Grayson's remarks. After he had concluded his remarks, Ben stated that he had not been satisfied with his relationship with Acme and intended to submit his resignation in the very near future. He then left Mr. Grayson's office.

The next day, December 12, Mr. Grayson asked Ben to step into his office for a few minutes. He apologized to Ben for his conduct of the previous day, remarking that he had had several things on his mind which had upset him and that he certainly had full confidence in Ben's abilities. Ben accepted his apology, remarking that he might have flown off the handle a little bit himself. The meeting ended on a cordial note.

On December 13, Ben Reed submitted his resignation and subsequently left the Acme Company on December 24, 1959.

Blair, Inc. (I)*

THE INFORMATION for this case was obtained from Mr. Burton L. Davis, a recent employee of Blair, Inc.

Burton Davis started work last September as a mechanical engineer in the Engine and Motor Division of the Blair Company, a large multiple-industry corporation. The division, with 400 employees, was the principal employer in Midland. Formed four years ago, the division designed and manufactured small gasoline-combustion engines used in lawn-mowers, motor scooters, snow throwers, portable saws, and power plants. Recently, the division had begun to turn out small electric motors. Division sales were currently $6 million.

Davis, seven years out of Purdue, had previously worked as an automotive engineer for two major automobile manufacturers and had excellent references from both. His salary at Blair was $950 per month.

He found that the engineering offices were new, of modern design, and air-conditioned. Supporting personnel in drafting, machine shop, and laboratory were adequate, and excellent physical facilities were available. Fringe benefits were at or above the industry level. For instance, Davis was promised a two-week vacation before completing a full year of service. His moving expenses were paid in full, in addition to $500 for an earlier trip to locate suitable housing. His travel expenses had also been covered when he came to Midland to interview the division chief engineer, Charles Lyons, and the corporate executive personnel director.

Burton Davis was assigned to the Design and Development Department (see Exhibit 1 for partial organization chart). Four of the six other engineers had no work experience with other employers (which was also true of the chief engineer) and had been with the company from two to thirteen years.

Davis was assigned a numbered space in the main parking lot and was given a decal for his car window. Only the first three rows in this lot were reserved by number. Employment was high at the time, and the only space available was one vacated by a draftsman who had just resigned. (See Exhibits 2 and 2A.)

Davis soon noticed that more than half of those who parked in the two parking areas adjacent to the engineering offices were people he would not have expected to have more favorable parking locations than

EXHIBIT 1
Blair, Inc. (I)
(partial organization chart Engine and Motor Division)

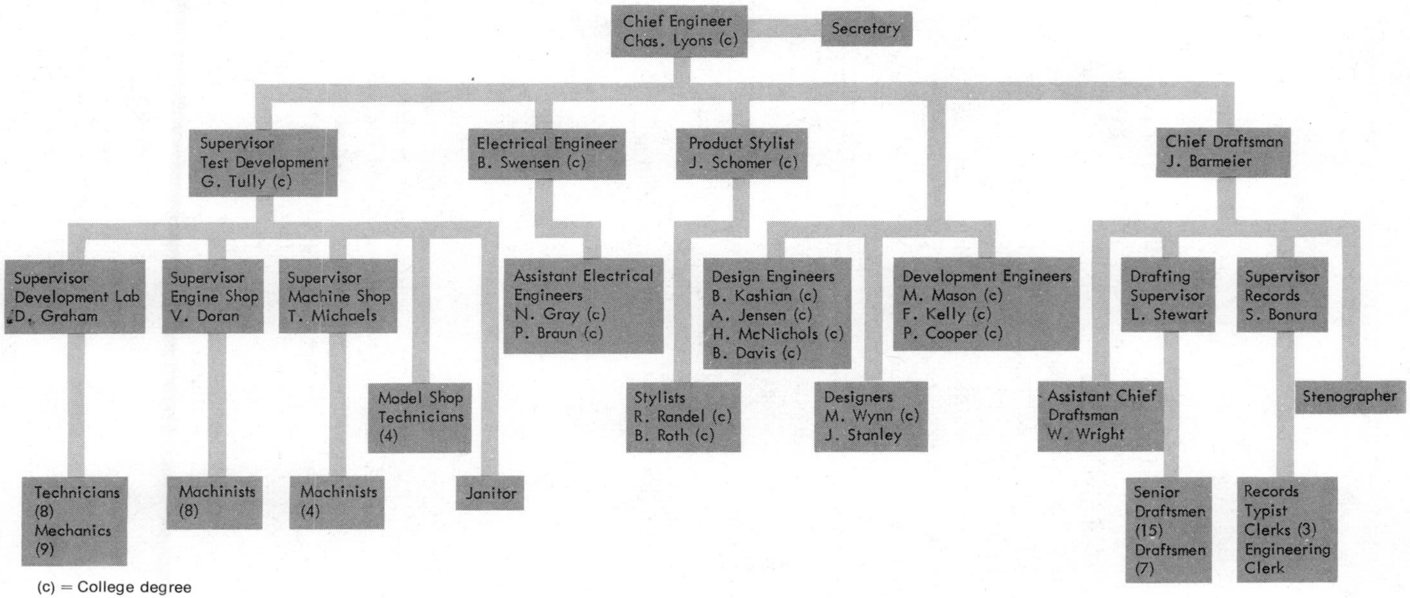

(c) = College degree

the engineers (see locations 6A and 6B, Exhibit 2A). Talking with his fellow engineers, he found they also thought it strange and had been irritated about it for some time.

The following personnel parked in these areas where space was reserved by name: C. Lyons, B. Swensen, J. Schomer, G. Tully, J. Barmeier, W. Wright, L. Stewart, S. Bonura, T. Michaels, V. Doran, and H. O'Brien. O'Brien was a disabled draftsman who used crutches—all agreed he deserved this location. Most engineers also agreed that Barmeier should park there; although his title was chief draftsman, he functioned almost as an assistant chief engineer and had been with the company for twenty years.

The engineering group felt strongly that Wright, Stewart, Bonura, Michaels, and Doran should not have parking privileges in a more desirable area than their own. Wright, assistant chief draftsman, supervised three drafting checkers and was seen constantly at Barmeier's elbow. The engineers called them "the Bobbsey twins." Stewart supervised some twenty draftsmen. In the engineers' view, his job consisted mainly of handing out timecards and paychecks. Draftsmen were allocated among the engineers and rarely changed assignments. Stewart usually asked the engineers to fill out job-rating sheets for the draftsmen since he had no basis for appraising their performance. Bonura supervised several office clericals. Michaels, of the Machine Shop, and Doran, of the Engine Shop, were called supervisors, but the engineering group felt that "foremen" was a more accurate term.

EXHIBIT 2
Blair, Inc. (I)
(index to plant layout [exhibit 2A])

1. Main office door—visitors only
2. Division administration
3. Entrance—all administrative and engineering employees
4. Entrance—factory employees
5. Entrance—engineering labs (not an employee entrance)
6. Parking—engineering personnel, reserved by name
7. Parking—administrative personnel, reserved by number
8. Parking—most of the engineers, reserved by number
9. Parking—most of the draftsmen, reserved by number
10. Parking—Burton Davis, reserved by number
11. Engineering gate—open all day
12. Truck loading dock
13. Paved empty space (could park eight cars)
14. Storage area (could park ten cars)
15. Storage area (could park five cars)
16. Storage area (could park ten cars)
17. Parking—supervisor of development lab, later
        supervisor of test and development also
18. Parking—engineering station wagon and pickup truck

Arnold Jensen (eight years with the company) and Paul Cooper (two years with Blair and two with Ellington Electronics) told Davis they were glad to find someone else concerned about this situation. Other engineers agreed but were reluctant to make an issue of it. One of them told Davis he might be considered a "rabble-rouser" if he talked too much about it.

From what Davis could determine, everyone had parked in the main lot until a few years back. Then two sections of grass were removed to make the small parking areas (6A and 6B in Exhibit 2A).

Since there wasn't room to include Lyons, Swensen, Schomer, Tully, Barmeier, and all the engineers, Lyons said that, rather than draw a line among them, he would not have any of the engineers park there. Instead, all "direct" supervisors were given reserved slots, which just

EXHIBIT 2A
Blair, Inc. (I)

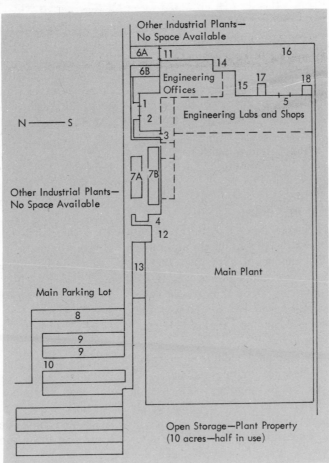

filled the space in the new area. Some engineers felt that Barmeier may have influenced this decision. Technically, the engineers were not "direct" supervisors, although they might have as many as ten people (draftsmen, typists, etc.) working under their control at one time.

Davis knew that every company had irritations with which one learned to live. However, as the weather grew worse, he walked through the unpaved gravel lot (which developed many holes in winter), plodded along the street (there was no sidewalk), and, still halfway from the entrance, watched others drive in, park near the engineering offices, and enter before he reached the door.

Other things began to disturb him about his position. He found that Barmeier and Wright, without his approval, changed drawings he had released from Engineering.

There were three blank boxes on each engineering drawing. The draftsman would initial the "drawn by" space; the checker, the "checked by"; and the engineer, the "approved by." Lyons usually also initialed the last box, which provided room for two sets of initials. A few months after Davis had started work, Wright started erasing the engineers' initials from the "approved" box, entered his own, and told the engineers to initial after the checker's in the middle box. Jensen and Davis immediately told Wright that he could put his own initials after the checker's, since he was supposed to be the checkers' supervisor and they were the engineers in charge of the project. Davis told Wright, "If you feel otherwise about it, let's go to Lyons right now." Wright immediately agreed to initial after the checker.

Some time after this incident, a sign reading "Authorized Personnel Only" appeared on the door to the blueprint records storage room where Bonura and the clerks worked. Barmeier told the engineering group that the purpose of this was to avoid disturbing the overworked print girls and that the sign applied to all draftsmen and engineers. Although the engineers protested, Barmeier refused to change his stand. Lyons came by during the argument and moved the group into the conference room. The engineers explained that they often needed information from a tracing; a quick glance was enough before returning it to the file. Under the new system, they would have to order a print and wait to get the information. Lyons agreed with the engineers. Davis, Jensen, and Cooper were particularly pleased. Jensen said later, "At last *we* won something around here."

It gradually became apparent to Davis that Lyons planned most of the engineering for his engineers. When assigning a new project he would suggest the handling of it in such detail that all chance of creative or original work was eliminated. He frequently went out in the drafting room and told layout draftsmen how he wanted things done. Sometimes he even failed to bring the responsible engineer in on the discussion.

No engineering meetings were held. The only regular meeting was a "production" meeting for which the division manager and his plant manager came to Lyons' office. Lyons was the only engineer in the meetings, although he often stepped out to get a drawing or to get a question answered from a design or developmental engineer whose project was under discussion at the time. On the rare occasions when an engineer *was* called into the meeting, it was without any advance warning, so that he was frequently unable to furnish the desired information on the spot. Barmeier, Wright, and Bonura sat in on all meetings. Since these were the only regular conferences, discussions inevitably went beyond production problems and dealt with new products and plans as well. The sales manager and the corporate director of engineering attended some of the meetings. To find out what was going on, the engineers relied on the grapevine or were forced to ask Barmeier, Wright, or Bonura. They rarely talked with Lyons except when he was giving them ideas on how he thought they should do their jobs.

Dissatisfaction grew among the engineers, although several still felt there was nothing to be gained by "stirring things up." Davis felt that if Lyons realized the extent of the developing morale problem he would try to do something about it.

One evening, he had an opportunity to talk to Lyons alone. He made it clear that he thought the situation was becoming critical. He told Lyons what he thought were the main points: The generally low status of the engineers and the feeling they had that they were not given enough responsibility. Davis pointed out that the parking situation was one of the main symbols of the engineers' status since it was a visible method of ranking. Lyons seemed uncomfortable throughout the discussion but said that he would think about it. Davis told Lyons that he was speaking only for himself but that he was sure his feelings were shared by most of the others. On leaving, Davis gave Lyons a reprint of an article on morale and suggested it might be of value.[1]

As months passed, no perceptible changes were made.[2] George Dunlop was hired to supervise the engineers, with the title of "Chief, Design and Development" and with the design and development engineers and the designers reporting to him. They had formerly reported directly to Lyons. (Dunlop parked in the engineering lot; Tully was moved to the rear with Graham, area #17 on Exhibit 2A—actually a more desirable spot, only 10 feet from a door.) Before Dunlop arrived, Lyons held a meeting with all salaried personnel to explain the decision to bring in a man from outside. He said that he thought the position could have

---

[1] A portion of the article is reproduced in Exhibit 3.

[2] During this period, Burton Davis typed a memo and circulated it informally among individuals in the division (see Exhibit 4, page 338).

been filled from within the company but that Edward King, the corporate director of engineering, thought that a man with considerable experience was needed. Davis considered it interesting that Lyons was only 34.

Dunlop was 48 years old and had worked as an executive engineer for National Motors, for Burling Aircraft, and for Duval Manufacturing. Lyons mentioned that people might wonder why a man with this background would come here. He explained that Dunlop liked small towns and enjoyed this type of work and that money was not that important to him. Davis commented later to Jensen that "executive engineer" at National Motors meant a big job and that Dunlop must have had a real setback somewhere along the way. The engineers considered it significant that Dunlop was placed in charge of seven engineers, with the draftsmen and technicians still reporting to others. Moreover, Barmeier was still next to Lyons, with no intermediary. They also noted that Dunlop had not been given the title of assistant chief engineer.

Several engineers with long experience with the firm believed they should have been candidates for the job. Other engineers thought Dunlop might become a useful go-between for them. They saw that Barmeier took care of *his* people and Tully took care of *his*. Perhaps the engineers now had someone to put in a few good words for them. Dunlop seemed, at first, to be a much better administrator than Lyons. At least, the engineers felt he "talked a good game." They began to tell him about things they felt needed improvement or correction. But, after two months, it became apparent that Dunlop had not recommended any changes to Lyons. It appeared to Davis and others that he was loathe to tell Lyons anything that might be disturbing. The engineers felt that he was "running scared."

Davis suggested to Jensen and Cooper that talking to Dunlop was not unlike a session with a psychiatrist. You talked about your problems and felt better even though nothing really changed. Whenever anyone returned from a talk with Dunlop, a colleague would ask, "Did you have a nice couch session?"

As the small group talked about their problems, the situation became almost unbearable to Davis. There was considerable talk of other jobs, and occasionally one of the men would have an interview with another firm. Finally, Davis, Jensen, and Cooper decided to approach Lyons in a group. They had decided that they would all leave anyway unless changes were made. This "group action" was distasteful to them, but they felt that it was the only way to get Lyons to realize he had a real problem to face. There seemed to be little to lose.

Following are some of the comments made by the engineers and Lyons as they talked in the chief engineer's office one evening after work:

ENGINEER: We feel a little silly talking about this, but since it does bother us and affects our morale, we feel you should know.

ENGINEER: The parking position ranks everyone, whether or not you be-lieve it does.

LYONS: Where you park doesn't have anything to do with the way I rank you.

ENGINEER: We feel that as highly paid college graduates who actually do the creative work, we should rank above "assistant chief draftsmen" and "foremen."

ENGINEER: Specifically, we feel that we should rank ahead of Wright, Stewart, Bonura, Doran, and Michaels.

LYONS: Do you feel you are better than those people?

ENGINEER: In terms of working for this company, yes. We would certainly be harder to replace. In any case, ranking is inevitable; we would like to think that you agree with us on where we rank.

LYONS: You know that you make much more money than those people, don't you?

ENGINEER: Yes, which is another reason for keeping the other symbols of rank in the same order.

ENGINEER: Salary is not a problem. We do not feel overpaid or underpaid in our present jobs.

ENGINEER: Whether or not *you* feel this is a problem, the fact that *we* feel it is a problem *makes* it a problem, by definition.

ENGINEER: The fact that parking ranks us in status actually affects our job efficiency as it relates to others. We have more trouble "getting things done" if we don't have the status to back it up.

ENGINEER: Saying that status symbols are unimportant doesn't make them go away. We live with status symbols all the time; unless they are distorted from the way most people expect to see them, they go unnoticed. Only when the sym-bol system gets out of line does it become a problem. This means that to have a smoothly functioning organization, an administrator has to consider status sym-bols and make every attempt to allocate them as his subordinates expect him to.

ENGINEER: Doran and Michaels are foremen, no matter what fancy names they are called. Stewart is the drafting supervisor and should rank under us, but Barmeier and Wright are doing engineering work. If you want to rank them above us that is your decision, but their titles should be changed. A chief draftsman and his assistant should never rank above any engineer. The situation is similar to the Army, where a master sergeant may have many years of experience and be valuable, but he does not outrank the greenest second lieutenant.

ENGINEER: We note that you have the closest space to the door in the lots near Engineering, and the division manager has the space closest to the door in the administration lot. Isn't it logical that the No. 2 ranking people have the next spaces, and so on down the line? That's the way almost everyone looks at it.

ENGINEER: We don't care *where* we actually park. The question is *who* parks where. If everyone had the same long walk, there would be no problem.

ENGINEER: Locating our parking spaces more conveniently without changing the relative status of the spaces will be no solution at all.

LYONS: But where can I find more parking space?

ENGINEER: We think there are a number of areas that could be used, but some effort would be required. There is unused space in front of the plant (13 in Exhibit 2A), or space could be made available by moving some of the stored ma-terials from the area east of Engineering (14, 15, and 16 in Exhibit 2A). Even if you can't find space for improved parking for everyone, engineers should park in that lot. Not necessarily the three of us, but *engineers.*

ENGINEER: The fact that you don't or can't trust us with more responsibility affects our morale and job interest also.

LYONS: But I do give as much responsibility as possible.

ENGINEER: But you act as if you don't really trust us.

LYONS: It's not that I don't trust you, it's just that I want to see the job done right.

As the talk ended, Lyons appeared to be disturbed and concerned. He said that he would think about what had been said and would see if there was anything that he could do.

Nevertheless, the three engineers were sure that Lyons had not really understood them. In spite of their emphasis on "not where, but *who,*" they sensed that the chief engineer believed that all they wanted was better, closer parking places. They felt he didn't understand their desire for more responsibility, either; he seemed to think they had all the responsibility they had a right to expect. They agreed that his comment on "doing the job right" demonstrated how little effect they had had.

They predicted that any solution that Lyons might devise would be unsatisfactory. They wondered if they should take any other steps or just wait and hope that Lyons had more understanding than they suspected. They realized that if the solution was unsatisfactory, it was the end of the road. They could hardly start the process all over again.

EXHIBIT 3
Blair, Inc. (I)

Indicator area	High morale exists when—	Low morale exists when—
1. The company	Lines of responsibility and authority are clear; coordination good; line staff teamwork generally productive; organization structure is flexible; managers can get to right official when necessary.	Authority overlaps; organizational structure is too complex; company has too many layers of review; communication breakdowns are frequent; reorganizations don't add up; committees interfere.
2. Company-division practices	Good rapport exists among managers; agreements are honored; men know where they stand and how they are doing; policies are clearly and quickly communicated; reward system is fair and current.	There's too much paperwork; managers have to beat the system; excessive rivalry exists among the departments; deadlines don't mean a thing; it is hard to get needed information; ideas die on vine.

EXHIBIT 3 *Continued*

Indicator area	*High morale exists when—*	*Low morale exists when—*
3. Decisions	Decisions are tied in well to policies and plans; managers get chance to participate in decision making; delegation is adequate; bad decisions are withdrawn when necessary; accountability is clear.	Decisions are too slow, poorly timed; subordinate has little chance to participate in the making of decisions; delegation is meager; decisions unduly influenced by tradition; real issues are evaded.
4. Leadership	Staff meetings are well run and produce results: boss keeps subordinates informed of policies and plans affecting them; men know the scope of their responsibilities; boss shows dignity and fairness.	Assignments and orders of boss are unclear; men have to work without knowing policy limitations; boss sets unreasonable deadlines; too many attempts are made at regimentation; standards fall.
5. Group climate	Team takes pride in its performance; men will go to bat for each other; professional aims, standards are high; grievances of a member are heard; overall quality of group output is high-grade.	Too many cliques exist; favoritism is shown some; work output is inadequate; one man dominates the group; bickering is common; there are recurrent rule violations; professional standards are low.
6. Job conditions	Managers find sufficient challenge in their jobs; abilities of men are utilized well; employees able to express their views; performance standards are realistic; workers get recognition when deserved.	It's difficult to get a job done; ideas put aside too often, too fast; men have to break rules to get action; boredom and restlessness are prevalent; pay scales lag behind the rates in other firms.
7. Status	Job privileges are modest but good; management is receptive to a man's views; talents are utilized; employees enjoy higher status in community because of their association with the company.	Favored few get recognition; opportunities for development are restricted; criticisms far exceed compliments; men must look out for themselves; firm has too many dead-end jobs.

Source: From Nathaniel Stewart, "You Can Keep Morale High," *Nation's Business*, March, 1963. Reprinted by permission.

EXHIBIT 4
Blair, Inc. (I)

Office Memo

ENGINE AND MOTOR ENGINEERING SECTION

To: "Supervisory" Personnel

Subject: Fitness Program

Going along with the present Washington administration's emphasis on hiking as a means of improving the fitness of the American people, it is suggested that those Blair employees now parking near the building exchange parking places with the Engine and Motor Section *Engineers.* The engineers are in splendid shape from their long hikes and feel that it is only fair to share this conditioning. After a suitable "building-up" period, a rotation system will be worked out to insure the retention of all the fitness benefits.

The Personnel Department

Bob Knowlton*

BOB KNOWLTON was sitting alone in the conference room of the laboratory. The rest of the group had gone. One of the secretaries had stopped and talked for a while about her husband's coming induction into the Army, and had finally left. Bob, alone in the laboratory, slid a little further down in his chair, looking with satisfaction at the results of the first test run of the new photon unit.

He liked to stay after the others had gone. His appointment as project head was still new enough to give him a deep sense of pleasure. His eyes were on the graphs before him but in his mind he could hear Dr. Jerrold, the project head, saying again, "There's one thing about this place that you can bank on. The sky is the limit for a man who can produce!" Knowlton felt again the tingle of happiness and embarrassment. Well, dammit,

---

* This case was prepared by Professor Alex Bavelas for courses in Management of Research and Development conducted at the School of Industrial Management, Massachusetts Institute of Technology, Cambridge, and is used with his permission.

he said to himself, he had produced. He wasn't kidding anybody. He had come to the Simmons Laboratories two years ago. During a routine testing of some rejected Clanson components he had stumbled on the idea of the photon correlator, and the rest just happened. Jerrold had been enthusiastic: a separate project had been set up for further research and development of the device, and he had gotten the job of running it. The whole sequence of events still seemed a little miraculous to Knowlton.

He shrugged out of the reverie and bent determinedly over the sheets when he heard someone come into the room behind him. He looked up expectantly; Jerrold often stayed late himself, and now and then dropped in for a chat. This always made the day's end especially pleasant for Bob. It wasn't Jerrold. The man who had come in was a stranger. He was tall, thin, and rather dark. He wore steel-rimmed glasses and had on a very wide leather belt with a large brass buckle. Lucy remarked later that it was the kind of belt the Pilgrims must have worn.

The stranger smiled and introduced himself. "I'm Simon Fester. Are you Bob Knowlton?" Bob said yes, and they shook hands. "Doctor Jerrold said I might find you in. We were talking about your work, and I'm very much interested in what you are doing." Bob waved to a chair.

Fester didn't seem to belong in any of the standard categories of visitors: customer, visiting fireman, stockholder. Bob pointed to the sheets on the table. "There are the preliminary results of a test we're running. We've got a new gadget by the tail and we're trying to understand it. It's not finished, but I can show you the section that we're testing."

He stood up, but Fester was deep in the graphs. After a moment, he looked up with an odd grin. "These look like plots of a Jennings surface. I've been playing around with some autocorrelation functions of surfaces —you know that stuff." Bob, who had no idea what he was referring to, grinned back and nodded, and immediately felt uncomfortable. "Let me show you the monster," he said, and led the way to the work room.

After Fester left, Knowlton slowly put the graphs away, feeling vaguely annoyed. Then, as if he had made a decision, he quickly locked up and took the long way out so that he would pass Jerrold's office. But the office was locked. Knowlton wondered whether Jerrold and Fester had left together.

The next morning, Knowlton dropped into Jerrold's office, mentioned that he had talked with Fester, and asked who he was.

"Sit down for a minute," Jerrold said. "I want to talk to you about him. What do you think of him?" Knowlton replied truthfully that he thought Fester was very bright and probably very competent. Jerrold looked pleased.

"We're taking him on," he said. "He's had a very good background in a number of laboratories, and he seems to have ideas about the problems we're tackling here." Knowlton nodded in agreement, instantly wishing that Fester would not be placed with him.

"I don't know yet where he will finally land," Jerrold continued, "but he seems interested in what you are doing. I thought he might spend a little time with you by way of getting started." Knowlton nodded thoughtfully. "If his interest in your work continues, you can add him to your group."

"Well, he seemed to have some good ideas even without knowing exactly what we are doing," Knowlton answered. "I hope he stays; we'd be glad to have him."

Knowlton walked back to the lab with mixed feelings. He told himself that Fester would be good for the group. He was no dunce, he'd produce. Knowlton thought again of Jerrold's promise when he had promoted him — "the man who produces gets ahead in this outfit." The words seemed to carry the overtones of a threat now.

That day Fester didn't appear until mid-afternoon. He explained that he had had a long lunch with Jerrold, discussing his place in the lab. "Yes," said Knowlton, "I talked with Jerry this morning about it, and we both thought you might work with us for awhile."

Fester smiled in the same knowing way that he had smiled when he mentioned the Jennings surfaces. "I'd like to," he said.

Knowlton introduced Fester to the other members of the lab. Fester and Link, the mathematician of the group, hit it off well together, and spent the rest of the afternoon discussing a method of analysis of patterns that Link had been worrying over for the last month.

It was 6:30 when Knowlton finally left the lab that night. He had waited almost eagerly for the end of the day to come — when they would all be gone and he could sit in the quiet rooms, relax, and think it over. "Think what over?" he asked himself. He didn't know. Shortly after 5:00 P.M. they had all gone except Fester, and what followed was almost a duel. Knowlton was annoyed that he was being cheated out of his quiet period, and finally resentfully determined that Fester should leave first.

Fester was sitting at the conference table reading, and Knowlton was sitting at his desk in the little glass-enclosed cubby that he used during the day when he needed to be undisturbed. Fester had gotten the last year's progress reports out and was studying them carefully. The time dragged. Knowlton doodled on a pad, the tension growing inside him. What the hell did Fester think he was going to find in the reports?

Knowlton finally gave up and they left the lab together. Fester took several of the reports with him to study in the evening. Knowlton asked him if he thought the reports gave a clear picture of the lab's activities.

"They're excellent," Fester answered with obvious sincerity. "They're not only good reports; what they report is damn good, too!" Knowlton was surprised at the relief he felt, and grew almost jovial as he said goodnight.

Driving home, Knowlton felt more optimistic about Fester's presence in the lab. He had never fully understood the analysis that Link was attempting. If there was anything wrong with Link's approach, Fester would probably spot it. "And if I'm any judge," he murmured, "he won't be especially diplomatic about it."

He described Fester to his wife, who was amused by the broad leather belt and the brass buckle.

"It's the kind of belt that Pilgrims must have worn," she laughed.

"I'm not worried about how he holds his pants up," he laughed with her. "I'm afraid that he's the kind that just has to make like a genius twice each day. And that can be pretty rough on the group."

Knowlton had been asleep for several hours when he was jerked awake by the telephone. He realized it had rung several times. He swung off the bed muttering about damn fools and telephones. It was Fester. Without any excuses, apparently oblivious of the time, he plunged into an excited recital of how Link's patterning problem could be solved.

Knowlton covered the mouthpiece to answer his wife's stage-whispered "Who is it?" "It's the genius," replied Knowlton.

Fester, completely ignoring the fact that it was 2:00 in the morning, proceeded in a very excited way to start in the middle of an explanation of a completely new approach to certain of the photon lab problems that he had stumbled on while analyzing past experiments. Knowlton managed to put some enthusiasm in his own voice and stood there, half-dazed and very uncomfortable, listening to Fester talk endlessly about what he had discovered. It was probably not only a new approach, but also an analysis which showed the inherent weakness of the previous experiment and how experimentation along that line would certainly have been inconclusive. The following day Knowlton spent the entire morning with Fester and Link, the mathematician, the customary morning meeting of Bob's group having been called off so that Fester's work of the previous night could be gone over intensively. Fester was very anxious that this be done and Knowlton was not too unhappy to call the meeting off for reasons of his own.

For the next several days Fester sat in the back office that had been turned over to him and did nothing but read the progress reports of the work that had been done in the last six months. Knowlton caught himself feeling apprehensive about the reaction that Fester might have to some of his work. He was a little surprised at his own feelings. He had always been proud — although he had put on a convincingly modest face — of the way in which new ground in the study of photon measuring devices had been broken in his group. Now he wasn't sure, and it seemed to him that Fester might easily show that the line of research they had been following was unsound or even unimaginative.

The next morning, as was the custom, the members of the lab, including the girls, sat around a conference table. Bob always prided himself on the fact that the work of the lab was guided and evaluated by the group as a whole and he was fond of repeating that it was not a waste of time to include secretaries in such meetings. Often, what started out as a boring recital of fundamental assumptions, to a naive listener, uncovered new ways of regarding these assumptions that would not have occurred to the researcher who had long ago accepted them as a necessary basis for his work.

These group meetings also served Bob in another sense. He admitted to himself that he would have felt far less secure if he had had to direct the work out of his own mind, so to speak. With the group-meeting as the principle of leadership, it was always possible to justify the exploration of blind alleys because of the general educative effect on the team. Fester was there; Lucy and Martha were there; Link was sitting next to Fester, their conversation concerning Link's mathematical study apparently continuing from yesterday. The other members, Bob Davenport, George Thurlow and Arthur Oliver, were waiting quietly.

Knowlton, for reasons that he didn't quite understand, proposed for discussion this morning a problem that all of them had spent a great deal of time on previously, with the conclusion that a solution was impossible, that there was no feasible way of treating it in an experimental fashion. When Knowlton proposed the problem, Davenport remarked that there was hardly any use of going over it again, that he was satisfied that there was no way of approaching the problem with the equipment and the physical capacities of the lab.

This statement had the effect of a shot of adrenalin on Fester. He said he would like to know what the problem was in detail and, walking to the blackboard, began setting down the "factors" as various members of the group began discussing the problem and simultaneously listing the reasons why it had been abandoned.

Very early in the description of the problem it was evident that Fester was going to disagree about the impossibility of attacking it. The group realized this and finally the descriptive materials and their recounting of the reasoning that had led to its abandonment dwindled away. Fester began his statement which, as it proceeded, might well have been prepared the previous night although Knowlton knew this was impossible. He couldn't help being impressed with the organized and logical way that Fester was presenting ideas that must have occurred to him only a few minutes before.

Fester had some things to say, however, which left Knowlton with a mixture of annoyance, irritation and, at the same time, a rather smug feeling of superiority over Fester in at least one area. Fester was of the opinion that the way that the problem had been analyzed was really typical of group-thinking and, with an air of sophistication which made it difficult for a listener to dissent, he proceeded to comment on the American emphasis on team ideas, satirically describing the ways in which they led to a "high level of mediocrity."

During this time, Knowlton observed that Link stared studiously at the floor, and he was very conscious of George Thurlow's and Bob Davenport's glances towards him at several points of Fester's little speech. Inwardly, Knowlton couldn't help feeling that this was one point at least in which Fester was off on the wrong foot. The whole lab, following Jerry's lead, talked if not practiced the theory of small research teams as the basic organization for effective research. Fester insisted that the problem could be approached and that he would like to study it for a while himself.

Knowlton ended the morning session by remarking that the meetings would continue and that the very fact that a supposedly insoluble experimental problem was now going to get another chance was another indication of the value of such meetings. Fester immediately remarked that he was not at all averse to meetings for the purpose of informing the group of the progress of its members — that the point he wanted to make was that creative advances were seldom accomplished in such meetings, that they were made by the individual "living with" the problem closely and continuously, a sort of personal relationship to it.

Knowlton went on to say to Fester that he was very glad that Fester had raised these points and that he was sure the group would profit by reexamining the basis on which they had been operating. Knowlton agreed that individual effort was probably the basis for making the major advances, but that he considered the group meetings useful primarily because of the effect they had on keeping the group together and on helping the weaker members of the group keep up with the ones who were able to advance more easily and quickly in the analysis of problems.

It was clear as days went by and meetings continued that Fester came to enjoy them because of the pattern which the meetings assumed. It became typical for Fester to hold forth and it was unquestionably clear that he was more brilliant, better prepared on the various subjects which were germane to the problems being studied, and that he was more capable of going ahead than anyone there. Knowlton grew increasingly disturbed as he realized that his leadership of the group had been, in fact, taken over.

Whenever the subject of Fester was mentioned, in occasional meetings with Dr. Jerrold, Knowlton would comment only on the ability and obvious capacity for work that Fester had. Somehow he never felt that he could mention his own discomforts, not only because they revealed a weakness on his own part, but also because it was quite clear that Jerrold himself was considerably impressed with Fester's work and with the contacts he had with him outside the photon laboratory.

Knowlton now began to feel that perhaps the intellectual advantages that Fester had brought to the group did not quite compensate for what he felt were evidences of a breakdown in the cooperative spirit he had seen in the group before Fester's coming. More and more of the morning meetings were skipped. Fester's opinion concerning the abilities of others of the group, with the exception of Link, was obviously low. At times, during morning meetings or in smaller discussions, he had been on the point of rudeness, refusing to pursue an argument when he claimed it was based on the other person's ignorance of the facts involved. His impatience of others led him to also make similar remarks to Dr. Jerrold. Knowlton inferred this from a conversation with Jerrold in which Jerrold asked whether Davenport and Oliver were going to be continued on; and his failure to mention Link, the mathematician, led Knowlton to feel that this was the result of private conversations between Fester and Jerrold.

It was not difficult for Knowlton to make a quite convincing case on whether the brilliance of Fester was sufficient recompense for the beginning of this breaking up of the group. He took the opportunity to speak privately with Davenport and with Oliver and it was quite clear that both of them were uncomfortable because of Fester. Knowlton didn't press the discussion beyond the point of hearing them in one way or another say that they did feel awkward and that it was sometimes difficult for them to understand the arguments he advanced, but often embarrassing to ask him to fill in the background on which his arguments were based. Knowlton did not interview Link in this manner.

About six months after Fester's coming into the photon lab, a meeting was scheduled in which the sponsors of the research were coming in to get some idea of the work and its progress. It was customary at these meetings for project heads to present the research being conducted in their groups. The members of each group were invited to other meetings which were held later in the day and open to all, but the special meetings were usually made up only of project heads, the head of the laboratory, and the sponsors.

As the time for the special meeting approached, it seemed to Knowlton that he must avoid the presentation at all cost. His reasons for this were that he could not trust himself to present the ideas and work that Fester had advanced, because of his apprehension as to whether he could present them in sufficient detail and answer such questions about them as might be asked. On the other hand, he did not feel he could ignore these newer lines of work and present only the material that he had done or that had been started before Fester's arrival. He felt also that it would not be beyond Fester at all, in his blunt and undiplomatic way — if he were present at the meeting, that is — to make comments on his [Knowlton's] presentation and reveal Knowlton's inadequacy. It also seemed quite clear that it would not be easy to keep Fester from attending the meeting, even though he was not on the administrative level of those invited.

Knowlton found an opportunity to speak to Jerrold and raised the question. He remarked to Jerrold that, with the meetings coming up and with the interest in the work and with the contributions that Fester had been making, he would probably like to come to these meetings, but there was a question of the feelings of the others in the group if Fester alone were invited. Jerrold passed this over very lightly by saying that he didn't think the group would fail to understand Fester's rather different position and that he thought that Fester by all means should be invited. Knowlton then immediately said he had thought so, too; that Fester should present the work because much of it was work he had done; and, as Knowlton put it, that this would be a nice way to recognize Fester's contributions and to reward him, as he was eager to be recognized as a productive member of the lab. Jerrold agreed, and so the matter was decided.

Fester's presentation was very successful and in some ways dominated the meeting. He attracted the interest and attention of many of those who had come, and a long discussion followed his presentation. Later in the evening — with the entire laboratory staff present — in the cocktail period before the dinner, a little circle of people formed about Fester. One of them was Jerrold himself, and a lively discussion took place concerning the application of Fester's theory. All of this disturbed Knowlton, and his reaction and behavior were characteristic. He joined the circle, praised Fester to Jerrold and to others, and remarked on the brilliance of the work.

Knowlton, without consulting anyone, began at this time to take some interest in the possibility of a job elsewhere. After a few weeks he found that a new laboratory of considerable size was being organized in a nearby city, and that the kind of training he had would enable him to get a project head job equivalent to the one he had at the lab, with slightly more money.

He immediately accepted it and notified Jerrold by a letter, which he mailed on a Friday night to Jerrold's home. The letter was quite brief, and Jerrold was stunned. The letter merely said that he had found a better position; that there were personal reasons why he didn't want to appear at the lab any more; that he would be glad to come back at a later time from where he would be, some forty miles away, to assist if there was any mixup at all in the past work; that he felt sure that Fester could, however, supply any leadership that was required for the group; and that his decision to leave so suddenly was based on some personal problems — he hinted at problems of health in his family, his mother and father. All of this was fictitious, of course. Jerrold took it at face value but still felt that this was very strange behavior and quite unaccountable, for he had always felt his relationship with Knowlton had been warm and that Knowlton was satisfied and, as a matter of fact, quite happy and productive.

Jerrold was considerably disturbed, because he had already decided to place Fester in charge of another project that was going to be set up very soon. He had been wondering how to explain this to Knowlton, in view of the obvious help Knowlton was getting from Fester and the high regard in which he held him. Jerrold had, as a matter of fact, considered the possibility that Knowlton could add to his staff another person with the kind of background and training that had been unique in Fester and had proved so valuable.

Jerrold did not make any attempt to meet Knowlton. In a way, he felt aggrieved about the whole thing. Fester, too, was surprised at the suddenness of Knowlton's departure and when Jerrold, in talking to him, asked him whether he had reasons to prefer to stay with the photon group instead of the project for the Air Force which was being organized, he chose the Air Force project and went on to that job the following week. The photon lab was hard hit. The leadership of the lab was given to Link with the understanding that this would be temporary until someone could come in to take over.

The Brewster-Seaview Landscaping Co.

NOTE: DO NOT READ this case until directed to do so by your instructor. It has been set up as a Prediction Case so that you can test your analysis by answering questions before reading the entire case.

PART I

DURING the summer of my freshman year in college, I worked for a small private landscaping company planting shrubs, seeding new lawns, cutting grass, and tending flower gardens. The company was located in my home town of Seaview, N.J., which is a rural community on the coast about 80 miles from Philadelphia. The company was owned and run by Joe Brewster, a 45 year old man who had lived in Seaview all his life. He had started the company some years ago and not only handled the paper work (payroll, bills, estimates, etc.) but also worked along with the crew six days a week.

The crew consisted of five guys ranging in age from 17 to 20 years. We all lived in towns around Seaview and had gone to the regional high school which was physically located in Seaview. Only two of us were attending college, but all had been hired personally by Joe following a short, informal interview. I can't be completely certain about the others, but I think all of us, and several others, sought the job because we needed work, enjoyed the outdoors, and had heard that Joe paid well and was an OK guy to work for. Working hours were from 8:00 A.M. to 4:30 P.M., with an hour off for lunch, Monday through Saturday. Once in a while we'd work overtime to help out some customer who had an urgent need. Each worker began at the same wage with the understanding that hard workers would be rehired the next summer at a higher wage. Several of the crew I was part of had been rehired under this policy.

Most of the customers we serviced lived in Seaview, knew Joe personally and seemed to respect him.

Joe owned one truck which he used to transport all of us, and necessary supplies and equipment, from job to job. Each morning, Joe, as we called him, would read off a list of houses that had to be completed that day. He would then leave it up to us to decide among ourselves who would do what task while at a particular house. We also were the ones who determined how long we would spend at each house by our work pace.

In doing the work itself, we were able to use our own ideas and methods. If we did a good job, Joe would always compliment us. If we lacked the necessary know-how or did a poor job, Joe was right there willing to help us.

At each house, Joe worked along with us doing basically the same work we did. He dressed the same as we did and was always very open and friendly towards us. He seldom "showed his authority" and treated us as equals. Although our work day was scheduled to begin at 8:00, Joe never became upset nor penalized us if we were ten or fifteen minutes late. Our lunch hour was usually an hour long starting anytime between 11:30 and 12:30 depending on what time we, the crew, felt like eating. Each member brought his own lunch to work and anytime during the day could take time off to go to the truck for a snack.

The crew itself became very well acquainted and we were always free to talk and joke with each other at any time and did so. We enjoyed each other's company, although we did not socialize after hours.

We also became very friendly with the customers. They were always eager to talk to us as we worked and Joe never objected. All in all, the job had a very relaxed, easy-going atmosphere. I, for one, felt little pressure to hurry, and like the others respected and liked Joe very much.

Prediction Questions

1. What will be the productivity, in terms of quantity and quality, of the work crew? Why?

PART II

The attitude we had toward the job was very high. We sometimes talked among ourselves about how we felt a sense of responsibility toward the job. While we talked and joked a lot while working, little horseplay occurred, and the talking and joking did not interfere with the work. We were always working steadily and efficiently, seeking to keep ahead of schedule. The days seemed to go fairly quickly and a lot seemed to get done. I know Joe said that our output was 15 percent above that which other landscaping companies experienced with summer crews.

We also took a lot of pride in our work. Feeling responsible for the job we did, we were constantly checking and re-checking every job to be sure it was perfect. We were always willing to work overtime for Joe when he needed us to do so.

Discussion Questions

1. What elements in the situation contributed to these positive results? Can you think of things which, if present, might have led to very different results? Explain how.

PART III

I returned the following summer to work for Joe because of the strong satisfaction I had with the job the summer before. So did the others. However, we were in for a surprise. Many things had changed. Joe had increased the number of workers to 10, hired another truck, and hired two young college graduates from Philadelphia as crew supervisors. His plan was to concentrate on the paper work and on lining up new customers, leaving the direct guidance of the two work crews to the new supervisors.

Joe had hired the two supervisors during the early spring, after interviewing a number of applicants. Both were young (23 and 24), from the city, and had degrees in agricultural management from Penn State, but had not known each other previously.

We "oldtimers" were assigned to one crew and 5 new workers were hired for the other crew. These new workers had little experience in landscaping. Except for the working hours, which were the same as during the previous summer, the two supervisors were told that they could run their crew in any manner they wished, as long as they kept to the schedule prepared by Joe.

No one on the crew had known the supervisors before. Joe had found them through ads in the paper. The supervisors didn't dress quite as informally as Joe did, perhaps because they didn't do as much actual physical work, but they did dress casually in dungarees and shirts, the same as the crew. Though we called the supervisors by their first names, they did some nit-picky things. For example, Joe never cared who drove the truck or who did what job; sometimes a crew member would drive and Joe would talk with the rest of us. But the supervisors always drove the truck and decided when we would eat. Nor did the supervisors help us unload the tools as Joe had done. They stood around and watched us.

Both supervisors refused to tolerate tardiness in the morning, and immediately set up a scheduled lunch hour which would remain the same throughout the summer. We were no longer allowed to go to the truck for a snack during the day and were constantly being watched over by our supervisor. The supervisors assigned us to specific tasks to be done at each job and told us how "they" wanted them to be completed. They also told us how much time we were to spend doing each job. They refused to let us talk to each other or to the customers (except about business) saying that it "only wasted time and interfered with our work." It was a more structured, more formal atmosphere than the summer before.

Prediction Questions

1. What kind of issues or problems are likely to develop during the second summer? Why?
2. How will productivity compare with that of the previous summer in terms of quantity and quality. Why?
3. What would have been your advice to the two supervisors about how they could best approach their new role?

PART IV

I was disappointed at the new set-up and a little bit surprised that Joe hadn't hired one of the more experienced members of the old crew as supervisor. But I figured it was necessary because of the increased volume of business so I tried to make the best of it. However, very soon my attitude and that of the rest of the old crew fell significantly. We began to hate the new supervisors and soon developed a great disinterest in the work itself. While I'm a person who usually is very conscientious and responsible, I have to admit that before long I, along with the others, began to put little care or concern into my work. The supervisors soon found it very difficult to get anyone to work overtime.

The new employees didn't react as strongly as we did, but I could tell that they weren't working with much enthusiasm, either.

I thought about talking to the supervisors but didn't because I'd only worked there the one year and figured that it was not my place to. The others were older than me and had worked there longer so I figured that they should, but no one did. Instead, we talked among ourselves and individually griped to Joe.

Joe didn't seem to know how to deal with our complaints. He passed them off by saying "Oh . . . I'll talk to the supervisors and straighten it out with them." But nothing changed, and in fact they seemed to clamp down more and push even harder. This only made us madder. Our work rate continued to fall.

Incidentally, throughout this period we had little social interaction with the supervisors but I noticed that they became more and more friendly with each other.

Meanwhile, the new crew's difficulties increased. Being new and inexperienced they couldn't do the work as easily as we could. Also the supervisors didn't, or couldn't, give them any adequate training. Their productivity went lower and lower. The supervisors were very upset and yelled at them, pushing them to get out their quota. We felt sorry for them and tried to help them; but we concentrated on reluctantly meeting our own quota.

I don't think Joe realized that the supervisors were not teaching the new crewmen. He was very busy and not around much, and I think he assumed that they were training the new men. I think he began to put pressure on the supervisors as the work rate fell, because things continued to get worse. We couldn't talk to customers, which surprised them. We couldn't even accept drinks. Production lagged greatly as compared to the previous summer and the two supervisors struggled to meet the schedule and deal with customer complaints about quality. By July 15th, the overall productivity of the company was 5 percent below "normal" and way below the previous summer.

As Joe became aware of this huge decrease in production he became very concerned and wondered what to do about it.

Discussion Questions

1. What caused the poor production condition during the second summer?
2. How might this situation have been avoided from the beginning?
3. What should Joe do now?
4. Do you think the supervisors could have effectively adopted Joe's style of leadership? What kind of problems might they have had if they did? How should they have conducted themselves?

Camp Zappa '73

THE IROQUOIS *Unit of Camp Zappa had been having some staff problems for quite some time. Rob, the educational resource counselor was not getting along with most of the other counselors. The stress and strain of having to put up with such an emotionally tense state of affairs coupled with the physical demands of a camp counseling job had taken a heavy toll on all the counselors, and drained away the very energies and spirit that they would have to use in order to try to come to a settlement among themselves. Things finally reached a boiling point when Rob, frustrated by not getting the respect and cooperation that he needed to conduct a co-ed evening program he had planned, staged a dramatic exit from the playing field. The campers and the rest of the counselors were left standing on the field with nothing to do except slap their arms and thighs to kill off invading, bloodthirsty mosquitoes. Susungi, his boss, had to act at once.*

Camp Zappa was established in the 1920s and over the years had grown into an organization with over 100 staff members. See Exhibit 1 (organizational chart). The low-paid staff virtually donated their summers to provide children from New York City with an experience of peer-group sharing and fun, challenges, and interests in a natural environment, an opportunity for educational help, and leadership development in a Christian atmosphere. Camp Zappa listed its major goals as follows:

1. To provide each child with an experience of real fun and fellowship through the method of shared decision making with his or her own age level and staff guidance.
2. To provide each child with the new experience and challenges that relate to the natural outdoor setting of camp life (i.e., woodsmanship, nature lore, camping, and so forth).
3. To provide help with reading motivation, educational deficiencies, cultural challenge and identity.
4. To provide experiences whereby city young people have opportunities to develop all their talents with respect to vocational aspirations, leadership development, responsibility, and so forth.

Every summer, campers from NYC ghettoes apply to spend a three-week period at camp. The campers are young and active; they have been waiting all year round to get away from the pressures of school and the sweltering summer heat of the city to go to camp and have some fun swimming in the lake and hiking in the woods as they did the year before. Upon arrival the 180 campers are divided into small units according to their age and sex. Each unit is headed by a small camp director (SCD) who supervises four cabin counselors, one educational resource counselor (ERC) and one counselor-in-training (CIT). The SCD is directly responsible to the assistant director (AD) of the same sex and in their turn, the ADs report to the camp director. Everybody from the SCD upwards is part of the supervisory staff (SS). The SS meets from time to time to evaluate how things are going and to recommend what changes, if any, ought to be made.

The cabin counselor is responsible for planning the program activities for his campers as well as ensuring their safety and welfare. The cabin programs are subject to the approval of the SCD and the AD. Cabin programs encompass most aspects of camp life from meals, kapers (clean-up duty), and naps — to swimming classes and overnight hikes into the woods. Sometimes the SCD and his counselors might plan to run interest groups in which campers would sign up to work with a counselor on a project. This is good for the campers because it provides them with the opportunity to work with a counselor other than their own cabin counselor and at the same time get to know campers from other cabins. Unfortunately, it is fairly common for a camper to sign up for an interest group because he wants to be with the counselor that is running the interest group and not necessarily because he is interested in the project.

The responsibilities of the ERC are not as clearly defined as those of the cabin counselor because the former does not have a cabin of his own. Over the years, the duties of the ERC have come to include helping to plan unit programs, providing program materials and replacing the cabin counselors on their days-off by "programming" with their cabins. Since he does not have a cabin of his own, the ERC usually complains about not being in touch with the kids. His feelings of alienation can be overcome by allowing him the opportunity to form his own interest group so that he may really begin to know some of the campers by working with them.

The SCD is responsible for the welfare of his unit and sees to it that counselors plan good programs for their cabins. He is responsible for maintaining discipline in the unit. He also works in conjunction with the counselors in planning evening programs for the whole unit.

The CIT of each unit is a helping shadow. He assists in various activities and often is given total responsibility for minor tasks and errands. It is hoped that he can learn from older counselors and prepare himself for a counseling or staff position in future years.

The camp administration usually requires all prospective counselors to report at camp for a two-week orientation program prior to the arrival of the first batch of campers for the first three-week camping session of the summer. The orientation program features rap sessions, group dynamics, role-playing, a general introduction to camp facilities and finally an overnight woods program. The purpose of the orientation is to enable the staff members to get to know one another so they can work together better in the subsequent summer months. The old staff members share some of their experiences from previous years so that the new counselors can begin to appreciate some of the problems that they will have to deal with in the course of the summer.

The counselors all arrived at camp on an evening in June in preparation for the summer of 1973. Susungi was to be the SCD of the Iroquois unit. This unit consisted of 32 boys aged between 13 and 15. The female counterpart to this age group, called Westward-Ho, was being headed by Maria, 20, a girl who was going to college at the University of Miami (Ohio). The rest of the camp consisted of four groups: 9–10 year old boys and girls and 11–12 year old boys and girls.

Susungi, 24, was a graduate student in engineering at the University of New Hampshire. He was a West African, born and raised in Tabenken, a small village in Cameroon. He had previously attended Bates College (Maine) for four years. He had been appointed SCD on the basis of his three years of previous camp counseling experience. Susungi described himself as being a basically easy-going individual.

The other Iroquois counselors were Tim, Pete, Phil, Rob, and Mel. Tim, 20, was a student at Miami (Ohio); he was a very aggressive and competitive individual. Tim and Susungi had been counselors of Iroquois the previous summer. Incidentally, Tim was Maria's boyfriend. Phil, 19, was a stout, muscular fellow who walked as if he were his own boss. Phil grew up in Philadelphia. He had graduated from high school but had neither been nor had any plans to go to college. Phil had been a CIT under Susungi a couple of years earlier but had risen to the rank of full counselor in the summer of '71. Pete, 22, had just graduated from The College of Wooster. He was born and raised in the Bronx. He wore a bushy, black, Ho-Chi-Minh type beard. He was rather talkative and generally pleasant. Rob, 21, was a graduate of Oberlin College. He was the ERC of the Iroquois. He wore a moustache and sideburns and was rather tall and lanky. In his job application form he had listed violin playing, yoga and transcendental meditation as his hobbies. He grew up in Worcester, Mass. Mel, 22, who grew up in Chicago, had just graduated from Amherst College and was planning to study business administration at the University of Chicago. Mel was a well-built taciturn fellow who was rather quietly sure of himself. Rob, Pete and Mel were rookie counselors, new to the camp. This was the group that Susungi met with on the first day of orientation.

The days went by quickly. Everybody had fun at the group dynamics sessions, rapping, role-playing and sizing one another up, checking out

EXHIBIT 1
Organization of Camp Zappa

A. Camp Organization

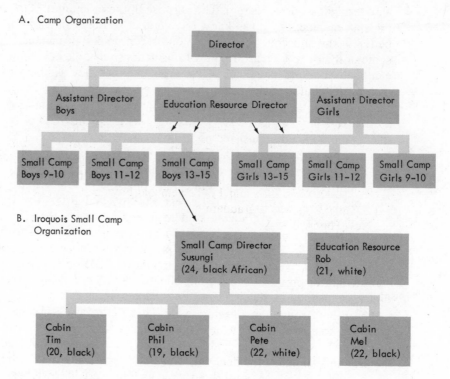

B. Iroquois Small Camp
   Organization

the girls, and so forth. By all indications things were going very well, at least for the Iroquois unit. The summer seemed very promising.

When time came for the woods program, Susungi and his crew decided to undertake a 50 mile hike on the Appalachian Trail instead of spending two boring days under a lean-to only a couple of miles in the woods. As they were preparing to leave, there was considerable debate among the counselors as to who would use the new packs and how much food each person would carry. Susungi suggested that those who wanted to use the new packs would have to carry a little more food since that was the only way to insure that the food wouldn't get squashed. Apparently that sounded reasonable to everybody since the solution was adopted without any complaints. The counselors were driven in a camp truck to Elisville, Conn., from where they were supposed to hike their way back on the Appalachian Trail to Camp Zappa which was located near Browndale, Mass. The total distance of about 50 miles was to be covered in 2½ days.

As the Iroquois "marauders," as they called themselves, made their hike along the trail, they began to know and open themselves to one another. Personality clashes began to emerge. Rob and Phil never seemed to work out. They spent a great deal of time quibbling about who could swim better, who was stronger and who could "whip whose ass." Rob complained that he was carrying the heaviest pack and deserved relief. The complaint was largely ignored because everybody felt the same way. As they hiked on and sweated their way up steep mountains, they seemed to become more and more irritable and tempers began to flare. At one rest stop Rob refused to help build a fire to cook the hamburgers because he had brought along a portable cooking unit, which he used alone. They spent the first night in the Mohawk Mountains in Connecticut. The following morning everybody got mad because Rob spread out his blanket and began performing his meditation exercises when everybody was ready to start. At one point there was a massive verbal attack against Rob from all but Susungi and Mel. Tim, Phil, and Pete were mad because Rob did not want to carry the canteen but wanted to drink the water in it. In the ensuing melee, they ended up throwing the canteen into the woods. Susungi retrieved the canteen and carried it the rest of the way. He later expressed his surprise at the fact that would-be counselors were behaving so much like campers, adding that if a bunch of campers did that in front of him he would probably bellow at them and threaten to "bury a combat boot up somebody's Eiffel tower" if they did not stop messing around. Under the circumstances he believed that that option was not appropriate. He decided not to do anything about the incident, reasoning that since the counselors were all grown-ups their behavior was probably just the result of fatigue-induced irritability which would all disappear soon after they reached camp and took a good rest.

Upon returning to camp, all the counselors were chanting "I want to be an Iroquois marauder," a very catchy chant, boasting that their hike was the longest that had ever been attempted at camp, and, what is more, had been accomplished in record time. None of them mentioned the fact that all but Susungi and Mel had wanted to hitch-hike the last four miles into camp. It was not easy for Susungi to finally convince them that it would be self-defeating to give up after such a brilliant 46-mile hiking record.

Susungi was disappointed with many aspects of the preparatory hike but held hopes that the counselors would become unified in their work with the campers.

On the first day of Session 1, Susungi slotted the campers into four cabins and assigned them to the four cabin counselors after trying as much as possible to avoid assigning potentially troublesome campers to the less experienced counselors. Two days later the campers were asked to sign up for one of what seemed to Susungi like a decent selection of interest groups. Tim's hobby and part-time college job was photography, so he decided to run a photography interest group. Mel had studied Kung-fu at Amherst and wanted to share his knowledge with anybody who was interested. Phil was excited about nature and ecology and wanted to expose the city children to as many aspects of nature and man's role in it as possible. Pete had been interested in Indian affairs since college. He had written a thesis on the historical significance of the Indian occupation of Wounded Knee. He wanted to set up a program on Indian lore, crafts and methods of survival. Rob wanted to run a Journalism interest group. This would involve teaching a little creative writing and these efforts would culminate in the production of a camp newspaper.

The campers divided themselves among the first four interest groups but no one signed up for the Journalism interest group. Rob was very disappointed. He took it as a personal rejection and was quite hurt. He and Susungi had a meeting and it was decided that Rob would float among the other four groups and help out when needed. During the first week he spent a couple of days with Pete's Indian program. Susungi noticed that friction was developing between Pete and Rob, but he was not sure of its exact cause. He had a feeling that it was a continuation of the "one upmanship" that he had observed during the training hike.

Arrangements were made for Rob to substitute for Mel on Tuesday, Mel's day off. On Tuesday afternoon Susungi noticed several of his unit's campers running around the unit lodge during the interest group period. When he asked them where they were supposed to be they said that they usually worked with Mel on the Kung-fu interest group, but Rob was there today and it was not much fun. He made them hold funny positions and meditate. They said that they had done enough of that during the afternoon rest hour. Susungi walked back to the Kung-fu interest group with the youngsters. Some of the others practiced their Kung-fu on the side. Susungi ordered everybody back into line and after participating in the exercises for a while finally left when he felt that order had been restored.

The other interest groups were running quite smoothly, but Rob could not provide any useful input; Tim's photography interest group was too specialized and since Rob did not know much about it there was little that he could do to help Tim. It was not possible for Phil and Rob to work together either, because Phil was highly individualistic and liked to run his own show. Furthermore, they had disagreed on several occasions on the Appalachian Trail and there was strong evidence that they had not come to an accommodation. The only times when Rob got a chance to do some work and feel useful was when he replaced the other counselors on their days off or when he assisted in the swimming instruction at the waterfront. Generally, he seemed to have plenty of free time to himself. The other counselors resented this because they felt that they were putting 24 hours a day and getting hell from the campers. It did not seem fair that Rob should be having things so easy.

The cabin counselors also complained about the "sleep-in" program. This was a system designed by Susungi and the other counselors whereby each counselor would have a few opportunities to skip breakfast and sleep late while another counselor or CIT watched over his campers at the breakfast table. The complaint was that Rob was taking too many sleep-in mornings since he had no cabin of his own to worry about. Susungi remembered that on a few occasions he had asked Rob why he missed coming to breakfast. Rob had replied that he was having colds and headaches in the mornings.

Susungi decided to have a talk with Rob and the other counselors. At the meeting the other counselors, including Mike, complained that Rob was lazy and was not doing anything to earn his summer pay; he was missing from a lot of unit activities and from the dining hall where they could use his relief to get away from the campers for a while. Rob charged that he had not been able to do anything because the other counselors would not let him be of any help in their cabin or interest group programs. The counselors only needed him to run silly errands, whereas he felt that he could be of more use to the whole unit. He declared that he was tired of trying to make himself accepted. Susungi felt that both sides had a legitimate grievance and that the best way to try to solve the problem was to find ways to make Rob feel useful. But how?

Susungi decided to have a meeting with Mr. Bob Adamn, the educational resource director (ERD) of the entire camp. At the meeting Susungi said that he was having some problems with his staff; since the ERC did not have any specific duties that kept him busy full-time, Rob was finding himself with a lot of free time and was being resented by the cabin counselors for it. Mr. Adamn said that he was aware of the problems that can result from having such a nebulous position in the staff set-up of the unit. He went on to suggest that Susungi should try to delegate some of the responsibilities of the SCD to Rob so as to make him feel more useful in the unit. Following this suggestion, Susungi decided to ask Rob to plan the Thursday night unit program. This was to be a co-ed program involving the girls of Westward-Ho, so Susungi talked to Maria about the plans.

Rob seemed pleased with the responsibility of planning a program for two units. On Wednesday, Susungi asked Rob about the Thursday night plans and all Rob said was that everything was under control. On Thursday morning Maria asked Rob what the female counselors could do to help; Rob said that all the girls needed to do was to show up at seven o'clock. The campers were asking their counselors and the counselors were asking each other about the big co-ed activity, but Rob was the only one who had the answers, and would not share them with anyone. After dinner everyone was told to meet on the field at seven o'clock.

Cabins started to arrive with their counselors before seven. The curiosity among the campers was high, but their counselors had few answers for them. When everybody was assembled on the field, Rob began to split them into co-ed teams and tried to solicit as little help from the other counselors as possible. As he posted the teams to various corners of the field it became apparent that they were going to do some kind of relay racing. Rob raced from corner to corner and from team to team trying to explain to the campers what he wanted them to do. The campers were getting restless and mosquito bitten as were the counselors. It became more and more difficult to organize the teams and keep them organized. Pete, Phil, Tim and a few of the female counselors, who had become totally suspicious of the whole evening program, resigned themselves to letting Rob run his show. Mel seemed to have a wait-and-see attitude. Susungi and Maria did not want to step in and take over because Rob would probably interpret this as an abrogation of his responsibilities, thus defeating the purpose of letting Rob plan and run his own evening program. Phil, however, made a derogatory remark about the whole show and Pete began to complain about the chaos. Rob, having heard these comments, dropped all the equipment for the relays and started yelling at the counselors, telling them that if they knew so much they might just as well run the program without him. He then pushed his way through the counselors and made his way to the cabin. Susungi had to decide what to do, and quickly!

The Captain's Table

NOTE: DO NOT READ this case until directed to do so by your instructor. It has been set up as a Prediction Case so that you can test your analysis by answering questions before reading the entire case.

PART I

THE CAPTAIN'S TABLE is located on a well traveled highway near two small cities in the eastern part of the country. Employing a total of about 40 people as waitresses, cooks, kitchen help, bartenders, and hostesses, the Captain's Table caters to businessmen entertaining customers and "dress-up dining" by residents of the area. It also has rooms available for wedding parties and other social functions. Overall, it is considered to be one of the best restaurants in the area.

The owner of the Captain's Table, Mr. Rogers, had bought the restaurant in 1945, and working closely with his manager, Bill Hayes, changed what was once a rather ordinary restaurant into a well-known and highly profitable enterprise. Over the years the business relationship between Mr. Rogers and his manager has developed into a social relationship. Both men belonged to the same yacht club, where they frequently entertained one another for dinner, as well as to the same church. On the job, Bill was given absolute authority to make decisions in Mr. Rogers' name.

Working closely with the manager was the head chef, Henry Plante, who often attended the informal meetings between Bill and Mr. Rogers where problems concerning the restaurant were discussed. With Mr. Rogers' approval, Bill and Henry had a business policy of allowing their employees the most freedom possible in the belief that this would produce a high degree of satisfaction and conscientiousness on the part of employees. As one of the waitresses exclaimed, "Working here is really a joy, everyone knows one another and gets along well. . . ."

In the kitchen, Henry exerted just enough authority to maintain discipline, but allowed the frequent blowoffs that come from the long hours and hot working conditions. His only real rule was to "treat the customer to the meal you would like to eat." His success was demonstrated by the many compliments he received from the customers. His standard reply to such compliments was to thank the customer, but explain that it was due to the contributions of his employees.

On several occasions when a well-known customer complimented him, Henry relayed the compliment to the rest of the kitchen help. This was well received and gave them great pride in their work. Said one employee about Henry, "I've worked in restaurants all my life, but here it's more than a job." It was the belief of many of the customers that it was Henry who made the restaurant a success.

In the dining room and lounge, Bill also allowed his employees considerable freedom, and encouraged them to make immediate decisions on their own without prior consultations. Said Bill, "My people are good, intelligent people, and I have complete faith in them." Under this policy the dining room personnel were allowed to fraternize with the kitchen help during the slow hours and even allowed to order drinks from the bar without fear of reprimand. When the monthly bar costs were tabulated Bill never questioned any of the employees' signed slips. He had said many times that as long as they did a good job, he didn't care how much they drank. High morale and customer satisfaction attested to the job they did and Bill saw no reason to change it. Interaction was high among all employees and nearly everyone was on a first name basis. Picnics and social events were arranged whenever possible to promote what was considered to be "one big happy family."

On several occasions when the work was slow and the day tedious, the kitchen help would play a game called "Air Raid." This would always produce lots of banter and joking as the help would bang on pots and pans and hide under the preparation table, in anticipation of flying meatballs and other food left over from the day. It was not unusual to see Henry as bombardier leading the battle and it usually ended by sending the waitresses to the bar with an order for beers for the "survivors." On Henry's day off, the dishwashers would help the cooks prepare the meals and someone else was designated as "honorary bombardier" during the "Air Raid" game.

A few months ago Bill retired and left the restaurant to live in Florida. Before he left Mr. Rogers ordered the restaurant closed for a day and gave a party for him with only employees and personal friends invited. Contributions of over $1,000 from the employees and a gold watch from Mr. Rogers with the inscription "To Bill, in appreciation for the many years of loyal service, 1945–1973" were given to him.

Discussion Questions

1. What kind of person should Mr. Rogers look for as a replacement for Bill? What criteria should he use in selecting a replacement? Why?

2. If you were Mr. Rogers, what are some of the questions you would ask applicants, interviewing for the manager's job, to help you judge their suitability?

3. What information would you be sure to give qualified applicants about the restaurant so that they too could make a judgment about whether they would fit in? Why?

PART II

Faced with the problem of replacing Bill, Mr. Rogers hired Mr. Robert Nielson. Nielson was a former maitre d' with extensive restaurant experience. He came highly recommended by the owner of another local restaurant. In an hour long meeting with Henry and Mr. Roberts, Bob was told of the working relationship between employees and the former manager. In addition, the excellence of the restaurant was heavily emphasized and his new and expanded duties explained. As maitre d' he was in charge of front of the house operations, but now he would be in charge of the entire restaurant. To this he replied, "I'm sure I can do a good job for you" and the meeting ended.

Although greeted with enthusiasm by everyone, only two weeks passed before Mr. Nielson began having problems with the help. As he constantly reminded people, "My name is Mr. Nielson, not Bill Hayes!"

As the new manager, one of Bob's first actions was to keep a careful record of all bar expenditures. When his first monthly tabulation showed over $500 in free drinks, he was overheard to say, "This place is unbelievably sloppy. It may have made money, but there is enormous waste. Five hundred dollars for drinks per month is $6,000 per year directly off of profits, not to mention the inefficiency of people who are not completely sober." He brought the matter to Henry's attention and blamed the kitchen for excessive drinking. "How can anyone do his work when he's half drunk?" he fumed in a fit of anger. Henry's only reply was that no one was going to tell him and his help how much they could or could not drink, and that he saw no reason to stop. The matter was dropped, but another problem arose on Henry's next day off.

As was the custom whenever Henry had a day off, several of the dishwashers pitched in to help prepare the meals in the kitchen. Due to an unpredicted noon time crowd, the kitchen ran short of clean dishes and service slowed, although not considerably. "As a matter of fact," one waitress mentioned somewhat sarcastically to another, "no one but an old fuss budget like him would have ever noticed it." Bob, however, saw matters differently. Storming into the kitchen, he demanded to know what was going on. When he saw the dishwashers working on the preparations, he became quite angry and yelled at them to get back to their own jobs because they were not getting paid to do the cooking. "No good lazy cooks" he muttered as he left the kitchen. With the dishwashers no longer helping out, the cooks staged a mini-slowdown in protest. For the rest of the day, there was constant friction with Bob barking orders like a marine drill sergeant, and the cooks ignoring them. The end of the night saw Bob extend the dining room hours from 9:00 until 10:00 P.M., with the cooks and kitchen help vowing to throw him out bodily if he came back into the kitchen again.

The next day, Henry had just entered the restaurant when Bob accosted him. In an emotional tirade, Bob blamed the whole mess on Henry, exclaiming that his lack of responsible leadership would no longer be tolerated. Henry sat quietly until Bob left, and then proceeded into the kitchen. When the dishwashers and cooks began talking all at once, Henry meekly threw up his hands and said "I've had it with him" and was gone for the rest of the day. Although business was conducted as usual, morale was at an all time low. When Henry failed to show up the following day, Bob became quite irritated and went in and out of the kitchen yelling at everyone in sight. Even the waitresses, to whom Bob had generally remained good-natured, came under his verbal abuses. Finally, with everyone's patience wearing thin, the day came to an end.

During the next few months, the situation deteriorated even further. Henry was in and out of the kitchen, morale was low, the cooks were preparing sloppy meals, and no one any longer took much pride in his job. As one of the waitresses remarked, "I used to like working here, but now I'm looking for another job." Several of the other employees began to express similar feelings. Bob, blaming the deterioration of morale and the gradual loss of business on Henry and the rest of the kitchen help, hired a new cook to speedup and improve the quality of the meals. Henry, feeling that he was being replaced went to Mr. Rogers and explained that although he had enjoyed working for him, he could no longer work under existing conditions, and was going to quit. Solemnly, Mr. Rogers sat back and listened to Henry, wondering what he should do.

Discussion Questions

1. What factors led to the problems that have now developed?
2. What assumptions did Bill, Henry, Bob, and Mr. Rogers have (a) about human motivation and (b) about leadership?
3. What options did Henry have when Bob Nielson began to push him? Why did Henry respond as he did?
4. What problems, if any, would have occurred if Mr. Nielson had been "another Bill Hayes" in his manner of fulfilling his role?
5. What should Mr. Rogers do now? Why?

The Carpenter Case*

Tom and Jane Carpenter are a young couple living comfortably in a New England town in the United States.

They have three children, Mary 11, Jerry 6, and Ann 3.

Tom works in the headquarters of a manufacturing company as an executive in the engineering department. He has an excellent salary and up until now has been satisfied with his job. A quiet, handsome man of about 36 years, he is intelligent, sensitive, ambitious and known as "a good family man." He has the respect of his colleagues and subordinates. The upper echelons of management regard him as a promising candidate for senior management in this company. Tom is considered a practical man, able to take the changes in life with a basic optimism and adaptability that appear to give him a maturity beyond his years. He likes the

---

* This case was prepared by Foulie Psalidas-Perlmutter, Ph.D., Clinical Psychologist, and is reproduced with her permission.

material wealth and comfort that his years of conscientious work have produced. He enjoys the status in his company which has an excellent name in its field, being considered one of the most progressive and future minded of U.S. companies of this type.

If Tom is the practical member of the family, Jane is the "dreamer." She is a pretty, energetic woman of 30, a good wife and mother and an active member of several committees and voluntary groups. She is strongly attached to both her family and her parents who are in their early 60s and live in a nearby town. She is sincerely interested in many good causes and always finds the time and energy to devote to them. While she is not a very practical woman by nature, her enthusiasm for her projects is admired by her many friends.

Tom and Jane married early and struggled together for several years until they were able to achieve the comfortable life they have now. Their marital life has been happy and more or less undisturbed, and through the struggle of their earlier years they were able to develop between themselves a rewarding relationship. Although they have travelled to several parts of the United States with and without the children, neither Tom nor Jane had travelled abroad until two years ago. At that time Tom, together with three other executives, was sent to Latin America to explore the possibilities of setting up four new plants in different countries of Latin America.

Both Tom and Jane have been feeling more and more relaxed in the past years, since many of their dreams have been realized. They have a good family, financial security and many friends. They are especially proud of their new home, recently finished. Jane has worked hard to find the furniture and the internal decorations they wanted and now her dream house seems completed. They have both been so far generally satisfied with their children, who are well adjusted to their present environment. There have been certain problems with Mary, who is a very sensitive and shy girl, and with Jerry who has had some difficulties adapting in school. But these were minor problems and they have not disturbed seriously the otherwise happy family life.

Despite this very satisfactory picture of family life, there have recently been more and more occasions when Tom and Jane have felt (each one without admitting it to the other) that something is "missing."

More and more, Tom thinks that his life has become a comfortable routine. The new tasks he is given have less "challenge" and "adventure." For a long while he has been satisfied that his career had a steady development through the years. The time of anxiety and uncertainty has passed, but also with it the time of excitement and the inner feeling of searching and moving. He had begun to feel that he needs a change and it was at that time that he was sent for two months to Latin America. Tom felt that this trip was one of the most interesting and rewarding events of his whole life. Being away for the first time from his family for such a long period, he missed them and he was disappointed because the wives were not allowed to accompany their husbands on that trip. But the prospects of building up their company in Latin America have been very attractive and he found that he liked to travel, to meet new people, to become acquainted with different ways of living, to be more a part of the "world" and of events outside of their hometown. The three other executives who took the trip with him had about the same feelings as he had. Each seemed to be a little weary of being "a little fish" at headquarters. The possibility of being a pioneer in the Latin American division to be created was an exciting prospect. Tom somehow felt reluctant to communicate to Jane all his satisfaction and his thoughts about that trip, as well as the facts that he was hoping to be chosen from among the executives to be responsible for setting up the plants in Latin America.

In a different way, but with the same feelings of restlessness and discontent, there are times now that Jane feels that the pleasant well organized life she has is lacking the excitement of unpredictability. She divides her time between many activities, but finds herself at times dreaming about the world outside of her hometown. She wonders, like Tom, at times whether their life has not become too settled, an almost unaltered routine, but unlike Tom, she checks herself by asking the simple question that after all, isn't this what life really is?

When Tom came home with the news that Mr. Abbott, the president of the company, had offered him the key position in the Latin American operation, she was pleased to hear of the high esteem his superiors had for Tom. Actually, Jane too had been wondering for some time what could be the result of Tom's trip to Latin America. Although she would have liked to have been able to go with him at the time, the idea that she would have had to leave the children for such a long time forced her to exclude absolutely the possibility of her going, even if the wives of the executives had been allowed to go with them. After that, she used to wonder at times whether the company would choose him, if the decision was made. At that time the idea of having to move to a new environment was not an unpleasant one.

Now that the offer was a firm one, with a high salary, cost of living expenses, opportunity for travel throughout Latin America, she began to have some fears. As Tom talked excitedly about the challenging tasks he would have, her fears seemed to increase. She began to feel more and more that they had little to gain from this experience as regards their family and their life. It was a big step forward in Tom's career, to be sure, but Jane felt that Tom would be successful wherever he was. On the present job, Tom and she shared so much time together, while in the new job, as she understood it, Tom would have to travel a great deal. She was very unhappy and ashamed about her fears as opposed to Tom's enthusiasm and obvious willingness to venture ahead.

One evening she sat down by herself and tried to figure out why this new job was not so attractive to her. There was some urgency for Tom to make up his mind within a week, and she felt the need to understand what this decision to move abroad meant for her and for her family.

She tried to be honest with herself. She had fears naturally about moving to a new environment which was strange and where people spoke another language. She knew that the climate was very different and she believed that the living conditions were likely to offer fewer comforts. She would be far from her friends and her old parents. Their furniture would have to be stored, and their new house rented or sold, since it was not clear how many years Tom would need to get the four new plants going.

She felt she would be isolated because she did not think that they could have a close contact with the local people for a long time. Whatever she had heard so far about the personality of the Latin Americans made her fear that close friendships would be difficult to achieve, at least for some time, because she had the impression that they were rather temperamental and unstable. Although she admitted to herself that this impression was based on hearsay and fiction, she somehow could not avoid believing it. She had also heard that there was a great deal of anti-American feelings in the country where they would first live. Furthermore, she wondered whether the sanitary conditions would be dangerous to the health of the children. The company had little experience in Latin America, so it would be likely that they would have to find their own way and learn, probably by hard experience, how to get along in these countries. She realized that what disturbed her more than anything else was probably the fact that Tom was going to have to travel a lot. Then she would probably have to face a great deal of the problems of their adaptation there alone, while up until this time they had always shared whatever problems they had to face and they supported each other in finding solutions. This also meant that Tom would see more places, meet more people, in general he would enjoy more, and probably get more satisfaction out of the whole experience than she and the children would. She was distressed to realize that she was already resentful towards him for that and angry because she could sense that, although he was discussing the problem with her, he had already made up his mind.

Jane kept these fears more or less to herself, but she did communicate to Tom her reluctance to go and gave as one of the main reasons her worry about the effect this move was going to have on the education of their children as well as on their health. One discussion went as follows:

JANE: Will the children lose a year or maybe even more going to inferior schools?

TOM: They will learn a new language—make new friends.

JANE: Who knows what kind of doctors there are . . .

TOM: Most of their doctors are trained in this country. Don't worry about it.

JANE: It will be all so new, so strange.

TOM: The children will adapt after a while and the experience will be good for them.

JANE: You'll be travelling quite a bit and I . . .

TOM: We'll both find this enriching, rewarding—not that I underestimate the difficulties involved, but we can overcome them and enjoy all the advantages of life abroad.

JANE (sigh): If you say so. . . .

Inwardly Tom was disappointed with Jane's negative reactions and the difficulties she seemed to be having. He had always believed her to be a woman of courage endowed with curiosity and interest for the world outside. In times of crisis previously in their life, she had always proved to be strong and supportive and she had always shown a spirit of adventure and willingness to go ahead. It was a painful surprise for him to realize that this spirit would operate only in the security of the familiar environment, while a more profound change seemed to appear to Jane as a great threat to herself and her family. He had hoped that she would back him in this decision which was so important to his career. Nevertheless, he maintained his confidence in her and he believed that she would change her mind in time. He called a Berlitz school nearby and made plans for both of them to take Spanish lessons.

When Jane's parents came to visit during this period of time, Jane told them of the company's offer to Tom. Her father, who had been ailing for some time, was visibly depressed by the news. Her mother said that this was going to be a great experience for them, "a chance of a lifetime," as she put it. Jane knew that her mother had always regretted not being able to travel abroad. Now she was thrilled that the children were given this opportunity and she promised to come and visit them in Latin America if Tom accepted the job. With her father ill, Jane doubted this very much.

Dinner with Mr. Abbott

A few days later, Tom's boss, Mr. Abbott, invited Tom and Jane for dinner, saying that he always talked over a new job abroad with both husband and wife, because he felt that it was very important to take into consideration how the wife felt. Jane had many fears about this dinner. First, she resented being "looked over" by Mr. Abbott, who until now had not really spent much time with them socially. Second, she did not want to reveal her doubts to Tom's boss, who had a reputation for making quick judgments about people, often not very favorable.

The dinner turned out to be a very pleasant one. Mrs. Abbott helped to put everyone at ease throughout the dinner, talking about her pleasant experiences abroad when Mr. Abbott was managing director of a subsidiary branch in Europe. Mrs. Abbott had enjoyed Paris and Rome, but she admitted that she knew little about life in cities like Buenos Aires or Rio.

Mr. Abbott finally turned to Jane and said: "Well, Jane and what do you think of Tom's new assignment?"

JANE: Oh—I don't know . . . I. . . .

MR. ABBOTT: I know you realize what a great opportunity this job will be for him. It's a greater challenge than anything he could get here, you know.

JANE: Well, you see, I. . . .

TOM: Jane is really a born traveller. I know that she is looking forward to this. She has already found out how she can take lessons in Spanish.

Mr. Abbott looked pleased.

MR. ABBOTT: That's really fine. You know, Tom, that ours is becoming an international company. There will be few opportunities for executives at headquarters whose overseas experience is limited. Our policy is to create a management team which could base its decisions on actual experience abroad. Of course, having the kind of wife who is willing to take the risk of going off to the jungle is quite an asset. You're a lucky man, Tom.

While Jane joined in the laughter, she was inwardly very angry. That night she and Tom had a quarrel:

TOM: Oh, boy, that evening really went beautifully!

JANE: Oh yeah? For whom?

TOM (surprised): Why, for both of us, of course. Don't you think so?

JANE (angry): Do you realize, Mr. Tom Carpenter, that you and Mr. Abbott talked as if you had already accepted the job? That everytime I opened my mouth you cut me right off?

TOM: I knew what you would do—ask questions, look hesitant, unsure. Mr. Abbott is not the kind of man you can level with. You have to sound enthusiastic, especially about company decisions.

JANE: And to whom, please, can I show my lack of enthusiasm about the "company's" decision to send me and my children to some godforsaken place?

TOM: For heaven's sake, Jane. What's the matter with you?

JANE (turning away, crying): I'm not going.

TOM: What? and ruin my career, a chance of a lifetime—for both of us? How will this make me look?

JANE: I'm just not ready to go.

TOM: You can just bet this opportunity will never be offered to me again.

Discussing the problem the next day with the children confused Tom and Jane more, because the children's reaction was not clear. Mary was unwilling to go, Jerry was frightened and Ann seemed excited. By now Jane was finding it difficult to sleep, and Tom said that a formal decision was required by next Monday.

They had a long weekend to think over the decision and give a final answer to Mr. Abbott on Monday.

The Case of the Changing Cage*

NOTE: DO NOT READ this case until directed to do so by your instructor. It has been set up as a Prediction Case so that you can test your analysis by answering questions before reading the entire case.

PART I

THE VOUCHER-CHECK filing unit was a work unit in the home office of the Atlantic Insurance Company. The assigned task of the unit was to file checks and vouchers written by the company as they were cashed and returned. This filing was the necessary foundation for the main function of the unit: locating any particular check for examination upon demand. There were usually eight to ten requests for specific checks from as many different departments during the day. One of the most frequent reasons checks were requested from the unit was to determine whether checks in payment of claims against the company had been cashed. Thus, efficiency in the unit directly affected customer satisfaction with the company. Complaints or inquiries about payments could not be answered with the accuracy and speed conducive to client satisfaction unless the unit could supply the necessary documents immediately.

Toward the end of 1952, nine workers manned this unit. There was an assistant (a position equivalent to a foreman in a factory) named Miss Dunn, five other full-time employees, and three part-time workers.

The work area of the unit was well defined. Walls bounded the unit on three sides. The one exterior wall was pierced by light-admitting north

---

* Data for the following case were taken from "Topography and Culture: The Case of the Changing Cage," *Human Organization,* vol. 16, no. 1 (1957), by Cara E. Richards and Henry F. Dobyns. Reproduced by permission of The Society for Applied Anthropology from *Human Organization,* vol. 16, no. 1 (1957).

windows. The west interior partition was blank. A door opening into a corridor pierced the south interior partition. The east side of the work area was enclosed by a steel mesh reaching from wall to wall and floor to ceiling. This open metal barrier gave rise to the customary name of the unit—"the voucher cage." A sliding door through this mesh gave access from the unit's territory to the work area of the rest of the company's agency audit division, of which it was a part, located on the same floor.

The unit's territory was kept inviolate by locks on both doors, fastened at all times. No one not working within the cage was permitted inside unless his name appeared on a special list in the custody of Miss Dunn. The door through the steel mesh was used generally for departmental business. Messengers and runners from other departments usually came to the corridor door and pressed a buzzer for service.

The steel mesh front was reinforced by a rank of metal filing cases where checks were filed. Lined up just inside the barrier, they hid the unit's workers from the view of workers outside their territory, including the section head responsible for over-all supervision of this unit according to the company's formal plan of operation.

Prediction Questions

1. Identify background factors important in influencing the emergent behavior of this group.
2. Predict the emergent system of the group; that is, its norms, activities, cohesiveness and so forth.
3. What would you predict is the level of group productivity and satisfaction? Why?

PART II

On top of the cabinets which were backed against the steel mesh, one of the male employees in the unit neatly stacked pasteboard boxes in which checks were transported to the cage. They were later reused to hold older checks sent into storage. His intention was less getting these boxes out of the way than increasing the effective height of the sight barrier so the section head could not see into the cage "even when he stood up."

The girls stood at the door of the cage which led into the corridor and talked to the messenger boys. Out this door also the workers slipped unnoticed to bring in their customary afternoon snack. Inside the cage the workers sometimes engaged in a good-natured game of rubber-band "sniping."

Workers in the cage possessed good capacity to work together consistently, and workers outside the cage often expressed envy of those in it because of the "nice people" and friendly atmosphere there. The unit had no apparent difficulty keeping up with its work load.

Discussion Question

1. Wherein were your predictions right and wrong? Analyze why.

PART III

For some time prior to 1952 the controller's department of the company had not been able to meet its own standards of efficient service to clients. Company officials felt the primary cause to be spatial. Various divisions of the controller's department were scattered over the entire twenty-two-story company building. Communication between them required phone calls, messengers, or personal visits, all costing time. The spatial separation had not seemed very important when the company's business volume was smaller prior to World War II. But business had grown tremendously since then, and spatial separation appeared increasingly inefficient.

Finally, in November of 1952, company officials began to consolidate the controller's department by relocating two divisions together on one floor. One was the agency audit division, which included the voucher-check filing unit. As soon as the decision to move was made, lower level supervisors were called in to help with planning. Line workers were not consulted, but were kept informed by the assistants of planning progress. Company officials were concerned about the problem of transporting many tons of equipment and some two hundred workers from two locations to another single location without disrupting work flow. So the move was planned to occur over a single weekend, using the most efficient resources available. Assistants were kept busy planning positions for files and desks in the new location.

Desks, files, chairs, and even wastebaskets were numbered prior to the move, and relocated according to a master chart checked on the spot by the assistant. Employees were briefed as to where the new location was and which elevators they should take to reach it. The company successfully transported the paraphernalia of the voucher-check filing unit from one floor to another over one weekend. Workers in the cage quit Friday afternoon at the old stand, reported back Monday at the new.

The exterior boundaries of the new cage were still three building walls and the steel mesh, but the new cage possessed only one door—the sliding door through the steel mesh into the work area of the rest of the agency audit division. The territory of the cage had also been reduced in size. An entire bank of filing cabinets had to be left behind in the old location to be taken over by the unit moving there. The new cage was arranged so that there was no longer a row of metal filing cabinets lined up inside the steel mesh obstructing the view into the cage.

Prediction Questions

1. How will the change effect the required and emergent systems?
2. What will be the consequences for productivity and satisfaction?

PART IV

When the workers in the cage inquired about the removal of the filing cabinets from along the steel mesh fencing, they found that Mr. Burke had insisted that these cabinets be rearranged so his view into the cage would not be obstructed by them. Miss Dunn had tried to retain the cabinets in their prior position, but her efforts had been overridden.

Burke disapproved of conversation. Since he could see workers conversing in the new cage, he "requested" Miss Dunn to put a stop to all unnecessary talk. Attempts by female clerks to talk to messenger boys brought the wrath of her superior down on Miss Dunn, who was then forced to reprimand the girls.

Burke also disapproved of an untidy working area, and any boxes or papers which were in sight were a source of annoyance to him. He did not exert supervision directly, but would "request" Miss Dunn to "do something about those boxes." In the new cage, desks had to be completely cleared at the end of the day, in contrast to the work-in-progress piles left out in the old cage. Boxes could not accumulate on top of filing cases.

The custom of afternoon snacking also ran into trouble. Lacking a corridor door, the food bringers had to venture forth and pack back their snack trays through the work area of the rest of their section, bringing this hitherto unique custom to the attention of workers outside the cage. The latter promptly recognized the desirability of afternoon snacks and began agitation for the same privilege. This annoyed the section head, who forbade workers in the cage to continue this custom.

Prediction Question

1. With this additional information, reaffirm or revise your previous predictions.

PART V

Burke later made a rule which permitted one worker to leave the new cage at a set time every afternoon to bring up food for the rest. This rigidity irked cage personnel, accustomed to a snack when the mood struck, or none at all. Having made his concession to the cage force, Burke was unable to prevent workers outside the cage from doing the same thing. What had once been unique to the workers in the cage was now common practice in the section.

Although Miss Dunn never outwardly expressed anything but compliance and approval of superior directives, she exhibited definite signs of anxiety. All the cage workers reacted against Burke's increased domination. When he imposed his decisions upon the voucher-check filing unit, he became "Old Grandma" to its personnel. The cage workers sneered at him and ridiculed him behind his back. Workers who formerly had obeyed company policy as a matter of course began to find reasons for loafing and obstructing work in the new cage. One of the changes that took place in the behavior of the workers had to do with their game of rubber-band sniping. All knew Burke would disapprove of this game. It became highly clandestine and fraught with dangers. Yet, shooting rubber bands *increased*.

Newly arrived checks were put out of sight as soon as possible, filed or not. Workers hid unfiled checks, generally stuffing them into desk drawers or unused file drawers. Since boxes were forbidden, there were fewer unused file drawers than there had been in the old cage. So the day's work was sometimes undone when several clerks hastily shoved vouchers and checks indiscriminately into the same file drawer at the end of the day.

Before a worker in the cage filed incoming checks, she measured with her ruler the thickness in inches of each bundle she filed. At the end of each day she totaled her input and reported it to Miss Dunn. All incoming checks were measured upon arrival. Thus, Miss Dunn had a rough estimate of unit intake compared with file input. Theoretically, she was able to tell at any time how much unfiled material she had on hand and how well the unit was keeping up with its task. Despite this running "check," when the annual inventory of "unfiled" checks on hand in the cage was taken at the beginning of the calendar year 1953, a seriously large backlog of unfiled checks was found. To the surprise and dismay of Miss Dunn, the inventory showed the unit to be far behind schedule, filing much more slowly than before the relocation of the cage.

Discussion Questions

1. Explain the emergent behavior and its consequences.
2. If you were Mr. Burke, what would you do now?

The Case of the Joint Meeting*

IT WAS TUESDAY, midway in an experimental course in Negotiations and the Resolution of Conflict, and the class was discussing problems faced by groups in disagreement. The professor, Hugh Spector, suggested that if groups see themselves in competition they will reenforce negative stereotypes of each other. As a number of students recalled situations which seemed to confirm the hypothesis, there was a reference to blacks as generally emotional, short tempered, vengeful and prone to using knives in a fight. A student responded with a laugh that this description was ridiculous and left him with an image of frightening looking blacks slinking around ready to pull out their switchblades at the drop of a hat. At this a white male student exclaimed indignantly, "But they do carry knives," and proceeded to tell a story he had heard about a recent incident. It involved one of his white male friends, who was also in the class. The friend was a member of an all white, male fraternity team that had been challenged to a game of touch football by an all black team of students. The game took place on a Saturday afternoon and had been underway for about 20 minutes when an argument developed between a black and white player following the completion of a play. As the tension between the two players had mounted, their voices rose and the black player brandished an open switchblade. The student reporting the incident said he thought that the black player was ready to use the knife. There had been some jostling, body contact and shouts, and then players scattered in panic in all directions. As the involved white student listened to his friend retell the story, he became increasingly agitated and finally interrupted to say that he had been plenty scared at the time and was now more frightened of blacks than ever.

Bubba Blair, the only black student in the class of 25, listened intently but quietly, as was his custom. When all eyes turned self-consciously to him, he said that he knew the guys they were talking about and he had heard the story differently. Since it was the practice for the class to learn from its own experience whenever possible, Professor Spector made the obvious observation that, "We have under our very noses an example of our hypothesis." Further discussion followed, with disagreement about what had happened on the football field. Blair seemed upset as his reports

* This case was prepared by Professors Allan Cohen and Herman Gadon of the Whittemore School of Business and Economics, University of New Hampshire.

of his friends' versions were attacked, though as usual he spoke in a soft, diffident way. Members of the class began to take sides.

Time was running out for the class period and Spector interrupted again to repeat that the class at that very moment had an example of a conflict of the kind of which he had been talking, presenting an opportunity to test the concepts of the course. He asked if the class were willing to carry on with the issue at the next meeting. There was a general murmer of approval when Bubba said he would be willing to bring some of his friends who had played in the game, and the class ended expecting to continue the discussion two days later.

Hugh Spector was pleased. First, the incident brought to life the learning that he wanted his students to acquire. Second, he was sincerely interested in this particular conflict and hoped to contribute something to its resolution. Third, he had general concerns about black-white relations and saw the coming confrontations as a way to get to issues vital to the campus.

Blacks at North Midwestern State University (NMSU) until recently had been a rarity. Traditionally 75 percent of the 10,000 member student body was largely undergraduate, white, Protestant, lower-middle to middle class, and rural, coming from within the predominantly white state.

People were generally politically conservative and on racial issues mildly prejudiced, mostly from lack of contact with blacks and other visible minorities. The census count of 1970 showed only 2,500 blacks among the state's 1.5 million residents, mostly concentrated in one urban center. For the most part students believed that everyone should have a fair chance to make his own place in the world. Many assumed that everyone did have equal chances and thus held blacks responsible for their lower incomes and standings. A substantial "liberal" element was much more sympathetic to minority issues. On the whole though, attitudes of the student body fairly reflected the attitudes of the majority of the administration, faculty and the 4,000 permanent citizens of the residential town of Smithton in which the university was located.

Until 1971 there had been only isolated pockets of student radicalism. When occasional voices of dissent rose, officials in the town and university responded nervously but not in retribution as nothing more than a noisy rally in front of the Administration Building had occurred, attended for the most part by the curious rather than the committed. NMSU was relatively quiet during that turbulent time in the lives of universities when there was stormy recognition of social issues, but many there felt socially responsible and anxious to do something to address needs they felt were legitimate. Consequently, like most northern colleges and universities, after prodding from liberal faculty members, NMSU had made an effort to bring blacks to its campus in the interest of providing them with new and previously unavailable opportunities for higher education.

By 1971 approximately 100 blacks had been enrolled in the university, mostly recruited from northern urban ghettoes in Chicago and Cleveland, and a few backward rural communities in the South. Bubba had come from a small town in Alabama.

The presence of blacks on the campus and in the town was largely a new experience. Black students had come to Smithton at a time when black self-consciousness was strong and rising in the country. "Black is beautiful" was still fresh and new. There was strong pressure among outnumbered blacks to stick together. Collective strength was seen by many blacks as necessary to cultivate pride and to provide for mutual support in a system in which they still felt that they were treated at best with condescension.

The university and town were populated with many people who saw themselves as having a conscience and being dedicated to the Constitutional premise that all men are created equal. They therefore supported recruitment of black students to uphold that belief. Many had been moved by the civil rights struggles of the 1960s.

On the other hand, a substantial number of students, with their beliefs in individualism, and lack of contact with minorities, resented the scholarship money and bending of admissions standards required to attract black students.

Both groups were poorly prepared to cope with blacks who seemed to prefer separation to acceptance as integrated members of the community. While university officials were working to integrate them into the ordinary routines of campus life, blacks were segregating themselves. The administration was increasingly facing unexpected dilemmas and crises precipitated by black students, such as a request by them for a special commons building furnished and maintained at university expense, from which whites were excluded. After black threats of picketing and boycotting of classes, a building was provided and student funds were channeled to a black organization. This caused much resentment among some white students who already were financially pressed. Because expected federal funds had not materialized in nearly the quantity necessary to provide sufficient support services to blacks, the administration was constantly struggling to find money.

Hugh Spector believed that much of the stress felt by blacks and whites on campus and the increasing number of unpleasant confrontations was directly traceable to inadequate communications between them. It was his opinion that negative stereotypes were consequently reenforced, increasing the polarization. Spector believed strongly that many of the problems he saw could be resolved if blacks and whites could only talk to each other in the right circumstances in order to test and disconfirm many of their prejudices. He believed that confrontation over real rather than imagined differences would result in increased trust and ultimately to solutions which would satisfy everyone.

He had acquired his beliefs through both past experience and study.

At one time in the early days of union organization he had been a consultant to a management team of negotiators, and helped achieve a settlement in a very difficult situation. On the campus and in the community he had become involved in helping individuals to talk more openly and directly with one another. Recently he had begun advising local groups on how to identify their self-interests, organize on their own behalf to pursue them, and talk constructively with authorities. He had helped to arrange meetings to both improve relations and to negotiate arrangements which better met the needs of the aspiring groups. He felt certain that his human skills were applicable to problems between blacks and whites, and was anxious to get them on campus together in a dialogue which would move them toward more understanding and thus contribute to better relations in the larger community. The unexpected opportunity presented by the presence of a scared white student and Bubba, a black student who would talk reasonably openly, pleased him. He hoped to help the coming encounter be a constructive one and was confident that he could handle whatever happened.

Before the next class meeting he reviewed in his own mind what he knew about all the students. Five of the 25 enrolled in the course were graduate students. One of them, Beth, whom he particularly respected, was studying to be a counselor. She was attractive, well-liked, sensitive, alert, outspoken, and intelligent. She often picked up things that he had missed in the class and he felt he could count on her. There were eight women in the class in all, and one black, Bubba Blair. Bubba and the two white male students who had precipitated the confrontation, Doug and Charley, were undergraduate business administration majors, as were most of the others. Doug was the one who said that he was threatened with a knife.

Doug, Charley, and Bubba had a direct stake in the affair. Others in the class seemed primarily interested in testing their ability to cope with the conflict, though some had apparently developed allegiances already.

Feelings in the class towards Bubba were difficult to ascertain. He usually spoke softly, seldom, and briefly, except for one instance early in the course when he had talked at some length about his own difficulty in participating in discussions because he felt inadequate and afraid of sounding foolish. His disclosure aroused a lot of sympathy, attracted support, and for a while seemed to bring other students closer to him. But his customary silence eventually made him a figure of mystery again and kept him relatively isolated. He dressed simply and kept to himself, though he shared a lot privately with Professor Spector. Spector knew, for instance, that Bubba found it difficult to oppose fellow blacks publicly, once they had arrived at a formal position, even when he strongly disagreed. Bubba said that he felt bound by loyalty and fear of isolation if he went his own way.

Doug and Charley were seen in the class as jocks, fraternity-types, social, light-hearted and light-headed but harmless. They generally came to class, as did most others, including the women, in conservative slacks, shirts, and loafers. Doug and Charley were often skeptical about the value of the course to themselves as future businessmen, yet remained interested in learning and had invested a lot of themselves in the previous class discussion about the affair on the football field. They seemed as anxious as Spector to have a satisfactory outcome for the coming meeting.

The class met next as usual at 9 A.M. on Thursday. Spector arrived early. Students filed in and settled themselves in their chairs, which were placed as was customary in a large circle to facilitate discussion. The usual chatter preceding the beginning of class filled the room. Spector thought that no one looked particularly keyed up besides himself. Doug and Charley arrived quietly and sat down together next to Professor Spector. Beth came in and sat in a chair across the room directly facing them. The noise subsided in the room and everyone seemed to be present except Bubba and his friends.

At several minutes after nine, the black students appeared in the doorway and moved jauntily to seats next to Beth. Though their eyes swept the room, they faced only each other, joking animatedly, and punctuating their conversation with loud staccato laughter. Bubba came first, dressed inconspicuously as always, followed by a tall, muscular, lean, handsome male with a flashing smile and alert, darting eyes, dressed in a yellow satin shirt open from the throat to mid-chest, tightly fitted hip-hugging jeans, and a black, silver-studded belt. He had a short, Afro haircut. Alongside him was a pudgy black male at least a head shorter, wearing a vivid purple, floppy wide-brimmed hat pulled down over one eye, a white dashiki, a necklace of animal teeth, red pants, and sandals. He was followed by a beautiful, slim but full-bosomed dark female, wearing skin-tight, electric-blue jeans, and a white blouse knotted in front, revealing a bare midriff to below the navel. They greeted Beth warmly with, "Hi, Sugar," and sat down.

Professor Spector started class by welcoming the visitors and explaining his hopes for a positive outcome. The blacks smiled at each other and Bubba identified his friends. His tall friend, Steve, was the player who was accused of pulling the knife. "Pudge" was a graduate student in the counseling program. He had seen the game. Pudge clowned and mugged constantly while being introduced. Linda was a personal friend who had not been at the game but wanted to come to the class.

Spector suggested that the session begin by Doug and Steve each telling what they thought had happened on the field, urging everyone to listen carefully so that the differences between the two versions were clear. He implored everyone to listen first for understanding and said that arguments should be avoided at least until the real differences had been established. He asked that responses at first be limited to requests for clarification.

Doug began his story. Steve interrupted frequently with sharp questioning which seemed to fit the ground rules but were in fact a kind of baiting. The early exchange went as follows:

DOUG: Steve was going out for a long pass and I brushed him as he went by to slow him down. I was defending short in the flat.

STEVE (with mock precision and a smile): What do you mean "brushed?" Describe a brush to me, will you? You mean you bushwhacked me on the blind side, huh?

Meanwhile, Pudge was singing tauntingly in the background: "A brush in the back is worth two in the hand."

DOUG (defensively): I didn't whack you in the back. You're exaggerating.

STEVE: I don't want to argue, boy. Just tell me what you mean by "brush." You mean like an elbow in my kidneys?

DOUG: I just brushed your shoulder as you went by.

STEVE: Where's your shoulder? Mine must be half-way down my back.

Pudge and Linda were laughing and slapping their thighs.

CHARLEY: What did you Negroes come here for anyway?

STEVE (wide-eyed): Negroes! Did you hear that? Any NE-GROES here, Pudge?

During this exchange Professor Spector listened and watched with growing apprehension. His own anxiety increased and he noticed rising tension in the students in the class. Spector also suddenly noted with alarm that Pudge was carrying a large clear plastic bag which contained a shredded material which looked suspiciously like marijuana. While Doug and Steve were talking, Pudge was elaborately rolling a cigarette, or a joint. Pudge lit up. Spector saw that many of the students had also noticed Pudge's activities and were looking at Spector — waiting, he thought, for a reaction from him. Hugh leaned imperceptibly forward to sniff, and with a sinking feeling, smelled what he was almost sure was "grass."

Pudge was leaning back now with a self-satisfied air after a hard, deep, hissing drag on the cigarette and a long, slow exhalation. He passed the cigarette to Beth, who looked at Spector defiantly he thought, took it and repeated the deep draw and slow, extended exhalation.

Spector remembered that only two days ago 12 students had been busted for possession of marijuana in a raid by town police. There were rumors that a young instructor was involved and would be asked to leave the university. The attitude of the university administration toward punishment for pot smoking was unclear but leaning toward expulsion under pressure from local and state police and public officials. They had been making a tremendous fuss about university toleration of drug use, and marijuana in particular, and the administration was under heavy fire.

Spector felt caught in a terrible bind. He had tenure and had been at the university for ten years. He was married, had a family of three children, and high monthly living expenses. On the one hand if he challenged the content of the pouch and it wasn't pot, he would make a fool of himself. If it was pot (he was almost certain that it was) and he didn't report it, he would become a conspirator and be vulnerable to being reported by a student. He could then be charged with collusion, presence while marijuana was smoked, or at best "softness," and would then expose both himself and the university to attack or prosecution. If it was pot as he suspected, and he did report it, he would be legally clear, but he would expose Pudge and Beth to suspension or expulsion and the university would face, he was certain, a new crisis with blacks and radical students. He was also worried about what would happen if he insisted that the smoking stop and there was a test of strength. What would he do if he said "stop" and was refused? Should he order Pudge and Beth to leave? What would happen if they wouldn't go? Could be physically force them out of the room? Would Steve pull a knife again? Should he himself leave the room?

The specter of the lost opportunity to bring people together to talk suddenly haunted him. He wondered if a dialogue could be maintained if he said nothing. He felt without being clear about it that this was a very critical test and he was fearful that if he didn't meet it adequately, he would expose himself, the class and the white community on campus to ridicule. He was sure that within hours after the class was over, the story would be widely known through the grapevine among a large number of students. But if he acknowledged that he noticed the smoking and tried to stop it, the class might explode and destroy the chance of human understanding. While Hugh raced through the alternatives in his head, Doug and Steve continued to spar, Steve taunting Doug, Doug attempting honest answers in indignation, and getting increasingly redder in the face. Spector felt immobilized and terribly uncertain about the correct thing to do yet he felt that he must do something quickly and that a great deal more than he had bargained for was hanging in the balance.

A Case of Prejudice?*

NOTE: DO NOT READ this case until directed to do so by your instructor. It has been set up as a Prediction Case so that you can test your analysis by answering questions before reading the entire case.

PART I

CAPTAIN BLAKE, an administration officer, arrived in Vietnam in May 1969 and was assigned to an Infantry Division. Immediately upon arrival at the Division base camp, he was interviewed by Colonel Roberts and Major Samuels. Colonel Roberts was in charge of Personnel and Administration, and Major Samuels was his assistant. Colonel Roberts advised Captain Blake that he was to be the Personnel Management Officer. Near the end of the interview, Colonel Roberts made the following remarks to Captain Blake:

ROBERTS: I am sure you will find your job interesting. As you probably know, the division has approximately 18,000 men. Since this is a one-year tour of duty, personnel turnover is a big problem. Captain Crawley, our last Personnel Manager, left for home yesterday, but he left you a good crew, so I'll expect good work.

BLAKE: I'll give it my best.

ROBERTS: One last thing and I'll let you go. Your office generates quite a few reports and other papers that must go to the "head shed." I expect those papers to be in good order when they hit my desk. I can't let papers go to my boss with errors in them. Crawley never seemed to be able to find a decent typist, so make that your first order of business. My clerk doesn't have time to retype work coming from other offices.

On that note, Captain Blake left. Upon arrival at the Personnel Management Office, he was greeted by his Personnel Sergeant, Master Sergeant Brown. Brown introduced him to the men, and gave him the normal orientation on what was taking place. This orientation ended with the following conversation between Brown and Blake:

BLAKE: Who is our typist?

BROWN: Right now, we don't have one. We just use anyone that is available.

---

* This case was prepared by Professors David A. Tansik and Richard B. Chase of the University of Arizona as a basis for classroom discussion and not to illustrate either effective or ineffective handling of an administrative situation. Presented at the Intercollegiate Case Development Workshop, University of Santa Clara, October 18–20, 1973. Used with permission of the authors.

BLAKE: Colonel Roberts seems to think we need a typist. Do you think you can find one in the next few days?

BROWN: No problem. I'll have one in a couple of days.

The next day, Sergeant Brown walked up to Blake's desk with Private Rogers, a tall slender Negro, and announced, "This is your typist, Captain. He will be present for duty in a couple of days. All new troops have to go through two days of Vietnam Orientation training before going on the job." Blake welcomed Rogers aboard and chatted briefly before Rogers returned to the Replacement Training Detachment.

The next day, Sergeant Brown and five clerks (D'Angelo, Smith, Fenney, Rayes, and Jones) approached Blake's desk, and the following took place.

BROWN: Captain, these gentlemen would like to talk with you.

BLAKE: Oh, what's up?

D'ANGELO: It's about the new man.

BLAKE: You mean Rogers?

D'ANGELO: That's right. We have a good group of guys here – we all work well together. In the past, we have been permitted to select the new clerks for this office, and we try to select guys who will fit in with the group. But Sergeant Brown didn't tell us that Rogers was for this office, he just asked us to find a good typist.

BROWN: I didn't know that it made any difference where he was to work – a typist is a typist.

FENNEY: It does make a difference. In addition to working as a team everyone in this office also lives in the same building.

D'ANGELO: That's right. Right now, we have a good group, and that's the main reason we get the job done so well.

BLAKE: Are you saying that Rogers won't fit in?

D'ANGELO: Right. He just won't fit in with this group.

BROWN: You mean he isn't your color, don't you?

D'ANGELO: No. That has nothing to do with it.

BLAKE: Don't you think we should at least give him a chance?

D'ANGELO: Frankly, no. Vietnam isn't exactly the best place to be, and the guys should at least be happy with the people they live and work with. That's why Captain Crawley always let us select the new men.

BROWN: This is nonsense. Why don't you just admit you are prejudiced?

D'ANGELO: That's not true.

BLAKE: I hate to break up the discussion, but we are about to miss dinner. Let's go eat and talk about this again tomorrow.

At this point, the men left, and the following conversation between Brown and Blake took place.

BROWN: This guy D'Angelo is a pain in the a--. He conned Captain Crawley into that bit about the men selecting new clerks for this office. If he wasn't the best clerk in the office, I would have gotten him transferred a month ago. He heads our assignment team, and that is a big job. (The assignment team interviewed and assigned all new arrivals, which averaged about 75 men per day.)

BLAKE: Do you think he is prejudiced?

BROWN: In this case, I think he is, but I haven't noticed any discrimination in the way he assigns new replacements to other units.

BLAKE: What do you think of the men selecting new clerks for this office?

BROWN: I have never seen it done that way before, and I don't really oppose the idea. But, in this case with Rogers, I don't think we should back down — I'd just tell them that's the way the ball bounces. Oh well, we had better go eat. Tomorrow is going to be a rough day.

BLAKE: You're right. I guess we do have a problem, and I'm not sure what the answer is.

Discussion Question

What should Captain Blake do? Why?

PART II

The following day, Blake returned to work, still unsure as to what was taking place. He was concerned about the issue of prejudice, but the opinion of the men that Rogers wouldn't "fit in" was equally interesting. About mid-morning, he decided to explore the situation. Blake called each man into his office individually and approached them as follows: "I would like to ask your assistance in a matter that concerns this office. You don't have to participate if you don't want to. But, if you are willing, I would like you to take a piece of paper and jot down your response to a few questions. Don't put your name on the paper, and when you have finished, just drop it in the box beside my desk." All 18 clerks volunteered to participate, and each was asked to answer the following five questions. (1) Is Rogers married or single? (2) What is his favorite sport? (3) What is his major hobby? (4) If he is assigned to this office, would you be willing to teach him the essentials of his job? (5) Do you think he would fit in with the rest of the crew?

After the last man had been interviewed, Blake tabulated the results, and found the following responses to each question:

1. Married: 3, Single: 12, Don't know: 3.
2. Basketball: 5, Baseball: 8, Swimming: 3, Track: 2.
3. Don't know: 18.
4. Yes: 12, No: 0. Don't know the job well enough to teach him: 6.
5. Yes: 14, No: 2, Don't know: 2.

Blake then sent for Rogers' personnel records. The records reflected the following:

1. Marital Status: Married.

2.   Sports Interest: Track.

3.   Major Hobby: Writing Poetry.

Shortly before closing time, Blake assembled the entire crew and made the following announcement: "Rogers completes training today, and I find no reason to interfere with his assignment to this office. He is a good typist, and that we need. He is married, likes track, and his hobby is writing poetry. Like most of you, I also missed two out of three of those questions. I don't know if he will fit in or not, but I ask for your cooperation in giving him a chance. With respect to selecting future clerks, the policy established by Captain Crawley will continue as long as it works."

There was no immediate reaction to Blake's announcement. Rogers reported for work the next day, and as time passed, it became obvious that he had indeed fit in with the group. Four months later, D'Angelo was nearing the end of his year in Vietnam. As part of a cross-training effort, Rogers was assigned as his understudy and successor as head of the assignment team. On his final day in the division, D'Angelo dropped by Blake's desk to say farewell. His parting comment was: "Rogers will never be a poet, but he is a darned good personnel clerk!"

Discussion Question

Analyze Blake's handling of the problem and explain the outcome.

Chuck, the Manager*

AT AGE 52, Chuck Fielding had spent many years as a successful engineer in various companies. He was well known in the fields of mechanical and aeronautical engineering. Chuck, however, wanted to get more involved in management. Therefore, when one of his old friends at Propwash, Inc., offered him a job as the head of the Production Engineering Department at their Thrust Division, Chuck enthusiastically accepted.

---

* From Robert E. C. Wegner and Leonard Sayles, *Cases in Organizational and Administrative Behavior,* © 1972. Reprinted by permission of Prentice-Hall, Inc., Englewood Cliffs, N.J.

Propwash, Inc., was a major aerospace firm. Chuck knew that if he did a good job in their Thrust Division, his future would be most promising.

The first thing Chuck realized was that the Thrust Division was far different from the rest of Propwash. Thrust was strictly in the business of developing and producing missiles and space vehicles. In 1956, Thrust had won the contract for a high performance ballistic missile. Numerous other contracts for additional space vehicles and missiles had been forthcoming, and Thrust Division had now grown to the point where sales were as large as the rest of Propwash combined.

EXHIBIT 1
Organization Chart for Propwash, Inc.

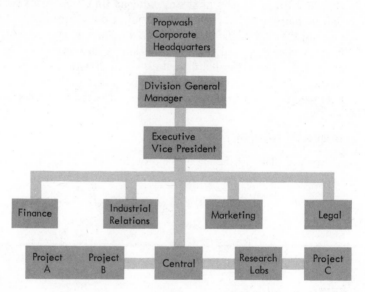

The division was organized on a Project basis normally in line with the governmental agency (Army, Navy, NASA, and so forth) supporting the Project. Thrust's general organization chart appears in Exhibit 1.

Primarily the projects were concerned with the design, development, testing, and production of a particular product. They also were concerned with improving the existing product and producing any logical follow-ons. The Central and Research organizations were concerned with the design, development, testing, and production, which was common to all or most projects, or alternatively with projects not yet sufficiently developed to be products. The Production Engineering Department was in Central.

PRODUCTION ENGINEERING

Fielding was amazed by what confronted him. The organization was in complete disunity. The engineers weren't engineering, and the department was the least popular in the company. A combination of events had led to this situation.

First, there was underutilization of manpower. Some of the men had no jobs to do. They were coming in and filling a desk, or inventorying labs, or just sitting about chatting. One of the most popular statements among the few younger engineers who had not as yet left was, "Where else can I be semiretired at the age of twenty-five?" Second, the men showed complete disgust with their technical leadership. Many of the men felt that the company "would buy a project for making gold out of cowdung if you talked fast enough."

Besides this, it appeared that this department was regarded as a joke by the majority of the other departments in the organization. Chuck quickly realized that many sections of the Thrust Division would not give his department any work at all. Soon after he accepted the job another project manager at his level said, "I'm sorry, Chuck. I can't give you any work. It's not your fault, I know, but I just can't trust the level of work I get from those people who work for you. Why, a year and a half ago one of them sent me a report, and I know some of the data he gave me was phony. Since then, when I've needed development work, I've gone to outside engineering companies."

Others told him that although the work was adequate, the time getting this work done was just too long to permit relying on Production Engineering.

Three years before Chuck took over, Grant Adams had been made manager of the Production Engineering group. He had received a Ph.D. from the University of California in Chemical Physics at the age of 23, and had worked for NASA in the Langley Research Center for about ten years prior to coming to work for Propwash. During this period he had written voluminous research monographs, and had become an outstanding voice in the early development on stress corrosion and fatigue in high-strength stainless steel alloys. In hiring Adams, Propwash followed a continuing policy of bringing outstanding minds into the corporation. Such minds presented the basis on which Propwash had built its eminence in the industry, and such names as Adams also helped when they appeared on proposals.

Adams, however, had a tremendous weakness for performing detailed studies. He would often accept jobs for the department, and become involved in the specific details of the study rather than in effecting a solution to the entire problem. Because of the tremendous rush to meet schedules in Project, the department frequently was late in issuing reports. The production groups found that they couldn't wait for reports, and therefore either did the work themselves or sent it all the way back down the work flow to Research.

Adams found that he was losing work. As he lost work, the supervisors of the groups under him became frustrated and angry. Soon they began going out to drum up business on their own, relying upon their own reputations within Propwash. However, the type of work each supervisor obtained varied considerably. Hence some got jobs which involved fairly basic research. On the other extreme, others were troubleshooting in the shops.

Eventually management became aware that Production Engineering was a bottleneck, that no work of significance was being accomplished, and Adams was transferred into Research in a staff capacity with a small lab and four assistants.

Adams was followed by a succession of three acting managers. Each lasted from two to three months. During this phase, the number of engineers fell from 100 to about 60. About 20 men resigned. The majority of the remainder either voluntarily transferred to other departments, or were asked to transfer. During this period the Production Engineering Department sank to its low point. The few budgeted man-hours for remaining research went to one or two of the faster-talking engineers who could convince the nontechnical acting managers that they had a good idea. On the other hand, most of the others were running about troubleshooting in the shops.

This was the situation when Chuck Fielding became manager.

FIELDING'S FIRST STEPS

His first step was to decide on the role of his department. He quickly learned that in the Thrust Division, Research was responsible for developing the fundamental concepts which eventually evolved into products. At some time his department would be consulted for input regarding materials, processes, and fabrication techniques. Ultimately the result of these efforts, both separate and joint, would be engineering reports. These would then be forwarded to the project or the central development group to build a prototype.

Although there might come a time when the implementation of the engineering report required that Fielding's department be consulted, he decided that troubleshooting in the shop was *not* desirable in that the individual projects had liaison engineers who were specifically responsible for eliminating causes of trouble in their project. But these liaison engineers resented the fact that the Production Engineering people were directly contacting the shops for such work. Invariably, if Production Engineering solved a problem, they claimed the credit. On the other hand, problems and failures were credited to the liaison engineers.

Chuck also found that pure research was outside of the jurisdiction of his department. First, it didn't have the personnel or equipment resources. Second, the people "up on the hill in Research" jealously guarded their realm in the company.

The role of his department was from applied research through development. He could characterize the flow of a project as:

pure
research

applied
research
and
development

prototype   product

Fielding's department interfaced with the several research groups on one side, and with the manufacturing engineers on the other. In the case of searching out trouble spots, he found it desirable to receive input from the liaison engineers and deal with their problems in a *consultative* manner, with the ultimate decision as the responsibility of the project liaison engineer.

DEALING WITH THE SUPERVISORS

As noted above, each supervisor in the Production Engineering Department was out drumming up business on his own. This resulted in tremendous instability in the relationship with the interfacing departments. Before Chuck had an opportunity to act on this problem, a situation arose that precipitated a change.

Ned Thomas was the supervisor of the metallurgy group. He was loud and vociferous, and always ready to get into a fight. Three months after he arrived, Chuck received an angry phone call from a project manager a full level above him who stated that Ned had been in his office that afternoon and attempted to negotiate a job with him. When he refused, Ned slammed a fist on his desk and called him an "s.o.b."

When Ned came back, Chuck called him into his office and asked why Ned had taken it upon himself to interact with someone at that level. Ned told Chuck to "mind his own damn business," and that he didn't intend to let "any damn manager mess up jobs I've spent weeks getting." Ned shouted rather loudly, and most of the people in the area heard him. After Ned stormed out, Chuck made arrangements to have him transferred out of his department.

From his previous jobs Chuck had become friendly with Mel Franks, a division manager at Propwash. Mel had been a driving, energetic technical manager. Two years ago, however, Mel had had a heart attack. After ten months of illness, he returned to a technical staff position. He was eager to perform in the Propwash environment, but his days of fighting the wars on the ladder of line management were over.

Mel was well liked, and knew almost everyone. He had many contacts, and some of these contacts were at a high level. He was easygoing, and willing to deal with people in a far more passive manner than the younger and more aggressive supervisors. Chuck made him his staff assistant, ostensibly as an administrator and personnel man.

Chuck then called in the supervisors and made it clear that new business would be cleared on the department level. It was all right for supervisors to meet with other supervisors in order to carry on new business or to discuss the old. It was not all right to go out to drum up new business. Mel had that job, and he would commit the department to new jobs.

DEALING WITH THE ENGINEERS

Mel moved adroitly in gathering new jobs. As this phase progressed, new assignments began to arrive. Chuck attempted to divide the labor so that junior engineers got assignments that would involve following a job from the early stages to the final report. Senior engineers either performed consultative work, or led a group of junior engineers. In this way, the young engineers were able to function in their field, gain useful experience, and were kept busy. On the other hand, senior engineers were able to use their experience and gain new experience leading the younger men.

Chuck also added a technical staff man to his personal staff. Recruited from another department at Propwash, Marty Hanson was a capable and intelligent senior staff engineer. He was able to provide Chuck with a strong measure of technical support in evaluating the work of the department.

The engineers were beginning to get work, and apparently felt that the work was meaningful. To further help this situation, Chuck attempted to reach an understanding with Research as to the approximate lines of jurisdiction. Then he embarked on a program of obtaining contracts from outside agencies, such as NASA, for projects within his agreed-on jurisdiction, and reached an understanding with Research on mutual support arrangement for such projects. By assigning engineers to outside assignments, he gave his men the opportunity to broaden their experience with outside contractors. In addition they had the opportunity to travel, which was a desirable fringe benefit for the men. At the same time Chuck began to encourage his people to attend more professional societies' meetings and to study toward advanced degrees.

CONCLUSION

As time went on, the Production Engineering Department greatly improved its operations. Chuck found that his control of the department was possible without crossing the natural jurisdictional lines which separated his department from interfacing departments. In turn, he found that these interfacing departments were more willing to deal with him on an equitable basis.

Mel was more capable than he could have expected in carrying on the day-to-day external relationships which were always necessary. Moreover, the supervisors grew to respect Mel's ability in these situations and looked to him for aid.

The supervisors quickly learned that Chuck meant business. They discovered that so long as they carried on their interactions with external departments and with the engineers within the parameters which Chuck had established, they would be permitted a great degree of autonomy in their relationships.

As productivity and morale of the PE department improved, Chuck Fielding's reputation grew. Early this year Chuck moved up to one level below the director of Central. The general feeling was that he would continue to move up.

Daniels Computer Company*

NOTE: DO NOT READ this case until directed to do so by your instructor. It has been set up as a Prediction Case so that you can test your analysis by answering questions before reading the entire case.

PART I

DANIELS COMPUTER Company's Memory Engineering Department was composed of four sections: magnetic, electronic, mechanical, and electrochemical. The customary development work undertaken by the department involved well-known principles of memory design. Each section carried on its phase of development in logical sequence, using the results of the previous section as a starting point. The members of each section were expert in their own fields. The sections were closeknit socially. The manager of the department left technical direction to section supervisors, reserving for his own responsibility the securing of essential services and maintenance of the development schedule. The department rarely failed to meet its schedule or technical requisites.

In July 1962, the Memory Department was assigned the development of a memory incorporating several new design concepts which had never been experimentally evaluated. The functioning of the special computer which was to incorporate the new memory depended upon the most advanced memory device possible within the limits of the new concepts. Development time was one-half the length of more routine developments.

The Memory Department manager selected the four most competent project engineers from the four sections to work on the special project. Each project engineer was directed to select five engineers and five technicians to work with him on the project. Because of time limitations and the unknown aspects of the new memory concepts, the four groups were to work on their own aspects of design simultaneously. Each team, remaining in the geographic confines of its home section, but independent of its former supervision, commenced immediately to test design schemes and components relevant to its own division of the technology. The project group members quickly became enthusiastic about their new assignment. The department manager left technical supervision to the project engineers of each group.

Prediction Worksheet

From what I know of the special project operation described in Part I, I would predict that:

1. The four project engineers (would) (would not) work well together to coordinate the work of their separate sections. (Note the reasons for your prediction.)
2. Enthusiasm among the members of the four special groups would (increase) (stabilize) (wane) as the project developed. (Explain why.)
3. Work on the special project would (progress smoothly) (be uneven, though satisfactory) as time went on. (Explain why.)
4. Social relationships will tend to be (project-wide) (special-group oriented). (Explain why.)

PART II

In late August 1962, the project engineers of the four special groups met for the first time to explore the technical prerequisites each had discovered. The goal of the meeting was to establish parameters for each group's subsequent design effort. It quickly became apparent that each group had discovered concept limitations within its own area which were considered by that group to be controlling. Inevitably, the position of any one group required considerable extra work by one or more of the others. The meeting concluded without compromise of original positions.

In the ensuing weeks all four groups worked desperately to complete certain design segments before complementary segments were completed in other groups. Haste was believed necessary so that the tardy group would have to reformulate its designs, basing them upon that which was already completed. Development of the new memory proceeded in this fashion until the project engineer of the slowest group proved experimentally and theoretically that several designs completed by other groups imposed technologically impossible conditions upon his area of design. A number of personal frictions developed between the groups at this time, with aspersions cast concerning the competence of out-group members. Even department members not formally involved in the special project became involved, siding with their section mates. Enthusiasm for the project on the part of group members waned.

PART III

On November 1, 1962, an engineer with considerable memory design experience was hired from outside the Daniels Company to become chief engineer for the special project. The four project engineers were directed to report to the new man. After examining the work of each group, the chief engineer indicated the basic approach to be taken in designing the new memory. Outstanding technical conflicts between groups were summarily dismissed by reference to the new approach. Each group was given a clear set of design instructions within the over-all design plan. Firm design time schedules, based on project group interdependence, were set. Frequent progress reports were required of each project engineer.

Prediction Worksheet

From what I know of the special project operation and the changes in that operation described in Part III, I would predict that:

1. The four project engineers (would) (would not) work well together to coordinate the work of their separate sections. (Note the reasons for your prediction.)
2. Enthusiasm among the members of the four special groups would (increase) (stabilize) (continue to decrease). (Explain why.)
3. The leadership style displayed by the chief engineer would be (functional) (dysfunctional) for total work group performance. (Explain why.)
4. Social relationships will tend to be (project-wide) (special-group oriented). (Explain why.)

PART IV

For several weeks after the chief engineer set the direction of the project, the project engineers vied with each other to see who could catch the chief engineer in error. Considerable time was spent in experimentation designed to find a weakness in the new design plan. Few problems in the plan could be found. The chief engineer defended his theoretical positions vigorously and continued to demand that schedules be met.

Schedules were met and the four groups worked simultaneously on related design aspects. Communication with the chief engineer grew in frequency. Communication directly between groups at all levels became common. Design limits were quickly discovered before the effort of other groups was needlessly expended.

The cohesion within technical groups became less pronounced, particularly among lower status engineers and technicians. Several lunch groups comprising members of several technical groups began to appear. Enthusiasm for the project was again expressed by the team members.

David Lannan: Street Singer*

. . . Well, I traveled 'round for many a year
Trying hard to figure this thing called fear,
Head hanging down and a frown on my brow
My fingers clenched in my pockets to the wrist
Thoughts confused and the words too few
To express the truths that I felt I knew
As I shuffled along digging the view
Of a crack in the back of somebody's shoe
Thru the memory of a love that I once knew
That ended before it began.

One trouble with me was indecision
I paced back and forth and kept repeatin'
Like a man that is stranded in a four wall prison
And slowly closing on his nonposition
I could feel my brow begin to sweatin'
I could feel my spine begin to tremblin'
Till I'd scream out loud "I've gotta make a decision,"
Then I'd jump in bed and pray for sleeping

---

* This case was prepared by Professor Allan Cohen of the Whittemore School of Business and Economics, University of New Hampshire.

And the very next morning I'd wake from dreaming
And start all over again. Oh-o-o, over again.

Oh how will all the colors make a new rainbow,
Turn all the men that ever lived into a stone to throw,
Cross an ancient ocean, someone once called space
Into the heart of heart of hearts, and make a golden race . . .†

David Rubinson and Friends, Inc. (DR&F), was a small company in the music business. They provided services ranging from recording production management, to securing recording contracts with large record companies, to music publishing administration. Their two most successful clients to date were The Pointer Sisters, in whom they had invested over $200,000 to develop, and Herbie Hancock, a jazz musician for whom they had provided important managerial and musical services. The Pointer's first album had sold over 500,000 copies, while similar success was achieved after three albums by Herbie Hancock. Each act had successfully toured the country, drawing large enthusiastic audiences. Though DR&F had produced records for other talented performers, for one reason or another few had been as successful, though Dvaid Rubinson himself had earlier been a well-regarded producer working for other companies and had a solid reputation.

Two of the "Friends" in DR&F were Jeffrey Cohen (27) and Bruce Good (30), ex-performers and songwriters who had struggled to earn a living through the San Francisco, Haight-Asbury heyday as part of a rock band and then as an acoustical act. Their earnings as musicians from 1965 to 1970 had averaged about $1,000 per year. They had survived by living communally, pooling earnings and contributions from relatives. They had met David Rubinson while he was a partner in Bill Graham's Fillmore Records, and though he had turned them down as performers, he took a liking to them and offered them jobs at $125 a week each as co-managers of Fillmore's music publishing company in 1970. DR&F split off and became a separate company in 1972.

While working with Fillmore, David Rubinson one day noticed an itinerant street singer in San Francisco who drew large crowds with his powerful voice and original songs. He approached the singer, David Lannan, and gave him a $10 bill. Lannan said he didn't need it; Rubinson gave him his card and said to drop by if he ever *needed* to make a record. Lannan described that meeting as follows: "I was singing with an ex-teacher of philosophy (a recognized Wittgenstein scholar) and a half-Chicano black. We accepted the $10 plus $11 more that other people gave us. We gave some away and spent the rest on food and wine the same day."

---

† Excerpt from "Morning" by David Lannan, Laze, ASCAP.

Several months later Lannan visited Rubinson. Rubinson's idea was to do an album recorded live in various locations throughout the city, including the stock exchange, a department store and the FBI building. Lannan was hesitant:

I never like to rush into things that are important for my life. I took six months to check DR&F out to see if they just wanted to make money off of me. For me business has to be mixed up with a family thing. I didn't want to just be a way of making money for them. I was, and am, into revolution, into changing all the misery in the world. I had been previously traveling with The Medicine Show, a group which did musical performances for prisoners, doing things like singing up to the seventh floor from the street by the county jail building, supporting draft resistance, taking acid and like that. So I wanted to be sure DR&F really cared about *me*, and I about them. It took me six months to decide. I finally agreed to sign a contract when Fillmore bailed me out of jail in San Luis Obispo. I was forced into a decision, usually the only way I ever get around to them. I was given $5,000 for signing. I remember their attorney saying something like "You'd better be worth this."

And one thing I didn't like was David pushing Jeffrey and Bruce on me as the producers of the album; my best highs came from working with him, and I thought that's what I would be doing. You see, I come from a background where people had very little and there was a lot of misery. My mother had incredible pain her last two-and-one-half years, going to the hospital once a week to be drained. Sometimes she'd be left lying in the hall with tubes coming out of her abdomen. My father was a working man, probably the most respected one in the area in Oklahoma where we lived. He was always president of his union and worked for the other men. So I feel very connected to the workers' point of view.

When David approached me while I was street singing I looked like a desert rat. I've heard he had been thinking of recording me without even asking; when I told him to negotiate with my "manager" he was shocked. I had a friend who was doing management work in Los Angeles; I had lived with him and his wife for one-and-one-half years. They were into swinging; I tried it but didn't dig it. So I'd do yoga while they balled. Swinging finally broke them apart. They were one of the most perfect couples I've known.

Here is how David Lannan was described in an article about him cutting a second album in Nashville:

David Lannan
— is what they called him, orphan child, when they adopted him.
— was born in Bartlesville, Oklahoma, in 1937.
— worked the zinc smelters and the Okie oilfields, where you didn't go out but you were drunk, and fought with broken glass.
— joined the Army on a snooker bet, was court-martialed for drunk-jumping an officer out of a barracks window.

—lived in the California desert with goats and chickens and a lady.

—made two babies, boy and girl, six years ago, three years ago, Sean and Megan.

—left home and went on the road.

—owns nothing but what's in the pack on his back.

—writes in his notebook, "Models: Gandhi, Will Rogers, Huey Long."

—sings in the streets; and, ever so occasionally, in studios . . .

"It was while I was watching the Chicago Democratic convention on TV," David Lannan says. "I felt I had to do something, to make contact with those people, and singing was the only way I could figure to penetrate the layers, so I went into downtown San Francisco and just started doing it."

"I began to go to the financial district, every morning, and sing to the people on their way to work. The faces! So bottled up and sad, first thing in the morning."[1]

David Lannan had finally agreed to do the original album, which was produced by Bruce and Jeffrey. A number of funny incidents which occured during the recording sessions in busy San Francisco locations were kept on the records. Though it received very favorable reviews, the album did not have large sales. David Lannan asked DR&F to hold his earnings and send him money periodically when he needed it. He had been advanced $5,000 and later was loaned a bit more, but the album's sales never even covered the advance. The money was quickly spent, partly on a long trip to India and Europe, which Lannan felt he needed to "get himself together."

Believing that David Lannan's talents had great potential, Rubinson, Cohen, and Good suggested a second album, recorded in Nashville with professional musicians, in order to showcase David's voice more effectively than the portably-recorded first one. Bill Graham put up the $5,000 necessary to go to Nashville, and they taped material which they considered to be outstanding. No record companies, however, would agree to release the album, partly because David Lannan would not go on tour to perform on stage, and the record companies believed that necessary to promote sales.

David did not believe himself ready to appear on stage, and wanted to "get himself together" first. Besides, he still had doubts about the motives and behavior of DR&F:

> I wanted to see if they were going to use the money they earned from me well, or just spend it on fancy things, like sports cars and furniture. I decided to move in with Jeffrey and his wife Bonnie, to see how the relationship would develop. I've been living in their place on and off for one-and-one-half years now and though I love them very much, and have seen Jeffrey go through very positive changes in that time, gaining lots of self-

---

[1] "Street Singer," by Craig Karpel, *Earth News*, April 1971.

confidence, I'm still not sure about DR&F. I don't mean that I don't like nice things, but they shouldn't be that important. You don't need six rooms worth of furniture when you live in three rooms.

Another problem is that David Rubinson now has so many walls built around him that I can't see him when I want to. When I go into their office I don't like the vibes. I can't get to him through his secretary and closed doors, and when I call, I wait at home all day without getting called back.

And he's earning plenty of money, more than he needs to live, but I don't like what I think he's doing with it. He should be creating brotherhood with it, just like a family. When I ask for money, just enough to live on, he shouldn't be treating me like some kind of investment which he's going to make money on. That's the only way I can do business.

I've been spending all this time working on getting myself pure inside, getting myself physically healthy so I won't have to lie in bed always sleeping or dragging my body along. I've gotten my eating and other needs to the minimum. I live out of my backpack so my expenses won't be too great. And recently I had said I'd need $500 to survive, but when I worked it out I was able to ask for only a $250 loan from David, to show him that I was working hard on getting ready and wouldn't blow it like I had before. He should see that I only ask for the minimum; he's only loaned me $750 so far.

Though things are coming together for me, I'm not in a hurry, because I believe that if something is to be, it will be available at different times. I'd like to go to Europe again, to live in France for two years maybe, do some playing with a group there, all as a part of preparing myself for going on stage. Then if things are right with DR&F, I could join them and we could work something out.

But I don't know; I don't keep lists of what bothers me about David, but for example when we were thrown out of the FBI building for singing and recording there, and the agent said, "Why don't you bums get a job," David went into a whole power ego number about how he was a recording industry executive earning $150,000 per year; that made me wonder.

At one point I thought I should connect up with someone else, so I got in touch with Joan Baez, because she was so idealistic with her antiwar activities. But she wouldn't see me, insisted I go through channels; when I wouldn't she asked me to stop calling her, so I don't know.

I don't want to hurry things, because when I'm ready it'll be so good that people will certainly come to hear it. I thought I might head down to Los Angeles and get in touch with the Rowan brothers, who I've always sensed I had a singing destiny with. I've known them since '69 and our circles stay in touch. They've only started to sing together on stage the last year or so—so it may be another year or two before we all sing together. I see all of this as part of getting ready, getting myself straightened out. I can't do it if things aren't right; I even left my wife, who was nice enough, because with her it wasn't dancing in the sky. I want myself to be pure and ready.

I was thinking of going down to Louisiana where I know some people who are very rich but totally unhappy. They just play games with each other, and don't know how to be real. Maybe I could help them somehow.

I do see signs that it may all start to happen here in the San Francisco area; more people here are beginning to see that there's more to life than the physical short stay on earth. The Aquarian Age may be arriving.

I realize that what I want is selfish—to please myself—but I want to help people over their pain and misery. Maybe when things work out I'll go back and live in the country, bringing what I've found to the people there. And if everything else fails, I can always go back there and raise goats.

David lived with Jeff Cohen of DR&F. Since joining DR&F Jeff had married, bought a Victorian house and completely restored it, furnishing it with period and modern pieces. A modest inheritance also allowed him to buy excellent stereo equipment and a used Alfa-Romeo sedan. The house had some spare rooms in it, and David Lannan had moved into a basement "apartment." He took occasional meals with Jeff and his wife, but usually cooked his own vegetarian food and then went to his room to sing or listen to music. Sometimes he stayed around to watch television or chat. Jeff liked David's presence and friendship but had mixed feelings about David's career "preparations":

David Lannan has an enormous talent. It is a vast one; it would be a wonderful gift to receive. I think he has a once-in-fifty-years-type of voice. He could be like Hank Williams to country music. He's that kind of person and I feel it a shame that his talent is not out and getting shared and heard by a lot of people. He has the power of taking any lyric and allowing it to become an archetypal situation. Hearing him can be a purifying experience. It could be freeing to witness any aesthetically pure art form. It's the same as dance or theater. Anything that is done as well as it can be done is a joy and inspiration to other people. The only way you can really help anybody is to be as free as you can possibly be at what you do so that people find out that there is something better and have something better to strive for. The Beatles in their excellence gave people something new to reach for: Yeah, it's OK to be young and it's OK to have long hair . . . it's excellent having that . . . and the world can get better.

David's got more of the spiritual than most people around, always willing to do his share and more to serve other people, making himself like a saint. I've also seen lately that he really is caught up in a lot of pictures in his head. He uses these to compare life to constantly, and his biggest problem is what he's holding onto the most: the idea of becoming saintly and living eternally. What he is constantly missing is the here and now, because he is comparing it to a picture he has of some ideal of perfection; most moments are compared to that, usually unfavorably. And then he is an optimist. In a different decade, David could be a real drifter or no good bum. He has a great potential for that; you can just see him breaking people's hearts right and left and saying, "Well, someday I'm going to get it, and I'm going to follow my dream," and then turning into a wino on the corner. I don't believe that's true of him now, but he's that personality type.

David has to have his own head together or he can't do anything at all until it's perfect. He has said that to me several times in those very words: He doesn't do anything until everything is perfect. He also has this thing about life in general with which I don't agree, a vision of the time when it *all* comes together. A blinding flash will suddenly make all the pieces fit together and everything will be absolutely right. He will know about everything and will attain sainthood or absolute purity. Then the world will come to love one another as brothers. He keeps looking for that big thing that's going to make it all change. In my experience it never happens that way. It happens daily a little bit at a time. He keeps putting off those moments and putting off those moments. He believes that the Aquarian Age is coming to San Francisco and that puts it off even further because then he has to wait for all the things to finally get together.

Jeff continued:

I don't personally think that he's ever going to change and decide that he wants to make it and get out and make the necessary steps to do so. He keeps assuring me that he's going toward that in his own way, but in four years I don't see him too many steps closer. I have tried not to pressure him into doing anything; he is free not to and it is OK with me and OK with DR&F because we don't really ever expect him to. I'll be surprised if he moves in that direction at all. In my experience in show business I have seen that the people who are involved and are artists don't really change that much. I think it's true that when someone frames out their game they tend to sleep in it a little while. David has been very strongly with his for a long time. He's not that light on his feet; with him it's heavy when change comes. I don't see him going towards "success."

I've seen great musicians break your heart because they weren't ready for success; if you go along with their craziness it's a waste of energy because people don't change that much. We have a great rock and roll band we could sign now if we would give them a bigger advance, but they only want it because they don't believe in themselves. We could afford the money, but won't give it because without confidence they won't make it anyway. If they sign with someone else for a bigger advance, that's OK, because they'll just blow it.

Even if David does get as pure as he wants to be, then there still will be problems. You don't find many pure people in the record business. There's scum in there; he's right. The worst pigs in the world are in the record business. He might be very strong in his trip and feeling very saintly, but you would have to be very, very strong to come up against those people without freaking after a while. It's hard to deal with company executives who know his record on a graph by the number—"50639 is pretty slow this week"—that sort of thing. I don't think he would accept the price he would have to pay.

I would like to believe that there is a way he can keep his purity and still transmit that voice to millions of people, but I don't know what it is. It would be fine with me if there were, but I just can't see it. I know how difficult it is and how much people are up against. Even when everything is going for them.

We had always told David that we would never push him into the grind of trying to succeed in the music business because he obviously wasn't the type. That was the agreement we had in the beginning: He would do what he wanted and we would do what we wanted and just let it go at that. And it was very obvious that he wasn't about to go on the road. When we took the Nashville album around to the different record companies we had to tell them that.

The way they merchandise records in the stores is by having artists on the road to arouse interest. It's really the only chance they have to sell records. It's a miracle if anyone can be a recording success without going on tour. What you have to do is make a record and then play Cleveland, Cincinnati, and Philadelphia, starting off with the little clubs, going around the circuit until people know who you are. Then maybe you can go back and start a concert tour. You build a following and those are the people who buy the records; it's a very gruelling life. And it was clear that David wasn't going to do that. It was only fair to inform the recording companies that he could not be depended on to follow up and merchandise his records. In every case that was the main factor in their turning him down. Their interest was to sell records.

You see, when David appeared on the stage he was just not as good as when he played on the streets. David Rubinson got him on to a program at the Fillmore one night and David Lannan was completely stiff and not communicative with the audience. He just stood up there and sang songs without paying much attention to what words came where or how long he was going on or any of the things that performers normally do. It was completely unstructured. He was a street singer; when you walk along the street you can sing the same song for eight hours and get personal contact with people. When you are down on eye level looking into someone's eyes it is different from standing up on stage and looking into 5,000 people's eyes.

In cutting the Nashville album the hardest thing to do was to get him to sing the songs the same way twice. We had trouble getting him to agree that it was all right to structure a song and put one verse after another, a chorus here, and an instrumental there, and a chorus here. These are pretty much standard things which you would expect anyone who paid much attention to music to be well aware of, but he wasn't at that time. I think he is more aware of them now.

At that time David was adding nothing constructive to the album except his voice and so the whole thing was formulated. It was: "Sing this verse here and sing that verse there and don't go up on that note, and can we run that one back again because you let go of the melody there." We do that only as much as it is needed. It is not a question of who is right and who is wrong, but a question of what works, so we would accept exactly as much as he would put into it.

I am not worried about how hard it would be to put a show together or to get a band together. I am struggling for his participation in the process, and I think these things can work themselves out. I know that in two to four weeks we could have a band that knew all the songs and we could put together a show that would work, and he could learn all the songs that way. I don't have any doubts.

I did have doubts when we were doing the Nashville album because it was a race against the clock. It was hard pressure getting him to work then.

I think he's getting used to his abilities and is more willing to work now. He fights off the idea of success. He doesn't even sing on the streets now at all; he's been out maybe two or three times in the last four months. David can't sing for money. He used to have a very difficult time accepting money on the street. He had a very pure idea of the scene and having it be for free. That's why David Rubinson wanted to really go overboard and give David Lannan money and all that, although he didn't really see any returns coming in. We never thought that the street singer album would sell any records; we had no illusions about it. It was a great album to make. When David Lannan goes out to sing for money in the streets he gets depressed and comes home in an hour. When he did it for free he used to go out and sing for eight or nine hours in a row.

The article on David Lannan's Nashville trip touched on this problem:

In the physical sciences there is something called the Heisenberg Uncertainty Principle which says that you can't take the measure of a thing without changing it: the thermometer cools the soup. Put a street singer in a studio to record him and he is no longer on the street. Meanwhile, Buck Owens is limosined to the streets of New York City so he can cut a record walking down them.

Vanguard picks a pair of street singers off the street and gives them $280,000. If they were to bank this and to live on the interest they could stay on the streets forever. Is that what they plan to do?

("I wonder if we've done the right thing," Jeff had said to me in the Nashville studio, as the 615 pickers stood there while David Lannan sang with his eyes closed, numbering the changes, ball pen on legal pads, 1155/4411/1155/4411/1541/1541/1541/1541, like track judges comparing stopwatch times.)

David Lannan plans to be on a hillside in Safford, Arizona, on Easter morning, as he has been on the last two Easter mornings, singing to the draft resisters who are prisoners there. If he makes any money from his record, he will use it to finance a medicine show, he and his friends traveling, making music, for free. "Every moment should be a medicine show," he says, and for that moment, it is.[2]

---

[2] "Street Singer", by Craig Karpel, *Earth News,* April 1971.

Jeff:

David fears success. Whenever it gets close he runs away. He constantly picks himself up and goes somewhere else when he thinks anything is happening. A record producer in Germany offered to make a record for him there and maybe get him on TV, etcetera. That happened shortly before David came back here to the United States; I assume he felt, "Maybe let's go see what's happening over there and maybe it'll be better at DR&F." So he came back and checked our scene out and was talking about this record he could make in Germany. It was, "Well, I can always do it someplace else; maybe I'll try over there and it will be more to my liking and more to my pace." He seems to be sort of locked in to that and is just refusing to accept responsibility for this moment of success.

It's interesting: When I started I had very high ideals about not making money and getting power but it doesn't seem to make sense to me to get caught up in ideals like that because all they do is keep you from doing what there is to get done. I think that David's ideals are keeping him from participating and to me participation seems to be the first order. DR&F has never been a rich company. I have no idea what it would be like if it were rich. We are in better shape now than we ever have been because we have two hit acts. But it costs a lot of money to keep those acts. The overhead is high and we're a small company.

When David Rubinson came to San Francisco he had some high ideals about starting an institute to give free seminars to anyone who wanted them on all aspects of the recording industry. He got the best people in each field — recording engineers, producers, attorneys, concert promoters, publishers — and brought them all together to give free seminars. He gave them free studio time and spent a lot of money on it himself; he couldn't get help from anyone else. He went to the National Academy of Recording Arts and Sciences and said, "Let's put up some money and maybe we could even build a building," and he went to all the major record labels and said, "Look, young people sooner or later are going to have to jump in and it would be better to train them to do it." The recording companies all passed. They are still like the small shop owner. It almost always boils down to one or two people making all the decisions. They just won't let go of that. The whole idea went down the drain.

I've seen David Rubinson on numerous occasions really go out on a limb to try to help other people in the industry get started, including Bruce and me. All that considered, he's not one to let a dollar slip through his fingers. He drives a hard bargain, though I have seen him turn down a million dollars worth of deals that he thought would be compromising. If he wanted to cash in he could have a long time ago. Specific groups have offered him vast amounts of money just to produce their record. All he would have to do is go into the studio, make the record, and he'd have twenty five or fifty thousand dollars, large amounts of royalties, and so on. He's been offered chances to manage groups that he didn't like in a number of quick cash deals. But his and our orientation is not solely making money; it's what we do because we enjoy doing it, and we're more than glad to, and demand that we do get paid for it. But that is clearly not our main motivation.[3]

I'm not apologetic any more for making money. If we hadn't accepted money for our services up to the time we found the Pointer Sisters there would be no way in the world that they could ever have occurred the way they did. It took $200,000 in order for them to happen and the money had to come from someplace. It came from David Rubinson's pocket, and if he hadn't been in business to get that kind of money the Sisters never would have made it because we had to support them for a while. We were able to work with them in a low-pressure way, allowing them to take two years to come up with a product while their formula got to where it is. It not only cost money initially but they have been a hit for over a year and it is only now they are starting to turn a profit. Up until recently it cost $100 to make $50 and it is impossible to function under that kind of circumstances unless you are in business. Otherwise you can have the highest ideals and you can't get anything done. The Pointer Sisters had been on the road and had even cut a record without any success; it took money and a lot of knowledge about the business and nitty-gritty work to get them to the point where they could be a hit.

On the day that we recorded David Lannan at the FBI building, David Rubinson was already hot from having gotten through being disappointed about the recording seminars he tried to run and other situations involved in his move from New York and Columbia Records. His work with Bill Graham was not panning out the way he hoped it would. Basically he wasn't getting the cooperation he needed because Bill was putting new energy into other things and didn't seem to have time for the record business. David had been very successful with four or five records on the charts when he came out to San Francisco, but didn't have any hits at that moment.

With all these things behind him, there we were making a record that he really wanted to make. He was coming along to see what was happening and to get involved and argue with people partly to deal with that side of getting the record made and partly to help make it an interesting record. The FBI director only saw a bunch of grubby "Peaceniks," as he referred to us, trying to stir up trouble. It turned out that they had had bomb threats that day. David Lannan walked in singing about peace and when the FBI Director turned off the tape recorder and tried to throw us out, he just kept on singing. The FBI Director was getting a little hot under the collar and began calling us names and suggesting that we ought to "get a job." This got under David's skin and hit his buttons, which made him freak. He said,

---

[3] In an article on the Pointer Sisters, one of whom had to be hospitalized for nervous exhaustion. Rubinson was quoted as follows: " 'None of the Pointers or I ever made a conscious decision to be an overnight sensation. . . . June, for example, never made a decision to stop being June Pointer and be June Pointer Sister, to deliver excellence every night and work 12 hours a day. And besides this she wants to go out and boogie too.' Rubinson is sure she won't be back performing at least for the rest of the year's dates. 'We're more concerned,' he said, 'that she lives how she wants, rather than say OK, get the hell back on the road.' " From "No Pause Till the End," by Len Epand, *Zoo World*, October 10, 1974.

"What do you mean, get a job? I make $150,000 a year. How much do you make?" When we left David Rubinson felt badly that he had lost control and thought that he had perhaps had blown it for all concerned. It was just something that happened. Of course David Lannan has been known to lose his temper and fly off and go incommunicado for a while too.

David Lannan has been my friend for several years and while I don't consciously hold anything back I suppose I haven't said some of this to him because I really don't believe he can change. He has always been welcome to stay here and when he shows up he does. We don't have to go through formalities. I don't think that any of us have talked about whether it is OK or not OK or anything like that. His girl friend who stays with him now once said that they would like to pay rent for the rooms while they had some money, because she was working at that time. I said that I would be glad to have $50 a month and she asked if they could pay $12.50 a week, which was fine. She paid for about three weeks and then they didn't have any money and didn't pay and I didn't ask for any. That was the only time any idea of rent came up. $50 didn't mean anything one way or the other; anyway, it had just been basically an open door. When we lived at our old place he would come and camp out in our backyard. Even when we lived in the country he would stay with us sometimes. He's always been welcome. One of his great charms is that he never has to worry too much about how he is going to survive in the world, because people are always going to bring him home to dinner or to stay. He has that quality about him. He's a joy to have around; he does all kinds of handy things when he's here.

It's not for me to force someone to play monopoly or poker or whatever. A guy comes and sits down with his chips and he's in the game, but if not he can still be a kibitzer. I think David would find he had a winning hand if he would play it.

Questions

1. How do David Lannan and Jeff each see themselves?
2. How does each see the other?
3. How does that affect the way they communicate with one another?
4. Which person do you feel closest to in preferences and values?
5. In what important ways do you differ from either or both of them in terms of ideals, career aspirations, interpersonal style, and so on?
6. As a manager, Jeff has the problem of trying to obtain maximum performance from a talented but reluctant "employee." What should Jeff do?

Defenses and the Need to Know*

Roger Harrison

THE PURPOSE of this paper is to discuss the ways we have of protecting our views of ourselves and others.[1] Specifically, it is intended to rescue the concept of "defensive behavior" from the ostracism in which it is usually held, to restore it to its rightful place as a major tool of man in adapting to a changing world, and to consider how defenses may help and hinder us in profiting from a learning situation.

Let us consider how we understand the world we live in, and particularly those parts of it concerning ourselves and our relations with other people. First of all, we organize the world according to *concepts,* or categories. We say that things are warm or cold; good or bad; simple or complex. Each of these concepts may be considered a dimension along which we can place events in the world — some closer to one end of the dimension, some closer to the other.

Actually, we can't really think without using these categories or dimensions to organize our thoughts. Any time we consider the qualities of ourselves, other persons, or events in the inanimate world, we have to use categories to do it. We are dependent for our understanding of the world on the concepts and categories we have for organizing our experiences. If we lack a concept for something which occurs in the world, we either have to invent one or we cannot respond to the event in an organized fashion. How, for example, would a person explain his own and others' behavior without the concept of love and hate? Think how much behavior would simply puzzle or confuse him or, perhaps, just go on by without really being perceived at all, for lack of this one dimension.

Concepts do not exist in isolation; they are connected to one another by a network of relationships. Taken all together, the concepts we use to understand a situation, plus the relationships among the concepts, are called a *conceptual system.* For example, we may say, "People who are warm and friendly are usually trusting, and hence, they are often deceived by others." Here we have a conceptual system linking the con-

---

* Taken from "Defenses and the Need to Know," by Roger Harrison, *Human Relations Training News,* vol. 6, no. 4 (Winter 1962–63). With permission of the editor, *Human Relations Training News.*

[1] This paper was stimulated by a lecture by Harrington Ingham and a paper by Abraham Maslow.

cepts of *friendly warmth, trust in others,* and *ease of deception.* Because concepts are linked one to another, the location of an event on one concept usually implies something about where the event is located on each of a whole network of concepts. It is thus almost impossible to take in a small bit of information about a characteristic of a person or event without its having a whole host of implications about other characteristics.

Images and stereotypes operate this way: when we discover that a person is a Negro, or a company president, a social scientist, or a husband, the information on these concepts immediately calls up a whole network of expectations about other characteristics of the person. In the case of stereotypes, these expectations may even be so strong that we do not check to find out whether our conceptual system worked accurately this time, but may even go to the other extreme of ignoring or distorting information which doesn't fit the conceptual system, so that the system may remain quite unaffected by disconfirming experiences.

The study of defenses, like the study of stereotypes, is the study of the processes that protect the organization of conceptual systems in the face of information and experiences which, if accurately perceived, would tend to break down or change the relationships among concepts in the system.

Why should conceptual systems be resistant to change? Actually, if they were simply intellectual exercises, they probably would not. In real life, conceptual systems come to have *value* attached to them. The values seem to be of two kinds: one kind I will call *competence value.* By the competence value of a conceptual system I mean its value for helping us to be effective in the world. After all, the conceptual systems we have were developed because we needed some way of making sense of the world; of predicting what kinds of results would follow from what kinds of causes; of planning what kinds of actions we needed to take in order to accomplish some desired result.

People have the conceptual systems they have because in some important situations the systems proved *adaptive* for them; by seeing the world in just this way they were able to get along better, to be more effective, to prepare better for what was coming next. For human beings conceptual systems are, in a very real sense, very nearly the most important survival equipment we have. Animals have instinctual patterns of response: complex systems of behavior that are set off without thinking in response to fairly fixed patterns of stimulation. Human beings have to do it the hard way, by developing systems of concepts that make sense of the world and then using these systems to make decisions as to what to do in each situation. Those conceptual systems that pay off over and over again tend to become parts of our permanent equipment for understanding the world and for deciding what to do in it. If we were to lose these systems we would become like ships without rudders; we would have lost our control systems and, with them, our chances of acting in an organized, intelligent fashion to meet our needs. This is what I mean by the *competence value* of conceptual systems.

Unfortunately, no conceptual system fits the world perfectly. In the interests of economy we simplify and leave things out as being unimportant: for example, we act as though relationships which are *statistical* (they are only true most of the time) are *necessary,* and hence true all of the time. On the rare occasions when the relationships don't hold, we tend to overlook it, rather than trying to understand why things didn't go as expected. We may, for example, conceptualize the qualities of decisiveness, aggressiveness, and masculinity as incompatible with a ready ability to express affection. This conceptual system may not change even when we are faced with the clear expression of affection on the part of a man about whose decisiveness and masculinity we have had ample evidence in the past. We simply pass it off as, "He's not himself," or, "He's not really showing affection," or even, "Deep down inside he isn't so decisive and masculine as he appears to be." We go through a lot of mental gymnastics to avoid seriously questioning a conceptual system which has proved useful in the past. So, frequently, the *last* alternative explanation we consider is, "It is perfectly possible for a man to express deep affection readily and still be decisive, aggressive, and masculine." Such an alternative would mean the significant alteration of a conceptual system.

The trouble is, you can't just alter one little conceptual system at will, and let it go at that. Concepts are too closely and complexly linked to change one or two relationships in isolation. One change leads to another, and pretty soon a major reorganization is going on. It may be, of course, that the reorganization may lead to substantial improvement in the person's understanding and effectiveness in the world, but in the meantime there may be considerable turmoil and confusion as the person questions relationships that once seemed solidly established and before new ways of seeing the world have been adequately tested and confirmed.

Of course, the more important the particular conceptual system in question is in making it possible for the person to meet his needs, the more strain and upset is involved in changing it. For example, one might believe that heavy objects fall more rapidly than light ones. The disconfirmation that would follow upon learning that all objects fall at the same rate would perhaps be uncomfortable, but only moderately so. Consider, on the other hand, the anxiety and stress which could be produced by the discovery that complying with another's demands does not always make the other like you and may, indeed, have the opposite effect. For a person who has put much reliance in his interpersonal relations on the techniques associated with such a conceptual system, its disconfirmation may have the dimensions of a major crisis in life.

So, much of the time we hang on to our not-so-accurate conceptual systems because they work for us most of the time, and to give them up would plunge us into mild or severe confusion without any real promise of eventually attaining a more accurate, effective reorganization. The picture does not look so good for improvement, and before I finish, it will look even bleaker.

There is another kind of valuing that goes on in placing events into conceptual systems, and I will call it *evaluation*. This is the well-known process of saying that some states of affairs are better and some are worse. For most conceptual systems, there is an element of evaluation; most concepts have a good end and a bad end, and we would rather see events come out on the good ends than on the bad.

Again, it is less important to see events come out well in some areas than in others. The closer we get to conceptual systems that are concerned with our *self-perceptions* and our important relationships with others, the more important evaluation becomes, and the more uncomfortably responsible we feel when events don't fall on the valued ends of the concepts. Thus, if we value love as against hate, and intelligence against stupidity, it becomes important to protect conceptual systems that organize the events so that we can see ourselves as brilliant and loving. People may desperately protect quite maladaptive, ineffective conceptual systems in order to maintain a favorable perception of self or others.

Sometimes *competence value* and *evaluation* compete for influence in the conceptual system. For example, some persons have led such difficult childhoods that it is only by seeing themselves as bad, worthless people that they can seem to make sense out of the awful things that people they trusted have done to them; at the same time, they have normal needs for self-esteem, and for seeing themselves at the valued ends of concepts. These people may experience considerable conflict between these two motivational influences on their conceptual systems.

These, then, are the "defenses." They serve to keep us from becoming confused, upset, and rudderless every time something happens contrary to our expectations. Frequently, they protect our liking for ourselves and others when we and they fail to live up to our ideals. Defenses give life more stability and continuity than could ever be justified by reference to the contingency and complexity of real events alone. Defenses keep our relations with others more pleasant and satisfying, protecting us from our own and others' anger, and helping us to go on loving people who are usually less than perfect and sometimes less than human.

At the same time, these same defenses block our learning, often dooming us to make the same mistakes over and over again. They make us blind to faults of our own we could correct, as well as those we can do nothing about. Sometimes they make us turn the other cheek when a good clout in the nose would clear the air and establish a new and firmer footing for an honest relationship. They can, in extreme cases, make so many kinds of information dangerous to our conceptual systems that we narrow and constrict our experiences, our feelings, and our thoughts, becoming virtual prisoners of our own protection.

I believe there is in each of us a kind of counterforce which operates in the service of learning. Let's call it a *need to know,* or a drive toward competence. We are used to thinking about physiological needs, and we recognize there are probably social needs, such as needs for love; but we often overlook the need for competence and knowledge. Yet it is in operation all around us. We see it in the baby when he begins to explore as soon as he can crawl; we see it again in the "battle of the spoon," where the child actually gives up the certainty of getting the food into his mouth for the less effective but exciting experiment of "doing it himself." We see this need again as the adolescent struggles to carve out for himself a life that is uniquely his own; and we see it reflected in continuing efforts to understand and master the world as adults. People who read history for pleasure, who have creative hobbies, or who voluntarily continue their education are all manifesting this drive toward competence and knowledge.

The need to know is the enemy of comfort, stability, and a placid existence. For its sake we may risk the discomfort of examining and revising our assumptions about groups and people; we may expose ourselves to the anxiety-provoking experience of "personal feedback," in which we often learn that others do not see us quite as we see ourselves; we place ourselves in groups where we know in advance we will be confused, challenged, and occasionally scared. Some of us expose ourselves to such situations more than once; to me, there could be no more convincing proof that the need to know is frequently stronger than the desire to maintain the comfort and stability of accustomed conceptual systems.

The discussion group thus frequently becomes a battleground between our desires to increase our competence and understanding, and to bolster our defenses. In this battle, we tend to take the side of the need to know and, like partisans everywhere, we malign, attack, and propagandize against the other side. Sometimes we forget that both sides are parts of a person, and that if either side destroys the other the person loses a valuable part of himself. This is particularly true in the case of defenses. We know from clinical practice and, I think, from personal experience and logic, that when a person's first line of defense becomes untenable, he drops back to another one, a sort of "second string" defense. Unfortunately, since we usually put our best and most adaptive defenses out in front, the second string is apt to be even less effective and reality-oriented than the first. To put it strongly, the destruction of defenses does not serve learning; instead, it increases the anxiety of the person that he will lose the more or less effective conceptual systems he has with which to understand and relate to the world, and he drops back to an even more desperate and perhaps unrealistic defense than the one destroyed. Though it may seem paradoxical, we cannot increase learning by destroying the defenses which block it.

What we can do is to create situations where people will not need to stay behind their defenses all the time. We can make it safe to sally forth from behind the moat, so to speak, secure in the knowledge that while we are exploring the countryside no one will sneak in and burn the castle.

People need their defenses most when they are most under threat and pressure. To make a mistake or become confused or admit to oneself that the world, ourselves, and others are not quite what we thought they were means that while we are revising or building new conceptual systems we will not be able to cope so well as before with the "slings and arrows" of a difficult situation. If we need every bit of competence we possess, we simply can't afford to give up conceptual systems which are tried but not perfect, in favor of exciting new ways of looking at things that are untested.

It is for this reason that I believe we cannot really begin to learn deeply from one another in a discussion group until we create relationships of mutual support, respect, and trust.

When we know that others will not place us in situations where we need every bit of our competence to cope with what is going on; when we know they will respect our own personal rate of growth and learning; when we know we have friends to help if we get into difficulties exploring new relationships, understandings, and behavior—then we can begin to look hard at the inadequacies in our ways of making sense of the world. We can examine those "exceptions to the rule" that we've always half expected might prove the rule inadequate; we can afford to really explore why ways of behaving that used to work fine are for some reason not producing satisfactions for us the way they used to, or why they seem to work with some people but not others; and we can really listen to the things people say that indicate they don't see us quite the way we see ourselves.

Out of this kind of exploration can come new and more effective conceptual systems, new ways of behaving that go along with them, and the excitement and pride that accompany increases in competence and knowledge. And when the excitement is over, and the new ways have been tested and integrated and have become habitual ways of seeing and behaving, I hope we will not be surprised to find that under conditions of stress we defend them against new learning just as strongly as we did the old. For these two partners go hand in hand: the need to explore and learn and the need to defend against disconfirmation and confusion. The challenge is to know how we can create conditions under which we can suspend one to enhance the other.

Dominion Acceptance Company Limited*

IN MAY 1973 Mr. B. L. Keast, Atlantic Regional Manager of Operations for Dominion Acceptance Company Limited, faced a number of personnel and operating procedures decisions directly affecting the operations of the Moncton, New Brunswick Branch of D.A.C. Earlier in the year changes in the management staffing of the Moncton Branch had been made and after three months the results of these changes were being evaluated in order to make adequate permanent changes in the Moncton operation. As the problems which had led to the changes had been of a particularly serious nature, it was imperative that Mr. Keast thoroughly examine the possible effects of any changes, as well as the causes of the problems arising earlier. In doing so he was compelled to consider the viewpoints of the Moncton Branch Manager, Mr. Ronald Snell, Snell's current Assistant Manager, Mr. Alex DeCoste, his previous Assistant Manager, Mr. Jerry MacDonald and the rest of the Moncton staff. In addition he recognized the importance of keeping the Moncton operation consistent with the other branches in his region as well as with National D.A.C. policy.

BACKGROUND

D.A.C. was one of the largest finance companies in Canada. Its primary business was the acceptance of conditional sales contracts from customers who had purchased consumer goods. D.A.C. then paid the retailer while the customer paid D.A.C. in monthly instalments. In addition to this retail financing, D.A.C. also made loans to firms to either begin or expand existing businesses. The company was entirely Canadian-owned, and operated on a national basis. Regional offices were located in five major Canadian cities, viz., Halifax, Montreal, Toronto, Winnipeg and Vancouver. Branch offices were located in most cities and some towns serving as district shopping centres. Atlantic region branch

---

* Case material prepared by Mr. William J. MacNeil under the direction of W. H. Cooper, Assistant Professor of Business Administration. St. Francis Xavier University, Antigonish, N.S., Canada. Reprinted by permission of Professor Cooper.

staff sizes varied from 3–40 depending on the population of the market being served and the amount of money loaned.

Corporate headquarters were in Toronto and functioned as a central policy making and administrative centre. Head office established specific policies and procedures regarding loans, branch control and reporting methods, as well as personnel policies and administrative procedures designed to ensure consistent coast-to-coast operations. To obtain consistency, D.A.C. had in 1968 prepared and distributed to each branch a detailed Procedures Manual which, in addition to the above policies, prescribed office procedures and provided detailed job descriptions for all branch positions. In the manual the policy of aggressively seeking new profitable accounts was stressed.

The Regional Manager of Operations (RMO) functioned as the intermediary between corporate headquarters and the branches in their respective regions. As with the Halifax RMO, all RMOs had as their primary source of information regarding branch operations the monthly statistics prepared for them by each branch. The format was prescribed by the Procedures Manual (including the due date of the third of each month covering the previous month's operations) and consisted of statistics on the number and dollar value of accounts, collections made, total branch expenses for the month and overdue accounts by age. As part of the computer analysis of branch operations, the RMO compiled this data into a regional report comparing all branches in the region and sent copies to each branch as well as to Toronto. Each branch manager could therefore regularly compare his performance against the other individual branches as well as with the region as a whole.

In his evaluation of branch operations and the resulting report Mr. Keast placed emphasis on the control of payments. The percentage of accounts 30 or more days late was the key evaluation variable and he expected the collection department in each branch to give special attention to such deficient accounts. The Atlantic region's average delinquency rate was 3 percent. Branch managers were generally quite sensitive about their office's delinquency rate and how their rate compared with other branches in the region, as shown in the monthly RMOs' report.

In addition to the monthly reports, the RMO conducted a yearly visit to each branch (without prior notice being given) to perform several kinds of inspection and audits. The RMO and his staff inspected the accounts and credit records, performed employee evaluations of the manager and assistant manager, and if time allowed, reviewed the manager's evaluations of the other staff members. As each manager hired his own staff and operated his branch with some autonomy, the results of the monthly and annual evaluations were of particular importance in judging the manager and his staff's ability.

THE FEBRUARY INSPECTION

Mr. Keast's inspection in June 1972 had rated the Moncton branch's overall performance as slightly below average. The July 1972 and sub-sequent monthly reports began to show a steadily increasing delinquency rate and a decrease in the dollar value as well as in the number of ac-counts. By January, 1973 the delinquency rate stood at 8 percent and the number of customer accounts had fallen from 3,500 in June 1972 to 3,000. This performance decline was significantly poorer than the other branches in southern New Brunswick. After repeated requests for ex-planations and unsatisfactory reponses, Mr. Keast decided to make his 1973 visit much earlier in the year, and hence on February 14 he arrived in Moncton at 7:15 A.M. Upon entering the airport terminal Mr. Keast and his staff assistant were surprised to find Mr. Snell queuing up for a ticket on the 7:35 A.M. departure for Toronto. An embarrassed Snell explained that he had some personal business in Hamilton, but that it was not urgent and could be delayed, particularly in light of the unex-pected annual inspection of the branch which was to be conducted that day.

Travelling to the branch from the airport Snell explained: "I've been finding it tough to do much to control our late accounts. We've a poor clientele, my assistant isn't qualified and the girls we've been getting to keep our account records up-to-date have not worked out. I know it makes the branch look poor but you know I've tried. I think in a couple of months we'll have the office turned around and be back among the regional leaders where we belong." Keast listened politely and expressed concern that something must be done soon to improve the Moncton operations. "If your staff is not up to the job, maybe we can fix that, but as far as customers go, you've got as good an economic area here as Scott does in Fredericton and Angus in St. John. Anyhow, you certainly have a lot more snow here than we do down in Halifax. Let's see how things are looking in the office." Arriving downtown, Keast and his assis-tant spent the next few hours going over the account cards and other financial records.

Things did not look good. Over 20 account cards had been found which were over 90 days past due (the January report had shown a total of 12 such accounts) and no note of contact between the office and the cus-tomer could be found for most of them for the past 60 days. The office was in disarray, the filing system in chaos, key records and papers took some time to locate and the customer account clerks seemed unfamiliar with much of the routine office procedure. Keast finished the morning going over the personnel files and noted that the turnover rates for clerical per-sonnel was high, absenteeism a problem and a key staff member (the ac-counts supervisor) had been fired a month ago and had not been replaced.

Leaving his assistant to tabulate the results of the morning's inspection, Keast took a by now very worried-looking Snell to lunch at Cy's. He intended to utilize lunch to do the performance appraisal and to suggest several courses of action that might be taken to remedy the Moncton problems. He was disturbed and somewhat surprised by what they had uncovered in their morning's work.

The bleak view of the Petitcodiac River at low tide which was visible from the restaurant window provided an appropriate backdrop to their luncheon conversation. Keast began: "Look Ron, you're over $5 million outstanding and $400,000 of that is overdue. We can't find half of what we're looking for in your records, and no one seems to know what they're doing. You admit yourself that things are out of hand." "But Mr. Keast, I've told you that I know we're having problems but I think it is up to me to solve them. I've been the manager here for eight years and I promise that within six months we'll have everything back to normal."

Toying with his lobster thermidor, Keast considered what he should and could do. He had certainly given Snell ample notice of dissatisfaction with the branch's operation, and the prospect for improvement seemed dim. On the other hand, Snell had a long record of satisfactory work with only one year of poor operation. He had been manager of the Moncton branch for eight years and had the longest stay of any branch manager in the region, as well as the longest service of any of the current staff at that branch. Keast thought that this visit had impressed on all the Moncton staff the alarm with which their performance was viewed by him. Weighing this, Keast advised Snell that "the inspection this morning has convinced me that changes have to be made. I think you knew this. You have worked well in the past but it looks to me that you may need some help in bringing the turn-around about." Snell agreed that he needed help. Keast continued: "My assistant worked at the Halifax branch before he became my assistant at Regional. You met him this morning. What do you think of him?" Snell responded in a noncommittal fashion saying, "He certainly seems efficient and gets right to the problem without fooling around. He seems fine. Why?" "Well, Ron, you suggested that Jerry MacDonald isn't doing his job the way you'd like him to. I'll see him this afternoon for his performance appraisal and I propose to offer him a field salesman position in Prince Edward Island. I would like to temporarily replace him with my assistant, Alex DeCoste." Stunned at this suggestion, Snell could only nod. He had half expected to be fired himself.

Before returning to the office Keast told Snell that this move was only temporary and would last for three months. At the end of that time he would return to Moncton and reinspect the branch. Both expressed the hope that the results would warrant a rerating of the branch from poor to at least satisfactory.

On returning to the office Keast spent half an hour with Jerry Mac-

Donald, explaining the reasons for the changes and his new responsibilities. Jerry was 40 years old and had once been the branch manager in Edmundston, New Brunswick, before coming to Moncton. His performance in Edmundston had resulted in his becoming assistant manager at the Moncton branch. Since then he had not shown much interest in becoming a branch manager again. He accepted the proposed change calmly. Keast then met with Snell and DeCoste and they discussed the changes that would have to be made in order to eliminate the current operating problems. DeCoste made several suggestions regarding collections, personnel training and new business, which were greeted with mild interest by Snell. They agreed to explore these idea more fully when DeCoste returned February 19 to assume his new duties. Keast and DeCoste then left the Moncton branch to catch their return flight to Halifax. On the return flight Keast impressed upon DeCoste the importance of getting the Moncton branch back in shape, not only for the sake of the branch's health, but also because other branch managers in the region were keenly interested in how Keast would handle the situation.

CHANGES

Returning the following Monday, DeCoste and Snell met briefly and exchanged pleasantries. Snell then formally introduced him to the rest of the staff, some of whom DeCoste had met the previous Wednesday. Most of the staff gave DeCoste a warm greeting. The staff consisted of three collection officers, a cashier/cash journal clerk and three file clerk/typists (a fourth had quit a week earlier). The accounts supervisor position remained unfilled. (See Exhibit 1 for an Organizational Chart of the Moncton Branch). Snell and DeCoste then returned to discuss the changes that needed to be made.

As with all the D.A.C. branches which had both a manager and an assistant manager, the Moncton manager's job description prescribed his primary duties as that of seeking new customers (both consumer and commercial), promoting sales and performing all public relations duties. These duties called for significant amounts of field work and as a result the daily supervision of office work was assigned to the assistant manager. DeCoste would assume all responsibilities for directing and appraising office personnel, and acting as liaison between the staff and the manager where necessary. In the Monday meeting the two men agreed that DeCoste would run the office as his job description indicated, but that any significant changes and decisions that DeCoste might make would be thoroughly discussed with Snell before making them.

On the afternoon of the 19th, DeCoste met with the collections staff and explained the changes to be made in the collection of past due and current accounts. The collection officers were to have all the accounts

EXHIBIT 1
Organization Chart: February 19, 1973

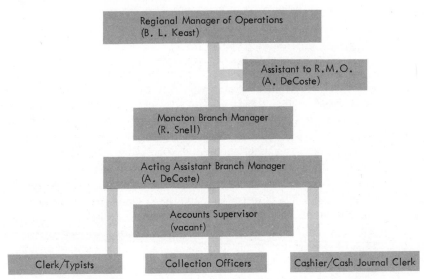

pulled which were 60 or more days overdue and resolve these accounts according to procedures set forth in the Procedures Manual. Once these were settled, they would then focus their attention on the next most critical group, the 30 to 60 days overdue accounts. It was agreed that these 250 accounts would be processed in two weeks time. DeCoste promised that a replacement for the previously fired accounts supervisor would be on the job within two weeks. In the meantime he designated the most senior of the officers as the temporary chief of this concerted effort.

That afternoon DeCoste met with the three clerk/typists and spent the rest of the day reorganizing the filing system and instructing them in the standard procedures for keeping account records current. This procedure consisted of the dating of all payments on the reverse of the customer's account card and the daily pulling of all account cards whose payments were due that day. These cards were then placed at the back of the "accounts payable" file. When accounts were paid the cashier/journal clerk noted this on the card and placed them in the "to file" box, to be filed by the clerk/typists. Two of the girls claimed to have never been trained in these procedures and made reference to account cards which had been handled somewhat carelessly in the past. It was hoped that this systematic customer accounts method would reduce the number of customer complaints.

By the end of February the office had begun to operate more smoothly than it had for some time. The office now had its full complement of staff, morale had improved, the number of uncollected overdue accounts had been reduced to 100 and DeCoste felt progress was being made. However, new problems were beginning to arise.

MARCH

The first problem arose at the end of the month. The February report was due March 3rd, which meant that the actual completion date would be Thursday, the 1st. It was DeCoste's responsibility to complete the task and on Wednesday he asked the staff (exclusive of Mr. Snell) to work overtime compiling data for the report. This request met with loud disapproval. The staff claimed that this had not been the practice for some time and when it had been, the staff had had to buy their own supper. Mr. Snell had ended the policy of D.A.C. paying for the dinner, claiming that it was too costly, and the evening work at months end ended shortly thereafter. The Procedure Manual stipulated that agreement to work overtime once a month was a condition of employment and that D.A.C. would pay for any expenses (including meals) incurred as a result.

Another problem related to an informal practice which had existed for some time. Between Keast's inspection visit and DeCoste's arrival as assistant manager, Snell had instructed all the staff that coffee breaks were to be eliminated. Snell continued to take a break twice a day in the coffee shop next door. On two occasions after his arrival, DeCoste accompanied Snell on his coffee break. On both occasions Snell belittled the staff, complaining about their ineptness, criticized his previous assistant manager and complained that after 18 years of service with the company they had forgotten about him. The staff began to sneak in thermoses of tea and coffee for use during Snell's regular visits to the coffee shop.

A third problem began occurring immediately after DeCoste's arrival. Arguments between staff members began to occur over who was to do what. Snell would hear these disputes, come out of his office and immediately direct the employees involved to do the tasks in the manner he indicated, all of this before DeCoste could act to resolve the dispute. On these occasions Snell referred to the need to run an efficient office.

An additional problem began during DeCoste's second week at Moncton. One of the collection officers approached him regarding a raise, pointing out that the last raise he had had was 18 months ago and it was for only $3 per week, raising him to $118. Alex checked the employee's personnel file and found he had not been appraised since the time of his last raise, despite the fact that it was D.A.C. policy to perform employee reviews annually on the anniversary of their employment. A raise seemed warranted to Alex as the officer was making $500 below the average for collection officers in the region with similar lengths of service, although there was a considerable range in salaries throughout the region. DeCoste approached Snell but was told that no raises would be granted until the rating of the branch was judged satisfactory by the RMO. He claimed the employee was being overpaid now and referred to the outstanding accounts problem. DeCoste responded "Look, Mr. Snell, I've examined all the personnel files for all our staff and have found the rates of pay to be well below the D.A.C. rates in the Atlantic region and our staff knows this. I think we need to catch up on our raises. I know Jerry MacDonald left this to you but you're too busy as it is and we're way overdue on the annual appraisals. As it is now, none of the staff knows why they have not had raises and that includes Jerry before he left." Snell's response was short and repeated his claim that no raises would be approved until the branch shaped up. DeCoste was sure that Keast had given Snell no directions regarding salary changes. After this conversation of the 27th Alex informed the employee that he was trying to get a raise of $10 a week approved and that a strong showing on the outstanding collections would improve his case.

Finally, DeCoste noted that he had inherited a staff who had grown accustomed to going to Snell with any operating problems. This practice had been tacitly approved by Jerry MacDonald, who had become used to having Mr. Snell in the office most of the time and left most matters of consequence for Snell to deal with. MacDonald had not, however, refrained from joining in on the jokes made about Snell on the rare occasions when he was out of the office.

THE MAY INSPECTION

During the February–April period the monthly reports showed the branch's improvement in its accounts collections. The delinquency rate for April 1973 was down to 4 percent and only one clerk/typist had quit. Some of the administrative and operations problems had been resolved but the problems of raises, office supervision by Snell and the coffee breaks prohibitions remained while the number of accounts had continued to fall. Keast had requested a private report from DeCoste regarding the Moncton operations and had received it at the end of April. In it he made observations regarding the various administrative and operating problems and also noted his own frustration in his current position.

Keast was to arrive on May 7 and the Moncton staff anticipated his arrival with varying mixtures of anxiety, hope, and fascination. Keast's own view of the May visit was one of realizing that there was more involved than the health of the Moncton Branch. Keast had tried to carefully consider all the factors regarding the Snell case in light of the current branch control system and the branch manager's job. Keast also had to keep in mind Snell's long service record, his welfare and that of the Moncton staff, as well as the health of the total Moncton operations and its place in the region. On the May 7, 7:30 A.M. flight he reviewed what he intended to say at that meeting. The weather had improved since his last flight to Moncton and he hoped the Moncton operation would continue to similarly improve.

Dundas Mechanical Contractors Ltd.*

DUNDAS Mechanical Contractors Ltd. was a medium sized firm employing some 200 men at peak periods. The company had been in business for over forty years and had an excellent reputation for quality work and service. The specialty of the company was plumbing, electrical and heating. Only rarely did they get involved with sprinkler systems. Like most companies, they had a complete sheet metal shop and seldom subcontracted any of their sheet metal.

For the past ten years Dundas had specialized in obtaining a large percentage of the plumbing and heating for the new industrial buildings being built in the west end of Toronto.

Bill Collins was the company's oldest foreman. He had started as an apprentice plumber 35 years ago, and had been managing jobs for the last 25 years. During most of Bill's tenure as a foreman, the plumbing jobs run by him had been a constant source of amazement to the company's management. The jobs run by Bill consistently made money and on the average he would run 5 to 10 percent under estimate. When he did not bring a job in on target it usually could be traced back to an error in the estimate or the suppliers failing to deliver.

This was even more surprising since Bill had never been considered outstanding management material. It was recognized that he had expert knowledge in the field of plumbing techniques but management had never considered that he possessed the qualities necessary for promotion to higher levels. In fact, the company's General Manager, Chief Estimator—plumbing, and three job Superintendents had all started in Bill's depart-

---

* This case originally was prepared by Prof. P. R. MacPherson of University of Guelph, Ontario, Canada, for a three day seminar for the Mechanical Contractors Association. It is reproduced with the author's permission.

ment as apprentices and had long since passed him on the promotional ladder.

One day just prior to Bill's retirement, the personnel manager, John Anderson, had asked "Bill, what's the secret of your successful job completion record?"

BILL: Secret? There's no secret. And its not my job record. The success for the jobs goes to the journeymen and apprentices. I'm only the catalyst. I usually have between 7 and 20 people on a job who like their work and for the most part they are all good at it.

JOHN: I'm sure there's more to it than that. There must be some actions you take which contribute to their success as journeymen and apprentices.

BILL: Well, basically I think it really boils down to how you treat the men. As I see it, men really don't need all the 'managing' I hear a lot of the younger foremen talking about. I just make sure that when they start, they get proper attention so they know the job and I thoroughly discuss the layout of the job and keep them up to date on any changes in the plans. Usually after they have had a chance to review the job I always ask them for suggestions and listen closely to their comments acting when and where I can see improvements. Another thing I do is always try to leave something for them to do on their own, it sort of enriches their work. After that, all I do is try to keep things rolling.

JOHN: What do you mean, keep things rolling?

BILL: It's just a lot of little things, really. For example, if the man is new, I quickly assess his ability and see that he is given work that he is most capable of doing. Usually I match good men together and the poor with the poor.

Incidentally, I came upon this idea a few years ago on a large industrial plant job where we were running pipe. The runs were 200' long and by accident I paired off four men in teams of two. Luckily for me I ended up with a good and a poor team. You say lucky, well this is what happened. The good team did a good day's work and in three days were almost a half day ahead of the other team. Finally the slower team must have felt it because they finally speeded up by organizing themselves better and caught up and we finished the job in less than the estimated time.

Other times in situations of this nature the poor team when finally realizing the real 'pro's' were going to do a day's work left the job.

JOHN: What about trouble makers?

BILL: Oh that's easy. I usually put them, whenever possible, to work by themselves. In so doing it is easy to evaluate and measure their progress.

JOHN: Bill, I'm still a little bewildered; how do you motivate your men, as very few leave you before a job is completed? Some I know from the names going through the office have been working for you on and off for several years.

BILL: Perhaps another little secret I have is planned jokes. For instance last week I went up to the second floor on an unscheduled inspection and found three men (new men) talking rather than working. I just about walked through them—I never really stopped—I just said as clearly as I could, "You guys here for a long time or a good time? Watch it, the painters are coming in, they'll be painting you with the building." A week later, in reviewing the progress on this section of the job, I found it to be on target so I went out of my way to compliment the group on their work.

On major work when it is finished I will inspect the work with the foreman if I'm acting as the general foreman or with the men (man) if the job only calls for a foreman. If a compliment is due I make a point of letting the men know I'm pleased.

JOHN: Bill, do you do any preplanning on your own before you start, and if so does it help you in your relationship with you and the men on the job?

BILL: Frankly John, I do a lot of preplanning. I carefully review the drawings as to the hours budgeted for the job and make my own estimates as to how many men I'll need and when. Usually I set up a schedule for each phase of the job on a weekly–hourly bar chart that I keep in the shack, and it is essential to have all the tools and material available at the right spot and at the right time and in the right quantities. When I first meet with the men on a new job to discuss it with them, the men are then assured of my confidence and ability because I can intelligently discuss the work layout because of my preplanning.

JOHN: What about the bar charts you talked about?

BILL: Oh, they are not really anything, just a weekly visual progress report that I have posted in the shack to let everyone know how we are doing. I think most men like to feel that they are accomplishing something. Incidentally, they (bar charts) work wonders if you have three crews each under a foreman, and doing essentially the same work. Last year, Pete, one of my three foremen on a job, was reviewing his progress and noticed he was a day behind Ed and Harry and walked out of the shack muttering that that won't last for long.

JOHN: Bill, do you ever make mistakes?

BILL: Sure I have and the first thing I do is admit it openly to them. After all, one has to be reasonable and fair. Only then will the men have any respect for you. Oh yes, I never 'knit pick' over the ten minute coffee breaks, and if a man finishes a job after four and it is getting close to quitting time, I generally tell him "that's a good day's work well done, pack-up. We'll start you on a new job in the morning." Sure, I lose a few minutes, but I generally gain more back the next day.

A few months after the above conversation, Bill retired. He was replaced as General Foreman by a young college graduate, George Brown, who had his journeyman's papers and whom the company was bringing along as a future executive. George had never run a major job before but had worked as a journeyman before returning to the local community college to obtain a diploma as an Industrial Technologist. He was regarded as a young man of good potential who could expect a bright future with the company. In his first week as General Foreman, George called a meeting of his three foremen on the job site, Al Blake, Jim Ogden, and Bob Ross.

GEORGE: The purpose of this meeting is to give you a briefing on what's expected of you on this job. I believe we can improve results considerably by proper planning and organizing. I have established weekly progress targets for each of you and for each of your men under your supervision. I have also divided the job into three areas and you will be responsible for the tools and materials and re-ordering stock. This way I can always pinpoint responsibility when things don't go right. You will each be responsible for the following up in your respective sections.

A year later, George was having lunch one day on the job site outside in the sun when he overheard two of his journeymen talking. They were sitting behind some crated heating units and obviously didn't realize he was there.

FIRST JOURNEYMAN: You know, Frank, I think I'll quit working when the job breaks down in Pickering. Ever since Bill Collins retired, I haven't really enjoyed working for Dundas, and so many of the old gang have either left the company or transferred to other departments. We have had eight different foremen in a year.

SECOND JOURNEYMAN: I know what you mean, Frank. I don't get a kick out of working anymore either. Most of the other people on the job seem to feel the same way. When Bill Collins was here it was more like we had a share in how the job went. Sure George Brown appears to be very smart and well organized, but he's a little too much like a machine.

George thought about the conversation when he returned to his office. He knew his results hadn't been good on this job, several times management would ask why he wasn't on target, but he hadn't been aware of any resentment toward him personally from the men. He hadn't been particularly harsh with anyone, and in fact, he had seen that several of the foremen who had worked for him received 25 cents above the rate. Morale should be good. He decided to compile some statistics to help him analyze the problem.

Job Site Results (year 1971)

	Turnover (percent)	Number
Planned estimated hours.................		30,000
Actual hours.......................		33,000
Employee Turnover:		
30 Journeymen......................	200	
3 Foremen.........................	125	
Requests for Transfer to Other Jobs:		
Foremen...........................		4
Journeymen........................		15
Number of One-Day Absences............		100

Question

If you were George Brown, what would you do?

The Eager New Lawyer and the Managing Clerk*

NOTE: DO NOT READ this case until directed to do so by your instructor. It has been set up as a Prediction Case so that you can test your analysis by answering questions before reading the entire case.

PART I

I WAS a lawyer with Messrs. Allan and Banes for 15 years and watched young lawyers come and go. Ours was a large Australian firm, employing 40 staff people. It was also one of the more prestigious firms, having established over the previous 50 years an enviable reputation for reliability and competency. I think the following case will give you some picture of a newcomer's introduction to our firm and to the profession of law.

Messrs. Allan and Banes had a reputation for conservatism, which reflected the influence of the partners, and, to a lesser extent, the nature of the work handled. There were eight partners in the firm: five specialized in corporation work, and the remaining three headed the departments of property, probate (wills and trusts) and common law (court cases such as motor-vehicle collisions).

Although the staff (that is, the nonpartners) numbered approximately 40 people, only about 15 actually handled legal work, the balance comprising women of various ages who performed secretarial and receptionist duties. These 15 people fell into two categories: those who were qualified attorneys, and those who were not. Those who were unqualified fell into two subcategories termed Managing Clerks and Articled Clerks. The distinction was important, because managing clerks could never advance, whereas articled clerks were generally younger people who had graduated from law school. After graduating it is necessary to work for a year in an attorney's office for the purpose of supplementing the more theoretical law school with some practical experience. At the conclusion of that year, and after satisfying certain further requirements (examinations, character) the articled clerk is admitted to the practice of law and finally becomes qualified as an attorney.

It was into this somewhat rarified atmosphere that Jack Bohnston stepped. He was young, eager, fresh from law school, and bursting with knowledge of the latest trends in law. In short, he knew a lot about what

---

* From Robert E. C. Wegner and Leonard Sayles, *Cases in Organizational and Administrative Behavior,* © 1972. Case edited slightly and restructured into a prediction case. Reprinted by permission of Prentice-Hall, Inc.

the law is, was, and ought to be. Now he was about to apply it. Nevertheless, Bohnston was not unmindful of the fact that he was fortunate to be doing his articles with Messrs. Allan and Banes and that the attorney to whom he was "articled" was Mr. McLloyd, one of the senior partners of the firm. McLloyd was in the corporation department.

, On his first day, Bohnston was advised by McLloyd that over a period of time he would be rotated through each department of the firm. This would enable Bohnston to gain some insight into the main branches of the law so that he would then be in a better position to assess the merits of each department and decide in which field to specialize. The first department was to be the property department; and in view of Mr. McLloyd's busy schedule, and the fact that he primarily operated in a different department, Bohnston was advised that he was to be placed under control and direction of Mr. Lawson.

Ned Lawson had been with Messrs. Allan and Banes for about ten years. He was sixty-three years of age, and due to retire in two years. Mr. Lawson was English, and had worked for an English firm of attorneys for some twenty years. He decided to leave England, and on his arrival in Australia found employment with Messrs. Allan and Banes. At no time had Lawson become or attempted to become an attorney; he was a managing clerk with considerable experience but no legal qualifications.

The building occupied by the firm was old, with large rooms and high ceilings. Lawson had one of the largest offices, and he liked the prestige and the privacy which accompanied it. He also appreciated the fact that he was well regarded in the firm because of his considerable practical experience, and that he was assigned a permanent secretary for his sole convenience.

After Jack Bohnston was shown around the offices of the firm by the partner in charge of the property department, and introduced to the other partners and staff, he met Lawson. After the usual introductory remarks, the property partner remarked to Bohnston that this was the room where he would work for the immediate future, and that in the first instance he was under control of Lawson, then himself, and ultimately Mr. McLloyd.

Discussion Questions and Predictions

1. What expectations is Lawson likely to have about the role that Bohnston should have? Explain your conclusion by reference to:
   a. Background factors
   b. Features of the Required System
   c. Lawson's self-concept
2. What expectations is Bohnston likely to have about his role? Explain your conclusion by reference to:
   a. Background factors

PART II

On that first day, and over the next couple of weeks, a series of events
occurred which greatly discouraged Jack Bohnston. These events or incidents were all of a very minor, almost petty nature.

As mentioned, Lawson's office was spacious, and in the middle of the
room stood his large desk. Bohnston's desk, situated in a far corner, was
more like a tiny table virtually surrounded by Lawson's filing cabinets. In
these first days Bohnston required very little secretarial assistance, but
when it was necessary, he was authorized by the property partner to use
Lawson's secretary. When he did this, he found that the work was seldom
returned to him the same day. Bohnston received few phone calls, and
held no conferences. Lawson's telephone rang continually, and he held
many conferences. During these conferences Lawson occasionally introduced Bohnston to the firm's client with the comment, "This is the
new articled clerk. I'm keeping an eye on him." More often, Bohnston
was studiously ignored. Lawson handled a heavy volume of work and
often requested Bohnston to assist him by performing minor and menial
tasks. These requests generally came at a time when Bohnston had other
work to complete; work assigned to him not only by the property partners
but also by the other partners.

Bohnston did not see any particular significance in these assignments.
But although he outwardly remained polite and courteous, the appropriate
role for the firm's most recent employee, inwardly he was frustrated and
disappointed and anxiously awaited the end of the year when his "penal"
servitude would end. He felt he was regarded as an idiot, capable only of
running errands; his lengthy and specialized training seemed of little use,
and he almost had to beg for his work to be typed. He received virtually
no recognition, prestige, or status. The work he was given seemed unimportant, but it often required reference to Lawson, an unqualified person
anyway, who gave advice in a grudging and abrupt manner if he gave it at
all. And when Lawson did pay attention he wanted to chat about his
family.

Each of the partners wanted his work to be done immediately, and thus
when Bohnston received several matters on one day, he succeeded in
satisfying none of the partners. Bohnston could not help comparing his

position with that of a close friend who, on graduating from law school, had decided not to do his articles and had gone straight into a corporation. This friend worked shorter hours, received three times Bohnston's salary, had his own office and secretary, not to mention other corporation fringe benefits.

About a month or so after Bohnston had joined Messrs. Allan and Banes, Bohnston approached Lawson about some matter and again was caught in a family-type conversation during which Lawson remarked that as he was approaching retiring age, Bohnston would be the last articled clerk he trained; indeed he had thought that the previous articled clerk he had trained would be the last.

Discussion Questions

1. What kind of relationship has emerged between Lawson and Bohnston? How do you account for it? In explaining, refer to the respective self-concepts of each and indicate how they are enhanced or diminished by the relationship.

2. What options are available to Bohnston in order to increase his learning and satisfaction?

PART III

Discussing Lawson's comments that night with a friend, Bohnston got a new insight, when his friend asked how he, Bohnston would feel if, at the close of his working years, with age catching up and perhaps his patience and tolerance slowing down, he was asked to train "just one last articled clerk." Bohnston imagined how he would feel! He understood then how he would feel about other matters — such as sharing an office and a secretary.

Along with this new view of Lawson, Bohnston reconsidered his own position. Although there was no question about his legal knowledge and ability, he realized that he was really very ignorant about the procedural aspects of the law. He also realized that this was precisely what Lawson possessed and that McLloyd, in placing him under Lawson, was well aware of Lawson's wealth of experience and hoped that it would be of help to him.

With these new perspectives of Lawson and of himself, Bohnston found everything very different over the next few weeks. He discovered that Lawson usually arrived an hour before the official starting time, and that if he himself also arrived during that hour Lawson was most affable and quite happy to discuss any current matters and to suggest alternative solutions to problems.

Bohnston now appreciated that during working hours Lawson did not have much time to do this. He still assisted Lawson; but Lawson explained not only what was to be done, but also the background of the matter and why it had to be carried out in a certain manner. Lawson provided Bohnston with technical aid and also gave him personal support. Occasionally a matter of Bohnston's did not develop as it should have, and if Bohnston had previously discussed it with Lawson, then Lawson would also attend the meeting with the property partner and would support Bohnston in the action he took and elaborate on the reasons. When the quantity of work that Bohnston handled increased, Lawson supported Bohnston's application for more secretarial assistance.

Thus Bohnston's attitude toward Lawson and the firm changed completely, but two matters still caused him some concern. The first arose from the fact that he still felt relatively deprived as compared to his friend who was employed by a corporation. The second matter that caused him concern arose from the fact that, notwithstanding the clear chain of command indicated to him at the outset, none of the partners observed this and he continued to receive work from them all. He really was not sure whose directives were to be followed or in what order.

Discussion Questions and Predictions

1. What kind of relationship has emerged as a consequence of Bohnston's changes in behavior? Why?

2. What are the blind spots of Lawson and Bohnston in the ways in which they perceive each other? How do you explain them?

3. What barriers still remain in the communications between Bohnston and Lawson?

4. What predictions do you now make about the future of the relationship between Bohnston and Lawson and the consequences for each in terms of their self-concepts, development and satisfaction?

The Eunice MacGillicudy/Marcus
Warren Case*

YOU HAVE been the Executive Director of Big Brothers and Big Sisters
of Ecclesville for the past year. The Agency is some 9 years old, having
started as a Big Brother Agency and added a Big Sister component approximately 2 years ago. The professional staff consists of four persons,
two men and two women. The two senior workers are Eunice MacGillicudy and Marcus Warren.

A Big Sister/Big Brother agency's historic function has been to recruit
adult volunteers and match them with children who have but one parent.
The adult volunteer acts as a friend and role model to the child to whom
he/she is matched. The Agency professional staff worker promotes the
adult volunteer with support services and helps the parent with problems
when asked.

Eunice, 32, has been with the agency for nearly four years and was the
first additional professional person hired by the previous Executive Director. She possesses both a BA and an MSW from State University and
had some three years professional experience prior to joining the Agency.
While her recorded caseload (matches) total 92, you have much reason to
suspect that not all those matches still exist because in reviewing her
files, at random, you have noticed that many matches have not been con-
tacted in nearly one year. There have even been some complaints from
mothers about Eunice's "unavailability." However, there is no question
regarding Eunice's commitment to the program and especially her skill in
developing community relations activities. Indeed, her caseload may be
suffering because of both her agency personal involvement and in community affaurs. Not only has she worked with groups of mothers, Big
Brothers and Big Sisters, and helped form a Local Council in a minority
area (unfortunately unsuccessful) but she is very active in the local chapter of NASW, sits on the Board of Ecclesville's Branch of the ACLU,
recently ran for the School Board (she lost by only a few votes), is a member of the Women's Political Caucus and undertakes volunteer therapy
work with teenagers. Through her efforts a distinguished local citizen
joined your Board and has arranged for a local trust for the past two

---

* This case was prepared by Lewis Reade and Marsha Klar, Big Brothers of America.
Reproduced with the authors' permission.

years. Chances are that through "the Eunice Connection" the $10,000 gift will be forthcoming again this year in November (it is now August) and will constitute approximately one ninth of your yearly income. If Eunice left the Agency and went to another social service the $10,000 would probably go with her.

Marcus Warren, 34, a black, joined the agency three years ago as the first minority professional. His background includes an undergraduate degree in journalism, four years in the Air Force as a personnel officer and he has completed all the course requirements for an MA in counseling psychology (an analysis of his innovative case work methods will constitute his thesis due next June). Marc is a sensitive and conscientious worker. His ability to develop rapport with the adults, children and parents he deals with is phenomenal. Treading a fine line, he expertly deals with both middle class people and the "street wise." He sees his military experience positively as providing him with organizational and administrative skills but has not become rigid because of it. He carries a caseload (matches) of some 70; each match is meticulously recorded and he has definite proof of personal (phone or visit) contacts at least once a month with each match. He has gladly offered to help the junior workers in learning to do their jobs well. In spite of all his abilities in working with matches, Marc has some difficulties working with the general public. He is proud of his work and if challenged (or sometimes even questioned) about his methods by the Board or an outside group he may get defensive. His knowledge of his real competence sometimes comes across as arrogance and you have had to smooth over some hurt feelings with United Way personnel as a result of a blowup by Marc at a Minority Involvement Seminar, where his methods were criticized. Then too, Marc is going through a painful separation with his wife, although the situation is eased by the fact they have no children.

Today you received notice that your LEAA proposal for a Juvenile Division/Court Related program has been funded for the next three years. The program includes the employment of a Program Supervisor and three workers who will handle referrals of boys and girls from single parent families at both the police contact and adjudicated level to your service. No similar program exists in Ecclesville and the entire operation must be developed from the ground up. This includes building relationships with police and courts officials, gaining local support in the center city minority communities from which most of the kids come, and developing the systems and procedures for processing and reporting on the matches made. There had been no secret for the past month that the grant would be made and that either Eunice MacGillicudy or Marcus Warren are the two candidates for the Program Supervisor's job which pays 25–30 percent more than they are presently earning. Word has gotten to you that Eunice has said that she will quit if she doesn't get the job and that Marc has said he'd seriously consider filing an action with the city Human Rights Commission if he is passed over.

The local Criminal Justice Agency (LEAA) has given you one week to name a Program Supervisor.

Evergreen Willows

EVERGREEN WILLOWS, a new convalescent home, had been in operation for several months. The large, one-story building, which had been specially constructed for its purpose, was divided into two identical wings, designated A and B wings. In the center of the building, separating the wings, was a large living room, a chapel, offices, and a middle wing which included the kitchen, patients' dining room, and employees' dining room. Each wing consisted of a nurse's station in the center with a corridor of patients rooms to each side.

Each nurse's station served the patients for its wing and each was under the direction of a Charge Nurse. Other nurses and nurse's aides worked under the Charge Nurse. Fom the opening day, each wing had been staffed separately. The Director of Nurses had assigned the more experienced older aides to "A" wing, where she planned to locate sicker patients. She assigned the less experienced aides to "B" wing which was to have patients who were more ambulatory. Except on rare occasions, A wing staff did not work on B wing, nor B wing staff on A wing.

The day shift on B wing consisted of one Charge Nurse and four nurse's aides. Normally the Charge Nurse was Jenny, a young registered nurse who had had no previous experience as a Charge Nurse before working at the Home. On her days off, she was replaced by Sue, a licensed practical nurse who worked part-time. The nurse's aides had rotating days off each week, so that, except when someone was sick and had to be replaced, the same aides were usually on duty at the same time. The B wing aides were of similar age and experience, having been hired at the same time. All lived in the local community and tended to see one another socially after hours.

Jenny's duties as Charge Nurse included dispensing medications, keeping charts and records up to date, and supervising the work of the aides. Actual patient care was the responsibility of the aides. Most of the

B wing patients were at least partially ambulatory. Caring for them involved assisting them in bathing, dressing, walking, and feeding, or, what nurses call "activities of daily living." The aides also liked to visit with the lonelier patients whenever time permitted. A number of the patients wandered around during the day, and it was often necessary for the aides to look for them, which consumed a great deal of time, considering the size of the building. Jenny, in giving her medications, ranged all over the building in search of patients, and was not always to be found on the wing.

From the opening of the home, Jenny had found that there was barely enough time in the day for the work she had to do. She did not give detailed instructions to the aides, and they developed their own routines in caring for the patients. One new aide even said that "it took her weeks before she felt she knew what she was supposed to be doing." Usually they would separate by corridor, each doing the work they saw needing to be done. All helped in passing out breakfast and dinner trays, feeding patients, and in answering lights when a patient called for assistance. All of the B wing aides kept busy, although sometimes there were complaints by some who felt they were "getting stuck" with the more unpleasant jobs because no one else would do them.

Nonetheless the atmosphere on the wing was friendly. The aides often spoke of how much they enjoyed the patients. While most of the aides had not sought a job working with older patients, even those who might have preferred a job in a hospital caring for younger patients, soon discovered that the "old folks" were interesting people. Consequently, there was much friendly contact between patients and aides as well as among aides and among patients. The patients enjoyed the atmosphere, although sometimes their families worried about the way they were allowed to wander about.

In contrast, A wing patients were for the most part bed-ridden, and required more actual nursing care. In fact, if a patient on B wing took sick, the Home's policy was to transfer that patient to A wing where there was a larger staff/patient ratio. The staff consisted of a Charge Nurse, Elizabeth, and two or three R.N.'s or L.P.N.'s and six aides. The charge nurse took care of duties at the nurse's station and drug room, while the other nurses dispensed drugs and did treatments. The nurse's aides did patient care. Many of the patients were unable to walk or stand, and helping them up to a chair involved heavy lifting. Fewer patients than on B wing were dressed, most wearing johnnies and bathrobes, and most remained in their rooms. Many of the patients who were confined to their rooms rang for the aides frequently throughout the day, often for only minor requests.

Elizabeth was an older, more experienced nurse than Jenny, and supervised the aides working under her in a strict manner. Each morning, the aides were paired in teams of two, and assigned to 16 specified patients. The assignments were standardized, and the A wing aides usually worked systematically and on a schedule to complete their work. There was little change from day to day, and patients were generally taken care of at the same time each day, and were accustomed to this. Working in teams of two gave each aide someone to assist her when lifting was necessary. Assignments included patients located far apart on the floor, but aides usually cared only for the patients on their assignment sheets. When another patient asked for assistance, they would often answer "Wait until your nurse gets here." Elizabeth kept a close watch on her aides and was very critical of the work they did. Sometimes she could be heard over the intercom saying something like, "Girls, there are five lights on A wing." She insisted that the girls maintain a professional relationship with the patients. While the atmosphere on the wing was far from homey, the sick patient received good technical care and their families felt a good deal of confidence in the quality of care provided on A wing.

The Administrator and Director of Nurses were cheerful and apparently well-liked by the nursing staff. They appeared at meetings held approximately every other week for in-service educational training or to up-date employees on issues of importance. Their response to the work

EXHIBIT 1
Evergreen Willows Floor Plan

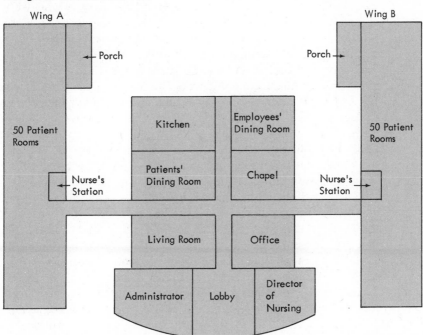

done by the nurses and the aides was favorable. However, they were rarely seen on the wings and they delegated a great deal of responsibility to the charge nurse.

After several months, the Director of Nurses announced at one of the in-service meetings that aides would now have assignments alternating them between the two wings. While she felt completely satisfied with the performance of both wings, she felt the aides should be more versatile and experienced with all types of patients.

When this new plan went into effect, a series of problems began to develop between the head nurses and aides of the two wings. B wing aides on A wing found themselves answering lights not belonging to their own patients, and falling behind in their own scheduled work. While working on one corridor, an aide would often forget those patients on the other corridor assigned to her, and those patients frequently had their lights on and unanswered for long periods of time. They complained to the head nurse when they had to wait. Thus the B wing aides were under constant criticism from Elizabeth, but when they tried to talk to her, they found she was not listening.

The help Elizabeth had from the other nurses allowed her more free time than Jenny had. She was often seen laughing and talking with the other nurses, but she did not socialize with the aides.

When on their own wing, the B wing aides now found they had to do even more work than usual. Most of the aides from A wing were lost on B, and needed much help in caring for the B wing patients. Nothing was written down and Jenny was too busy or not around to help them, so the responsibility of orienting them fell to the wing B aides.

Stating that there was "nothing to do" on B wing, a few of the A wing aides took frequent coffee breaks. The regular aides from B wing could not find them when they needed help, or did not have the time to go to the employees dining room to get them. One incident on B wing occurred when an aide was assisting a patient to bed, and the patient slipped to the floor. There was no one nearby, nor did anyone answer the emergency light when the aide called. The aide had to leave the patient to get help. When this situation was reported to Jenny she reprimanded the wing A aide who was not on the floor where she was supposed to be and recommended to the Director of Nurses that she be fired. It was the decision of the Director that she "should be entitled to a second chance." The situation did not improve.

A great deal of resentment developed among the nursing staff. Several of the aides, including those considered to be the best workers, quit, or began looking for other jobs. The attitude of the Administrator and Director of nurses was one of little concern. In the words of the Director of Nursing: "We have many applicants for each vacancy. Anyone can be replaced. Our turnover rate of employees here is better than in most nursing homes."

The Expense Account*

SAM SWANSON was in a predicament. Last week Sam went down to the branch plant in Baltimore. When he came back, he filled in his expense sheet and was about to hand it in when Bill Wilson and Jack Martin stopped by. The following conversation took place:

BILL: Come on, wrap it up: it's time for some coffee.

JACK: Sam, we've given you the honor of buying us coffee today.

SAM: Okay, fellows, I accept the honor—but wait until I add that 30 cents to my "swindle sheet" so that I can get paid for it.

BILL: How much are you charging the company for that Baltimore trip?

SAM: Wait, let's see—it comes out to a total of $142.

JACK: $142! My gosh, Sam, you've made some boner. Let's see what you have there.

SAM (handing sheet to Jack):   What should it be? I thought I put everything down.

BILL: Seven of us have been going to Baltimore for over three years now, and none of us has ever been lower than $150—and most of the time, it's above $160.

JACK: To start off with, Sam, you have only $2.75 for limousine to the airport. Most of us put down the taxicab rate of $5.50. You don't have any transportation back from the airport—what about that? Those two items alone add up to $8.25. That'll make your total $150.25.

SAM: Betty picked me up at the airport. The regulations on the back say I can't charge for that.

BILL: She had to buy gas, and there's wear and tear on the car.

JACK: Didn't you buy someone lunch or dinner while you were there? Your expense account will stand one or two of those.

SAM: Actually, fellows, everyone was buying me lunch or dinner. I didn't get much of a chance to spend money.

BILL: Gosh, Sam, do something with that expense account—don't turn in $142. That'll make the rest of us look pretty bad. Bring it up to $150 anyway, or we'll be in for a rough time.

JACK: I agree; fix it up, Sam. But first let's get that cup of coffee.

While drinking coffee, Jack and Bill explained their philosophy: While away from home on business you are really spending twenty-four hours a day on the job and only getting paid for eight hours; therefore, the extra expenses are warranted. They also pointed out that there are some hid-

---

* Prof. Rossall J. Johnson, author. From a research project on decision making: "Conflict Avoidance through Acceptable Decision," *Human Relations,* vol. 27, no. 1, 1974. Reproduced with the author's permission.

den costs to the individual—getting clothes cleaned, maintaining luggage, the cost of a baby-sitter so your wife can leave the house while you are away, and other little items which add up.

When Sam came back from coffee, he reexamined his expenses. If he charged $5.50 taxi fare to and from the airport, he would be just at the $150 mark. But he really didn't spend this money, so it didn't seem right to put that on the expense sheet.

Sam was new with the company—three months. He was getting along very well with the other men. He also recognized that if they did not like him, they could make his work rough—maybe get him into a spot where he couldn't do his job.

Questions

What should Sam do? (Check only one.)

_____ 1. Charge cab fare to and from the airport, so that the total is $150.25.

_____ 2. Charge cab fare from the airport (when his wife picked him up), making a total of $147.50.

_____ 3. Charge limousine fare from the airport to make a total of $144.75.

_____ 4. Make no change; hand in expense for $142.

_____ 5. Ask his supervisor what he should do.

Explain briefly the reason for your decision.

The Fairford Library

THE CITY of Fairford is a relatively small "old mill town" city of 15,000 people. Most of the families in the area have lived there for many generations. The only new people in the area are those whose families have been transferred here by one of the major local manufacturers. In fact, most of the people in the city departments have worked there for most of their lives.

At the city's library, Miss Clark had been the Librarian for 37 years, until her retirement in 1965, and had worked at the library for a total of 58 years. Mrs. Foster, the assistant Librarian, had worked at the library ever since she had graduated from high school. She was planning on retiring within the next year or two. Mrs. Little, in her early 50s, had worked at the library for almost 15 years, and Mrs. Arnold, about 55 years old, had worked at the library for almost as long.

All of these ladies had worked together for many years and virtually all decisions were made with joint consultation. Even the hiring and firing decisions were made by all. They chose their hours, their preferred days off, and whenever they decided that they would like a special day off, they immediately arranged their schedules to make it possible. During this period the work load and atmosphere was very relaxed and friendly. It was so friendly that during off hours the ladies would telephone one another to chat. If they arrived late for opening the library, no one really cared. If they had errands to do, they were free to attend to them.

EXHIBIT 1
Library Floor Plan

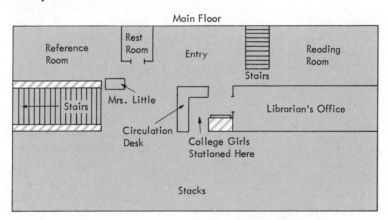

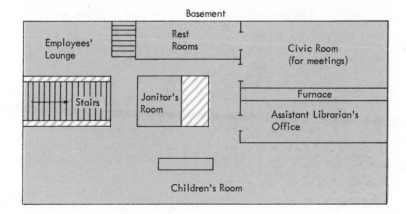

The Board of Trustees and the City Manager made all of the important decisions, and the ladies were not given the official responsibility for decision making although they often took it upon themselves to make day-to-day decisions.

After Miss Clark retired, the library was renovated and expanded to include the basement as a part of the library. A new Librarian was hired by the trustees, and given the decision making responsibilities. He took the office upstairs. Mrs. Foster, the Assistant Librarian, acquired a newly created basement office in which she could take charge of ordering and cataloguing books (see Exhibit 1 for floor layout).

She liked this office very much because she was out from under the "eye" of the Librarian and not visible to the public. Mrs. Foster liked her job and often enjoyed reading some of the more interesting books that she cataloged. She had worked here for so many years, and felt that she had the most power in the library personnel structure. After all, she knew many people and knew just where every book was to be found. She said that while she would like to be the Librarian, she did not want the tension that would surely go along with it. She felt very secure where she was and did not see any reason to change. She enjoyed the way of life which the work provided her.

Mrs. Arnold, the Children's Librarian, had a nice room adjoining Mrs. Foster's office. The desk in the Children's Room was placed so that patrons could be seen at the desk by Mrs. Foster if Mrs. Arnold was not in the room. This arrangement also provided the two ladies with a better opportunity for chatting back and forth. Mrs. Arnold always seemed busy even though the Children's Room was usually in disorder with uncharged books on the desk and scattered around. It would have taken only an hour a day to keep it neat. Mrs. Foster always was reprimanding Mrs. Arnold about the state of messiness, but Mrs. Arnold ignored Mrs. Foster's complaints.

Mrs. Little, the Reference Librarian and circulation overseer, worked upstairs. Although she was supposed to assist people in finding books and reference materials and do minor bookkeeping, she spent most of her time keeping an eye on the other employees and reporting back to Mrs. Foster.

A Mrs. Hoffe worked at the circulation desk. She was about 35 years old and new to the area. She was very easy to get along with, and everyone in the library enjoyed working with her.

Two college girls, who had started while still in high school, also worked there. Their work varied, but they interacted with all of the library personnel. They were well liked by the other employees, worked quickly and efficiently, and were given much responsibility.

After they had completed all of their work plus any other work that anyone else had that needed to be done, they would chat and joke with

Mrs. Hoffe, read magazines or send someone downstairs to get refreshments. The college girls and Mrs. Hoffe knew what they were doing and could handle almost any situation. They knew that they were valuable staff.

The group of older ladies consumed time by working at a slow pace and chatting throughout the day, often leaving work undone until the next day. The group of younger women worked efficiently and joked around only after getting the work done. Much friction developed between the two groups.

During the five years after Miss Clark retired, three Librarians were hired. In each case, there was so much conflict between the Librarian's objectives and those of the trustees and older staff that the Librarian soon decided to find employment elsewhere. For example, Mr. B's policy was to run the library on a military basis, exert tyrannical rule over employees, and override decisions made by trustees. Because of the great turnover in Librarians, the Assistant Librarian (with the trustees behind her) virtually ran the place.

When the trustees selected the fourth Librarian, Mr. Fischer, everyone felt that he would stay longer than others since he had brought his family with him to the area. He was about 35 years old, had a Master's Degree in History and one in Library Science, and several years experience in actual library work. However, he immediately found that many of his progressive objectives were not in harmony with the objectives of the older staff. Two of these objectives were to reorganize the library so that it became an information center for the whole community, and to have the employees of the library be more involved in getting the community interested in the library. Rather than back off, he pushed his objectives more strongly, and sought to determine why the conflict existed.

Ever since he first started work, Fischer had shown more interest in and friendliness to Mrs. Hoffe and the college girls. He soon established a favorable relationship with them. During the time that he was trying to find out why his ideas, based upon his experience in large city libraries, were rejected, he found that he was supported by Mrs. Hoffe and the college girls. Soon he began to use the three of them as a liaison between the "old guard" and himself rather than going directly to the older ladies. He found that whenever he mentioned a change in the system, the older ladies rejected his ideas immediately, often talking behind his back and poking fun at him.

For example, when he suggested that they get out into the community to find ways to give greater service; they would accuse him among themselves of just wanting to socialize instead of working. Similarly, when he would be at meetings with school personnel or town officials the ladies would attack him for not being "at work." In talking to their friends and the public they claimed he "goofed off" a lot.

Mr. Fischer judged productivity by how quickly the employees completed their assigned tasks, how neatly the tasks were done, how closely they followed his instructions, and whether or not they were easily distracted from their duties. The lack of respect on the part of the older women became so great that he found that whenever he mentioned the disorder that the Children's Librarian had created or the general lack of productivity of the older ladies, they were resentful. He soon began avoiding them.

The not-so-permanent personnel and Mrs. Hoffe respected his authority and his person to a high degree. Mr. Fischer found that he only had to mention something that he would like done and either Mrs. Hoffe or one of the two college girls would drop everything else and do it. It got so that he would discuss any changes that he would like with them, getting their opinions and suggestions as to how they would go about it.

Business communication between the groups declined. The older ladies' productivity level fell even lower as they spent more and more time complaining amongst themselves.

Although the Library's written policy gave Mr. Fischer the final say in hiring and firing decisions, he had to move with caution because the trustees had the final power. He considered firing the Assistant Librarian, Mrs. Foster, moving the Children's Librarian upstairs to work on circulation, and giving the job of Children's Librarian to Mrs. Hoffe. He believed this would help since when she had to replace Mrs. Arnold in the children's room, Mrs. Hoffe had proved herself by doing a better job. She kept the room neater, and kept uncharged books off the desk and put away.

Mr. Fischer believed all of his ideas were plausible, but he was beginning to be perplexed as to how to go about applying them.

The Foster Creek
Post Office Case*

THE UNITED STATES Post Office in Foster Creek, New York, is a small, first-class office serving a suburban community of 11,000. Normally, the post office employs eleven people—a postmaster, an assistant postmaster, six carriers (including one parcel-post truck driver), and three clerks.

Each postal employee's job requirements are minutely subdivided and explicitly prescribed by the *Post Office Manual*—a large, two-volume publication of the U.S. Post Office Department in Washington, D.C. There is a "suggested" rate per minute, and/or day for sorting and delivering letters, of which every postal employee is well aware. The work is highly prescribed, routine, and repetitive, with little basis for the development of individual initiative. Although each man contrives a few little tricks (which he may or may not pass along to his fellow workers) for easing his *own* work load, there is little incentive for a postal employee to attempt to improve any part of the mail delivery system *as a whole*. Each man performs pretty much as he is expected to perform (nothing more or less). Roger, the assistant postmaster, clearly verbalized this attitude, "The inspectors can't get us if we go by the book [manual]."

The irregular, unannounced visits by the district postal inspectors arouse a strange fear in *all* employees at the Foster Creek Post Office. Although each of the eleven employees is fairly well acquainted with the inspectors, there is something disturbing about the presence of a man whose recommendations may mean the loss of your job. The security of their position in the post office is highly valued by employees of Foster Creek, some of whom are no longer young and must provide for their families. It is customary, therefore, to see an entire post office staff snap to attention and work harder at the arrival, or possibility of arrival, of a postal inspector.

Larry, the Foster Creek postmaster, had a philosophy regarding the affairs of his office which was: "Keep the patrons and the inspectors happy." Outside of this requirement and an additional one which made it imperative that each employee punch in and off the time clock at the exact

---

* This case was written under the supervision of Alvar O. Elbing. Names of people and places have been disguised.

From *Behavioral Decisions in Organizations* by Alvar O. Elbing. Copyright © 1970 by Scott, Foresman and Company. Reprinted by permission of the publisher.

appointed time (this requirement was primarily for the ease of book-keeping), each man could do his job pretty much as he wished. The clerks reported at 6 A.M. to sort the day's mail into different stacks for the carriers who arrived at 7 A.M. The carriers then "cased" (further sorting according to street and number) their letters and usually were "on the road" by 9 A.M. They were required to be back in the office at 3:30 P.M., if possible, for further casing, and at 5 P.M. all the carriers went home.

In the summer months when the mail is relatively light and the weather is clear, each carrier easily finishes his route (including time allowed for a half-hour lunch break) by 1:30 P.M. It is standard procedure for the men to relax at home for two hours before reporting back in at 3:30 P.M. In the winter, on the other hand, with snow piled high in the yards, each carrier can no longer take the shorter route across the yards, and the men often finish long after 3:30 P.M. Larry is well aware of this procedure and says: "It all balances out, and in the hot summer they can use the extra hours to take it easy."

At 3:30 P.M. (or so) the day's big social event takes place at the post office. With the cry of "Flip for Cokes," all the employees except Jane, the one female clerk, match dimes to see who will be the day's loser and provide cokes for the others. This daily gaming is one of the many examples of the free and frequent sociability which exists among the ten male employees. Although the office's formal organization is detailed by postal regulations (see Exhibit 1), owing to the similar socioeconomic status and interests of the employees, the post office atmosphere is very relaxed and informal (see Exhibit 2). Many of the men bowl together; they go to the same church; and they often attend high school graduations and funerals affecting the families of their co-workers.

EXHIBIT 1
Foster Creek Post Office Formal Organization

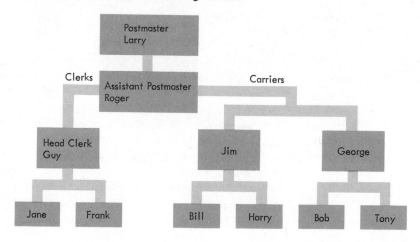

On payday (every Friday), each of the ten male employees contributes 50 cents of his paycheck to "the fund." This fund is used for coffee and donuts, to provide sick employees with flowers and "get-well" cards, and to purchase a ham to be shared at work during Christmas time.

Other important parts of each day are the regular morning and afternoon conversations. In the morning, the talk invariably turns to news items in the morning's paper. In addition, the men often talk about "those politicians in Washington" and the possibility of a postal pay raise. In the afternoons, the men relate any interesting experiences from the day's rounds. These experiences range from dog bites to coffee with an attractive female patron.

EXHIBIT 2
Foster Creek Post Office Informal Organization

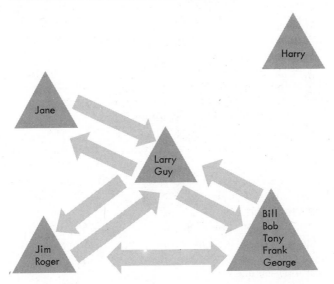

In general the 11 employees of the Foster Creek Post Office enjoyed their work. They comprised a close-knit team doing similar and somewhat distasteful work, but, as George, a senior carrier, put it, "We get good, steady pay; and it's a lot easier than digging ditches."

In mid-June 1968, Larry filed a request for a carrier to replace a regular Foster Creek carrier who had died suddenly. At 7 A.M. on Monday, July 8th, Harry reported for work as a permanent replacement.

Harry was a tall, skinny man with thinning hair, long fingers, and wire-rimmed eye glasses. He appeared to be in his fifties. He seemed nervous and shy, and when Larry introduced him to the Foster Creek regulars, Harry stared at the floor and said only "Hi!" Initial opinions of this new carrier were mixed. Jim, another senior carrier, probably best expressed the employees' sentiments when he said: "He's not too friendly — yet — he's probably a little nervous here — but *man* can he case mail!"

Harry was an excellent caser. For 27 years he had been a clerk in the main post office. The attitudes and work environment in big city post offices differ markedly from those in smaller offices (as Larry was quick to point out when any of Foster Creek's employees complained). In the city post offices, where competition for the few available positions is extremely keen, a man must not only be very competent but most follow the postal regulations *to the letter*. As Harry said quietly to Roger upon his arrival at Foster Creek, "Things were just too pushy in the city. And besides, my wife and I wanted to move out here in the country to have a house and garden of our own to take care of."

Harry had a well-kept and attractive house and garden. It was apparent that Harry loved to take care of his lawn and garden, because he spent all day Sunday working on it. As a member of the Foster Creek Building and Loan Association, Larry knew that Harry had purchased the property with cash.

On Wednesday, Harry's third day at work, the opinions regarding Harry had become more concrete. As Jim said: "Harry's strange. He thinks he's better than all of us, coming from that city office. He never talks to us or says anything about himself. All he does is stand there and case mail, but *man* is he fast at that!"

The first real problem arose on the fourth day. Harry had learned his route well enough so that he, too, was able to finish by 1:30 P.M. His ability to case and "tie out" (gathering the mail in leather straps) his mail so quickly put him on the road by 8:30 in the morning — ahead of the other four carriers.

On this Thursday afternoon Harry reported back to the post office at 1:15, having finished his entire route. Upon seeing this, Roger's first reaction was to say, "Go home and have some lunch, Harry. Relax at home for a little while."

Harry replied, "I've had my lunch. There are letters on my case. I've got to do them now. I've got to do my job." Having said this, he began to case the several hundred letters which had piled up since the morning. He finished these quickly, and then went on and cased all the mail which was lying on the other four carriers' cases. When the four regular carriers returned at 3:30 P.M., they were, to say the least, surprised.

Bill, the youngest and least energetic of the carriers, thanked Harry. However, Jim and George in particular were very angry. They grumbled about having a "newcomer" interfere, with his "city tricks" and "fancy casing." They were especially angry that Harry had violated the 3:30 rule. They were determined that he would not be the one who would make them lose their precious privileges, and they complained to Larry about Harry. The postmaster told Harry to case only his own mail, and to take it easy when walking his route in the future.

The next day, Friday, was payday. Each man contributed his share to "the fund." Harry refused. "I don't drink coffee," was his only answer. No one pushed the matter further, although discontent over Harry had developed among all the employees.

As the next week passed by, Harry appeared to sink into an even deeper shell. He punched in at 7 A.M. and punched out at 5 P.M. In between, he neither looked at nor spoke to any of the other employees. He continued to report back into the office before 3:30, case all his own mail, and then sit on the stool in front of his case reading magazines. Larry was worried primarily about Harry's exposure to the public as he sat at his case reading, and so on Friday of Harry's second week, Harry's and Bill's cases were switched (see Exhibit 3).

When each of the carriers reported in on Friday afternoon, Bill was told that his case was moved so as to give him more room to handle his quickly growing route (which, in part, was true). Harry said nothing about the switch, but went straight to work in his new location.

During Harry's third week at the post office, Larry began to worry even more about his behavior. Although the carrier was hidden from the public now, a postal inspector could catch Harry reading at his case very easily.

On Thursday, July 18th, Larry's worst fears were realized. An inspector came to the Foster Creek Post Office. As he walked in, Harry was sitting quietly at his case, reading as usual. The inspector looked at Harry, then at Larry.

Larry explained that Harry had an easier route than the other car-

EXHIBIT 3
Foster Creek's Post Office Layout

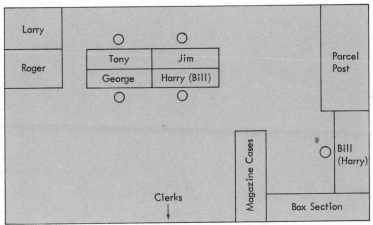

riers. Because of this and his ability as a caser, Harry was able to finish
his route more easily. Larry pointed out that he did not know what to say
to the carrier, for he had finished all his *required* work. The inspector
suggested that Larry readjust the routes to give Harry more houses to
deliver and more mail to case. This was attempted but Jim, George, and
Tony reacted unfavorably.

Full Speed Ahead

"WELL, if you insist, I can't stop you," Professor McRow concluded,
"but I do not think you can get into the MBA program at this time. If
you can, it will be all right with me."

McRow peered out from his eyeglasses, and looked at the student
standing in his office. Max Weber, a first semester economics student,
had informed him that he wished to transfer from the economics department to the University's Master of Business Administration program.

Weber had visited McRow several times before to discuss his misgivings about the economics program. Weber had asserted he felt largely
inadequate for the courses. McRow had assured him he was mistaken and
that his discomfort was typical of most graduate students. McRow's
words had little effect; Weber's impatience and concern grew as each
week passed.

He had felt uncertain about graduate work in economics before he had
come to the university. He had debated between the MBA and MA
economics programs and had chosen the latter, but by July of the previous summer he had come to feel he had made a mistake. He had discussed a possible switch with friends to obtain their reactions to such an
idea.

"That would be a surprise," remarked Jim Brock. "After all, all I ever
see you read is economics."

Another friend registered her opinions more strongly. "Max, that's
the most frivolous thing I've ever heard," said Ann Cole. "My god, two
weeks into the MBA program and you'll want to switch into the botany
department!"

Weber listened to McRow, his friends, and his family, but in the end
he decided to transfer. Rushing about the campus, he completed the nec-

essary paperwork in about a day, and he joined his first MBA class, Professor Taylor's marketing course, on a Thursday afternoon, the fourth week of the semester.

The next few days he spent buying books, picking up syllabi and beginning the long catch up process. Weber attended his first statistics and accounting classes on Monday, and on the following day he attended his first session of Professor Probier's class in organizational behavior.

The class was broken up into three discussion groups and Professor Probier assigned Weber to group "B" which consisted of Alex Hamilton, Bill Fast, Mike Graff, Linda Harkness, Ed Kubek and Henrietta Chase. Weber pulled up a chair, sat down, and decided to himself he would be an active and contributing member to group B. As a "no-nonsense" type of person, he decided to enter the discussion "full speed ahead," quickly trying to solve the problems contained in the case studies selected by the professor.

Ten minutes after he had joined B, however, Weber wanted to ask Professor Probier if he could not join another group. He did not like what he saw or heard.

Group B was in the throes of a minor crisis. It had neither a group leader nor a policy for rewarding (grading) individual performance. The group members were discussing among themselves what they should do. Weber was distressed by this situation. The other groups, as far as he could discern, had apparently resolved these issues long ago and were now working on the day's assignment. Weber decided he should try to do something about the situation.

"I kind of think we should work on the case before us," he said. "If none of you really care to see Probier on a regular basis, I'll be willing to do it until you can come up with a final solution." Weber was thinking to himself this would pick him up a few extra grade points, and besides, he wanted to get down to business.

The group continued to talk about the group leader issue—to death as far as Weber was concerned. "Talk, talk, talk," he thought to himself, "Parkinson was right after all. Work does expand to fill the time allotted." By the end of the class the group had decided Alex Hamilton should continue to serve as spokesman on a "permanent" basis but subject to change.

When class was over, Weber did not pause to linger with his fellow group members, but chose instead to dash out of room 301 as quickly as possible. "Aaagh," he groaned to a fellow dorm resident, "these people are incredible! They can't make up their minds about anything."

"I think they're afraid to offend one another," he continued, "so they end up not accomplishing anything at all. It looks like I'm going to have to do some prodding and pushing of my own if anything is going to get done in that class."

During the next few weeks Weber found himself doing a large amount of "prodding and pushing." "I think we're getting off the track" became a favorite expression with him. He did not hesitate to interrupt and try to change the direction of conversation when he felt it necessary.

He soon sensed his tactics were unpopular but this did not stop him. He believed Ed Kubek and Bill Fast were especially unfriendly toward him, but Weber told himself he did not care. As far as he could perceive, these two men were not making a sufficient contribution to the group so their opinions did not matter. He found Linda Harkness agreeing with him many times, and Hamilton often solicited his advice and comments. Weber felt that as long as he had the attention of these two influential members his position was secure.

Yet, certain signals began to crop up which indicated his position of influence in the group was declining. Weber found that members of the group no longer looked at him when they talked to him. Fast would look at Hamilton when answering a question from Weber. Harkness would do the same or look out the window. Graff looked at a wall or at Kubek. Weber found himself talking less. Members of the group would casually remark they did not like his choice of words when he expressed himself. Fast especially disliked the work "thrash" which Weber used when he wanted to settle a difference of opinion with another member of the group; "I don't think we 'thrash' anything out here," remarked Fast. "We get along pretty well and discuss things without having to 'thrash' them out as you like to say."

Weber recognized his position was on the decline, but he did not know how to arrest that decline. Increasingly the other group members ignored him. The group did not respond to any of his feeble efforts to bring the problem into the open. The most he could elicit from the group was a polite "you are more task oriented than the rest of us."

Weber found this kind of reply unsatisfactory. He suggested that if the group wanted to get at the roots of their differences, then they should bring their journals (required by the instructor as a data base for a term paper on the group's experiences) to class and read their entries to one another. The response to this proposal was unenthusiastic.

"I don't think that's such a good idea."

"Let's not do that."

"Yeah, let's not."

Weber felt stymied. Fortunately for him Professor Probier assigned the members of each group to evaluate one another. He also requested each group to list its norms or standards of behavior. Finally, Weber had the opportunity to get a long smoldering problem out into the open.

The results of the evaluation were largely what he expected. Voted least liked and most threatening, Weber was also voted by the group as being unhelpful, though Hamilton gave him a high rating. There were also a few unpleasant surprises. People whom he thought would have rated him highly in some categories gave him singularly low grades. Harkness, whom Weber had regarded as his greatest ally, viewed him as a threat and put him at the top of her least liked list.

"Obviously, we have some problems here," Weber leaned back in his chair and folded his hands on top of his head. "I've kind of felt there's been something wrong, but I need feedback from you people if I'm going to do anything about it."

The members of the group opened up, and while not harsh in their words, they made it clear to Weber he had not been subscribing to their norms. They told him all members were to be treated alike and with equal respect. Furthermore, they informed him that the individual's self-expression and development came first and the assigned tasks second. Weber had, they felt, tended to dominate the conversation too much. He was prone to cut people off; people who had ideas to express too.

For Weber this may have been the most fruitful class of the semester. The problem was out in the open, and he could now begin to work on it. He told the group he was unwilling to sacrifice his task-oriented nature but that he would try to maintain a lower profile. Over the next few classes he deliberately talked less and asked more questions. He tried to change his role to that of a coordinator who sometimes plays the devil's advocate.

Weber continued to concentrate on getting the job done in class, and the group came to expect him to fulfill a task role. The group saw him as a prodder, "our old task master" as Bill Fast would phrase it. And Weber had to admit to himself that he felt most comfortable in that role. He considered himself ill-suited to play what he called deprecatingly "touchy-feely." He preferred to deal with the facts or problems devoid of the human equation. Hamilton's open and informal leadership style was more focused on expression of feelings than he would have preferred, but allowed him to concentrate on getting the jobs done.

Over the next few weeks, Weber found himself liking the members of the group more than he had in the past. Moreover, he felt the group liked him better and that the group was working more effectively as a unit. This new unity became apparent when it came time to write a group analysis of two cases "Mr. Haws" and "Chuck, the Manager." Every member participated in the task, especially Mike Graff and Ed Kubek, whom the group had criticized previously for not participating enough. As for Weber, he succeeded in retaining a task-oriented position, but he participated relatively little in the conversation the group had on the project. The group met one night in a conference room to discuss the paper. Weber automatically went to the blackboard and began to write down people's comments. He tried to give the members an outline on the board, and he did not express many opinions of his own. Largely he fielded questions, which he hoped would give the discussion a direction and a definite scope.

The meeting went well. An instructor passing by commented that he was impressed, and the group was pleased with his remarks. Weber was tempted to take it as a personal compliment, for he was the one at the blackboard. The group ended the meeting happy with the results. Fast, who had been critical of Weber, praised Weber for the job he had done.

Weber felt he was now at last making progress in gaining both group acceptance and friendship. "I didn't care for you at all at first," Kubek remarked a few days later. "You came on pretty strong. But you've changed, and you aren't so bad after all."

Weber and Harkness wrote the final draft of the Chuck–Haws analysis and Professor Probier gave the group a 90 percent on the paper. The group decided to give each member an equal share of the grade since all members had participated in the task. Professor Probier, however, found this unacceptable and insisted the group divide the grade on a proportionate basis.

"Why?" asked Hamilton, the group spokesman. "We all contributed to the output."

"Yes, why can't we divide it up equally?" Weber questioned. "Like Alex said, everyone did something for the paper. I helped to write the final draft, but Alex wrote part of the rough draft, and Henrietta did the typing."

"I think you're avoiding the issue," answered Probier.

"No we're not," Weber replied a little more emphatically than he would normally. He felt most members had contributed fairly. But he and the group also realized he had spent more time rewriting the paper than the others. He was worried. A discussion on how to divide up the grade might create friction. This was the last thing he wanted. He had worked hard to improve his standing in the group, and told himself he was not about to let Professor Probier undo any of the good he had accomplished. In fact, he wrote the defense explaining the group's position, and he was as happy as any other member to see Professor Probier acquiesce to the group's desires.

Weber generally was satisfied with his position in the group. He thought he had overcome the old hurdles. He now had good relations with the other members. Harkness was more cordial to him. Graff suggested Weber and he play paddle ball, and Weber developed friendly relations with Kubek and his wife. While not the most influential member of the group, Weber decided he was willing to trade off the opportunity for further influence for more popularity. His main goal became to preserve the status quo.

This "era of good feeling" did not last long for Weber. He began to experience trouble with the group shortly after the completion of the

Chuck–Haws analysis. The next assignment was to write a case. The group chose Ed Kubek's proposal, and Kubek wrote a rough draft. A meeting to discuss the paper was held; Kubek provided more information, but the meeting ended with little accomplished. Graff wrote another rough draft but the group did not feel this second version was adequate.

The task of rewriting and producing a final draft fell into Weber's hands almost by default. Kubek and Graff had written enough. Harkness was ill, Hamilton would be away, and Chase and Fast said they would be unable to help. To Weber, it seemed no one wanted to have anything to do with the paper.

Neither did Weber. He had helped to write the previous paper and believed it was someone else's turn. The case write-up promised to take even longer than the previous paper. He had already fallen behind in his other courses, and he had put more than 20 hours into his assistantship that week. This set him back even further. By Friday he found himself tired but faced with a case which the group admitted was far from complete.

That weekend he drove to his parents' home in Lancaster to write the case. Weber also drove to Danford to work on it with Kubek, and by Sunday evening he had finished what he felt would be an acceptable final draft.

On Monday he turned the case over to Hamilton, who had offered to type the paper. Weber asked the members of the group to read the draft before it was turned in to Professor Probier.

For the most part no one seemed interested in the paper. "I'm sure it's all right, Max," commented Henrietta Chase. "The last job you did turned out really well." Fast was also unwilling to read it. "We've worked on that thing long enough; I don't want to start picking things apart now."

Interest in the case, however, mounted when Weber explained how he and Kubek had decided to end it. "I don't think that's the way we should do it," said Hamilton. "I think we should change it so it will help our analysis." Chase and Fast agreed, and with Hamilton and Weber the four of them went to the student snackbar to discuss the case further.

At the cafeteria the conversation turned to matters unrelated to the case. Weber wished to clear the matter up, so while the other members ate lunch he stepped outside to look for Kubek. Finding Kubek in the Social Science computer terminal room, Weber brought him back to the snackbar, and in a short time a final change was made which was acceptable to everyone.

Professor Probier returned the case with a grade of 93 percent a week later. The group was pleased with the result, and as was the custom, the grade was divided up equally.

This time Weber held strong misgivings about an equal distribution of the grade. He believed Kubek and he had spent more time on it than the rest and deserved a higher grade.

Yet he did not express this view to Alex Hamilton. "I'm going to leave it up to you and Ed about what to do about the grade," Hamilton said to Weber. Weber turned to Kubek. "I think we should divide it equally," said Kubek. "That's fine with me," Weber answered.

Weber was not pleased with this outcome. He had griped to both Kubek and Hamilton before class that he felt he had been saddled with the paper. He had hoped Hamilton would take the initiative and recommend to the group that Kubek and he receive higher shares of the grade. Instead, Hamilton had passed the decision to Weber. Since Kubek wanted an equal distribution ("It's not worth fighting over," he had told Weber earlier), Weber felt he could not insist on a higher grade. He did not trust how the group would respond, and did not want to open the issue for the professor's scrutiny. The matter was closed.

Placed in an awkward position before the group, Weber had chosen to let the matter rest. Weber walked away after class feeling he had been cheated.

"They left me to write the paper," he complained to a fellow MBA student from another group, "but they didn't make any effort to see how it turned out. They just assumed everything would be OK. They forgot it was their paper, too."

"I do not know who was responsible for that paper's success," he concluded, "but I think I do know who would have been held responsible if it had been a failure."

At the time of this incident, new groups were being formed in the class. Weber was assigned to a group which contained some of the members of the old group. Despite his displeasure about the paper's outcome, he was happy to find himself surrounded by familiar faces. But at the first meeting no one displayed any interest in the day's assignment. With Thanksgiving approaching, most members wanted to relax and discuss their plans for the holiday.

With no one eager to begin the task Weber found himself filling the vacuum of leadership. He asked questions and tried to direct the conversation. He kept notes and delivered a report with which he was dissatisfied to the class. He had found this session especially frustrating, for no one seemed to want to help him to get the job done.

When classes resumed after Thanksgiving, Weber decided he would do as little as possible for his group. "I'm tired of playing secretary and doing everybody else's work. It's not worth it."

He talked less in class. He stopped taking notes. His mind began to wander in class and his notebook filled with doodles. In one class Fast remarked, "Max doesn't seem to be with it at all today."

Fast was right, but Weber was simply grateful the semester was drawing to a close. Exhausted, he hoped he would never have to sit in on another organizational behavior class for the rest of his stay at the university.

Home Economics*
or
At Last! An Application of the
Dismal Science to Everyday Life

Christopher R. Sprague and Linda G. Sprague

WE ADDRESS primarily that audience familiar with remarks such as:

> Hey, Mom, "Godzilla Meets Mussolini" is on at eleven-thirty. Can I stay up?

> I'll go to bed as soon as I finish my dumb English homework.

> *Your* mother never made *you* go to bed in the middle of the "International Miss Dill Pickle" Pageant.

> It's not *fair!* I went to bed at eight last night, so why should I have to go to bed at nine tonight when I'm not even tired?

> Everyone in my class is watching "A Xenobiologist Looks at the 50s' on PBS tonight at ten. Why can't I stay up?

While our primary audience consists of those blessed with in-house progeny, we think that our research will be of interest to any who have ever harbored doubts about Economics[1] as a living presence in ordinary life.

---

* Reproduced with the permission of the authors. Christopher R. Sprague is an Associate Professor of Decision Sciences and Management at the Wharton School, University of Pennsylvania. Linda G. Sprague is an Associate Professor of Operations Management at the Whittemore School of Business and Economics, University of New Hampshire. The authors and their two children, James and Barbara, live in Cambridge, Massachusetts.

[1] Some familiarity with economics is assumed. If you cannot obtain a copy of "The Last Definitive Article about Economics" by C. R. Sprague, D. N. Ness, W. B. S. Crowston, and J. McIntyre, 1970 (surreptitiously distributed), any reputable elementary text will do. The authors are partial to Samuelson, at least in part because he is a charming person.

Our concern here is the age old problem of bedtime for children. As can be seen from the authors' biographical sketch on the first page of this article, we have particularly severe problems in this regard since bedtime regulations must often be enforced by a baby-sitter.

Approaches to the bedtime problem range from the Prussian (every night at 7:30, no exception) to the Progressive (let them keel over when they're sleepy enough). We had chosen a middle ground; regular bedtime, later on weekends, dispensations for special events. This last point—exception to the general rules—occasioned the arguments suggested by the quotes at the beginning of this article; the resulting harangues cost us incalculable mental anguish, not to mention many hours, each week.

Having exhausted rationality, we decided to apply the science of last resort—Economics. Why not, we thought, *sell* stay-up time to our children at some reasonable rate (say a penny a minute)? Two practical considerations stopped us: first, our children have wildly different attitudes towards money—one is a miser, the other a spendthrift; second, what could we do about gifts? Birthdays, for example, would surely result in local inequities and Christmas presents could easily become the occasion of overtired children.

In spite of these problems, we felt that the basic idea was sound, so like many a government, we created a currency. Our currency unit, called the CHRON, is usable *only* to buy time for staying up. The remainder of this paper discusses aspects of the CHRON economy and its results in our experimental universe.

HOW THE CHRON SYSTEM WORKS

Every Sunday, each child receives an allowance of 270 CHRONS. They may spend their CHRONS however they like to buy stay-up time. The basic price is one CHRON per minute after 9:05 P.M.[2] Each child signs out on the way to bed and keeps a running tally of the CHRON balance.

Promoting the General Welfare—Taxes and Rebates   Like any government, we choose to exercise our taxing authority to promote the general welfare. Specifically, the rates for time change as follows:

9:05–10:05 P.M.	1 CHRON/minute (base rate)
10:05–11:05	2 CHRONS/minute
11:05–whenever	3 CHRONS/minute

These rates are halved if there is no school the following day. So, a child

---

[2] Any who wonder about the :05 are invited to try instituting a CHRON system beginning on the hour in a household with three television sets.

who goes to bed at 11:15 on Saturday night is charged:

$$60 \text{ minutes @ } \tfrac{1}{2} = 30$$
$$60 \text{ minutes @ } 1 = 60$$
$$10 \text{ minutes @ } 1\tfrac{1}{2} = \underline{15}$$
$$105 \text{ CHRONS}$$

The purpose of the differential rates is to encourage early bedtimes before school without precluding occasional late evenings during the week.

CHRONS unused in any week are carried over to the next week, making it possible to save up for a special occasion.[3] Exhibit 1 is an example of the CHRON tally sheet.

EXHIBIT 1
CHRON Tally Sheet (sample)

Date	Balance	Bed	Used	Left
Sunday 11/17	358	9:25	20	338
Monday 11/18		9:10	5	333
Tuesday 11/19		9:20	15	318
Wednesday 11/20		9:30	25	293
Thursday 11/21		10:05	60	233
Friday 11/22		10:05	30	203
Saturday 11/23		11:15	105	98
Sunday 11/24	368	11:05	180	188

Special Regulations—Monetary Policy A persistent problem has been what to do when friends visit until late at night or possibly overnight. Some concession is clearly required, but it must be equitable for the other child. Our solution is to charge the child with the guest at half the prevailing rate, crediting the other child with the same number of CHRONS. This of course results in the creation of CHRONS; but inflation is not an issue since the currency is not thereby debased.

When a child is away overnight, the charge is a flat 30 CHRONS. When a child is out late by choice, regular rates apply. When a child is out "officially" (with us at a play, for instance), CHRONS begin at regular rates 15 minutes after arrival home.

Free Market CHRONS The children may trade CHRONS with one another for any consideration they choose. Recent CHRON sales have gone at 1¢ each, but nonmonetary swaps are also occasionally made.

---

[3] What is described here is the "Cambridge CHRON"; an earlier version, the "California CHRON," was essentially the same except for the triple price after 11:05, but with only half carryover for unused CHRONS. The system was revised to permit CHRON build-ups for late-show horror movies, beauty pageants, and other such major events.

RESULTS: LIFE IN THE CHRON ECONOMY

We used the CHRON system in 1972–73, abandoned[4] it in 1973–74, and returned to it in October 1974 (with the variation explained in footnote 3). To put it briefly, we are satisfied with the system.

Effective implementation required that we make our objectives plain. This was not as simple as it sounds: "going to bed on time" is an inadequate description of what we are trying to achieve.

Basically, we want the children to get enough sleep to maintain their health. However, we recognize that considerable variation over time is entirely possible within that objective. For instance, eight hours of sleep one night and ten the next is entirely consistent with the overall goal. Further, we know that other objectives can frequently conflict with "enough sleep," at least temporarily. Staying up to read a good book or to watch a TV show may have substantial educational value. And, staying up late now and then just for the fun of it is not inherently wrong if sufficient sleep is obtained overall.

Our children essentially understand what we are trying to do, and we believe that they are not unusual in this regard. The problem has always focused on sorting out the conflicts on a case-by-case basis. It was as irritating for the children as it was for us when we were in the position of making detailed judgments practically on a daily basis—with the added problem of maintaining equity ("You let James stay up last night!" or "Barbara was up until midnight when Suzie was here!").

The CHRON system places "operational control" in the children's hands; they make their own judgments about when and why to stay up. But they make these decisions in the context of the overall policies which we have established through the rate-setting mechanism.

Are they getting enough sleep? Yes. We have two ways of assessing this: (1) their general health is fine; (2) we have a running record (see Exhibit 1) which is always available for inspection. Of course, we have experienced minor aberrations, the most notable being a Late-Late Show Godzilla Festival. But the system is self-correcting: using 300 CHRONS in one shot runs the balance low enough to force early bedtime on subsequent nights.

An extremely attractive feature of the system has been the shift from nightly quibbles to occasional policy sessions. Debates about base rates, carry-over, guest credits, and the like, are preferable to the seemingly endless hassles we experienced without the CHRON system. And we should point out that our children understand the operation of the system

---

[4] We would like to claim that this was for experimental control. In fact, we were so disorganized in 1973–74 that we never got around to drawing up a Tally Sheet. This year-long hiatus did, however, provide us with a reference point for evaluation.

well enough to bring up challenges that required considerable discussion and thought to work out. Of course, we have had to forego the use of bed-time as a disciplinary mechanism. On balance, we do not regret the loss.

Those who wonder at what age children can understand Economic concepts should know that we began this system when James was 11 and Barbara was 9. Two weeks after the system went into effect, they discovered a key gap in the system—we had failed to properly define "bed-time." It is now defined as "ready for bed and in bed, perhaps reading, but definitely not watching TV.",

The Tally Sheet (Exhibit 1) shows a phenomenon which has persisted since the introduction of the system—a CHRON backlog. Each child maintains a build-up of about 100 CHRONS; if this is used up, it is quickly returned to that level so that there is always a cushion for unexpected events.

EVOLUTION AND EXTENSIONS

The CHRON Economy can accept considerable variation: as the children grow older, we will be able to change the base rate and/or the weekly CHRON allowance to reflect changes in their needs. As an example, we are now working on the problem of baby-sitting—what to do when one of the children accepts a job which will require staying up late. (For now, this is being handled under a "guest credit" arrangement.)

Professor David B. Montgomery of Stanford University has extended the principles of ECHRONOMICS by developing a system to allocate TV-watching time; the unit of currency in his system is the VGP (Viewing Garbage Programs). His attempt to integrate the VGP with the CHRON has met with limited success.

We have described this system and our results with it in the hope that others may also find it useful. Our experience with it has been at least as successful as many industrial systems with which we are familiar. It also has the distinction of being a system which has actually been implemented.

Hovey and Beard Company*

NOTE: DO NOT READ this case until directed to do so by your instructor. It has been set up as a Prediction Case so that you can test your analysis by answering questions before reading the entire case.

PART I

THE Hovey and Beard Company manufactured wooden toys of various kinds: wooden animals, pull toys, and the like. One part of the manufacturing process involved spraying paint on the partially assembled toys. This operation was staffed entirely by girls.

The toys were cut, sanded, and partially assembled in the wood room. Then they were dipped into shellac, following which they were painted. The toys were predominantly two colored; a few were made in more than two colors. Each color required an additional trip through the paint room.

For a number of years, production of these toys had been entirely handwork. However, to meet tremendously increased demand, the painting operation had recently been re-engineered so that the eight girls who did the painting sat in a line by an endless chain of hooks. These hooks were in continuous motion, past the line of girls and into a long horizontal oven. Each girl sat at her own painting booth so designed as to carry away fumes and to backstop excess paint. The girl would take a toy from the tray beside her, position it in a jig inside the painting cubicle, spray on the color according to a pattern, then release the toy and hang it on the hook passing by. The rate at which the hooks moved had been calculated by the engineers so that each girl, when fully trained, would be able to hang a painted toy on each hook before it passed beyond her reach.

The girls working in the paint room were on a group bonus plan. Since the operation was new to them, they were receiving a learning bonus which decreased by regular amounts each month. The learning bonus was scheduled to vanish in six months, by which time it was expected that they would be on their own — that is, able to meet the standard and to earn a group bonus when they exceeded it.

Prediction Question

What will the new hook-line do to productivity and satisfaction?

PART II

By the second month of the training period trouble had developed. The girls learned more slowly than had been anticipated, and it began to look as though their production would stabilize far below what was planned for. Many of the hooks were going by empty. The girls complained that they were going by too fast, and that the time study man had set the rates wrong. A few girls quit and had to be replaced with new girls, which further aggravated the learning problem. The team spirit that the management had expected to develop automatically through the group bonus was not in evidence except as an expression of what the engineers called "resistance." One girl whom the group regarded as its leader (and the management regarded as the ringleader) was outspoken in making the various complaints of the group to the foreman: the job was a messy one, the hooks moved too fast, the incentive pay was not being correctly calculated, and it was too hot working so close to the drying oven.

PART III

A consultant who was brought into this picture worked entirely with and through the foreman. After many conversations with him, the foreman felt that the first step should be to get the girls together for a general discussion of the working conditions. He took this step with some hesitation, but took it on his own volition.

The first meeting, held immediately after the shift was over at four o'clock in the afternoon, was attended by all eight girls. They voiced the same complaints again: the hooks went by too fast, the job was too dirty, the room was hot and poorly ventilated. For some reason, it was this last item that they complained of most. The foreman promised to discuss the problem of ventilation and temperature with the engineers, and he scheduled a second meeting to report back to the girls. In the next few days the foreman had several talks with the engineers. They and the superintendent felt that this was really a trumped-up complaint, and that the expense of any effective corrective measure would be prohibitively high.

The foreman came to the second meeting with some apprehensions. The girls, however, did not seem to be much put out, perhaps because they had a proposal of their own to make. They felt that if several large fans were set up so as to circulate the air around their feet, they would be much more comfortable. After some discussion, the foreman agreed that the idea might be tried out. The foreman and the consultant discussed the question of the fans with the superintendent, and three large propellor-type fans were purchased.

Prediction Question

What will be the impact of the fan decision on morale, and relations with the foreman?

PART IV

The fans were brought in. The girls were jubilant. For several days the fans were moved about in various positions until they were placed to the satisfaction of the group. The girls seemed completely satisfied with the results, and relations between them and the foreman improved visibly.

The foreman, after this encouraging episode, decided that further meetings might also be profitable. He asked the girls if they would like to meet and discuss other aspects of the work situation. The girls were eager to do this. The meeting was held, and the discussion quickly centered on the speed of the hooks. The girls maintained that they would never be able to reach the goal of filling enough of them to make a bonus.

The turning point of the discussion came when the group's leader frankly explained that the point wasn't that they couldn't work fast enough to keep up with the hooks, but that they couldn't work at that pace all day long. The foreman explored the point. The girls were unanimous in their opinion that they could keep up with the belt for short periods if they wanted to. But they didn't want to because if they showed they could do this for short periods they would be expected to do it all day long. The meeting ended with an unprecedented request: "Let us adjust the speed of the belt faster or slower depending on how we feel." The foreman agreed to discuss this with the superintendent and the engineers.

The reaction of the engineers to the suggestion was negative. However, after several meetings it was granted that there was some latitude within which variations in the speed of the hooks would not affect the finished product. After considerable argument with the engineers, it was agreed to try out the girls' idea.

With misgivings, the foreman had a control with a dial marked "low, medium, fast" installed at the booth of the group leader; she could now adjust the speed of the belt anywhere between the lower and upper limits that the engineers had set.

Prediction Question

What will be the impact of the dial control decision on productivity and satisfaction?

PART V

The girls were delighted, and spent many lunch hours deciding how the speed of the belt should be varied from hour to hour throughout the day. Within a week the pattern had settled down to one in which the first half hour of the shift was run on what the girls called a medium speed (a dial setting slightly above the point marked "medium"). The next two and one-half hours were run at high speed; the half hour before lunch and the half hour after lunch were run at low speed. The rest of the afternoon was run at high speed with the exception of the last forty-five minutes of the shift, which was run at medium.

In view of the girls' reports of satisfaction and ease in their work, it is interesting to note that the constant speed at which the engineers had originally set the belt was slightly below medium on the dial of the control that had been given the girls. The average speed at which the girls were running the belt was on the high side of the dial. Few, if any, empty hooks entered the oven, and inspection showed no increase of rejects from the paint room.

Production increased, and within three weeks (some two months before the scheduled ending of the learning bonus) the girls were operating at 30 to 50 percent above the level that had been expected under the original arrangement. Naturally the girls' earnings were correspondingly higher than anticipated. They were collecting their base pay, a considerable piece rate bonus, and the learning bonus which, it will be remembered, had been set to decrease with time and not as a function of current productivity. The girls were earning more now than many skilled workers in other parts of the plant.

Prediction Question

How will other personnel react and why?

PART VI

Management was besieged by demands that this inequity be taken care of. With growing irritation between superintendent and foreman, engineers and foreman, superintendent and engineers, the situation came to a head when the superintendent revoked the learning bonus and returned the painting operation to its original status: the hooks moved again at their constant, time-studied designated speed, production dropped again, and within a month all but two of the eight girls had quit. The foreman himself stayed on for several months, but, feeling aggrieved, then left for another job.

Discussion Questions

1. What parallels can you see between the case and this class session.
2. What conclusions can be drawn from this case about leadership, motivation and change.

Irwin Manufacturing Company*

IN AUGUST of 1964, B. A. Warner, personnel director of the Irwin Manufacturing Company, was trying to decide what action he should take with regard to Dan Johnson, an employee of the company. Johnson had submitted an acceptable suggestion but, before submitting the idea, had given it a trial run, thus violating a long-standing rule that no change could be put into effect without the prior approval of the engineering department.

Irwin Manufacturing Company produced electrical equipment and was located in a large city in the Midwest. It had been formed in 1919 by Mr. A. B. Baker, father of the present president and grandfather of two of the vice presidents. The company organization is shown in Exhibit 1. The company had a reputation for being a "good place to work." Employees were not unionized. Most of the company's products were mass produced to very close tolerances. They were sold in 48 states by a sales force numbering almost 400. These salesmen worked out of 53 company-owned branches and sold on commission. Home office employment was in the neighborhood of 1,300.

Dan Johnson had started with Irwin as a drill-press operator in 1953, shortly after arriving in Chicago from his former home and birthplace, Kentucky. Irwin was the first place to which he had applied, and he was offered the job on the spot. During his time with Irwin, he had received frequent pay increases. Exhibit 2 contains a record of Johnson's wage progress.

In 1958, five years after Johnson joined Irwin, he was promoted to setup man in the newly formed spring department. This department came

---

* From Bergen, G. and Haney, W. *Organizational Relations and Management Action,* McGraw-Hill Book Company, New York, N.Y., 1966. Copyright, Northwestern University. Reproduced by permission.

EXHIBIT 1
Irwin Manufacturing Company: Partial Organization Chart

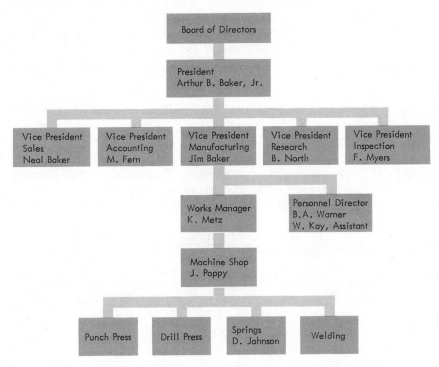

about as a result of a large government contract. After the contract expired, the volume of Irwin's regular products had expanded enough to make it unnecessary to transfer Johnson back to his job as drill-press operator. As setup man, he was responsible for the setting up of the automatic equipment in his department as well as the supervision of the ten female spring loopers who also worked in the department. The springs were automatically formed by machine. They were then moved to benches where spring loopers, using special pliers, formed the ends.

EXHIBIT 2
Irwin Manufacturing Company (selected data on Dan Johnson)

Personal: 38 years old, married, two children. 1 year high school.

Salary:	*Effective date*	*Hourly wage*	*Effective date*	*Hourly wage*
	4/29/53	$1.60	5/1/59	$2.35
	8/26/53	1.70	1/3/60	2.45
	11/18/53	1.80	1/18/61	2.55
	6/3/54	1.90	9/30/61	2.65
	12/15/54	2.05	8/12/62	2.80
	9/18/57	2.15	2/10/63	2.90
	3/29/58	2.25	11/1/63	2.95

Johnson also operated a special-purpose engine lathe designed to manufacture heavy-duty springs. This engine lathe was not in constant use. When needed, it was usually scheduled for reasonably long runs.

In reviewing Johnson's personnel folder, Warner noticed that this was the third time he had violated the same rule. Other details concerning Johnson are noted in Exhibit 3. Dan's latest violation was a serious one, according to company engineers. If it had not been detected, serious damage might have resulted.

Johnson's idea concerned the forming operation of a certain heavy-duty spring—performing it in one step rather than two, thus eliminating one complete job element. He designed a special tool bit to accomplish the form. Before submitting his suggestion, Dan decided to try out his idea. He ran 5,000 of these heavy-duty springs. After inspecting them and seeing nothing wrong with the results, he moved them to the assembly area, where they would eventually become parts of machines which sold for $250.

They remained unnoticed in the assembly area for almost a week, until it came time to use them in final assembly. At this point, an inspector observed the difference and placed a stop order on the parts, pending investigation. Product engineers were called in, and they immediately called for Joe Poppy, Johnson's immediate supervisor. When Poppy expressed ignorance of the situation, Johnson was called in. He readily admitted making the change and commented, "Why, only yesterday, I mailed in the suggestion form." This occurred on the eighteenth of the month. Dan was told to return to his department until disposition of his case had been determined.

Company engineers explained to Warner that they could not be sure at the time if Johnson's idea was a good one. They feared that his form job set up a stress concentration that might fail under repeated loadings. They further explained that if this were so, it was fortunate that the inspector had caught the mistake. Otherwise, the springs would have been assembled into machines, which could develop trouble in the field and require expensive servicing.

On the afternoon of the eighteenth, Warner asked Bill Kay, a personnel assistant, to interview Johnson to learn more about his background. Bill Kay's comments follow:

> A very likable, sincerely motivated worker. . . . Realizes he did wrong. When reminded that he had previously been warned about trying ideas out without approval, he expressed regrets and could offer no explanation. He said he was only sorry he didn't have more of an education, as he would like to study spring engineering and design. He also related an unhappy experience that happened to him about a month ago. As one of the engineers was walking through the department, Dan had stopped him and inquired if there were any books he could borrow to explain the theory of spring design. The

engineer replied, "What would a hillbilly like you want with a book? Stick to your comic books and leave the technical publications alone." Dan said he didn't mention the incident to anyone, but he thought the girls in the department had overheard the engineer's remarks. He would not give the name of the engineer. Dan said his home life was fine. He spent two evenings a week in Boy Scout activities and bowled on another night in the company league. When asked why he had refused to attend foremanship training classes, he said he hated to spend another evening away from his family. Dan ended the interview with the hope that he would be given another chance.

Bill Kay

Late in the next day, Kay interviewed Joe Poppy. Poppy said he was in favor of firing Johnson. He explained that only this morning, his boss,

---

EXHIBIT 3
Irwin Manufacturing Company (comments on back of personnel record card)

Date	Comment
6/15/58	Discussed importance of not initiating changes without approval. While walking by, noticed Dan grinding tool bit. Upon inquiring, learned he was trying out a new idea. Carefully explained the function of the suggestion system. *Joe Poppy*
2/9/60	Ran 11,000 defective parts. Failed to use lubricant. Said he was experimenting and couldn't understand why the lubricant was needed. *J. Poppy*
9/15/60	Offered chance to attend foremanship training. Refused. *K. Metz*
9/16/62	Same as comment of 9/15/60. *K. Metz*
10/8/62	Ran 6,000 defective springs. Failed to use specified tool bit for cutoff. His own design resulted in a burr. Warned he would not get another chance. *J. Poppy*
9/18/63	Offered chance to attend foremanship training. Refused. *B. Warner*

EXHIBIT 4
Irwin Manufacturing Company (suggestion record—Dan Johnson)

Date	Award	Date	Award
6/15/58	$10.00	12/18/62	$15.00
8/11/59	5.00	2/12/63	25.00
9/6/59	15.00	8/2/63	15.00
3/4/60	20.00	1/14/64	10.00
7/21/61	5.00	2/16/64	10.00

Note: No record of the total number of suggestions submitted is available, as the suggestor only identifies himself if he wins an award.

Karl Metz, had "chewed him out" about Johnson. Neal Baker, vice-president and sales manager, had heard about the incident and called Metz on the carpet. Mr. Baker had expressed horror at the thought that 5,000 defective machines might have gone out to customers. Poppy also said Johnson did a fairly good job as supervisor of women but that he could no longer tolerate his constant experimenting.

Warner was reviewing the case after lunch on the nineteenth, in preparation for a meeting with Poppy and Metz to decide Johnson's fate, when the phone rang. It was Ralph Brown, product engineer, who reported that Johnson's idea was thoroughly sound. Based on this evidence, he was recommending a $50 suggestion award.

Warner hung up the phone wondering what effect this should have on his decision. Company policy provided that even if Johnson were discharged, he would still be in line for the award.

The Job Change*

THE SARAZAN Manufacturing Company, leading producer of water meters, is owned and managed by one of New England's oldest families. The company employs approximately 500 people. In the middle 1960s the factory moved from an old four-story building in South Boston to a new modern two-story building in a new industrial center located in Lexington.

Because of the demand for temporary additional help necessitated by the move, four college students were employed as stock clerk's assistants. I was one of these students. Our duties were to organize and pack stock which included raw materials, machine parts, and subassembly parts.

During the period of time I was working at Sarazan I got to know several of the employees quite well. Among these was a fellow named Stan who had been with the company for about seven years. When Stan first started he drove a chisel (fork-lift truck) for approximately a year, but had spent the rest of his time with the company as a stock clerk. In this job he

---

* From Robert E. C. Wegner and Leonard Sayles, *Cases in Organizational and Administrative Behavior,* © 1972. Reprinted by permission of Prentice-Hall, Inc., Englewood Cliffs, N.J.

checked incoming stock, prepared production orders, and brought stock to the elevator for delivery to the appropriate department.

His method of handling day-to-day activities was quite simple — and he did his job exceedingly well. The production orders were given to him from the production control office. These orders were always for a specific period of time, usually several days. On the given date for a particular order Stan assembled the materials and delivered them to the various departments. On the rare occasions when a foreman came to the stock room to request some specific material, Stan had them fill in the necessary forms. After he checked out his supply, he called the particular foreman and informed him of how much of what he wanted was available and indicated to the foreman when he would be able to deliver it. Stan felt himself in control of his daily activities, and had the reputation of a very energetic and efficient worker. He was happy and easygoing, and it was a pleasure to deal with him.

As the new plant neared completion, it was learned that additional drivers would be needed to move materials in the new factory. Since Stan had retained his driver's rating, he was sent to Lexington as a driver. This was at the beginning of my third week of employment. One week later I also was transferred to the new plant. When I arrived, I found that there were four chisels, one in shipping and receiving, and the other three under the stock-room foreman's supervision. These three chisels were responsible for (1) moving stock to and between work areas, and (2) arranging stock and stacking pallets in the stock area.

Stan was driving one of these chisels, which was smaller than the other two and could turn in the aisles. Since his truck was also capable of reaching higher than any of the others, he was called on to do odd jobs that could not be done by others.

In his new job Stan was supposed to receive orders only from his boss, the stock-room foreman. But, because of the rush nature of the work on the new plant, Stan often received orders from many other people. While driving through the plant, going to or coming from a particular job, it was not unusual for another worker or foreman to stop him and request that he move something. At the beginning, Stan usually acceded to their wishes even though it often cut into his schedule. As a result of this, Stan was often bawled out by his supervisor for not getting back on schedule from a given job.

When Stan tried to explain the situation, his supervisor said, "Well, who do you think you're working for anyway, me — or those other guys in the plant. You do what I say, and nothing more." After this, Stan would not do the various odd jobs the other foremen requested of him. This often caused conflict with these foremen, for they thought Stan was trying to sabotage their efforts to get their jobs done. When Stan tried to explain what his boss had told him, the other foremen would dismiss this by saying, "Yes, but our main job here is to get operations going as efficiently and as quickly as possible. You've got that special chisel, and you should be helping us no matter what your boss says!"

Despite all this, and knowing Stan's good nature, I had expected to find him relatively satisfied with his new job. After all, he was working at the new plant—which had more prestige than working at the old plant; he had an interesting job in that he was called on to do many different tasks; and because of the job change, his salary had been slightly raised.

To my surprise, however, I found that Stan was a totally different person than the fellow I had known at the old plant. He was sullen, uncooperative, and did less work than he had done as a stock clerk. He would often ignore a request to do a job; and if he did consent he was very impatient and reckless, often banging into things and dropping and damaging materials. He was continuously complaining and would readily associate himself with any group that was currently expressing dissatisfaction. His foreman indicated that unless Stan's behavior improved rapidly he would be dismissed.

John Higgins:*
An American Goes Native in Japan

In the fall of 1962, Mr. Leonard Prescott, vice president and general manager of the Weaver-Yamazaki Pharmaceutical Company Ltd. of Japan was considering what action, if any, to take regarding his executive assistant Mr. John Higgins. In Mr. Prescott's opinion, Mr. Higgins had been losing his effectiveness as one who was to represent the U.S. parent company because of his extraordinary identification with the Japanese culture.

The Weaver Pharmaceutical Company was one of the outstanding concerns in the drug field in the United States. As a result of extensive research it had developed many important drugs and its product lines were constantly improved, giving the company a strong competitive ad-

* Reprinted from *Stanford Business Cases* 1963, vol. 1 with the permission of the publishers, Stanford Graduate School of Business. Copyright © 1963 by the Board of Trustees of the Leland Stanford Junior University.

vantage. It also had extensive international operations throughout many parts of the world. Operations in Japan started in the early 1930s, though they were limited to sales activities. The Yamazaki Pharmaceutical House, a major producer of drugs and chemicals in Japan was the franchise distributor for Weaver's products in Japan.

Export sales to Japan were resumed in 1948. Due to its product superiority and the inability of major Japanese pharmaceutical houses to compete effectively because of lack of recovery from war damage, the Weaver Company was able to capture a substantial share of the market for its product categories. In order to prepare itself for increasingly keen competition from Japanese producers in the foreseeable future, the company decided to undertake local production of some of the product lines.

From its many years of international experience, the company had learned that it could not hope to establish itself firmly in a foreign country until it began manufacturing locally. Consequently, in 1953 the company began its preliminary negotiations with the Yamazaki Company Ltd., which culminated in the establishment of a jointly owned and operated manufacturing subsidiary. The company, known as the Yamazaki-Weaver Pharmaceutical Co. Ltd. of Japan, was officially organized in the summer of 1954.

Initially, the new company only manufactured a limited line of products. However through the combined effort of both parent companies, the subsidiary soon began to manufacture sufficiently broad lines of products to fill the general demands of the Japanese market. For the last several years, importation from the United States had been limited to highly specialized items.

The company did a substantial amount of research and development work on its own, though it was coordinated through a committee set up by the representatives of both parent companies to avoid unnecessary duplication of research effort. The R&D group at the subsidiary had turned out a substantial number of new products, some of which were marketed successfully in the United States and elsewhere.

The management of the Weaver Company looked upon the Japanese operations as one of the most successful international ventures it had undertaken. It felt that the future prospect looked quite promising with steady improvement in the standard of living in Japan.

The subsidiary was headed by Mr. Shozo Suzuki, as president and Mr. Leonard Prescott as executive vice president. Since Mr. Suzuki was executive vice president of the parent company and also was president of several other subsidiaries, his participation in the company was limited to determination of basic policies. Day to day operations were managed by Mr. Prescott as executive vice president and general manager. He had an American executive assistant, Mr. Higgins, and several Japanese directors who assisted him in various phases of the operations. Though several other Americans were assigned to the Japanese ventures, they were primarily concerned with research and development and held no overall management responsibilities.

The Weaver Company had a policy of moving American personnel around from one foreign post to another with occasional tours of duty in the international division of the home office. The period they spent in a country generally ranged from three to five years. Since there were only a limited number of Americans working in the international operations of the company, the personnel policy was rather flexible. For example, it frequently allowed a man to stay in a country for an indefinite period of time, if he desired to. As a result of this policy, there were, though few in number, those Americans who had stayed in one foreign post over ten years.

The working relationship with the Japanese executives had been generally satisfactory, though there had been a number of minor irritations, which the companies believed were to be expected from any joint venture. The representatives of both parent companies were well aware of these pitfalls and tried to work out solutions to these problems amicably.

Mr. Leonard Prescott arrived in Japan in 1960 to replace Mr. Richard Densely who had been in Japan since 1954. Mr. Prescott had been described as an "old hand" at international work, having spent most of his 25 year career with the company in its international work. He had served in India, the Philippines and Mexico prior to coming to Japan. He had also spent several years in the international division of the company in New York. He was delighted with the challenge to expand further the Japanese operations. After two years of experience in Japan, he was pleased with the progress the company had made and felt a certain sense of accomplishment in developing a smooth functioning organization.

He became concerned, however, with the notable changes in Mr. Higgins' attitude and thinking. Mr. Higgins, in the opinion of Mr. Prescott, had absorbed and internalized the Japanese culture to such a point where he had lost the United States point of view and orientation. He had "gone native," so to speak, in Japan which resulted in a substantial loss of his administrative effectiveness as a bi-cultural and lingual executive assistant.

Mr. Higgins was born in a small Midwestern town. After completing his high school education there in 1950, he went on to attend a large state university nearby, where he planned to major in accounting. During his junior year at college, he was drafted into the Army. After his basic training, he was given an opportunity to attend the Army Language School for an intensive training in a foreign language, providing that we would extend his period of enlistment for another year. Since he had taken much interest in foreign languages, primarily German and Spanish during his high school and college days, he decided to volunteer for this assignment, knowing that the Army would decide the language for him to study. He was enrolled in a Japanese language section with several others. After fifteen months of intensive training in the language, he was assigned as an interpreter and translator to the Intelligence Detachment in Tokyo.

Shortly after he arrived in Tokyo, he was selected to do more intensive work with Japanese and he attended an advanced course emphasizing reading and writing. By the time he completed the program, he was able to read newspapers, and political and economic journals of a fairly sophisticated level. His assignment at the Intelligence unit consisted primarily of going over Japanese newspapers and periodicals and translating those parts which were of interest to the United States Army. While he was in Japan, he took evening courses in the Japanese language, literature and history at a well-known Japanese university in Tokyo. At the same time, he acquired many Japanese friends whom he visited quite frequently in his off-duty time. He thoroughly fell in love with the Japanese culture and determined to return to live in Japan for some time.

Immediately upon his release from the Armed Forces in 1957, he returned to college to resume his education. Though he had thought seriously about majoring in Japanese, upon close examination, he decided against it for several reasons. First of all, he felt that majoring in the language would limit his career to teaching or to specialized forms of government service, neither of which he wanted. Secondly, this would mean many more years of intensive graduate study leading to a terminal degree. Finally, he was desirous of using the language as a means rather than as an end in itself. For these reasons, he decided to finish his college work in business management.

In 1958 he graduated from the university with honor and took a position as a management trainee with the International Division of the Weaver Pharmaceutical Company. The company had a policy of assigning new international trainees to domestic operations for a period of six months to get them acquainted with the overall company operations. They then were given six months to a year training at the international division of the company in New York prior to an assignment overseas. In the fall of 1959, Mr. Higgins, having successfully completed both of the training programs, was assigned to the Japanese operations as executive assistant to the general manager, Mr. Richard Densely.

He was pleased with his first overseas assignment. He was anxious to return to Japan not only because of his interest in the Japanese language and culture, but also for the opportunity to do something about improving the "Ugly American" image many Americans had created in Japan.

Because of his ability of the language and his intense interest in Japan he was able to assess the attitude toward the United States of far broader segments of the Japanese population than was possible for many. He noted that Americans had a tendency of imposing their value systems, ideals and thinking patterns upon the Japanese, because many of them were under the illusion that anything American was universally right and applicable. They did not, in his opinion, show much desire to understand and appreciate the finer points of the Japanese culture. Generally their adaptations to the Japanese culture did not go beyond developing a taste for a few typical Japanese dishes or learning a few simple Japanese sentences. He had felt indignant on numerous occasions over the inconsiderate attitudes of many Americans he had observed in Japan and was determined to do something about it.

His responsibilities as executive assistant under Mr. Densely covered a wide scope of activities ranging from trouble shooting with major Japanese customers, attending trade meetings, negotiating with the government officials, conducting marketing research projects and helping out Mr. Densely in day to day administration of the firm. Mr. Densely was well pleased with Mr. Higgins' performance and relied heavily upon his judgment because of his keen insight into Japan.

When Mr. Prescott took over the Japanese operations in 1960, he found Mr. Higgins' assistance indispensable in many aspects of the operations. For the next two years, he depended much upon Mr. Higgins' advice on many difficult and complex administrative and organizational problems. Mr. Prescott found him to be a capable administrative assistant and staff member.

However, Mr. Prescott began to note a gradual change in Mr. Higgins' basic values and attitude. Mr. Higgins, in Mr. Prescott's opinion, had become critical of the company's policy in managing the Japanese operations and Prescott became increasingly apprehensive of his effectiveness as an executive assistant. He attributed this change to his complete emotional involvement with the Japanese culture, with a consequent loss of objectivity and identification with the U.S. point of view. Mr. Prescott mentally listed a few examples to describe what he meant by Higgins' "complete emotional involvement" with the culture.

In the summer of 1961, Mr. Higgins married a Japanese girl whom he had met shortly after he returned to Japan. His wife was an extremely attractive and intelligent woman by any standard. She had been graduated from the most prominent women's college in Japan and had studied at a well-known Eastern university in the United States for a brief period of time. Shortly after their marriage, Mr. Higgins filed a request through Mr. Prescott with the personnel director of International Division in New York, asking to extend his stay in Japan for an indefinite period of time. The personnel director approved the request upon consultation with both Mr. Densely and Mr. Prescott. Mr. Prescott noted that marriage was a big turning point for Mr. Higgins. Until that time, he was merely interested in the Japanese culture in an intellectual sense, but since his marriage he was observed to have developed a real emotional involvement with it.

He and his wife rented an apartment in a strictly Japanese neighborhood and he was often seen relaxed in his Japanese kimono at home. He was also observed to use the public bath, a well-known Japanese institution. His fluent Japanese combined with a likeable personality and interest in the Japanese culture won him many friends in the neighborhood. Everyone, including small children greeted him with a big smile and friendly gestures addressing him as "Higgins-san" whenever they saw him.

His mode of living was almost entirely that of a typical Japanese. He seemed to have completely integrated himself with Japanese life. He was invited to weddings, neighborhood parties and even to Buddhist funerals. On these occasions, he participated actively and fulfilled whatever part was required by the customs and traditions.

The Weaver Pharmaceutical Company had a policy of granting two months home leave every two years with transportation paid for the employee and his family. When Mr. Higgins' turn came, he declined to go home even on vacation on the ground that his parents were already dead and his brothers and sisters were widely scattered throughout the United States. Consequently, he did not feel he had any home ties in the United States. He and his wife took his two months leave and visited many of the remote historical sites throughout Japan.

None of these points by itself disturbed Mr. Prescott greatly. However, he was afraid that accumulations of these seemingly insignificant factors would tend to distort Higgins' cultural orientation and identification, thereby losing his effectiveness as a bi-lingual and cultural representative of the American parent company. In administrative relationships, there have recently been a number of incidents which tended to support Mr. Prescott's anxiety over his attitude. A few of the specific examples were these.

In performing his responsibilities as executive assistant Higgins had taken on many of the characteristics of a typical Japanese executive. For example, Mr. Higgins was reported to spend a great deal of time in listening to the personal problems of his subordinates. He maintained close social relationships with many of the men in the organization and he and his wife took an active interest in the personal lives of the employees. They even had gone as far as arranging marriages for some of the young employees.

Consequently, many of the employees sought Mr. Higgins' attention to register their complaints and demands with the management. For example, recently a group of middle management personnel approached Mr. Higgins concerning the desirability of more liberal fringe benefits. These were particularly in the areas of company-sponsored recreational activities such as occasional out-of-town trips and the acquisition of rest houses at resort areas.

On another occasion, the middle management personnel registered their objections concerning a recent company policy of promoting personnel based upon merit rather than length of service and education, the two most important criteria in traditional Japanese approach. Shortly after Mr. Prescott took over the Japanese operations, he was appalled with Japanese promotion practices and decided to change these to a merit system. In the process, he consulted with Mr. Higgins as to its applicability in Japan.

The latter objected to the idea, saying that the Japanese were not quite ready to accept what he considered a radical approach. Since Mr. Prescott did not see it as a radical concept, he went ahead and announced the policy. At the same time, he installed an annual review system, whereby every one of the management personnel would be evaluated by his immediate superior and this would constitute an important basis for promotion.

The Japanese objections were primarily based upon the ground that their traditional personnel practices were so different from those of the United States, that a mechanical imposition of the U.S. method would not work in Japan. The system, had as Higgins expected, created many undesirable problems. The Japanese group contended that Mr. Prescott, not understanding the language, was not aware of the magnitude of the anxiety and insecurity the policy had caused. Because of the traditional superior-subordinate relationship characterized by distance, fear, and obedience, they were not willing to take these problems directly to Mr. Prescott. Therefore they asked Mr. Higgins to intercede on their behalf by reporting their feelings to Mr. Prescott.

Mr. Prescott felt that though it was helpful to have Mr. Higgins report back to him the feelings and opinions of the middle management personnel, which otherwise might never come to his attention, he did not appreciate the latter's attitude in so doing. In these cases, Mr. Higgins' sympathy was with the Japanese group and he usually insisted that these demands were reasonable and well justified, according to the Japanese standard and traditions. Mr. Prescott found it necessary to deal with Mr. Higgins on these demands instead of being able to work with him as it had been in the past. His perception had been so colored that Mr. Prescott became hesitant to ask Mr. Higgins' opinions on these matters. Lately, whenever Mr. Prescott proposed a change in administrative procedures which might be contrary to Japanese traditions or culture, Mr. Higgins invariably raised objections. In Mr. Prescott's thinking, there were dynamic changes taking place in traditional Japanese customs and culture and he was confident that many of the points Mr. Higgins objected to were not tied to the cultural patterns as rigidly as he thought they might have been. Besides, Mr. Prescott thought that there was no point for a progressive American company to copy the local customs and felt that its real contribution to the Japanese society was in bringing in new ideas and innovations.

To substantiate this point, he learned that some of his Japanese subordinates were much more susceptible to new ideas and were willing to try them out than Mr. Higgins. This fact has convinced Mr. Prescott that Mr. Higgins was too closely and overly identified with the traditional pattern of the Japanese culture, not sensing the new and radically different development taking place in Japan.

Moreover, two recent incidents raised some doubts in Mr. Prescott's mind as to the soundness of Mr. Higgins' judgment, which he, heretofore, had never questioned. The first incident was in connection with the dismissal of Mr. Nomogaki, chief of subsection in the Purchasing Department. In the opinion of Mr. Prescott, Mr. Nomogaki lacked initiative, leadership and general competency. After two years of continued prodding by his superiors including Mr. Prescott himself, he has shown little interest, if any, in self-improvement. As a result, Prescott had decided to dismiss him from the organization. Both Higgins and Takahinshi, personnel manager of the subsidiary, objected vigorously on the ground that this had never been done in the company. Besides, in Japan the management was required to live with a certain amount of incompetent executives as long as their honesty and loyalty were not questioned. They further claimed that the company was partially responsible for recruiting him initially and had kept him on for the last ten years without spotting his incompetency, thus it was not completely fair to require Mr. Nomogaki alone to take the full burden. Mr. Prescott, unimpressed by their arguments, dismissed him after serving proper notice.

A few weeks later, Mr. Prescott learned quite accidentally that Mr. Nomogaki was re-employed by one of the other subsidiaries of the Japanese parent company, the Yamazaki Pharmaceutical Co. Ltd. Upon investigation, he found, to his surprise that Messrs. Higgins and Takahinshi had interceded and arranged for him to be taken back without informing Mr. Prescott. For understandable reasons, Mr. Prescott did not appreciate their action and confronted Mr. Higgins with this, who in turn told Mr. Prescott that he had done that which was expected of a superior in any Japanese company.

Another incident was in connection with his relationship with the government. In Japan, the government plays a substantially greater part in business and economic activities than it does in the United States. It is important for companies to maintain a good working relationship with government officials of those agencies which have control over their activities. This is particularly true of foreign subsidiaries. Because of many complicated intricacies, government relations had been entrusted to Mr. Higgins and his two Japanese assistants.

Mr. Prescott had observed a basic difference in the view with which he and Higgins looked upon practices of this sort. Prescott, knowing the differences in business ethics in various countries, accepted some of these activities as a necessary evil but felt that they had to be kept to the minimum in order to preserve the overall integrity of the company. Whereas Mr. Prescott felt, Mr. Higgins had become a willing participant in the system without much reservation or restraint.

Mr. Prescott believed these problems to be quite serious. Mr. Higgins had been an effective as well as efficient executive assistant and his knowledge of the language and the people had proved invaluable. On numerous occasions, his American friends envied Prescott for having a man of his qualifications as an assistant. He also knew that Mr. Higgins had received several outstanding offers to go with other American companies in Japan.

Prescott felt that Higgins would be far more effective could he take a more emotionally detached attitude toward the Japanese people and culture. In Mr. Prescott's view, the best international executive was the one who retained a belief in the fundamentals of the U.S. point of view while also understanding foreign attitudes. This understanding, of course, should be thorough or even instinctive, but it also should be objective, characterized neither by disdain nor by strong emotional attachment.

He was wondering how he could best assist Mr. Higgins to see his point of view, so that they could collaborate more effectively in fulfilling their administrative responsibilities.

Discussion Questions

1. What are the significant characteristics of Mr. Higgins' attitude? Of Mr. Prescott's attitude?
2. What do you think are the underlying causes for changes in Mr. Higgins' attitude?
3. Do you agree with Mr. Prescott's definition of an "effective" international executive? How would you go about developing a man of these qualities?
4. What objectives should Mr. Prescott have in working with Mr. Higgins?
5. What actions should Mr. Prescott take?

Laird's Lament

MY NAME is Jenny Barker and I want to tell you about an experience I had working as a waitress my senior year in high school.

I was 16 at the time and decided, in early September, to get a job because I had nothing to do and all my friends were working. When I saw an ad in the paper, placed by a restaurant that was within walking distance of my home, I decided to apply there.

The place was called Laird's Steak House, and was a small, quality restaurant. It was owned and operated by Mrs. Martinelli (Mrs. M), aided by her son, Bob, his wife Alice, Mrs. M's daughter Marie and occasionally Marie's husband, Victor. Victor usually managed a larger family restaurant in the next town and only dropped in occasionally. Bob acted as host and fill-in cook, while Alice, Marie and Mrs. M took turns hosting.

When I applied for the job, I had to talk to Bob and Alice as well as Mrs. M. Mrs. M struck me as grumpy, but artificially sweet to the customers. She made a big point about being nice to the customers, and also kept emphasizing cleanliness. When I finally got the job, she didn't give me any other instructions. She just gave me the menu and told me to memorize it, completely.

Bob and Alice actually did most of the interviewing. At first I didn't think I had much of a chance at the job. They kept talking about the fact that I was too young to serve beer, and that they were reluctant to hire me because of that fact. Eventually, I got the job because, as they said, they really needed someone. They said they would call me each week whenever they needed me.

I must say, I didn't feel very welcomed at Laird's right from that interview on. Mrs. M made me feel like an intruder in her family, and obviously favored the other waitresses who had worked there for several years.

The staff consisted of a night and day dishwasher, two cooks who rotated day and night shifts, and nine waitresses. The waitresses were: (1) Sally, a young wife; (2) Becky, a girl three years my senior whom I had known vaguely most of my life as a popular upperclassman (she was voted prettiest in her graduating class); (3) Shelly, Becky's friend, an attractive blonde; (4) Susan, a 23 year old who was the most experienced and best waitress of the bunch and (5) Dot, a middle-aged mother who seldom worked nights. There were two other day-time waitresses whom I never met.

All of these girls were attractive and seemed to me to put on airs, flirting with the customers and trying to act very sophisticated. I felt rather artless by comparison; Susan even nicknamed me "kid." Having worked at Laird's for several years, they all knew the routine by habit and had developed a close relationship among themselves. In addition, they sometimes worked for Victor in the larger restaurant and had a close social relationship with Bob, Marie, Alice, and Victor, going to the same weddings, and so forth. Susan was the most respected and the informal leader of the group, while Marie was glamorous, outgoing and often talked with customers while they waited for meals.

The group did a lot of fooling around with one another and even kidded openly with Bob, Alice, and Marie. They were encouraging and friendly with Nancy, Susan's sister (who was also a high school senior in training as a waitress), but seemed snobby and insincere toward me. I didn't make friendships with any of them while I was there. I would sometimes stand near them when several were talking, but they never drew me into the conversation. Once in a while I'd try to start a conversation myself, but I never got very far. Their outside interests seemed different than mine. Also, with some, I couldn't even say, "did you have a nice weekend?" I felt that they would think, "what is this punk up to."

I felt like an outsider from the beginning and that never really changed. It's funny, because I'm a person who likes to please others and I'm always able to fit in with groups. In school, I'm seen as talkative, aggressive and something of a leader. The only other time something like this ever happened to me was when I joined the cheerleader squad. That was a group with a lot of status in my school, and when I joined them I sort of held back and was quiet at first.

One of the things that the waitresses did was to stand back of the counter together smoking cigarettes whenever there was a free minute. I didn't smoke, so I worked during my free minutes for lack of anything better to do. Besides, I didn't feel free to take breaks since I was new and couldn't feel as sure of my job as they did. My attempts at joking with Bob or Marie seemed feeble and formal. I always felt they compared me with Becky, and Shelly or even Nancy who was older looking than I was and much like Susan in appearance and personality.

Mrs. M watched me closely. She seemed cold and critical, which made me feel even younger and more inexperienced compared to the others. Otherwise she ignored me as a person. Her only comments were complaints which she'd pass on through Bob. She did comment favorably on Becky's smile, Susan's efficiency, and Shelly's popularity with the customers, but she never complimented me. I know I did a good job because Marie revealed several times that the clientele was pleased with me, too. Mrs. M's slight criticisms ("wipe that up") and attitude made me feel further degraded. Though I did my work well, the only encouragement I got were remarks like "Busy night, good job," from Marie as she sped by. Being the youngest and newest and not part of the clique, I felt on the bottom of the totem pole.

As time passed, I decided that the group was closely knit and found it easier to make no effort to exert myself to become a part of it. My relations were formal. I would go to work at 4:30, set up, wait for the people to pour in and busy myself doing the best job possible. The customers seemed satisfied and pleased with me and I enjoyed the interaction with the public. I felt relaxed and outgoing with the customers, many of whom were regulars. Though my salary was $1.30/hour, I averaged $10 to $15 per night in tips working for 5 hours.

There were two shifts to the job—11 to 3:30 (which I never did) and 4:30 to 9:30. From 3:30 to 4:30 the restaurant closed to prepare for the dinner crowd. At 4:30 I was required to go to the back room, put the salad-dressing buckets on ice, get rolls, salads, silverware and coffee ready. I always worked the back section, which had booths and was the last to be filled with customers (see Exhibit 1). The coffee machine was located in the back and was an added responsibility for me. Since Susan handled the section with tables next to my section, I helped her with salads and soda when she was busy. She, in turn, served beer to my customers for me. Otherwise there was little interaction between waitresses. The waitress in front operated from her section alone. Each waitress was required to give her order to the cook and while the order was prepared,

EXHIBIT 1
Laird's Steak House Floor Plan

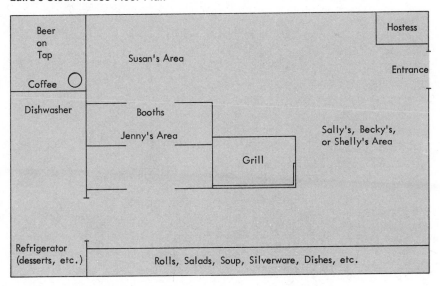

served salad, rolls, and beverages. The cook prepared the order over an open charcoal grill, then called our names out.

One thing I noticed was that Susan was more friendly than the others. She was nice to me when we were alone. When we were with the others, she would ignore me and make no effort to include me in the conversation. She seemed to be more interested in the topics the others wanted to talk about.

One cook was a middle-aged family man and the other a young Puerto Rican named Reggie. The former was friendly and fatherly, but Reggie was temperamental and derogatory. He often reprimanded me harshly in front of everyone, saying that he could not read my writing. One night he played a practical joke in the backroom by sticking spaghetti up his nose, which I felt in *very* poor taste, not in keeping with Laird's standards. I found Reggie to be immature, yet his remarks often upset me ("Christ, you're dumb and ugly"). Nevertheless, he never showed his worst side to Mrs. M, and frequently talked about "the old lady" behind her back.

The night dishwasher, a young black named Bill, with a wife and two children, was relatively new on the job. He and I became good friends and in my spare time I talked with him. One day Mrs. M came in the dishroom and reprimanded me harshly, saying I looked cheap talking to Bill. This particularly bothered me because no customers were in the restaurant and they could not have seen me if they were. To me, the girls looked more "cheap" smoking together at the back counter within sight of customers, but I said nothing. This seemed to confirm Mrs. M's attitude toward me. Her dislike of me and the superiority of the experienced older girls was a threat to my sense of adequacy. Their smoking really bothered me!

While the other girls seemed to be having fun and seemed satisfied, I felt excluded and unhappy. I often was pressured to work weekends because the other girls did not want to; this made me feel "stuck" doubly, because whenever they wanted a night off, I was expected to fill in. Their lack of appreciation made me feel even more inferior, even though I usually didn't mind working weekends. The weekends generally were busy, went quickly and tips were especially good. Nevertheless, I still felt extremely tense under Mrs. M's watchful eye and was never quite sure what Bob, Alice, or Marie actually thought of me. Our relationships were formal and limited to, "hello, how are you?" I often felt flustered when Reggie needled me, but I always got my job done.

On two consecutive weekends in February I had to go away. I was quite worried since I had never asked for time off, even though the other girls often did so. After several days of pondering, Mrs. M and Bob consented. I wondered how they felt about this, whether they thought I was taking advantage of them or what. They must have been irritated because after the second weekend, they never called me to come into work again.

I suppose I could have called and asked, but I didn't know who was supposed to, so I didn't. . . .

Well, that's the story. I respected that gang because they were attractive, popular girls, but I sure didn't like the way they worked. They certainly were less than conscientious about keeping things clean, despite Mrs. M's making such a big thing about it. But at least I fulfilled my responsibilities; I get a better feeling when I act in a responsible manner. I didn't treat Mrs. M discourteously the way they did, talking about her behind her back when she was so nice to them! That seems unfair! But, it was rough to feel so unwelcomed and to always be the outsider.

Discussion Questions

1. What factors contributed to the situation experienced by Jenny?
2. How does she see herself?
3. How do others see her?
4. What could she have done to make the situation more satisfying to herself?
5. How would you explain Susan's behavior when alone with Jenny?

*Larry Ross**

THE CORPORATION is a jungle. It's exciting. You're thrown in on your own and you're constantly battling to survive. When you learn to survive, the game is to become the conqueror, the leader.

"I've been called a business consultant. Some say I'm a business psychiatrist. You can describe me as an advisor to top management in a corporation." He's been at it since 1968.

I started in the corporate world, oh gosh — '42. After kicking around in the Depression, having all kinds of jobs and no formal education, I wasn't equipped to become an engineer, a lawyer, or a doctor. I gravitated to selling. Now they call it marketing. I grew up in various corporations. I

* From S. Terkel, *Working.* Copyright © 1972, 1974 by Studs Terkel. Reprinted by permission of Pantheon Books, a division of Random House, Inc.

became the executive vice president of a large corporation and then of an even larger one. Before I quit I became president and chief executive officer of another. All nationally known companies.

Sixty-eight, we sold out our corporation. There was enough money in the transaction where I didn't have to go back in business. I decided that I wasn't going to get involved in the corporate battle any more. It lost its excitement, its appeal. People often ask me, "Why weren't you in your own business? You'd probably have made a lot of money." I often ask it myself, I can't explain it, except . . .

Most corporations I've been in, they were on the New York Stock Exchange with thousands and thousands of stockholders. The last one — whereas, I was the president and chief executive, I was always subject to the board of directors, who had pressure from the stockholders. I owned a portion of the business, but I wasn't in control. I don't know of any situation in the corporate world where an executive is completely free and sure of his job from moment to moment.

Corporations always have to be right. That's their face to the public. When things go bad, they have to protect themselves and fire somebody. "We had nothing to do with it. We had an executive that just screwed everything up." He's never really ever been his own boss.

The danger starts as soon as you become a district manager. You have men working for you and you have a boss above. You're caught in a squeeze. The squeeze progresses from station to station. I'll tell you what a squeeze is. You have the guys working for you that are shooting for your job. The guy you're working for is scared stiff you're gonna shove him out of his job. Everybody goes around and says, "The test of the true executive is that you have men working for you that can replace you, so you can move up." That's a lot of boloney. The manager is afraid of the bright young guy coming up.

Fear is always prevalent in the corporate structure. Even if you're a top man, even if you're hard, even if you do your job — by the slight flick of a finger, your boss can fire you. There's always the insecurity. You bungle a job. You're fearful of losing a big customer. You're fearful so many things will appear on your record, stand against you. You're always fearful of the big mistake. You've got to be careful when you go to corporation parties. Your wife, your children have to behave properly. You've got to fit in the mold. You've got to be on guard.

When I was president of this big corporation, we lived in a small Ohio town, where the main plant was located. The corporation specified who you could socialize with, and on what level. (His wife interjects: "Who were the wives you could play bridge with.") The president's wife could do what she wants, as long as it's with dignity and grace. In a small town they didn't have to keep check on you. Everybody knew. There are certain sets of rules.

Not every corporation has that. The older the corporation, the longer it's been in a powerful position, the more rigid, the more conservative they are in their approach. Your swinging corporations are generally the new ones, the upstarts, the *nouveau riche*. But as they get older, like duPont, General Motors, General Electric, they became more rigid. I'd compare them to the old, old rich—the Rockefellers and the Mellons—that train their children how to handle money, how to conserve their money, and how to grow with their money. That's what happened to the older corporations. It's only when they get in trouble that they'll have a young upstart of a president come in and try to shake things up.

The executive is a lonely animal in the jungle who doesn't have a friend. Business is related to life. I think in our everyday living we're lonely. I have only a wife to talk to, but beyond that . . . When I talked business to her, I don't know whether she understood me. But that was unimportant. What's important is that I was able to talk out loud and hear myself—which is the function I serve as a consultant.

The executive who calls me usually knows the answer to his problem. He just has to have somebody to talk to and hear his decision out loud. If it sounds good when he speaks it out loud, then it's pretty good. As he's talking, he may suddenly realize his errors and he corrects them out loud. That's a great benefit wives provide for executives. She's listening and you know she's on your side. She's not gonna hurt you.

Gossip and rumor are always prevalent in a corporation. There's absolutely no secrets. I have always felt every office was wired. You come out of the board meeting and people in the office already know what's happened. I've tried many times to track down a rumor, but never could. I think people have been there so many years and have developed an ability to read reactions. From these reactions they make a good, educated guess. Gossip actually develops into fact.

It used to be a ploy for many minor executives to gain some information. "I heard that the district manager of California is being transferred to Seattle." He knows there's been talk going on about changing district managers. By using this ploy—"I know something"—he's making it clear to the person he's talking to that he's been in on it all along. So it's all right to tell him. Gossip is another way of building up importance within a person who starts the rumor. He's in, he's part of the inner circle. Again, we're back in the jungle. Every ploy, every trick is used to survive.

When you're gonna merge with a company or acquire another company, it's supposed to be top secret. You have to do something to stem the rumors because it might screw up the deal. Talk of the merger, the whole place is in a turmoil. It's like somebody saying there's a bomb in the building and we don't know where it is and when it's going to go off. There've been so many mergers where top executives are laid off, the accounting department is cut by sixty percent, the manufacturing is cut by twenty percent. I have yet to find anybody in a corporation who was so secure to honestly believe it couldn't happen to him.

They put on a front: "Oh, it can't happen to me. I'm too important." But deep down, they're scared stiff. The fear is there. You can smell it. You can see it on their faces. I'm not so sure you couldn't see it on my face many, many times during my climb up.

I always used to say—rough, tough Larry—I always said, "If you do a good job, I'll give you a great reward. You'll keep your job." I'll have a sales contest and the men who make their quota will win a prize—they'll keep their jobs. I'm not saying there aren't executives who instill fear in their people. He's no different than anybody walking down the street. We're all subject to the same damn insecurities and neuroses—at every level. Competitiveness, that's the basis of it.

Why didn't I stay in the corporate structure? As a kid, living through the Depression, you always heard about the tycoons, the men of power, the men of industry. And you kind of dream that. Gee, these are supermen. These are the guys that have no feeling, aren't subject to human emotions, the insecurities that everybody else has. You get in the corporate structure, you find they all button their pants the same way everybody else does. They all got the same fears.

The corporation is made up of many, many people. I call 'em the gray people and the black—or white—people. Blacks and white are definite colors, solid. Gray isn't. The gray people come there from nine to five, do their job, aren't particularly ambitious. There's no fear there, sure. But they're not subject to great demands. They're only subject to dismissal when business goes bad and they cut off people. They go from corporation to corporation and get jobs. Then you have the black—or white—people. The ambitious people, the leaders, the ones who want to get ahead.

When the individual reaches the vice presidency or he's general manager, you know he's an ambitious, dedicated guy who wants to get to the top. He isn't one of the gray people. He's one of the black-and-white vicious people—the leaders, the ones who stick out in the crowd.

As he struggles in this jungle, every position he's in, he's terribly lonely. He can't confide and talk with the guy working under him. He can't confide and talk to the man he's working for. To give vent to his feelings, his fears, and his insecurities, he'd expose himself. This goes all the way up the line until he gets to be president. The president *really* doesn't have anybody to talk to, because the vice presidents are waiting for him to die or make a mistake and get knocked off so they can get his job.

He can't talk to the board of directors, because to them he has to appear as a tower of strength, knowledge, and wisdom, and have the ability to walk on water. The board of directors, they're cold, they're hard. They don't have any direct-line responsibilities. They sit in a staff capacity and they really play God. They're interested in profits. They're interested in progress. They're interested in keeping a good face in the community—if it's profitable. You have the tremendous infighting of man against man for survival and clawing to the top. Progress.

We always saw signs of physical afflictions because of the stress and strain. Ulcers, violent headaches. I remember one of the giant corporations I was in, the chief executive officer ate Gelusil by the minute. That's for ulcers. Had a private dining room with his private chef. All he ever ate was well-done steak and well-done hamburgers.

There's one corporation chief I had who worked, conservatively, nineteen, twenty hours a day. His whole life was his business. And he demanded the same of his executives. There was nothing sacred in life except the business. Meetings might be called on Christmas Eve or New Year's Eve, Saturdays, Sundays. He was lonesome when he wasn't involved with his business. He was always creating situations where he could be surrounded by his flunkies, regardless of what level they were, presidential, vice presidential . . . It was his life.

In the corporate structure, the buck keeps passing up until it comes to the chief executive. Then there ain't nobody to pass the buck to. You sit there in your lonely office and finally you have to make a decision. It could involve a million dollars or hundreds of jobs or moving people from Los Angeles, which they love, to Detroit or Winnipeg. So you're sitting at the desk, playing God.

You say, "Money isn't important. You can make some bad decisions about money, that's not important. What is important is the decisions you make about people working for you, their livelihood, their lives." It isn't true.

To the board of directors, the dollars are as important as human lives. There's only yourself sitting there making the decision, and you hope it's right. You're always on guard. Did you ever see a jungle animal that wasn't on guard? You're always looking over your shoulder. You don't know who's following you.

The most stupid phrase anybody can use in business is loyalty. If a person is working for a corporation, he's supposed to be loyal. This corporation is paying him less than he could get somewhere else at a comparable job. It's stupid of him to hang around and say he's loyal. The only loyal people are the people who can't get a job anyplace else. Working in a corporation, in a business, isn't a game. It isn't a collegiate event. It's a question of living or dying. It's a question of eating or not eating. Who is he loyal to? It isn't his country. It isn't his religion. It isn't his political party. He's working for some company that's paying him a salary for what he's doing. The corporation is out to make money. The ambitious guy will say, "I'm doing my job. I'm not embarrassed taking my money.

I've got to progress and when I won't progress, I won't be here." The shnook is the loyal guy, because he can't get a job anyplace else.

Many corporations will hang on to a guy or promote him to a place where he doesn't belong. Suddenly, after the man's been there twenty-five years, he's outlived his usefulness. And he's too old to start all over again. That's part of the cruelty. You can't only condemn the corporation for that. The man himself should be smart enough and intuitive enough to know he isn't getting anyplace, to get the hell out and start all over. It was much more difficult at first to lay off a guy. But if you live in a jungle, you become hard, unfortunately.

When a top executive is let go, the king is dead, long live the king. Suddenly he's a persona non grata. When it happens, the shock is tremendous. Overnight. He doesn't know what hit him. Suddenly everybody in the organization walks away and shuns him because they don't want to be associated with him. In corporations, if you back the wrong guy, you're in his corner, and he's fired, you're guilty by association. So what a lot of corporations have done is when they call a guy in—sometimes they'll call him in on a Friday night and say. "Go home now and come in tomorrow morning and clean out your desk and leave. We don't want any farewells or anything. Just get up and get the hell out." It's done in nice language. We say. "Look, why cause any trouble? Why cause any unrest in the organization? It's best that you just fade away." Immediately his Cadillac is taken away from him. His phone extension on the WATS line is taken away from him.[1] All these things are done quietly and—bingo! he's dead. His phone at home stops ringing because the fear of association continues after the severance. The smell of death is there.

We hired a vice president. He came highly recommended. He was with us about six months and he was completely inadequate. A complete misfit. Called him in the office, told him he was gonna go, gave him a nice severance pay. He broke down and cried. "What did I do wrong? I've done a marvelous job. Please don't do this to me. My daughter's getting married next month. How am I going to face the people?" He cried and cried and cried. But we couldn't keep him around. We just had to let him go.

I was just involved with a gigantic corporation. They had a shake-up two Thursdays ago. It's now known as Black Thursday. Fifteen of twenty guys were let go overnight. The intelligent corporations say, "Clear, leave tonight, even if it's midweek. Come in Saturday morning and clean your desk. That's all. No good-bys or anything." They could be guys that have been there anywhere from a year to thirty years. If it's a successful operation, they're very generous. But then again, the human element creeps in.

---

[1] Wide area telecommunications service. A prerogative granted important executives by some corporations: unlimited use of the telephone to make a call anywhere in the world.

The boss might be vindictive and cut him off without anything. It may depend what the corporation wants to maintain as its image.

And what it does to the ego! A guy in a key position, everybody wants to talk to him. All his subordinates are trying to get an audience with him to build up their own positions. Customers are calling him, everybody is calling him. Now his phone's dead. He's sitting at home and nobody calls him. He goes out and starts visiting his friends, who are busy with their own business, who haven't got time for him. Suddenly he's a failure. Regardless what the reason was — regardless of the press release that said he resigned — he was fired.

The only time the guy isn't considered a failure is when he resigns and announces his new job. That's the tipoff. "John Smith resigned, future plans unknown" means he was fired. "John Smith resigned to accept the position of president of X Company" — then you know he resigned. This little nuance you recognize immediately when you're in corporate life.

Changes since '42? Today the computer is taking over the world. The computer exposes all. There's no more chance for shenanigans and phoniness. Generally the computer prints out the truth. Not a hundred percent, but enough. It's eliminated a great deal of the jungle infighting. There's more facts for the businessman to work from, if the computer gives him the right information. Sometimes it doesn't. They have a saying at IBM: "If you put garbage in the computer, you'll take garbage out." Business is becoming more scientific with regard to marketing, finance, investments. And much more impersonal.

But the warm personal touch *never* existed in corporations. That was just a sham. In the last analysis, you've got to make a profit. There's a lot of family-held corporations that truly felt they were part of a legend. They had responsibilities to their people. They carried on as best they could. And then they went broke. The loyalty to their people, their patriarchy, dragged 'em all down. Whatever few of 'em are left are being forced to sell, and are being taken over by the cold hand of the corporation.

My guess is that twenty corporations will control about forty percent of the consumer goods market. How much room is there left for the small guy? There's the supermarket in the grocery business. In our time, there were little mama-and-papa stores, thousands and thousands throughout the country. How many are there today? Unless you're National Tea or A&P, there's just no room. The small chains will be taken over by the bigger chains and they themselves will be taken over . . . The fish swallows the smaller fish and he's swallowed by a bigger one, until the biggest swallows 'em all. I have a feeling there'll always be room for the small entrepreneur, but he'll be rare. It'll be very difficult for him.

The top man is more of a general manager than he is an entrepreneur. There's less gambling than there was. He won't make as many mistakes as he did before in finance and marketing. It's a cold science. But when it comes to dealing with people, he still has to have that feel and he still has to do his own thinking. The computer can't do that for him.

When I broke in, no man could become an executive until he was thirty-five, thirty-six years old. During the past ten years there've been real top executives of twenty-six, twenty-seven. Lately there's been a reversal. These young ones climbed to the top when things were good, but during the last couple of years we've had some rough times. Companies have been clobbered and some have gone back to older men. But that's not gonna last.

Business is looking for the highly trained, highly skilled *young* executive, who has the knowledge and the education in a highly specialized field. It's happened in all professions and it's happening in business. You have your comptroller who's highly specialized. You have your treasurer who has to know finance, a heavily involved thing because of the taxation and the SEC. You have the manufacturing area. He has to be highly specialized in warehouse and in shipping—the ability to move merchandise cheaply and quickly. Shipping has become a horrendous problem because costs have become tremendous. You have to know marketing, the studies, the effect of advertising. A world of specialists. The man at the top has to have a general knowledge. And he has to have the knack of finding the right man to head these divisions. That's the difficulty.

You have a nice, plush lovely office to go to. You have a private secretary. You walk down the corridor and everybody bows and says, "Good morning, Mr. Ross. How are you today?" As you go up the line, the executives will say, "How is Mrs. Ross?" Until you get to the higher executives. They'll say, "How is Nancy?" Here you socialize, you know each other. Everybody plays the game.

A man wants to get to the top of the corporation, not for the money involved. After a certain point, how much more money can you make? In my climb, I'll be honest, money was secondary. Unless you have tremendous demands, yachts, private airplanes—you get to a certain point, money isn't that important. It's the power, the status, the prestige. Frankly, it's delightful to be on top and have everybody calling you Mr. Ross and have a plane at your disposal and a car and a driver at your disposal. When you come to town, there's people to take care of you. When you walk into a board meeting, everybody gets up and says hello. I don't think there's any human being that doesn't love that. It's a nice feeling. But the ultimate power is in the board of directors. I don't know anybody who's free. You read in the paper about stockholders' meetings, the annual report. It all sounds so glowing. But behind the scenes, a jungle.

I work on a yearly retainer with a corporation. I spend, oh, two, three days a month in various corporate structures. The key executives can talk to me and bounce things off me. The president may have a specific problem that I will investigate and come back to him with my ideas. The reason I came into this work is that all my corporate life I was looking for somebody like me, somebody who's been there. Because there's no new problems in business today. There's just a different name for different problems that have been going on for years and years and years. Nobody's come up yet with a problem that isn't familiar. I've been there.

Example. The chief executive isn't happy with the marketing structure. He raises many questions which I may not know specifically. I'll find out, and come back with a proposal. He might be thinking of promoting one of his executives. It's narrowed down to two or three. Let's say two young guys who've been moved to a new city. It's a tossup. I notice one has bought a new house, invested heavily in it. The other rented. I'd recommend the second. He's more realistic.

If he comes before his board of directors, there's always the vise. The poor sonofabitch is caught in the squeeze from the people below and the people above. When he comes to the board, he's got to come with a firm hand. I can help him because I'm completely objective. I'm out of the jungle. I don't have the trauma that I used to have when I had to fire somebody. What is it gonna do to this guy? I can give it to him cold and hard and logical. I'm not involved.

I left that world because suddenly the power and the status were empty. I'd been there, and when I got there it was nothing. Suddenly you have a feeling of little boys playing at business. Suddenly you have a feeling—so what? It started to happen to me, this feeling, oh, in '67, '68. So when the corporation was sold, my share of the sale was such . . . I didn't have to go back into the jungle. I don't have to fight to the top. I've been to the mountain top. (Laughs.) It isn't worth it.

It was very difficult, the transition of retiring from the status position, where there's people on the phone all day trying to talk to you. Suddenly nobody calls you. This is a psychological . . . (Halts, a long pause.) I don't want to get into that. Why didn't I retire completely? I really don't know. In the last four, five years, people have come to me with tempting offers. Suddenly I realized what I'm doing is much more fun than going into that jungle again. So I turned them down.

I've always wanted to be a teacher. I wanted to give back the knowledge I gained in corporate life. People have always told me I'd always been a great sales manager. In every sales group you always have two or three young men with stars in their eyes. They always sat at the edge of the chair. I knew they were comers. I always felt I could take 'em, develop 'em, and build 'em. A lot of old fogies like me—I can point out this guy, that guy who worked for me, and now he's the head of this, the head of that.

Yeah, I always wanted to teach. But I had no formal education and no university would touch me. I was willing to teach for nothing. But there also, they have their jungle. They don't want a businessman. They only want people in the academic world, who have a formalized and, I think, empty training. This is what I'd really like to do. I'd like to get involved with the young people and give my knowledge to them before it's buried with me. Not that what I have is so great, but there's a certain under- standing, a certain feeling . . .

Mega-Watt

MARTY was a graduate of a four-year college where he majored in in- dustrial engineering. Upon graduation, he accepted a position on a com- pany-wide training program with Mega-Watt, a large industrial equipment producer. The company was divided into several departments in several different geographic locations, and each department produced its own product. This program allowed him to view the operations of two different departments in two different locations before deciding on a permanent position with the company. The various work assignments included ex- posure to various work areas such as materials, control supervision, quality control, and engineering. Marty's job reviews were generally good. In fact, on his supervision assignment he was so well liked by his em- ployees that on his last day on the job they got together and gave him a farewell party even though he had had a part in the firing of one employee whose work he had diagnosed as inadequate. From Marty's perspective, too, that assignment had been a satisfying experience. He found that he enjoyed the role of supervisor, and felt reassurance from the fact that his own technical knowledge proved to be sufficient to allow him to accu- rately evaluate the employee's performance as a draftsman.

Upon graduation from the training program, he accepted a position as area supervisor (screw machine parts) in the Quality Control Section of the Switch and Gear Department. It was his job to maintain control over product quality in his area. His goal was to insure that the area did not ship substandard products and that the dollar loss due to producing bad products was minimal. He was, in theory, given complete authority to carry out the duties of his position.

The Quality Control Section of the Switch and Gear Department was a relatively new organization, having been instituted about three years prior to Marty's appointment. The Section manager, Marty's immediate supervisor, was John Sullivan. John, too, had been a graduate of the company's training program a number of years before. After several years experience in other Departments, he was appointed manager of the Quality Control Section when the section was first established. Due to various problems, including membership on a management committee concerned with maintaining the plant's nonunion status, John Sullivan had been able to give only limited attention to the screw machine area of the Section and the area had had only limited success. John expected Marty to make significant gains quickly so that the Quality Control Section would get a greater amount of recognition within the Department. John's supervisor, Edward Wilson, had hired Marty. This was company policy—any employee in an exempt salary position had to be hired and fired by an individual who was two levels higher than he on the management ladder. In spite of this formal arrangement, John had considerable influence on the employment status of his employees.

Each supervisor in the Quality Control Section had his own area of responsibility and one or more inspectors to help him obtain data on the condition of various manufacturing processes within that area. The data received from the inspectors, combined with a knowledge of statistical techniques, should enable the supervisor to perform his job effectively.

Socially the supervisors got along well with each other. They played cards together during lunch breaks. It was customary for any one of the supervisors to buy a round of coffee for the others. John Sullivan, however, was not involved socially with the supervisors—his office being somewhat removed from their work areas.

Marty's area of responsibility was the screw machine area which he took over from Jack Simms when Jack succeeded in getting a position in Engineering. The screw machine operators were highly skilled employees with considerable experience and longevity with the company. Their operating supervisor was Joe Nilson, whose boss was Adam Winn. (See Exhibit 1.)

Joe Nilson and Adam Winn were older men of extensive supervisory experience. They had both risen from the ranks, but supported management's efforts to make certain that the employees of Mega-Watt had no reason to embrace unionism.

The operation of the screw machine was such that once the machine was set up it would continue producing identical parts. During that time, the operators merely fed more raw materials into the loading tubes to keep the machine supplied. After a length of time, the machine tended to get out of adjustment. If the operator failed to check the output periodically several thousand bad parts could result.

Many different parts were produced on each machine. One of Joe Nilson's responsibilities was to schedule the work so that each machine was kept busy. Since the employees were paid on a piece rate incentive

EXHIBIT 1
Organizational Chart: Switch Gear Department

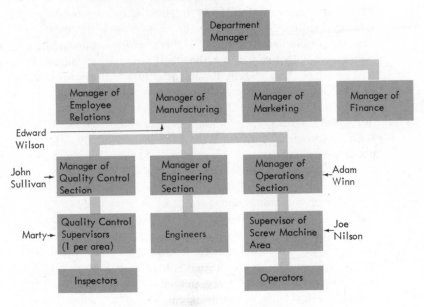

system for each piece produced, and since idle machines produced no saleable products, scheduling was an important function.

Marty had had one prior assignment in Quality Control for about six months, while he was on the training program. He was not, however, familiar with the operation of automatic screw machines. He was eager to embark on this new assignment. His job ratings had been good, and he considered his present position a "stepping stone" into management. Despite his inexperience, he appeared extremely self-confident in his ability to do a good job.

Marty was soon to find out, however, that the operators were not as eager as he to change their ways. Many of the suggestions Marty made to improve quality and reduce losses also tended to make extra work for the operators and slow down production somewhat. When Marty tried to exert his authority, he found that he met resistance from both Joe Nilson and Adam Winn.

Marty's boss, John Sullivan, sympathized with him, but insisted that he must make gains using diplomacy. For about a year and a half, Marty tried to improve the quality of the manufacturing processes using diplomacy with the operators and Joe Nilson. He made some gains, but they were neither significant enough nor fast enough to satisfy John Sullivan.

Marty became discouraged. His morale began to drop to that of the other Q.C. supervisors. He started looking for another job—first within the company, then on the outside. His job performance continued to be unacceptable. Edward Wilson began to pressure John Sullivan for results. John decided that something had to be done, but wondered what had gone wrong.

Metropolitan Steel Company*

IN SEPTEMBER 1945, Donald Roy obtained a job as a radial drill press operator in a machine shop of the Metropolitan Steel Company. About that time, Roy had a conversation with a friend, Orvis Collins, who was employed as a production worker in a nearby factory. Roy and Collins exchanged reports of their early work experiences. When they found that both their jobs were paid on a piecework basis, Collins told Roy about his introduction to piecework when he first started work:

ORVIS COLLINS: The shop superintendent told me that he considered it important to get in with the right people at the beginning and drew a folder out of his desk from which he read a poem about thinking. The title of the poem was something like "If We Only Think." The thesis of the poem was that if we give thought to each of our daily actions, we get along better with other people.

He then read an essay, "The Crooked Stick," which appeared to have been clipped from some advertising matter. The point of the essay was that there are crooked sticks in every woodpile, and that they are more trouble than they are worth. He said he thought it would be a good thing if we could find some way to make those people who are troublemakers see that being troublemakers is not to their own advantage.

He *then* explained the incentive system and said that it was a fair system because each man was paid with regard to the amount of work he did, and not simply for being on the job. He said if I worked hard, in a couple of months I would be earning $1.50 an hour. He added, however, that some people are not interested in giving their best to the company and therefore do not earn as much as some of the more unselfish ones.

---

* Reprinted from P. R. Lawrence, and J. A. Seiler, *Organizational Behavior and Administration,* rev. ed. (Homewood, Ill.: Richard D. Irwin, Inc., 1965) with permission of the publisher.

Collins then related to Roy a conversation he had had soon afterward with Bob, one of the workers at the factory:

BOB: Well, I suppose you've been up to see Heinzer [the superintendent]. Gosh, I remember when I went up to see him.

COLLINS: What did you talk about?

BOB: It was a hot August afternoon, and we all sat around there in a big circle. Heinzer did the talking. He just went on and on about the company, and what a good place the company is to work at, and how democratic it is here, and how everybody can talk to anybody he pleases about any gripe, and how he wanted to hear about it if there was anything we didn't like. He just went on and on.

COLLINS: What else?

BOB: He told us about how the piecework system was set up so that nobody could hang on anybody else's shirttail. He said it was every man for himself. He said: "You've got your friends, sure; but you're not going to give them anything unless they give you something in the way of a bargain in return."

He went on this way: "Now, say that you want to buy a suit, and you have a friend who is in the clothing business; you might go in and say: 'Look here, Ted, I'm looking for a suit, and I want to pay about $25 for it. What have you got?' Ted shows you what he has in stock, and you're pretty well satisfied with one for $30. You say: 'I'll come in Monday with the money, Ted,' and you go out. But while you're walking down the street, you see this other suit in the window. Just the same suit Ted offered you for $30, but this outfit only wants $25. All right, young man, which suit do you buy?"

Heinzer looked right at me, and I knew what he was getting at. So I thought for a minute and said: "I'd buy the $30 suit and lose the extra $5.00 if I could help a friend."

Heinzer didn't know what to say. He took off his straw hat and wiped his forehead with his handkerchief. Then he said: "But that isn't good business, young man."

I said: "When it comes to buying a suit from a friend or from some other fellow, I'll buy from a friend, and I don't care about business." (We knew we were both talking about piecework.)

Heinzer thought for a long time; then he said: "But that's not the way the world is run. Now, what would you do if you were walking down the street with your wife and met another fellow? And this friend was wearing a suit identical with the one you had on, and your wife was with you and his wife was with him, and your wife said to this fellow: 'Why, that's just like Bob's suit. How much did you pay for it?' And the fellow said: 'I paid $25 for it at such and such a store and bought my wife a new hat with the $5.00 I saved by not trading at our mutual friend's store.'" (He had fancy names for all these people worked out and everything, and you could tell he had been working up this story for a long time; but I'll bet this was the first time he had to use it this way.)

I said to Heinzer: "Whoa, just a minute; my wife wouldn't say such a thing. My wife isn't selfish. She would want me to do the right thing by my friend." That ended Heinzer's talk.

He just said: "I guess that'll be all for today, boys." As we walked out, he said to me: "That's all right, son. I like a man who can give a straight answer." Like heck he does. That was just some more psychology stuff. He took a course over at ———— University on psychology, and now everything is psychology to him. He thinks that this psychology bunk he learned is giving him a big advantage over guys who don't know it. Always trying to get the best of the other guy! They can take all the psychology in the world, and you know what they can do with it as far as I'm concerned, because there's nothing that can beat good, old-fashioned honesty.

Roy found that his own experiences were somewhat similar to Collins'. When Roy was hired, a personnel department clerk assured him that the radial drill operators were averaging $1.25 an hour on piecework. Since Roy had had no previous machine-shop experience, and since a machine would not be available for a few days, he was advised to spend some time watching Jack Starkey, a radial drillman with a great deal of seniority and skill.

One of Starkey's first questions was: "What have you been doing?" When Roy said he had worked in a Pacific Coast shipyard at a rate of pay over $1.00 an hour, Starkey exclaimed: "Then what are you doing in this place?" When Roy replied that averaging $1.25 an hour wasn't bad, Starkey exploded.

JACK STARKEY: Averaging, you say! Averaging?

DONALD ROY: Yeah, on the average. I'm an average guy, so I ought to make my buck and a quarter, that is, after I get on to it.

STARKEY *(angrily):*   Don't you know that $1.25 an hour is the *most* we can make, even when we *can* make more? And most of the time, we can't even make that. Have you ever worked on piecework before?

ROY: No.

STARKEY: I can see that! Well, what do you suppose would happen if I turned in $1.50 an hour on these pump bodies?

ROY: Turned in? You mean if you actually did the work?

STARKEY: I mean if I actually did the work and turned it in.

ROY: They'd have to pay you, wouldn't they? Isn't that the agreement?

STARKEY: Yes! They'd pay me — once. Don't you know that if I turned in $1.50 an hour on these pump bodies tonight, the whole damn methods department would be down here tomorrow? And they'd retime this job so quick it would make your head swim! And when they retimed it, they'd cut the price in half, and I'd be working for 85 cents an hour instead of $1.25!

It took a while for Roy to find out exactly what Starkey was talking about, but he learned a little more about what Starkey meant from Joe Mucha, the day man on his machine. Mucha shared Roy's job repertoire and kept a close eye on Roy's production. On November 14, the day after Roy first attained quota, Mucha advised: "Don't let it go over $1.25 an hour, or the time-study man will be right down here! And they don't waste time, either. They watch the records like hawks. I got ahead, so I took it easy for a couple of hours."

Mucha told Roy that he had noticed that Roy had made $10.01 the day before and warned him not to go over $1.25 an hour. He told Roy to figure the setups and the time on each operation very carefully so that he would definitely not total over $10.25 in any one day.

Starkey spoke to Roy after Mucha left. "What's the matter? Are you trying to upset the apple cart?" He explained in a friendly manner that $10.50, for example, would be too much to turn in, even on an old job. "The turret-lathe men can turn in $1.35," he said, "but their base rate is 90 cents, and ours is 85 cents."

Starkey warned Roy that the methods department could lower prices on any job, old or new, by changing the fixture slightly or changing the size of drill. According to Starkey, a couple of operators (first and second shift on the same drill) got to competing with each other to see how much they could make. They got up to $1.65 an hour, and the price was cut in half. From then on, they had to run that job themselves, as none of the other operators would accept it.

According to Starkey, it would be all right for drill pressmen to turn in $1.28 or $1.29 an hour, when it figured out that way, but it was not all right to turn in $1.30 an hour.

Several weeks after Roy started working, two operators staged the following conversation for his benefit:

ED: That guy (pointing across the room) is the greatest rate buster in the shop. Give him a job he can make a nickel on, and he'll break his back for the company.

MIKE: That's no lie. He's ruined every job on that machine. They've cut him down to the point where he has to do twice the work for half the pay. A few more like him would ruin this shop. [Roy later learned from the timekeeper that this "rate buster" had a very high "take-home."]

ED: It's guys like that who spoil the shop for the rest of us. Somebody ought to take a piece of Babbitt and pound some sense into his thick skull. That's the only kind of treatment a guy like that understands.

MIKE: We're handling him the best way as it is. The only way to handle those bastards is not to have a thing to do with them. That guy hasn't got a friend in the place, and he knows it. You can bet your life he thinks about that every time he comes to work.

Roy noticed that, with one exception, all the men who seemed to be called "rate busters" ate lunch apart from the work group and from each other. (When Collins attempted to strike up a friendship by "hanging around" a rate buster's machine, he was told: "Why the hell don't you get out of here and let a man work? There's enough guys around here who've got enough in their pockets so they can afford to spend their time and the company's gassing with you. I can't. I'm a poor man.")

The one rate buster who did eat with the rest of the men was John. Aggressive in his dealing with his fellow workers, John was at any time prepared to defend his views. For this reason, he was often the center of heated agruments. These arguments were usually political in nature, and on such subjects as whether Russia had any part in winning the war, whether Roosevelt planned to become a dictator, or whether workmen had the right to strike. In the behavior of the group, there was often notice-able an attempt to draw John out, to bait him. John often became wildly excited in the course of these discussions, to the amusement of the group. Following is an example of one of these discussions:

SWEDE: Not all unions are rackets.

JOHN: The guys who run them all are racketeers. I don't need anybody walk-ing around telling me where I'm going to work and why.

SWEDE: Without a union, the boss tells you where you're going to work; and if you don't like it, you can't open your mouth.

JOHN: If you don't like it, you can get out. Put yourself in the position of the employer. Do you want somebody coming and telling you whom you can hire and whom you can't?

SWEDE: The point is, I'm not an employer. I'm an operator, and I want to get just as much as I can out of it.

JOHN: That's just it. The union is for the guy who doesn't want to work. The guy who wants to work doesn't have any trouble. My grandfather worked without union protection, and I can work without union protection.

HANK: Where did he work? Down on the farm? *(Laughter from the group.)*

JOHN: You guys make me sick! The way you loaf around here, you're stealing just as much as if you walked up to F. E. Berrett[1] and stuck a gun in his ribs.

BILL: The trouble with a gun, John, is that they can run you in for it.

Roy found that, unlike the rate busters, most of the other operators seemed to have time to "burn." One evening, Ed Sokolsky, one-time second-shift operator on Starkey's drill, commented on a job the latter was running:

ED SOKOLSKY: That's a gravy job. I worked on those, and I could turn out nine an hour. I timed myself at six minutes.

ROY: Really? At 35 cents apiece, that's over $3.00 an hour!

SOKOLSKY: And I got ten hours;[2] I used to make out in four hours and fool around the rest of the night.

Sokolsky claimed he could also make over $3.00 an hour on the two

---

[1] President of Metropolitan Steel Company.

[2] During this period, some workers were working a ten-hour shift, some an eight-hour shift.

machines he was presently running, but he could turn in only $1.40 an hour or, occasionally, $1.45 or $1.50 for the two machines together. He said that he always "made out" for a ten-hour shift by 11:00 o'clock, that he had nothing to do from 11:00 to 3:00, and had even left early, getting someone to punch his timecard for him.

"That's the advantage of working nights," said Sokolsky. "You can make out in a hurry and sit around, and nobody says anything. But you can't get away with it on day shift with all the big shots around. Jack has to take it easy on these housings to make them last eight hours, and that must be tough."

Old Pete, another old-timer, confided to Roy: "Once, when they had timed me on some connecting rods, I could have made $20 a day easy. I had to run them at the lowest speed on the machine to keep from making too much. I had a lot of trouble once when I was being timed, and they gave me $35 a hundred. Later, they cut it to $19.50 a hundred, and I still make $9.50 a day."

Roy's own first "spare time" came on November 18. That day, he made out with such ease on the pedestals that he had an hour to spare. To cover the hour, he had to poke along on the last operation, taking twice as much time to do forty-three pieces as he ordinarily would. A few days later in the washroom, before Roy started work, Willie commented on Roy's "gravy" job, the pedestals:

WILLIE: The methods department is going to lower the price on the pedestals; there was some talk today about it.

ROY: I hope they don't cut it too much. I suppose they'll make some change in the jigs?

WILLIE: They'll change the tooling in some way. Don't worry, when they make up their minds to lower a price, they'll find a way to do it.

However, in March, Roy experienced a sudden increase in skill and found himself capable of making out early on jobs other than the pedestals. With this increase of skill, Roy found the pedestals quickly fading as the supreme contributors of "gravy." For example, on March 22, Roy stalled along, turning out only 89 casings, which he added to his kitty of 40 for a turn-in of 129. Mucha had a kitty of 13, and Roy figured that the 116 pieces left would just do Mucha tomorrow. Although the shift did not end until 11:00, Roy finished his last piece about 9:30 and started cleaning the machine about 10:00 o'clock. Roy noticed that Tony, who worked beside him, was also through early, standing around his machine. "This is the earliest you've made out, isn't it?" Tony asked. "That's the kind of job I like. Then I can go at it and enjoy it."

On April 7, Roy was able to enjoy four hours of "free time." He turned out 43 connecting rods in the four hours from 3:00 to 7:00, averaging nearly 11 an hour. At 7:00 o'clock, there were only 23 pieces left in the lot, and he knew there would be no point in building up a kitty for Monday if Mucha punched off the job before Roy got to work. Roy could not go ahead with the next order (also a load of connecting rods) because the rules made presentation of a work order to the stock chaser necessary before material could be brought up. So he was stymied and could do nothing the rest of the day. He had 43 pieces and added 11 from yesterday's kitty to turn in for a total 54. He sat around the rest of the evening, and none of the bosses seemed to mind.

Roy also found, about this time, that he was receiving quite a bit of unasked-for "help." For example, one night, he had just started work on a new job, calling for outside hex cuts on a housing ring. The layout department had laid out the cuts, each equidistant from the others. Jake said to Roy: "I'll let you in on a little secret. You put on your smooth jaw vise, and I'll show you how to cut those babies in no time." Jake had made a plug which slipped inside the housing. He set the cutter and took the cuts off the finished surface of the plug. By eliminating the surface gauge, he had cut the job down so that Roy was making well over $4.00 an hour. Roy turned in the job for $1.10 after loafing 5.3 hours. (Since he was a new man, $1.10 was "tops" for him on this job.) Jake was very secretive about the plug and made Roy return it to him as soon as he had finished. He stowed it in his tool locker, saying: "Forget you ever saw this thing until you need it again." After that, Roy found that each group had a collection of special cutting tools, jigs, and fixtures which were carefully concealed from members of the incentive department. These tools were usually made on company time. Through the use of such devices, many operations could be performed in a fraction of the time allowed for them.

Another night, when Roy came to the cage to punch off rework, the time-cage girl said: "You don't want to punch off rework yet, do you?" and suggested that he should get a start on the next job before punching off rework. On still another occasion, Art, the foreman, was at the time cage when Roy punched off the day work of rereaming and on to the piecework of drilling. Art came around to Roy's machine shortly after. "Say," he said, "when you punch off day work onto piecework, you ought to have your piecework already started. Run a few, then punch off the day work, and you'll have a good start. You've got to chisel a little around here to make money."

Roy once accidentally turned in a job for twice his "rate" as set by the group. The foreman caught the job ticket before the timekeeper had punched it and called it to the attention of one of the setup men, who returned it to Roy with the admonition to be more careful. Roy altered the card so that he was paid his "usual rate."

Roy was repeatedly warned to watch out for time-study men. Gus told him that a girl hand-mill operator had been discharged a year ago when a time-study man caught her running one job while punched in on another.

The time-study man came over to the girl's machine to time a job, only to find the job completed and the girl running another.

Time-study men were a favorite topic of conversation. One day, Roy was present when Starkey was giving some detailed advice to Tennessee, another relatively inexperienced man, in ways of coping with the time-study man:

STARKEY: If you expect to get any kind of a price, you got to outwit that s.o.b.! You got to use your noodle while you're working, and think your work out ahead as you go along. You got to add movements you know you ain't going to make when you're running the job. Remember, if you don't screw them, they're going to screw you! Every movement counts!

Another thing, you were running that job too damn fast before they timed you on it. I was watching you yesterday. If you don't run a job slow before you get timed, you won't get a good price. They'll look at the record of what you do before they come around and compare it with the timing speed. Those time-study men are sharp!

TENNESSEE: I wasn't going very fast yesterday. Hell, I was going as slow as I could without wearing myself out slowing down.

STARKEY: Well, maybe it just looked fast because you were going so steady at it.

TENNESSEE: I don't see how I could run it any slower, I stood there like I was practically paralyzed!

STARKEY: Remember those guys are paid to screw you, and that's all they got to think about. They'll stay up half the night figuring out how to beat you out of a dime. They figure you're going to try to fool them, so they make allowances for that. They set the prices low enough to allow for what you do.

TENNESSEE: Well, then, what chance have I got?

STARKEY: It's up to you to figure out how to fool them more than they allow for.

TENNESSEE: The trouble with me is, I get nervous with that guy standing in back of me, and I can't think.

STARKEY: You just haven't had enough experience yet. Wait until you have been here a couple of years, and you'll do your best thinking when those guys are standing behind you. I was timed once on some levers like the ones you're running. I got a price of $4.00 a hundred, and I could make about $2.00 an hour. But I didn't run them the way they were timed. When the time-study man came around, I set the speed at 180. I knew damn well he would ask me to push it up, so I started low enough. He finally pushed me up to 445, and I ran the job later at 610. If I'd started out at 445, they'd have timed it as 610.

Then I got him on the reaming, too. I ran the reamer for him at 130 speed and .025 feed. He asked me if I couldn't run the reamer any faster than that, and I told him I had to run the reamer slow to keep the hole size. I showed him two pieces with oversize holes that the day man ran. I picked them out for the occasion. But later on, I ran the reamer at 610 speed and .018 feed, same as the drill, so I didn't have to change gears.

Then, there was a burring operation on the job, too. For the time-study man, I burred each piece after I drilled and reamed, and I ran the burring tool by automatic feed. But afterwards, I let the burring go till I drilled 25 pieces or so, and I just touched them up a little by holding them under the burring tool. I used to make out in five hours, easy, on that job.

Always keep in mind the fact that you can't make money if you run the job the way it's timed. They time jobs just to give you your base rate if you kill yourself trying to make it, no more. You've got to get the job timed below the speeds and feeds you can use later. Whenever a piece is timed at maximum speeds and feeds, there's no hope! You have as much chance as a snowball in hell!

TENNESSEE: Yeah, but what if they make you speed it up to maximum speed? What are you going to do then?

STARKEY: You got to be tough with them. Remember, those guys don't know their ass from a hole in the ground as far as these machines are concerned. When they tell me to speed up to about what I figure I can run the job, I start to take my apron off and tell them: "All right, if you think it can be run that fast, you run it!" They usually come around. You should have seen Ray Ward when he was working on the drill presses. Ray knew his drills. He'd burn up a drill every four or five pieces when they were timing him, and say the speed was too high for the tough stuff he was running. Tough stuff, my ass! They'd lower the speed and feed to where he wasn't burning up the drills; then afterwards, he'd speed up and cut through that tough stuff like cheese.

TENNESSEE: What I want to know is, how in hell could Ward burn up the drills like that? You can't just burn up a drill when you feel like it.

STARKEY: It's in the way you grind the drill. Ray used to grind his own drills, and he'd touch them up before they timed him. The wrong kind of a grind will burn up a drill at a lower speed than the drill can take if it's ground right for the job. There are all sorts of ways to skin a cat, and Ray knew 'em all. He could start with the head or the tail or any one of the four feet. Ray knew all the tricks!

I used to have to laugh at the way he got up a sweat when they were timing him. He'd jump around the machine like a monkey on a string, with the sweat just pouring off him. His shirt used to get soaking wet, and he'd have to wring it out afterwards. And when they finished timing him, he'd stagger away from the machine a little, like he'd given everything he had in him. But of course, it got to a point where he wasn't fooling anybody any more, except maybe some new time-study man who came along, and the time-study department would have him tipped off about Ray.

I never did see Ray sweat a drop when he was actually running a job; he was always about forty pounds overweight, the laziest guy I ever did see. He'd move a box up to the machine and putter around all day like he was making mud pies or something.

Roy noticed, however, that with all this elaborate strategy, even the canniest operators often gave their best in a timing duel, only to get "hopeless" prices for their pains. These jobs were usually called "stinkers" by the men. From the day Roy first came to the shop, he heard a lot of talk about these stinker jobs. Al McCann (the man who probably made quota most often) said he gave a new job a trial; if it was no good, he took his time. After that, Roy noticed that whenever McCann worked on the chucks, he apparently made little effort to make out.

Mucha said of a certain job: "I did just one more than you did. If they don't like it, they can do it themselves. To hell with them. I'm not going to break my back on stuff like this. I could have made out, but why kill myself for day rate?"

Old Pete, the multiple man, said: "I ran some pieces for twenty-five minutes to see how many I could turn out. I turned out twenty at 1.5 cents apiece [72 cents an hour]. So I smoke and take it easy. I can't make out."

Roy noticed that when Sokolsky, one of the better operators on the line, was working on an operation on which he could not make out, he did not go at his task with much vigor. He either poked around or left his machine for long periods of time; and Paul, the setup man, seemed always to be looking for him. Steve, the superintendent, was constantly bellowing: "Where in hell is Ed?" or "Come on, Ed, let's have some production around here!" One night, Roy heard him admonishing Sokolsky: "Now, I want you to work at that machine till 3:00 o'clock. Do you understand?"

Roy watched with real interest when Starkey and the men who worked his machine on the other shifts were assigned a major job they regarded as poorly priced — an item called a hinge base. Roy observed them working on the hinge bases off and on for over nine months. During the period, three men worked second shift on Starkey's machine, in the following sequences: Sokolsky, Dooley, and McCann. When Starkey and Sokolsky first started working on hinge bases in December, Roy noticed that they did not seem to be doing very well. Sokolsky cursed intermittently and left his machine for long period of time. The foreman would find the machine idle and would bellow about it. Sokolsky began to call the piece a "stinker."

Sokolsky seemed to have continual trouble with his jig, a revolving piece attached to the side of the table. Two disks seemed to stick together, and he was always (every day or so) using the crane to dismantle the jig (a very heavy one). He sanded the discs and oiled them, taking several hours for the cleaning operation. Steve did not seem to like it. Whenever Paul found the jig torn down and Sokolsky away somewhere, he would yell: "Where the hell's Ed?" in a provoked manner.

In February, Roy was told by Sokolsky that he and Starkey were turning out about twenty-four pieces in a ten-hour period, that the job had been timed several times, but no raise in price had been given. The two men were asking for a price of 38 cents. Sokolsky said they could turn out three an hour; but until they got a decent price, they would turn out two an hour. Toward the end of that evening, Roy noticed that Sokolsky was sitting on a box doing mothing, his machine idle.

ROY: What's the matter? Did they stop the job on you?
SOKOLSKY: I stopped it, I don't feel like running it.

In March, Dooley took over the night shift on Starkey's machine. One night, while he was working on hinge bases, Dooley admitted he could barely make out on the job, but "Why knock myself out for day rate? We're doing three an hour or less until we get a better price!"

In August, after McCann started working on the hinge bases, he told Roy they had gotten a price raise on the hinge bases, from 23 to 28 cents, and another to 31 cents.

AL MCCANN: But it's still not high enough. As it is now, we can make exactly 94 cents an hour. We're trying to get 35 cents. We can turn out one piece in exactly sixteen minutes. That's not four an hour. We've been giving them three an hour.

One night, Gil, the foreman, sat or stood behind McCann for at least an hour, and Roy could see McCann did not like it. He worked steadily but with deliberate slowness, and did not look at Gil or speak to him.

But one night late in August, McCann told Roy that he (McCann) was making out on the hinge bases, that he had gotten disgusted Friday, speeded up the tools, and turned in thirty-one pieces for earnings of $9.60 on an eight-hour shift.

MCCANN: It was easy, just as easy as the frames. Now, I'm kicking myself all over for not doing it before. All I did was to change the speed from 95 to 130. I was sick of stalling around all evening, and I got mad and decided to make out and let the tools burn up. But they made it all right, for eight hours. What's the use of turning in 94 cents an hour when you can turn in $1.25 just as easy? They'd never raise a price you could make 94 cents on, anyhow. Now, maybe they'll cut it back.

After Roy had been on the job for several months, he noticed that while he didn't mind the work, he did find that when he was doing a job on which he wasn't trying to make out, the time seemed to drag. Roy found himself struggling to attain quota "for the hell of it" because it was a "little game" and kept him from getting bored. In addition to escaping the monotony of factory labor by playing a game, Roy found that fast, rhythmical work seemed less tiring.

Dooley watched Roy set up for the frames one night and remarked: "You can make out on that if you want to break your neck." "Breaking his neck" was a welcome relief from the monotony of carefully pacing his work. Roy was so sleepy he could hardly keep his eyes open before he started on the frames; but at 11:00 o'clock, he felt bright and wide awake.

Slow jobs seemed to wear Roy out far more than the fast ones. Roy mentioned this to John, one of the other operators, who said: "That's the way with me. I've got to keep my mind occupied, or I get bored; it wears me out. I can't stand around, either. When I am going hell-bent for election on a good piecework job, the evening passes very swiftly, and I don't realize that I am tired until it is all over. On those day work jobs, I get so bored I could stand in the aisle and yell."

In his conversations with the men in the shop, Roy found that rate cutting was the most frequent subject of conversation. In spite of the fact that both union and management had made strong guaranties that rates would not be cut, the workers were unconvinced. Leonard Bricker, an old-timer in the shop, maintained that management, once bent on slashing a piecework price, would stop at nothing.

LEONARD BRICKER: Take these $1.25 jobs. One guy will turn in $1.30 an hour one day. Another fellow will turn in, say, $1.31 or $1.32. Then the first fellow will go up to $1.35. First thing you know, they'll be up to $1.50, and bang! They'll tear a machine to pieces to change something to cut a price.

SWEDE: Pay it by the hour, or pay it by the job, that little man in the straw hat won't pay you any more than he has to.

MIKE: They won't cut the rate on this job, but what's to prevent them from changing the casting a little and giving it another number? Then it's a different job, and they'll set a lower rate on it. Piecework is like leading a goat around with a carrot. You give the goat a nibble, but you never let him have a real bite.

Roy noticed, however, that he had never heard any of the men mention any specific examples of either direct or indirect rate cutting. On one occasion, a worker spoke about management plans to "put the screws" on certain jobs and claimed that there had been several recent instances of

EXHIBIT 1
Metropolitan Steel Company: Production Piecework Hours Worked (by ten-cent earnings intervals)

Earnings per Hour (in cents)	Period I November through February		Period II March through August		Total November through August	
	Hours Worked	Per- cent	Hours Worked	Per- cent	Hours Worked	Per- cent
Unknown*	66.4	11.4	37.5	4.9	103.9	7.7
5–14	3.0	0.5	–	–	3.0	0.2
15–24	13.5	2.3	37.5	4.9	51.0	3.8
25–34	37.8	6.5	12.0	1.6	49.8	3.7
35–44	93.0	16.0	57.1	7.4	150.1	11.0
45–54	74.0	12.8	70.5	9.1	144.5	10.6
55–64	43.1	7.4	14.6	1.9	57.7	4.3
65–74	36.8	6.3	27.0	3.5	63.8	4.7
75–84	49.0	8.5	8.7	1.1	57.7	4.4
Total under 85 cents	416.6	71.7	264.9	34.4	681.5	50.4
85–94	39.1	6.7	12.1	1.6	52.1	3.8
95–104	9.7	1.7	9.8	1.2	19.5	1.5
105–114	3.8	0.7	14.1	1.8	17.9	1.3
115–124	18.0	3.1	65.0	8.4	83.0	6.1
125–134	93.2	16.1	403.1	52.3	496.4	36.7
135–174	–	–	1.5	0.3	1.5	0.2
Total 85 cents or over	163.8	28.3	505.6	65.6	670.4	49.6
Total	580.4	100.0	770.5	100.0	1,351.9	100.0

* All "unknown" hourly earnings fell below the base rate level of 85 cents per hour.

rate cutting. Roy asked which jobs had been cut. When the worker could not name one, the steward standing nearby said: "Shut up, you make me sick—always crying before you are hurt."

After Roy had worked at the shop for a little over ten months, he decided to take a look at what he had done in that time. Each day, he had jotted down some notes about his production and earnings. When he added it all up, he found that he had worked 1,851 hours, 1,351 of which were "production piecework" hours. The remaining 500 hours were taken up with time study, rework, and setup. In 670 (50 percent) of the production piecework hours, he had made out. That is, he produced enough pieces of work to "earn," at the piece rates for the kind of work done, the 85-cent per hour "base rate" which he was guaranteed for every hour spent on the job.

Roy's hourly earnings on production piecework varied from $0.09 to $1.66. Exhibits 1 and 2 show the spread of hourly earnings for the various

EXHIBIT 2
Metropolitan Steel Company: Production Piecework Hours Worked (by ten-cent earnings intervals)

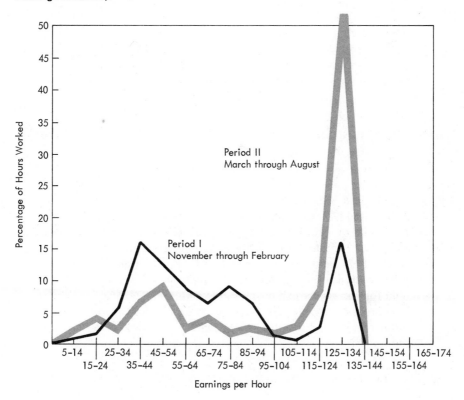

jobs. Roy divided the ten months into two periods in order to separate out the initial learning period from the period when he had attained a little higher level of skill.

Although he did not keep a complete record of the hourly earnings of Mucha on the radial drill, Roy frequently jotted down Mucha's output for the day, and found that Mucha's figures ran fairly close to his own. Furthermore, it was Roy's opinion that his record during the second period was not out of line with that of other operators in the shop. Of the men on the same shift with Roy, doing the same kind of work, McCann, Starkey, Koszyk, and Sokolsky could all turn out greater volume than Roy and, in his opinion, were his betters in all-around skills. Seven were below him in these respects, but only three of them (Smith, Rinky, and Dooley) had worked long enough to be much a part of the group. Roy thought he was about average in both skill and work assigned to him.

During the last two months of the period (July and August), Roy estimated that he had "goofed off" an average of over two hours on the days when he made out. Since these make-out days represented 46 percent of all days he worked, he figured that if he had wanted to be a rate buster, he could have made on the average an extra $1.58 a day.

Multi-Products, Inc.*

"THE AVERAGE young fellow today has no concept of how to beat a competitor and how to squeeze money out of every dollar," Richard B. Haws, president of Multi-Products, Inc., of Los Angeles, California, said in February 1959 to Bertram Stace, an old friend and stockholder. "It's not really their fault—they've just had lousy training over the past 20–30 years, as far as the acceptance of responsibility and of being held accountable for the stewardship of a job is concerned. If we ever begin to have a depression as we did back in 1929 to 1931, God knows how the industries of this country would suffer. Just look at the way they waste money. . . ."

Mr. Haws's career, 1902–56

"I was born in 1902, the son of poor parents," Mr. Haws continued. "One day when I was a small boy I was sitting in our hometown drugstore and the wealthy owner of a pottery (his son lost all of it) came in and sat down beside me. He talked to the druggist and then he turned to me and said, 'No use talking to you, you'll never have any money.' I will never forget those words. I don't resent them—they were the greatest driving force in my life. If they've been before my eyes once, they've been before them five million times."

Picking up his office copy of *Who's Who,* Mr. Haws showed Mr. Stace that he had attended college for three years, worked as a salesman in a local business for another five, and then moved to New York in 1929 to sell for the Lawton Machinery Company. "We were living in a nice apartment and had all our money in the market when the crash came. I went to our landlord and asked him to let me break the lease, but he pointed out that he needed money more than ever now and refused. I went home to think about it and then returned and pleaded with him to let us move to one of his cheaper apartments. Finally he agreed. He moved us the next day and that night brought up a new lease for me to sign. I looked him in the eye and said, 'Oh no. When you moved us out of that first apartment, you broke the lease. We're moving out of here tomorrow.' That's the sort of sharp thinking—in that case born out of financial necessity—that young fellows don't seem to use today. They certainly don't learn it in business schools."

Mr. Haws thought his Lawton Machine Company days had been an invaluable experience. "Young fellows today are soft—they don't believe me when I tell them that my wife often would wait for my phone call in the late afternoon to see if I'd sold a machine. If so, I'd have enough money for her to buy food for supper! Those were the days when we were ashamed to admit we had lost an order. We were paid straight commission; anyone could ask for a raise but all you got was 'Go out and sell some more machines.' I remember the sales manager used to say, 'Any salesman can come in, push the desk in my lap and call me a S.O.B. as long as he produces—but he'd better keep on producing.'

"When I was with Lawton, I met a young statistician whose head was full of ideals and up in the clouds, but he was dead broke. I suggested he sell machines until he found another job. I showed him the sales pitch and sent him off with a machine under his arm. The next day he was back saying he couldn't take it. I told him anybody could sell machines and if he couldn't he had no guts. He stuck with it two months until he got another statistical job. You've got to have guts and imagination to get someplace. A friend of mine who was president of a large company put it this way, 'If I have a guy around me who hasn't been in jail, I have a weak man!'

"It was during my time with Lawton that I realized I wanted a nice house, expensive car, fine clothes—the things that money can buy. I decided then and there I had the ants in my pants to want excitement and to get all or nothing. If you know what you want and what you can afford, it's pretty easy to set up a program for yourself. I've tried to get others to do the same, but they don't. It's pretty difficult for a young man or a student because he's not had the business experience to see what you can get out of life, and what money will buy. But then, even older men don't do it. Take my associate Joel Dennis. He's happy to earn about $15 an hour, save up for a new expensive camera, throw on a $47 suit of clothes that doesn't fit properly, and just lead that sort of life. Maybe he's happy, but he doesn't have the ants in his pants I do. . . ."

Mr. Haws told his friend that he decided he didn't aspire to be a Lawton sales manager, but rather wanted a "show of my own" and was willing to pay for the necessary experience. He had left his $18,000 Lawton job to work first for a large company as a $6,000-a-year procedures man and later for a medium-sized company as a financial officer. During his stay with the second company he was given warrants and stock. When he left he had about 27,500 shares which had cost him some $12,000; by 1959 these shares were worth over $1 million. In 1953 he became president of a small manufacturing company, and four years later he was asked to head Multi-Products, Inc.

Multi-Products, Inc., 1946–56

Mr. Haws's friend, Mr. Stace, was a stockholder in Multi-Products, Inc., and knew something about its early history from published records. The company was founded by Earle M. Cave in January 1946 to make a consumer item. By 1951 the company had lost some $500,000 on five years' sales of $625,000 and Mr. Cave started a new line. During the next two years Multi-Products expanded into two related and one unrelated lines through acquiring three small companies. The company's 1954 statements showed a net profit of about $290,000 on $5.7 million sales, a net worth of $3.3 million, and an accumulated deficit of $80,000; however, the auditors "were unable to form an opinion as to the overall results of operation" because management had decided to defer certain expenses totaling $375,000.

The next year, Mr. Stace recalled, the company ran into difficulties. The June 1955 quarterly report showed a six months' profit of about $60,000 on about $2.7 million sales, but when the annual report came out there were losses of about $3.6 million on $6 million sales.

Early in 1956 the company underwent litigation. Mr. Stace recalled the basic issues were whether the net income for the period ending June 30, 1955, were overstated and both income statement and balance sheet invalid and whether at the time the quarterly report was issued management knew the company was operating at a loss. The testimony showed that four entries, labeled "management adjustments" by the disapproving controller, had turned a $300,000 March quarter loss into a $60,000 profit before the statement was forwarded to the company's banks. The court ruled that the June profit had been overstated by almost $1 million owing to improper deferment of certain expenses, calculation of the cost of goods sold on the basis of cost formulae rather than by using the cost system, and failure to establish reserves for anticipated losses.

In court Mr. Cave said that accounting, especially details such as divisional operating data or cost entries, was beyond his "purview of operation," interest, or knowledge. He stated that he relied completely on the judgment of Mr. Bangs, vice president of finance, on all accounting matters, and on the auditors on all financial questions pertaining to the company statements. He said that in general "it was not my custom to have any contact whatsoever with the people at the working level, such as Mr. Land or Mr. Heyden (assistant controllers). If I had identified myself at any time with the minutiae between the juniors below any of the vice presidents, then I would have been totally unable to have kept my proper purview of the overall operation of the company and longer term planning of the company. I stayed expressly away from all matters which fell totally below the vice presidential levels." He said the first time he had "any conception" of the losses was when the new auditors showed him the 1955 financial statements in February 1956 after his return from a vacation. Besides, over $2 million was due to auditors' adjustments.

Both Mr. Cave and the Multi-Products, Inc., counsel stressed that investors bought the company's stock on the basis of its potential long-term growth, not the statements, and so it would not have materially mattered one iota if the six months' statement ending March had shown a profit or a small loss. According to published reports, Mr. Cave never owned over 2 percent of Multi-Products, Inc., stock and did not speculate.

After losing $4 million on $5.9 million sales in 1956, the firm faced financial disaster. Only selling a large block of shares at $2 a share to an investment fund in January 1957 avoided bankruptcy. (Mr. Stace ruefully recalled that the stock back in 1952 had sold for $42 a share.) New directors and a new management, including Mr. Haws, were brought in, and the division making products unrelated to the other lines was sold.

Multi-Products, Inc., under Mr. Haws's management, 1957–59

Mr. Haws explained to Mr. Stace that since coming to Multi-Products, Inc., he had concentrated on three areas: organization, acquisitions, and employee motivation and compensation.

Organization   "For about the first month after I joined Multi-Products, Inc., I just watched operations and got the feel of the situation," Mr.

Haws said. "Then I went to work on our organization. There were 51 people in the accounting department. I called in the head of the department and told him to move the people into another room. He protested there was only room for 12 there and I said, 'That's right, by tomorrow you'll only have 12 people in your department.' I also called in the head of the merchandising department and showed him a new room with space for three people and the secretary. He had to reduce his staff from 11. Quality control had seven people and a secretary. I told the superintendent he would have two people including himself to do all the scheduling, the expediting and control. The department heads said this was impossible. I said, 'All right. I will stay after five o'clock tonight and want you to come in and tell me if you're man enough for the job or else resign.'

"Actually, volume had grown much better than I anticipated, and we still have only 12 people in the accounting department. Goes to show there were a lot of people sitting around on their hands doing nothing. You know, a partially employed person is the most ineffectual person in the business; he is inaccurate, lazy, and — worst of all — keeps other people from working.

"About March I took the department heads to dinner at the hotel. I told them what I was trying to do, put up a sales and profit chart, and said, "We'll start work at 8:15 in the morning, and not 8:45 or whenever you seem to feel like wandering in.' The treasurer broke in with, 'Let's take a vote on it.' I said, 'Fine, but if anyone votes against the proposal, I'll accept his resignation.' There was no vote.

"After the meeting the treasurer said, 'You certainly got off easy.' I replied, 'No, I had to listen to you. That's enough anguish for one evening. I don't have enough cash on me, so come in tomorrow morning and you can get your check.' I fired him right there; he was 45 years old but as yet he had not learned that organization conduct was more important than personal convenience."

In reorganizing the company, Mr. Haws said he decided whom to let go almost on a replacement basis. "Who cares about accountants, salesmen, shop foremen, or treasurers? But purchasing agents, merchandisers, and engineers are rather important to you. You have to know where to start a fight and where not to. You must move slowly because you have not possession of all the facts. . . ."

Acquisitions and New Business   The company needed to generate sufficient new business to utilize the large loss carry-forward generated since December 31, 1955. "The fundamental reason for our being in business is to utilize the tax losses," Mr. Haws explained. During 1957 he revamped the product line, acquired two small companies making similar products, and reduced the size of the loss to about $470,000 on sales of $3.7 million. By June 1958 the company showed earnings of $75,000 on sales of about $2 million, but much faster profit generation was needed. Mr. Haws started to diversify.

The first acquisition was the Seward Company which was obtained through an exchange of stock in July 1958. Shortly before, Seward had invested in a relatively large amount of new fixed assets. By changing the write-off period from three years to ten, Multi-Products maximized the immediate profit and thus effectively deferred the tax loss carry-forward beyond its normal expiration date. The extra profit was recorded as deferred income on the statements and was included in income for tax purposes only. By February 1959 Multi-Products had protected almost $1 million of its tax loss.

The other two unrelated businesses were bought in October 1958 and January 1959 on an "incentive" basis. Mr. Haws explained, "The man who owned the first one foresaw estate problems and wanted to sell the business for $1.5 million, its asset value. I said I would offer him $2 million if I could have it my own way with less than 30 percent down. I paid him $500,000 and picked up $400,000 of the company's cash the next day. In order to make up the $1 million balance of his original $1.5 million asking price, he will receive two thirds of the after-tax profit without limit of time. Obviously, if there are never any profits, he will never get any more than the down payment already made. Over the next five years, if his two-thirds share of the profits generate more than the $1.5 million asking price, he gets his excess up to the full $2 million offer. The business is currently producing after tax profits of $40,000 a month. I was talking to the seller the other day about putting out his fancy profit-sharing ideas, Cadillacs, hotel suites, and other perquisites, and he said he wouldn't work so hard without them. I replied, 'You scare me to death! You've only got $500,000 for your company so far and that's *all* you get if you don't produce profits.' I paid $25,000 down for the second business, which had $280,000 in cash, and made a similar incentive arrangement for the rest of the sales price.

"In other words, I am giving these men an incentive to continue to produce profits and thus am much more sophisticated than others using similar formulas. Some are good at this sort of thing. They pay an inflated cost above the company's net worth as a *contractual* obligation, which puts ether on the balance sheet as goodwill or some other evasive term, and they have to amortize the ether over a stipulated period on their operating statement, which adversely affects profits and gives their stockholders an untrue picture of earnings. On the other hand, I give the seller the full purchase price above asset value *only* if he earns it.

"I can't understand acquiring a company to add to your losses. Men who contractually overpay must be either awfully young or look too far into the future. Look at this article in today's *Wall Street Journal*[1] about Mr. Zeckendorf's company. Real estate is the safest investment in an inflationary economy and Webb & Knapp's assets have grown from $7 mil-

---

[1] *The Wall Street Journal*, February 9, 1959, p. 1.

lion in 1945 to $210 million in 1957, yet it lost money last year; the common stockholders have never received a dividend, and the preferred is $60 in arrears. When that happens, something is really wrong! Anytime you increase assets, your return on investment should increase proportionately. There's no point in getting big just for bigness' sake. Under my incentive system, we know the management of the purchased company will work hard to show a profit and not allow earnings to show a decreased return on investment."

Employee Motivation and Compensation   "The problem that really concerns me the most is turning young men into cost- and profit-conscious executives, who are worried about getting sales, controlling costs, setting profitable prices, and spending the company's money. I put a young man in charge of a division. He'd go out and buy some steel. If it were too brittle, would he tell the purchasing department to send it back? Heavens no! He'd just put it in inventory! Same with capital equipment. He'd buy some machinery, and if it didn't work, he'd put it to one side and forget about it, and not even try to get salvage value out of it. Another division head was losing $120,000 but was very indignant when I called him into the office to hear what he was going to do about it because he thought we could just borrow money from a bank. I said, 'You've got 60 days to turn this situation around. I've got no place in the company for a loser.'

"I've got another fellow who came in and said, 'It has been just 14 months since my last raise.' I said, 'What do you want to talk about?' He replied, 'my raise.' And I said, 'The length of time has no relation as to whether you get a raise or not.' I added that he was reviewed a few months ago, at which time he told me about how many letters he wrote but didn't tell me what business he had brought into the house and the profit that he had earned. He replied, 'I worked hard,' and I said, 'I don't know about that. We've got working rules that you start work at 8:15; you're here at 8:30 or 8:45, and during the baseball season you're at the ball park. Sure, I know that you tell the secretaries that you are calling on a customer, but I just happen to know that you were at the baseball game. You come back tomorrow and tell me how much business you have brought in, and how much profit you have made for the company, and whether you are earning the salary you have.'

"Engineers are far too loyal to what they call their 'professional ethics.' A company may have a contract to do something, but the engineer will see that he could do it just that much better. The customer didn't ask for it, the specifications didn't ask for it, and if we do it, we won't be able to make a profit or deliver on time. But because of this professional idealism, the engineer goes ahead and does it anyway, with the result that we lose money, the customer is mad because we are late, and perhaps it doesn't work any better than it would have anyway.

"All the other professions — doctors, lawyers, teachers — except the engineer have to collect their bills. Ninety-nine percent of the latter are living off somebody else's money. If you ask them what have they contributed to earn their money, they get insulted. And if I suggested I wasn't going to pay them unless they contributed to the company, they'd quit. It's never seemed to dawn on some of them that they have to earn their keep.

"Dr. Collins is an example. I noticed that he had more and more unexcused absences and was coming in at 9:00 to 10:00 A.M. and leaving at 3:00 P.M. so I inquired around and learned he was discussing setting up his own company. I called him in the next day and said, 'Let's let our hair down. I'm not going to have this sloppy behavior.' He said, 'You never said anything about my working Saturdays and Sundays when we set up that new division,' to which I replied, 'No, I didn't say anything about my doing it either, but that's why we pay you a good salary. When are you going to leave?' He asked me when I wanted him to and got the reply, 'Tomorrow.' He said, 'I'd hoped you'd let me stay around until I get my company going. Anyway, my time ought to be my own.' And I said, 'O.K. fine, I'll give you a check tomorrow and you'll have all the free time you want.' You know, he's got a wife, two kids, is buying a home, but doesn't recognize the security he owes his family judging by the way he treated his job. His company never got off the ground and now he's broke and looking for a job. I'd like to help him, but my responsibility ended when he transferred his loyalties.

"Expense accounts and perquisites are another problem. Some fellows never put a limit on their hotel bill, so of course they get the most expensive room in the house. I just stopped three executives from leaving in the company plane at 3:00 P.M. instead of 5:00 P.M. They just wanted to get to their destination in time for supper; they hadn't thought that their salaries cost the company $55 an hour, or $110. Another young fellow came in here and said the company should give him a country club membership for entertaining customers. I said, 'No. You may be entertaining five customers now, but soon it will be fifteen people because in fact the company would be paying for your wife's and kids' weekends at the club.'

"You find this lack of cost-consciousness at all levels of the organization. Take those three girls out there, who are executive secretaries and assistants and are paid from $450 to $550 per month. I told them, 'I have a fetish against coffee breaks, which I think are the doom of American industry. Just get a few people around a coffee machine, and I'll bet three out of five of them will have something to gripe about. You are being paid enough money to know that this really does cost money. I don't want coffee drunk at the desk, but if you want to drink coffee, you can check in and out on a time clock and be paid an ordinary clerical salary.' I also asked them to exert their influence on the other girls to try and stop this coffee break business.

"About a week later I went past the coffee machine and found one of the three girls there talking to another secretary. She asked me if I would like a cup of coffee and I said I couldn't afford it. She said, 'Oh, I would be glad to spend the 10 cents.' And I said, 'That's not the point. The company can't afford the time.' So I put in an order to cut her salary $50 per month. That brought all three girls into my office, saying it was a very unfair thing to do. I said, 'I wasn't unfair. Here's a girl who violated an order that I had given. . . .' I then pointed out that I am not running a charitable organization, but running a business, and I can't allow any individuals to destroy the organization. So she has $50 less a month.

"In short I guess people don't realize—and perhaps I didn't either when I was an employee—that you buy manpower the same way you buy productive machinery. You must get a return for your investment.

"We have constant reviews and checks to be sure we're getting a return. Those with an annual salary of $6,000 or less get a semiannual review, while those over $6,000 get an annual one. If the supervisor doesn't recommend a raise, the man has 90 days to correct the faults found. If he does not correct them, he is out. Of course, when I let a man go, the supervisors often come in and really squawk; however, they are more careful the next time when writing their appraisals.

"There are several ways I check on the supervisors' evaluations. I sometimes call in a supervisor and make up fictitious stories about how I never saw so-and-so at work, or how I always see him coming in at 9:00 o'clock in the morning. Then I ask him if he is afraid to put a complete evaluation on somebody. Then I start in on another man. I make him defend all his recommendations. Sometimes they just plain collapse—the supervisors can't really defend their recommendations. They have to have a really good look at what each man does and not just say the whole department has done well. Also, I'll pick out three or four cards sent to me by the personnel department on people coming up for review, and I'll walk around their departments in the morning and at 4:45 in the evening. You can really get an idea of how hard a person works by doing that a couple of times for three or four days. You pick up enough information to justify your comments, and my objections to the supervisors often hit near enough home."

Future Plans   Mr. Haws's long-term objective for the company was to utilize the tax loss carry-forward through more diversification, but he told Mr. Stace that his personal objective was to leave Multi-Products, Inc., after another year or so. "I've really worked myself out of a job; I don't do a darn thing except read *The Wall Street Journal* and look for new acquisitions." His contract, which he—but not the company—could cancel, was up in 1961; his salary was about $35,000 with a $17,500 a year consulting fee guarantee for five years after leaving the company, and he had 60,000 of the 113,000 outstanding warrants at $2 a share. The stock was selling for $9 a share in February 1959.

In summing up his career, Mr. Haws felt he had learned to take calculated risks and win, but that young men with whom he worked did not do so. "If I ever had $5,000 in the bank, I'd be mad because it is not earning me a penny. When I am 60 or 65, I don't want to be a total dependent on somebody else, as nine-tenths of these people are destined to be. I offered 5,000 shares of the company at $2 apiece to one young man, and he said, 'I'll let you know in a while. I've got to think it over.' I said, 'I'll give you ten seconds to decide and those ten seconds have just passed, and the offer is off.' Heavens, a young man should have jumped at a chance like that!"

Nolim (A)*

PETER DE JONG re-read his father's letter as he sat in his New York office. In part the letter read:

> The sudden death of Max makes the situation in the coal company critical. As you know, Max has been handling most of the day-to-day management even though our partnership has always been 50/50. Each year my businesses have grown increasingly more difficult for me to handle alone. I think, Peter, that the time is ripe for you to come home and take a part in the business. If I ever needed your help, now is the time. The coal company would be an ideal place to begin. I plan to buy the 50 percent share from Max's wife and that way we would have full control. You could run the business in just the way that Max did, although I would have to spend time with you initially to help teach you the business. . . .

The suddenness of the letter made Peter unsure of how he should reply. It was the first time his father has asked him for help. Until that moment he had not given a thought to returning to Holland. Peter enjoyed living

* This case was prepared by George Taucher under the direction of Professors Herman Gadon and Quinn McKay as the basis for class discussion rather than to illustrate either effective or ineffective handling of an administrative situation. Copyright 1972 by l'Institut pour l'Etude des Méthodes de Direction de l'Entreprise (IMEDE), Lausanne, Switzerland, reproduced by permission.

in the United States. The future seemed bright at the International Oil Company where Peter had spent most of the previous year. Promotions had come rapidly and at 23 he was clearly ahead of his age group. Peter had done a variety of marketing jobs including running a large training service station on a major turnpike junction. As satisfying as his progress had been, Peter was not sure that he would stay at International over the long term. Already the politics of corporate life were apparent. Some of his colleagues on the international coordination staff "had particularly sharp elbows," Peter noted.

For these and other reasons, Peter was less and less attracted to large corporations and more toward an entrepreneurial situation where "he could be his own man." He already had his eye on a small TBA (tires, batteries and accessories) distributorship in Philadelphia that was having financial troubles. He felt that what he had learned in petroleum marketing at International would enable him to turn the situation around. Furthermore, recent anti-trust rulings in favor of independent distributors in the TBA business had clearly given the distributorship a favorable environment. In short, he saw the possibilities of developing a major growth business. Peter felt that his contacts at International would serve him in good stead. Indeed, John Weber, the International Oil Personnel Director was favorable to the idea and had even offered to support him with part of the capital needed. Peter often referred to Weber as "his American father." Weber had hired Peter and had befriended the young Dutchman. Peter was often a guest at the Weber house. One of the things Peter resolved to do before he replied to his father was to talk to John about the letter.

Peter de Jong had a remarkably varied life for his 23 years. A solitary boy and only son, Peter was raised strictly — contrasted even more by the way his three sisters were "spoiled" by their father. At 15 Peter had his first major disagreement with his father. This was to begin a period in which he was away from home, except for short visits, for the next eight years. Peter was doing well in school and his teacher recommended that he continue on and get his *abitur*.[1] Peter very much wanted to go to one of the top boarding schools in The Netherlands. Although this would have been socially and financially acceptable, Johann de Jong refused saying that the local school was adequate and that Peter should continue to live at home. While his father felt that education was important, he also thought it should be highly focused on making Peter a better businessman. After a confrontation, that included threats by Peter to leave home, Johann compromised. Peter would take a business apprenticeship program with an old army colleague of Johann. This man was known by Johann to have the same conservative, patriarchal view as himself.

---

[1] Preparation for University, e.g., High School, Matriculation, A levels.

Peter spent the next three years away from home learning the shipping supply business, enjoying earning his own way for the first time. Finishing the program at 18, Peter went to England at the recommendation of his father's friend to study at the University of Hull and to perfect his English. However, after a few months, Johann de Jong sent his son a letter telling him he believed that Peter was "wasting his time" in a provincial English University and should gain practical business experience. Peter was to report to the headquarters of the International Oil Company in London "immediately."

This decision had its origin in a business trip to the United States where Johann was strongly influenced by talks he had with an executive who suggested that his company, International Oil, offered both excellent experience and a scholarship program to American universities. Peter felt that he had to comply since he had no funds of his own although he felt he was gaining from his work in Hull. The London experience, however, was unfortunate from every point of view and Peter returned home to Friesland within a few months.

Back at home, Peter was able to convince his father that a university degree was important to future business success. Accordingly, Peter enrolled in the three year Commercial University Program in Amsterdam — supported financially by his father. Objections on his son's "playboy" life style led Johann to cut off his financial support in the second year. As Johann put it in his confrontation with his son, "I fulfilled my part of the contract by giving you money for your university studies. You failed to live up to your part. Therefore I don't feel that I should continue to support you." Peter returned to his second year and sold newspapers and other door-to-door items to support himself, assisted from time to time by his mother who was able to send a few guilders. Remarkably, he finished the three year program in two years. Johann came to the graduation and there was a moving reconciliation.

After graduation, Peter entered the management trainee program at International Oil in New York through his father's connections. Even there, the going was less than smooth initially. Discovering that his salary as a Dutchman was less than half of that of his American colleagues in the program, Peter quit in disgust and was tending bar in Baltimore when International decided to re-hire him as a regular employee. From there, Peter moved rapidly up the corporate ladder.

Turning over his father's offer in his mind, Peter realized how little he knew about his father's businesses. True to his analytic training in business school, Peter wrote down what little he knew.

Nolim: An oil distribution company in retail, heating oil, lubes and agricultural markets. There were 80–100 retail outlets of substantial potential. An exclusive contract with the International Oil Company for all sales in Friesland. Sales were growing rapidly in all areas corresponding to the rapid growth in Europe in general. Peter knew the Dutch market was growing at well over 10 percent at the time.

The Coal Company: A traditional coal distribution company with declining sales, though a move into heating oil was offsetting the decline somewhat. Facilities, including docks, were modern.

The Austin Distributorship: Recently started, Peter knew that this operation was still in the red. Job van Gelden, who had married Peter's sister, was running the distributorship for Johann.

The Mercedes Distributorship: Had been established for a number of years and was doing very well as far as Peter knew.

Peter estimated the sales at about fl 15 million for all the companies, guessing that Nolim made up about half of that total. Peter did not have the slightest idea about the profits or financial structure of the companies. He did know, however, that the company had been incorporated two years earlier with the assistance of Paul Van Rijn, his brother-in-law, an Amsterdam lawyer who had married his older sister. He knew that Paul was thinking of taking up legal practice in Friesland so that he could devote more time to the companies.

Peter knew that the most important fact about the family companies was his father. Johann had often said, while sitting around the family dining room table: "I never want these companies to grow so big that I can't handle all of the details myself." Peter knew this to be a guiding force and few of the employees had much, if any, authority for independent decision making.

Johann de Jong, at 66, was in every sense a self-made man. Having left the family farm after a dispute with his father, he made his own way without much of a formal education. Promotion to officer level in the army led to important connections. An early venture in the hotel business ended in bankruptcy and it took years to pay off the debts even though there were no legal requirements to do so. A restart as an oil salesman led to many years of hard work and finally the founding of his own oil distributorship. Prior to World War II, growth was very slow and success meager. After the war, however, the recovery changed the climate dramatically and growth and profits came more easily. Even under prosperous conditions Johann continued to eat, sleep and live his business.

Peter thought more about the man he might be working with. He had never had much of a personal life with his father. For one thing Johann was seldom able to tear himself away from the business and when at home discussions were usually business oriented. Then, too, Johann was already 43 when his son was born. Peter felt close to his mother; the fact that she was 18 years younger than her husband enabled her to relate to Peter more easily than did Johann. Peter's oldest sister was by his father's previous marriage, and Peter always sensed an underlying tension between his mother and half sister. The household was ruled with an iron hand and Johann never permitted open conflict in the family. Disputes, however small, were swept under the rug.

Johann became an important figure in Friesland and was tempted to go into politics; he decided at the last moment to stick to his business. Johann had come a long way from being a farmer's son to one of the most important businessmen in Friesland. Still he maintained much of the sturdy ethics of Friesland—strong religious conviction, honor and stolid moderation in his life style.

Peter de Jong put down his father's letter and gazed out of his window across the skyline of New York.

Power and the Ambitious Executive*

By Robert N. McMurry

THE METHODS *of holding top-management power in a company strike many people as devious and Machiavellian. They involve calculated alliances, compromises, and "deals"—and often they fly in the face of practices advocated by experts on organizational behavior. From the standpoint of the beleaguered and harassed executive, however, there may be no substitute for them—if he wants to survive at the top.*

The most important and unyielding necessity of organizational life is not better communications, human relations, or employee participation, but power. I define *power* as the capacity to modify the conduct of other employees in a desired manner, together with the capacity to avoid

* From *Harvard Business Review,* November–December, 1973.© 1973 by the President and Fellows of Harvard College; all rights reserved.

having one's own behavior modified in undesired ways by other employees. Executives must have power because, unfortunately, many employees resent discipline; to these employees, work is something to be avoided. In their value systems "happiness" is the ultimate goal. For the organization to be made productive, such persons must be subjected to discipline.

Without power there can be no authority; without authority, there can be no discipline; without discipline, there can be difficulty in maintaining order, system, and productivity. An executive without power is, therefore, all too often a figurehead — or worse, headless. The higher an executive is in his management hierarchy, the greater his need for power. This is because power tends to weaken as it is disseminated downward.

Gaining and keeping power

If the executive owns the business, that fact may ensure his power. If he does not, and sometimes even when he does, his power must be acquired and held by means which are essentially political. Of critical importance, since most of his power is derived or delegated, his power must be dependable. Nothing is more devastating to an executive than to lose support and backing in moments of crisis. It is for this reason that the development of continuing power is the most immediate and nagging concern of many professional managers.

How can chief executives and other managers who possess little or no equity in a business consolidate enough power to protect their jobs and enforce their dictates when necessary? The eight recommendations which follow are the fruit of 30 years of observation of a great number of executives managing a variety of enterprises.

A number of these conclusions conflict with the findings of other writers. The most that can be said in defense of my recommendations is that they did not spring from an ivory tower. They are based on strategies and tactics employed by demonstrably successful executives who lacked financial control of their enterprises. The executives were working pragmatists. Their prime criterion of a desirable course of action was: Will it work? While the strategies presented here are not infallible, they have proven their worth more often than not in the hard and competitive world of business.

1. The executive should take all the steps he can to ensure that he is personally compatible with superiors.

In the case of the chief executive, this means compatibility with the owners and/or their representatives, such as bankers, lawyers, and family members; in the case of other managers, senior executives and owners are the key groups. The point is that though a manager may have all the skills, experience, and personal attributes his position requires, if his values and goals are not reasonably consonant with those of the persons who hold power and he is not acceptable to them personally, his tenure will probably be brief.

To protect against subsequent disillusionment and conflict, the prospective manager should, before he joins the company, endeavor to become acquainted with his prospective superior or superiors informally. This could be done at dinner with them, on the golf course, or on a trip. At such a meeting he can learn his superior's values, standards, prejudices, and expectations. If any significant evidence of incompatibility emerges, he should call off negotiations—incompatibility tends to worsen rather than improve with continued contact.

If at all possible, the manager's wife should meet the superior, also under informal conditions, since compatibility with her can play an important part in the new man's acceptance. Likewise, if it can be arranged for the manager's wife to meet the chief's wife, early in the course of negotiations, that should be done. Compatibility between these two can be very advantageous; incompatibility can be fatal.

2. Whether he comes to the company from outside or is being promoted from within, the executive should obtain an employment contract.

While many owners and senior executives protest that they never make such agreements and that it is against their policy to do so, the prospective manager must insist that every policy is subject to change and that he will not accept the position without one. A failure to win out at this most critical juncture can be fatal to him. The reason is not so much that failure strips him of any vestige of job security and power but that it indicates to those in command that he is somewhat docile and submissive and probably can be pushed about at their whim.

This is particularly true where the executive's primary assignment is to salvage and rehabilitate a sick or failing operation or to initiate and pioneer a new and radically different field of activity that no one in the business knows much about. The compensation may be alluring, the status attractively elevated, and the challenge exciting. But the risks have to be great. If worse comes to worst and the executive is removed, he will have a tidy sum to carry him over the six months or longer that he needs to find a new job.

3. On taking a major assignment, the executive should obtain from his superiors a clear, concise, and unambiguous statment in writing of his duties, responsibilities, reporting relationships, and scope of authority.

Such a document is absolutely essential if the manager is not later to make the humiliating and frustrating discovery that the parameters of his job have been changed, often with no notice to him. He may have been

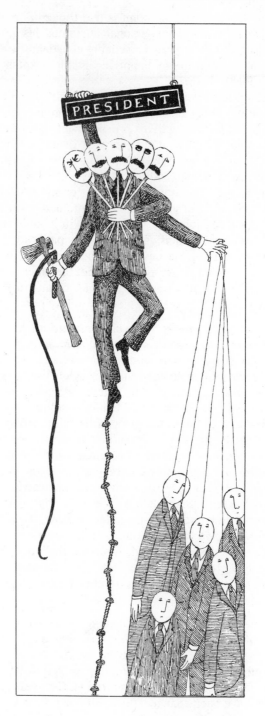

led to believe at the outset that he had certain responsibilities and commensurate authority to carry them out. Later he may learn that he has no such authority and that some of the people who were to report to him in effect do not do so. He may discover that figuratively he has been castrated; all of his authority has been taken from him, leaving him powerless. If, when he protests, he cannot substantiate his charges with a written commitment, he is likely to be told, "You have misunderstood our original agreement."

4.   The executive should take exceptional care to find subordinates who combine technical competence with reliability, dependability, and loyalty.

As many a top executive has learned to his sorrow, he is constantly vulnerable to sabotage by his underlings. This is especially the case where he comes in from outside and "does not know where the bodies are buried." It is for this reason that he should be so careful in the choice of his immediate subordinates.

In theory, each superior, regardless of his level in the management hierarchy, should have a strong, competent number-two man who is ready and willing to step into his place should he be promoted, retire, leave the company, or for any reason be unable to continue to function. Some executives do just this. But in practice the policy can be hazardous, at least in terms of the senior man's job security.

An aggressive, ambitious, upwardly mobile number-two man is dangerous to any chief, weak or strong. For one thing, the number-two man is often very difficult to control. He has his own personal array of goals and objectives which may or may not be consistent with those of his superior and/or the company. Since he is usually inner directed and a man of strong convictions, it is often difficult to divert him from the course which he has set for himself and which he sincerely believes to be best for him (and secondarily for the company). The risk is considerably lessened if the chief has only one strong subordinate, for then it is easier to watch and constrain him.

Moreover, since the strong subordinate tends to be an individualist, he is more apt to find himself in conflict with his peers. He has a compulsive need to achieve *his* goals regardless of the needs or expectations of the others or of the welfare of the enterprise as a whole. Not only may his influence be seriously divisive, but he tends to fragment the enterprise, to induce a centrifugal effect in it. This is why such businesses as advertising and consulting are so notoriously prone to fragmentation; they attract too many entrepreneurs.

Strong, decisive, qualified men are rarely willing to remain for more than a brief time in a secondary role. Their impatience is accentuated if, for any reason, they do not respect their superior or feel frustrated in their careers. Sometimes they conclude that their greatest opportunity lies not

in seeking advancement by moving to another company but by undermining and eventually supplanting their present superior.

In consequence, the politically astute top executive seeks subordinates who not only have the requisite technical skills but who are also
to some degree passive, dependent, and submissive. Their "loyalty" is
often a euphemism for docility. They tend to be security-conscious and
prone to form a dependent relationship with their chief. If the chief has
held his position for many years, this building of a submissive group has
usually taken place slowly by a process of trial and error. But when
he comes in from outside or takes over as the result of a merger, he is
often prone (and is usually well advised) to bring his own associates with
him or to give preferment to men whom he knows and has worked with
previously.

*5. A useful defensive tactic for the executive is to select a compliant
board of directors.*

Of course, the chief executive is the one most immediately concerned
with this ploy, but second- and third-level managers, too, may have a
vital interest in this matter. In recent years, changes in directors' responsibilities have made it somewhat more difficult to stack the board
in the old-fashioned sense. But its membership and operation can still
be influenced in a significant way.

Inside directors tend usually to be more malleable than outside
directors. Few will be courageous enough to cross swords with the
chief executive. While board members by law are the stockholders'
representatives and thus are the holders of ultimate power in the business,
in practice this is often little more than a polite fiction. In many instances
they have largely abdicated their management or even corporate supervisory responsibilities.

Sometimes the directors are too busy to interfere in operations. Not
infrequently they have little equity in the business and, hence, are dis-
interested in it. Sometimes they have been chosen principally because
they are "big names" who add status and respectability to the company
but can devote little time to its affairs. Much as some observers and
authorities dislike such tendencies, they are the realities. The top-management group that knows how to use and exploit power will make sure
that it, too, enjoys the blessings of a compliant board.

*6. In business, as in diplomacy, the most important stratagem of
power is for the executive to establish alliances.*

The more alliances the executive can build, the better. He can establish
several kinds of relationships:

With His Superiors He can make personal contact with and sell himself to the owner of the business or, where the ownership is widely
diversified, to the more influential stockholders. One chief executive I

know has luncheon once each month with the widow of the founder of his company. As long as she is convinced that he is a "wonderful man," he has both power and tenure.

Where banks, insurance companies, or mutual funds have a controlling voice in the company, the executive can seek to ingratiate himself with their key executives. If certain of his directors are unusually dominant, he does everything he can to win their favor and support. This does not necessarily mean that he is obsequious and sycophantic in his relationships with them. On the contrary, he may regularly stand up to them and confront them directly.

The key to success in a relationship of this nature is the ascertainment of the other person's expectations. If the man or woman whose support he hopes to win likes tigers, he is a tiger; if the person prefers a mouse, he restrains his more aggressive impulses. Above all, he studies each person's prejudices and values and is careful never to offend them.

With His Peers   The adroit manager also builds allegiances with others at his own level. While these people may not be direct sources of power to him, they can often be valuable as supplementary means of support and intelligence. Included among his contacts should be prominent industry figures. Since government intervention in business is increasing daily, acquaintance with senators, congressmen, and major department heads in government can also be helpful. (The owners of a company doing business with the Defense Department will think twice before sacking an executive who is on intimate terms with the Secretary or his deputy.)

One good means of ensuring support from peers is to identify common goals and objectives toward which all can strive. An even more powerful step is to find a common enemy—an antibusiness government official, let us say, or a hostile labor leader. Often influential rivals for power or even disgruntled subordinates can be neutralized by being taken into groups having common goals or enemies.

With Subordinates   I have already mentioned the importance of selecting dependent subordinates in whose selfish interest it is to support their chief. Such persons may also be useful as sources of internal intelligence. The information they provide is not always completely accurate or reliable, but it can be crosschecked against data from a variety of other sources.

7.   The executive should recognize the power of the purse.

He knows that the best control he can exercise over his subordinates is fiscal. Hence he seeks as quickly as possible to position himself where he approves all budgets. Nothing is as effective in coping with a recalcitrant staff as the power to cut off financial support for their projects. On the other hand, nothing so often promotes gratitude and cooperation as fiscal support of subordinates' favorite projects.

8. The executive should understand the critical importance of clear and credible channels of communication upward from all levels of his personnel and downward from him to them.

Without such channels the executive is an isolate who does not know what is transpiring in his enterprise. His commands will be heard only partially by his subordinates; they will be infrequently understood and rarely acted on. He should recognize that many of his staff have strong motives to keep the truth from him and to block or distort his downward communications.[1]

To overcome deficiencies of communication, the executive must learn not to depend too much on his hierarchy of assistants (many of whom are not communication centers at all, but barriers to it). Where possible, he will address his people directly, conducting periodic "State of the Company" reports to them and encouraging direct feedback from them by soliciting anonymous questions and expressions of dissatisfaction. He must supplement his formal channels of upward and downward communication by all available means, such as work councils, opinion polls, interviews with natural leaders, and community surveys.

Personal style

The place of a chief or other top executive in a business in which he has little or no equity is somewhat analogous to that of a diplomat working in an unfriendly, if not openly hostile, country. He may have much overt status and prestige, but he has little real power. He needs to accomplish certain goals, but he has little true leverage to apply to those people whom he seeks to influence. In view of this, he sometimes finds it necessary to use indirect, oblique, Machiavellian stratagems to gain his ends.

Observation of many politically astute executives in action indicates that most of them utilize supplementary ploys in coping with and influencing owners, associates, employees, and other groups. They know that an executive-politician must:

• Use caution in taking counsel—He may take the views of others into account, but he knows the decisions must be his. Advice is useful, but unless its limits are recognized, it can easily become pressure.

• Avoid too close superior-subordinate relationships—While he must be friendly with his subordinates, he is never intimate with them. His personal feelings must never be a basis for action concerning them. His door may be "open"—but not too far.

---

[1] For a fuller explanation of this point, see my article "Clear Communications for Chief Executives," HBR March-April, 1965, p. 131.

• Maintain maneuverability—He never commits himself completely and irrevocably. If conditions change, he can gracefully adapt himself to the altered circumstances and change course without loss of face.

• Use passive resistance when necessary—When under pressure to take action which he regards as inadvisable, he can stall. To resist such demands openly is likely to precipitate a crisis. Therefore he initiates action, but in such a manner that the undesired program suffers from endless delays and ultimately dies on the vine.

• Not hesitate to be ruthless when expedient—No one really expects the boss to be a "nice guy" at all times. If he is, he will be considered to be a softy or a patsy and no longer deserving of respect. (A surprisingly large segment of the population has a strong need to be submissive. Hence these people are more comfortable under a ruthless superior. This can be clearly seen in the rank and file of many labor organizations.)

• Limit what is to be communicated—Many things should not be revealed. For instance, bad news may create costly anxieties or uncertainties among the troops; again, premature announcements of staff changes may give rise to schisms in the organization.

• Recognize that there are seldom any secrets in an organization— He must be aware that anything revealed "in confidence" will probably be the property of everyone in the establishment the next morning.

• Learn never to place too much dependence on a subordinate unless it is clearly to the latter's personal advantage to be loyal—Although some people are compulsively conscientious, most are not. Most give lip service to the company or the boss, but when the crunch comes, their loyalty is exclusively to themselves and their interests.

• Be willing to compromise on small matters—He does this in order to obtain power for further movement. Nothing is more often fatal to executive power than stubbornness in small matters.

• Be skilled in self-dramatization and be a persuasive personal salesman—He is essentially an actor, capable of influencing his audiences emotionally as well as rationally. He first ascertains his audience's wants and values. He then proceeds to confirm them, thus absolutely ensuring his hearer's acceptance of his message.

• Radiate self-confidence—He must give the impression that he knows what he is doing and is completely in command of the situation, even though he may not be sure at all.

• Give outward evidence of status, power, and material success— Most people measure a leader by the degree of pomp and circumstance with which he surrounds himself. (This is why the king lives in a palace and the Pope in the Vatican.) Too much modesty and democracy in his way of life may easily be mistaken for a lack of power and influence. For example, most subordinates take vicarious pride in being able to say, "That's my boss who lives in the mansion on the hill and drives a Rolls Royce."

• Avoid bureaucratic rigidity in interpreting company rules — To win and hold the allegiance of his subordinates, an executive must be willing to "bend the rules" from time to time and make exceptions, even when they are not wholly justified.

• Remember to give praise as well as censure — Frequently, because he is under pressure from his superiors, he takes out his frustrations on his subordinates by criticizing them, sometimes unreasonably. He must remember that, if their loyalty is to be won and held, they merit equal amounts of praise and reassurance.

• Be open-minded and receptive to opinions which differ from his — If he makes people feel that anyone who disagrees with him is, ipso facto, wrong, his power will suffer. Listening to dissent is the principal means by which he can experience corrective contact with reality and receive warning that the course he is following will lead to trouble. Also, openness to disagreement helps him to use his power fairly — or, more accurately, use it in a manner that will be perceived as fair by subordinates.

Conclusion

The position of a top executive who has little or no equity in the business is often a perilous one, with little inherent security. If things go well, his tenure is usually ensured; if they go badly, all too often he is made the scapegoat. Since many of the factors that affect his performance are beyond his control, he is constantly subject to the threat of disaster. His only hope for survival under these conditions is to gain and retain power by tactics that are in a large measure political and means that are, in part at least, Machiavellian.

Such strategies are not always noble and high-minded. But neither are they naive. From the selfish standpoint of the beleaguered and harassed executive, they have one primary merit: they enhance his chances of survival.

Ricard Company (A)*

THE C. E. RICARD Company Ltd., established in 1953, specializes in canning food products. Sales are on a contract basis under the label of the purchasing companies. The organization, originally centered on a single individual, has gradually developed in a form of management by participation.

HISTORICAL BACKGROUND

The company had begun modestly enough when its founder, Mr. Claude Ricard, had had a chance to get started in the canning business as supplier to a food-products firm. The business was progressing (with sales of $2.6 million and profits of $45,000 in 1960) when Mr. Ricard died, seven years after launching it.

After a short period of uncertainty, the task of managing the firm was turned over to a relative of the founder, Mr. Robert Beaulieu, who had joined the company not long before. After holding steady for some years, sales and profits forged ahead when additions were made to the plant. Recently, after eight years at the head of the firm, the general manager decided to triple the cannery's production capacity. This decision was prompted by rapid growth in demand and more particularly by the prospect of a large contract with a well-known firm in the food industry. One year after the new plant opened, sales had climbed to $7.4 million, while profits had reached $390,000. Sixty employees had worked for Ricard at the time of the founder's death; there were now two hundred.

This growth had been accompanied by a series of far-reaching changes within the firm. The founder's death had left it utterly disorganized; Mr. Ricard had been the heart of the business, and no one was prepared to take over from him. Mr. Beaulieu, to whom the reins of management were entrusted, had no experience in this area, and had worked for the company for only six months.

Mr. Beaulieu had a high-school diploma in commercial studies. He had begun his career as an office clerk in a firm of moderate size, and had risen to the position of purchasing manager, but saw little hope of further

---

* This case was prepared by Professor Pierre Laurin, University of Montreal, as a basis for class discussion. Presented at the Intercollegiate Case Development Workshop, University of Santa Clara, October 18–20, 1973. Copyright © 1973 by the Ecole des Hautes Etudes Commerciales de Montréal., and used with permission.

promotion. It was at this point that Mr. Ricard had offered him a position in his company, with the prospect of eventually becoming operations manager.

Paradoxically enough, Mr. Beaulieu felt that his lack of experience had been useful to him in his new job. He began by hiring foremen (the company had never had any before) and unhesitatingly went to them when he had problems, acknowledging his own inexperience and requesting their advice. By this means, Mr. Beaulieu noted, he was able to obtain excellent cooperation from his men. Adopting a similar attitude with suppliers and customers, he found both groups willing to cooperate with him to the fullest possible extent, since the continued existence of the company was in their own interest. In this fashion he obtained valuable advice on means of regulating inputs of raw materials into processed food products and other important technical matters. He also found that he made many friends.

A position was created for a deputy manager, to help Mr. Beaulieu with his duties. Another step the manager took at an early stage was to engage a firm of consultants to develop a standard cost system for him, in order to make it easier to evaluate the performance of each of the company's product lines. Mr. Beaulieu called in another firm of consultants some years later, to set up an organizational structure that would be compatible with rapid growth.

A systematic task analysis was carried out, and one of the first conclusions arrived at was that the deputy manager should be appointed to the position of production manager. At this time the deputy manager had recently been replaced by an engineer, Roger Dubois. With the assistance of the firm of consultants, subsequent years were devoted to solving production problems and exploring prospects for growth, which Mr. Beaulieu suspected might be little short of breathtaking. A market study submitted exactly ten years after Mr. Beaulieu took over confirmed his fondest hopes: the possibilities were extensive, notably in the eastern United States. "We realized, however," Mr. Beaulieu said, "that for expansion on the scale we were contemplating, our managerial team would not be enough. We decided to add a whole new level of management and to recruit from outside."

ORGANIZATION

The newly created positions were those of sales manager, purchasing manager, and administrative services manager. At this stage, a sales manager and a purchasing manager had been hired. Appendix A and Appendix B show the company's organizational chart and provide some information about the managerial staff.

The production manager's job included all the responsibilities normally

APPENDIX A
Organizational Chart of The Ricard Company Ltd.

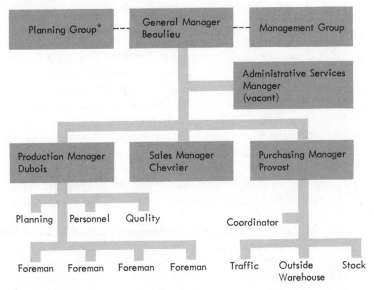

* Not yet organized.

APPENDIX B
Information about the Managers of The Ricard Company Ltd.

Name	Position	Age	Length of Time with Ricard	Education	Former Position
Robert Beaulieu...	General manager	37	11 years	High-school diploma	Purchasing manager, small company
André Chevrier....	Sales manager	53	1 year	B.A.* studies in administration	Marketing manager, large, well-known firm
Roger Dubois......	Production manager	38	5 years	B.A., chemical engineering	Production consultant, firm of consultants
Marcel Provost....	Purchasing manager	34	8 months	Agronomist, M.B.A.†	Consultant, government agency

* Bachelor of Arts.
† Master of Business Administration.

associated with that position, but in this particular instance there were two factors that were exceptionally critical. Quality was one, since all products were rigorously inspected by the companies whose labels appeared on the cans. Production process control was the other, since Ricard could only survive as long as it was financially advantageous for other companies to buy from it rather than preparing their own products.

The production manager was a young engineer, whose motivation sprang from an interest in directing operations in a systematic fashion. He had previously worked for a large firm, but had been attracted by the potential challenge offered by a company like Ricard. At the outset he knew nothing whatever about the way the company operated, but as he himself said, "a good administrator does not have to have a thorough knowledge of the technical side."

Purchasing had a highly important position in the firm, both because raw materials were a major cost item and because competition for supplies was keen. Prices tended to fluctuate markedly in response to variations in the availability of different food items. On the one hand, outlays for raw materials and stocks had to be kept to a reasonable level; on the other hand, continuity of production had to be maintained, and opportunities for increased sales had to be seized when they appeared. To maintain a balance among these various forces was a somewhat delicate business.

The purchasing manager, Marcel Provost, was an ambitious young man who admitted frankly that he had been attracted to that position in particular because he had recognized it as the crux of the whole operation. "It was even more critical than sales," he said, "because we were in a seller's market, and the company's success depended on efficiency in purchasing." Three factors had brought him into the company: his desire to be at the decision-making centre of a dynamic enterprise, his interest in working in the food industry, and the open-mindedness of the general manager.

Sales, for its part, held something of a privileged position in the business in view of the fact that all production was sold in advance, as the sales manager himself acknowledged. The major problem the company faced was diversifying the clientele, so as not to be excessively dependent on one customer who accounted for a large percentage of sales figures. Recent efforts in this direction had met with success, but care had to be taken not to outrun Production's ability to increase plant output. The tactic had therefore been adopted of approaching potential customers with a view to paving the way for possible future sales.

Sales contracts were negotiated at very high levels. A contract was sometimes the result of negotiations lasting a year or more on the subject of the financial advantage that a company might expect from buying from Ricard.

The sales manager, Mr. Chevrier, had a confident air about him and conversed readily but with discretion. He had held high positions in large companies, but had been attracted to Ricard, he said, by the great possibilities that the industry had to offer, and by the determination of the men at the top to take advantage of them. The personality of the general manager and his management philosophy were major elements in this latter factor.

This management philosophy was well illustrated by the role that the management committee had come to assume. This committee, which consisted of the general manager and the other three managers, convened once a week; meetings lasted for several hours. The general manager defined the committee's functions as noting current problems and working as a team in an effort to find solutions.

In the first place, Mr. Beaulieu considered it important for all of them to be acquainted with the problems of each sector, given the critical degree of interdependence among sectors in the company. To take a simple example, the sales personnel could not promise deliveries without knowing whether adequate supplies of raw materials would be forthcoming. Similarly, the production department had to be kept up to date on orders and supply conditions in order to be in a position to prepare the mix of products according to specifications.

It was also the committee's task to scrutinize current results and apply appropriate corrective measures as needed. When any manager had a problem, all the managers were mobilized to help solve it.

The general manager's function within this committee, as he himself saw it, was to act as a moderator, guiding the discussion and clarifying the situation when problems were raised. He explained: "for instance, if a production problem is brought up, it is up to me to point out the implications of that problem for the business as a whole and to induce the others to reach a decision and act on it. We co-decide, so to speak. I contribute my ideas on the same footing as the others. If it happens that B . . . 's idea is best, it is my responsibility to say that it is best. If there is any one who disagrees, he has to be given additional information. It may turn out that he was right to disagree. I admit that this procedure is cumbersome and not always effective, but I believe in it."

Mr. Beaulieu had hopes that the committee would feel free to discuss problems of all kinds at some future date, but at present problems involving personalities were too delicate to handle. He acknowledged that it might be hard on someone to be shown to be wrong in the presence of three other people, but in his view it was preferable for problems to be discussed by four people together than in one-to-one situations.

Mr. Beaulieu's view of the matter was based on a deeply rooted conviction that a leader must share responsibility with his subordinates to the greatest possible extent. "As far as I am concerned," he stated, "a leader must be able to lead his men and delegate a maximum of authority. He should give his subordinates as much responsibility as possible. I am against one-man rule. A leader should be flexible and give his men a chance to express their views. I don't believe in being autocratic; I believe in dialogue and participation."

Mr. Beaulieu did not deny that a leader's task is to accept responsibility and direct his followers. He compared his function as a leader of men to the work of a teacher, whose influence is owing to the confidence he inspires and the guidance he provides, and who adds an element of coherence to the ideas and efforts of others.

The other three managers regarded this philosophy as a highly important element in the organizational lives. They were unanimous in expressing respect for the general manager's enlightened outlook.

The sales manager, Marcel Provost, reacted most positively to the participation concept. He explained that the main reason why he had come to Ricard was the prospect of "having a full share in all decision-making." He saw Mr. Beaulieu as a coordinator who did not attempt to unduly exert his influence as general manager. "One of the other managers," he said, "might very well become the leader on some major issue."

Mr. Provost considered that the committee still had some distance to go in the direction of greater efficiency. He admitted that a group approach might well slow down the decision-making process, and was devoting some thought to possible improvements in the discussion procedure. "However," he said, "it would be a mistake to try to achieve faster-moving discussions at the expense of quality."

Mr. Provost also had some comments to make on the problems that the delegation of authority might imply for the general manager. "The delegation of power means a gain for the subordinates. I imagine that this consideration must play a major part in the general manager's thinking. In any case, I came to Ricard because it was the only company I knew of where the general manager was willing to run the risk of delegating authority to young university graduates who were eager to build something worthwhile."

The production manager, Roger Dubois, had been with the company for five years. In his view, the virtue of the new management formula lay in the fact that it enabled the managers to establish an unprecedented type of subtle working relationships with the general manager. "I am an engineer, and my training taught me to operate logically. There was a certain amount of conflict when I worked as deputy manager; I thought he was too concerned with growth and not concerned enough with building a sound internal organization. I had trouble selling my point of view. Provost's arrival made a difference, fortunately; it seems to be easier to get my point of view across; we are more on the same wavelength. Things go much better now that the four of us work things out together. Before, when the director and I worked alone, there was no avoiding that superior-inferior relationship."

The sales manager, André Chevrier, spoke confidently of the part he played in the Ricard Company. The fact that he spent most of his time selling Ricard products to some of the largest firms in the world was an essential source of gratification for him. He expressed admiration for Mr. Beaulieu; "In fact, I idolize him," he said with a laugh. He was impressed by the general manager's receptiveness to other people's ideas and his ability to learn quickly. As an example, he pointed to Mr. Beaulieu's exhaustive knowledge of all aspects of the company's operations and all the details of their interrelationships.

CURRENT PROBLEMS

The new plant had now been open for five months. In the general manager's opinion, the period of adjustment to the new machinery and new methods had been long enough, and it was time for the plant to settle into a normal operating routine. First and foremost, he said, it was crucial to achieve once again the high standard of quality on which the company's business had been built. And secondly, additional efforts had to be made to obtain better utilization of raw materials and higher output. The general manager pointed out that there were substantial amounts of money to be recovered. All this meant that the managers would be called upon to demonstrate initiative and alertness in solving the problems that arose in their respective areas. Mr. Beaulieu was by far the best informed of all of them about the various factors at work, but he now wanted to withdraw to some extent from day-to-day issues to devote more of his time to planning.

Ricard Company (B)*

ON THE BASIS of several months' experience, the managers of the Ricard Company agreed that the system of management now in effect within the organization was basically satisfactory, but they also stressed that the system was not functioning as well as it should be, and that corrective measures were needed. They all thought that the following episode had subjected the system to its most severe test to date.

THE INCIDENT

The problem had to do with sizable losses that Production had been suffering for some time. The question was raised at one of the management committee's weekly meetings.

The four managers were seated at a rectangular table, two on each side. The meeting began as usual with exchanges of information about the week's activities. The general manager's comments demonstrated his extensive knowledge of the company's operations. Usually he would state his point of view somewhat as follows: "If I may intervene, on the basis of my experience with such-and such, I think that . . . "

After reviewing the purchasing situation, the meeting turned to production. The sales and purchasing managers requested explanations of the various figures in the weekly production report. At one point the general manager mentioned that the percentage of rejects was still running at a very high level as a result of the fact that the proportion of water in the cans was incorrect; he also pointed out that the ratio of raw materials to finished products was inadequate in terms of yield. He concluded by turning to Dubois, the production manager, and asking: "Now, how do you intend to correct this?"

Dubois answered somewhat evasively. Provost, the purchasing manager, added a comment. Then the general manager took up the thread again, asking in a conciliatory manner: "Well, now, what should we do? We have devoted a lot of time to solving problems of $100 and $200. Here we have a problem of $2,000 to $4,000 a week, and we can't get an answer; we're told 'it will correct itself'."

---

* This case was prepared by Professor Pierre Laurin, University of Montreal, as a basis for class discussion. Presented at the Intercollegiate Case Development Workshop, University of Santa Clara, October 18–20, 1973. Copyright © 1973, by the Ecole des Hautes Etudes Commerciales de Montréal and used with permission.

The production manager mentioned some equipment he thought the plant required, and the discussion became technical for a time. Dubois estimated that it would be at least six weeks before he would be able to correct the situation. This brought a reaction from Provost: "But during that time we will be losing $2,000 a week." It was clear that the general manager shared this sentiment.

Dubois then explained what the trouble was, while the general manager listened closely, interrupting on occasion to ask for clarification of certain points, as did Provost.

"In any case," the general manager said at the end of the exchange, "the important thing is to make sure that the problem is getting enough attention. Do you need any help? Shall we put some extra people on to it? Six more weeks of this is going to wreck your budget."

Dubois replied that there was a certain type of pump that he had to find, that various pieces of equipment had to be checked over, etc. The general manager retorted, "what I am asking you gentlemen is, what shall we do to handle a problem of this nature? We have been getting bad results for ten weeks now, and according to Roger [Dubois] we can look forward to six weeks more of the same. The problem is that it is costing us $2,000 a week. I am wondering if we're going about this in the right way, and if not, is there anything that can be done about it."

Dubois listed several possible corrective measures that might solve the problem. While he was speaking, Provost went to the blackboard in the front of the room and sketched a diagram showing the points raised by Dubois. At the end of Dubois' summary, Chevrier, the sales manager, concluded, "well, what we have to do is put on the pressure to get this equipment as soon as possible."

MARCEL PROVOST: Maybe it's a matter of men rather than a matter of equipment.

ROBERT BEAULIEU: Perhaps we should ask Company X [Ricard's largest customer] to lend us a man for a certain length of time.

After half an hour of such exchanges, Provost asked, "Is it a problem of know-how or a problem of time? I mean to say, do we know what has to be done, only it's going to take a while? Or don't we have any ideas?"

ROBERT BEAULIEU: What is the problem exactly?

ROGER DUBOIS: There is too much lean meat in the cans.

ROBERT BEAULIEU: Is that it?

ROGER DUBOIS: Yes, this is giving us too much weight per can.

MARCEL PROVOST: O.K., that's the problem, but what causes it?

ROGER DUBOIS: It may be the weighing of the raw materials. (Provost, who was still at the blackboard, made another entry on his diagram.) Then, it may be incorrect regulation of water content. Then, our floor losses[1] may be too high throughout the whole production process.

---

[1] "Floor" losses: losses of raw materials resulting from handling.

Various possibilities were discussed during the next half hour. Provost repeated his earlier question: "Is the difficulty that we don't have the know-how, or do we know what to do about it?" (His diagram now had three parts: problems, causes, solutions. The central part was the most filled in).

Dubois suggested that the problem might also be the result of inadequate coordination among the three sectors of the firm. This question was discussed at some length, and finally the managers concluded that the problem was solved for the future. All appeared satisfied with the discussion, but the general manager added: "I want dates; I want to know what is going to be done; and [addressing Dubois] if you need help, you will get it."

ROGER DUBOIS: If the problem is in the weighing of the raw materials . . . (he went on to explain the activities and costs that would be inherent in the process of obtaining information at this preliminary stage in production).

ROBERT BEAULIEU: What we really have to do is pinpoint the source of the problem.

ROGER DUBOIS: If the weighing were really the cause, we wouldn't really be losing anything. It would work out, or at least it could work out at some point.

MARCEL PROVOST: Let me see if I grasp this, Roger, what is your main problem?

ROGER DUBOIS: Losses of raw materials. This can cost us up to three-quarters of a cent per can.

ROBERT BEAULIEU: X number of cases at three-quarters of a cent per can comes to $1,700 a week. At $1,700 a week we could put somebody on it full time. Is there any way of straightening it out in less than six weeks?

The others checked the general manager's calculations over for themselves. Some of his figures were challenged, but Beaulieu produced records to show that they were correct. All agreed that the loss was serious. There was a long silence, and then the production manager returned to his initial consideration: "What is needed is a pump, but I can't tell yet exactly what to buy."

MARCEL PROVOST: But in the meantime you can station a man to keep an eye on floor losses.

ROGER DUBOIS: We will lose a lot anyway. A pump is the thing.

ROBERT BEAULIEU: All right, about these floor losses, will you be in a position to give me something on this?

ROGER DUBOIS: I have taken it up with Company X. They are helping me find the right pump.

ANDRÉ CHEVRIER: Maybe it would be possible to rent one.

ROGER DUBOIS: It's a special pump; it's not the kind of thing you can rent.

MARCEL PROVOST: About this other point, the weighing of the raw materials, what can be done about that?

Various aspects of the point that Provost had raised were discussed at length. Dubois made a point of refuting most of the suggestions that were put forward on the grounds of technical considerations. He insisted repeatedly that in his opinion the crux of the matter lay elsewhere. At one point in the discussion, the sales manager got up to leave. The general manager called to him with a smile, "Our discussion doesn't interest you, eh, André?"

Finally agreement was reached on the feasibility of making random spot checks of the weighing of the raw materials, and certain individuals were selected for the job. Then the general manager went on, "These floor losses, now, what are we going to do?" [Addressing Dubois] "You can order your pump by tomorrow?"

ROGER DUBOIS: No, I can't have the pump by tomorrow. I'll have to station a man out there with a shovel.

MARCEL PROVOST: "Was there any way of knowing that this pump was going to be needed?"

Dubois admitted that there had been some lack of foresight involved. When questioned about the feasibility of obtaining the pump as soon as possible, Dubois replied in terms of the technical features of the particular pump in question and pointed out the necessity of having detailed specifications. Finally, he promised to give the matter his undivided attention, and the general manager went on to a different subject. The meeting had been going on for three hours.

EVALUATION OF THE MEETING

The main protagonist in the incident, Roger Dubois, the production manager, had the following comments to make on what had happened at the meeting: "I went over the whole business with Robert [Beaulieu] afterwards. The others don't realize that in engineering it is impossible to operate by picking up the telephone and setting everything up for the next day. Take all that business about ordering a pump, for instance. You have to have detailed specifications; you have to be sure to order exactly what you want. I thought it would take six weeks before I could find the right kind, the right specifications, etc. In the mind of the general manager, I could have sent somebody to get all that information, but he didn't say so. The other committee members were afraid of meddling in my area of responsibility. If the general manager had said to me, 'I would like you to go and make it your business to find the pump you need' I would have gone. If he had said that to me, I would have done it. Basically, the problem is that on the one hand they were afraid to get involved in my area of responsibility, while on the other hand they wanted a pump first thing tomorrow morning."

Dubois also had doubts about the contributions that the other managers at the meeting had made to the subject under discussion. "Take this business of writing down alternatives on the blackboard, for example. That was the business of Production, not the management committee. They came up with two or three possibilities, whereas when I got together with my production staff next day we came up with fifteen. We wasted two hours during the management committee meeting because it was a production problem. In a discussion of that kind, they were putting me on the spot with all sorts of questions that I was not prepared to answer. We're in the middle of reorganizing, I don't have the experience. I couldn't handle that kind of a discussion before conferring with my men in Production."

In spite of his doubts, however, Dubois preferred, on balance, to see matters discussed at the management committee level rather than with the general manager. He added, "I had the impression that they were putting pressure on me to solve everything right away, but they weren't really. They were trying to help me handle my problem."

The general manager, for his part, was dissatisfied with the way the meeting had gone because he felt that progress had not been made fast enough. He had felt impelled to take up the problem again the next day with the production manager. He said, "I am dissatisfied because the problem has been around for several weeks already. There it was in plain sight, and now I am told that it will be six weeks before it can be solved. Reaction time is too slow. The other managers don't seem to see how serious this problem is. I understand that Roger is overloaded with work, but the way he bombarded us with vague reasons left me flabbergasted. I told him afterwards that I was not convinced that it would take six weeks. I told him that it would be entirely in order for him to take his car and go and buy a pump, or send someone else to do it" [normal delivery time would be six weeks]. "I have the impression that he doesn't want to be helped. He's afraid that I will accuse him of not doing his job properly if I bail him out."

The general manager stated that for the past two days he had been working in the factory on certain production problems to take some of the load off Dubois. He considered this state of affairs as temporary. "I prefer to delegate authority. I can't go out myself and buy the pump and come back and say, 'Here, I've found the pump.' That would destroy our spirit of teamwork. But at the same time, we're not in business to prove a theory."

Provost, the purchasing manager, said that he had a lot of sympathy for Dubois, because he himself had a background of training in technology, and also knew from experience what it meant to be responsible for production. He had invited Dubois to his house shortly after the meeting and had assured him of his assistance in solving the problem. Provost held himself responsible for the problem to some extent because raw materials were purchased in accordance with his specifications. He thought that the meeting had been useful because it was important for the sales manager to acquire some insight into production problems before accepting any new orders. As for decision-making on particular issues, he considered the process somewhat cumbersome, but felt that the committee should continue, since the opinions of all four managers were needed to reach decisions. He identified the source of the problem in these terms: "We were psychologically unprepared for a problem of this nature. We had fallen into the habit of assuming that difficulties would be settled quickly, whereas in planning for the new factory we should have assumed that we would have to expect to go on operating at a loss for a longer period of time."

The only manager whose evaluation of the meeting was definitely positive was Chevrier. According to him, the meeting might not have been very effective, but nevertheless it had been useful because it had pointed up the urgency of a serious problem. As far as he was concerned there was no such thing as perfection, and he considered it futile to imagine that there might be.

GENERAL CONSIDERATIONS

This production problem left a lasting impression on the new management team. As the general manager put it, "the production problem that we are grappling with at the moment has given me a good deal to think about. It is all very well to sit down around a table, participate and so forth, but when there are urgent problems to be dealt with, a time comes when action must be taken. We are not here to demonstrate a philosophy of management. Before this problem arose, the questions we dealt with had to do mainly with means of reaching our objectives. It was smooth. But this was the first time we had had such a critical problem to solve. . . . As general manager I have to see to it that the problem is corrected; otherwise radical action will be necessary. If there were incompetence at some point, a decision would have to be made, but it would be a joint decision. We all have our strengths and weaknesses. In the future we will have to take advantage of the strengths and compensate for the weaknesses more quickly than we have done so far."

This experience had also caused the general manager to think about the fact that in his opinion his subordinates tended to turn to him far too much, in spite of his preference for delegating authority. "I believe in group management. I think that management on a team basis is feasible. I would not even object if someone else took the lead on a particular occasion. Unfortunately, my authority is much greater than I would like it to be. For example, the action that has been taken to date on this production problem is the result of my intervention. I would like Roger [Dubois] to take more responsibility; I would like him to make more suggestions."

Mr. Beaulieu also expressed the wish that the purchasing manager would depend less on him to settle pressing day-to-day problems. "As I told him when he joined the company, 'your main responsibility is buying hogs' feet on the best possible terms.' Not much glory in that, but it is important for the company. I would like to have less influence in questions of that sort. Even so, Provost is more independently-minded than Dubois, and I'm not complaining."

Provost, for his part, suggested that it might be dangerous if some of the managers did not "pull their weight" in the team, but said that such was not the case at present. In his view, one of the basic problems brought out by the incident was the question of how to use everyone's talents to best advantage. He also offered some thoughts on the financial side of the problem:

"I am not sure that Robert [Beaulieu] sees all the implications of this problem," he said. "The losses that we have sustained mean a serious cash-flow problem, and this in turn raises the issue of financing. In my opinion, too much stress has been put on short-term financing. This throws an unwarranted strain on our liquidity position."

Provost reflected, however, that the experiment was still in its early stages, and that the group would learn from experience. He thought it was entirely possible that one of them might develop into an informal leader — perhaps the general manager, perhaps one of the others. In the latter case, the two should be able to divide their responsibilities in such a way as to benefit the company to the greatest possible extent.

Robert F. Kennedy High School*

ON JULY 15, 1970, David King became principal of the Robert F. Kennedy High School, the newest of the six high schools in Great Ridge, Illinois. The school had opened in the fall of 1968 amid national acclaim for being one of the first schools in the country to be designed and constructed for the "house system" concept. Kennedy High's organization was broken down into four "houses" each of which contained 300 stu-

---

* This material was prepared by Assistant Professor John J. Gabarro as a basis for class discussion rather than to illustrate either effective or ineffective handling of an administrative situation. Copyright © 1974 by the President and Fellows of Harvard College, reprinted by permission.

EXHIBIT 1
Robert F. Kennedy High School

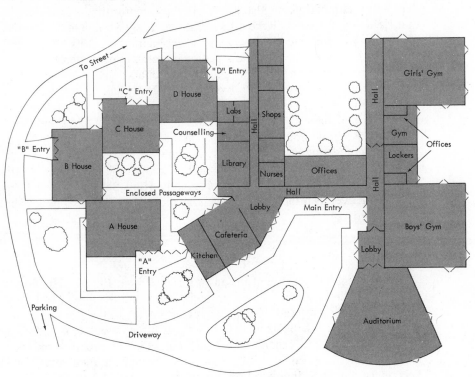

dents, a faculty of 18 and a house master. The Kennedy complex was especially designed so that each house was in a separate building connected to the "core facilities"[1] and other houses by an enclosed outside passageway. Each house had its own entrance, class rooms, toilets, conference rooms and house master's office. (See Exhibit 1 for the layout.)

King knew that Kennedy High was not intended to be an ordinary school when it was first conceived. It had been hailed as a major innovation in inner city education and a Chicago television station had made a documentary on it in 1968. Kennedy High had opened with a carefully selected staff of teachers, many of whom were chosen from other Great Ridge Schools and at least a dozen of whom had been especially recruited from out of state. Indeed, King knew his faculty included graduates from several elite East and West coast schools such as Stanford, Yale, and Princeton, as well as several of the very best midwestern

---

[1] The core facilities included the cafeteria, nurses' room, guidance offices, the boys' and girls' gyms, the offices, the shops, and auditorium.

schools. Even the racial mix of students had been carefully balanced so that blacks, whites and Puerto Ricans each comprised a third of the student body (although King also knew — perhaps better than its planners — that Kennedy's students were drawn from the toughest and poorest areas of town). The building itself was also widely admired for its beauty and functionality and had won several national architectural awards.

Despite these carefully and elaborate preparations, Kennedy High School was in serious difficulty by July of 1970. It had been wracked by violence the preceding year, having been twice closed by student disturbances and once by a teacher walkout. It was also widely reported (although King did not know for sure), that achievement scores of its 9th and 10th grade students had actually declined during the last two years, while no significant improvement could be found in the scores of the 11th and 12th graders' tests. Thus, the Kennedy High School, which King was taking over as principal, had fallen far short of its planners' hopes and expectations.

David King

David King was born and raised in Great Ridge, Illinois. His father was one of the city's first black principals and thus King was not only familiar with the city, but with its school system as well. After two years of military service, King decided to follow his father's footsteps and went to Great Ridge State Teachers College from which he received his BEd in 1955 and his MEd in 1960. King was certified in Elementary and Secondary School Administration, English and Physical Education. King had taught English and coached in a predominantly black middle school until 1960 when he was asked to become the school's assistant principal. He remained in that post until 1965 when he was asked to take over the George Thibeault Middle School, a large middle school of 900 pupils which at the time was reputed to be the most "difficult" middle school in the city. While at Thibeault, King gained a city-wide reputation for being a gifted and popular administrator and was credited with changing Thibeault from the worst middle school in the system to one of the best. He had been very effective in building community support, recruiting new faculty and in raising academic standards. He was also credited with turning out basketball and baseball teams which had won state and county middle school championships. King knew that he had been selected for the Kennedy job over several more senior candidates because of his ability to handle tough situations. The superintendent had made that clear when he told King why he had been selected for the job.

The superintendent had also told him that he would need every bit of skill and luck he could muster. King knew of the formidable credentials of Jack Weis, his predecessor at Kennedy High. Weis, a white, had been the superintendent of a small, local township school system before becoming Kennedy's first principal. He had also written a book on the "house system" concept, as well as a second book on inner city education. Weis had earned a PhD from the University of Chicago and a divinity degree from Harvard. Yet, despite his impressive background and obvious ability, Weis had resigned in disillusionment, and was described by many as a "broken man." In fact, King remembered seeing the physical change which Weis had undergone over that two year period. Weis' appearance had become progressively more fatigued and strained until he developed what appeared to be permanent black rings under his eyes and a perpetual stoop. King remembered how he had pitied the man and wondered how Weis could find the job worth the obvious personal toll it was taking on him.

History of the School

1968–1969   The school's troubles began to manifest themselves in the school's first year of operation. Rumors of conflicts between the housemasters and the six subject area department heads were widespread throughout the system by the middle of the first year. The conflicts stemmed from differences in interpretations of curriculum policy on required learning and course content. In response to these conflicts, Dr. Weis had instituted a "free market" policy by which subject area department heads were supposed to convince head masters of why they should offer certain courses, while head masters were supposed to convince department heads of which teachers they wanted assigned to their houses and why they wanted those teachers. Many observers in the school system felt that this policy exacerbated the conflicts.

To add to this climate of conflict a teacher was assaulted in her classroom in February of 1969. The beating frightened many of the staff, particularly some of the older teachers. A delegation of eight teachers asked Weis to hire security guards a week after the assault. The request precipitated a debate within the faculty about the desirability of having guards in the school. One group felt that the guards would instill a sense of safety within the school, and thus promote a better learning climate, while the other group felt that the presence of guards in the school would be repressive and would destroy the sense of community and trust which was developing within the school. Dr. Weis refused the request for security guards because he believed that symbolically they would represent everything the school was trying to change. In April a second teacher was robbed and beaten in her classroom after school hours and the debate was rekindled, except that this time a group of Spanish-speaking parents threatened to boycott the school unless better security measures were instituted. Again Dr. Weis refused the request for security guards.

1969–1970 The second year of the school's existence was even more troubled than the first. Because of cutbacks ordered during the summer of 1969, Dr. Weis was not able to replace eight teachers who resigned during the summer and it was no longer possible for each house to staff all of its courses with its own faculty. Dr. Weis therefore instituted a "flexible staffing" policy whereby some teachers were asked to teach a course outside of their assigned house and students in the 11th and 12th grades were able to take some elective and required courses in other houses. During this period, Chauncey Carver, one of the housemasters, publicly attacked the move as a step toward destroying the house system. In a letter to the *Great Ridge Times,* he accused the Board of Education of trying to subvert the house concept by cutting back funds.

The debate over the flexible staffing policy was heightened when two of the other housemasters joined a group of faculty and department chairmen in opposing Chauncey Carver's criticisms. This group argued that the individual house faculties of 15 to 18 teachers could never offer their students the breadth of courses that a school-wide faculty of 65 to 70 teachers could offer and that inter-house cross registration should be encouraged for that reason.

Further expansion of a cross registration or flexible staffing policy was halted, however, because of difficulties encountered in the scheduling of classes in the fall of 1969. Several errors were found in the master schedule which had been preplanned during the preceding summer. Various schedule difficulties persisted until November of 1969 when the Vice Principal responsible for the scheduling of classes resigned. Mr. Burtram Perkins, a Kennedy housemaster who had formerly planned the schedule at Central High assumed the scheduling function in addition to his duties as housemaster. The scheduling activity took most of Perkins' time until February.

Security again became an issue when three sophomores were assaulted because they refused to give up their lunch money during a "shakedown." It was believed that the assailants were from outside of the school and were not students. Several teachers approached Dr. Weis and asked him to request security guards from the Board of Education. Again, Dr. Weis declined but he asked Bill Smith, a Vice Principal at the school, to secure all doors except for the entrances to each of the four houses, the main entrance to the school, and the cafeteria. This move appeared to reduce the number of outsiders in the school.

In May of 1970 a disturbance occurred in the cafeteria which appeared to grow out of a fight between two boys. The fight spread and resulted in considerable damage to the school including the breaking of classroom windows and desks. The disturbance was severe enough for Dr. Weis to close the school. A number of teachers and students reported that outsiders were involved in the fight and in damaging the classrooms. Several

students were taken to the hospital for minor injuries but all were released. A similar disturbance occurred two weeks later and again the
school was closed. The Board of Education then ordered a temporary
detail of municipal police to the school despite Dr. Weis' advice to the
contrary. In protest to the assignment of the police detail, thirty of
Kennedy's 68 teachers staged a walkout which was joined by over half
the student body. The police detail was removed from the school, and an
agreement was worked out by an ad hoc subcommittee of the Board of
Education with informal representatives of teachers who were for and
against assigning a police detail. The compromise called for the temporary
stationing of a police cruiser near the school.

King's First Week at Kennedy High

Mr. King arrived at Kennedy High on Monday, July 15th and spent
most of his first week individually interviewing the school's key administrators (see Exhibit 2 for a listing of Kennedy's administrative staff as of
July 15th). He also had a meeting with all of his administrators and department heads on Friday of that week. Mr. King's purpose in these
meetings was to familiarize himself with the school, its problems, and its
key people.

His first interview was with Bill Smith, who was one of his Vice Principals. Mr. Smith was black and had worked as a counselor and as a Vice
Principal of a middle school prior to coming to Kennedy. King knew that
Smith had a reputation for being a tough disciplinarian and was very
much disliked among many of the younger faculty and students. However, King had also heard from several teachers, whose judgment he
respected, that Smith had been instrumental in keeping the school from
"blowing apart" the preceeding year. It became clear early in the interview that Smith felt that more stringent steps were needed to keep outsiders from wandering the buildings. In particular Smith urged King to
consider locking all of the school's 30 doors except for the front entrance
so that everyone would enter and leave through one set of doors only.
Smith also told him that many of the teachers and pupils had become fearful of living and working in the building and that "no learning will ever
begin to take place until we make it so people don't have to be afraid anymore." At the end of the interview, Smith told King that he had been approached by a nearby school system to become its director of counseling
but that he had not yet made up his mind. He said that he was committed
enough to Kennedy High that he did not want to leave, but that his decision depended on how hopeful he felt about its future.

As King talked with others, he discovered that the "door question"
was one of considerable controversy within the Faculty and that feelings
ran high, both in favor of the idea of locking all the doors as well as against

it. Two of the housemasters in particular, Chauncey Carver, a black, and Frank Czepak, a white, were strongly against closing the house entrances. The two men felt that such an action would symbolically reduce house "autonomy" and the feeling of distinctness that was a central aspect of the house concept.

Chauncey Carver, master of "C" House, was particularly vehement on this issue as well as on the question of whether students of one house should be allowed to take classes in another house. Carver said that the flexible staffing program introduced the preceeding year had nearly destroyed the house concept and that he, Carver, would resign if King intended to expand the cross-house enrollment of students. Carver also complained about what he described as "interference" from department heads in his teacher's autonomy.

Carver appeared to be an outstanding housemaster from everything that King had heard about him—even from his many enemies. Carver had an abrasive personality but seemed to have the best operating house in the school and was well liked by most of his teachers and pupils. His program also appeared to be the most innovative of all. However, it was also the program which was most frequently attacked by the department heads for lacking substance and not covering the requirements outlined in the system's curriculum guide. Even with these criticisms, King imagined how much easier it would be if he had four housemasters like Chauncey Carver.

During his interviews with the other three housemasters, King discovered that they all felt infringed upon by the department heads, but that only Carver and Czepak were strongly against "locking the doors" and that two other housemasters actively favored cross-house course enrollments. King's fourth interview was with Burtram Perkins who was also a housemaster. Perkins was a black in his late forties who had been an assistant to the principal of Central High before coming to Kennedy. Perkins spent most of the interview discussing how schedule pressures could be relieved. Perkins was currently involved in developing the schedule for the 1970–1971 school year until a Vice Principal was appointed to perform that job (Kennedy High had allocations for two Vice Principals and two assistants in addition to the housemasters. See Exhibit 2).

Two pieces of information concerning Perkins came to King's attention during his first week there. The first was that several teachers were circulating a letter requesting Perkins' removal as a housemaster because they felt he could not control the house or direct the faculty. This surprised King because he had heard that Perkins was widely respected within the faculty and had earned a reputation for supporting high academic standards and for working tirelessly with new teachers. However, as King inquired further he discovered that Perkins was greatly liked within the faculty but was also generally recognized as a poor house-master. The second piece of information concerned how Perkins' house compared with the others. Although students had been randomly assigned to each house, Perkins' house had the largest absence rate and the greatest number of disciplinary problems in the school. Smith had also told him that Perkins' drop-out rate for 1969–1970 was three times that of any other house.

While King was in the process of interviewing his staff he was called on by Mr. David Crimmins, Chairman of the History Department. Crim-mins was a native of Great Ridge, white, and in his late forties. Crimmins was scheduled for an appointment the following week, but asked King if he could see him immediately. Crimmins said he wanted to talk with King because he had heard that a letter was being circulated asking for Perkins' removal and that he wanted to present the other side of the argument. Crimmins became very emotional during the conversation, and said that Perkins was viewed by many of the teachers and department chairmen as the only housemaster who was making an effort to maintain high aca-

EXHIBIT 2
Administrative Organization, Robert F. Kennedy High School,
Great Ridge, Illinois

Principal	David King, 42 (black)
	BEd; MEd, Great Ridge State
	College
Vice Principal	William Smith, 44 (black)
	BEd, Breakwater State College
	MEd (Counseling), Great Ridge
	State College
Vice Principal	Vacant – to be filled
Housemaster, A House	Burtram Perkins, 47 (black)
	BS; MEd, Univ. of Illinois
Housemaster, B House	Frank Czepak, 36 (white)
	BS, Univ. of Illinois
	MEd, Great Ridge State College
Housemaster, C House	Chauncey Carver, 32 (black)
	AB, Wesleyan Univ.
	BFA, Pratt Institute
	MAT, Yale University
Housemaster, D House	John Bonavota, 26 (white)
	BEd, Great Ridge State College
	MEd, Ohio State Univ.
Assistant to the Principal	Vacant – to be filled
Assistant to the Principal (for Community Affairs).	Vacant – to be filled

demic standards, and that his transfer would be seen as a blow to those concerned with quality education. He also described in detail Perkins' devotion and commitment to the school and the fact that Perkins was the only administrator with the ability to straighten out the schedule, and that he had done this in addition to all of his other duties. Crimmins departed by saying that if Perkins were transferred, that he, Crimmins would personally write a letter to the regional accreditation council telling them how badly standards had sunk at Kennedy. King assured him that it would not be necessary to take such a drastic measure and that a cooperative resolution would be found. King was aware of the accreditation review that Kennedy High faced the following April and he did not wish to complicate the process unnecessarily in any way.

Within 20 minutes of Crimmins' departure, King was visited by a young white teacher named Tim Shea who said that he had heard that Crimmins had come in to see him. Shea said that he was one of the teachers who organized the movement to get rid of Perkins. Shea said that he liked and admired Perkins very much because of his devotion to the school but that Perkins' house was so disorganized and discipline so bad that it was nearly impossible to do any good teaching. Shea added that it was "a shame to lock the school up when stronger leadership is all that's needed."

King's impressions of his administrators generally matched what he had heard about them before arriving at the school. Carver seemed to be a very bright, innovative, and charismatic leader whose mere presence generated excitement. Czepak seemed to be a highly competent, though not very imaginative administrator, who had earned the respect of his faculty and students. Bonavota, who was only 26, seemed very bright and earnest but unseasoned and unsure of himself. King felt that with a little guidance and training Bonavota might have the greatest promise of all. At the moment, however, he appeared to be a very uncertain and somewhat confused person who had difficulty simply coping. Perkins seemed to be a very sincere, and devoted person who had a good mind for administrative details but an almost total incapacity for leadership.

King knew that he would have the opportunity to make several administrative appointments because of the three vacancies which existed. Indeed, should Smith resign as Vice Principal, King would be in the position of filling both Vice Principalships. He knew that his recommendations for these positions would carry a great deal of weight with the central office. The only constraint that King felt in making these appointments was the need to achieve some kind of racial balance among the Kennedy administrative group. With his own appointment as principal, the number of black administrators exceeded the number of white administrators by a ratio of two to one, and as yet Kennedy did not have a single Puerto Rican administrator even though a third of its pupils had Spanish surnames.

The Friday Afternoon Meeting

In contrast to the individual interviews, King was surprised to find how quiet and conflict-free these same people were in the staff meeting that he called on Friday. He was amazed at how slow, polite, and friendly the conversation appeared to be among people who had so vehemently expressed negative opinions of each other in private. After about 45 minutes of discussion about the upcoming accreditation review, King broached the subject of housemaster–department head relations. The ensuing silence was finally broken by a joke which Czepak made about the uselessness of discussing that topic. King probed further by asking whether everyone was happy with the current practices. Crimmins suggested that this was a topic that might be better discussed in a smaller group. Everyone in the room seemed to agree with Crimmins except for Betsy Dula, a young white woman in her late twenties who was chairman of the English Department. She said that one of the problems with the school was that no one was willing to tackle tough issues until they exploded. She said that relations between housemasters and department heads were terrible and it made her job very difficult. She then attacked Chauncey Carver for impeding her evaluation of a non-tenured teacher in Carver's house. The two argued for several minutes about the teacher and the quality of the experimental Sophomore English course that the teacher was giving. Finally, Carver, who by now was quite angry, coldly warned Mrs. Dula that he would "break her neck" if she stepped into his house again. King intervened in an attempt to cool both their tempers and the meeting ended shortly thereafter.

The following morning, Mrs. Dula called King at home and told him that unless Chauncey Carver publicly apologized for his threat, she would file a grievance with the teachers' union and take it to court if necessary. King assured Mrs. Dula that he would talk with Carver on Monday. King then called Eleanor Debbs, one of the school's Math teachers whom he had known well for many years and whose judgment he respected. Mrs. Debbs was a close friend of both Carver and Mrs. Dula and was also Vice President of the city's teachers' union. He learned from her that both had been long-term adversaries but that she felt both were excellent professionals.

She also reported that Mrs. Dula would be a formidable opponent and could muster considerable support among the faculty. Mrs. Debbs, who was herself black, feared that a confrontation between Dula and Carver might create tensions along race lines within the school even though both Dula and Carver were generally quite popular with students of all races. Mrs. Debbs strongly urged King not to let the matter drop. Mrs. Debbs also told him that she had overheard Bill Smith, the Vice Principal, say at a party the preceding night that he felt that King didn't have either the stomach or the forcefulness necessary to survive at Kennedy. Smith further stated that the only reason he was staying was that he did not expect King to last the year. Should that prove to be the case, Smith felt that he would be appointed principal.

Shape Up or Ship Out:
The Confessions of a Head Resident

HUXLEY HALL is a men's residence hall at Upstate University, housing some 130 students. The building consists essentially of three and one-half floors, with the basement and first floor being regarded as a single administrative unit. Each floor has one Resident Assistant (RA), an undergraduate, whose main functions are to be helpful to students, to help build community on the floor, and to see that University and hall rules generally are complied with. The staff is coordinated by me, Marvin Katz, the head resident (HR). I am a graduate student in the Counseling Program, 33 years old, interested in becoming an administrator in an educational setting. I have overall responsibility and accountability for the functioning of the entire residence hall, so my HR job offers good career preparation to me.

Huxley has acquired a distinctive reputation over the years, deriving from the fact that an inordinately large proportion of varsity athletes reside there. In the past, Huxley has been the scene of legendary feats of drinking, noise and destruction. Terms such as "jock house" and "zoo" are frequently applied to Huxley, and not entirely without justification.

This year, from the very beginning, the third floor of Huxley seemed intent upon carrying on that tradition. Led by a core group of *macho* football and hockey freshmen, a sizeable group began terrorizing the rest of the third floor (and other parts of the university community) starting in September, when the first floor candy machine somehow found its way up to the third floor. The following sorts of incidents have become the rule rather than the exception: loud conversations and shouting; blaring stereos and televisions as late as 4:30 A.M.; breaking windows, light globes and bottles; ripping bannisters off the wall; slamming doors; playing hockey in the halls (often with real pucks); throwing darts at people's doors; physical intimidation of people wishing to sleep or study; and staging water fights with fire extinguishers. In addition, there have been many instances of dope smoke wafting in the hallway, and flagrant violations of parietal hours.

The Principals

Dan, the third floor RA: A junior at Upstate U., an enthusiastic, sensitive person, always willing and ready to help anyone on the floor; honest and open when dealing with people, although not especially articulate; tending to identify very personally with his job as RA; quick to encourage students to stand up for their own rights on the floor, but ready to stand up for those not "ballsy" enough to do so for themselves; reasonable, doesn't go around trying to think up picky ways to catch people breaking rules; likely to ask people in a nice way, rather than give orders.

Frank: about 6'1", 220 pounds, freshman football player, on scholarship; inactive this season due to injury; incredibly loud person; frequently drinks heavily and becomes even louder; generally liked, even by those who wish he would disappear; has been involved in at least forty notable incidents, mostly involving late night noise; is one of the leaders of a rowdy group, the fringe members of which often do the real damage.

Jim: an excellent freshman hockey player; responsible directly or indirectly for much of the $300 damage bill thus far incurred by the third floor; has been the main offender in tampering with fire safety equipment; used to take special pleasure in taunting Dan, the RA; has his own cult of hero worshippers who support and encourage him in noise, destruction and hazing the RA.

Dick: a late arrival on the trouble scene; had little to do with the floor until his girlfriend broke up with him; is closely associated with Frank's group, but independently has flagrantly violated parietal hours, intimidated other students on the floor, endangered others with fireworks, caused extensive and intentional damage for which he refuses to own up, and been involved in several minor dope violations; marginal football player.

Sheldon: has a particularly grating way about him, which has led to bitter relationships with the RA and several other students of the floor; not generally liked; has mainly been associated with late night rowdiness, use of fire extinguishers, intimidation, fireworks, and parietal violations; a marginal hockey player.

Prior Attempts to Cope with Situation

From the outset, Dan, as RA, tried to keep a lid on the situation by talking with individuals and groups on the floor. He kept the rest of the staff informed of developments and asked for their advice and support on many occasions. Dan wrote up "incident reports" on individuals involved in flagrant rule violations, or continually involved in normal violations. When the talking did not seem to work, several of the main protagonists were brought before the hall judiciary council for various offenses. This solution proved unworkable, however, as peer pressure became too great, and the council expressed its desire to be spared judicial functions, for fear of reprisal. I, Marv, chose instead to concentrate on organizing social functions. I held dorm meetings, floor meetings, small group meetings, and individual meetings in an attempt to get the differences resolved. Most of the students saw an irreconcilable conflict between the rowdies and the rest. The rowdies had no particular investment in resolving conflict, since their behavior was paying off in good fun. While threats of punishment seemed to have some effect, when the hall judiciary proved ineffective, expectations began to develop that nothing serious would happen to the offenders. This happened despite the fact that two very active rowdies were evicted from the hall by the campus-wide Student Judicial Board (SJB), for conduct occurring outside of Huxley.

As the second semester progressed, the situation worsened; rowdies began increasingly to regard the RA's warnings as mere harassment and retaliated with provocative behavior toward Dan and increased intimidation of other complaining students. At the end of February, I met individually with six rowdies, including the four principals, and informed them that their behavior had gone beyond permissible limits. I asked for their commitments to shape up, keep each other in line, or ship out. This began a series of incidents directed primarily at Dan, the RA. Windows were broken, doors slammed, bottles broken, fire extinguishers discharged, firecrackers set off, and apples splattered against Dan's door, and no one knew for certain who was responsible.[1] Dan became increasingly more irritable, alternately angry and despondent as the semester wore on.

The end of spring vacation brought fresh supplies of fireworks, thanks to Sheldon's trip to Florida. One Tuesday, a pack of about two dozen firecrackers was dropped down the stairs from the third floor to the first, narrowly missing one student. On Wednesday, I returned from a class in conflict management to find the fire trucks in front of Huxley Hall. Apparently, someone had blown apart a ceiling fixture with a firecracker, and the smoke set off the fire alarm. Dick's door was also kicked in. I called a floor meeting that night. A hushed crowd listened to me outlaw hall games (which might lead to damage in the corridor), announce that any-

---

[1] At the end of each semester, damages to a dormitory for which responsibility is unknown, are apportioned equally to all residents by the Business Office.

one caught with firecrackers would be prosecuted to the fullest, and issue a general warning that action would be taken on further rule violations.

The Proverbial Last Straw

On Friday afternoon, Dan came in to see me, slumped into a beanbag chair. With an air of resignation, he said, "I can't take it anymore. I've got to leave." It turned out that a variety of events had occurred during the night between 12:30 and 2:00 A.M. The corridors were filled with marijuana smoke, clearly emanating from Frank's room and from Dick's room. Sheldon had been openly entertaining a woman in his room in violation of parietal hours. When Dan asked him to close the door, Sheldon gave him grief. Dan then told him to see the woman out of the hall; Sheldon and the woman left; but after waiting a few minutes for Dan to leave, returned. Frank staggered in drunk dragging a huge road sign; when Dan told him to get rid of it, in no uncertain terms, a fellow football player-friend intervened to tell Dan what an incompetent RA he was. A heated argument ensued and the two came close to blows. Dan finally walked away and went to bed. Unable to sleep, he opened his door a few minutes later to find Frank's friend poised to urinate on his door.

The Heat of Battle

I arranged an instant meeting with my boss, the University Director of Residential Life, who, upon hearing the most recent story, became furiously angry. I asked for, and received, authorization to offer the chief trouble makers on the floor the option of voluntarily moving to another residence hall immediately or being taken before the campus-wide Student Judicial Board. Within the hour the offer was made to the four principals. Jim claimed that he had kept in line since his last warning and that it would be unfair to include him. Dan had to agree that he knew of no recent offenses by Jim, so Jim was quickly reinstated.

The Brewing Storm

Word spread like wildfire through Huxley Hall. Rumors were running rampant as to who and what and why. The three "victims" and their supporters were outraged. "Why? What have we done that is so serious? How could you do such a thing without any warning?" The cauldron brewed throughout the day, Saturday. Around 10:30 that evening, I paid a visit to the third floor. Someone had bought a keg, and groups of students were engaged in heated debate around the recent developments. Immediately, they descended upon me for explanations. I tried to escape by saying that all would be explained at a general dorm meeting to be held the following night, but I gradually got dragged into discussing some of the essential points of the matter with various groups of students. Around midnight, I announced that all sides would have an opportunity to be heard, and that if I could be persuaded that my decision had been unwise I would not hesitate to reverse it. I also suggested the possibility of bringing in a third party expert to moderate the proceedings on Sunday, and this idea met with some enthusiasm. With that I escaped, knowing that I could not let the matter drop there.

Late that night as I took stock, here's how I summarized the situation:

1. Frank, Dick and Sheldon know that they've caused trouble and done some damage, but I think only now are they beginning to realize how serious the situation is. I think they are now getting an inkling of how others are really feeling, and how much they have upset Dan and others. They have really not seen it before; their response was, "Somebody must be out to get us; why is it happening to us." They actually believe that they have not had fair warning.

2. I think Frank, Dick and Sheldon really want to stay. They apparently realize it would not be easy to move into a strange dorm, perhaps with a stranger as a roommate, for the last six weeks. Also, it could be embarrassing to them trying to explain the change in location to parents and friends.

3. As Head Resident, I don't have a lot of direct power. For example, I can't levy fines or the like. I've got to rely on persuasion and social pressure. I could take the case to the Student Judiciary Board; but short of making a federal case and getting them expelled from school, which I think I could do, I see that as shirking my responsibilities. Also, if the SJB didn't expel them and just issued a warning, the RA's would feel let down, and I'd look silly.

4. I don't see that the athletic coaches would be of any help. They don't pay any attention to an athlete's dorm life unless it affects the player's performance on the field. To convince them that Frank and the others were about to be expelled would require me to take it to the SJB and by then it would have so much momentum it couldn't be stopped. And if they are evicted from the dorm by SJB they would automatically lose their athletic scholarships and not be able to play.

5. I'm really not certain what the rest of the 35 guys on the floor are feeling, nor that they have all the facts. I've heard several say that "they've had it" and want to move out, yet some are the same people who today have been saying that my action is very sudden. Also, so many guys in this dorm won't speak up at the general meetings, that I find it is hard to judge what support I can expect from the other residents if I insist that the three (Frank, Dick, and Sheldon) move out. I

do think the residents could do more to stand up to these four and make them behave.

6. Also, at least two people are critical of my letting Jim stay, saying that he set off the firecracker Wednesday night. I don't know if they're right or not. That reminds me, I'm not sure that all four are seen alike by the other residents; and I think Sheldon is the bigger problem for Dan.

7. The RAs would certainly back me. They'd like to get rid of those bastards at once. Certainly Dan's about done in, yet he's no quitter. I talked to him about changing floors, but he won't go for it. He needs my backing. I don't know how he'd feel if we took them back even with strong assurances that they would behave.

8. I don't dislike them individually, except for Sheldon. Most of all, I don't want to come out looking like a marshmallow, but neither do I want to just swing the axe. If I could get some real assurances that they'd shape-up and that the floor would police them, I'd be willing to have them stay.

As best I can determine, my objectives now are:

1. To change a disruptive pattern of behavior on the third floor which is inimical to the educational purpose of the University and inconvenient or even dangerous for other students.

2. To give support and protection to Dan, the RA, who I feel has been the object of more abuse than any human being deserves to receive and who is obviously at the end of his rope.

3. To have the residents of Huxley Hall feel that the principals have been fairly dealt with—not necessarily agree with the decision, but agree that a reasonable person in my position might well have arrived at the same decision.

4. To avoid jeopardizing the legitimacy of my authority and thereby lend credence to the notion that if they push, I'll back down.

I've told everyone we're going to have a floor-wide meeting tomorrow evening to discuss all of this but I'm really concerned about how that meeting will go. I expect that almost all of the 35 guys will show up; how the hell do I control it? Maybe I should get an outsider in to help since I am no longer seen as a neutral. I wish I had an oracle who could help me work out an effective approach!

EPILOGUE

NOTE: DO NOT read this epilogue until you have thoroughly an-alyzed the case and developed an effective approach for Marvin to follow!

Subsequent to the ending of the case, a number of events occurred:

1. Marvin decided to talk to the professor of his course in conflict management. He hoped he could persuade the professor to sit in on the Sunday night meeting and act as a third party expert to moderate and facilitate the proceedings.

2. The professor listened attentively to Marvin's presentation of the situation and raised a number of questions. However, he felt un-comfortable about acting as a facilitator at the Sunday meeting, for the following reasons:

   a. It seemed as if Marvin was tossing the buck to him, and this was neither appropriate nor likely to contribute to Marvin's growth and effectiveness as Head Resident.

   b. He was not convinced that a group confrontation was the best approach to take in this situation.

   c. He sensed that Marvin wasn't clear in his own mind whether he was willing to work for a resolution or really ready to lay down the law and make unilateral decisions.

3. Marvin and his professor continued to discuss alternatives, and even-tually concluded that Marvin needed more data on how people felt and perceived things.

4. Marvin also came to the conclusion that the general meeting was not a good setting in which to attempt to gather more data, because:

   a. Past experience indicated that too many residents would not speak out in the large meetings.

   b. Historically, his role in the large meetings had been more one of controlling than one of listening.

5. Marvin decided that the best first step would be to talk to everyone individually. Upon his return to the dorm, he left a note on every-body's door asking them to see him as soon as possible. Throughout Sunday he talked to nearly everyone, and found that:

   a. Few had the facts clear.

   b. Few were at either extreme. That is, only one or two were ada-mant about kicking out the trouble makers, and only one or two felt that they were being unfairly treated. Most were willing to have them stay if there were some guarantee that their behavior would change.

6. With this additional data, Marvin once again sat down with his pro-fessor to discuss what to do. They explored several alternate ways of

conducting the meeting. Eventually, Marvin decided that he'd like to allow the four to stay in the dorm if strict conditions could be spelled out, outlining very precisely what guidelines they could and could not transgress. The professor suggested that one way to have the dorm group participate in spelling out those conditions would be to divide the total group into small groups of five or six with each small group responsible for working out the rules for a particular aspect of dorm life (noise, destruction, and so forth).

7. Marvin conducted the Sunday night meeting in this manner. This led to the development of a written contract which all four signed (see Exhibit 1).

8. The ultimate results were positive:

   a. The dorm residents came to realize, from the Sunday night discussion, that Dan could not be expected to do it all alone. Several came to him and said just that, offering their support. This was a great help to Dan's morale.

   b. The residents began to act in ways that were supportive of Dan, exerting social pressure on the four to shape up or ship out.

EXHIBIT 1
Contract Worked Out by Small Groups of Dorm Residents

Date:_____

CONTRACT

In consideration of being allowed to remain as a resident of Huxley Hall, the undersigned hereby agrees to abide by the following conditions and guidelines:

Noise

1. The regular Huxley Hall quiet hours of 11:00 P.M. to 7:00 A.M., Sunday through Friday, and 2:00 A.M. to 9:00 A.M. on weekends, must be observed.

2. Loud conversations, running into corridor walls, pounding on walls and doors, slamming doors, and other boisterous conduct which is disturbing to floor residents is prohibited (during quiet hours).

3. Individual room doors should be kept closed during quiet hours when engaging in any noisy activity, including without limitation, card games, stereo or television playing, wrestling.

4. Shouting out the windows of Huxley Hall after quiet hours begins is prohibited.

In each of the above cases, failure to respond immediately to a request to bring conduct within the limits of what is permissible shall constitute a breach of contract.

5. Use of fireworks — inside the hall or out the windows — is absolutely prohibited, and shall constitute a breach of this contract.

6. Playing of hall games of any kind at any place in Huxley Hall's public areas shall constitute a breach of this contract and shall in addition carry an automatic $5.00 fine.

EXHIBIT 1 (Contd.)

Damage
1. Intentional or reckless damage caused by the undersigned, including bottle breaking, is absolutely prohibited and shall constitute a breach of this contract.
2. Tampering in any way with fire safety equipment, including without limitation extinguishers, heat and smoke detectors, and alarm boxes is strictly prohibited and shall constitute a breach of this contract.
3. Marijuana smoking: A flagrant violation of University policy against marijuana smoking, i.e., being caught smoking, shall constitute a breach of this contract. Three incidents of suspected smoking shall also constitute a breach.

Parietals
Three incident reports or one flagrant violation of the University policy on parietal hours, i.e., failure to respond to a staff member's request to conform with the policy, shall constitute a breach of this contract.

Miscellaneous
1. Staff members should be treated with the respect due their positions.
2. Students in the hall are responsible for controlling their guests and the uses to which their rooms are put; violations of hall rules by those for whom students are responsible may result in breach of this contract.
3. Presence of the undersigned in an area where rules are being violated may be misconstrued as participation — stay away from trouble.
4. IN ALL CASES, BREACH OF THIS CONTRACT IS TO BE DETERMINED BY THE HEAD RESIDENT AFTER CONSULTATION WITH ALL INTERESTED PARTIES. THE TEST TO BE USED IS THAT OF REASONABLENESS AND CONSIDERATION FOR THE MUTUAL RIGHTS OF STUDENTS, STAFF AND THE UNIVERSITY.

   THE UNDERSIGNED AGREES TO VACATE HUXLEY HALL IN PROPER ORDER WITHIN TWENTY-FOUR HOURS OF THE TIME THAT WRITTEN NOTICE THAT A BREACH OF THIS CONTRACT HAS BEEN COMMITTED.

Date:_____ Signature:_____

Shay's Hardware

SHAY's Hardware Store is a family operated business located in a small New England town. Harold Shay and his wife have run the business for over 30 years and have been able to earn a modest living from it. Harold and his wife are getting old however, and for about the past 10 years the bulk of the operation has been left in the hands of their son Ray.

Ray Shay has worked in his father's store ever since he was old enough to sweep floors. He has spent most of his life learning the business from the inside and when he took over, Shay's was left in capable hands. Married and in his early thirties, Ray was ambitious, energetic and extremely skilled with his hands. He was able to save Shay's from the fate of most small town stores. Seeing that they would be unable to compete with the prices of larger, more diversified stores in the cities, he concentrated on providing services to go along with the products. Shay's engaged in almost any activity associated with the business; painting, plumbing service, TV repair, antenna installation, landscaping, appliance service and anything else Ray could do. Everybody in town knew Ray to be reliable and reasonable in price and most people called Shay's when they needed something fixed before going somewhere else.

During most of the year, the jobs he undertook were on a small scale and he was able to handle them on his own. Harold and Mrs. Shay operated the store while Ray was out on call.

Sam Welch, 18, also worked at the store, part time during the school year and full time during the summer. He had now worked for the Shay's for almost three years. During the school year he stayed mostly at the store, taking orders from Harold, doing most of the heavy work and occasionally helping Ray. Shay's busy season was during the summer when he would work with Ray full time and a younger boy would be hired at the store.

For a high school student, working for Shay's was an extremely good summer job and Sam knew it. While most of his friends spent the summer in a factory or restaurant doing the same things day after day, he would be outdoors doing something different practically every week. Furthermore, Ray was a good natured boss and the two got along quite well.

Sam was also quite handy, eager to learn, and Ray enjoyed teaching him. They became good friends. As Sam grew more skillful Ray would give him more and more responsibility, even to the point where he would be sent on some jobs alone. Ray had even promised him a permanent job after graduation and Sam was seriously considering taking it.

A recent summer was a particularly busy one at Shay's as a result of Ray's decision to expand the Paint Department. He was hoping that if he could employ kids of Sam's age at summer wages and train them to paint houses people would hire Shay's instead of costlier professional painters. The idea worked well. During the spring he contracted to paint several houses to be done over the summer months. The volume was heavy enough that he could keep two extra helpers employed full time painting houses with Sam which would leave him free to concentrate on other jobs.

Ray hired two of Sam's classmates, Jeffrey Brown and Jack Meredith, on Sam's recommendation. Both were enrolled in college for the fall semester and were willing to work cheap. They agreed to work for $2.50 per hour compared to Sam's wage of $3.15. Both had some experience painting houses; in fact more than Sam did. Sam was excited about their employment. He was really looking forward to spending the summer with two of his best friends, while continuing to help Ray.

The first job went quite smoothly. Under Ray's supervision Sam learned quickly, as usual, while Jeff and Jack needed no help at all. Jack was extremely fast and did a good job on clapboards, while Jeff was especially capable on trim and windows. Sam was able to hold his own but was a little slower than the other two. Ray was confident that the three could handle all of the houses he had contracted and that they could be trusted to be left alone for extended periods.

One day early in July, Ray was installing a TV antenna and fell off the roof. Luckily it was a one-story house and he landed on his feet. Unfortunately, he suffered a severe back sprain and had to remain in bed for a couple of weeks.

Many of Shay's services had to be temporarily curtailed but Ray was reluctant to end his profitable house-painting venture. The boys had done well so far under his minimal supervision and he was confident that Sam could handle the responsibilities. With Harold's approval, he sent word to Sam to take over and keep the job going.

Things went smoothly for the next two weeks as Sam really didn't have to exercise any of his authority. Jeff and Jack really didn't have to be told what to do. The procedure had become almost routine. Between the fussy homeowners and the constant supervision of the "sidewalk superintendents" there was little time to goof off. Once in a while they would have a few beers on a hot afternoon, or spray the garden hose on each other. Sam, who took part in these activities, was sure that Ray would not have minded.

During the first week of August they started work on Austin Miller's house. Mr. Miller was president of the local bank and owned one of the largest houses in town. The Millers also had a huge, tempting swimming pool in the back yard. Jack particularly had been looking forward to this job because he had been dating Mr. Miller's daughter, Kathy, for some time. While Mr. and Mrs. Miller were gone most of the time, Kathy usually had several friends over and they often spent the whole day sunning themselves by the pool.

Under the circumstances it became increasingly difficult for the three to concentrate on their work (especially when they were in sight of the pool) and to make matters worse the weather turned unbearably hot. Kathy invited them to spend their lunch breaks by the pool. Sam soon noticed that every day the lunch period seemed to get longer and work periods shorter and less productive. It wasn't long before the work got behind schedule.

At first Sam was a willing participant and took as much time off as the other two, but it soon became apparent to him that they would not be able to finish the house in the allotted three weeks unless they got to work. He also knew that Ray would be out of bed in a few days and would probably be around for inspection. Sam wanted him to be pleased at their progress.

He was reluctant to order his friends around, especially in front of the girls. Most of the time he was able to end the lunch breaks by using gentle persuasion. He would say something like "Hey, I guess it's time to get back to work," and hope that Jack and Jeff would follow him. After a while this method became less and less effective as the two would work when they chose and paid little attention to Sam. Sam felt more and more anxious and helpless.

One afternoon Sam was finishing a small piece in the front of the house while Jack and Jeff went around to the other side to begin a new section. After he finished his end he went around to the side to find nothing done, two paint brushes hardened in the sun, and no sign of Jack or Jeff. He soon found them playing volley ball with the girls by the pool.

Sam finally lost his temper and started yelling at them ordering them to get back to work. The two found this amusing and Jack replied, "Sure pal, soon as we win two out of three." Seeing that the situation was hopeless Sam went back to work and they joined him half an hour later.

That Friday Mr. Miller went to the store and complained to Harold that the boys had been working on his house for two weeks and it wasn't even half finished. Harold told him that Ray was coming back to work Monday and would find out what the problem was. When Harold told him of the complaint, Ray decided that a surprise visit would provide him with the best answer.

Ray arrived at the Millers about one o'clock Monday afternoon, just in time to catch Jack and Jeff in one of their extended lunches at the pool while Sam was working alone. When Ray found Jack and Jeff he nearly fired both of them on the spot but instead he told them to either get to work or go home. He was also furious at Sam.

"I made you the boss here and it was up to you to get this job done. Is this how you run an operation by letting your workers loaf all day? If they wouldn't work you should have told me right away and I would have straightened them out. I thought you were more responsible than this."

The Slade Company*

RALPH PORTER, production manager of The Slade Company, was concerned by reports of dishonesty among some employees in the Plating Department. From reliable sources, he had learned that a few men were punching the time cards of a number of their workmates who had left early. Mr. Porter had only recently joined the Slade organization. He judged from conversations with the previous production manager and other fellow managers that they were, in general, pleased with the over-all performance of the Plating Department.

The Slade Company was a prosperous manufacturer of metal products designed for industrial application. Its manufacturing plant, located in central Michigan, employed nearly 500 workers, who were engaged in producing a large variety of clamps, inserts, knobs, and similar items. Orders for these products were usually large and on a recurrent basis. The volume of orders fluctuated in response to business conditions in the primary industries which the company served. At the time of this case, sales volume had been high for over a year. The basis upon which The Slade Company secured orders, in rank of importance, were quality, delivery, and reasonable price.

The organization of manufacturing operations at the Slade plant is shown in Exhibit 1. The departments listed there are, from left to right, approximately in the order in which material flowed through the plant. The diemaking and setup operations required the greatest degree of skill, supplied by highly paid, long-service craftsmen. The finishing departments, divided operationally and geographically between plating and painting, attracted less highly trained but relatively skilled workers, some of whom had been employed by the company for many years. The remaining operations were largely unskilled in nature and were characterized by relatively low pay and high rate of turnover of personnel.

The plating room was the sole occupant of the top floor of the plant. Exhibit 2 shows the floorplan, the disposition of workers, and the flow of work throughout the department. Thirty-eight men and women worked in the department, plating or oxidizing the metal parts or preparing parts for the application of paint at another location in the plant. The department's work occurred in response to orders communicated by production schedules, which were revised daily. Schedule revisions, caused by last-minute order increases or rush requests from customers, resulted in short-term volume fluctuations, particularly in the plating, painting, and shipping departments. Table 1 outlines the activities of the various jobs, their interrelationships, and the type of work in which each specialized. Table 2 rates the various types of jobs in terms of the technical skill, physical effort, discomfort, and training time associated with their performance.

The activities which took place in the plating room were of three main types:

1. Acid dipping, in which parts were etched by being placed in baskets which were manually immersed and agitated in an acid solution.
2. Barrel tumbling, in which parts were roughened or smoothed by being

EXHIBIT 1
Manufacturing Organization

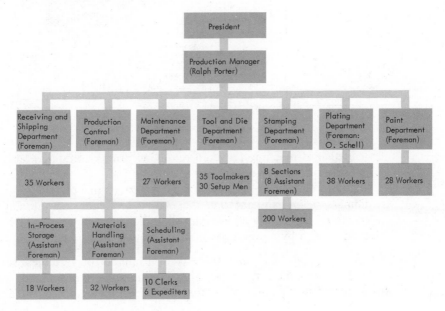

EXHIBIT 2
Plating Room Layout

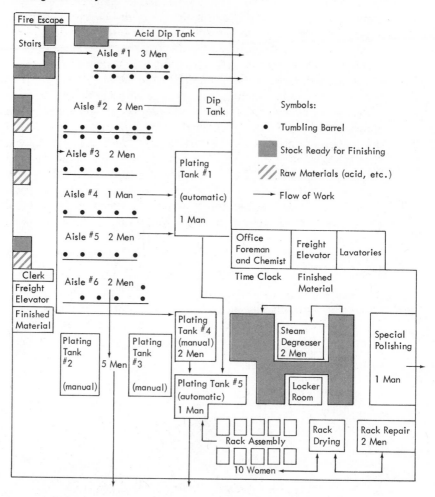

loaded into machine-powered revolving drums containing abrasive, caustic, or corrosive solutions.

3. Plating – either manual, in which parts were loaded on racks and were immersed by hand through the plating sequence; or automatic, in which racks or baskets were manually loaded with parts which were then carried by a conveyor system through the plating sequence.

Within these main divisions, there were a number of variables, such as cycle times, chemical formulas, abrasive mixtures, and so forth, which distinguished particular jobs as they have been categorized in Table 1.

The work of the plating room was received in batch lots whose size averaged a thousand pieces. The clerk moved each batch, which was accompanied by a routing slip, to its first operation. This routing slip indicated the operations to be performed and when each major operation on the batch was scheduled to be completed, so that the finished product could be shipped on time. From the accumulation of orders before him, each man was to organize his own work schedule so as to make optimal use of equipment, materials, and time. Upon completion of an order, each man moved the lot to its next work position or to the finished material location near the freight elevator.

TABLE 1
Outline of Work Flow, Plating Room

Aisle 1: Worked closely with Aisle 3 in preparation of parts by barrel tumbling and acid dipping for high-quality* plating in Tanks 4 and 5. Also did a considerable quantity of highly specialized, high-quality acid-etching work not requiring further processing.

Aisle 2: Tumbled items of regular quality* and design in preparation for painting. Less frequently, did oxidation dipping work of regular quality, but sometimes of special design, not requiring further processing.

Aisle 3: Worked closely with Aisle 1 on high-quality tumbling work for Tanks 4 and 5.

Aisles 4 and 5: Produced regular tumbling work for Tank 1.

Aisle 6: Did high-quality tumbling work for special products plated in Tanks 2 and 3.

Tank 1: Worked on standard, automated plating of regular quality not further processed in plating room, and regular work further processed in Tank 5.

Tanks 2 and 3: Produced special, high-quality plating work not requiring further processing.

Tank 4: Did special, high-quality plating work further plated in Tank 5.

Tank 5: Automated production of high- and regular-quality, special- and regular-design plated parts sent directly to shipping.

Rack assembly: Placed parts to be plated in Tank 5 on racks.

Rack repair: Performed routine replacement and repair of racks used in Tank 5.

Polishing: Processed, by manual or semimanual methods, odd-lot special orders which were sent directly to shipping. Also, sorted and reclaimed parts rejected by inspectors in the shipping department.

Degreasing: Took incoming raw stock, processed it through caustic solution, and placed clean stock in storage ready for processing elsewhere in the plating room.

* Definition of terms: *High or regular quality:* The quality of finishes could broadly be distinguished by the thickness of plate and/or care in preparation. *Regular or special work:* The complexity of work depended on the routine or special character of design and finish specifications.

TABLE 2
Skill Indices by Job Group*

Jobs	Technical Skill Required	Physical Effort Required	Degree of Discomfort Involved	Degree of Training Required†
Aisle 1	1	1	1	1
Tanks 2–4	3	2	1	2
Aisles 2–6	5	1	1	5
Tank 5	1	5	7	2
Tank 1	8	5	5	7
Degreasing	9	3	7	10
Polishing	6	9	9	7
Rack assembly and repair	10	10	10	10

* Rated on scales of 1 (the greatest) to 10 (the least) in each category.
† Amount of experience required to assume complete responsibility for the job.

The plating room was under the direct supervision of the foreman, Otto Schell, who worked a regular 8:00 to 5:00 day, five days a week. The foreman spent a good deal of his working time attending to maintenance and repair of equipment, procuring supplies, handling late schedule changes, and seeing that his people were at their proper work locations.

Working conditions in the plating room varied considerably. That part of the department containing the tumbling barrels and the plating machines was constantly awash, alternately with cold water, steaming acid, or caustic soda. Men working in this part of the room wore knee boots, long rubber aprons, and high-gauntlet rubber gloves. This uniform, consistent with the general atmosphere of the "wet" part of the room, was hot in the summer, cold in winter. In contrast, the remainder of the room was dry, relatively odor-free, and provided reasonable stable temperature and humidity conditions for those who worked there.

The men and women employed in the plating room are listed in Table 3. This table provides certain personal data on each department member, including a productivity-skill rating (based on subjective and objective appraisals of potential performance), as reported by the members of the department.

The pay scale implied by Table 3 was low for the central Michigan area. The average starting wage for factory work in the community was about $1.25. However, working hours for the plating room were long (from 60 hours to a possible and frequently available 76 hours per week). The first 60 hours (the normal five-day week) were paid for on straight-time rates. Saturday work was paid for at time and one half. Sunday pay was calculated on a double-time basis.

As Table 3 indicates, Philip Kirk, a worker in Aisle 2, provided the data for this case. After he had been a member of the department for several months, Kirk noted that certain members of the department tended

TABLE 3: Plating Room Personnel

Location	Name	Age	Marital Status	Company Seniority (in years)	Department Seniority (in years)	Pay per Hour	Education*	Familial Relationships	Productivity Skill Rating†
Aisle 1.........	Tony Sarto	30	M	13	13	$1.50	HS		1
	Pete Facelli	26	M	8	8	1.30	HS	Louis Patrici, uncle; Pete Facelli, cousin	2
	Joe Iambi	31	M	5	5	1.20	2 yrs. HS	Louis Patrici, uncle; Tony Sarto, cousin	2
Aisle 2.........	Herman Schell	48	S	26	26	1.45	GS	Otto Schell, brother	8
	Philip Kirk	23	M	1	1	.90	College		‡2
Aisle 3.........	Dom Pantaleoni	31	M	10	10	1.30	1 yr. HS		2
	Sal Maletta	32	M	12	12	1.30	3 yrs. HS		3
Aisle 4.........	Bob Pearson	22	S	4	4	1.15	HS	Father in tool and die dept.	1
Aisle 5.........	Charlie Malone	44	M	22	8	1.25	GS		7
	John Lacey	41	S	9	5	1.20	1 yr. HS	Brother in paint dept.	7
Aisle 6.........	Jim Martin	30	S	7	7	1.25	HS		4
	Bill Mensch	41	M	6	2	1.10	GS		4
Tank 1.........	Henry LaForte	38	M	14	6	1.25	HS		6
Tanks 2 and 3..	Ralph Parker	25	S	7	7	1.20	HS		4
	Ed Harding	27	S	8	8	1.20	HS		4
	George Flood	22	S	5	5	1.15	HS		5
	Harry Clark	29	M	8	8	1.20	HS		3
	Tom Bond	25	S	6	6	1.20	HS		4
Tank 4.........	Frank Bonzani	27	M	9	9	1.25	HS		2
	Al Bartolo	24	M	6	6	1.25	HS		3
Tank 5.........	Louis Patrici	47	S	14	14	1.45	2 yrs. college	Tony Sarto, nephew; Pete Facelli, nephew	1
Rack assembly	ten women	30–40	9M, 1S	10 (av.)	10 (av.)	1.05	GS (av.)	six with husbands in company	4 (av.)
Rack mainte-nance {	Will Partridge	57	M	14	2	1.20	GS		7
	Lloyd Swan	62	M	3	3	1.10	GS		7
Degreasing	Dave Susi	45	S	1	1	1.05	HS		5
	Mike Maher	41	M	4	4	1.05	GS		6
Polishing	Russ Perkins	49	M	12	2	1.20	HS		4
Foreman.......	Otto Schell	56	M	35	35	na	HS	Herman Schell, brother	3
Clerk..........	Bill Pierce	32	M	10	4	1.15	HS		4
Chemist	Frank Rutlage	24	S	2	2	na	2 yrs. college		6

* HS = high school; GS = grade school.   † On a potential scale of 1 (top) to 10 (bottom), as evaluated by the men in the department.

‡ Kirk was the source of data for this case and therefore in a biased position to report accurately perceptions about himself.

to seek each other out during free time on and off the job. He then observed that these informal associations were enduring, built upon common activities and shared ideas about what was and what was not legitimate behavior in the department. His estimate of the pattern of these associations is diagrammed in Exhibit 3.

The Sarto group, so named because Tony Sarto was its most respected member and the one who acted as arbiter between the other members, was the largest in the department. The group, except for Louis Patrici, Al Bartolo, and Frank Bonzani (who spelled each other during break periods), invariably ate lunch together on the fire escape near Aisle 1. On those Saturdays and Sundays when overtime work was required, the Sarto group operated as a team, regardless of weekday work assignments, to get overtime work completed as quickly as possible. (Few department members not affiliated with either the Sarto or the Clark groups worked on week ends.) Off the job, Sarto group members often joined in parties or weekend trips. Sarto's summer camp was a frequent rendezvous.

Sarto's group was also the most cohesive one in the department in terms of its organized punch-in and punch-out system. Since the men were regularly scheduled to work from 7:00 A.M. to 7:00 P.M. weekdays,

EXHIBIT 3
Informal Groupings in the Plating Room

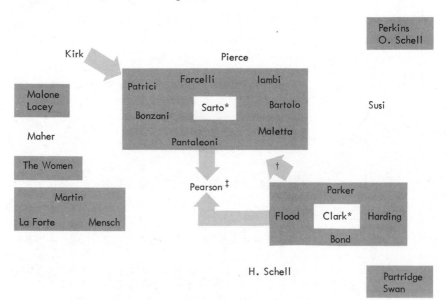

* The white boxes indicate those men who clearly demonstrated leadership behavior (most closely personified the values shared by their groups, were most often sought for help and arbitration, and so forth).

† While the two- and three-man groupings had little informal contact outside their own boundaries, the five-man group did seek to join the largest group in extraplant social affairs. These were relatively infrequent.

‡ Though not an active member of any group, Bob Pearson was regarded with affection by the two large groups.

and since all supervision was removed at 5:00 P.M., it was possible almost every day to finish a "day's work" by 5:30 and leave the plant. What is more, if one man were to stay until 7:00 P.M., he could punch the time cards of a number of men and help them gain free time without pay loss. (This system operated on week ends also; at which times members of supervision were present, if at all, only for short periods.) In Sarto's group the duty of staying late rotated, so that no man did so more than once a week. In addition, the group members would punch a man in in the morning if he were unavoidably delayed. However, such a practice never occurred without prior notice from the man who expected to be late and never if the tardiness was expected to last beyond 8:00 A.M., the start of the day for the foreman.

Sarto explained the logic behind the system to Kirk:

> You know that our hourly pay rate is quite low, compared to other companies. What makes this the best place to work is the feeling of security you get. No one ever gets laid off in this department. With all the hours in the week, all the company ever has to do is shorten the work week when orders fall off. We have to tighten our belts, but we can all get along. When things are going well, as they are now, the company is only interested in getting out the work. It doesn't help to get it out faster than it's really needed—so we go home a little early whenever we can. Of course, some guys abuse this sort of thing—like Herman—but others work even harder, and it averages out.
>
> Whenever an extra order has to be pushed through, naturally I work until 7:00. So do a lot of the others. I believe that if I stay until my work is caught up and my equipment is in good shape, that's all the company wants of me. They leave us alone and expect us to produce—and we do.

When Kirk asked Sarto if he would not rather work shorter hours at higher pay in a union shop (Slade employees were not organized), he just laughed and said: "It wouldn't come close to an even trade."

The members of Sarto's group were explicit about what constituted a fair day's work. Customarily, they cited Herman Schell, Kirk's work partner and the foreman's brother, as a man who consistently produced below that level. Kirk received an informal orientation from Herman during his first days on the job. As Herman put it:

> I've worked at this job for a good many years, and I expect to stay here a good many more. You're just starting out, and you don't know which end is up yet. We spend a lot of time in here; and no matter how hard we work, the pile of work never goes down. There's always more to take its place. And I think you've found out by now that this isn't light work. You can wear yourself out fast if you're not smart. Look at Pearson up in Aisle 4. There's a kid who's just going to burn himself out. He won't last long. If he thinks he's going to get somewhere working like that, he's nuts. They'll

give him all the work he can take. He makes it tough on everybody else and on himself, too.

Kirk reported further on his observations of the department:

As nearly as I could tell, two things seemed to determine whether or not Sarto's group or any others came in for weekend work on Saturday or Sunday. It seemed usually to be caused by rush orders that were received late in the week, although I suspect it was sometimes caused by the men having spent insufficient time on the job during the previous week.

Tony and his group couldn't understand Herman. While Herman arrived late, Tony was always half an hour early. If there was a push to get out an extra amount of work, almost everyone but Herman would work that much harder. Herman never worked overtime on week ends, while Tony's group and the men on the manual tanks almost always did. When the first exploratory time study of the department was made, no one in the aisles slowed down, except Herman, with the possible exception, to a lesser degree, of Charlie Malone. I did hear that the men in the dry end of the room slowed down so much you could hardly see them move; but we had little to do with them, anyway. While the men I knew best seemed to find a rather full life in their work, Herman never really got involved. No wonder they couldn't understand each other.

There was quite a different feeling about Bobby Pearson. Without the slightest doubt, Bob worked harder than anyone else in the room. Because of the tremendous variety of work produced, it was hard to make output comparisons, but I'm sure I wouldn't be far wrong in saying that Bob put out twice as much as Herman and 50 percent more than almost anyone else in the aisles. No one but Herman and a few old-timers at the dry end ever criticized Bobby for his efforts. Tony and his group seemed to feel a distant affection for Bob, but the only contact they or anyone else had with him consisted of brief greetings.

To the men in Tony's group the most severe penalty that could be inflicted on a man was exclusion. This they did to both Pearson and Herman. Pearson, however, was tolerated; Herman was not. Evidently, Herman felt his exclusion keenly, though he answered it with derision and aggression. Herman kept up a steady stream of stories concerning his attempts to gain acceptance outside the company. He wrote popular music which was always rejected by publishers. He attempted to join several social and athletic clubs, mostly without success. His favorite pastime was fishing. He told me that fishermen were friendly, and he enjoyed meeting new people whenever he went fishing. But he was particularly quick to explain that he preferred to keep his distance from the men in the department.

Tony's group emphasized more than just quantity in judging a man's work. Among them had grown a confidence that they could master and even improve upon any known finishing technique. Tony himself symbolized this skill. Before him, Tony's father had operated Aisle 1 and had trained Tony to take his place. Tony in his turn was training his cousin Pete. When a new finishing problem arose from a change in customer specifications, the foreman, the department chemist, or any of the men directly involved would come to Tony for help, and Tony would give it willingly. For example, when a part with a special plastic embossing was designed, Tony was the only one who could discover how to treat the metal without damaging the plastic. To a lesser degree, the other members of the group were also inventive about the problems which arose in their own sections.

Herman, for his part, talked incessantly about his feats in design and finish creations. As far as I could tell during the year I worked in the department, the objects of these stories were obsolete or of minor importance. What's more, I never saw any department member seek Herman's help.

Willingness to be of help was a trait Sarto's group prized. The most valued help of all was of a personal kind, though work help was also important. The members of Sarto's group were constantly lending and borrowing money, cars, clothing, and tools among themselves and, less frequently, with other members of the department. Their daily lunch bag procedure typified the common property feeling among them. Everyone's lunch was opened and added to a common pile, from which each member of the group chose his meal.

On the other hand, Herman refused to help others in any way. He never left his aisle to aid those near him who were in the midst of a rush of work or a machine failure, though this was customary throughout most of the department. I can distinctly recall the picture of Herman leaning on the hot and cold water faucets which were located directly above each tumbling barrel. He would stand gazing into the tumbling pieces for hours. To the passing, casual visitor, he looked busy; and as he told me, that's just what he wanted. He, of course, expected me to act this same way, and it was this enforced boredom that I found virtually intolerable.

More than this, Herman took no responsibility for breaking-in his assigned helpers as they first entered the department, or thereafter. He had had four helpers in the space of little more than a year. Each had asked for a transfer to another department, publicly citing the work as cause, privately blaming Herman. Tony was the one who taught me the ropes when I first entered the department.

The men who congregated around Harry Clark tended to talk like and copy the behavior of the Sarto group, though they never approached the degree of inventive skill or the amount of helping activities that Tony's group did. They sought outside social contact with the Sarto group; and several times a year, the two groups went 'on the town' together. Clark's group did maintain a high level of performance in the volume of work they turned out.

The remainder of the people in the department stayed pretty much to themselves or associated in pairs or triplets. None of these people were as inventive, as helpful, or as productive as Sarto's or Clark's groups, but most of them gave verbal support to the same values as those groups held.

The distinction between the two organized groups and the rest of the department was clearest in the punching-out routine. The women could not work past 3:00 P.M., so they were not involved. Malone and Lacey, Partridge and Swan, and Martin, La Forte, and Mensch arranged within their small groups for punch-outs, or they remained beyond 5:00 and slept or read when they finished their work. Perkins and Pierce went home when the foreman did. Herman Schell, Susi, and Maher had no punch-out organization to rely upon. Susi and Maher invariably stayed in the department until 7:00 P.M. Herman was reported to have established an arrangement with Partridge whereby the latter punched Herman out for a fee. Such a practice was unthinkable from the point of view of Sarto's group. It evidently did not occur often because Herman usually went to sleep behind piles of work when his brother left, or, particularly during the fishing season, punched himself out early. He constantly railed against the dishonesty of other men in the department, yet urged me to punch him out on several emergency occasions.

Just before I left The Slade Company to return to school after 14 months on the job, I had a casual conversation with Mr. Porter, the production manager, in which he asked me how I had enjoyed my experience with the organization. During the conversation, I learned that he knew of the punch-out system in the Plating Department. What's more, he told me, he was wondering if he ought to "blow the lid off the whole mess."

Smokestack Village, Inc.

THOMAS J. BRONSTON, Chairman of the Board of Trustees and General Manager of Smokestack Village, was worried about the developing problem between his employees and Karl Olson, the man he wished to have replace him as General Manager.

Smokestack Village was a tourist attraction located near the Continental Divide in central Colorado. It offered visitors a large railroad museum and daily excursion rides on old railroad lines. The museum had over 40 steam locomotives on display and many other exhibits relating to the days of steam railroading. The excursion rides were operated during the summer and fall months over 26 miles of track winding through a valley high in the Rockies. It had been founded by Miles E. Smith, a semiretired railroad buff, with Mr. Bronston's assistance in arranging financing.

Mr. Smith served as General Manager during the early years of slow growth. When he was unexpectedly killed in an automobile accident, Mr. Bronston tried to find someone to take care of the day-to-day operating responsibility. This included short-range planning, ordering supplies, handling the finances and coping with "nosey Federal inspectors." When unsuccessful in finding someone he considered satisfactory, he reluctantly took on the task himself. This meant closing up his own business as an investment counselor and moving from Denver to Grenoble, which was closer but still 45 miles from Smokestack Village.

He had been General Manager for the past five years. During that time, the museum had started running the excursion trains, and the many engines that had been sitting around the turntable rusting had been stored undercover during the winter and restored on a regular basis. Attendance had tripled over the five-year period. He now felt that it was time for "new blood" in management and he was informally looking for a replacement. The long commute was also getting to him.

Assistant Manager Jim Harris, 28, was in charge of restoration, painting, lawnmowing and ticket sales. Working for him were three girls who sold tickets and staffed the exhibit cars. Also under his direction were five high school boys who worked around the locomotive displays, painting, restoring the engines to their original looks, lawnmowing, weeding, sweeping walks, and doing trackwork. Jim spent most of his day making sure the boys were working and not goofing-off from what they considered to be "just a summer job in which you put in your 40 hours."

Contact between Harris' crew and a crew that operated the excursion trains was limited because of the physical layout of Smokestack Village and the jobs they did. The train crew spent the day either in the station or up the line while the museum crew was working around the display engines a distance away.

Sven Olson was in charge of the train crew and was also the engineer on the train. Sven was a veteran of fifty years' service as an engineer for the Great Western Railroad, and he knew his business. The other employees used to joke that he knew more about railroads than they would ever have time to forget. At 75, he was still capable of working longer and harder than most of the other employees 55 years younger than he.

Ned Bronston, 17, the son of Mr. Bronston, was the fireman. He lived with Sven in the bunk car parked near the enginehouse. It was the first summer working at Smokestack Village for both of them, although Ned had spent many days at Smokestack with his father over the years.

Working with them were three other employees who had worked at Smokestack Village in the past. Bob Johnson, 30, had worked for the Village for four years as conductor for the passenger train in the summer and in the office in the winter.

The brakemen were Al Stanhope, 18, and Peter Townshend, also 18. They had worked at Smokestack for the past two summers on the museum crew and it was their first summer on the train.

The five of them became fast friends. They worked well together and enjoyed each other's company both during and after work. It was not unusual for them all to go out to dinner at the end of the day, or sit around the bunk car half the night talking about railroads. Al and Peter kept sleeping bags at the bunk car and frequently stayed overnight.

Al, Peter, and Ned, with Sven's consent, traded jobs occasionally; Ned worked as brakeman while Al or Peter fired the engine. Frequently Sven would allow the fireman to run the engine while he fired. Most railroads allowed this, and Mr. Bronston knew that with Sven in the cab, nothing could go wrong. The practice allowed for the training of future engineers. Mr. Bronston only asked that the train leave and arrive in the Village on time. How this was to be done was left up to the five of them. They found it best to work as a team; each of them knew the other's job well enough from the practice of switching jobs to know what to expect from the others. Arguments were few and far between.

The day started for Sven and Ned at 8:30 A.M. Being fireman, Ned had many duties to tend to before the engine could be run that day. The fire had to be rebuilt from the day before, lubricators filled, water worked out of the cylinders and the engine coaled. The coal dock was 75 yards from the enginehouse, and this gave Ned an opportunity to run the engine a bit. If he had time and the engine warranted it, he would polish the engine, wiping oil and cinders from the boiler and wheels.

While Ned was working on the engine, Sven would be preparing a sumptuous breakfast for the two of them. He would also boil a large pot of coffee for Bob, Al, and Peter, who would arrive at ten. Breakfast started at 9:30, and the train crew would join them at 10:00 for a half hour of railroad talk. The talk usually turned to girls, sports, and movies; the breakfast hour was enjoyed by all.

At 10:30 it was time to take the engine and passenger cars down to the station in preparation for the first run, leaving at 11:00. Mr. Bronston would be waiting on the platform for the train's arrival. He would climb into the cab to talk with Sven about the engine. He would inquire as to whether the engine was running well, the coal supply was lasting and any other details related to the operating department. Satisfied that all was going well, he would head back to his office.

Mr. Bronston felt that he had a responsible crew working on the train. There was an unstated understanding between him and the train crew that as long as things went smoothly, he would not interfere in their routine. Sven worked hard with the train crew drilling them on railroad procedures and safety measures. Running a railroad is serious business, and they all knew it. Fooling around could not be tolerated when 800 people were on the train. There were instances where local kids had tried to derail the train by placing ties and spikes on the track. Al and Ned had managed to catch the culprits and they were turned over to the State Police.

The arrival of the train back in Smokestack Village after the first trip

EXHIBIT 1

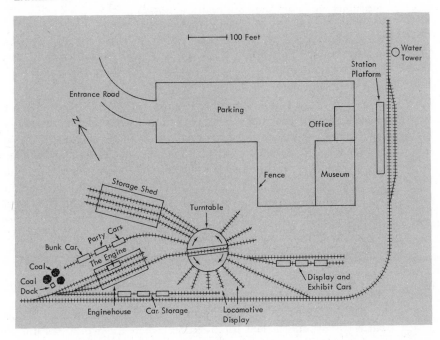

marked the beginning of lunch for both the museum and train crews. Ned would buy lunch for Sven and himself and return to the engine. One of them stayed on the engine at all times. After eating, Sven would climb down off the engine and wander around talking with visitors while other visitors would climb into the cab for a look around and maybe a chance to blow the whistle.

Two more trips would be made before the end of the day at 6:00 P.M. It took Ned about an hour to shut down the engine for the night. If the train crew was going out to dinner together, they would all pitch in to get the work done, otherwise Sven would start dinner for Ned and himself while Bob, Al, and Peter would head home for dinner.

There were times when the engine needed major repair due to some malfunction. When this happened, the museum crew would join the train crew in repairing the locomotive. Sometimes the work would take all night—nobody complained. It had to be done if the train was to run the next day. Sven and Ned would work with the crews until midnight and then retire. If they were to function the next day, they needed their sleep. The two of them put in the hardest day of all the employees.

Each morning at 3:00 A.M. Ned would wake up and go out to the engine to check the water level, steam pressure, and the fire which was left burning from the day before. The engine had a habit of building up steam pressure when left unattended and this led to difficulties the next morning, the worst being a boiler explosion.

In doing this, Ned violated federal law which requires that railroad employees not work more than 16 hours followed by a 10-hour rest period. Ned was well aware of this law, but chose to ignore it. Smoke-stack Village would have had to hire a night hostler to watch the engine, and this was costly. So he did it himself.

Employees turned in their timecards each Wednesday. They were to write down the hours they had worked and what they had done. Average pay for the museum and train crews was $1.60 an hour. Bob earned a higher wage since legally the responsibility of the train and the hundreds of passengers was his and his higher pay was justified. The train crew only put in for a 44 hour week, although 50 and 60 hours of actual work was not unusual. They never asked for pay for the nights they worked re-pairing the engine. Working on steam engines was considered a privilege. Al, Peter, and Ned spent many evenings working on one engine in the exhibit area that was their favorite. They had painted the engine and spent many hours hunting through the storage shed and spare parts boxcars looking for gauges, valves and other parts to replace ones missing from the locomotive. They didn't ask to be paid for this.

The museum crew, for the most part, did the same thing with their time-cards. They only asked for overtime when the work was not with the engines. They had a few pet projects that they also worked on after hours; for example, they had been painting the railroad name on the sides of the passenger cars, doing one side of one car an evening.

During the times when the two crews were working in the evenings, Jim Harris and Sven were never around. The evening projects were the idea of the employees involved and they wished to do it on their own. Mr. Bronston, on his daily inspection tours of the grounds, would only offer suggestions as to what might look better or more realistic. The final deci-sions were left up to the crews. The two groups stayed to themselves most of the time. The only time the two crews worked together was when the engine that Al, Peter, and Ned were working on had to be lettered. The museum crew stenciled the engine for the three of them to paint. The museum crew had offered to do the job and the offer was gladly accepted. Once the job was done, the two crews went back to the original format of working by themselves.

The museum crew's attitude of it being "just a summer job . . ." changed during the month of June. Once the lawnmowing and trackwork and other tasks were done, they were permitted to work on the engines, which was much more interesting and enjoyable to the point that they stayed late on their own time.

Sven had one son, Karl, 50, who lived in Wyoming. Karl was a suc-cessful mechanical engineer with a long list of patents to his credit. He had been involved in the production of a sound movie projector for a large camera producer, and his expertise had helped send a man to the moon. He had started many engineering consulting firms with clients like NASA, the armed services, the automobile industry suppliers, and railroads. He had sold his businesses over the past few years and was now in semiretirement, taking on consulting work out of his home when he wanted.

During the month of June, he made several trips to Smokestack Village and the area with his wife, Henrietta, to visit his father. He would ride in the cab of the engine and Ned would sometimes let him sit in the fireman's seat. Karl considered this a privilege and was grateful to Ned. Sven and Karl got along quite well. Karl never interfered with Sven's work, realizing that he was in the presence of one of the best and most well known engineers in the country.

It was not long before Karl was seen in the office with Mr. Bronston discussing Smokestack Village. Karl had many ideas on how to increase patronage at the museum. He knew some people in the TV advertising business and he arranged for low-cost TV commercials to be aired in major cities of the area.

Karl started spending more and more time at the museum. Mr. Bronston, realizing that Karl had plenty of spare time that might be put to constructive use at Smokestack Village, asked him if he would be interested in becoming a trustee. Karl accepted the offer, and he and his wife moved into a local motel for an indefinite stay.

Prior to Karl's becoming a trustee, Mr. Bronston had asked Ned what he thought of Karl. Ned couldn't think of anything negative at the time and told his father that he would get the other employees' reactions. The museum crew didn't have much contact with Karl, only Jim knew who he was and he thought Karl was OK. The train crew had only known Karl for a month at that point, and didn't register any complaints about him either. They knew that Mr. Bronston was looking for a replacement, but since Mr. Bronston had left the operating department to them and didn't interfere, they didn't care who was the boss. In the next two weeks they would all have reason to care after all.

Karl, now a trustee, began to make his appearance in the bunk car every morning at 9:00 to start issuing orders. The train crew started to grumble that they didn't need this intrusion in their morning routine. Karl no longer allowed the morning coffee break. The work that Al, Peter, and Ned did in the evenings was now to be done in the morning starting at nine. Ned, having to work on the engine, couldn't participate. Ned's work in the morning was under constant fire from Karl. As a result, the "extra bit" Ned did polishing the engine was neglected. Karl also ordered that the engine and train be ready in the station at 10:15 each morning. Sven and Ned were incensed at this. It meant getting up earlier and rushing breakfast on what they considered to be their own time. Sven was also told by Karl that when the engine was moved even a foot, he had better be at the throttle or Karl would find a new engineer. Ned was no longer allowed to run the engine to the coal dock and the firemen were not allowed to run the engine on the mainline. At lunch time, Ned could no longer leave the engine to get lunch for Sven and himself from the cafeteria in the station. They were both to stay on the engine at all times during the day. The conductor and brakemen were not subjected to the same restriction, and this caused hard feelings between the engine and train crews. When Sven had asked Karl how he was to get lunch, Karl told him to bring a sandwich with him in the morning. Sven told the four men he worked with to ignore Karl. Mr. Bronston had given Sven his orders and those were the ones to follow. Karl seemed careful not to give orders when Mr. Bronston was around.

The employees began to look around to see if Karl was watching, and if he was, to do it his way. Nobody dared cross him. But the trips allowed the train crew a chance to get away from Karl and do things their own way. Once the train left the station, they would stop looking over their shoulders to see if Karl was watching. Bob got in the habit of signalling Sven to start when Karl was nowhere in sight, while Al and Peter would walk the length of the train to see if Karl had gotten on while they weren't watching, and if so tell the engine crew through a prearranged hand signal. If Karl was on the train, the trip would be slower and the whistle wasn't blown as much, which upset Sven because he felt that the people had paid for a train ride and he was going to give them a ride they would never forget.

Mr. Bronston had told the employees that Karl had been made a trustee, but had not made any mention of any authority that Karl might have when dealing with employees. The Smokestack Village Board had 15 trustees on it. They were all known by the employees and many of them came to Smokestack on weekends to look around. They frequently asked the employees how projects were coming, but never ordered anyone around. For the most part, they were fund-raisers for the organization and policy makers. On one trustee's visit, he asked one of the museum crew workers to wear cleaner clothes because the employees were in the limelight. It was the only incident where a trustee, other than Karl, confronted an employee all summer.

Karl had made it understood that anyone who didn't do as he said would be fired. The way he gave orders, the message was clear: "Do it my way, or you're out."

Morale hit bottom. Employees came to work at nine and left at five. Before, when the engine needed repair, Jim had asked who would like to stay late to help fix the engine and the museum crew would head for the phone to call home to cancel dinner or their girlfriends to cancel dates.

This was no longer true. Sven and Jim had to plead with the museum crew to stay and they would agree only if it were understood that they were free to leave if Karl showed up. Ned and Al and Peter would stay, even if he did show, because they needed the engine. The timecards started to show exactly how many hours each employee worked. Fifty and 60 hours was not unusual, and the payroll was doubled with the overtime.

About two weeks after Karl's appointment as a trustee, Mr. Bronston was made aware of the payroll increase by his secretary, Jean, who handled the payroll accounts. Jean, the employees' "second mother," offered no explanation, although she did know what was happening. Mr. Bronston decided to accept Sven's standing invitation for dinner in the bunk car with Ned and himself. The conversation that night finally turned to Karl. Sven related some of the incidents that made him angry with his son, Karl. Ned, at Sven's insistence, let it be known that Karl was ruining a good working environment. Employees were rebelling by "misplacing" valuable locomotive tools and parts, painting and restoration work was slowing down, and little jobs, such as picking up trash, were not being done. If Mr. Bronston wanted the stencilling and lettering of the passenger cars finished, he would have to order it finished on Smokestack Village's time. Ned also stated that he, and most of the other workers, felt it difficult to follow two bosses. They were all at a loss as to whose orders to follow: Karl's, as he was always around the grounds, or Mr. Bronston's, who was the boss even when he was working in the office.

Mr. Bronston thanked the two of them for dinner and got in his car for the 45 minute trip home. As he drove he reflected upon the situation. Karl looked like a man capable of taking his place. He had plenty of spare time that he was willing to devote to the Village and was a successful businessman with many connections in the railroad industry. Karl would make the Village his life, something that Mr. Bronston didn't want to do. Living in Grenoble, a poor mill town, wouldn't bother Karl as he didn't have any children and didn't much care what his wife thought. Ned had overheard Karl tell Sven that his wife had cancer, "so she'll be gone soon."

The present circumstances cast a doubt in Mr. Bronston's mind as to whether he could entrust Karl with the Museum. The next trustees' meeting would be in October. He knew he would have to stay on until then as General Manager when Karl might take the job. Now if he could figure out a way to keep peace until then . . .

The Suburban Ski Shop Dilemma

THE SUBURBAN SKI SHOP, located ten miles outside of Metropolitan City in the heart of the suburbs, was a well known and quite prosperous store. Although the shop was open year 'round, selling tennis equipment during the summer months, their busiest time occurred between October and February. During this period it was necessary to hire five or six extra people beside their year round staff of five employees. I was hired in September along with several other seasonal workers, but was told that they would be needing one person to stay on after their peak season. Because I had had quite a bit of past experience in this field of work, they asked me to consider the offer. I told them I would think seriously about their proposition but was unable to commit myself since I was unsure of how my schedule for school would work out.

On October 1 the entire seasonal staff appeared at the shop for a brief training session to help familiarize us with the equipment, clothing and selling processes such as the operation of the cash register, sales slips, returns, guarantees, and so forth. After this session the group was invited back to Sally's house (the manager) for refreshments and to give us the opportunity to get to know the people we would be working with. Several times during the course of the day Sally had mentioned the fact that it was very important to develop good relationships among all employees. At times we would be working under great pressure and a congenial atmosphere would help relax not only ourselves but the customers as well. Everyone agreed that friendly relationships would, at least, promote smoother functioning of the shop and provide pleasant working conditions. After an hour or so of socializing with the other employees, it became quite evident that Sally had made an effort to hire people she thought would get along and work well together. Almost all of the employees were in their twenties, college students or graduates, friendly, and with similar interests—the main one being skiing, of course. Sally then gave us our schedules for the following weeks but noted that they were subject to change if someone needed a day off or became ill.

The first week was rather hectic and confusing in terms of really getting to know the operations of the shop; there were still a number of small details which I had to familiarize myself with. However, I was not alone and managed to catch on quickly because of my experience. The majority of mistakes made were due to ringing up the wrong amount on the cash register or mismarking the price on items brought out from the stock room. Ordinarily there wouldn't be any problem, but when the store became crowded mistakes were made in trying to work faster than one accurately could. It seemed to me during these busy times that Sally was nowhere to be found. She would either have to make a fast trip to the bank for change, have an important meeting with some manufacturer, or similar circumstances. This left the rest of the employees on their own as far as running the store was concerned. Often I would be asked what to do when certain mistakes were made because I was the most familiar with these processes. When Sally would balance the books at night these mistakes would be discovered, and she could identify the person who had done it by the initials on the saleslip. The following day Sally would confront the guilty employee and ask what had happened. As we quickly discovered, Sally was an extremely bright and efficient person with good skills in her type of managerial position. However, she was a little short on patience when her employees had "off days" or made even small mistakes. In other words, she expected the rest of us to be as she was, and even though we tried to the best of our abilities, no one really seemed to meet her standards completely.

As the season progressed, all the employees became quite close, seeing each other outside of work maybe once or twice a week. We often discussed the difficulties we had in pleasing Sally, which seemed to upset most of the employees. I could understand their point, but felt they didn't know Sally's side of the story. I had gotten to know Sally rather well since she generally ate her lunch or dinner when I had my break. She was only in her mid twenties, having been sent to the east from the main store in Colorado, to start a new business. She spent so much time at work that she hadn't been able to meet many people in the area. So, for lack of outside activities the ski shop had become her main concern, and all her efforts were put into making sure she did an excellent job. On occasion she would discuss the business with me in relation to the employees. She felt that if they slacked off the slightest bit or made mistakes, the business would go down the drain. I tried to explain to her that we all tried our best but we were human and subject to mistakes. However, Sally insisted that at this point the business was in no financial position to cover mistakes made in undercharging a customer or mismarking the price on items for sale.

The rest of the employees were aware that Sally questioned me about their job performance. There were no bad feelings, but they often asked me what Sally said about them. I told them about the financial problem facing the company, hoping this would explain Sally's anger as well as ease the feelings between the two groups. Several days after their latest questioning I overheard Stan, (the stock boy) and a few other kids talking. Stan was explaining his ingenious plan to rip-off ski equipment. The stock room was in the back of the building with the employee parking lot right behind it. When you wanted a pair of boots or something, all you would have to do was tell Ward. The plan was simple: When you were ready to go home he'd slip the boots out the back door of the stockroom and into your car while you were saying goodbye to Sally and the other employees. I heard them mumble, "Well, if Sally thinks we make the shop lose money by making mistakes on the register, she hasn't seen anything yet." Later I told Stan that I had heard his plan, and although I'd never say anything to Sally, I certainly wouldn't advise doing it. Sally often went into the stockroom and it would be too easy to get caught.

A week later I was in the stockroom getting some items for a customer. As I passed the back door I put down my order and looked outside to see if it was snowing. I opened the door just in time to see Stan putting a $90 jacket and a pair of $80 boots into one of the cars. I was so startled I just stood there watching him when he turned around and saw me. He smiled sheepishly, said all the kids were in on this and asked if I wanted him to get me some new boots too.

What should I do?

If I tell Sally, they will be reprimanded or even fired. This late in the season they would not get other jobs. If they weren't fired our relationships would become unbearable—I would be seen as a traitor. If I don't tell Sally; I am their accomplice. She'll eventually lose her job through mismanagement since a lot of expensive stock will be missing.

Thomas Motor Company Case*

THE THOMAS MOTOR COMPANY was a Plymouth-Dodge agency in Brownville, Michigan. The company was founded in 1927 by Mr. Edward P. Thomas. Until his unexpected death in September 1954, Mr. Thomas had been an active, respected citizen of the community and a successful businessman. Mr. Thomas's eldest son, John, succeeded to the presidency of the company.

John Thomas graduated in engineering from Mid-State University in

* From *Organizational Behavior: Cases and Readings,* by Austin Grimshaw and John W. Hennessey. Copyright © 1960 by McGraw-Hill, Inc. Used with the permission of McGraw-Hill Book Company.

1947 and went to work as a salesman for Industrial Chemical Company in a nearby region. It had always been understood that he would take over the reins of the Thomas Motor Company when his father retired. John and his family returned to Brownville immediately after the elder Thomas's fatal heart attack.

John Thomas learned much about the business in a short time. In the first 13 months, he made very few administrative changes and he was guided chiefly by the recommendations of the experienced men who had worked for his father.

The Thomas Motor Company had two major divisions: sales and service. The service division had an auto-service center located downtown with the showrooms and main office. The truck-service center had its shop on the outskirts of town, about ten blocks from the main office.

The truck-repair shop regularly employed a service manager, four mechanics, a cashier-bookkeeper, and a parts man (although in late 1955 the latter was scheduled to be drafted into the service in six weeks and no replacement had yet been obtained).

The foreman and service manager of the truck center was Mr. Titus Nolan. He had been with the company since it was organized in 1927. His job included talking with customers regarding the cost and time of each job and assigning the work to the mechanics. Nolan also worked on the trucks himself when time allowed, although he had worked more closely with the men in the past than he now had time to. His ability as a foreman and a first-rate mechanic was widely respected; also Nolan was known as a quiet, unassuming man who, in the other mechanics' words, "takes things as they come and doesn't easily get excited."

The other truck mechanics were Bob, Jim, Ralph, and Dexter, an apprentice. (Their ages were 34, 32, 36, and 24, respectively.) In late 1955, Bob and Jim had been working in the shop about ten years. Ralph Turner had been employed by the Thomas Motor Company for the past 15 months. Dexter had been there for one year.

Ralph had previously worked in his father's trucking company, doing maintenance work on the trucks in their own shop. However, they did not have enough work to use their own shop profitably all of the time, as it developed, and so its use was discontinued. As a result, Mr. Turner and Ralph decided that Ralph would go to work for Mr. Thomas, and his father would send all of his truck repair and maintenance work there. This was quite a large account, and one the Thomas Company was happy to obtain.

When Ralph first came to work he asked to do the repairs on his father's trucks. Mr. Nolan said that Ralph could do this as much as was practicable. About two months later, Mr. Nolan had an opportunity to talk to the senior Turner about his agreement. Nolan explained that the usual method of working in the shop involved each man's becoming more or less of a specialist on certain kinds of jobs and being assigned to these kinds of repairs as much as possible. Nolan felt that this led to increased efficiency and better workmanship. Also, he explained that since Mr. Turner's trucks were serviced at uneven intervals — sometimes two or three trucks at a time, sometimes none — he felt that Mr. Turner could be better served if the repairs were handled in the usual way by different men. Mr. Turner accepted this proposal.

Mr. Nolan passed the word on to Ralph. Ralph said he could see the logic of this and would accept "anything you decide upon." Nolan said at a later time that he expected this reaction from Ralph, because Ralph seemed to be getting along so well with the job and with the other men in the shop. He was "a very cooperative employee," in Nolan's words.

The mechanics were paid the going union-scale wage for their craft, and the only pay differentials were based on seniority. Dexter, new to the trade, was paid considerably less than the others.

Mr. Nolan considered Bob, Jim, and Ralph about equal in overall skill as mechanics, but Bob was the fastest man in the shop, with Jim a close second. Ralph was somewhat slower, and of course Dexter was a good deal slower because of lack of experience.

When a job was taken into the truck shop, the customer was usually told what the labor cost would be when he left the truck. From past experience the mechanic could usually judge fairly well whether he was losing too much time in the job, or whether he was going to finish on schedule or ahead of time. He tried to get ahead of the job he was doing so he could go across the street for coffee about 10 A.M. and again at 2:30 P.M. It was also an unwritten law that if a mechanic was not ahead on his job, he would not be able to go for coffee. Bob and Jim were almost always able to go, and Ralph was rarely able to go.

Dexter was almost always assigned to help one of the other mechanics. He would go for coffee if the man he was working with was able to go. Mr. Nolan, the parts man, and the cashier almost always went. These coffee sessions were looked upon as pleasant social occasions.

About August 1955, Ralph Turner began to make mistakes in his work, which Nolan attributed to haste on Ralph's part. Nolan checked the men's work carefully, and he was usually able to catch errors in the shop. However, several of Ralph's mistakes were not caught and proved to be quite serious. The first incident involved his not allowing enough clearance on a valve job. This customer returned about a week later very angry; and, although the garage did the work again free of charge, it lost a very good account.

At this time, Nolan talked to Ralph and told him to slow down and take his time even if he ran over the time that the job usually took. Ralph complained that the shop was too dirty and that this was the reason he made mistakes. He had been able to keep his own shop very clean and free from dirt when he worked for his father. Nolan replied that it wasn't possible to keep this shop as clean as Ralph's previous one because there wasn't sufficient spare time but that he felt the shop was as clean as most shops of this type. Ralph was a good deal more careful and worked at a slower rate for a couple of weeks. During this time he was never able to take a coffee break.

Nolan also noticed that Ralph had gradually shown, since he stopped working exclusively on his father's trucks, an increasing tendency to be interested in what other mechanics were doing on his father's vehicles when they were in the shop for repair. Several times Nolan had spoken to Ralph when the latter was found, during the lunch hour, tampering with a Turner truck on which one of the other mechanics was assigned to work. Nolan did not take this very seriously nor did he speak to Ralph, except mildly, because he felt it showed simply that Ralph was "eager and just solicitous about those old Dodge friends of his."

About two months later, in October 1955, Ralph failed to replace the rubber retainer in a set of hydraulic brakes he was repairing. The mistake very nearly caused a serious accident, and another account was lost. Nolan again appealed to Ralph to slow down. Ralph said that he was finding it very difficult to work with Dexter. (Nolan had been assigning Dexter to help Ralph for the previous three weeks.) Ralph said that Dexter seemed only bent on getting out for coffee. He felt that Dexter was not skillful enough to be working as fast as he tried to. He stated, "Dexter only wants to push me, not to learn from me."

Nolan replied he would have Dexter work with Bob or Jim but that he had wanted him to learn from all the men. Ralph agreed to be as careful as possible and to work more slowly.

About this same time, Ralph told his father that he had come to feel that the other mechanics had a prejudice against him. He said he could hardly work with the roar of the radio they had going at all times, either baseball or music. He had asked Bob to turn it off when Bob went out for coffee. Bob had given him a blank look and a grunt and turned it off for a couple of days.

Ralph continued, "The radio seems to be on louder than ever now. They never even think about me enough to turn it down when they go out for coffee. Furthermore, I think they are the kind that would talk about me behind my back, especially Dexter."

Nolan kept a close watch on Ralph's work. He recounted the whole problem to John Thomas when he came by one day in December 1955.

Nolan concluded by saying, "Ralph certainly is a changed man since we first hired him. In fact, if I weren't concerned about our losing the Turner account, I'd fire Ralph right now. We just can't afford his attitude and his errors. As it is, I'm afraid he's going to quit, and we'll lose the account anyway."

Two Head Nurses:
A Study in Contrast*

IN EXTERNAL features Floor A and Floor B are very similar. Each has about 30 private and semiprivate beds. On each floor medical patients and surgical patients are cared for by graduate nurses, student nurses, nurses aides, and maids.

Floor A

On Floor A, people speak in hushed voices. Conversation is at a minimum. Miss Smith, the head nurse, spends almost all her time at her desk. She gives instructions firmly and unambiguously. The nurses go from room to room caring for patients in a businesslike impersonal manner, and there is little give-and-take between them and the patients.

A. THE HEAD NURSE   Miss Smith's supervisor said of her: "Miss Smith is of the old school. She's really very stern and rigid. She runs an excellent floor from the standpoint of organization and system. It's beautifully organized. She has all her supplies in perfect condition, but she can't handle human relations. Her graduates claim that she treats them like students, watches everything they do, checks up on them all the time, and won't allow them any responsibility. The students claim that Miss Smith gives them only routine, only the small details."

It is generally agreed that Miss Smith is fair and not arbitrary. For example, she makes a conscious effort to grant nurses' requests for time off whenever possible, but is strict and uncompromising with nurses who violate regulations. She is uniformly courteous in a formal manner. The following conversation with a member of the dietary department is typical: "I am calling for Miss Wilson, a patient in Room 413, a diabetic case. She would like coffee with every meal. Is that all right? Thank you."

She observes the same rather starchy courtesy whether the pressure of work is relaxed or at its height, and expects the same formal courtesy from her subordinates.

B. THE ASSISTANT   Miss Smith delegates almost no authority to Miss Green, her assistant. When Miss Smith is on the ward, Miss Green shares floor duty with the other nurses and does not work at the desk. When Miss Green is in charge, there is a marked change in the atmo-

---

* We are indebted to Professor George Strauss for this case.

sphere. People talk to each other more naturally, and sit around when the work is slack. There is also considerable confusion on the ward.

C. GRADUATE NURSES   The attitude among the younger graduates toward Miss Smith's supervision is expressed in the following quotations:

> Miss Smith runs a very strict floor, and the nurses resent her because she treats them like students.

> When I came here, Miss Smith checked up on everything I did, and that was hard to adjust to. You felt you were a student all over again.

> Miss Smith is off, and the doctors who come here are in a more sociable frame of mind. The whole atmosphere seems to relax. Often we have a nurses' aide mix up a pitcher of lemonade and we have it sitting right down at the desk. If you tried that in the daytime, Miss Smith would have a stroke. When Miss Smith is on, she absolutely does not tolerate any smoking. But when she's off, we all stop and smoke and have coffee.

> I don't pay any attention to Miss Smith any more, and I don't think the other girls do either. You just let what she says go in one ear and out the other. At first it bothered me, and I think it annoyed most of the other girls that she treated us like students. All I say is, 'Yes, Miss Smith,' and go ahead and do what I would have done anyway. We sit around and talk to each other when the work is done, and if Miss Smith asks us to be a little quiet we lower our voices, but we don't attempt to slink around or anything. There was a tendency to do that for a while, but you soon get over that.

The attitude of the older nurses is different as the following quotations show:

> I like working with Miss Smith. I know a lot of the girls complain about her because she's fussy and checks on them. Personally I'd rather work on this floor than anywhere else for exactly that reason. Everything here is done properly. The doctors prefer this floor because this is where the patients get the best care. The other nurses aren't impressed by that. They insist they wouldn't work here because Miss Smith is a fussbudget. They don't seem to care whether the patients get good care or not.

> I picked this floor because I liked the supervision here. I've worked with Miss Smith while I was a student and I knew what to expect. I honestly feel I still need a responsible person nearby to supervise. I need guidance, and therefore I prefer to work on a floor where there is a fairly strict supervisor. On some of the other floors things are too slipshod. Everything is hodgepodge, and it drives me crazy. I like things done in an orderly fashion, and it bothers me very much when everything is slipshod. I don't mean the atmosphere, I mean Miss Smith. She doesn't believe in relaxation at all. As for myself, I prefer to work hard and get it done with and then relax. I can see Miss Smith's point. After all, you have these sick people here and they have to be taken care of. She's got to lay down the law to us to a certain extent. I keep telling my husband how lucky he is to be in his kind of work. Everything in his place is buddy-buddy. But I guess in hos-

pitals it just can't work that way. The head nurse has to be strict in order to get the work done. Isn't that right?

Some of the girls are lovely to work with, but others just aren't good at supervising. They don't know how to express themselves. Now when Miss Smith is on, it is altogether different. She knows how to get things done the first time.

D. STUDENT NURSES   Miss Smith keeps her students under rigid discipline, and they complain to their supervisor that she gives them only routine work and doesn't allow them to take any responsibility. They feel they learn much less than on other floors. The students ask few questions either of Miss Smith or of the graduate nurses. They rarely talk to anyone.

E. RELATIONSHIPS AMONG WORKERS   All relationships on Floor A tend to be formal and impersonal. There is very little give and take or development of camaraderie. Nurses' aides complain that the nurses never teach them anything. Miss Smith divides up the work equably and assigns it clearly, and there is no complaint that some members of the group are slack in carrying out their duties. Yet when Miss Smith is off the floor there is evidence of antagonism among the different workers. The aides say that if they had problems they would take them up with their housekeeping supervisor.

F. PATIENT CARE   The relationship between nurses and patients is rather formal and distant. Patients remain in their rooms, and very few walk about on the floor. Requests by patients and visitors are taken care of promptly and efficiently. The charts are in excellent order, but there is some evidence of slipups in nursing care. In one case, a patient was given the wrong drug and had a severe reaction. During the period when the ward was observed there were three instances of postoperative fever. Once when an intern removed a drainage catheter and forgot to replace it, the error was not corrected for five hours.

Floor B

The atmosphere on Floor B is warm and informal. There is a good deal of gossiping and good-natured horseplay, and the girls discuss their problems with one another.

A. THE HEAD NURSE   Miss Rogers, the head nurse, spends only about two-thirds of her time at her desk, and the rest of the time she is on the ward helping with patient-care and chatting informally with workers and patients. She often consults individual nurses, or the entire nursing staff about problems and changes. She expressed her attitude toward supervision as follows:

> The hospital has changed since I graduated. At that time it was just losing the old military discipline and becoming more reasonable in its approach. The present way is much better, on the whole, than the old. I find

that if you give people a break, they are more likely to pitch in and help you when you're in a jam. I never could stand this old military discipline stuff.

Miss Rogers is informal in her relationship with her subordinates. Her way of giving an order is typified in this quotation:

> Do you want to go to the pharmacy for me? Gee, that would be swell. Again, when telephoning central supplies, Miss Rogers will say: Is this you, Betty? Listen, you poor kid, this is me again. I'm sorry, but we've got to have two sets of trays. I thought I'd tell you because if I send the aide down, the poor kid won't get it right.

On the other hand, when the ward is under pressure, Miss Rogers tends to give her answers in an offhand, somewhat distracted way.

B. THE ASSISTANT   Miss Rogers deliberately divides authority with her assistant, giving her the jobs of ordering drugs and supplies and superintending the cleaning. She consults her when making decisions. When she is absent, the assistant carries on supervision much as Miss Rogers does. There is little difference in the atmosphere on the ward whether Miss Rogers or her assistant is in charge.

C. GRADUATE NURSES   One of the graduate nurses on Miss Roger's floor said: "On this floor anybody can speak up whenever she feels like it, and we get along together fine. The girls on this floor are very good to work with. Miss Rogers is an excellent head nurse, and there is good spirit."

This is rather typical of the attitude of the younger nurses. The older nurses feel somewhat differently:

> Miss Rogers is a very nice person, and all the girls have been lovely to me. But I don't think the organization is as careful as it used to be, and that's why a lot of mistakes are made. It's very easy to forget to give medicine, for instance. It happened to me. Since each nurse is responsible for her own patients, nobody checks up to see whether you've actually given a patient what he's supposed to have. Nobody tells you how you're getting along. I don't know whether I'm doing a good job or not. Maybe I'm forgetting things. Maybe patients complain about me. If so, I never hear of it. I just have to guess that I'm doing all right. I wish that sometimes somebody would come along and check up, and let me know when I do things wrong, and how I can improve myself. I feel that being out so long, I must have plenty of room for improvement.
>
> Sometimes I work down on Miss Rogers's floor. I was down there last week, and it was exasperating. I had to go down to the drug room myself twice during the morning, and I know that some of the other nurses had to do that too. Well, that's foolish. If the drugs were checked properly in the first place, all the drug orders would have gone down at the same time. That would never happen on Miss Smith's floor because she runs it in a very orderly and systematic way. I don't get any joy out of working on Miss Rogers's floor because things are done just too sloppily.

D. STUDENT NURSES   Miss Rogers said that she enjoys teaching, but has some problems in maintaining discipline. Students seem to be accepted as an integral part of the social group. They take part in informal discussions and are free to ask any questions they wish.

E. RELATIONSHIPS AMONG WORKERS   The relationship among the different groups of workers on Miss Rogers's floor is easy and informal. Some of the nurses' aides address Miss Rogers by her first name, and she calls them by nicknames. There is a strong spirit of camaraderie throughout the ward. On the other hand, Miss Rogers does not assign tasks to each worker in a clearcut specific way, and consequently there is some tendency to shirk certain tasks. As one nurses' aide put it:

> They just expect all of us to get the work done. If one person lies down on the job, it would mean that the other person does that much more. Evidently they don't stop to think who does what. We've got a little bit of jealousy. A good boss could straighten it out.

The nurses' aides on Miss Rogers's floor say that if they had a problem they would first take it up with her.

F. PATIENT CARE   The relationship between patient and workers on the ward is easy and informal. The patients are part of the social group. They wander in and out of their rooms. At times they join in the chatting of a group of nurses, and even run small errands for the nurses. The nurses call them by their first names.

When the work is heavy, however, Miss Rogers and the nurses tend to be brusque with the patients. They do not always meet the patients' requests or those of their visitors promptly. Charts are not maintained with scrupulous care.

Although some of the older nurses feel that the loose supervision is likely to result in slipups in nursing care, none were noted during the period of observation.

Patients who once have been on Floor B not infrequently ask that they be sent there again at the time of a second admission. Some doctors also request that their patients be admitted to this floor because of the good psychological care which they receive.

The Ultimate Frisbee Team's Dilemma

HARRY, Jere, George, and Bob L. were students at Centerville University who enjoyed playing Ultimate Frisbee, a game requiring two teams of seven. Since it was hard to round up fourteen players every time they wished to play, they decided to start a regular frisbee team. Their hopes were to get some potentially good frisbee players together and teach them how to play Ultimate. They realized they would need to publicize the team and one of them, Jere, spoke to a reporter from the school newspaper and a short article appeared about the team (see Exhibit 1). In the interview Jere stated, "The team is open to all students, especially girls." Any of the four could have spoken to the reporter, but Jere took the initiative. Jere also announced a practice through the newspaper. Eleven people came to that initial practice: Jere, Fred, Roger (Fred's roommate), Jim H., Jean, Bob L., George, Pete C., Pete R., Paul, and Harry. Jere took their names, addresses, and telephone numbers and announced that practices would be held at 4 P.M. on Tuesdays and Thursdays (at a time which was convenient for Jere). It wasn't clear why Jere should be the one to decide this, but since he was taking names, he was the one asked by the newcomers.

At the second practice some new people showed up: Chas, Alex, Bert, Gene, (all of whom lived together), Bob M., Linda, Sharon, and Jack. However, some people from the first practice didn't come because they had conflicting classes. Jere took these new people's names and toyed with the idea of taking attendance, but nothing came of it because, as he said to his roommate, "I didn't want to turn people off or make them feel they had to come." However, many players made a mental note of who was there and who wasn't. Different people came and went like this at each practice thereafter.

Jere and several others knew how to play Ultimate and spent the first few practices teaching the others. Jere dominated the direction of these early practices, but after a short time the rest of the players were as good and some even better. Everyone had a lot of fun learning and playing. Jack and Chas were two players who stood out at practice. Jack, a grad student, was calm and collected, never got angry and always played fairly. Chas had been the captain of his high school football team and always organized the team he was on, deciding who should play and who should sit out.

Jere dealt with much of the administrative work, such as announcing to the school radio and newspaper where and when practices would be held. No one asked Jere to do this, but attendance was sporadic and he hoped to get new people to fill the gaps at practice. However, response to the newspaper and radio announcements was minimal; consequently, Jere felt there should be an organizational meeting at night which hopefully would generate interest and attract more players. At the next practice Jere announced the meeting and explained that it was also to set-up officers, dues, and so forth. Jack had 200 flyers printed up and he and Chas posted them around campus.

Jere came to the meeting late and found that strong opposition had developed against dues and against organization in general. Jere tried to explain that in order to receive funding from the University or to use University vehicles the team must be organized with officers and a constitu-

EXHIBIT 1
The *Centerville News*, March 1, 1974

'ULTIMATE FRISBEE' ARRIVES WITH SPRING
By Janice M. Dupre

Springtime is just around the corner and for Frisbee lovers it's time to warm up the old throwing arm.

This spring a group of frisbee enthusiasts are trying to get together a frisbee team at Centerville University (CU). Originator of the team is Jere Harris.

Many people are familiar with the frisbee as simply a plastic disc used for throwing around on a beach.

But, there is an official game played with a frisbee. It's called Ultimate Frisbee and it's like soccer in many ways.

"In Ultimate Frisbee there are seven players per team on the field. There is a kick off, but you can't run with the frisbee in your hand," explains Harris. "It's an extremely fast game with two twenty-four minute halfs."

According to Harris, a Middle

States Frisbee League is now being formed by a student from Amerion College. Colleges that already have teams and will hopefully be joining the league include: Western Reserve, Ohio Wesleyan, Wayne University, and Clarke. One of the best frisbee teams in the area is the New Hampton College team.

In past years individuals from CU have gotten together to play other schools, but there never has been an official team.

"I've been playing frisbee all my life, but I never heard of Ultimate Frisbee until a friend of mine told me about the game last year. It's really a fast moving game with lots of collisions because the frisbee is always in the air with everyone diving for it," said Harris, a junior Hospital Administration major.

Ultimate Frisbee is by no means a

EXHIBIT 1 (contd.)

gentle game. At this moment Bob LaPointe, future co-captain of the forming CU team has a dislocated shoulder from a frisbee game he recently played in.

The friend that introduced the game to Jere Harris last year was a graduate of Columbia High School in New Jersey. It was at Columbia where the first game was played.

"The Columbia High team can beat any team in the nation," said Harris. "They won over thirty games at the national tournament held in Michigan last year. Columbia High School also publishes the Ultimate Frisbee rulebook."

Each year a national frisbee tournament is held at Copperhopper, Michigan. Hundreds of Ultimate Frisbee teams from the U.S. and Canada come to take part in the tournament. The game of Frisbee is not confined to North America, it's very popular overseas and according to Harris is just being introduced to Red China.

So far the CU Frisbee team composes about ten members. Harris is hoping to get the team off the ground and start practicing soon. He is planning to announce practices as soon as he can arrange a time in the indoor track and as soon as the weather gets nice.

"Frisbee is open to women" stresses Harris, "to play you don't have to be a super frisbee thrower, you just have to be able to throw and catch the frisbee and to run."

Along with all the food, energy, and political crises there is also a frisbee crisis. Frisbees are made with plastics and since there is a plastic shortage the frisbees are an endangered species. Harris said that the major Frisbee companies such as Whamo, are urging people to buy their frisbees now because soon they will be hard to come by.

But until that time comes, Frisbees will continue to fly in the sky on warm spring days at Centerville.

---

tion, saying that the sports director for the University had told him this. A vote on dues barely passed whereupon several members left the meeting vowing they had quit. Jere followed them into the hall pleading with them to be sensible, but could overhear two other members saying, "So what, we don't need them anyway." A debate ensued for a few minutes and Jere called an end to the meeting, putting off a vote on a captain because he feared it would create further division among the team, since either Jere, Jack, or Chas might have made a good captain. Many new people who had shown up to the meeting explained they couldn't make practices as currently scheduled. Jere shrugged and said he'd try to set up alternative practices; however, this was never done.

A new group of players arrived after about ten practices: Stan, Reggie, Mark, Bill T., and Howie. They always came and left together and often played on the same team. They were good players and talked about the coming games and their anticipated role in them. Reggie asked Jere at his first practice, "Do you think I'll start the first game?" Jere just shrugged.

By this time over 20 people had come out for the team, including 3 girls. (See Exhibit 2.) The players fell into five friendship groups as shown in Exhibit 3. As practices continued, they became hard and competitive and a lot of the fun which had been evident in the beginning seemed to disappear. One day Jere enraged Sharon by taking the frisbee away from her and throwing it himself. She started to walk off the field but Jere called her back and the two had an argument right out in the middle of the field, where everyone could see and hear it. She stayed at practice, but was silent the rest of the day.

As the date for the first game drew near, all of the dues money was

EXHIBIT 2

Name	Attendance†	Initial Appearance	Ability†	Age	Class	Showed Up for Bus
Jack	regular	2d practice	A	23	Grad	XX
Fred	regular	1st practice	A	19	Fresh	XX
Jere......	regular*	1st practice	B	20	Jr.	XX
Jean	regular	1st practice	C	19	Soph	XX
Harry....	regular*	1st practice	A	21	Sr.	
Roger....	sporadic	1st practice	B	21	Sr.	XX
Reggie ...	regular	10th practice	A	18	Fresh	XX
Mark	regular	10th practice	A	18	Fresh	XX
Howie ...	regular	10th practice	A	18	Fresh	XX
Stan	regular	10th practice	A	19	Fresh	XX
Paul	sporadic	1st practice	B	19	Soph	
Jim H. ...	regular	1st practice	A	19	Jr.	XX
Chas.....	regular	2d practice	A	20	Soph	XX
Gene	sporadic	2d practice	B	20	Soph	XX
Bert	sporadic	2d practice	B	19	Soph	
Sharon...	regular	2d practice	C	20	Jr.	
Linda	sporadic	2d practice	C	18	Fresh	XX
George...	regular*	1st practice	A	19	Soph	XX
Bob L....	sporadic	1st practice	B	19	Soph	XX
Bob M. ..	sporadic	2d practice	B	20	Jr.	XX
Pete C. ..	sporadic	1st practice	B	19	Fresh	XX
Bill T.....	regular	10th practice	C	19	Soph	XX
Alex	sporadic	10th practice	C	19	Soph	
Pete R....	sporadic	1st practice	C	18	Fresh	XX

* Founders of the team.
† Based on Jere's "mental notes."

used to rent a 15 seat bus for the 50-mile trip to the other school. The day before the game about 12 people attended a meeting to discuss travel plans. Jack brought a letter written by Sharon. It was addressed to the team but started:

> Dear Jack:
>
> The incident at this afternoon's practice was the last straw, but I would like to impress, far from the only one. I'm writing this to you because you are the only one on the team who ever gave me any encouragement or made me feel like a real live person, and not a bumbling incompetent.
>
> I joined the frisbee team because I enjoy playing vigorous frisbee in the comradeship of others, and to develop my own skill and confidence, but none of these are achievable under the present conditions.
>
> How can I enjoy and concentrate on the game, when not a minute goes by that I must force myself to ignore and rise above degrading and humiliating sexist treatment? It's often said that a female, be it a filly race horse or me on the frisbee team, must be three times as good as a male in order to be considered equal. Nothing truer has ever been said. Even Jere, who's practiced with me so much and encouraged my progress, turns overtly sexist in the presence of his teammates. Certainly the issues are not completely imagined in my mind—ask the other female players.
>
> I am not against competitiveness as long as the competition element stimulates constant improvement. But when point-making takes priority over the freedom to make mistakes or try new things, then I think something is wrong. Maybe, if anyone cares you could let them in on this. . . .

With this Sharon announced her resignation from the team. The letter was received with much debate by the team and some players refused to read the letter. Jack sided with the opinions stated in the letter and was joined in this opinion by many of the original members, including the two remaining girls. Jere remained silent, unable to side with one view or the other.

Obviously some choice had to be made as to who would go on the bus. Group D insisted on "Sending down the best 15," in which case all of them would go. Group C said, "Take those who have come to the most

EXHIBIT 3
Subgroups (with spokesperson listed first)

Group A: Jere, Harry, Bob L., George
Group B: Chas, Gene, Alex, Bert
Group C: Jack, Jean, Linda, Sharon, Jim H.
Group D: Stan, Reggie, Mark, Howie, Bill T.
Group E: Fred, Roger, Pete C., Paul
All the rest are independents, coming under no group.

EXHIBIT 4
Comparative Lists for Going
to the Game

Jack's List	Group D's List
Jere	Reggie
Jack	Mark
Fred	Howie
Jean	Stan
Roger	Paul
Jim H.	Jere
Sharon	Jack
Linda	Fred
Bob L.	Roger
George	Jim H.
Harry	Chas
Paul	Gene
Pete R.	Bert
Chas	George
Gene	Harry

practices." Jere felt that this was the fairest solution, but it was hard to implement since no one was sure as to who had attended how many practices.

Jere, Jack and Stan sat down and wrote up several lists of 15, (See Exhibit 4) but none were acceptable to all of the groups. Jere put off making any decision; several people got quite sore. Jere felt caught in the middle, and it was not something he could shrug off. He tried to act as the moderator of the dispute, but kept saying, "Does anyone have any ideas?" Argument continued and people began to leave very upset with no decision reached. Jere felt that he had been responsible for letting the scene get out of hand.

The day of the game came and 19 people stood outside near the bus. Everyone wondered what to do. Some expressed the opinion that a captain should be elected to make the decision.

Discussion Questions

1. What are the norms exhibited by the Ultimate Frisbee players?
2. What factors influenced Jere's behavior?
3. Should the Ultimate Frisbee team be "open to all students, especially girls"?
4. Why isn't the Ultimate Frisbee team more of a cohesive unit than it is?
5. How can the team resolve the dilemma which it now faces?

The White Company*

NOTE: DO NOT READ this case until directed to do so by your instructor. It has been set up as a Prediction Case so that you can test your analysis by answering questions before reading the entire case.

PART 1

THE WHITE COMPANY was one of some 80 electroplating plants in the city of Detroit which applied nickel and chromeplating to automobile parts. Price competition among these eighty plants was very intense.

The company had a nonunion work force which fluctuated between 15 and 50, depending on orders from the auto manufacturers. Few personnel records were kept. There was a standard policy of firing anyone who showed any interest in unionism. Hiring and training practices were not formalized, and the number of workers varied widely from day to day, depending upon contracts. There was practically no job training. No more than a few minutes was spent in pointing out workers' duties and in introductions to co-workers.

The work was mostly unskilled, and the company employed many manual work methods instead of the semiautomatic equipment found in other companies. It used a number of practices designed to cut costs: (1) repairs were neglected and workers were expected to make up for this mechanical ineffectiveness, (2) personal (work) equipment was not quickly replaced . . ., (3) many safety practices were neglected . . . (4) hiring and training were fitted with a situation of high turnover, so that new workers were given little training and fired if they did not quickly learn to turn out a standard amount of production . . ., (5) overall wages were so low that the most highly paid workers received only average union wages for the industry and the workers did not receive the usual union fringe concessions.

The workers in the plant could be categorized into two main groups: high-turnover personnel, and long-service employees. The backgrounds of the workers in the plant were quite different for longer service people as compared to high-turnover workers. High-turnover personnel tended to be either part-time workers, such as students, or relatives and friends of long-service workers; experienced workers who were on strike elsewhere or temporarily laid off; or finally, young newcomers to the labor

---

* Information for this case was taken from W. J. Goode and Irving Fowler, "Incentive Factors in a Low Morale Plant," *American Sociological Review,* vol. XIV, no. 5 (1949). Also in William J. Goode, *Explanations in Role Theory* (New York: Oxford University Press, 1973) pp. 319–29. Reproduced by permission of the authors and publisher.

market. The five longer service personnel were different in many respects but had in common a quite desperate need for a job, either because they had physical handicaps which would make them unemployable in many places, or, in the case of women, because they had to support dependent husbands. Some of the long-service workers had been with the plant since its beginnings. Almost all of them could perform nearly every task and could substitute for an absent worker.

Predictions

From what I know about the White Company, I would predict that:

a. Worker productivity would be (high) (moderate) (low). Explain the reasons for your prediction.

b. Satisfaction in the plant would be (high) (moderate) (low). Explain the reasons for your prediction.

PART 2

The long-service employees under pressure from management initiated a work pace which the high-turnover group had to follow. Those who did not follow such a pace were exposed to reprimand by word, gesture, or look from the long-service workers. If they continued this lack of cooperation, informal pressures on the foremen by the key workers would eventually cause their discharge. Because of the timing aspects of electroplating frequent bottlenecks occurred. However, these bottlenecks did not necessarily mean delays in production. They rather meant that at such times the key workers would attack the bottleneck with increased energy and, with the spontaneously induced help of the high-turnover personnel, would erase the difficulty. If this in turn produced a piling up of units at a later phase of the plating process, then the key personnel utilized the same practices and again the bottleneck was relieved. According to an expert in the industry, the White Company's level of worker productivity was running only 12 to 14 percent below those firms that had invested in semiautomatic equipment. The company was "financially successful against strong competition."

Morale in the plant was low. "Workers exhibited considerable animosity toward the owners as well as the production manager," and "among the workers themselves."

Postprediction Analysis

Refer to your predictions at the end of Part 1. How closely do they match the information above? Do inaccuracies in your predictions reflect inadequate analysis? If so, explain the analytical failure. If not, what additional information would you have needed in Part 1 to improve your predictive accuracy and how would you have used that information?

Work Group Ownership of an Improved Tool*

THE WHIRLWIND Aircraft Corporation was a leader in its field and especially noted for its development of the modern supercharger. Work in connection with the latter mechanism called for special skill and ability. Every detail of the supercharger had to be perfect to satisfy the exacting requirements of the aircraft industry.

In 1941 (before Pearl Harbor), Lathe Department 15–D was turning out three types of impeller, each contoured to within 0.002 inch and machined to a mirrorlike finish. The impellers were made from an aluminum alloy and finished on a cam-back lathe.

The work was carried on in four shifts, two men on each. The personnel in the finishing section were as follows:

1. *First Shift* — 7 A.M. to 3 P.M. Sunday and Monday off.
    a. Jean Latour, master mechanic, French Canadian, forty-five years of age. Latour had set up the job and trained the men who worked with him on the first shift.
    b. Pierre DuFresne, master mechanic, French Canadian, thirty-six years of age. Both these men had trained the workers needed for the other shifts.
2. *Second Shift* — 3 P.M. to 11 P.M. Friday and Saturday off.
    a. Albert Durand, master mechanic, French Canadian, thirty-two years of age; trained by Latour and using his lathe.
    b. Robert Benet, master mechanic, French Canadian, thirty-one years of age; trained by DuFresne and using his lathe.
3. *Third Shift* — 11 P.M. to 7 A.M. Tuesday and Wednesday off.
    a. Philippe Doret, master mechanic, French Canadian, thirty-one years of age; trained by Latour and using his lathe.
    b. Henri Barbet, master mechanic, French Canadian, thirty years of age; trained by DuFresne and using his lathe.
4. *Stagger Shift* — Monday, 7 A.M. to 3 P.M.; Tuesday, 11 P.M. to 7 A.M.; Wednesday, 11 P.M. to 7 A.M.; Thursday, off; Friday, 3 P.M. to 11 P.M.; Saturday, 3 P.M. to 11 P.M.; Sunday, off.
    a. George MacNair, master mechanic, Scotch, thirty-two years of age; trained by Latour and using his lathe.

---

* This case was written by Professor Paul Pigors and is reprinted with his permission.

    b. William Reader, master mechanic, English, thirty years of age; trained by DuFresne and using his lathe.

Owing to various factors (such as the small number of workers involved, the preponderance of one nationality, and the fact that Latour and DuFresne had trained the other workers) these eight men considered themselves as members of one work group. Such a feeling of solidarity is unusual among workers on different shifts, despite the fact that they use the same machines.

The men received a base rate of $1.03 an hour and worked on incentive. Each man usually turned out 22 units a shift, thus earning an average of $1.19 an hour. Management supplied Rex 95 High-Speed Tool-Bits, which workers ground to suit themselves. Two tools were used: one square bit with a slight radius for recess cutting, the other bit with a 45-degree angle for chamfering and smooth finish. When used, both tools were set close together, the worker adjusting the lathe from one operation to the other. The difficulty with this setup was that during the rotation of the lathe, the aluminum waste would melt and fuse between the two toolbits. Periodically the lathe had to be stopped so that the toolbits could be freed from the welded aluminum and reground.

At the request of the supervisor of Lathe Department 15–D, the methods department had been working on his tool problem. Up to the time of this case, no solution had been found. To make a firsthand study of the difficulty, the methods department had recently assigned one of their staff, Mr. MacBride, to investigate the problem in the lathe department itself. Mr. MacBride's working hours covered parts of both the first and second shifts. MacBride was a young man, twenty-six years of age, and a newcomer to the methods department. For the three months prior to this assignment, he had held the post of "suggestion man," a position which enabled newcomers to the methods department to familiarize themselves with the plant setup. The job consisted in collecting, from boxes in departments throughout the plant, suggestions submitted by employees and making a preliminary evaluation of these ideas. The current assignment of studying the tool situation in Lathe Department 15–D, with a view to cutting costs, was his first special task. He devoted himself to this problem with great zeal but did not succeed in winning the confidence of the workers. In pursuance of their usual philosophy: "Keep your mouth shut if you see anyone with a suit on," they volunteered no information and took the stand that, since the methods man had been given this assignment, it was up to him to carry it out.

While MacBride was working on this problem, Pierre DuFresne hit upon a solution. One day he successfully contrived a tool which combined the two bits into one. This eliminated the space between the two toolbits which in the past had caught the molten aluminum waste and allowed it to become welded to the cutting edges. The new toolbit had two advantages: it eliminated the frequent machine stoppage for cleaning and regrinding the old-type tools; and it enabled the operator to run the lathe at a higher speed. These advantages made it possible for the operator to increase his efficiency 50 percent.

DuFresne tried to make copies of the new tool, but was unable to do so. Apparently the new development had been a "lucky accident" during grinding which he could not duplicate. After several unsuccessful attempts, he took the new tool to his former teacher, Jean Latour. The latter succeeded in making a drawing and turning out duplicate toolbits on a small grinding wheel in the shop. At first the two men decided to keep the new tool to themselves. Later, however, they shared the improvement with their fellow workers on the second shift. Similarly it was passed on to the other shifts. But all these men kept the new development a closely guarded secret as far as "outsiders" were concerned. At the end of the shift, each locked the improved toolbit securely in his toolchest.

Both DuFresne, the originator of the new tool, and Latour, its draftsman and designer, decided not to submit the idea as a suggestion but to keep it as the property of their group. Why was this decision made? The answer lies partly in the suggestion system and partly in the attitude of Latour and DuFresne toward other features of company work life and toward their group.

According to an informational bulletin issued by the company, the purpose of the suggestion system was to "provide an orderly method of submitting and considering ideas and recommendations of employees to management; to provide a means for recognizing and rewarding individual ingenuity; and to promote cooperation." Awards for accepted suggestions were made in the following manner: "After checking the savings and expense involved in an adopted suggestion [the suggestion committee] determined the amount of the award to be paid, based upon the savings predicted upon a year's use of the suggestion." "It is the intention of the committee . . . to be liberal in the awards, which are expected to adequately compensate for the interest shown in presenting suggestions." In pursuance of this policy, it was customary to grant the suggestor an award equivalent to the savings of an entire month.

As a monetary return, both DuFresne and Latour considered an award based on one month's saving as inadequate. They also argued that such awards were really taken out of the worker's pockets. Their reasoning was as follows: All awards for adopted suggestions were paid out of undistributed profits. Since the company also had a profit-sharing plan, the money was taken from a fund that would be given to the workers anyway, which merely meant robbing Peter to pay Paul. In any case, the payment was not likely to be large and probably would be less than they could accumulate if increased incentive payments could be maintained over an extended period without discovery. Thus there was little in favor of submitting the new tool as a suggestion.

Latour and DuFresne also felt that there were definite hazards to the group if their secret were disclosed. They feared that once the tool became company property, its efficiency might lead to layoff of some members in their group, or at least make work less tolerable by leading to an increased quota at a lower price per unit. They also feared that there might be a change in scheduled work assignments. For instance, the lathe department worked on three different types of impeller. One type was a routine job and aside from the difficulty caused by the old-type tool, presented no problem. For certain technical reasons, the other two types were more difficult to make. Even Latour, an exceptionally skilled craftsman, had sometimes found it hard to make the expected quota before the new tool was developed. Unless the work-load was carefully balanced by scheduling easier and more difficult types, some of the operators were unable to make standard time.

The decision to keep the tool for their own group was in keeping with Latour's work philosophy. He had a strong feeling of loyalty to his own group and had demonstrated this in the past by offering for their use several improvements of his own. For example, he made available to all workers in his group a set of special gauge blocks which were used in aligning work on lathes. To protect himself in case mistakes were traced to these gauges, he wrote on them: "Personnel [sic] Property – Do not use. Jean Latour."

Through informal agreement with their fellow workers, Latour and DuFresne "pegged production" at an efficiency rate that in their opinion would not arouse management's suspicion or lead to a restudy of the job, with possible cutting of the rate. This enabled them to earn an extra 10 percent incentive earnings. The other 40 percent in additional efficiency was used as follows: The operators established a reputation for a high degree of accuracy and finish. They set a record for no spoilage and were able to apply the time gained on the easier type of impeller to work on the other types which required greater care and more expert workmanship.

The foreman of the lathe department learned about the new tool soon after it was put into use but was satisfied to let the men handle the situation in their own way. He reasoned that at little expense he was able to get out production of high quality. There was no defective work, and the men were contented.

Mr. MacBride was left in a very unsatisfactory position. He had not succeeded in working out a solution of his own. Like the foreman, he got wind of the fact that the men had devised a new tool. He urged them to submit a drawing of it through the suggestion system, but this advice was not taken, and the men made it plain that they did not care to discuss with him the reasons for this position.

Having no success in his direct contact with the workers, Mr. Mac-Bride appealed to the foreman, asking him to secure a copy of the new tool. The foreman replied that the men would certainly decline to give him a copy and would resent as an injustice any effort on his part to force them to submit a drawing. Instead he suggested that MacBride should persuade DuFresne to show him the tool. This MacBride attempted to do, but met with no success in his efforts to ingratiate himself with DuFresne. When he persisted in his attempts, DuFresne decided to throw him off the track. He left in his lathe a toolbit which was an unsuccessful copy of the original discovery. At shift change, MacBride was delighted to find what he supposed to be the improved tool. He hastily copied it and submitted a drawing to the tool department. When a tool was made up according to these specifications it naturally failed to do what was expected of it. The workers, when they heard of this through the "grapevine," were delighted. DuFresne did not hesitate to crow over MacBride, pointing out that his underhanded methods had met with their just reward.

The foreman did not take any official notice of the conflict between DuFresne and MacBride. Then MacBride complained to the foreman that DuFresne was openly boasting of his trick and ridiculing him before other workers. Thereupon, the foreman talked to DuFresne, but the latter insisted that his ruse had been justified as a means of self-protection.

When he was rebuffed by DuFresne, the foreman felt that he had lost control of the situation. He could no longer conceal from himself that he was confronted by a more complex situation than what initially he had defined as a "tool problem." His attention was drawn to the fact that the state of affairs in his department was a tangle of several interrelated problems. Each problem urgently called for decision that involved understanding and practical judgment. But having for so long failed to see the situation as a whole, he now found himself in a dilemma.

He wished to keep the good will of the work group, but he could not countenance the continued friction between DuFresne and MacBride. Certainly, he could not openly abet his operators in obstructing the work of a methods man. His superintendent would now certainly hear of it and would be displeased to learn that a foreman had failed to tell him of such an important technical improvement. Furthermore he knew that the aircraft industry was expanding at this time and that the demand for impellers had increased to such an extent that management was planning to set up an entire new plant unit devoted to this product.

X Company*

Background

THE X COMPANY was situated in a town in Northern Italy. It had more than 3,000 employees and was very well known in the highly competitive national and international market as a producer of radio sets and amplifiers. The company's top management had the reputation of always having taken much interest in relationships with their employees.

A personnel department had been established ten years before. In recent years, as the company expanded, the wages of workers in various departments had been revised several times, generally following the request of the Union Committee to adjust them to reflect prevailing living costs. It was a company policy to maintain wages at slightly above the area average.

In the past two years the mechanization process adapted to various operations was intentified and modern assembly lines were now in several departments. In the department for assembly of Super-Radio sets (which was the most modern model and the one produced in greatest volume) new lines had been installed at the end of last year.

Former Method of Assembly

Before the new assembly concept was adopted, the final assembling of the Super had been carried out, for three years, by eight crews of 4 men each, plus 16 inspectors. All of these employees were men. Each assembly man completed a separate series of complicated operations, before the work was moved to the next stage. Each stage required about 20 minutes. The stages were not divided into elementary standardized operations and the work was still of an artisan character. Management planned that as time went by, workers would learn more than one stage of the assembly, which would give them the right to a special classification involving a small wage increase.

The workers were paid on an individual piece rate basis, which had been calculated on the times of skilled workers purposely chosen. The engineers considered that 100% was maximum efficiency. The average efficiency of the department was about 91–92% under a system in which

---

the piece rate incentive premium started after 70% of standard was exceeded. This was exceeded only in very exceptional cases when workers achieved 105–110%, but normal variations were between 80% and 100%. Generally, the workers seemed to be satisfied with their situation, as they felt there was an opportunity to develop new and varied skills.

Experimental Period

The first conveyor belt introduced into Super-Radio assembly, was partly mechanized. It was moved by the workers as their operations were completed. The new conveyor belt was first operated by a group of skilled workers during the experimental period, but they were gradually replaced by other workers of the assembly department. Work was originally on an experimental basis. Incentive wages were not paid during the experimental period because the new standards were under study and it was necessary to have an adequate trial.[1] When the experimental phase was over those employees who had been working for a longer time under the new assembly method had completed seven months of training, while those who had been working there for less time averaged approximately two months of training.

A group incentive system was introduced on the basis of the new times, and computed on the total number of Super-Radios produced on an assembly line. Two parallel lines were installed.

Description of the Super-Radio Assembly Line

The new lines had 28 stages timed for 300 seconds each. After every three stages there was an inspection carried out by a man who served both lines. The inspection of the unit output of each stage involved 100 seconds. The assembly work required a few standardized repetitive hand operations; however, the degree of skillfulness required at each stage of the assembly and inspection operations was different. The workers had been formerly placed four at a bench with a shelf on which they put the sets when these were completed. They were now carrying out the operations assigned to them at a small individual bench, which was perpendicular to the belt, and on which the set was placed for movement when each stage was finished (see draft of the layout·of the final assembly lines, old and new, in Exhibit 1).

Near the main assembly lines there were other work stations at which the assembly operations of the subgroups feeding the main lines were done. The production of these subassemblies, however, was carried out for stock because between the side lines and the main ones there was a

---

[1] Workers received their former individual average pay during this period.

pool of material corresponding to a day's production of the main line. Most of these assembly operations were individual, but a few steps were completed by groups of workers, in successive phases. These side operations involved a certain amount of skill in assembling and in regulating.

Work methods on the Super assembly line for each individual operation were specified in detail by the engineers. Each worker (at the main or at the side lines) was required to repair the defective production which was attributable to him. The time allowed for each operation took this into account. It included, in fact, an adjustment for scrap calculated on the basis of the scrap made during the trial period when the times were under study. The recovery of scrap was included in the responsibilities of assembly workers.

For remuneration, the assembly workers on the main assembly lines were paid on the basis of a group piece rate incentive while those working at the side lines, who were carrying out individual operations, were paid on the basis of individual efficiency. Daily production determined by the number of coupons handed in to the supervisor at the end of each day, and not on the number of machines actually produced.[2] Piece rate earnings on each line were the same for all workers assigned to it.

Near the regular workers on each line were some qualified substitutes who occasionally were inserted in the line by the foreman, when he felt this was necessary to balance the flow of work. The piece rate incentive for the substitutes was equal to that of the other workers when they were on the line.

The skilled workers assigned to inspection, some of whom had formerly worked on assembly, derived one-half of their earnings from each line but received a higher base rate than assembly workers. Their total pay was therefore somewhat higher than assembly men on either line.

Output of the Department after the Introduction of the Assembly Lines and before the Strike

In the first months after the introduction of the assembly lines, the time-study engineers noticed a general decrease in the efficiency of the

---

[2] Before the introduction of the assembly lines the foreman was aware that considerable discrepancy existed between the number of coupons delivered and the number of sets actually produced. Often in the last two days of the month the workers remained nearly idle, having already produced the number of machines estimated in the original plan. A slowing down in work occurred also at the end of each day, in the last two hours, although the number of machines produced was the required one, and the average efficiency was quite satisfactory.

Super assembly line. Production dropped to an average of 80% of the efficiency estimated. Management tried to obviate this by creating an extra production bonus, designed to encourage the assembly workers to increase their efficiency, but the results were not satisfactory. Efficiency was in fact, stabilized at an average of about 80%, with slight variations from day to day. Throughout this period the workers raised complaints because of what they referred to as the "tighter work times."

The Union Committee, on behalf of the workers, asked management at this time to increase work time allowances, but management refused. The engineers tried to persuade the Union Committee on a basis of their observations and calculations that the times had actually been increased. The Union Committee insisted on a restudy of work times. As one of the workers said: "You have tightened the times and because of this we are unable to go above our present 80% efficiency. We lose too much, if you do not increase the times. We should be entitled to more money since the Company is making millions out of the Super-Radio sets."

EXHIBIT 1
Assembly Line Layouts: "Super-Radio" Assembly Department

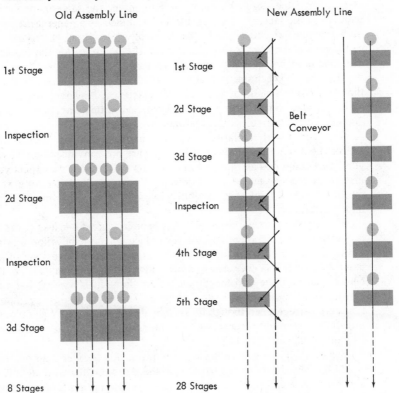

The Strike

At the beginning of February the department went on strike. The strike took place suddenly. Management did not expect it, and workers did not respond to pleas by the Union Committee to return to work while it negotiated with management. The personnel manager, to whom responsibility was given for settling the strike found it difficult to clarify the reasons for its occurrence and to work on a proposal which, in his opinion, might be accepted as a strike settlement. On March 6, after 12 meetings with Union representatives, workers in the Super-Radio department were still on strike.

Part of the minutes of a meeting attended by Dr. Bollini, the Union Committee and several representatives of the assembly department appointed by their fellow workers is reported below:

The Committee raised at the start the problem of time allowances. They asked for a revision of times and for an increase of 20% for the workers of the Super-Radio assembly department.

BOLLINI: If you think that management should give 20% extra to the workers assigned to Super-Radio assembly without giving the same increase to the other workers in the factory, this ought to be examined as a general problem, and not as a problem concerning only the assembly department. Everyone works and everyone has the right to get the increase. If you are raising the problem because of a unique technical issue, let's talk about it further.

MOTTINI: The point is that the individual piece rate incentive, before the time cut, allowed many of us to get 95% efficiency. Now with the time cut we are no longer able to reach these percentages, and in this way, instead of getting the amount we got before, we get *less* and we work *more*.

BOLLINI: I wish to clarify two points: one concerns the times on the new line. I have submitted the figures to you. If you are not convinced, you have a right to your own opinion. The other point concerns the fact that we expect you to agree that technological change is a good thing for everyone. Let's hope we can agree on this at least. I think that our efforts to improve the department's efficiency are quite reasonable.

RENZI: We say that production has been increased because of the time cut. It is true that some technical revision took place when the new line was introduced. However, we cannot accept having the workers put in a position of getting less money. Nobody has ever said to the workers "do more than 90%" but they did it before, and now they no longer succeed in doing it. If we say that a time is not correct you should get it restudied again. Somehow you always find that your times are correct, even though for us they do not work out. We don't even ask for a restudy any more because we have already told you that we do not like your way of calculating standards.

FERRARI: The work we have got to do now is heavier than before.

CARLI: We have started working at the assembly line with an 80% efficiency, and every day different people from management are putting pressures on us to get more. Before, with the same work we were getting 93–94%. We could breathe before, now it is no longer possible. We have "flying control" now. Before the work was done more conscientiously and accurately. Now, while they take the last breath out of us, they accuse us of working less in order to get increases from management.

FERRARI: When the engineers come and ask how is "our morale," this makes me think that they have a guilty conscience!

BERARDELLI: The workers at the Super assembly argue that they are now compelled to work at a very high speed, and that the work itself is difficult if we perform it as the time-study engineers want us to.

GIUSTETTO: We perspire, we sweat, we have hangovers, we have upset stomachs, we have feelings and emotions and we're not going to let you make machines out of us. When you talk about the time allowance you talk about it for a minute. We talk about a lifetime. We're not going to work on a watch time basis that hasn't got no feelings.

SEHERTI: If we don't stand up and fight we'll become robots. We want to be able to talk to the guys next to us sometimes. The way we're set up now we're nothing but machines.

BOLLINI: Let us see one problem at a time. There is a general question: the production increase and the financial capacity of the company. I have already answered these points. Here is a problem we have got to face in connection with all departments as soon as we can. We have got to be competitive. Costs have got to come down. I am willing to talk further about them with our engineering people. But let us see what they are. There is the time standards problem. In connection with this you can submit complaints each time you feel there is a problem, but the complaints must be specific and detailed. So far we feel we've studied the times you've complained about and they are all right. No change in them can be justified. Then as you say, there is the problem of the assembly line, itself. You're exaggerating about the work on the line. It's just a matter of getting used to the change.

The meeting described above was followed by other meetings, attended also by other members of top management, but no concrete results were achieved. The discussion always covered the same points.

1. What problems are the Company facing in the Super-Radio Assembly Department?
2. How do you explain them?
3. What choices does the Company have?

INDEX

This book has been set in 10 and 9 point Times Roman, leaded 2 points. Chapter titles are in 16 point Palatino, and chapter numbers are in 54 point Weiss Series II. The size of the type page is 27 by 45½ picas.

Managerial
Leadership
(Chapter 11)

Managerial
Leadership
(Chapter 11)

Required
Two-Person
Work
Relationship
(Chapter 9)

Consequences
• *Productivity*
• *Satisfaction*
• *Development*

Consequences
• *Productivity*
• *Satisfaction*
• *Development*

Emergent
Interpersonal
Processes
and Outcomes
(Chapter 10)

Required
Group Behavior
(Chapters 3-6)